Newly Revised Program Prepares Students For Family Living and Adult Responsibilities

Comprehensive Teaching and Learning Package

*Welcome to **Married and Single Life** — A complete program designed to help you prepare your students for family living and adult responsibilities. Developed to reinforce positive and thoughtful approaches to life, every component emphasizes realistic examples and relevant activities. Discussion and action-based activities help students learn to ask and answer the tough questions they face now and in the future.*

This newly revised and expanded program includes four major components.

STUDENT TEXT helps students analyze the major questions revolving around their individual and family roles now and in the future.

TEACHER'S ANNOTATED EDITION helps you lead students through the text and provides you with extensive guides and suggestions for teaching.

TEACHER'S CLASSROOM RESOURCES BOX provides hundreds of plans and activities to help your students master content and develop basic skills, reference materials and reproducible masters to save you hours of preparation time. Plus full-color transparencies to enliven your classroom presentations.

STUDENT WORKBOOK contains ready-to-use activity sheets and study guides for each chapter, designed to help students extend their learning and strengthen their academic skills.

Color Transparency Pkg.
Married & Single Life
Extending the Text
Married & Single Life
Student Workbook TAE
Married & Single Life
ABCNews InterActive Videodisks Correlation
Married & Single Life
Balancing Work and Family
Married & Single Life
Testing Program
Color Transparency Pkg.
Married & Single Life
FAMILY AND CONSUMER SCIENCES PROFESSIONAL DEVELOPMENT SERIES
Dealing with Sensitive Issues
Responsible Relationships
Married & Single Life
Lesson Plans
Married & Single Life
Student Workbook
Married & Single Life
Building Life Skills
Married & Single Life

Student Text

This completely revised and expanded favorite presents a positive approach to developing life skills: communications, conflict resolution, decision making and management.

Topics are discussed in logical sequence. Students begin by thinking about themselves in the present, then consider what their lives will be like as they become adults. A new unit on the middle years and the later years has been added at the end of the book.

The text emphasizes the importance of personal goals and strong personal values. Personal responsibility and a realistic view of life are seen as the keys to adult living.

- Controversial topics are viewed objectively.
- All chapters integrate higher order thinking skills.
- Interesting language makes the material easy to read.

A special section address the joys and problems of single living.

Special text highlights help you give your students more guidance.

Balancing Work and Family...

New to this edition, these features focus on the challenges that today's families face as they juggle the many demands on their time and energy.

A Slice of Life...

Case studies present specific examples and questions to help students think through problems.

I Can...

Positive features give students confidence by discussing ways to handle certain situations. First-person accounts tell how someone dealt with such a situation. Questions and activities involve students in the solution.

Sidelight...

Interesting and factual information extends students' knowledge so that they can make more thoughtful decisions.

Reaching Out...

Two-page spreads at the end of each unit show teens reaching out. Students will see the benefits of involvement with others. Questions suggest ways in which they, too, can make a difference.

Reaching Out

Tracy reaches out to the members of her blended family.

Tracy "It took time to get used to the idea of moving in with a whole new family — a stepfather, stepbrother, and stepsister. My mom and dad had fought a lot, so I expected the same thing to happen with Tim. He's quieter than my father, though, so he didn't yell to make his point. I liked our new house, and Tim, who works in construction, turned the basement into two extra bedrooms. At first everything seemed awkward, but I decided to make a real effort to get along. I shared my music tapes and tried to be open with my new family. Sometimes it didn't feel natural, but it got easier once we all relaxed. Even though it feels a bit crowded at times, we are starting to feel like a real family."

I CAN ◆◆ Resist Pressure

Angeline felt that she had lost control of her own will until she learned some techniques that helped her do what she wanted to do instead of going along with others.

"At first I thought it would never work. I learned how to say "no" in my independent living class, but it didn't sound easy. I guess I was too used to just giving in all the time.

"I decided to start with Clark. When he asked me for my homework for the umpteenth time, I stood firm, looked him straight in the eye, and said, 'Not anymore, Clark. I don't feel right about it. I hope we can still be friends anyway.' I said it calmly and without smiling. I wanted him to get the message straight.

"Clark was taken back by my answer. He even pushed me a little more. I just told him I had to meet Dee, and I left. He never asked me for my homework again. He has been a little distant since then. I don't know whether we'll ever be good friends again or not, but if he was just using me, I guess I don't need that kind of friendship."

- What techniques did Angeline use that were helpful to her?
- How can you say "no" and attempt to keep a friendship at the same time?
- Describe some other situations in which these techniques might be useful.
- Do you need to learn to be more assertive about saying "no"? Think of some times when you should have said "no" in the past. How would you handle similar situations differently in the future?

Friends may at times exert positive peer pressure. Alexis was very shy and had a difficult time developing relationships until she became part of a child development class. Her classmates were very concerned about her and made an extra special effort to include her in everything. In class discussions, a common response was, "We want to know what you think about this, Alexis." They were a group of encouragers exerting a positive influence on Alexis's social development.

Friends may step in, exert pressure, and prevent major crises as well. Friends don't let friends get involved in things that may be immoral, dangerous, or illegal. How can you and your friends be a positive influence on others?

Peer pressure can be positive. Have you ever encouraged a friend to learn a new skill? This kind of pressure is helpful to people.

A Slice of Life

After graduating from high school, Celeste found a job in a plumbing and heating supply store. She did typing and filing and answered the phone. The pay was low, but it was a job. Celeste and two friends shared expenses on an apartment until one got married and the other moved out of town. Celeste could not manage the rent herself, so she returned to her family home.

It seemed strange to be home again. She had been on her own long enough to feel independent, but now she had to answer to her parents again. She wanted to save money for a new car, but they wanted her to pay them rent. She had always lived there for free before. After Celeste left home, the number of laundry loads her folks washed went down. Now the number was up again. Celeste assumed they would wash her clothes as usual. Celeste did not understand the tense atmosphere that was developing in her home. It had never been there before.

Thinking It Through

- Why is home life different for Celeste now?
- How do you think her parents feel about having Celeste home again?
- What suggestions do you have for Celeste and her parents?

◆ Managing as a Single in the Family Home

When singles continue to live in the family home as young adults or they return to the family nest after a time away, new rules may be needed. Parents generally want a young adult to be taking on responsibility. If the young adult is going to school, there will be fewer expectations. If he or she has a job, how ever, parents are right to expect som of expenses. In both situations ho jobs should be shared. The young a have some expectations too. More is usually one of these. Since the you son is living at home, parents often f they still have some say. To work all of t ground rules need to be set up. The fol suggestions ought to be included in a w contract between the parents and y adult:

- List responsibilities, such as clea laundry, and food preparation.
- Set a schedule for paying expenses, as rent, phone bills, electricity, heat, food.
- Discuss acceptable limits of behav such as the handling of privacy and re tionships outside of the family unit.
- Set a time limit for living at home, bas on the reason for being there.

When young adults live in the family home, a written contract should spell out the rules. What topics should be covered?

Babies who live in homes filled with tension are apt to be more fussy and demand more attention than those whose homes are relaxed and loving. Children who grow up in families where hugs and kisses are abundant are usually more open about showing their deeper feelings than those where family members keep their distance.

In addition to the emotional climate, factors such as family size, position in the family, relationships with brothers and sisters, and parenting styles affect personalities of family members. The family is the major communicator of culture to its members. Finally, it is within the context of family that most people develop their viewpoints on everything from food likes and dislikes to politics and religion.

◆◆◆ Erikson's Theory

Theories on personality development show how strong the family influence is. According to psychologist Erik Erikson, personal development takes place in a series of stages. Each builds on the one before and can provide a solid base for the next. He suggested that each of these life stages includes a central problem that must be solved before personal development can continue. Preparation for each new task occurs during the previous stage and is worked out gradually. Erikson believed that each stage combines forward-moving urges pushing against forces working against them. The person involved decides

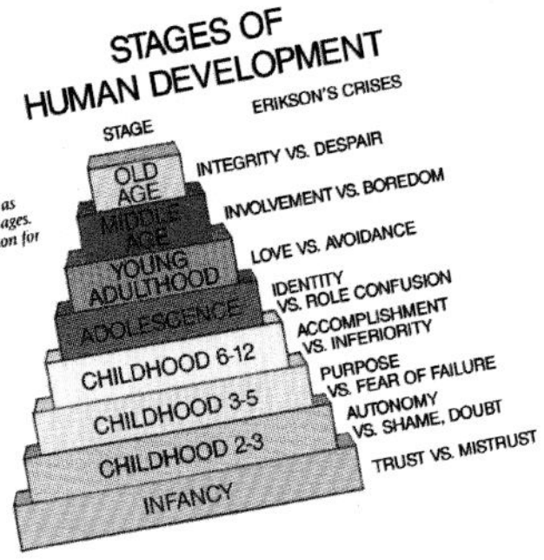

According to psychologist Erik Erikson, personalities develop as people go through different stages. Each stage builds a foundation for the next.

SIDELIGHT

Communication Etiquette

Knowing what to do in social situations helps you feel confident. The rules that describe proper behavior are called etiquette. The rules of etiquette are useful when you face new situations.

- A *firm*, but not crushing, handshake shows confidence and friendship and can be extended by both males and females. A handshake is an appropriate end to a job interview. It is also often used during introductions. When making introductions, give the names of both people. Mention the key person first, the one you wish to honor. An introduction can be stated like this: "Miss Davis, I would like you to meet my stepfather, Mr. Warden. Dad, this is Miss Davis, my soccer coach."
- When using the telephone, remember to time your use so that others have a chance to use the phone too. When you take a message for someone, write it down and make it complete. You can say: "Bob is not here right now. May I take a message?" Include a phone number if possible. If you reach a wrong number, apologize rather than hang up in someone's ear.
- In any social situation, if you are not sure about what to do, follow the cues of someone whose knowledge you respect.

◆◆◆

◆◆◆ Skills for Effective Communication

Good communicators know the importance of choosing an appropriate time and place for important conversations. No wise employee asks for a raise when the boss complains of a splitting headache. No smart student asks the science teacher for extra time on an assignment immediately after another student breaks six beakers in the chemistry lab. Although you cannot always control time and place, some messages will be much more effective when you do.

When the time and place are right for meaningful conversation, do so with straight talk. Say how you feel simply and honestly. If you are discussing a sensitive issue, open by saying, "I feel uneasy." This reduces tension and invites the other person to understand.

As you have read, communication involves listening too. Many people have learned not to listen to others. They may want to do all the talking or simply spend time thinking of what to say next. This is talking *to*, rather than *with*, the other person. Learning to talk *with* someone means learning to respond to another's remarks. This is the give and take that makes conversation flow. You won't have to worry about what to say next if you listen and respond to what you hear.

Some people talk to each other instead of with each other. Which of these situations is illustrated here? How might the situation be changed for the better?

Teacher's Annotated Edition

***The Teacher's Annotated Edition** puts the teaching aids you've asked for right at your fingertips. The bound-in Teacher's Manual helps you plan your course and your students' learning. Teaching annotations are overprinted on every page of the teachers' edition to help you guide students through the content.*

Chapter Opener questions help you introduce each chapter.

Discussion ideas enhance student involvement.

Activity ideas help you add variety to in-class and outside projects.

Problem Solving activities ask students to do some evaluating and find solutions.

Life Management Skills engage students in management-oriented activities or discussion.

Work and Family situations involve students in learning to balance work and family life.

More About provides tidbits of information that you can use to expand content in the student text.

Photo Focus helps you turn the text photographs into teaching/learning opportunities.

Answers to the chapter review questions, conveniently located, make it easier for you to evaluate students' learning.

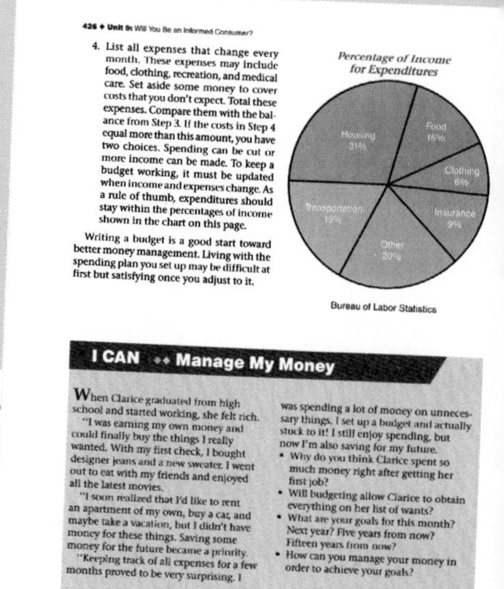

426 ◆ **Unit 9:** Will You Be an Informed Consumer?

4. List all expenses that change every month. These expenses may include food, clothing, recreation, and medical care. Set aside some money to cover costs that you don't expect. Total these expenses. Compare them with the balance from Step 3. If the costs in Step 4 equal more than this amount, you have two choices. Spending can be cut or more income can be made. To keep a budget working, it must be updated when income and expenses change. As a rule of thumb, expenditures should stay within the percentages of income shown in the chart on this page.

Writing a budget is a good start toward better money management. Living with the spending plan you set up may be difficult at first but satisfying once you adjust to it.

Percentage of Income for Expenditures

Bureau of Labor Statistics

I CAN ◆◆ Manage My Money

When Clarice graduated from high school and started working, she felt rich.

"I was earning my own money and could finally buy the things I really wanted. With my first check, I bought designer jeans and a new sweater. I went out to eat with my friends and enjoyed all the latest movies.

"I soon realized that I'd like to rent an apartment of my own, buy a car, and maybe take a vacation, but I didn't have money for these things. Saving some money for the future became a priority.

"Keeping track of all expenses for a few months proved to be very surprising. I was spending a lot of money on unnecessary things. I set up a budget and actually stuck to it! I still enjoy spending, but now I'm also saving for my future.

- Why do you think Clarice spent so much money right after getting her first job?
- Will budgeting allow Clarice to obtain everything on her list of wants?
- What are your goals for this month? Next year? Five years from now? Fifteen years from now?
- How can you manage your money in order to achieve your goals?

More About Interest on Savings. Two kinds of interest are available on savings accounts. They include simple and compound interest. Simple interest is paid only on the principal. Compound interest is paid on the principal plus any simple interest accumulated on the principal. Interest = principal × rate × time (i = prt).

Problem Solving. Have students respond to the following problem: George borrowed $600 from the bank to buy a CD player. He agreed to repay the loan in 2 years at an interest rate of 11%. How much interest will George have to pay? (i = prt; I = 600 × 0.11 × 2; I = 132; George will pay $132.00 in interest.)

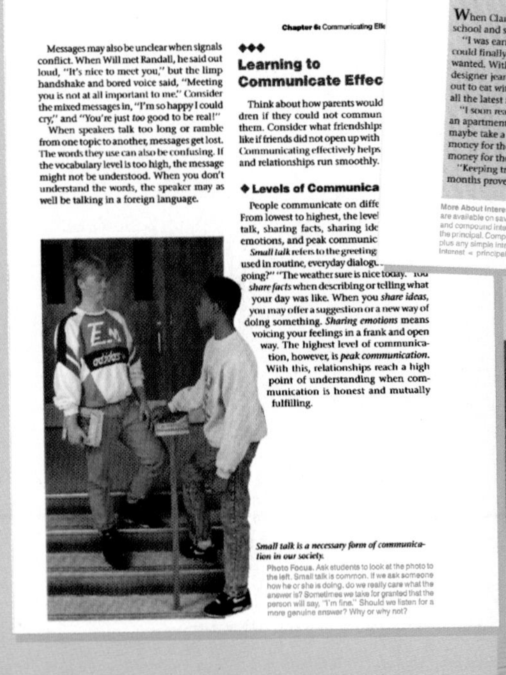

Chapter 6: Communicating Effe

Messages may also be unclear when signals conflict. When Will met Randall, he said out loud, "It's nice to meet you," but the limp handshake and bored voice said, "Meeting you is not at all important to me." Consider the mixed messages in, "I'm so happy I could cry," and "You're just *too* good to be real!"

When speakers talk too long or ramble from one topic to another, messages get lost. The words they use can also be confusing. If the vocabulary level is too high, the message might not be understood. When you don't understand the words, the speaker may as well be talking in a foreign language.

◆◆◆

Learning to Communicate Effec

Think about how parents would dren if they could not commun them. Consider what friendships like if friends did not open up with Communicating effectively helps and relationships run smoothly.

◆ Levels of Communica

People communicate on diffe From lowest to highest, the level talk, sharing facts, sharing ide emotions, and peak communic

Small talk refers to the greeting used in routine, everyday dialogu going?" "The weather sure is nice today." You *share facts* when describing or telling what your day was like. When you *share ideas*, you may offer a suggestion or a new way of doing something. *Sharing emotions* means voicing your feelings in a frank and open way. The highest level of communication, however, is *peak communication*. With this, relationships reach a high point of understanding when communication is honest and mutually fulfilling.

Small talk is a necessary form of communication in our society.

Photo Focus. Ask students to look at the photo to the left. Small talk is common. If we ask someone how he or she is doing, do we really care what the answer is? Sometimes we take for granted that the person will say, "I'm fine." Should we listen for a more genuine answer? Why or why not?

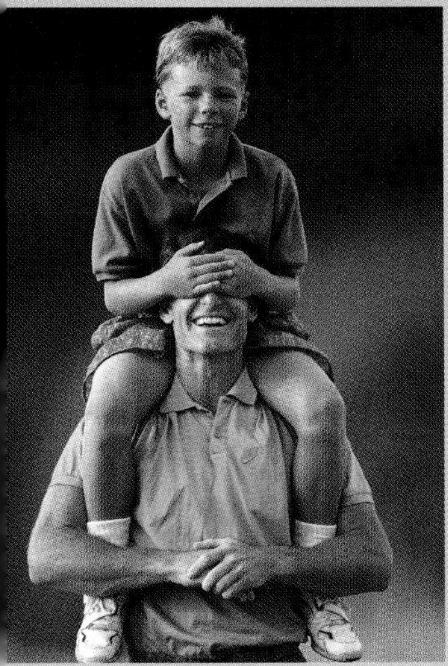

CHAPTER 21

Review

Answers
Testing Your Memory
1. Entering marriage with thought of change is unwise since this is likely to cause resentment.
2. Any three: talk about feelings; ask questions; speak gently; listen to your partner; consider timing.
3. Making a decision alone doesn't require consulting someone else. Making a decision with a partner requires thinking of the other person's feelings and knowledge. Both must agree on what the issue is. Compromise may be needed to reach agreement.
4. Couples need to divide responsibilities based on the strengths, skills, interest, and time available to do the work.
5. Any five: never allow abusive behavior; do not ignore problems; count to ten; communicate; place value on the other's point of view; attack the issue, not the person; discuss one problem at a time; learn to compromise; learn to apologize; forgive and forget.
6. Any five from the list on page 302. Students may suggest other ways.

Summarizing the Chapter

- Marriages are successful because people make an effort.
- Accepting your spouse means not having a plan to change him or her.
- Good communication is vital to a healthy marriage.
- Making decisions together helps self-esteem.
- Sharing responsibilities is common in marriages today. This keeps one partner from being overburdened.
- Conflicts in marriage should be resolved as they come up.
- Time must be allowed in marriage for each other and for friends.
- Intimacy and sexual contact are two different things in marriage, but they affect each other.
- When you marry, your in-laws become your family too.

Testing Your Memory

1. Should you plan to change your spouse's annoying habits? Explain your answer.
2. List three suggestions for communicating in marriage.
3. How does decision making with a partner differ from making a decision by yourself?
4. Describe how a couple might divide responsibilities.
5. List five ground rules for resolving conflicts in marriage.
6. List five ways to be thoughtful in marriage.
7. Explain the difference between intimacy and sexual contact.
8. Why are friends needed by a married couple?
9. How can too much closeness with in-laws be a challenge for some married couples?

308

Thinking Critically

1. Explain why it is often hard to talk about a sensitive issue with someone you are very close to.
2. Sometimes struggling through hard times makes people stronger. This may even strengthen the bonds in marriage. Why do you think this is often true?
3. Power comes with controlling the money in a marriage. Why is this true? Do you think finances should be handled by one or both partners? Explain your answer.

Taking Action

1. Interview a married couple (or just one partner) who are both employed. Find out how they divide duties, including child care, cooking, cleaning, laundry, yardwork, shopping, household maintenance and repairs, auto care, and bill paying. How did they decide on this?
2. In groups create and perform skits about the following situations. Use good communication techniques to solve the problems.
   a. The husband and wife have set up a list of responsibilities for each of them to do. One of them, however, is not following through, leaving many jobs for the other to do.
   b. One partner spends so much spare time in outside activities that they have little time together as a couple. The other partner is unhappy about this.

Making Decisions

When Leslie and Torrence were first married, they often went out of the way to do thoughtful things for each other. Sometimes it was just a simple compliment or a loving hug. Other times it was a candlelight dinner or some special surprise. Six years and two children later, the thoughtfulness seems to have been lost along the way. Leslie has the feeling that it doesn't even bother Torrence. It does bother her. She feels the distance growing between them.

What mistakes have Leslie and Torrence made? What do you think is ahead for them? How might this situation be changed?

7. Intimacy is the closeness that comes from deep, personal conversation, loving gestures, and displays of affection. Intimacy may be part, but not limited to, sexual contact between marriage partners.
8. Friendships are necessary for good emotional health.
9. Too much closeness with in-laws can cause resentment among marriage partners. Couples need time to themselves in order to carry on their roles as spouses first and married children second. They need to be clear and firm about their needs when dealing with in-laws.

Thinking Critically
1. Answers will vary. Point out that fear of hurting someone often makes it difficult to discuss sensitive issues.
2. Answers will vary. Resolving problems in a healthful manner gives couples a sense of accomplishment.
3. Answers will vary. Emphasize that marriages may be strengthened when both partners work through financial matters together.

309

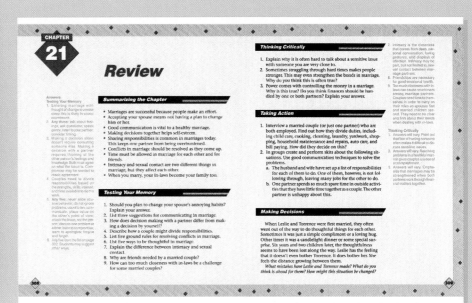

Convenient *Answers* for the Chapter Review

CHAPTER 1

Your Personality

Chapter Challenge

Resources. Refer to the Teacher's Resource Book and Student Workbook for materials related to this chapter.

Look for These Answers . . .

- Why is every person in the world unique?
- What factors influence one's personality?
- Explain Erikson's theory of personality development.
- What are self-concept and self-esteem?
- How does a person build self-esteem?

Look for These Terms . . .

- adolescence
- assertiveness
- culture
- environment
- extroverts
- heredity
- introverts
- personality
- self-concept
- self-esteem

16

All the girls were gathering by the track for their first practice of the season. This was Abigail's first year on the team. As a matter of fact, she had just transferred in from a school in another state.

"How long have you been on the team?" Abigail asked the girl beside her.

"She can't hear you," Pat said. "Salina is hearing impaired. She won't know what you say unless you get her attention first and speak directly at her."

"I see," Abigail replied as she moved closer to Pat.

A few more girls arrived. As they did, some left for different parts of the field. When Chelsey joined the group, she greeted everyone and welcomed Abigail to the team. "I heard you are a good sprinter, Abigail," she said. "We need you." Then Chelsey touched Salina on the arm. While Salina watched, Chelsey's fingers signed a greeting and message to her. Salina smiled and signed back. "Salina and I are going over to the long-jump pit," Chelsey said. "We're going to rake it out."

As they walked away, Abigail asked, "Where did she learn that?"

"She taught herself," Pat replied. "She's about the only one who can have a conversation with Salina."

"Sounds like a lot of work to me," Abigail said. "I wonder why she bothered to learn."

After a long pause, Pat looked at Abigail and said, "I guess that's just the kind of person she is. Maybe that's why everyone likes her so much."

Chapter Opener. Ask students to read the opening scenario to the chapter. Ask the following questions: How would you describe the personalities of each teen in the scenario? How do you think Salina feels about Chelsey? Why is Chelsey one of only a few who can communicate with Salina? What enables Chelsey to be the way she is?

Realizing Your Uniqueness

Bubbly, somber, shy, moody, friendly, mischievous, pessimistic, happy, sad: Do any of these words describe people you know? Do any of them match you? Personalities cannot be described in just a few words. It takes many.

Personality is the sum of all characteristics that make a person unique. You have your own distinct personality. Although others may have some similar traits to yours, no one else in the world has exactly the same combination of characteristics that you have.

The word "personality" is derived from the Greek word "persona," which means mask. Many people show the world only certain sides of themselves. They keep other traits hidden from view, as though behind a mask. Other people tend to be more open.

Personality is a very complex concept. Like a puzzle, personality is seen by others as a total impression of who a person is. At the same time, the personality puzzle is made up of many pieces. These may be viewed separately for greater understanding. No personality, however, may be completely described in terms of just one piece of the puzzle.

17

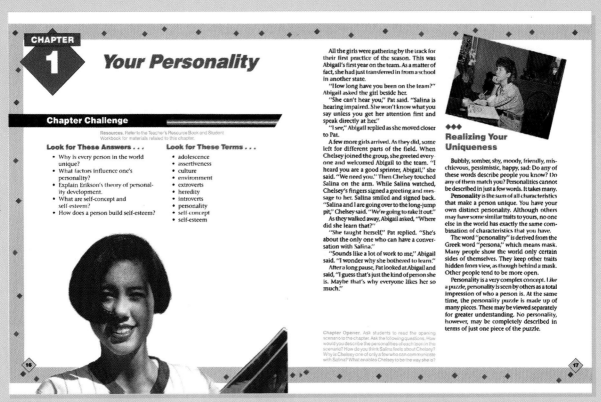

Easy to use annotations for *Resources, Chapter Opener, Activity, and Discussion*

Teacher's Classroom Resources

More than 600 pages of extras in convenient-to-use booklets to help you help your students.

- Student Workbook/Teacher's Annotated Edition
- Balancing Work and Family
- Responsible Relationships
- Building Life Skills
- Dealing with Sensitive Issues
- Extending the Text
- Lesson Plans
- Testing Program
- ABCNews InterActive™ Videodiscs Correlation
- Color Transparencies Package

Program Components

Textbook	
Student edition	0-02-643000-2
Teacher's Annotated Edition	0-02-643001-0
Workbook	
Student Workbook	0-02-643002-9
Teacher's Annotated Edition*	0-02-643004-5
Teacher's Classroom Resources Box	
Balancing Work and Family*	0-02-642942-X
Responsible Relationships*	0-02-643008-8
Building Life Skills*	0-02-643006-1
Dealing with Sensitive Issues*	0-02-642798-2
Extending the Text*	0-02-643007-X
Lesson Plans*	0-02-643005-3
Testing Program*	0-02-643010-X
ABCNews InterActive™ Videodiscs Correlation*	0-02-643015-0
Color Transparency Package*	0-02-643011-8

*These components are included in the Teacher's Classroom Resources

For more information, contact your nearest regional office or call toll-free 1-800-334-7344.

Northeast Region
Glencoe / McGraw-Hill
15 Trafalgar Square #201
Nashua, NH 03063-1968
603-880-4701 • 800-424-3451
Fax: 603-595-0204
(CT, MA, ME, NH, NY, RI, VT)

Mid-Atlantic Region
Glencoe / McGraw-Hill
P.O. Box 458
Hightstown, NJ 08520
609-426-5560 • 800-553-7515
Fax: 609-426-7063
(CD, DE, MD, NJ, PA)

Atlantic-Southleast Region
Glencoe / McGraw-Hill
Brookside Park
One Harbison Way, Suite 101
Columbia, SC 29212
803-732-2365 • 800-731-2365
Fax: 803-732-4582
(KY, NC, SC, VA, WV)

Southeast Region
Glencoe / McGraw-Hill
6510 Jimmy Carter Boulevard
Norcross, GA 30071
770-446-7493 • 800-982-3992
Fax: 770-446-2356
(AL, FL, GA, TN)

Mid-America Region
Glencoe / McGraw-Hill
936 Eastwind Drive
Westerville, OH 43081
614-890-1111 • 800-848-1567
Fax: 614-899-4905
(IN, MN, OH)

Great Lakes Region
Glencoe / McGraw-Hill
846 East Algonquin Road
Schaumburg, IL 60173
708-397-8448 • 800-762-4876
Fax: 708-397-9472
(IL, MN, WI)

Mid-Continent Region
Glencoe / McGraw-Hill
846 East Algonquin Road
Schaumburg, IL 60173
708-397-8448 • 800-762-4876
Fax: 708-397-9472
(IA, KS, MO, ND, NE, ND)

Southwest Region
Glencoe / McGraw-Hill
320 Westway Place, Suite 550
Arlington, TX 76018
817-784-2113 • 800-828-5096
Fax: 817-784-2116
(AR, LA, MS, NM, OK)

Texas Region
Glencoe / McGraw-Hill
320 Westway Place, Suite 550
Arlington, TX 76018
817-784-2100 • 800-828-5096
Fax: 817-784-2116
(TX)

Western Region
Glencoe / McGraw-Hill
709 E. Riverpark Lane, Suite #150
Boise, ID 83706
208-368-0300 • 800-452-6126
Fax: 208-368-0303
Includes Alaska
(AK, AZ, CO, ID, MT, NV, OR, UT, WA, WY)

California Region
Glencoe / McGraw-Hill
15319 Chatsworth Street
P.O. Box 9609
Mission Hills, CA 91346
818-898-1391 • 800-423-9534
Fax: 818-365-5489
(CA, HI)

Glencoe Catholic School Region
Glencoe / McGraw-Hill
25 Crescent Street, 1st Floor
Stamford, CT 06906
203-964-9109 • 800-551-8766
Fax: 203-967-3108

Canada
McGraw-Hill Reyerson Ltd.
300 Water Street
Whitby, Ontario
Canada L1N 9B6
905-430-5000 • 800-565-5758
Fax: 905-430-5020

DoDDS and Pacific Territories
McGraw-Hill School Publishing Company
1221 Avenue of the Americas
13th Floor
New York, NY 10020
212-512-6218
Fax: 212-512-6050

International
McGraw-Hill Inc.
International Group
1221 Avenue of the Americas
28th Floor
New York, NY 10020-1095
212-512-3641
Fax: 212-512-2186

FCS 91260-1

GLENCOE
McGraw-Hill

P-4/96

Teacher's Manual

Married & Single Life

Sixth Edition

Sixth Edition

Teacher's Manual

Married & Single Life

Audrey Palm Riker
Holly E. Brisbane

GLENCOE
McGraw-Hill
New York, New York Columbus, Ohio Mission Hills, California Peoria, Illinois

Contributors

Mark Bregman

Ann Branch, M.Ed.
Home Economics Teacher
Jefferson High School
Alexandria, Minnesota

Cover photos from Stock Market CD 2

Glencoe/McGraw-Hill
A Division of The ***McGraw-Hill*** *Companies*

Printed in the United States of America

Send all inquiries to:
Glencoe/McGraw-Hill
3008 W. Willow Knolls Drive
Peoria, IL 61614-1083

ISBN 0-02-643000-2 (Student Text)

ISBN 0-02-643001-0 (Teacher's Annotated Edition)

1 2 3 4 5 6 7 8 9 10 RRDW 00 99 98 97 96

Contents of Teacher's Manual

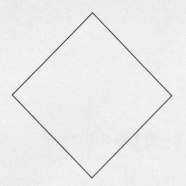

Introducing the Sixth Edition

This Sixth Edition of *Married and Single Life* builds on the strengths of previous editions and continues to offer a flexible, comprehensive framework for family living courses. At the same time, the text has been revised and expanded to reflect changing family concerns and current realities and challenges. It answers the kinds of questions today's young people have about preparing for family living and adult responsibilities.

How has *Married and Single Life* changed? In this new edition you will find:

- More pages.
- New *Balancing Work and Family* features.
- New chapters on *The Middle Years* and *The Later Years.*
- More than 100 new photos.
- Thought-provoking features in every chapter and at the end of every unit.
- Updated text throughout, with changes that reflect current trends and concerns.
- Improved and expanded support materials.

In some ways, *Married and Single Life* has not changed. Although improved, it is still the flexible complete program you need for teaching and learning.

- **Flexible.** The text is designed for flexibility in teaching. Chapters are self-contained so you can pick the ones you need to suit the course you are teaching.
- **Complete.** A glance through the table of contents will show that the text covers a wider range of topics than ever before.
- **Teaching.** *Married and Single Life* maximizes teaching effectiveness. The supplements put hundreds of discussion and activity ideas at your fingertips and at the same time provide ready-to-use worksheets, handouts, tests, color transparencies, and more. The easy-to-use Teacher's Classroom Resources box will save you hours of preparation.
- **Learning.** The text's clear and readable style is easy for students to handle, and the use of relevant examples makes the material come alive. The text is packed with information that teens need and with examples that they can relate to.

The *Married and Single Life* program includes these components:

- **Student Text.** The core of the program is this 512-page book.
- **Teacher's Annotated Edition.** This component contains the Teacher's Manual that you are reading now and annotations throughout the text.
- **Student Workbook.** The student study guides and activity sheets in this softbound book are designed to stimulate learning.
- **Teacher's Classroom Resources box.** Turn to this component for a variety of booklets offering lesson plans, resources, handouts, worksheets, reproducible masters, tests, teaching suggestions, and color transparencies.

On the following pages, you will find more information about each of these components as well as suggestions for using them effectively.

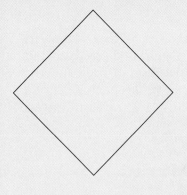

Getting Acquainted with the Student Text

At the heart of the *Married and Single Life* program is the student textbook. It is a logically organized resource of information, visual reinforcement, and special features that help to make learning a worthwhile experience.

◆◆◆

What Does the Text Contain?

As you teach with *Married and Single Life,* you will see that the information it contains is relevant to all people, not just those in your class. This is the kind of material that you will wish you had studied as a teen and that you will want your own children to read.

Those who encounter troubled teens every day know that individuals and families need help. They need to know about themselves, how to get along with others, and how to improve their own conditions as well as those of others. It is with these thoughts in mind that the writing of the Sixth Edition of *Married and Single Life* has developed.

The text is, of course, very discussion-oriented. Without trying to tell readers what to do, it carefully prods them to take directions that involve responsibility and concern for others. Although serious topics are not avoided, the emphasis is positive. Teens can learn to deal with tough situations in positive ways and with the right attitudes.

The text for *Married and Single Life* has a future perspective. It begins with the present and carries students through an analysis of each of the major questions that they are likely to encounter in the future. The text is divided into ten units, each one dealing with an important question. Thirty-three chapters combine to make these units.

◆ Unit One: What About You?

Before students can look ahead, they must get a handle on the present. That is what this unit is about. In the five chapters of the unit, students take a close look at themselves. They examine their personalities, thinking about why they are what they are. They also consider development, with a focus on the special concerns of teens. One chapter has been devoted to character so that students can explore what it means to be mature and what qualities are linked with good character. To round out their study of themselves, a chapter on health is included before students take a glimpse into the future at the close of the unit.

◆ Unit Two: What Skills Do You Need?

A successful future is much more likely to become reality when people possess certain skills that can help them along the way. Four critical skills are covered in the four chapters of this unit. They are communication, decision making (along with problem solving), handling conflict, and learning to manage. Armed with these skills, your students will be ready to take on the questions posed by each of the units that follow. With careful thought, study, and preparation, they will be able to move toward a brighter future.

◆ Unit Three: What Are Families Like?

Families are complicated today. Students need to understand what families are like so they can be comfortable with whatever family situation they may be in now and in the future. They need to be equipped with specific information on how to make family life positive. In the first chapter of this unit, students learn about the different patterns of family living, including the family life cycle. The second chapter deals with techniques for making families strong. What students take from this chapter they can apply to family life now and also when they build their own families later on. This is critical, not only to them as individuals but also to the condition of society. In the last chapter of this unit, a very important one, students take a look at the major challenges that families face today and learn ways to cope with them.

◆ Unit Four: How Can You Handle Relationships?

This unit has high impact on students at this point in their lives. It also has strong relevance to their futures. In four chapters students examine relationships, moving from friendships, to dating, to love and commitment, to sexuality. Students are encouraged to take a thoughtful, caring approach to handling relationships at every level.

◆ Unit Five: What About Single Life?

At some point in time single living is experienced by nearly everyone. With this edition of *Married and Single Life*, this topic is given the attention it deserves. With a unit all its own, single living is addressed positively but with careful consideration of the concerns that single people have. Management of a successful single lifestyle is the focus of this unit.

◆ Unit Six: Is Married Life for You?

The question posed by this unit has important implications for students. Simply asking the question should help them begin to see that marriage is a choice and also one that must be made carefully. The nuts and bolts of the marriage process are covered in the first of the four chapters. Here students learn about laws and customs that deal with marriage. The heart of the unit is contained in the next two chapters. In one, students take a close look at what to think about before entering into a marriage. In the other, they learn what it takes to make a marriage successful. Because so many people are challenged by divorce today, the last chapter covers this as well as remarriage and the creation of blended families.

◆ Unit Seven: Will You Become a Parent?

Like the last unit, here is a question aimed at making students realize that they have an important decision to make. Parenthood is a choice, not an obligation or a casual circumstance. In the first of four chapters, students consider the seriousness of making the decision to parent. They examine readiness as well as methods for planning. The next two chapters deal with reproduction and child development. The unit ends with an important chapter on responsible parenting. Not only does this chapter tackle guidance and discipline, but it also covers the whole range of parental responsibility, including the need to promote social, moral, and emotional development in children.

◆ Unit Eight: What Will Your Life's Work Be?

This is, of course, one of life's major decisions. The two chapters in this unit lead students toward finding the right career and then functioning well on the job. Given the need for professionalism and ethics in today's work world, these topics are also included.

◆ Unit Nine: Will You Be an Informed Consumer?

This unit helps students focus on managing their own futures as consumers. First, students learn about money management, including checking accounts and different kinds of savings options as well as buying on credit. In the second chapter, they gain buying know-how, with a focus on what to be wary of in the marketplace. The last chapter of the unit surveys what they need to know about the major expenses people have in life.

◆ Unit Ten: What Lies Ahead?

To round out the series of questions students must address in thinking about their own futures, this unit focuses on the middle years and the later years. Students learn about the physical, mental, emotional, and social changes that people experience as they grow older. The two chapters in the unit explore the rewards and challenges of the middle and later years, and give guidelines for preparing early for retirement.

◆◆◆

What Are the Elements of the Text?

◆ Unit Opening Pages

Each unit opens with a color photo that symbolizes the content of the unit. A list of the chapters in the unit appears on the right-hand page of the unit opener spread.

◆ Chapter Opening Pages

The first two pages of each chapter have been designed to prepare students to read the chapter and to spark their interest. The components included are:

- **Chapter Challenge.** Under this heading are two items. Student objectives are listed under "Look for These Answers." Students should read these and be prepared to find the answers as they read the chapter. Vocabulary terms are listed under "Look for These Terms." When the terms are defined within the chapter, they are printed in boldface type for easy reference. A definition is given, as well as examples or further explanation when needed. Phonetic pronunciation guides are included for terms that are difficult to pronounce.
- **Opening Scenario.** The text of each chapter begins with a short scenario. In general, these are brief glimpses into real-life situations. They demonstrate one or more of the concepts in the chapter and provide food for thought. You may want to read these with students and have a class discussion that prepares them for reading the chapter. Note that discussion questions are suggested in the annotation below each scenario in the Teacher's Annotated Edition of the text.

◆ Writing Style

Distinctive headings divide the chapter into topics and subtopics. The text itself is written at a comfortable reading level for high school students. Explanations are clear and concise and go beyond just theory. Students are provided with the practical information they need. This gives the text depth and usefulness. Examples are realistic and carefully worked into the text in the appropriate places.

◆ Visual Elements

Married and Single Life is packed with hundreds of color photographs and drawings. The illustrations and fresh, contemporary design provide visual and personal appeal for students. Illustrations have been selected not just for interest, however. They have been coordinated with the text to teach as well.

- Photographs show teens and others in realistic situations. The photos reinforce the text and help students improve their observation skills.
- Captions are more than just informative. Many ask questions to help students review facts, apply text concepts, and develop higher-level thinking skills.
- Drawings make learning concrete by clearly illustrating those ideas that cannot be portrayed by text alone.
- Charts summarize or present certain information in an organized format.

◆ Features

The text for *Married and Single Life* includes more than 90 features throughout the chapters and at the end of each unit. The features extend the content of the text and offer ample opportunity for thought and discussion. Features are of the following types:

- **A Slice of Life.** These are case studies developed to complement one or more key ideas in the chapter. Every chapter has at least one case study. At the end of each case study, you will find some probing questions listed under the title, "Thinking It Through." Students must draw upon their reading of the text as well as their own critical thinking skills to respond to these questions.
- **Sidelight.** As extensions to the text, these features provide additional information for students. The information stands out, providing opportunities for additional discussion and easy reference.
- **I Can.** Young people today need opportunities to see that they can succeed in life, even in small ways. These features are designed to show in first-person format how other teens have tackled sometimes tough situations and succeeded. Questions at the end of each feature take students into the example and then channel them into relating the situation to their own lives.
- **Balancing Work and Family.** These features focus on the challenges that today's families face as they try to juggle the many demands on their time. Students learn about the importance of setting aside quality time for family members, of teamwork in the family, of compromise, and of using time effectively. The features suggest strategies for successful coping in the home and on the job. Each feature ends with questions that encourage students to explore what they have read and suggest other ways of dealing with specific family problems.
- **Reaching Out.** These features appear at the end of each of the ten units of the text. The primary objective is to help students see that reaching out to others is an important part of getting along in life. Reaching out does not necessarily mean doing something grand. People can reach out to each other in many ways. These features show how ten young people reach out to others. The first-person accounts also explain how these young people have had an effect on others. The topics for these features include reaching out to a peer in need; to friends in conflict; to an unemployed parent; to peers about responsible sexuality; to a single parent; to members of a blended family; to a friend in crisis; to customers in an after-school job; to the neighborhood through a community project; and to an elderly neighbor. At the end of each unit feature, students are encouraged through questions to examine how they might reach out themselves in similar ways.

◆ Chapter Review Pages

Each chapter ends with a two-page review section. This material can be used to help students better understand the chapter, to check how well students have mastered chapter content, and to help them prepare for the chapter test. The components are:

- **Summarizing the Chapter.** This is a list of the main points covered in the chapter.
- **Testing Your Memory.** These are objective questions based on information presented in the chapter. (Answers are provided beside the questions in the Teacher's Annotated Edition of the text.)
- **Thinking Critically**. Critical thinking skills are needed to respond to these questions. Students must go beyond the text, examining their own opinions and using their reasoning abilities to come up with answers. (Although answers to these questions will generally vary, some points to emphasize with students are provided in the answer key beside the questions in the Teacher's Annotated Edition of the text.)
- **Taking Action.** You may wish to assign one or more of these activities to students to help them do further exploration. These activities are designed to help students reinforce, apply, and extend chapter learning.
- **Making Life Choices.** Each review section has a short case study that presents a situation in which a decision must be made. Students are asked to respond. They must evaluate what is going on in the situation and suggest a decision. These are excellent for class discussion or for writing exercises.
- **Using Your Journal.** Journal-writing activities in the review encourage students to use a private journal to explore their thoughts on a variety of the issues covered in the text. Students are told in the Chapter 1 activity that the journal is for their own use and that they will not be asked to show what they write to anyone. The idea here is to encourage students to be honest with themselves about sensitive issues and to use their journals to explore ways of dealing with personal problems.

◆◆◆

What's in the Back of the Book?

The reference materials in the back of the *Married and Single Life* text are:

- **Glossary.** The Glossary defines all of the chapter vocabulary terms. Pronunciation guides are included for difficult terms. Students can use the glossary to quickly review their understanding of new terms.
- **Index.** A complete alphabetical index provides easy reference to the subject matter.

We welcome comments from teachers and students on this and other Glencoe Family and Consumer Sciences publications. Address your letters to:

Director of Family and Consumer Sciences
Glencoe/McGraw-Hill
3008 W. Willow Knolls Drive
Peoria, IL 61614

Using the Teacher's Annotated Edition

The book in your hands is the Teacher's Annotated Edition (TAE) of the *Married and Single Life* text. The Teacher's Manual at the front of the TAE, which you are now reading, provides information about the text and all its components. Included in the manual is a Scope and Sequence Chart. It shows how major themes are woven throughout the text. You will find it useful for:

- Planning your course.
- Sequencing courses.
- Emphasizing particular course themes.
- Correlating *Married and Single Life* to your curriculum.

The TAE also includes annotations for teacher use printed at the bottom of each text page. These annotations are of eight different types, as explained below:

- **Chapter Opener.** To introduce the chapter, refer to these discussion questions that pertain to the scenario that begins each chapter. After students have read the scenario or you have read it together, use these questions to guide students into thinking about some of the points that will be covered in the chapter.
- **Discussion.** Some ideas for discussion are presented here in question format.
- **Activity.** These are activities you may want to try in class. Some may be accomplished in a short time. Others may require some outside time and preparation. Some are suggested as group activities.
- **Problem Solving.** These are generally activities with a problem theme. Students are asked to do some evaluating and find solutions.
- **Life Management Skills.** These are discussion ideas or activities with a life management theme. Students are asked to come up with management techniques that would be useful in the situation described.
- **Work and Family**. Whenever relevant, students are asked to respond to situations that deal with balancing work and family life.
- **More About.** The text can be expanded with information provided in these annotations. Sometimes an idea for increasing students' understanding is also included with the information. Occasionally a reference to another part of the text is provided here.
- **Photo Focus.** With these annotations you can focus attention on a particular photo in the text. Discussion can be generated by the questions suggested.

The TAE also provides answers to two question sections, "Testing Your Memory" and "Thinking Critically," on the review pages of each chapter.

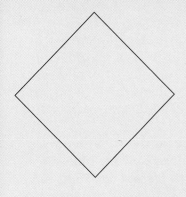

Using Other Program Components

◆◆◆

Student Workbook

The *Married and Single Life* Student Workbook provides a variety of well-planned, ready-to-use activity sheets for each chapter. They are designed to help students master the text content, extend their learning, apply basic academic skills, and strengthen higher-level thinking skills.

Study guides are also provided in the workbook. These can be used to guide students' reading and/or to review the chapter concepts in preparation for tests.

Directions for the guides and activity sheets are easy to follow with a minimum of teacher guidance. The 8½" x 11" sheets are perforated so that they can be easily detached and turned in for checking. (You may want to ask students to keep their completed assignments in a folder or notebook.) Answers to Student Workbook activity sheets and study guides are found in a special teacher's edition of the Student Workbook.

Please note that the *Married and Single Life* Student Workbook is designed as a consumable workbook for use by one student. Reproduction of these sheets for classroom use is a violation of copyright.

◆◆◆

Teacher's Classroom Resources

The Teacher's Classroom Resources box contains a variety of resources that complete the *Married and Single Life* program. The key features of the TCR are described here. For a better understanding of what the box contains, see the TCR itself.

◆ Booklets

A complete package of supplemental materials comes to you in a format that is easy to access and use. Separate booklets, most with perforated, tear-out pages, give you many options for planning, teaching, and assessing. The booklets included in the Teacher's Classroom Resources box are:

- **Student Workbook TAE.** An annotated edition of the workbook, showing answers in place.
- **Balancing Work and Family**. A new booklet that addresses issues students will encounter when they move out into the workplace, but that also recognizes students' needs for many life manage-

ment skills in order to cope with the demands of school, work, family, and so on. Many of the worksheets present scenarios that ask students to offer solutions for the problems presented.

- **Responsible Relationships.** A new booklet that offers students opportunities to explore relationship issues and develop skills in dealing with the different people in their lives.
- **Building Life Skills.** Worksheets designed to give students practice with the following skills: communicating; conflict resolution; coping; decision making; management; and problem solving.
- **Dealing with Sensitive Issues.** Material that helps you discuss issues such as depression, teen suicide, abuse, sexuality, and more. Background information is provided along with teaching strategies designed for sharing and discussing sensitive material with your students.
- **Extending the Text.** Reproducible handouts that provide supplementary information for students, expanding on chapter topics for in-depth learning. Others are activity-oriented.
- **Lesson Plans.** Chapter-by-chapter lesson plans offer lists of all the resources in the TCR and the Student Workbook that can be used for teaching a particular chapter. In addition, the lesson plans offer a variety of activity ideas for introducing the lesson, teaching the lesson, completing the lesson, and evaluating students. The activities include reteaching activities for use with students who may be struggling and need special help, and enrichment activities for students with extra ability who need supplemental work.
- **Testing Program.** A complete set of chapter and unit tests in reproducible format. Matching, true-false, multiple choice, and essay items are included. An answer key is included at the back of the booklet.
- **ABCNews InterActive™ Videodiscs Correlation.** Shows how the videodiscs can be used with *Married and Single Life* and with other family and consumer sciences titles published by Glencoe/McGraw-Hill.

◆ Color Transparencies

This package provides almost 50 ready-to-use transparencies in full color. Included in the package is a booklet of specific teaching suggestions to help you make the most effective use of each transparency. You will find the transparencies a valuable tool for introducing topics, reinforcing concepts, sparking discussion, and developing higher-level thinking skills. This package can also be purchased separately from the Teacher's Classroom Resources box.

◆ ABCNews InterActive™ Videodiscs

The *ABCNews Interactive™ Videodiscs* offer nonjudgmental explorations of the following issues: Violence Prevention; Teenage Sexuality; Drugs and Substance Abuse; Alcohol; Tobacco; AIDS; and Food and Nutrition. For each topic, the program offers a videodisc accompanied by a guidebook with barcoded lesson plans, a print directory, and software. ABC News anchor Ted Koppel provides the on-screen editorial structure. A correlation showing how the videodiscs can be used with *Married and Single Life* is included in the TCR.

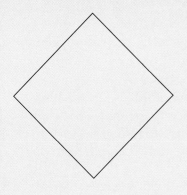

Teaching with Married and Single Life

When teaching with the *Married and Single Life* text, you are likely to use classroom discussion as a common teaching technique. Stimulating discussions seldom just happen. They require some effort for success, through planning and skilled leadership.

◆◆◆

Preparing for Discussions

Before you can have a worthwhile classroom discussion, several factors should be considered:

- **Climate.** The best discussions take place when class members are willing and eager to participate. If students do not know each other well, they may be reluctant to participate in the discussion, particularly if the subject matter is sensitive. You may want to use ice-breaker activities to help students get used to expressing their opinions and feelings. They are more likely to talk freely if they know each other fairly well and have built a feeling of trust in the classroom. To move in this direction, one teacher hands out index cards and asks students to write several things about themselves that people probably don't know. These are then placed in a basket, drawn out, and read. Students must then link a classmate with the descriptions on each card. As a result, students learn more about each other and have the opportunity to become closer.
- **Consideration.** An attitude of respect is imperative for good discussions. Students must realize that each person is entitled to his or her opinion. It is okay to disagree. It is not okay to make personal attacks. Allow for humor as long as it does not take a disrespectful direction.
- **Content.** Discussion topics must be worthwhile and relevant. A lively discussion is not likely to result if students have no interest in, or understanding of, the subject. You will want to be sure that students have the background information they need and that the topic has been clearly presented.

If you are planning a discussion on a controversial topic, exercise some caution. Talk to your principal first to see how this should be handled. If special measures must be taken, such as a letter home to parents, he or she can advise you of this.

◆◆◆

Choosing a Format for Discussion

Perhaps the most common format for discussion occurs when the teacher stands before the class and leads the entire group in discussion via questioning. This is fine, but you may want to try something different on occasion. For example:

- Sit down within the group so that you are not as much of an authority figure and so that students can talk more easily with each other rather than just with you.
- Arrange chairs so that students face each other to encourage exchanges. Perhaps a circle would work.
- Form small groups for separate discussions. This may be less intimidating to some students. Be sure to make groups accountable for their discussions. That is, they must report back the results of their discussion in some way. A secretary, for example, could be appointed to take notes on the discussion.

  Use different techniques to form groups. You might have students number off, divide them alphabetically, or put birth months together. Never allow students to form groups themselves by a choosing technique that turns into a popularity contest. This can be devastating to those who are unchosen or selected last.
- Divide into two teams to debate an issue, or have two students present opposing views to the class.
- Select a panel to discuss the topic before the large group. Follow with questions.

◆◆◆

Managing a Discussion

This is the most challenging part – facilitating a good discussion. What techniques can you use to make it go well? Keep these pointers in mind:

- Be enthusiastic. This can be infectious. If students sense your interest in the topic, they are more likely to follow your lead.
- Give students time to respond. Some students need more time than others to put their thoughts together. If the quickest responders and the most aggressive ones always get recognition, more reflective students will be deterred from participating.
- Try to involve everyone. You may want to say something like, "Let's get many opinions out in the open," or "Jeff has shared his opinion with us. Now let's hear some others."
- Use good questioning. Questions should not be answerable by "yes" or "no." Formulating key questions ahead of time will help.
- Encourage students to use critical thinking skills. Although questions at all levels are appropriate at times, those at the higher levels are more challenging. Students can be encouraged to identify cause and effect; make inferences; recognize other points of view; analyze decisions; recognize bias, propaganda, assumptions, values, and stereotypes; compare and contrast; make predictions; analyze behavior; make generalizations; draw conclusions; and form hypotheses.
- Occasionally appoint a student discussion leader. This gives students a chance to develop leadership skills and to experience the discussion process from the teacher's point of view.
- Evaluate the results. Some discussions will be more successful than others. Take a few minutes to reflect on what worked and didn't work for you and your class. You may even want to ask for feedback from your students. This will help you move toward even better discussions in the future.

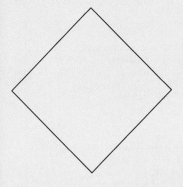

Scope and Sequence Chart

This chart shows how major themes are woven throughout *Married and Single Life*. You will find it useful for:

- Planning your course.
- Sequencing courses.
- Emphasizing particular course themes.
- Correlating *Married and Single Life* to your curriculum.

SCOPE AND SEQUENCE

	Chapter 1 Your Personality	Chapter 2 Your Development
COMMUNICATION SKILLS		• Early language development
COPING WITH CHALLENGES	• Rebuilding self-esteem after troubled times	• Dealing with negative emotions
DECISION MAKING/ PROBLEM SOLVING		• Development of formal thinking • Deciding on plans to overcome negative emotions
FAMILY STRENGTH	• Positive family influences on personality, self-concept, and self-esteem • Spending quality time with family members	• Family as stimulus for intellectual development • Family as training ground for social skills • Family as provider of emotional skills
HANDLING RESPONSIBILITY	• Guidelines for building one's own self-esteem	• Recognizing and dealing with negative emotions • Developing one's own values and standards for behavior
HEALTH AND WELLNESS	• Building blocks of emotional and mental health • Self-concept • Building self-esteem	• Physical and intellectual development • Basic needs for good emotional development • Dealing with emotions
MANAGEMENT SKILLS		• Managing negative emotions
RELATIONSHIP SKILLS	• Being assertive • Positive attitude	• Socialization • Handling anger constructively
SOURCES OF HELP		• Talking emotional problems over with others • Professional counselors
VALUES AND GOALS	• Changing bad habits	• Moral development • Moral choices • Religious principles as a moral guide

Chapter 3 Your Character	Chapter 4 Your Health	Chapter 5 Your Future
• Listening to others		
	• Managing stress • Addiction	
• Responsibility and decision making • Decisions and code of ethics • Deciding on ranking values	• Decisions affecting wellness and healthy lifestyle	• Deciding what one wants from life • Setting goals to accomplish desired lifestyle
• Caring for Family • Developing a positive attitude	• Seeking help for family problems • Making time for family meals	• Being a responsible family member
• Building a strong code of ethics • Becoming responsible for self and for others • Making well thought-out decisions, acting on them, and living with the results	• Practicing habits that promote wellness • Learning positive ways of handling stress • Saying "no" to tobacco, alcohol, and drugs	• Setting goals for oneself • Taking control of one's own life
	• Good hygiene • Nutrition • Sleep and exercise • Defense mechanisms • Handling stress • Tobacco, alcohol, and drugs • Eating disorders	• Maslow's five basic human needs
	• Stress management skills • Developing a good eating plan	• Guidelines for taking control of one's own life
• Becoming unselfish • Positive and negative attitudes • Showing respect and empathy		• Being a responsible family member
	• Talking stress over with adult or friends • Alcoholics Anonymous • Counseling and self-help groups	
• Code of ethics • Choosing and ranking values	• Wellness and healthy lifestyle	• Choosing goals for future as adult • Relating goals to values • Values and lifestyle choices

SCOPE AND SEQUENCE	Chapter 6 Communicating Effectively	Chapter 7 Making Decisions
COMMUNICATION SKILLS	• Verbal and nonverbal communication • Barriers to communication • Levels of communication • Attitudes for effective communication • Skills in timing, straight talk, and active listening	
COPING WITH CHALLENGES		• Peer pressure • Problem-solving skills
DECISION MAKING/ PROBLEM SOLVING		• Effects of decisions • Steps in decision making • Approaches to decision making • Using decision-making skills to solve problems • Analyzing problem by breaking it into parts
FAMILY STRENGTH	• Using good communication to create understanding of each other's problems and needs • Sharing ideas and emotions to build stronger family bonds	• Helping members learn to make decisions
HANDLING RESPONSIBILITY		• Making decisions for oneself • Considering effects of decisions on others • Accepting responsibility for and dealing with consequences of decisions • Resisting impulse decisions
HEALTH AND WELLNESS		
MANAGEMENT SKILLS		• Using decision-making process and problem-solving skills
RELATIONSHIP SKILLS	• Positive verbal and nonverbal communication • Importance of communication in relationships • Showing empathy • Effective communication skills; includes timing, straight talk, and active listening • Etiquette for introductions and the phone	• Considering decision's possible effects on others
SOURCES OF HELP		
VALUES AND GOALS	• Becoming a good communicator	• Weighing values in decision making • Importance of decision making in achieving goals

Chapter 8 Handling Conflict	Chapter 9 Learning to Manage	Chapter 10 Patterns of Family Living
• Importance of communication in settling conflicts • Poor communication as cause of conflict	• Brainstorming ideas in a group • Written plan for group endeavors	• Entertainment technology's effects on family communication
• Preventing conflict • Negative and positive approach to handling conflict • Learning to compromise to settle conflict	• Being resourceful to make up for resources that are limited or lacking	• Stepfamilies • Dealing with changes throughout family life cycle • Dealing with changing roles in middle years • Dealing with changes caused by retirement and aging
• Arriving at compromise	• Deciding on goals • Deciding on plan to achieve goals	• Decisions involving readjustment during empty nest stage • Elderly's housing choices
• Family conference to air complaints and settle differences • Openly discussing grievances with family members • Compromise	• Teamwork in the family	• Establishing feelings of trust and interdependence in early years of marriage • Support and care for family members with problems
• Preventing conflict • Positive resolution of conflict	• Setting and achieving personal goals • Being resourceful • Acting as responsible member of a group	• Responsibilities of parenthood • Caring for one's parents in later years
• Physical and emotional injuries caused by violence		• Health problems related to aging • Nutrition for elderly • Effects of loneliness and depression on elderly • Domestic violence
	• Setting goals • Recognizing and utilizing resources • Five-step planning process • Managing within a group	• Adjusting to changes throughout family life cycle
• Preventing conflicts with others • Seeing others' points of view • Learning tolerance • Learning to compromise • Controlling one's temper	• Working in a group	• Negotiation and adjustment in stepfamilies
	• Mentors	• Medicare • Community centers
• Differing values as cause of conflict with others	• Setting long- and short-term goals • Developing a plan for achieving goals	• Setting new goals when children grow up and leave home

SCOPE AND SEQUENCE	Chapter 11 Living in a Family	Chapter 12 Facing Family Challenges
COMMUNICATION SKILLS	• Talking and listening to each other to form family bonds • Openly discussing disagreements • Showing affection with words and actions	• Showing empathy • Talking over problems • Showing grieving persons you care
COPING WITH CHALLENGES	• Adjusting to changing roles in the family	• Stress in dual-earner families • Unemployment • Stress of moving to new area • Serious illness or disability of family member • Alcoholism and other addictions • Family violence and abuse • Suicidal tendencies • Death of loved one • Coping skills
DECISION MAKING/ PROBLEM SOLVING	• Joint discussions to decide on ways to solve problems	• Coping skills for dealing with problems • Deciding ways to balance work and family
FAMILY STRENGTH	• Commitment; putting family first • Communication and understanding • Spending time together • Demonstrating affection and appreciation • Establishing family traditions • Shared beliefs • Sharing memories	• Being supportive • Sharing workloads • Working together to deal with life's challenges • Sharing memories of a deceased loved one
HANDLING RESPONSIBILITY	• Working to play a positive role in one's family	• Sharing family workload • Developing coping skills
HEALTH AND WELLNESS	• Family as provider of emotional needs	• Emotional effects of unemployment • Effects of alcoholism • Effects of abuse and neglect • Signs of suicidal feelings
MANAGEMENT SKILLS		• Scheduling and planning for dual-earner families • Using coping skills
RELATIONSHIP SKILLS	• Showing empathy • Openly discussing feelings and problems • Openly demonstrating appreciation and affection • Giving sincere compliments	• Being supportive • Becoming informed about challenges others face in order to offer understanding and support
SOURCES OF HELP	• Professional counselor • Minister • Family support systems	• Alcoholics Anonymous • Child welfare agencies • Shelters for battered women • Counselors • Suicide prevention centers • Community mental health centers • Welfare assistance
VALUES AND GOALS	• Prioritizing family's welfare and happiness	• Setting priorities for how time is best spent • Dealing positively with life's challenges

Chapter 13 Friendships	Chapter 14 Dating	Chapter 15 Love and Commitment
• Sharing feelings • Openly talking over differences • Showing caring through words and actions	• Practicing social talk • Open and honest discussion	• Long talks • Open and frank discussion of feelings and needs
• Peer pressure	• Shyness • Peer pressure • Date rape • Ending relationships	• Broken relationships • Jealousy
	• Determining dating readiness • Choosing who to date • Ending a relationship	• Deciding if it is lasting love • Determining readiness for commitment
	• Parental concerns about dating	• Love of family members
• Resisting peer pressure • Holding up one's end of friendship	• Practicing responsible freedom in dating	• Committing oneself to a relationship
	• Dealing with financial limitations	
• Making other person feel important • Standing by friends in times of trouble • Being trustworthy	• Showing courtesy • Being oneself • Sharing thoughts and experiences	• Assessing compatibility • Thoughtful gestures • Talking
• Values and friend choice • Peer pressure versus personal values	• Determining qualities wanted in a date	• Values and intellectual love • Effects of commitment to relationship on life goals

SCOPE AND SEQUENCE

	Chapter 16 Sexuality in Relationships	Chapter 17 The Status of Singles
COMMUNICATION SKILLS		
COPING WITH CHALLENGES	• Consequences of teen pregnancy • Resisting sexual involvement • Peer pressure • Handling desire	• Economic difficulties • Being thrust into singlehood after death of spouse or divorce
DECISION MAKING/ PROBLEM SOLVING	• Deciding on abstinence or sexual activity	• Choosing singlehood • Delayed marriage
FAMILY STRENGTH		• Security of family nest
HANDLING RESPONSIBILITY	• Understanding risks of sexual involvement • Resisting pressure to become sexually active • Not pressuring partner into sexual involvement • Learning to handle desire • Making commitment	• Learning to be self-supporting
HEALTH AND WELLNESS	• Sexually transmitted diseases	• Personal fulfillment • AIDS
MANAGEMENT SKILLS		• Establishing independent lifestyle
RELATIONSHIP SKILLS	• Thinking of others, not just self-gratification • Learn to understand one's own feelings and those of opposite sex	• Cooperation and consideration in joint living
SOURCES OF HELP	• Health clinics for those with STDs	
VALUES AND GOALS	• Self-esteem and sexuality • Concern for others and sexuality • Moral conscience and sexuality	• Desire for independence and freedom • Career involvement • Desire for financial stability

Chapter 18 Successful Single Living	Chapter 19 Marriage Customs and Laws	Chapter 20 The Decision to Marry
• Meeting new people • Developing mutually agreed-on ground rules for shared living arrangements	• Discussing expectations • Written prenuptial agreements and marriage contracts • Oral wedding vows	• Discussing convictions, expectations, and lifetime goals
• Managing finances • Developing relationships • Fulfilling desire for children • Shared living arrangements • Single parenthood		• Interfaith marriage • Interracial marriage
• Choosing housing • Developing new relationships	• Deciding on prenuptial agreement or marriage contract	• Choosing marriage partner • Deciding to marry • Deciding on roles in marriage • Deciding on having children; if, when, how many
• Setting ground rules when adult offspring move back in with parents	• Developing marriage contract to outline and clarify important concerns	• Marriage partners with shared interests, values, goals, and convictions • Parental approval of marriage
• Balancing monthly income and expenses • Saving money for future • Contributing fair share of workload and expenses in shared living arrangements	• Meeting all legal requirements for marriage	• Getting to know prospective mate and oneself before marriage • Planning and budgeting a wedding
• Safety • Maintaining good eating habits • Fulfillment and contentment for emotional health	• Consanguinity and genetics	
• Financial planning and management • Managing shared living arrangements • Managing as single parent	• Acquiring all the documents and meeting all requirements for marriage • Marriage contracts and prenuptial agreements	• Planning and preparing for a wedding • Budgeting a wedding
• Seeking out new friendships in new community • Setting up ground rules when entering shared living arrangements	• Agreeing on what is wanted out of and expected in a marriage before entering into it	• Compatibility with prospective mate's family and friends • Sharing interests, goals, and convictions with future partner • Agreeing on role expectations
• Big Brother/Big Sister program • Support groups	• City or county clerk • Clergy	• Religious and professional counseling
• Planning for a secure financial future • Fulfilling desire for children • Finding a purpose in life	• Establishing marital expectations • Meeting legal requirements for marriage	• Interests; mutuality of and importance of • Desired qualities in partner • Shared lifetime goals • Convictions; religious and worldly • Desire for children • Role expectations

SCOPE AND SEQUENCE

	Chapter 21 Successful Marriage	Chapter 22 Divorce and Remarriage
COMMUNICATION SKILLS	• Making list of division of responsibilities • Discussing feelings openly, but calmly • Listening and giving understanding and helpful feedback • Showing affection	• Talking over problems • Explaining divorce in ways a child can understand
COPING WITH CHALLENGES	• Handling finances • Resolving conflicts • Sexual compatibility • Getting along with in-laws	• Marital problems • Divorce or separation from spouse • Divorce or separation of parents • Being a non-custodial parent • Blended families
DECISION MAKING/ PROBLEM SOLVING	• Joint decision making • Deciding on roles and division of responsibilities	• Working at saving a marriage • Ending a marriage • Custody of children
FAMILY STRENGTH	• Displaying affection and showing thoughtfulness • Making time for each other • Getting along with in-laws • Non-interference in adult offsprings' lives	• Both parents helping children adjust to divorce, giving them plenty of love and reassurance • Blended families learning to trust, accept, adjust, compromise, and pull together
HANDLING RESPONSIBILITY	• Sharing responsibilities for cooking, household chores, shopping, child care, and paperwork • Commitment	• Working to save a troubled marriage • Helping children adjust to divorce
HEALTH AND WELLNESS	• Intimacy and affection • Sexual compatibility	• Emotional effects of divorce • Rebuilding self-esteem • Marital problems and work performance
MANAGEMENT SKILLS	• Managing household finances • Joint decision making • Plan for division of responsibilities	• Starting life over after divorce • Adjusting to life in blended family
RELATIONSHIP SKILLS	• Accepting each other • Dealing with problems as they arise • Compromise • Thoughtfulness and not taking each other for granted • Making time for each other	• Compromise • Applying what is learned from failure of first marriage to future relationships • Learning to adjust, accept, and pull together in blended families
SOURCES OF HELP	• Marriage encounter or enrichment groups	• Marriage and family counselors • Self-help groups • Family and friends
VALUES AND GOALS	• Making a commitment	• Weighing the pros and cons in a marriage • Setting new goals after divorce

Chapter 23 Parenting Decisions	Chapter 24 Becoming a Parent	Chapter 25 Parenting the Young Child
• Discussing whether and when to have children	• Discussing health care and diet with doctor	• Infants' crying • Development of language skills
• Infertility • Teenage parenthood • Unplanned pregnancy	• Complications during pregnancy	• Dealing with temper tantrums
• Deciding to become a parent • Choosing a contraceptive method • Decisions about unplanned pregnancy	• Deciding on childbirth methods	
• Grandparents helping care for children • Father taking more active role in parenting	• Father's support of mother in preparing for birth and birth process	• Bonding with both parents • Encouragement, reinforcement, security, and love
• Sharing household and child care responsibilities • Changing lifestyle to take on parenting role • Making personal and financial sacrifices for children • Responsibility and contraception	• Having good prenatal care and nutrition during pregnancy • Avoiding tobacco, alcohol, and drugs during pregnancy	• Providing a nurturing environment • Learning about patterns of development in order to understand behavior, provide for needs, and recognize problems
• Emotional readiness for parenthood • Age and pregnancy • Contraception • Infertility • Health problems in teen pregnancy	• Reproductive systems • Conception • Genetics • Signs of and testing for pregnancy • Prenatal development • Health care during pregnancy • Problem pregnancies • Drugs, alcohol, and tobacco • Sexually transmitted diseases • Birth process	• Physical, intellectual, social, and emotional development—birth to preschool
• Financial planning for raising children	• Preparing for birth	• Using knowledge about child development as parenting tool
• Being emotionally ready for parenthood		• Young children spending time with peers • Games as play for preschoolers • Understanding child's patterns of development in order to better deal with behavior
• Educational programs for teenage parents • AFDC • Women, Infants, and Children (WIC) program	• Genetic counseling	
• Desire for children • Values and contraception • Education and teenage parenthood • Unplanned pregnancy and adoption	• Working at having healthy pregnancy to help ensure healthy baby	• Moral development

SCOPE AND SEQUENCE

	Chapter 26 Responsible Parenting	Chapter 27 Finding the Right Career
COMMUNICATION SKILLS	• Language development • Explaining reasons for rules and discipline • Listening and paying attention to children	• Discussing career with those in the profession • Letter of application and resume • Job interview—attitude, behavior, questions, and answers
COPING WITH CHALLENGES	• Children with special needs • Child abuse • Parenting problems	• Paying for education and training
DECISION MAKING/ PROBLEM SOLVING	• Choosing toys appropriate to age and ability • Deciding on rules and appropriate discipline • Choosing child care	• Choosing and planning for a career • Deciding where to go for education and training
FAMILY STRENGTH	• Building a nurturing environment • Family working together to give extra encouragement to child with special needs	• Finding a job that meshes with family life
HANDLING RESPONSIBILITY	• Meeting child's physical, social, intellectual, and emotional needs • Providing guidance and discipline • Preparing child for unsafe situations • Choosing child care that provides nurturing, safe environment	• Choosing appropriate career • Making plans and choices needed to achieve desired career • Finding financing for education and training • Applying for a job
HEALTH AND WELLNESS	• Physical needs of infants and children • Building child's self-esteem	• Work and self-esteem
MANAGEMENT SKILLS	• Using knowledge about child's development as parenting tool	• Analyzing self and values when selecting a career • Exploring career opportunities • Setting long- and short-term goals • Planning for education and training • Arranging to finance education or training • Getting a job
RELATIONSHIP SKILLS	• Providing social experiences • Providing behavior guidelines	• Making a positive impression in job interview
SOURCES OF HELP	• Social service agencies • Hospital services • Counseling • Support groups • Child care classes • Child welfare agencies • Libraries	• Publications with career information • People involved in chosen field • School guidance counselor • Scholarships • Government-sponsored financial aid and educational programs
VALUES AND GOALS	• Moral development • Parental goal of child with healthy self-esteem and self-confidence	• Work ethic • Values and career choice • Short- and long-term goals in career planning

Chapter 28 On the Job	Chapter 29 Managing Your Money	Chapter 30 Buying Know-How
• Listening to directions • Constructive criticism	• Discussing money management in shared household	• Listening to or reading ads carefully • Reading labels and warranties • Reading consumer magazines • Discussing products and businesses with others
• Losing a job • Discrimination • Sexual harassment	• Financial problems	• Problems with a purchase
• Deciding career goals • Deciding to change jobs • Deciding to relocate	• Deciding on spending plan • Investment decisions • Deciding when and how to use credit • Solving financial problems	• Deciding where to make purchase • Deciding on product or brand to buy
• How moving affects families • Impact of work on family life	• Married couple making financial decisions as team	
• Improving skills and knowledge to advance on the job • Considering others when deciding to relocate • Being dependable • Being a willing worker • Using constructive criticism to better oneself • Ethical behavior	• Developing a wise spending plan • Saving for emergencies and future • Using credit wisely	• Becoming informed about products and services • Comparing products, services, and prices • Saving sales receipts, labels, and guarantees • Resisting impulse buying • Knowing rights as consumer and what to do if they are violated
• Gaining knowledge, improving skills, and watching for opportunity to advance on job • Using commuter time productively • Balancing work and home life	• Planning a budget and sticking to it • Saving money • Managing a checking account • Making investments • Wise use of credit	• Evaluating advertising, researching product, and comparison shopping before buying
• Positive attitude • Dependability • Willingness to work • Tolerance • Honesty and ethical behavior	• Making joint financial decisions • Compromise	• Resisting high-pressure sales techniques
• Unemployment compensation • Equal Employment Opportunities Commission	• Consumer credit counseling services • Attorneys • Welfare office	• Consumer magazines • Better Business Bureau • Consumer protection agencies
• Setting and revising goals for developing career • Being a good employee • Ethics and professionalism	• Setting financial goals and budgeting for them • Using credit to help achieve long-term goals	• Effects of values and goals on spending • Getting the most for one's money • Environmental awareness

SCOPE AND SEQUENCE

	Chapter 31 Making Consumer Decisions	Chapter 32 The Middle Years
COMMUNICATION SKILLS	• Reading consumer publications, ads, labels, warranties, leases, and purchase agreements	• Establishing ground rules for adult children who return home and for elderly relatives to move into their child's home
COPING WITH CHALLENGES		• Dealing with transition • Demands made on "sandwich generation" • Adjusting to changing family circumstances
DECISION MAKING/ PROBLEM SOLVING	• Choosing housing • Buying a car • Choosing insurance	• Midlife reassessment • Career changes • Learning new skills
FAMILY STRENGTH		• Adapting to "empty nest" • Becoming a grandparent • Adult children returning home • Care of elderly relatives
HANDLING RESPONSIBILITY	• Making housing choices • Checking for quality and comparison shopping before buying • Making a will • Getting insurance to protect self, family, possessions, and property	
HEALTH AND WELLNESS	• Nutrition and meal planning • Health insurance • Health Maintenance Organizations	• Dealing with menopause • Need for regular exercise, balanced diet, regular checkups
MANAGEMENT SKILLS	• Evaluating housing before renting or buying • Research, evaluation, and comparison shopping before buying • Using creativity and imagination to help cut expenses	• Planning for retirement
RELATIONSHIP SKILLS		
SOURCES OF HELP	• Community events and recreation areas • Medical and legal clinics	
VALUES AND GOALS	• Home ownership as goal • Saving money on purchases, energy, and recreation • Furnishing home in stages • Car ownership as goal • Protecting self and family with insurance	• Seeking a new and challenging career • Continuing education for the sake of learning • Financial security as a goal

Chapter 33 The Later Years
• Establishing rules when older person moves in with grown children
• Dealing with ageism • Link between emotional health and person's interests • Adjusting to retirement • Living on a fixed income • Dealing with death of partner
• How to spend time after retirement • Dealing with financial problems • Dealing with transportation problems • Making housing decisions
• Adjustments when older person moves in with grown children
• Political and economic power of older people • Writing a living will
• Greater longevity of population • Physical aspects of aging • Mental and emotional aspects of aging • Diseases and disorders associated with old age • Depression associated with loss
• Meals on Wheels • Community centers • Social Service Agencies • Respite care programs • Hospice movement
• Living independently as long as possible

NOTES

NOTES

Married & Single Life

Sixth Edition

Teacher's Annotated Edition

Married & Single Life

Sixth Edition

Audrey Palm Riker   Holly E. Brisbane

GLENCOE
McGraw-Hill

New York, New York   Columbus, Ohio   Mission Hills, California   Peoria, Illinois

Contributors

Janis Meek, M.S., CFCS
Home Economics Teacher
Warren County High School
Warrenton, North Carolina

Linda R. Glosson, Ph.D., CFCS
Home Economics Teacher
Wylie High School
Wylie, Texas

Vicki K. Hornung, M.S.
Home Economist and Teacher
United Local Schools
Hanoverton, Ohio

Carolyn S. Morse, M.S.
Home Economics Teacher
Booker T. Washington High School
Houston, Texas

Sharon S. Smith, Ph.D., CFCS
Consultant
Long Beach, California

Mark Bregman

Janet McGrath

Kathryn Spitznagle

Cover photos from Stock Market CD 2

Glencoe/McGraw-Hill

A Division of The **McGraw-Hill** *Companies*

Previous copyrights 1988 and 1984 under the title *Married and Single Life* and 1976 and 1970 under the title *Married Life* by Audrey Palm Riker and Holly E. Brisbane.

Printed in the United States of America

Send all inquiries to:
Glencoe/McGraw-Hill
3008 W. Willow Knolls Drive
Peoria, IL 61614-1083

ISBN 0-02-643000-2 (Student Text)

1 2 3 4 5 6 7 8 9 10 RRDW 00 99 98 97 96

ISBN 0-02-643001-0 (Teacher's Annotated Edition)

1 2 3 4 5 6 7 8 9 10 RRDW 00 99 98 97 96

Contents

UNIT 2

UNIT 3

WHAT ARE FAMILIES LIKE?.........138

UNIT 4

HOW CAN YOU HANDLE RELATIONSHIPS?

UNIT 5

WHAT ABOUT SINGLE LIFE? 238

UNIT 6

UNIT 7

WILL YOU BECOME A PARENT?..326

UNIT 8

WHAT WILL YOUR LIFE'S WORK BE? 390

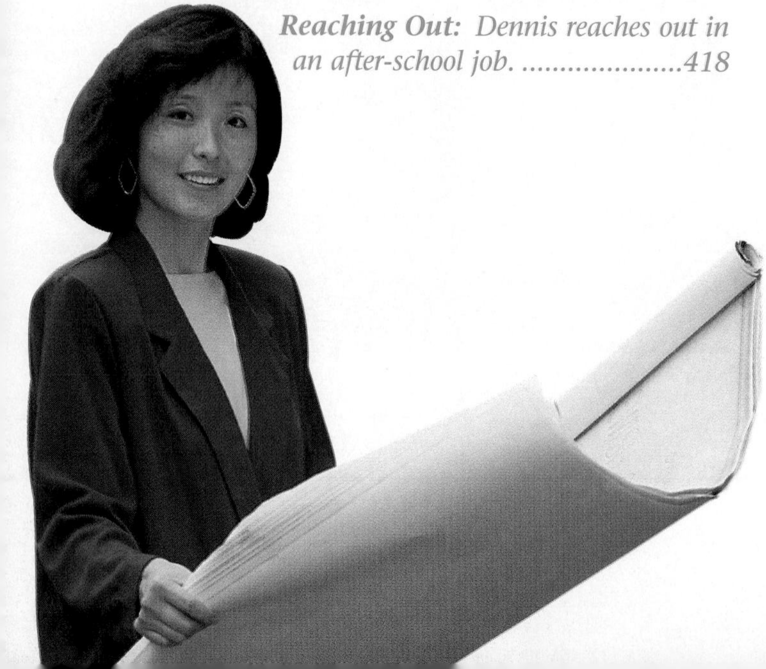

UNIT 9

WILL YOU BE AN INFORMED CONSUMER?....................................420

UNIT 10

UNIT

1

What About You?

CHAPTER

CHAPTER 1

Your Personality

Chapter Challenge

Resources. Refer to the Teacher's Classroom Resources box and Student Workbook for materials related to this chapter.

Look for These Answers . . .

- Why is every person in the world unique?
- What factors influence one's personality?
- Explain Erikson's theory of personality development.
- What are self-concept and self-esteem?
- How does a person build self-esteem?

Look for These Terms . . .

- adolescence
- assertiveness
- culture
- environment
- extroverts
- heredity
- introverts
- personality
- self-concept
- self-esteem

The track team was gathering by the track for its first practice of the season. This was Abigail's first year on the team. As a matter of fact, she had just transferred in from a school in another state.

"How long have you been on the team?" Abigail asked the girl beside her.

"She can't hear you," Pat said. "Salina is hearing impaired. She won't know what you say unless you get her attention first and speak directly at her."

"I see," Abigail replied as she moved closer to Pat.

A few more team members arrived. As they did, some left for different parts of the field. When Chelsey joined the group, she greeted everyone and welcomed Abigail to the team. "I heard you are a good sprinter, Abigail," she said. "We need you." Then Chelsey touched Salina on the arm. While Salina watched, Chelsey's fingers signed a greeting and message to her. Salina smiled and signed back. "Salina and I are going over to the long-jump pit," Chelsey said. "We're going to rake it out."

As they walked away, Abigail asked, "Where did she learn that?"

"She taught herself," Pat replied. "She's about the only one who can have a conversation with Salina."

"Sounds like a lot of work to me," Abigail said. "I wonder why she bothered to learn."

After a long pause, Pat looked at Abigail and said, "I guess that's just the kind of person she is. Maybe that's why everyone likes her so much."

Chapter Opener. Ask students to read the opening scenario to the chapter. Ask the following questions: How would you describe the personality of each teen in the scenario? How do you think Salina feels about Chelsey? Why is Chelsey one of only a few who can communicate with Salina? What enables Chelsey to be the way she is?

Realizing Your Uniqueness

Bubbly, somber, shy, moody, friendly, mischievous, pessimistic, happy, sad: Do any of these words describe people you know? Do any of them match you? Personalities cannot be described in just a few words. It takes many.

Personality is the sum of all characteristics that make a person unique. You have your own distinct personality. Although others may have some traits similar to yours, no one else in the world has exactly the same combination of characteristics that you have.

The word "personality" is derived from the Greek word "persona," which means mask. Many people show the world only certain sides of themselves. They keep other traits hidden from view, as though behind a mask. Other people tend to be more open.

Personality is a very complex concept. It is like a jigsaw puzzle, made up of many different pieces that fit together to form the whole. Each piece of your personality puzzle is one of your characteristics. Someone who wanted to describe your personality would have to identify all of the pieces. Do you think that anyone could do that? Could you?

Discussion. Using the opening story, have students share ideas about why people tend to like someone like Chelsey. In what ways does she reach out to others? What are some other ways that individuals can reach out to others?

◆◆◆

Personality Traits

When Bud moved to Westport High School, it wasn't long before he had a circle of friends. He was outgoing. He smiled at people and struck up conversations with them. Corinne's experience was different. When she arrived she did not seek out companionship. She adjusted to the new school by observing what was going on. Eventually, she became close to a couple students in one class, and they became good friends.

Bud and Corinne represent two classic personality types — the extrovert and introvert. **Extroverts** (EKS-truh-vurts) like to be around people and communicate with them. **Introverts** (IN-truh-vurts) find satisfaction in being alone. They do not require as much interaction with others as extroverts do. Although most people are a blend of both of these, they still tend to lean in one direction or the other. Both are positive personality types unless carried to either extreme. If an extrovert becomes overbearing and an introvert cannot function with others at all, then there is a problem.

As you read earlier, many words describe personality traits. Trying to list them all would be difficult. Where do they all come from? Why did you develop some and not others? Read on and you will see that there are many reasons why you are the way you are.

Extroverts enjoy reaching out to others while introverts are more likely to keep their feelings to themselves. Most people have characteristics of both personality types.

Discussion. Write the words *extrovert* and *introvert* on the board. Ask students to identify characteristics of each type and list their responses. Discuss with students the positive and negative qualities of each type. Ask why, as a society, we need a variety of personality types.

Activity. Have students list five words they would use to describe their own personalities. Share anonymous examples and have the class guess the right person. Ask students to name one or two traits that make each person in the class unique.

◆◆◆

Influences on Personality

The personality puzzle is made of many different qualities. Heredity and environment determine what pieces go into each individual's personality puzzle.

◆ Heredity

Certain traits are passed from parents to children at birth. This is your **heredity** (huh-RED-uht-ee), the qualities that you have inherited. For as long as he can remember, Ty has known that he has natural dancing ability. He can feel the rhythm of the music so clearly, and any dance style comes easily to him. Ty's mother has taught dance classes for years. They both know where Ty's ability came from.

Ty's skill is easy to trace. Many qualities that people inherit are not as easy to see, nor do they point directly to a parent. Heredity is complicated. Some qualities can move down

SIDELIGHT

Influences on Personality

Although the family is a primary influence on your personality, many other factors affect you too. Think about how each of the following has affected your personality:

- **Gender.** Are you male or female? What effect does this have on your personality?
- **Race.** How does your ethnic origin affect who you are?
- **Skills.** What skills do you have? What are your strengths and weaknesses? Are they hereditary? What effect do they have on you?
- **Inherited Qualities.** Besides gender, race, and skills, what other inherited qualities do you have?
- **Beliefs.** Do you have any strong beliefs, perhaps through religious training, that help shape your personality?
- **Friends.** Who are your friends and what qualities do they bring out in you?
- **School.** Who have you known and what have you learned that made a difference to you?
- **Home.** Where do you live? What neighborhood, city, and state? Does this have an effect on your personality?
- **Culture.** What customs and rules do you follow? How do these affect you?

◆◆◆

A person whose parents read a lot for pleasure is more likely to enjoy reading too. Is that a result of heredity or environment?

Activity. Ask students to choose and prepare a brief report on a well-known person who is either an extrovert or introvert. Have them provide examples to defend their positions and offer reasons why the person has developed the particular personality type.

Problem Solving. Have students work in small groups to research and report to the class on a trait that is thought to be genetically inherited. Have them use the library and other available resources to present facts and their own reactions.

from previous generations. This explains why some children often have qualities that are quite different from their parents.

Are people locked in by their heredity? If Leslie is shy by nature, must she remain so the rest of her life? What do you think?

◆ Environment

Your **environment** (in-VY-run-munt), or surroundings, also influences what you are like. This is different for each person. Like the ripples in a pond, the environment may be thought of as a set of circles, all surrounding the same center, the individual. The inner circle contains the family. Experiences within the family help shape the personality of every individual. The next circle goes beyond family to include friends and associates at school, at work, and in the community. Culture (KUL-chur) is also part of this circle. Your **culture** teaches you beliefs, customs, skills, habits, traditions, and knowledge common to those in the community where you live. Your personality will be affected by what you learn. The outer circle represents the larger world environment. The state of the nation and world you live in affects your personality in many ways.

All of these influences make people different — different in personality and different in the ways they relate to others. Even identical twins, who have the same hereditary makeup, will not be the same because of external influences and the way they react to them.

◆ The Family Influence

The family is the most influential environmental factor in shaping personality. Every family has its own emotional climate, to which even the very young baby is sensitive.

Balancing Work & Family

Quality Time

How much of the time you spend with your family is "quality time"? *Quality time* is a term used to describe meaningful interactions between people with few distractions. (Watching a football game together on television is *not* an example of quality time.) Quality time provides a chance for family members to catch up on each other's news, to plan for future events, or just relax together.

Parents are usually very busy providing for their family, making meals, doing household chores. For children and teens, schoolwork and outside activities seem to fill up the day. Many families simply don't set aside quality time for the family to be together. Yet shared time strengthens both the family as a whole and each person in it.

Here are some tips to try in your family:

- ◆ Try to make a habit of getting together to talk when everyone gets home in the evenings.
- ◆ Make it a priority to eat breakfast or dinner together regularly.
- ◆ Work out a plan for a parent to spend time alone with one child each week. Just taking time for each other will help you stay close.
- ◆ Plan short trips, so the family can spend time together away from home.
- ◆ Choose a night as family night, when you all play a favorite family game, or watch a favorite movie together.

Think About It

1. What positive influences might quality time have on family members?
2. What are some ways families can limit distractions during quality time?

More About Personality. Point out that psychologists have studied the influences of heredity and environment on personality by comparing identical twins separated at birth and raised in different homes. You might assign students to find and report on such studies.

Activity. Divide students into small groups and have them report on one custom or tradition from another culture. Have each group explain the meaning and practice of the custom and how it might affect personality.

Babies who live in homes filled with tension are apt to be more fussy and demand more attention than those whose homes are relaxed and loving. Children who grow up in families where hugs and kisses are abundant are usually more open about showing their deeper feelings than those where family members keep their distance.

In addition to the emotional climate, factors such as family size, position in the family, relationships with siblings, working life of parents, and parenting styles affect personality. The family is the major communicator of culture to its members. Also, it is within the context of the family that most people develop their viewpoints on everything from food and entertainment to politics and religion.

◆◆◆

Erikson's Theory

Theories on personality development show how strong the family influence is. According to psychologist Erik Erikson, personal development takes place in a series of stages. Each builds on the one before and can provide a solid base for the next. He suggested that each of these life stages includes a central problem that must be solved before personal development can continue. Preparation for each new task occurs during the previous stage and is worked out gradually. Erikson believed that each stage combines forward-moving urges pushing against forces working against them. The person involved decides

Erikson's Stages of Development

Stage	Age	Central problem to be solved	Outcome if not mastered
Infancy	birth to 1	develop trust	mistrust
Early Childhood	1 to 3	develop autonomy	shame, doubt
Middle Childhood	3 to 5	develop initiative	guilt
Late Childhood	6 to 11	develop industry	inferiority
Adolescence	12 to 18	develop sense of identity	role confusion
Young Adulthood	19 to 30	develop intimacy	isolation
Middle Adulthood	31 to 60	develop generativity	self absorption
Maturity and Old Age	61 to death	develop integrity	despair

Life Management Skills. Using Erikson's personality scheme above, have pairs of students invent and act out situations in which one partner reacts with trust, the other with mistrust; one with approval, the other with criticism; etc. For example, siblings might debate a lost possession, a parent might set a curfew for a teen, or two friends might date the same person. Have the pairs act out results, and reward the best efforts. Have students brainstorm ways to turn mistrust around.

which tug will win out. Only by wrestling with the crisis of your present life stage, can you hope to master it and move on to meet the next one.

For example, in Erikson's first stage infants develop either a basic trust or mistrust of those around them. How much they gain in either direction depends on how well their needs for love, comfort, and food are met by adults who take care of them. Trust leads to a healthy attitude toward life in general. From this foundation, the child develops a feeling of security and an idea that the world is a safe and friendly place. Of course, mistrust can occur if negative conditions exist.

In the second stage the toddler, by learning to walk and talk, gains a sense of independence. If adults punish or discourage these early efforts, feelings of shame and doubt can be the unhappy result.

From ages three to five, children raised in homes with approval and support have a sense of get-up-and-go. They try out new things, expand knowledge, learn sex roles, and learn what is right and wrong. Of course, the opposite is also possible. Children from homes marked by disapproval and criticism may get the idea that they cannot do anything right.

Later, school-aged children have a chance to form good study and work habits. This makes them feel confident about themselves and what they can do. Feelings of failure and inferiority result if they do not succeed and receive praise for their efforts.

The stage of life between childhood and adulthood is known as **adolescence** (add-uhl-ES-uhns). In this stage individuals search for personal understanding about self: Who am I? What should I be doing? How well can I do it? The opposite direction for teens is to remain immature and dependent by not taking advantage of chances for personal development.

Older adolescents and young adults seek physical and emotional closeness with others to avoid isolation and loneliness. Middle-aged adults must find ways to remain productive and helpful to society. If not, they may become bored and self-centered.

Older adults continue to learn and seek satisfaction with a well-lived life. During the later years, healthy people view aging and dying as a normal part of life. If not, depression and despair may result.

As you can see, many of these stages are affected by what happens within the family. A troubled family may not be able to provide the support that developing children need. When this happens, personalities are affected in the negative ways just described. Personality disorders are not easy to change. This does not mean it cannot be done. When you have the need and desire to make positive changes, you can do it. Some people are able to identify their own weaknesses and work to overcome them. Others, when the problem is deeply rooted, seek professional help to work things through.

Growing up in an emotional climate that is supportive and loving helps a child develop a positive personality.

Discussion. Ask students how they think a child's self-esteem is affected in these situations: a parent yells at a small child repeatedly for touching boxes on the shelves at the grocery store; a parent becomes angry when his or her seven-year-old strikes out twice in a baseball game; an adult caretaker allows a three-year-old to roam outdoors freely without supervision; adults never allow a child to do things on his or her own; a caretaker strikes a child every time he or she wants to show disapproval.

Your Self-Concept

Just as others form a view of your personality, you also have an image of yourself. This is called your **self-concept.**

The foundation of self-concept is laid by early childhood experiences. Young children form a view of themselves based on the way they are treated by family members. They may see themselves as good or bad, smart or dumb, nice or mean. These opinions of self form the basis of self-concept.

Your self-concept is continually changing. Satisfying success experiences contribute to a positive self-concept, while depressing, defeat experiences build a negative self-concept. Your self-concept adjusts itself according to what happens to you.

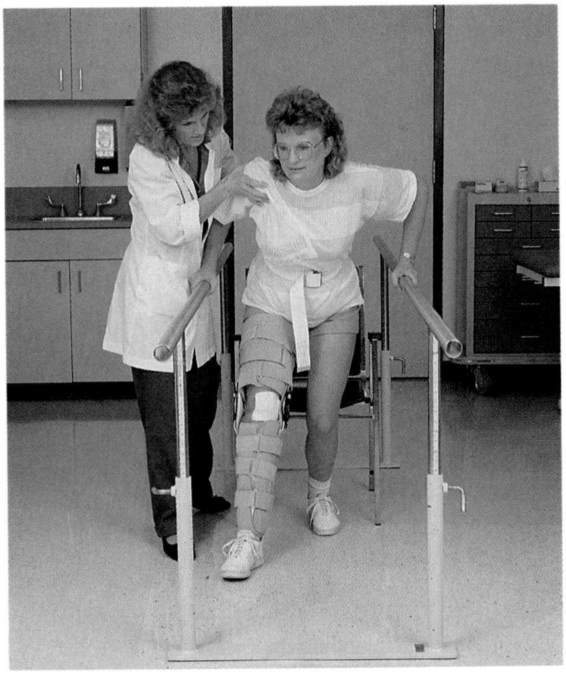

Your self-concept can change according to the successes and defeats you have. When you accomplish things that make you feel good, you will have a positive self-concept.

Activity. Ask students to write down any three memories from early childhood that immediately come to mind. Then ask them to connect those memories to their self-concept. Were the memories positive or negative? How did they affect the student's self-concept?

Your Self-Esteem

While self-concept is the way you see yourself, **self-esteem** (self-is-TEEM) is the way you feel about yourself. Mark likes to try new things. Not everything goes just right all the time, but he doesn't worry about his mistakes. For him, they are just learning experiences. When he helps out at the community center, he leads the young children in games. They like to be around Mark because they sense he cares about them. How would you describe Mark's self-esteem?

Sometimes people make the mistake of thinking that if only they were rich, handsome, or beautiful, everything would be wonderful. Often the people who seem to have everything, however, are the most unhappy. If you think of the celebrities you have read about, you will note that many have had difficulties in life. What does this mean? It means that self-esteem is based on something other than appearance and material possessions. Then what is it based on?

Self-esteem can be high, low, or anywhere in between. A high self-esteem occurs when certain emotional needs are met — needs for identity, security, acceptance, purpose, and self-worth. When it is low, these needs are not met.

Having a sense of identity means knowing who you are. You realize your strengths and accept your weaknesses. While in touch with your roots, you are still able to branch out to achieve your personal aims.

When security needs are met, a person feels safe. A calm emotional climate promotes this feeling. Clear expectations and involvement in decision making also help.

Discussion. Have students think of well-known personalities who seem to have everything. Do these celebrities seem happy or not? Ask students to bring in articles or other resources that support their arguments.

SIDELIGHT

Habits

Habits, the behavior patterns that become part of your routine, can be good or bad. They concern your schedule, grooming, and the way you do things. Try making a list of your habits, both good and bad. If you want to make a change, plan to replace the bad habit with a good one. Be committed. Make yourself use the new habit consistently. Eventually, the new, and preferred, habit can become as much a part of your routine as the old one was.

◆◆◆

The need for acceptance is met whenever people feel a sense of belonging. They feel liked and accepted by others. Belonging comes through links to family, teams, friends, and other groups. When people feel accepted, they feel free to participate.

With a sense of purpose, you work to achieve what is important. This gives motivation to your day and adds meaning to your life. Some life experiences can threaten your sense of purpose. These include absence of family responsibility, loss of job, illness, disability, and old age.

Having a sense of self-worth means believing you deserve love, respect, and attention. Children learn to feel worthy when they receive praise and encouragement; children who are deprived of these learn to think of themselves as no-good.

Activity. Ask students to list five things that would make them feel positive about themselves and five things that would make them feel negative about themselves. Have them share examples and brainstorm ways to turn the negative things around.

As you can see, self-esteem builds in many ways. To function well in the world, you need a good self-esteem. It can help you move forward in life with enthusiasm and pleasure. It can help you do and be what you want.

◆ Building Self-Esteem

Sometimes, for whatever reasons, life gives you some hard knocks. Self-esteem may suffer. Does this mean you have to give in and give up? Of course not. You can help build your own self-esteem back up in several ways:

- **Accept yourself.** You don't have to be like anyone else. If all people were alike, that would be boring. Because people are so different, you will never be able to please everyone, so don't even try. Remember that normal means being up sometimes and down others. Remember too that normal also means being good at some things and not at others, and that's okay.

People who reach out to help others are more likely to have a high self-esteem. Why do you think this is true?

Life Management Skills. Ask students to list three specific new skills and three specific ways to reach out to others that could boost their self-esteem. If possible, have each student carry out one item on the list and report results. Reward the students' efforts.

• **Forgive yourself.** Everyone makes mistakes. Everyone has to learn to take criticism. This does not mean you are unliked. It simply means you are not perfect, and who is?

• **Learn a new skill.** Find something you like to do and then do it. Share it in some way with others if you want to. Self-esteem grows when you accomplish things, and even more when others recognize what you do. Choose something that is realistic for you. Not everyone can be a star volleyball player. If you can be good at auto mechanics, needlepoint, or raising chickens, go for it.

• **Reach out to others.** When you do, others will respond. Look especially for those with a need. You might try volunteer work or simply helping someone in your family or neighborhood. Choose from all age categories. Someone needs you. If you reach out, your efforts will be appreciated, and you will have less focus only on yourself.

• **Be positive.** Practice making positive choices. Decide to trust rather than to worry. Choose liking over disliking. Laugh rather than cry. Compliment rather than criticize. When things are tough, try once more rather than give up. Give more than you take. Participate instead of watching from the sidelines. Navigate with the current instead of stagnating in the way things have always been done. Be a plus, not a minus. Smile too.

• **Be assertive.** You are not a doormat. You have the right to your opinion and your feelings. **Assertiveness** (uh-SURT-iv-ness) means speaking up for yourself without offending others. Be comfortable with saying what you think in an honest and considerate manner. If you need to say "no," do so with confidence and without apology. When you see a problem, work to correct it. Respect comes to those who do.

A Slice of Life

Why did she get herself in these situations all the time? Regina kept trying to figure it out, but she could never quite come up with an answer.

It had just happened again. Leisha had called and begged her to make crepe paper flowers for the homecoming dance. It would take hours — hours that Regina did not have to give. Oh well, she would try to adjust her part-time hours at work and her study time. Maybe she could do it.

At least this would be better than selling candy bars door-to-door. She had done that twice for a club she belonged to, and she hated every minute of it. Regina disliked anything that had to do with sales, but they said they needed her help.

As Regina sighed, the phone rang. "Uh oh, what do they want this time?" she thought.

Thinking It Through

- Can you pinpoint Regina's problem? What is it?
- How can Regina solve her problem?
- Have you ever found yourself in Regina's situation? What did you do?

Discussion. Discuss with students what is meant by the statement, "You learn from your mistakes." Ask students to list mistakes that they have made that have helped them learn. Have students ask their parents what mistakes they made while growing up and how they learned from them.

Activity. Ask students to act out situations in which they need to be assertive. How would they handle the following situations: you are sitting with a group of friends who are discussing a very controversial topic and you feel differently about it; two classmates at school are saying negative things about your best friend's parents; your company just cut health benefits and you aren't happy with this change.

CHAPTER 1

Review

Summarizing the Chapter

- Every person is an individual with unique characteristics.
- Personality is the combination of characteristics in a person as perceived by other people.
- Personality is influenced by hereditary and environmental factors.
- The family is the greatest environmental influence in personality development.
- The image you have of yourself, or self-concept, may be positive or negative, according to successes and failures experienced.
- Self-esteem is the way you feel about yourself and results from needs being met — needs for identity, security, acceptance, purpose, and self-worth.
- There are many ways to build your own self-esteem if you are willing to try.

Testing Your Memory

1. Why is every personality unique?
2. Distinguish between the introvert and extrovert personality types.
3. Name and explain two main influences on personality.
4. List four aspects of family life that can affect the personalities of family members.
5. What is the basis for Erikson's theory?
6. How does a person's self-concept develop?
7. List and explain four ways to build your own self-esteem.

Answers
Testing Your Memory

1. There are many characteristics that make up a personality. These come together in many different ways to create unique personalities.
2. An *extrovert* likes to be around people and communicate with them. An *introvert* finds satisfaction in being alone, not needing as much interaction with others as an extrovert does.
3. *Heredity:* the qualities that are passed on to a person genetically from parents. *Environment:* the influences that come from your surroundings, including family, friends and associates, and the world.
4. **Any four:** emotional climate, family, size, position in the family, relationships with brothers and sisters, parenting styles.
5. Erikson's theory is based on the idea that personal development takes place in a series of stages, each one building on the one before and providing a solid base for the next.
6. Self-concept is rooted in early childhood experiences. A view of self develops based on the way people are treated by family members.
7. **Any four:** accept yourself; forgive yourself; learn a new skill; reach out to others; be positive; be assertive.

Thinking Critically

1. To what extent are people limited by their heredity? Explain your answer.
2. If people put you down, should you believe what they say? What is a better approach?
3. Who is more likely to follow along with the crowd regardless of the crowd's behavior, someone with high or low self-esteem? Why?
4. What effect does appearance (body image) have on self-esteem? Analyze how society influences a person's body image.

Taking Action

1. Write a script for a puppet show. Include dialogue to reflect the self-esteem of the characters, showing their needs for identity, security, acceptance, purpose, and/or self-worth. Present the puppet show to the audience of your choice.
2. Conduct a survey to determine preferred positions in the family, that is, the oldest, the youngest, the middle child, and the only child. What advantages and disadvantages did you find for each position?
3. For one week, try not to say anything negative about yourself. Share how you did with fellow classmates.

Making Life Choices

Mr. Underwood walked by the living room and looked in. There was Jess in front of the television again. "How can he spend so much time there?" Mr. Underwood wondered to himself. "That's all he does. No friends. No activities. Every day it gets harder and harder to talk to him. He just doesn't seem happy — not with himself or with anything else." Mr. Underwood sighed and moved quietly away.

What do you think is wrong with Jess? If you were Mr. Underwood, what would you do? Can Jess do anything to help himself?

Using Your Journal

At the end of each chapter you will be invited to record some of your thoughts in your private journal. Your journal might be a notebook, a diary, even a computer disk. Whatever form it takes, your journal is for your own use — you will not have to show it to other people. In this chapter you have read about self-esteem. Use your journal to write about your own self-esteem. List the things you like, and dislike, about yourself. Then write down some actions you could take to help you feel better about the things you dislike.

Thinking Critically

1. Answers will vary. Point out that determination enables people to go beyond certain hereditary limitations.
2. No. Believe the people you trust and think positively about yourself.
3. People with low self-esteem probably would because they are less likely to have confidence in themselves.
4. Usually a person who is comfortable with his or her own appearance will have a higher self-esteem. Answers about society will vary.

CHAPTER 2

Your Development

Chapter Challenge

Resources. Refer to the Teacher's Classroom Resources box and Student Workbook for materials related to this chapter.

Look for These Answers . . .

- What physical changes occur during puberty for females and males?
- How can intellectual development be enhanced?
- What factors affect social development?
- What is needed for good emotional development?
- Describe some common emotions and how to handle them.
- Explain moral development.

Look for These Terms . . .

- emotions
- maturity
- modeling
- phobias
- puberty
- role model
- socialization
- values

Looking in a mirror was always discouraging. Even his reflection in a glass windowpane was cause for a pang of concern.

Jerome not only wondered when, but he also wondered if. His grandfather said it would happen — to just be patient. That wasn't easy when you were sixteen and still looked like a high school freshman. In fact, sometimes people thought he was.

"Are you staring in the mirror again?" Reggie asked. Jerome's older brother was home from college. Reggie looked great. His skin had cleared up. He was several inches taller than Jerome. Besides that, he had muscles, and he actually needed to shave every day. "You know, Jer, that mirror's not going to change anything. Only time will. Mark my words. Things will be different in a year or two."

Jerome smiled. He guessed they were all right. Time would tell, and if things didn't work out exactly the way he wanted, well, he would just have to make the best of it. Maybe shooting a few baskets would make him feel better. Jerome grabbed his basketball and headed for the door.

Chapter Opener. Ask students to read the opening scenario to the chapter. Ask the following questions: Why do young people sometimes have concerns about their development? How does Reggie help Jerome with his feelings? What signs do you see that Jerome's attitude is a positive one?

Photo Focus. Have students look at the photo at the left. Ask them how the teen is helping the child develop. How will she benefit as well?

The Process of Change

Adolescence is marked by change. Changes come in all areas of development — physical, intellectual, social, emotional, and moral. Reaching **maturity** (muh-TUR-uht-ee) means that full development has taken place. Each area of development does not reach maturity at the same time. For example, a person could be physically mature yet never be emotionally mature. It depends on what happens in that person's life.

The road to adulthood is sometimes a bumpy one. Jerome is typical of young people, both male and female, who struggle with the changes they are experiencing. In each area of development people move along at different rates. While one teen can't wait to see some signs of physical maturity, another is painfully dealing with maturity that arrived too early. A little knowledge, some understanding, and a sense of humor can all help during this time.

Personal development is a continual process of change and challenge. Each stage in the process builds on the one before. When all goes well, each stage provides a solid base for the next. This is true in all areas of development.

Physical Changes

Physical changes are the most apparent part of personal development. Growth during childhood years is slow but steady, with occasional spurts along the way. Between the ages of eleven and thirteen (sometimes earlier), **puberty** (PYOO-burt-ee) begins. Sexual development occurs during puberty. In addition, physical growth generally races ahead for two or three years before tapering off in the middle or late teens.

In females puberty is marked by the first menstrual period. On the average, American females have their first period at age twelve or thirteen. This may also occur normally as early as age nine or as late as seventeen.

The first signs of sexual maturity in males appear at about age twelve. The sexual organs begin to develop. During puberty, height may increase as much as four to six inches in one year.

Physical growth may be uneven and cause worry about body proportions. The top part of the face grows faster than the lower. Head, hands, and feet speed on to adult size well ahead of slower growing arms and legs. Increases in shoulder breadth and trunk size take place last. That is why many teens seem lean and awkward for a time.

Other changes occur as well. Body hair grows coarser, darker, and longer in both sexes. Sweat glands work overtime. Fat deposits relocate. The systems for breathing and digesting food increase in size and capacity. The male's voice begins to deepen. Worries about acne, body odor, and hair are common during these years.

By age sixteen most adolescents look physically mature. Although many continue to grow slowly for several more years, the extreme differences that show up between eleven and fourteen even out during the late teens.

When thinking about body growth and development, remember that typical patterns do not fit everyone. Great physical differences may be noticed when comparing any two teens. For example, an early maturing male may complete all puberty changes before a slower developing female, even though the opposite is usually true.

Most teens go through a period of concern about their bodies as they move toward maturity. Worries about size and proportion may be troubling until the teen realizes that differences in people make them interesting. The true measure of a person's worth, after all, is not in body type. It goes much deeper. Part of maturity is learning to recognize this.

Your Intellectual Development

Much like physical growth, intellectual development moves along in set patterns from infancy. These stages generally follow the same sequence. The child must successfully complete each task before the next one can be mastered.

Unlike physical development, however, the stages of intellectual progress do not unfold naturally. The child must be stimulated to learn the numbers, letters, shapes, and colors that will be so important for later learning.

Activity. Have students tape a long sheet of paper beside a full-length mirror. Tell them to look at themselves in the mirror as they trace their image on the paper. Tape the papers on the wall, and have students stand against their image. Did they overestimate or underestimate their body size? Which parts? Ask students to focus not on how they want to look but on how they would like to feel about their looks. What steps can they take to change their body image?

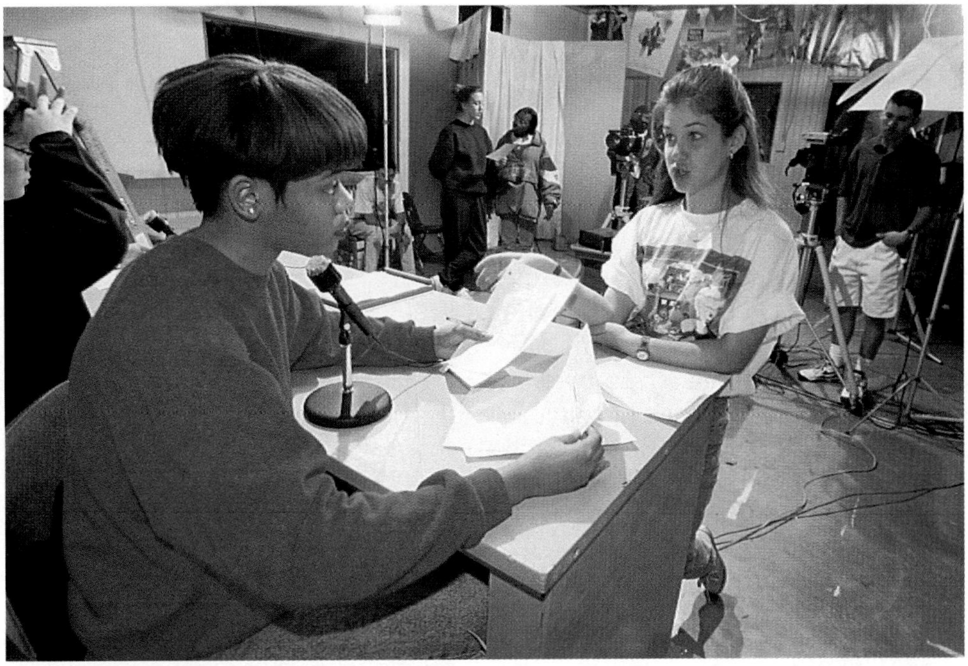

Formal thinking enables you to examine the world around you, question the ideas of others, and consider many possible solutions to a problem.

In fact, the process may speed up as the result of enriching experiences at home or in a stimulating nursery or preschool setting. In contrast, delays in intellectual development may occur during a prolonged illness or when a child is neglected or abused.

Jean Piaget, a famous psychologist, explained the stages of normal intellectual development. During early infancy babies pay full attention to their own bodies and their own needs. They are the center of their own universe. Gradually they discover things and people outside themselves. As they learn to talk, they begin to understand basic categories, such as people, animals, numbers, and relationships. An advanced level of intellectual activity, called formal thinking, sets in at about age eleven or twelve.

Formal thinking opens the mind to the real world. It allows you to keep track of many ideas at the same time and to reason logically. This expanded talent also reminds you that others share the same brain power. It lets you consider possible results of one decision as compared with another. You begin to notice the links that connect ideas and events. You may begin to question ideas that you once took for granted. You can cement your conclusions into personal beliefs or discard them as no longer valuable. In practical terms, you begin to develop the mental skills to manage the important parts of your life.

To develop good judgment and increased mental ability, you must practice thinking. By facing life's problems and working them through, you can actually improve your mental power. Some people keep their thinking sharp by reading mystery stories or by solving crossword puzzles. Others find challenges in games, career demands, or chosen fields of study.

More About Your Development. One factor that makes teenagers more anxious about sexuality is stereotypes, or assumptions about how boys and girls are supposed to act or look. Have students write down the heading "Males Do" or "Females Do" according to their gender, and list what they were told while growing up about what people of the same sex are typically supposed to do. For example, "boys play sports" or "girls play with dolls." Are there stereotypes on their lists? Are they true? If not, how can they be changed?

◆◆◆

Developing Socially

At first your personality was very simple. As a baby, you cooed when happy and cried when uncomfortable. In dealing with the world around you, you began to learn and to understand. You also started to discover how to relate to other human beings. This is the **socialization** process.

This process does not occur in the same way for every individual. Because each person has so many different experiences, the way each develops socially is not the same, even though certain patterns may be similar.

Signs of socialization may be seen throughout infancy and early childhood. Even newborn infants often make response sounds when parents talk to them. The eight-month-old who cries because big sister is crying may be demonstrating early signs of sympathy. Children who imitate what adults say and do are practicing their social skills by pretending to be grown-up.

The family is the first, and most influential, training ground for social skills. Family members serve as a link, connecting with the past and preparing for the future. From the family, the child receives a name, a place to live, a language, and a culture. Youngsters learn to get along in their particular part of the world. This means learning how to dress, how to speak, and what to eat in order to fit in and be accepted in the social group.

In large part, you learn to get along by watching those with whom you live. When adults and older siblings show children what to say and do, the process is known as **modeling**. The person imitated is known as a **role model**. Very early in life, children copy their parents. Later, they look to friends, teachers, and other adults who impress them. Young adolescents may borrow an expression from a favorite teacher or an action from a TV star.

Discussion. Ask students to cite examples of any national or global event that may have had an impact on their intellectual development. What did they think about the event? Why did it affect them?

Young people learn from role models. Are there any dangers in this?

Role models can be good or bad, depending on whether the imitated behaviors are desirable, legal, and constructive. Unfortunately, some people imitate everything about a role model based on one trait that they find admirable. The danger, of course, lies in the assumption that everything is worth imitating when, in fact, it may not be.

Effective social skills are based on the image people have of themselves. With a positive self-concept, young people feel confident enough to find ways to get along with others and to be accepting. They are able to give as well as take and follow as well as lead. These social skills are essential for healthy relationships in family, career, and all aspects of life.

Problem Solving. Divide students into small groups and assign each a different age of child development — twelve months, eighteen months, etc. Have the groups research and report on a child's emotional characteristics at that age and explain any reasons why they have them.

◆◆◆

Emotional Development

Have you ever thought that someone was very immature acting? What did that actually mean? Chances are, the person was not in control of his or her emotions.

Emotions are feelings experienced in reaction to thoughts, remarks, or events. They are automatic responses that are neither right nor wrong. Reactions to emotions, however, can be right or wrong. As you grow through childhood and adolescence, you learn to handle the many emotions that you feel. You learn to respond to them, ideally in ways that are not destructive to yourself and others. In order to do this well, several basic needs must be met along the way. They are:

- **Security.** Children who are anxious about their own well-being are less trusting and prone to feeling anger, frustration, and fear.
- **Acceptance.** Without this, children have trouble understanding and accepting others. They find it harder to love.
- **Companionship.** People need friendship. Putting limits on this need means not learning how to relate to others.
- **Success.** If a child seldom knows success, the feelings of failure and inadequacy are likely to prevail.
- **Opportunity.** When children do not have chances to try new things, they may be fearful and unhappy.

It shouldn't be hard for you to see what could happen to a person whose needs have not been met in these areas. The greater the problem, the greater the chance that a person will experience more negative emotions and have trouble dealing with them.

Good emotional development hinges in part on having childhood opportunities to try new things and experience success. What else is needed?

If you tried to make a list of emotions, it would be a long one. Not only are there many, but they also come in different forms. For example, you may feel one form of love for your parents, another form for a good friend, and still a third for someone very special. Emotions are found in degrees, ranging from quite mild to very strong. For example, Patti felt happiness in the form of contentment when she worked on a cross-stitch pattern she liked. She felt happiness in the form of joy when her brother came home from the army.

Emotions are very changeable. Affection can blossom into love, sadness can slide into grief, and fear can build into terror. It is even possible to experience several different, even opposite, emotions at the same time. Mixed emotions such as love and hate or happiness and sadness are often generated by intense life experiences.

Some emotions are very common ones. A closer look at these may help as you move toward maturity.

Activity. Have students list three people they perceive as current positive role models and three negative role models. Ask them to include their reasons why. What personality traits make for positive and negative role models?

Discussion. Discuss with students how social skills can be hampered because of the environment the child is raised in. What kind of negative social skills might a child learn? What about an only child? How might his or her social skills be different from that of a child who has several siblings?

◆ Anger

People feel anger in different degrees and act on it in different ways. Learning to handle anger constructively is a sign of maturity. Violent reactions are unacceptable. Any reaction that hurts others is a poor choice. Closing anger up inside can be hard on you. That's why talking calmly about what is bothering you can help. Working through angry feelings by putting your energy into some constructive activity is a good idea.

◆ Fear

As long as fear does not prevent you from doing things you want or need to do, it is okay. Actually, fear can be good if it keeps you from doing something foolish. Many fears in adolescence are based on a concern about what others will think. Asking someone for a date is a typical teen fear. The asker worries about everything from appearance to rejection in such situations. When you have fears like this, ask yourself if it really matters what others think. In the long run, missed opportunities are likely to be more of a disappointment.

Anxiety is one form of fear. Practically everyone feels anxiety from time to time and usually for a good reason. Typically, students are anxious before giving an oral report in class. This too is based on a concern about what others think. Good preparation will often help lessen anxiety. When you know what is going to happen and you have planned ahead what to do, you will be less anxious.

Phobias (FO-bee-uhs) are extreme fears. They cause people to fear such things as airplanes or close spaces. These can be overcome. Often it takes only strong determination.

◆ Depression

Hasn't everyone said it at one time or another: "I just feel depressed today." Depression comes in all degrees. Sometimes when you feel down, you don't even know why. Mood swings typically mark the adolescent years. Taylor describes his feelings. "I can be on top of the world. Then, for no reason, I suddenly drop. When I'm down, I'm not much fun to be around. The one thing I do know is that before long I'll feel better." Like Taylor, many teens experience sudden mood swings on a regular basis.

Most of the time, gloomy moods decrease and become easier to handle as you get older. You can help this process along by not blaming yourself or others for every mood slump. Allow yourself to have them. Since they are normal, you don't need to worry. Learn to manage them too. When you feel down, do something that fits your mood. Go for a walk by yourself. Find a quiet spot and look through last year's yearbook. Talk to a friend. Before long, you will find yourself thinking about things that will lift your spirits.

When you feel angry, it is easy to say things that hurt others. How can you prevent this?

Life Management Skills. Have students think of ways to deal with anger in the following situations: A friend is going out with your boyfriend or girlfriend behind your back; a friend has strong opinions about lots of things and this really makes you mad; a friend or sibling has made a promise to help you out and lets you down; a classmate is spreading lies about you; a parent disciplines you for something your sibling did.

A Slice of Life

The last time Danielle was supposed to give an oral report, she stayed home on that day. The time before that she had actually almost fainted. Her knees shook so much that she could barely stand up. Her hands shook too. In fact, she lost her place three times because she couldn't hold her paper still. Danielle was fed up with this situation. She was ready to make some changes.

Danielle formed a three-fold plan of action. She would come at this problem via perception, practice, and preparation.

To begin with, Danielle decided that she must change the way she perceived her problem. Instead of always telling herself how bad it would be, she started to think about the positive side. Everyone else had to give oral reports. They all survived. Some of them were nervous too. Nervousness is normal. Speaking before others is a challenge. Once she learned to handle it, it would be useful to her. Danielle erased the negative thoughts from her mind, replacing them with positive ones. The next step was practice. She would start in little ways. Raising her hand to speak in class was first. She would also practice speaking in front of a mirror at home. She visualized herself as confident and controlled while practicing.

The last step was preparation. This would be carried out at the time she had to make a speech. She would research her topic well and start with clear notes on cards. Practicing the particular speech many times would be part of her preparation.

The first test of Danielle's plan came several weeks later. She was ready. Although she was still nervous, everything went better than it ever had before, and she knew the next time would be better yet.

Thinking It Through

- Can you add any other suggestions to Danielle's plan of action?
- Why do you think Danielle's plan worked?
- Is there anything about Danielle's approach that could be carried over to other challenges in life?

◆ Inferiority

Clint's feelings of inferiority were evident to everyone but him. He was quick to criticize others because something inside him said that this made him look better. Actually, it made him look bad. Whenever he was criticized, he was upset. Clint always seemed to be seeking approval from others. He felt inadequate without it. Sometimes he envied others, not realizing that he had his own strengths. This made him feel sorry for himself.

Problem Solving. Have small groups of students research causes of depression, such as psychological or life-event factors. Ask them to act out skits in which one student is depressed and another offers information about causes and ways to combat depression.

Activity. Have students compile a "mental health survival guide" to be made available to the student body. The guide should include community resources for teenagers suffering from extreme emotional disorders, the services offered, and any costs involved.

Feeling down sometimes and up others is typical during the teen years. How should one deal with this?

When your mood is low for whatever reason, it is easy to get down on yourself. Usually this is temporary. If you find that too much of your thinking goes this way, stop and think about all that you do well. Make a list if you need to. Switch your thoughts from yourself to someone else. A new focus will eliminate much of the pressure you put on yourself.

◆ Extreme Emotions

Although it doesn't happen to most people, once in awhile an emotion becomes overwhelming. Some people have been known to wash their hands many times a day to remove feared germs or refuse to leave the safety of their homes. This is an extreme form of anxiety. A person suffering from severe depression has intense feelings of despair that do not go away. When emotions become so overpowering that a person cannot function normally, help may be needed. If talking to someone does not solve the problem, a professional counselor has the expertise to find solutions.

Work and Family. Sometimes people who have extreme feelings, such as anger or impatience, may find it hard to function well in their work and family environments. How might these feelings hurt their relationships with others? How might people handle these extreme feelings?

◆◆◆

Developing Morally

Moral development means learning to recognize the difference between right and wrong. All of life goes easier when you have a clear set of personal rules to live by. Moral and intellectual growth are usually linked. Even so, a person's moral awareness may not develop as fast as mature thinking. This explains why some very smart people are sometimes selfish and dishonest.

Many psychologists believe that moral growth, like physical development, moves forward in a series of stages matched to chronological ages. For example, at age seven children do as they are told to avoid punishment or to win praise or reward. Gradually, each individual develops a set of values. **Values** are the beliefs and feelings about how important someone or something is to you. At first, a child's values may be a reflection of the parents' views on right and wrong. Older youths learn to cherish values for their own reasons as a result of personal experiences.

Life Management Skills. Have students create strategies based on values to deal with the following: a friend confides that he or she shoplifted an expensive item; you arrive at a classmate's party where people are using drugs; a friend confides in you that he or she has been sexually abused.

Part of the maturing process is developing your own moral code. Many people are guided in this by their religious beliefs as well as by the rules of society.

During adolescence, moral choices become more complicated. Questions of right and wrong become shaded by conflicting values and points of view. You may reexamine certain childhood convictions in the search for greater independence and maturity. You will also look outward to society's rules of morality and relate this to your own code. You will grow and change and become your own person.

For many young people a spiritual base serves as a positive force that gives purpose and direction to life. Religious principles provide a basic outlook to guide daily actions. A strong belief in something outside yourself supplies an anchor for the stormy times. Most people want to be fair and reasonable in their dealings with others. They want the internal security of a clear moral code and a peaceful conscience.

◆◆◆

The Family Influence

As you can see, development is a complicated process. There is one force in particular that has a profound effect on every individual's development— the family. Whether physical, intellectual, social, emotional, or moral, every kind of development is aided when family support is present. A strong family provides the environment that people need to reach their potentials. This, in turn, provides a strong society.

SIDELIGHT

Developmental Tasks for Teens

According to educator and behavioral scientist Robert J. Havighurst, teens must accomplish certain tasks in order to find happiness and success in life. Think about which of these tasks you are close to achieving:

- To have new and more mature relationships with peers, both male and female.
- To adopt socially approved masculine or feminine adult roles.
- To accept your physical self.
- To become emotionally independent.
- To define your own philosophy about family living.
- To choose and prepare for an occupation.
- To adopt a set of standards for behavior.
- To become socially responsible.

◆◆◆

Activity. Have students make a list of morally wrong choices in their opinions and another list of the right choices. Discuss why each thinks each choice is morally wrong and morally right. You may even debate some of these issues.

Discussion. Discuss with students how their parents and others have influenced the choices they have made. If their parents weren't there, on what would they have based their moral decisions?

CHAPTER 2

Review

Answers
Testing Your Memory

1. Physical, intellectual, social, emotional, and moral development.
2. **Any three:** body proportions; acne; body odor; hair; body size.
3. Families provide a link to the future. Children imitate family members at first and learn how to get along with others by watching those they live with.
4. Role models are good if the behavior copied is desirable, legal, and constructive. If not, the role model is bad.
5. Security, acceptance, companionship, success, and opportunity.
6. **Any one for each:** *Anger* — put your energy into a constructive activity. *Fear* — don't worry about what others think, plan ahead, or be determined. *Depression* — don't blame yourself, manage your down times, or talk to someone. *Inferiority* — think about all you do well or focus on others.
7. Adolescents are moving toward independence and trying to set up their own moral code based on childhood convictions, society's rules, and their own attitudes. Some conflicts and questions may occur during this process.

Summarizing the Chapter

- Personal development is a continuous process of change and challenge.
- Puberty brings about rapid increases in height, weight, and sexual development.
- The ability to do formal thinking expands the intellectual capacity of adolescents.
- Through family interaction, individuals develop social skills that enable them to get along with other human beings in society.
- Good emotional development hinges upon the meeting of certain needs during childhood.
- Negative emotions can be managed.
- Moral development gives an increased awareness of right and wrong, making life more productive and satisfying.

Testing Your Memory

1. Name five areas of personal development in which changes and challenges arise.
2. List three concerns that teens have about physical development during adolescence.
3. Explain how the family affects a child's social development.
4. Are role models good or bad? Explain your answer.
5. List the five needs that must be met for good emotional development.
6. Describe a technique for dealing with each of the following emotions: anger; fear; depression; inferiority.
7. Why do moral choices become more difficult during adolescence?

Thinking Critically

1. What advice would you give to a friend who is concerned about his or her physical development?
2. Imagine you had to start life all over. If you could choose, would you rather be a rich orphan or a poor but well-loved child?
3. What childhood fears can you remember feeling? Can you remember an experience that led to one of these fears?

Taking Action

1. Watch a television show that features children in a family setting. What did you observe in the environment that would help children develop fully?
2. Name your favorite role model from childhood. Write a paragraph that tells why you admired this person.
3. Make a collage of pictures, cartoons, and/or words to represent emotions. Illustrate as many dimensions of emotion as possible.

Making Life Choices

Jean is the middle child in a family with three children. As Jean sees it, her older sister has everything. Not only is she pretty, but she also gets good grades and has a nice boyfriend. Her younger sister got the talent in the family. She is athletic and has a drawer full of medals that she has collected. People really like her too. Jean yearns for things to be different for her and wonders why it turned out this way.

Do you think Jean's analysis of her situation is realistic? What problems might Jean have if she continues to think the way she does? If you were Jean, what would you do?

Using Your Journal

As you have just read, adolescence is a time of change — physical, intellectual, social, and emotional. Use your journal to write about some of the changes that are happening in your life. List the changes that you see as positive, and those that you see as negative. Then write down your thoughts about how you can best deal with the negative changes. What can you do to feel better about them?

Thinking Critically

1. Answers will vary but may include the idea that patience and acceptance are useful when dealing with physical development.
2. Answers will vary but students will need to examine which is more important, material possessions or love.
3. Answers will vary.

CHAPTER 3

Your Character

Chapter Challenge

Resources. Refer to the Teacher's Classroom Resources box and Student Workbook for materials related to this chapter.

Look for These Answers . . .

- What are the signs of moral maturity?
- On what is your personal code of ethics based?
- How are values selected and ranked?
- How do attitudes reflect character?
- In what ways can teens learn to assume responsibility?

Look for These Terms . . .

- character
- code of ethics
- empathy
- integrity
- prejudice
- respect
- stereotyping
- volunteerism

She felt very uncomfortable. Her skin color was different from everyone else's in the room. Why had she even decided to come tonight anyway? She didn't really belong here. Alisha wished that she had at least brought a friend with her. There was security in numbers.

After the meeting, people began to walk around, talking with friends and getting acquainted. Alisha's discomfort, which had faded somewhat during the program, began to return. Just for something to do, she walked over to the refreshment table to get a glass of punch. This was better than standing around doing nothing. She stood by the table drinking the punch as one young woman brushed beside her. Alisha's cup nearly spilled, but the young woman only gave her a scornful glance and hurried away.

Alisha had about decided to leave. This was a disappointment, because she had come with so much enthusiasm, so much hope that she could make a contribution to this group. She turned to head for the door and came face to face with Rona.

"Hello. My name's Rona Samuelson. I'm so glad you came tonight. If you have some time, I'd like to introduce you to some of the people in our organization. Tell me what got you interested in our group."

Rona put her hand lightly on Alisha's arm and began to lead her back into the group. The two were already deep in conversation. They were a contrast in appearance, but now that didn't matter anymore.

Moving Toward Maturity

Your **character** is your moral maturity. This type of maturity has little, if anything, to do with age. It has everything to do with what kind of person you are, your actions, your personal code of ethics, your attitudes, and your ability to assume responsibility.

Actions, not ages, reflect moral maturity. Some fourteen-year-olds are more mature in a moral sense than some forty-year-olds. For example, a teenage son who unselfishly cares for his younger sister while their father is out drinking and gambling with friends shows more maturity than the father. The father's actions are self-centered and irresponsible, yet the son's actions speak of selflessness and compassion.

Chapter Opener. Ask students to read the opening scenario to the chapter. Ask the following questions: What race is each young woman? (Note that students may use their own backgrounds to attribute a race to each person; however, the scenario gives no indication of this. The young women could be any combination of two different races.) Have you ever felt the way Alisha did, that is, out of place in a group? Why? What do you think about Rona's handling of the situation? Suppose Rona had not shown up. What would have happened? Would you have decided to leave as Alisha was about to do?

Most young people want to be mature, fair, and honest. Not only do they want a set of standards to live by, but they also want something to stand for and something to believe in.

Reaching the highest level of moral development, to become a person of character, is a challenge for anyone. There are several milestones that signal progress toward maturity. With maturity comes:

- The ability to control and find constructive outlets for strong emotions.
- Acceptance of opposing points of view.
- The initiative to do unpleasant or difficult tasks.
- A willingness to act without expecting reward or acknowledgment.
- The patience needed to delay gratification (personal satisfaction and pleasure) when necessary or wait for long-term reward.
- Determination, in other words, the ability to "hang in there" when problems arise.
- Assertiveness in working for positive change and acceptance of things that cannot be changed.
- Dependability through the honoring of promises and commitments.
- The ability to admit mistakes rather than make excuses.
- The ability to think and act independently.
- Peripheral vision — that is, the ability to see situations as a whole, from all angles.

Much of maturity involves becoming more unselfish. Life offers many choices between getting what you'd like to have and fulfilling the needs of others. Inside everyone is an immature child who keeps insisting "Me! Me!" At some point that child has to learn to make choices based on the welfare of others if true maturity is to be reached.

Mature people can be counted on to make a difference without expecting any reward. What are some other characteristics of maturity?

Discussion. Ask students: What influences help shape *character?* Why do negative influences make it harder to develop a strong character? Is character unchangeable, or can one work hard to strengthen and improve character? What steps can one take to change?

Activity. Have students list different examples of someone they know, such as peers, parents, relatives, and other adults, who exemplify each quality of moral maturity listed above. Have them explain their choices and show how the person is an apt role model.

◆◆◆

Your Personal Code of Ethics

Having a strong personal **code of ethics** (ETH-iks) means having a clear set of rules or principles to guide your actions and decisions. For example, one principle might be: "I believe that all people are worthy of respect no matter what they look like or how they act." Do you agree or disagree? Most people do have some beliefs or principles that guide them, although they may not be conscious of them.

A code of ethics serves as an internal security force. Your conscience nags you promptly when you break your own rules. You must tell the truth to yourself and others. You must admit the unpleasant things about yourself. You must hold yourself responsible for your own mistakes, admit the harm that you might have caused, and try to make up for it. Through a strong personal code of ethics, you can influence people and circumstances. You can know the satisfaction of having control of your life.

When Cheryl's stepmother let her have the family car for the evening, she was thrilled. It was new and sporty — and red, her favorite color. Two hours later it was scratched and had a small dent on the back right side. It was Cheryl's fault. She bumped a car in a parking lot. The damage was slight, and there was none to the other car. She wondered whether her stepmother would notice. Then she had a funny feeling inside.

What do you think was going on in Cheryl's mind? She was trying to decide whether or not to admit her error. She knew that her stepmother would be upset. If the damage was discovered later, however, Cheryl would either have to lie or explain why she kept it a secret. This would make matters worse. Admitting her mistake now would be better. This was the honest approach. Cheryl's ethical code guided her toward an answer. Would you have made the same decision?

When faced with a dilemma, your personal code of ethics will help you make the right decision.

Problem Solving. Ask students to write a brief paragraph about a mistake they may have made in their personal lives. Were they torn about how to resolve the mistake? What did they do? Did they take responsibility for the mistake? If not, do they regret it?

Life Management Skills. Have students offer concrete examples of how values affect each of these: what you read, how you use your spare time, what you buy, what you save, and what you throw away. What values are brought into play by each of these actions?

You can work on strengthening your own personal ethics now. Remember that the happiest and most productive adults are those who select personal rules for living, practice them, and depend on them in times of stress. They learn to say, "In this type of situation, I will act this way for this reason." Making on-the-spot, and important, decisions will be much easier when you are armed with a code to live by.

What do you value? How important is your education to you?

Your Values

In general, your code of ethics reflects your set of values. Remember that values show how you feel about the importance of people and things in your life. Real values are seen in daily living. They affect what you say and do, what you read, how you use your spare time, how you treat others, what you buy, what you save, and what you throw away. Learning to prize your values and live by them takes time, effort, and practice. Values that receive only "lip service" are meaningless.

In thinking about values, you will have to compare them to see which ones are most important to you. You will rank them in order of importance. In certain situations, two or more worthwhile values may come into conflict. When this happens, it is reassuring to rely on your ranking of values to aid in makeing the choice between one value and another.

◆ Choosing Values

Deciding what your values will be and how to rank them may not be easy. Most people learn basic moral values at home from their families. Other strong sources of values include religious organizations, television and other media, and friends. Could any of these sources influence you in the wrong way? For example, a friend who values excitement might want you to try shoplifting with him. He might find a challenge and a thrill in it. In this case, you have a choice to make. Do you choose his value of excitement or some other value that is more important to you? You will encounter influences all the time. How can you be sure the values you put high on your list are the right ones?

Activity. Have students list one value that has had an impact on them. Ask them to explain in writing how the value is reinforced for them at home, on TV, in the media, or by a close friend. How does the particular value affect the way they act toward others?

Discussion. Discuss with students how their values have changed over the years. What has persuaded them to change their values? What values are most important to them now? List student responses on the board and encourage students to add to the list as more ideas occur to them.

The answer to this question is not a simple one. See if this helps. When you are deciding what to value, ask yourself: Could this be harmful or destructive in any way to me or to anyone else? If it could, then it probably doesn't belong on your list of values. Since shoplifting is illegal and causes higher prices for everyone, the lure of excitement should not win out.

In general, people agree on the basic issues of right and wrong. These are established in society and have changed very little over the years.

◆◆◆

Your Attitudes

Attitudes reveal your character to other people. They reflect your values. Certain attitudes tend to be constructive forces in relationships, while others are destructive in nature.

◆ Integrity

People with **integrity** (in-TEG-ru-tee) are honest. Honesty means so much to them that they will tell the truth, even when lying would be an easy way out. People of integrity do not lie to protect themselves or to get their own way. They keep their word. Promises are made with care, because they are meant to be kept. Commitments bring a heavy sense of responsibility to people with integrity.

◆ Respect

Along with integrity, the attitude of respect is a positive force in relationships. When you **respect**, you show honor and esteem for others. Look for things to like in people. This will help you show sincere regard for them. Take an interest in their interests and activities; listen to their ideas and beliefs. Even when their beliefs are different from yours, you can show respect by listening. This in no way will diminish the strength of your beliefs; in fact, it can actually strengthen your convictions.

Balancing Work & Family

Positive Attitude

What's the secret to successfully managing life's challenges? Many people would say that a positive attitude is the most important quality you need. A can-do approach will help you in school, at home, at work, and when you have your own family.

You can start now, by practicing how to think positively—and communicating this attitude to your family. The trick is to turn negatives into positives. If you see something as a burden, it will become one. If you turn it into a positive experience, you may even find that it's enjoyable.

For example, parents are often tired after a long day at work. Yet, when they arrive home, they need to listen to family stories, prepare dinner, and maybe help with homework. Here's how a positive attitude can help.

Point out that those after-work responsibilities—dinner, homework and so on—are a great way for the family to spend time together. Parents don't have to do everything themselves. Not only does this take pressure off of the parent, it turns responsibilities into enjoyable activities for the whole family.

Family members who communicate a can-do attitude show anything is possible if their family works together. That's the power of positive thinking.

Think About It

1. What benefits does a positive attitude bring?
2. What are some other ways you can communicate a positive attitude?

Discussion. Ask students how they feel about people who lack integrity. Have they ever had a friend who they thought was honest but who turned out to be dishonest? After the dishonesty came to light, what happened to the friendship?

Activity. Point out to students that many people have different opinions and beliefs. Even though someone has a different belief, you can respect that person by at least listening to what he or she has to say. Have students act out situations in which their opinions differ from another's. Have them show how they would deal with this yet still maintain respect for each other.

A Slice of Life

"Hey, Tricia, here's your notebook! Thanks, you're a lifesaver!" Travis called as he joined the group of students about to enter the chemistry lab. Tricia tucked the notebook away.

Throughout lab, Tricia's thoughts wandered to Travis. They had known each other for over four months now, and it had been a great four months! He was so much fun to be with and so thoughtful of her. Even her parents approved of Travis. They said that he was a "nice young man" and "came from a good family." It was nice to have her family approve of a friend for a change.

"So what if he isn't perfect?" she thought. "What's wrong with helping him a little with his chemistry? I'm sure that he could have done his lab report on his own if only he had less to do." She nudged the worrisome thoughts to the back of her mind.

Tricia was a good student and had always worked hard for her A's and B's. She was an honest person and took pride in her achievements. Sharing her work with Travis, she supposed, was not exactly the right thing to do, but then again, helping someone else couldn't be altogether wrong, could it?

Two days later they were having their weekly lab quiz. When Mr. Hilliard was called to the office to answer the phone, Travis passed Tricia a note. "What formula did you use for number nine?" the note read.

Thinking It Through

- What values do you see in Tricia's thoughts and actions? Are there any conflicts?
- What do you think Tricia will do about Travis's note? Why?
- Does cheating have any harmful effects? How can this help a person decide where to put it on the value scale?
- If you were in Tricia's position, what would you do, and why?

◆ Empathy

Which of these responses to a troubled friend shows empathy? "Chin up; you'll do better on the next test," or "You look down about your grade; it must have been a hard test." If you said the second one, you are right. **Empathy** is seeing another person's point of view. With empathy, you show the other person that his or her feelings are real and you understand them. The first statement above says, "You shouldn't feel as you do." The second one says, "I see how you feel and I understand." People of character learn how to lend this type of support to others.

More About Character. One component of empathy is the ability to assume the perspective of another person. Sometimes by listening and understanding the other person's point of view, the person will be encouraged. Divide students into teams of three and have one partner verbalize a real or fictional personal problem to another. The other person should act out the problem from the partner's point of view with the third person. The "person with the problem" should judge the accuracy of the dramatization.

◆ Prejudice

Two related destructive attitudes are prejudice (PREJ-ud-us) and stereotypical thinking. **Prejudice** is an unfair or biased opinion. Prejudicial feelings are most often linked to religion, politics, and race or ethnic origins. Prejudiced people are those who judge others and analyze situations according to a very limited perspective. Because of their limited view, they do not see many truths or factors which may be relevant. This leads to incorrect opinions and unfair actions.

If you feel prejudice toward others, examine the reasons why. Are you merely mimicking the attitude of someone else? Look for the facts and become knowledgeable. This may change your attitude.

◆ Stereotyping

One of the greatest sources of prejudice is the practice of stereotyping. **Stereotyping** means prejudging people on the basis of personal characteristics or group associations. Examples of stereotypical quotes include "dumb blonde," "absentminded professor," and "tough, macho male." Obviously, all blondes are not dumb; neither are all professors absentminded, nor all males tough and macho. Stereotypes form the basis of some serious ills in society — racism, sexism, and ageism. While stereotypes are clearly illogical and immoral, they are difficult to change. People who have formed habits of thinking in stereotypes do not want to reexamine their ideas. They may suffer from low self-esteem and unconsciously hope to build up their own images by making others look bad. The greatest danger of stereotypical thinking is the limitation it places on a person's potential.

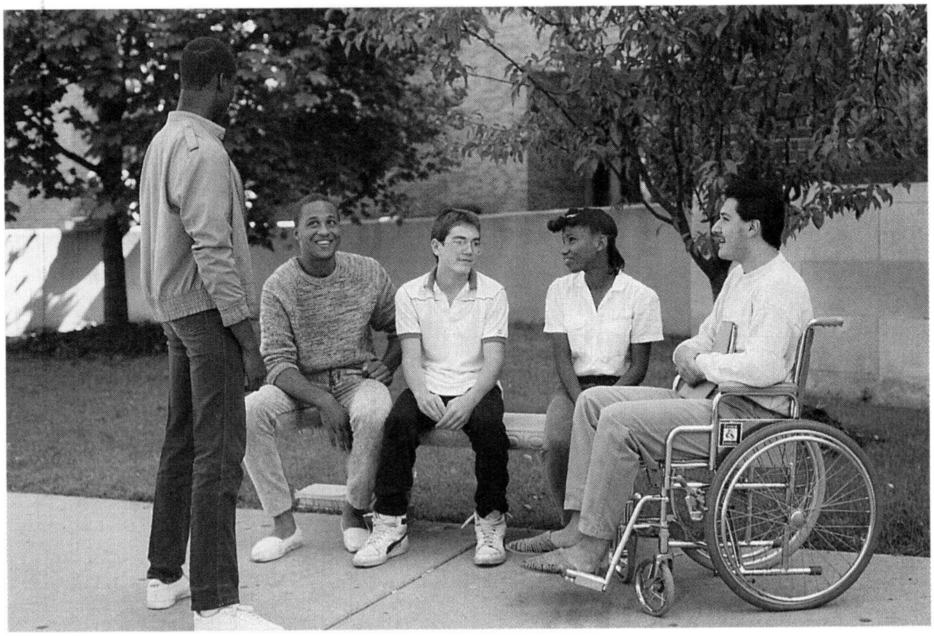

Those who are prejudiced lock out certain people and experiences from their lives. What are the potential losses when they do this?

Problem Solving. In the society we live in today, there is much prejudice among racial, religious, and political groups. Ask students to list some positive ways that communities can try to eliminate this problem. Can a group of people make the difference or does it take a whole community working together?

Activity. Have students bring in a newspaper or magazine article that contains an example of a stereotype. Ask them to explain why they selected it. Is the stereotype fair or unfair to any group of people? What are examples of positive stereotypes? Are they fair or not?

What stereotypes do people sometimes have about elderly people? What do you think about this?

◆◆◆

Taking on Responsibility

A sure sign of maturity is a person's willingness and desire to be responsible. Teens who are moving in this direction feel responsibility for themselves, their family and friends, and their community. They care.

Becoming a caring person brings rewards to the individual as well as benefits to society. Helping others gives a feeling of satisfaction and strengthens self-esteem. Skills are often learned or refined, which can transfer to a career. As society benefits from the efforts of caring citizens, the world becomes a better place to live.

◆ Responsibility for Self

"I made this mess, so I'll clean it up."

"I'll stay home and study tonight, so I can go to the movie tomorrow night."

"I made a mistake; I'm sorry."

Discussion. Students have many responsibilities as teenagers. Ask students what some of those are. As they mature, how will those responsibilities change? What new responsibilities might they take on as an adult? Are they more accountable for their actions in handling those responsibilities as adults?

Words like these are frequently spoken by responsible teens. Character develops as they take on responsibility for their actions, their mistakes, their successes and failures, and their decisions.

Becoming responsible means you must learn to do four things:

- Develop your ability to think clearly.
- Begin to make well thought-out decisions.
- Learn to act on your own decisions.
- Be willing to live with the results of your actions.

◆ Family and Friends

Young people of character care about their families and friends. Angel cooks at home and helps care for her younger brother. Brett folds the laundry and runs errands. Randy took care of the neighbors' house and yard while they were on vacation. Becky helped a friend move into an apartment. All of these young people feel a sense of responsibility to their families and friends. It shows in their actions.

Activity. Ask students to interview their family members or close friends to find out responsibilities they have to themselves and their family members. When did they take on these responsibilities and when did they change?

I CAN ◆◆◆ Make Improvements

Change is always possible. Deon made this discovery in his life.

"My problems started in little ways. No one was home most of the time, so I spent a lot of hours on the street. If you want trouble, you can sure find it there. At first a couple buddies and I got caught for vandalism. Later the charges were breaking and entering. When I got involved with a gang, things got more serious. An assault charge was added to my record.

"Deep inside I didn't feel good about any of it. My family was hurting too. Several people tried to reach me, but I didn't have any use for them. It wasn't until my best friend died in a gang fight that I started to question my whole way of living.

"Getting out wasn't easy. Once a gang gets hold of you, they like to hang on, but I decided to try. There were some tough moments, but my uncle helped me, and I made it.

"Today I think differently. The things I care about are different. I've got some hope for my future now, and I actually feel good about myself. Maybe the best part is that eventually I'd like to help others get back on track. That's my goal anyway."

- What do you think led Deon to delinquency?
- How would you describe his character before and after?
- Have Deon's values changed? Explain with specifics.
- If Deon could make dramatic changes, could you change your character in some way if you wanted to? Are there any changes you would like to make?

◆ Community

Citizenship shows a person's concern for community. Harry Jenkins at 75 proudly tells that he hasn't missed voting in an election for over 50 years. He always says, "If you didn't vote, then don't complain." What is his point?

Responsibility to community can be shown in many ways. Taking care of your property is one. Following laws is another. Making your community a better place to live is still another.

Today's teens have concerns of far greater scope than generations before. Their sense of responsibility to community has expanded to the global community. Social problems, such as hunger, poverty, pollution, and the plight of the homeless, are not restricted by boundary lines or nationality. The needs are felt by human beings everywhere.

Life Management Skills. Ask students to write a description of a peer who is involved in any aspect of community service. Have students find out how the person became involved, what he or she does, and evaluate the values involved in such action. How might students relate this to their own lives?

More About Gangs and Violence. In some cities gangs are a serious problem. Teens can counteract the situation in many ways. They can: make a pact with themselves and others to keep the peace; report what they see to authorities; join or create a peer conflict-resolution group; reject violence in the media; stay away from drugs; and join a neighborhood crime watch in the school or community.

When people take responsibility for what goes on in the community, everyone benefits. What can you do to make your community a better place in which to live?

Every community has volunteer groups already in place and volunteer resources ready to provide information. You may be able to get ideas by looking in the yellow pages of your telephone directory under "Volunteer Services" or "Social Service Organizations." Through volunteering, teens can prepare for their roles as responsible citizens and leaders in the very near future. Moreover, the attitude of caring returns to those who reach out by making them feel good about themselves.

Volunteering helps you as well as others. How are these young people benefitting themselves and their community?

◆ Volunteerism

Today, community caring is often voluntary in nature. **Volunteerism** is the practice of offering services of one's own free will. Many teens today are working to save the environment through ecological awareness programs and recycling centers. Others donate time to serve the special needs of disabled children, the elderly, the homeless, and other teens.

Life Management Skills. Have each student choose and research a different program or organization utilizing teen volunteers. What services does the program offer and what duties does the volunteer perform? What values are highlighted by the work?

Photo Focus. Ask students to look at the photo above. These students appear to be happy doing volunteer work. Ask students if they have ever volunteered to do work in their community. If so, what organization and what type of work was it?

SIDELIGHT

Leading Questions

Q: Who is a *leader*?
A: A good leader is a person who helps members of a group move toward common, worthwhile goals.
Q: What personal qualities does an effective leader usually have?
A: Effective leaders are confident, yet cooperative. They are assertive, yet caring, enthusiastic, dependable, and energetic. They are organized and still flexible.
Q: What are the most common leadership styles?
A: There are two main styles of leadership:

- In the *directive approach,* the leader tells group members what to do. Directive leaders make group plans, assign tasks, oversee members in the completion of tasks, and evaluate results.
- In the *participatory approach,* the leader involves the group members in decision making. Plans are made following democratic processes; members volunteer for tasks and work together to complete and evaluate.

Q: Which leadership style is best?
A: The best approach to leadership depends upon the task, the qualities of the leader, and the makeup of the group. In general, highly intelligent leaders with workable plans that are already well-developed do best in directive settings. Where all ideas of group members are needed to arrive at the best plan, a participatory approach is better.
Q: Why are leadership skills important?
A: Leaders are people who see that things get done. Leaders are needed in every aspect of life — from family, school, and work groups to those in religion, politics, public service, and civic affairs.

◆◆◆

More About Volunteering. Help your students see that volunteerism comes in many different degrees. Some people almost make an unpaid career out of volunteering, giving hundreds of hours to their causes. Although this is commendable, not everyone has this kind of time to give. Volunteer efforts can be made singly or in a group. People can join an existing group or start their own efforts with a friend or with many others. They could begin with something as simple as a resolution to pick up loose garbage in the neighborhood whenever it is spotted. Students may have other ideas in addition to these: tutoring children; visiting and helping the elderly; coaching in a summer sports program for children; hospital work; and rehabilitating the neighborhood. Make sure students understand that although volunteer work does not provide income, there are many other benefits to be gained.

CHAPTER 3

Review

Answers
Testing Your Memory

1. Any three from the list on page 42.
2. A clear code of ethics can help you make the right decisions on the spot.
3. Your actions reveal what your true values are.
4. Ask yourself if your actions could be harmful or destructive to you or anyone else. If the answer is "yes," your values are headed in the wrong direction.
5. People with integrity are honest, they do not lie to protect themselves or get their own way, and they keep their word.
6. People who think in stereotypes do not want to reexamine their ideas. They may have a low self-esteem.
7. Caring for others gives a person a feeling of satisfaction and strengthens self-esteem. Skills are gained and can sometimes be transferred to a career. The world becomes a better place.
8. **Any four:** ecology; disabled children; the elderly; the homeless; needs of other teens.

Summarizing the Chapter

- Your character reflects your moral maturity.
- Maturity is not based on age, but on actions.
- A personal code of ethics provides rules for living.
- Ranking your values helps you decide which ones are most important to you.
- Attitudes are reflections of character for others to see.
- Attitudes of respect, integrity, and empathy are constructive forces, while prejudice and stereotypical thinking are destructive attitudes.
- Becoming responsible means learning to think clearly, to make sound decisions, to act on your decisions, and to live with results.
- Volunteerism offers opportunities for people to learn caring behaviors and take on responsibility.

Testing Your Memory

1. List three signs of maturity.
2. How can having a code of ethics help you?
3. How can you distinguish between values that are real and those that receive only "lip service"?
4. What will help you choose the right values?
5. Describe three characteristic behaviors of people with integrity.
6. Why do some people form the habit of thinking in stereotypes?
7. What benefits can be gained from caring for others?
8. Name four types of causes in which volunteers are needed in most communities today.

Thinking Critically

1. Select three milestones of mature behavior from those listed on page 42. Give an example for each of these from your own experiences.
2. If you had to write a code of ethics for all people to follow, what principles would you include? Discuss these in class and see if you can agree on five.
3. What basic values do you think society agrees on?
4. How can prejudices be eliminated?

Taking Action

1. Develop a written personal code of ethics. List guiding principles or rules by which you live and make decisions.
2. Read a short story or novel of your choice. Select two characters for comparison of maturity levels. List examples of mature and immature behaviors for each. Write a summary statement to draw conclusions.
3. Complete this sentence: "I was honest (or respectful) when I ..."

Making Life Choices

Michael had always believed in letting people make their own decisions. When he made mistakes, he learned from them. He didn't usually make the same mistake twice. He began to question his own beliefs, however, when it involved his younger sister Linda. At thirteen, she was getting involved with the wrong group of young teens. He didn't know if he could stand by and watch her make mistakes in this case. He knew what this crowd did, but his parents did not.

What is the purpose of a code of ethics? Are there ever justifiable reasons for not following one's code of ethics? What would you do if you were in Michael's place?

Using Your Journal

You have just read that a sign of maturity is accepting responsibility for self, for family and friends, and for community. How willing have you been to accept more responsibility? Use your journal to record things you have done that point to your growing sense of responsibility. Do you feel you could do more? Write down ideas for showing your growing sense of responsibility for those around you.

Thinking Critically

1. Answers will vary.
2. Answers will vary.
3. Answers will vary. Students may turn to religious principles and societal laws to find answers.
4. Answers will vary but may include that the process begins with each individual and the way that person influences others, especially future generations.

CHAPTER 4

Your Health

Chapter Challenge

Resources. Refer to the Teacher's Classroom Resources box and Student Workbook for materials related to this chapter.

Look for These Answers . . .

- Why is wellness important?
- What factors contribute to wellness?
- What is stress?
- What defense mechanisms are used in response to stress?
- How can stress be managed?
- What are the threats to wellness?

Look for These Terms . . .

- defense mechanisms
- Food Guide Pyramid
- hygiene
- nutrition
- stress
- wellness

Sasha watched as her grandmother breathed into the machine. The emphysema had gotten so bad that her grandmother had to use the machine several times a day.

When Sasha's grandmother had finished with the machine, she took a few deep, raspy breaths and then lit a cigarette.

"But, Grandma, you can barely breathe. Why are you having a cigarette?" Sasha asked.

"I know I shouldn't, Sasha, but I get so upset when I have to use that breathing machine. This calms me down."

"If you didn't smoke, you might not need that machine, and you wouldn't have to be calmed down," Sasha replied.

"I know, dear, that makes sense, but I guess good sense has never been part of my thinking when it comes to smoking. If it had, I guess I would have given it up when I was turned down for that insurance company job. They only wanted nonsmokers. That would have been a good job, Sasha, but I let it get away."

"I know, Grandma. I'm sorry it worked out that way."

"Sasha, don't let my troubles go for nothing. Remember what happened to me, and you do better. It's not worth it, child; it's just not worth it."

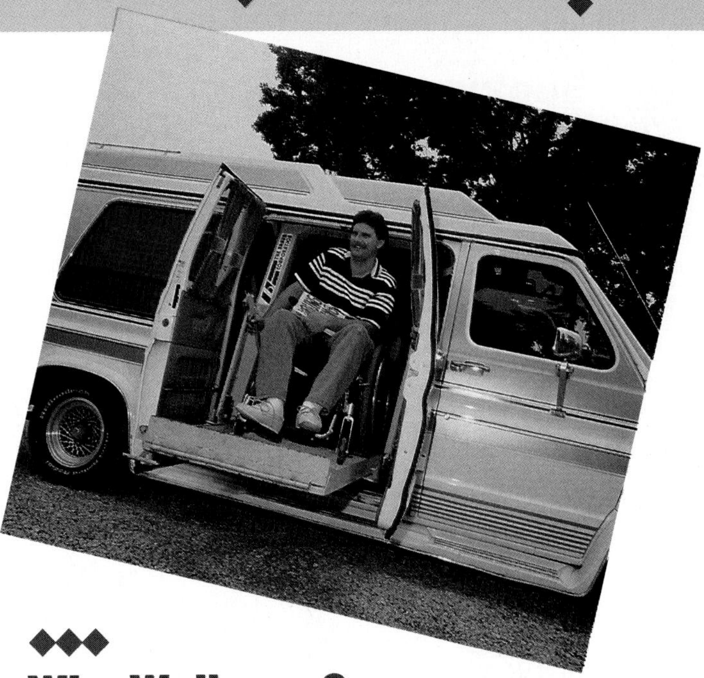

Why Wellness?

When is the right time to think about health — when you are sick or before you become sick? In the past people dealt with illness when it occurred. They may not have had the time or the knowledge to do otherwise. Today people know much more about health. They are aware that good health practices can often prevent or postpone many illnesses or decrease their severity. Although people must still deal with illness when it occurs, much more emphasis is placed on staying well in the first place. This is what wellness is all about.

Good health includes more than just a healthy body. It includes your emotional well-being too. Often the two work hand in hand. The better your physical state, the better your emotional state and vice versa. If one suffers, the other is soon to follow.

Chapter Opener. Ask students to read the opening scenario to the chapter. Ask the following questions: What inconsistency do you see in the grandmother's behavior? Why has this occurred? Do people think about the future when they choose harmful habits or behavior? Why? Do you think Sasha will listen to her grandmother's warning?

Work and Family. Point out to students that people who must combine work and family obligations often have very busy schedules. Ask them what impact this can have on health. What precautions should people take to maintain good health in such circumstances?

Life Management Skills. Have students contact the American Cancer Society and Heart Association to receive health prevention guidelines. What preventive measures do they practice? Why does taking an active role in staying healthy also boost self-esteem?

◆◆◆

Seeking Wellness

Wellness is a way of living each day that includes choices and decisions based on healthy attitudes. It comes as a result of good hygiene, proper nutrition, plenty of rest, regular exercise, and emotional stability. By attending to each of these, you can feel good, look your best, and get the maximum enjoyment out of life.

Balancing Work & Family

Making Time for Meals

Busy family members with busy schedules may be tempted to grab a snack, stop in at a fast food place, or skip meals altogether. Yet people on the run need the nutrients that well-planned meals can bring. Here are some ways families can work together to eat well.

- **Plan ahead.** As a family, sit down together each weekend and plan the meals for the week. Figure out who will be home for which meals, then decide what those meals should be.
- **Share the load.** Decide who will take responsibility for each meal. If you know ahead of time that you're cooking that spaghetti dinner on Wednesday, you can plan your other activities around that commitment.
- **Cook in quantities.** Many foods freeze well or will keep in the refrigerator for a few days. Cooking extra usually takes no more time and provides for future meals. Brainstorm creative uses of leftovers with your family.

Think About It

1. What are some other ways families can work together to make sure they eat well?

◆◆◆

Good Hygiene

Good **hygiene** (HY-jeen) means practicing cleanliness. Doing so will help you keep your body in good condition and also help keep you from catching the germs that lead to illness. Not every society and culture follow the same rules for cleanliness. Not every skin type needs the same care. You need to determine what is best for you.

Germs are commonly spread by hand. Washing your hands regularly with soap reduces the risk of spreading germs. Regular bathing not only makes you more presentable to others but it also keeps you healthier. Good oral hygiene is important too. Proper tooth care from an early age will enable you to keep your teeth working well for you in the years ahead.

◆◆◆

Proper Nutrition

When you eat the right food for proper health and development, you are following good **nutrition**. Eating nutritiously becomes natural with a little know-how and with the help of the Food Guide Pyramid.

The **Food Guide Pyramid**, shown on the facing page, is a guide to help you choose the foods you need every day. The pyramid divides foods into five basic groups:

- Bread, cereal, rice, and pasta
- Vegetables
- Fruits
- Milk, yogurt, and cheese
- Meat, poultry, fish, dry beans, eggs, and nuts

For each group, you are advised to eat a certain number of servings each day.

Activity. Ask students to report on their skin and hair type and dental condition. What grooming regime is appropriate for them? How often should they carry it out? Could they take steps to improve their grooming habits?

More About Acne. Studies have shown that there is no strong evidence to support beliefs that chocolate and fried foods cause acne. Things that can cause or aggravate the condition are: hormonal changes, certain cosmetics, extreme heat and humidity, as well as certain habits such as resting the chin on a hand.

The Food Guide Pyramid

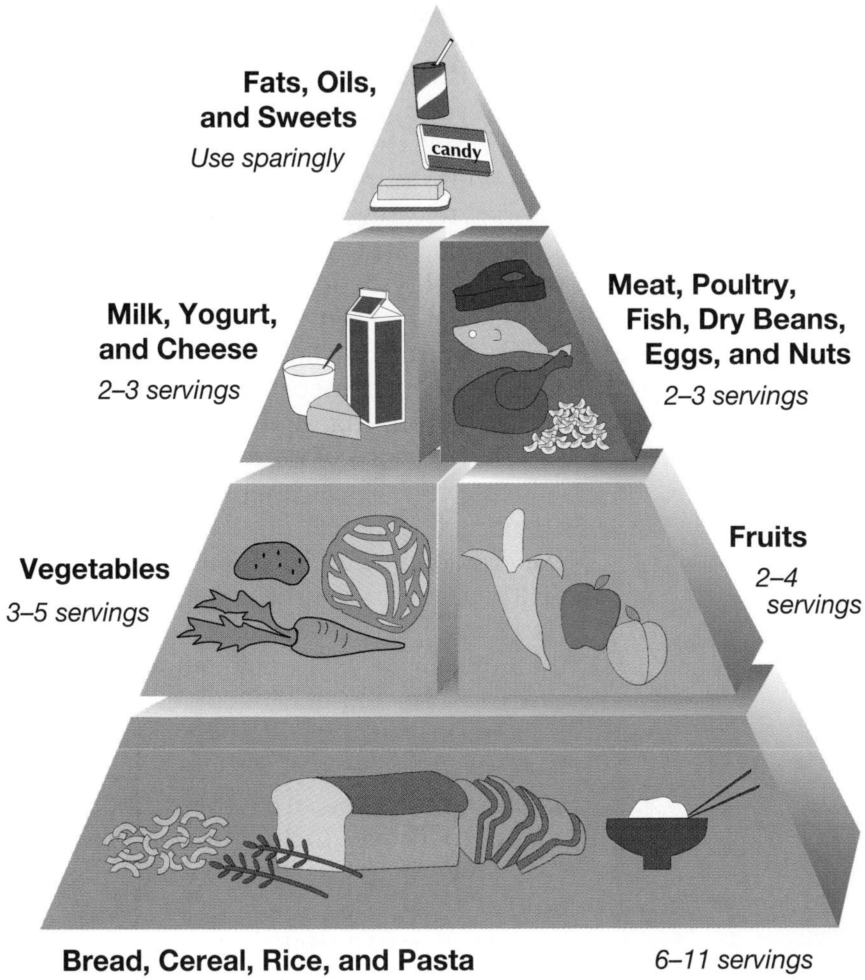

Sample serving sizes:

Bread, cereal, rice, and pasta
1/2 cup cooked cereal, rice, or pasta
1 slice of bread

Vegetables
1 cup raw leafy vegetables
1/2 cup cooked vegetables
3/4 cup vegetable juice

Fruits
1 medium apple, orange, or banana
1/2 cup cooked or canned fruit

Milk, yogurt, and cheese
1 cup milk or yogurt
2 ounces processed cheese

Meat, poultry, fish, dry beans, eggs, and nuts
1 egg
2-3 ounces cooked lean meat, poultry, or fish
1/2 cup cooked dry beans

The Food Guide Pyramid is a simple guide to healthful eating. You'll get the nutrients you need if you eat the suggested number of servings from each group each day.

The way the food groups are arranged on the pyramid is significant. At the base of the pyramid is the food group from which you need the most servings each day. As you go up the pyramid, the number of servings you need goes down.

At the very tip of the pyramid you will see fats, oils, and sweets. Foods high in these substances tend to be low in nutrients and high in calories. You should try to limit your intake of foods that are high in fat and sugar and focus on foods in the five basic groups instead.

The list to the right of the pyramid gives examples of serving sizes. As you can see, serving sizes are quite small, so you don't have to eat a lot of food to meet your daily requirements.

Another way to make sure you eat right is to study the nutrition labels on any prepared foods that you buy. These labels list the major nutrients found in the food, the amount of fat, and the percentage of daily requirements that the food provides.

Good nutrition makes for a healthy body as well as a healthy mind. By eating a balanced diet from the five main food groups, you give your body all the fuel it needs to function. This is vital to total wellness.

Life Management Skills. Have students keep a diary of everything they eat for one week and then share their diaries with the class. Have students suggest ways to make over diets for better nutrition, good health, and high energy benefits.

More About Nutrition. Vegetarians need to figure out how to obtain the needed nutrients from fewer foods. Vegetarians who eat eggs, cheese, and milk will find it easier to obtain all the nutrients. Those who eat plant foods only need to combine complementary foods to get the high-quality protein they need.

◆◆◆

Plenty of Rest

Your body needs rest in order to operate efficiently. Most people require eight to ten hours of sleep each night. Women require more than men, and teens require more than adults. Teens are in various stages of growth and require extra sleep to grow properly.

Establishing a regular sleep routine is another big plus. Going to sleep and waking up at about the same times every day sets a regular sleep pattern for your body. Your body, in turn, develops regular working and resting cycles, so it functions more efficiently. Short rest periods may help make up for lost sleep, but a regular sleep routine is best. Loss of sleep affects your mind, your eyes, your mood, and your appearance.

The type of exercise you choose is not important. Exercising regularly is. In what ways do you get exercise each week?

Discussion. Ask students to share examples of sleeping patterns. Do any have insomnia or other sleep disturbances? If so, have they consulted health professionals? What are steps to insure a good night's sleep?

◆◆◆

Regular Exercise

Exercise is habit forming. Those who exercise at a young age are more likely to continue to be active throughout life. Exercise helps your body run more smoothly, burns excess calories, releases stress, improves posture and appearance, and improves your attitude and mental agility. Besides all of this, it feels good — especially when you do something you enjoy. Running, walking, skiing, biking, aerobics, tennis, baseball, football, basketball, soccer, swimming, and racquetball are all wonderful forms of exercise.

Before you begin an exercise program, have a complete physical to be safe. Choose an exercise you like, and do that for a minimum of 30 minutes four times a week. Daily exercise is even better. For variety choose more than one activity. Think about what comes easily to you. You may like that the best.

Be sure to warm up with light exercise first. Walking and stretching are good. Repeat this *after* exercising too so that your body has a chance to recover. Including a warm up and cool down with exercise can help prevent injury.

When Jose first started running, he hated it. He was a little overweight, and he could only run a short distance before he was out of breath. With determination, however, he stuck with it. He read about running and talked to runners before getting involved. That way, he was careful not to do anything that would cause injury. Now that he is in condition, he runs distances and feels wonderful. Each week is a new challenge as he tries to improve his distances and his times.

Activity. Have students visit an exercise gym. Have them interview a fitness instructor of the gym to find out what exercise program is good to start with. Ask them if they are involved in such a program and how they think this helps a person stay fit.

I CAN ♦♦ Be Healthy

For some people the idea of good health means nothing until they discover what it is like to feel good. This is what happened to Mary.

"I had read it in magazines. My health teacher taught it to us. Even some of my friends were into health, but for a long time I didn't pay any attention.

"Then one day I just turned my life around. I was tired — literally. I was also overweight, and I just didn't want to do anything except sit around all the time. Boredom had set in too.

"Bicycling saved me. I found a friend who likes to bike. We started going on short trips and eventually long ones. I discovered that by eating right, I could do better. Now I eat lots of carbohydrates, you know, pasta — in every form. I've also cut way back on fat. Nutrition labels tell you how much fat things contain. I know I'm not supposed to have over 55 grams of fat each day, so I strive to keep under that. It's different for young males, 72 grams. One slice of pizza can have 6 grams of fat, so now I eat two slices instead of four. Cutting down on red meat has also helped me eliminate fat.

"It's amazing how good I feel now. I'm trimmer, firmer, energetic, and more mentally alert. Good health is a way of life for me now."

- What are the advantages of a healthful lifestyle?
- What motivated Mary to choose a healthier way of living?
- Is there anything you need to do to live a healthier life? How can you motivate yourself?

♦♦♦

Emotional Health

Your emotional health is just as important to your total wellness as physical health. Studies indicate that a positive attitude is a factor in controlling the frequency and severity of illnesses. People with a positive attitude have less stress. They have learned how to control it.

What is stress? When something causes you to have physical, mental, or emotional strain or tension, you have **stress.** Not all people react the same way. Some can handle more pressures than others. When stress does occur, it shows in many ways. From your own experience, you may be able to add to this list of the signs of stress: tight muscles; upset stomach; headaches; fingernail biting; sleeplessness; increased heart rate; fast breathing; fidgeting; lip biting; and rashes. When stress is ongoing, physical illnesses, such as ulcers or heart trouble, can result. Emotional problems may also occur. A person may be anxious, fearful, or depressed. Some even turn to alcohol or other drugs as a means of temporarily covering up the stressful feelings. This, of course, only compounds the problem.

Activity. After reading the chapter, have students list three to five issues or situations that cause the most stress in their daily lives. Have them evaluate why these things cause stress and list one step for each that could help alleviate stress.

More About Handling Stress. Negative emotions and stress suppress the immune system; some studies report that laughter and feelings of trust and hope will help you feel better. When people laugh, they let go of anxiety, fear, embarrassment, hostility, and anger.

Some people have stress when they must speak before a group. This can be overcome with effort.

◆◆◆

Defense Mechanisms

When people experience stress, they react in all sorts of ways. **Defense mechanisms** are reactions to stressful situations. Some are positive and some negative. Do you see yourself in any of these?

- **Attacking Directly.** Tackling a problem head-on is fine as long as you do so calmly. Jo Ellyn was bothered by her friend's habit of changing plans at the last minute without telling her. She decided to bring this up in conversation when the time seemed right. This seemed better than starting an argument when she was upset.
- **Redirecting.** Redirecting enables a person to turn negative emotions like irritation, anger, aggression, and frustration into worthwhile efforts. Homework, sports, music, hobbies, and volunteer work represent desirable examples of redirecting.
- **Daydreaming.** Most people get lost in their thoughts now and then. Mattie likes to think about romantic situations. As long as she does not replace the real world with her fantasies, this is okay.
- **Compensating.** This can be either negative or positive. When Arianna feels inferior to her friends who have more money, she talks about everything new she has. This is negative because boasting is boring. When Travis left the soccer team due to a knee injury, he joined the newspaper staff instead. This was positive since it gave him something constructive to take the place of his loss.
- **Denying.** When faced with a stressful situation, Blake often uses denial. For example, his mother asked, "Who spilled soda on the carpet?" Even though he did spill it, Blake immediately responded, "Not me!" The attempt is to avoid anything negative that might come from admitting responsibility.

Problem Solving. Have students suggest better ways to handle the following: When Dionne arrives at Ellen's party, Ellen thinks Dionne's outfit makes her look terrible and tells her so in front of a crowd; when Bobby picks a fight with someone at a small party, Lila loses her temper and tells him he needs help — in front of his friends.

Problem Solving. Ask students to review the defense mechanisms listed and write a brief example, either real or fictional, to illustrate each. For each negative mechanism, have students offer an alternative way to resolve the situation.

Daydreaming can be pleasant. If this young woman finds she enjoys daydreaming more than real life, however, she has a problem.

A Slice of Life

Mr. Smithers was looking him straight in the eye. He wanted the paper now. It was due today.

Clay squirmed a little. "I just forgot," he said matter of factly.

"That's no excuse, Clay," Mr. Smithers replied. "You've known about this assignment for two weeks."

Clay was feeling the pressure. "Hey, I would have done it, but I was sick last night. Besides that, my dad asked me to run some errands for him, and I had to do them . . ."

"I want you to stop this right now, Clay," Mr. Smithers interrupted.

Clay turned and stormed from the room. "Okay, okay, so I'll do it in study hall. I never understood what you wanted in that paper anyway. You didn't even explain it to our class."

Thinking It Through

- Identify the defense mechanisms that Clay used.
- Do you see any inconsistencies in Clay's responses?
- What do you think Mr. Smithers thought about Clay's comments?
- What advice do you have for Clay?

Observers usually see right through this defense mechanism, if not right away, then later on. Blake's word then becomes questionable all the time.

Sometimes denial is helpful. People who must cope with tragedy, for example, may use denial to give themselves some time to recover. This is a common approach to dealing with death.

Discussion. Discuss the following with students: As a child, every time Karen did something wrong her parents attacked her in some way. Sometimes they used words to punish her. Sometimes they even hit her. All of this was painful for Karen. In time she learned to try to avoid the pain by not admitting her mistakes. Often she tried to put the blame elsewhere — on her sister, a friend, or a circumstance. This became a defense mechanism for her. Ask students why this happened and what they can learn from it. Is there a solution for Karen now that she is seventeen?

• **Forgetting.** Some people "forget" what hurts them. A child who sees a pet killed by a car may blot the image from memory. Like denial, this can save the painful reality for a time when it can be handled. Sometimes people who tuck a traumatic experience away from memory continue to suffer from it in some way. They may decide to seek professional counseling to help them retrieve and deal with the memory.

Forgetting is used by some as an excuse. Pete claimed that he forgot to do a project when the due date arrived. People did not believe him, and they were right.

• **Regressing.** With regression, people act as they did when they were much younger. Childlike traits, such as crying, whining, calling names, and throwing and breaking things, are used. This behavior, which is viewed as immature, is not respected by others.

• **Blaming.** Jacqueline always looks for someone to blame for her own errors or poor decisions. When her team loses, it's the referees' fault. If something goes wrong at work, a fellow employee was the problem. If her grade is low, the teacher's explanation was poor. People who constantly blame others are tiresome. Others easily see through this defense mechanism.

• **Transferring.** Eric picked a fight with his younger brother after his father grounded him for the weekend. This is transferral. Taking out anger or frustration on an innocent bystander is unfair. Only when it turns anger away from the object person to a safer target, such as a pillow or punching bag, is it useful.

• **Converting.** People who turn a problem or emotion into physical ailments are using conversion. For example, Tess developed a stomachache every time she had to get up in front of a group. This was very real and only went away after she learned to deal with her fear.

• **Idealizing.** Vick had such a high opinion of himself that his actions and words were a real bore to everyone. People who place excessive value on themselves, other people, or possessions are practicing idealization.

• **Rationalizing.** When Lara was not asked to go to the homecoming dance, she told everyone that she really did not want to go and she would probably have to work that night anyway. The truth was that she did want to go, but she felt that an excuse was better than admitting that she had not been asked. People usually don't believe such excuses and don't respect the people who make them.

• **Giving Up.** When everything seemed to be going wrong, Norm felt like giving up. He did not feel like trying anymore. Running away seemed like a solution to him. With support and encouragement from friends, he was able to overcome this reaction. Later he realized that running away from problems does not solve them.

◆ Stress Management

As you can see, people respond to stressful situations in many ways. A little stress in life is inevitable. It may even be useful at times, as it pushes you to do better and accomplish more. Much of the time you brush small stresses aside. At some point, however, anyone can feel overloaded by stress.

How can you control the feelings you have each day so that stress does not get out of hand? Stress management skills can help. Here are some suggestions:

• **Keep a positive attitude.** Everything looks a little better when you look at the bright side.

• **Accept the fact that there are things you cannot control.** Make the best of each situation.

• **Take a step back.** Breathe deeply, clear your head, and then decide how to react or not react to a given situation.

Activity. Have students act out: keeping a positive attitude when disappointed by a test grade; dealing with an uncontrollable situation, such as a family move; saying no to pressure to use alcohol; sharing a family problem with a friend. How do these techniques help manage and reduce stress?

Life Management Skills. Point out that most families need to use stress management techniques when trying to balance work and family responsibilities. Ask students to give examples of ways the techniques listed here would help people balance work and family.

• **Plan ahead.** A little organization on the front end can save stress later on.

• **Learn to say "no."** Try not to take on more than you can handle. Refuse to do anything that violates your personal values.

• **Trust an adult friend.** Talk to an adult, perhaps someone other than your parents, who will listen without judging you and then help you sort through your stresses.

• **Develop friendships.** A good friend will want to listen to you and help with problems.

• **Spend some time alone.** Whether you spend it reading a magazine, playing basketball, or watching a movie, take time to unwind. Focus on the pleasure of an activity rather than how well you do.

• **Relax.** Learn some relaxation techniques. Long, slow breathing is one. Concentrating on relaxing each muscle in your body one at a time is another.

• **Exercise.** Not only is this good for your physical health, it keeps your emotional health stable too.

• **Develop a sense of humor.** This can take the pressure off many situations.

◆◆◆

Threats to Wellness

Wellness can be threatened by poor nutrition, lack of rest and exercise, and stress. It can also be threatened in other ways.

◆ Tobacco

Everyone knows that the use of tobacco is a threat to health. Yet although the percentage of adult Americans who smoke has been dropping for some years, tobacco use among teens has been increasing. In all, some 3 million teens smoke or chew tobacco. Some smoke because of peer pressure. Others think that smoking will make them look more grown up. Few teens who start using tobacco think about the consequences of their decision.

You can relieve stress by taking time out to do something that helps you unwind.

Discussion. Discuss with students why people who smoke don't do as well physically in sports. Ask students if they know of someone who started smoking and several years later developed physical problems.

Life Management Skills. Have students organize a class or school "smokeout." Publicize the date well in advance, and, if possible, offer small prizes to every smoker who refrains that day. Smokers might want to start a "quitters" support group.

Whatever excuse a teen may find to smoke or chew tobacco, it is not valid. Here are the reasons why. Smoking and chewing can cause cancer, hypertension, emphysema, headaches, gum and tooth decay, wrinkled skin, and reduced energy levels.

If these reasons are not enough, consider some others. Smoking is unacceptable today in many places. Many homes, businesses, and public buildings do not allow smoking. Some people avoid those who smoke. Job candidates even lose out because they smoke. Moreover, secondhand smoke is harmful to others.

Both cigarettes and chewing tobacco are physically addicting. Your body ultimately feels a need for the nicotine. This addiction makes quitting harder. If you don't want to get yourself in any of the difficult situations that smokers today face, then just don't start. It's your decision. Only you can make it.

◆ Alcohol

Two good reasons exist for not drinking alcohol. Number one, it is a harmful drug. Number two, it is illegal for those who are underage. Alcohol devastates the lives of individuals and their families every day. The problems begin with that first drink.

Alcohol has physical effects. The immediate ones include hangovers, headaches, and blackouts. Dependency and serious health problems can result with continued use.

Alcohol reduces the flow of oxygen to the brain, which impairs balance and judgment. As a result, some 10,000 young people die each year in alcohol-related accidents. These include car and swimming accidents as well as injuries from fights. Alcohol reduces inhibitions, so people do things they normally wouldn't do. This includes trying sex and other drugs. The results may be sexually transmitted diseases, pregnancy, and drug addiction.

SIDELIGHT

Help For Addictions

When people have serious problems with addictions, whether smoking, alcohol, or other drugs, they need help. Many people begin by trying to overcome the problem alone or with the help of family and friends. This is a start. It may be effective. If not, other help is needed.

Counselors and self-help groups are a good resource for any problem. Often hospitals, churches, community agencies, and hot lines provide services. Teens can check with school counselors to find out what resources are available.

People who smoke can often quit on their own. It isn't easy, but it is possible. A gradual approach may work. Finding substitute activities helps. Some people have success with over-the-counter products.

Alcoholics Anonymous (AA) is an excellent resource for people with drinking problems. Families, including teens, can also participate in programs designed to help them deal with the drinker's problem. Many communities have treatment centers that work with alcoholics and their families. Look in the yellow pages of your telephone directory under "Alcoholism."

Many of the same programs that treat alcoholism deal also with other drug problems. Look in the yellow pages of your telephone directory under "Drug Abuse and Addiction — Information and Treatment."

◆◆◆

Activity. Have students contact the National Council on Alcoholism for recent statistics on teen drinking dangers. Have them cite the statistics in a letter to a friend, real or fictional, who has a drinking problem. The letter should persuade the friend to stop.

More About Drinking. Drinking alcohol carries with it many risks. Statistics show that 10,000 young people ages 16-25 are killed each year in alcohol-related accidents of all kinds. The highest number is for auto accidents, with swimming accidents and injuries in fights following.

Teens who party where alcohol is present, whether they drink or not, run the risk of legal problems. Athletic and academic careers can be ruined when this happens. Although teens think it won't happen to them, it often does.

Problems with alcohol do not affect just the person who drinks. Friends and particularly the family also pay a painful price. You will read more about this in Chapter 12.

◆ Other Drugs

Like alcohol, other drugs also alter judgment, reduce inhibitions, and are addictive. They affect your mind and body. They threaten your total wellness, both immediately and long-term.

Results of drug use range from sterility to reduced mental capacity to death. Drugs offer long-term problems in exchange for short-term highs. They do not solve problems; they create them. Just like smoking, the easiest way to stop is never to start. If you are in charge of your own life, you can say "no" when it comes to drugs.

◆ Eating Disorders

Eating disorders are another threat to wellness, usually for teens and young adults. Females are particularly affected, although males — especially athletes — are victims as well.

Anorexia nervosa (an-uh-REX-ee-uh ner-VOH-suh), or self-starvation, is caused by an obsession with thinness combined with psychological problems. People who suffer from this disorder eat so little food that they become profoundly thin even though they think they look good. Malnutrition, fatigue, depression, and menstrual problems can result with this disorder.

Bulimia (buh-LIM-ee-uh) is another eating disorder marked by a pattern of eating in large quantities and then ridding the body of the food in some way. Self-induced vomiting, laxative abuse, and severe dieting are all techniques used. Like anorexia, bulimia also has complicated psychological causes. Malnutrition, fatigue, depression, and menstrual abnormalities can result. Eroded tooth enamel, muscle weakness, dehydration, and heart, kidney, and bowel problems are other long-range effects.

For both disorders, a qualified counselor is usually needed. If untreated and the problem becomes severe, death can result in either situation.

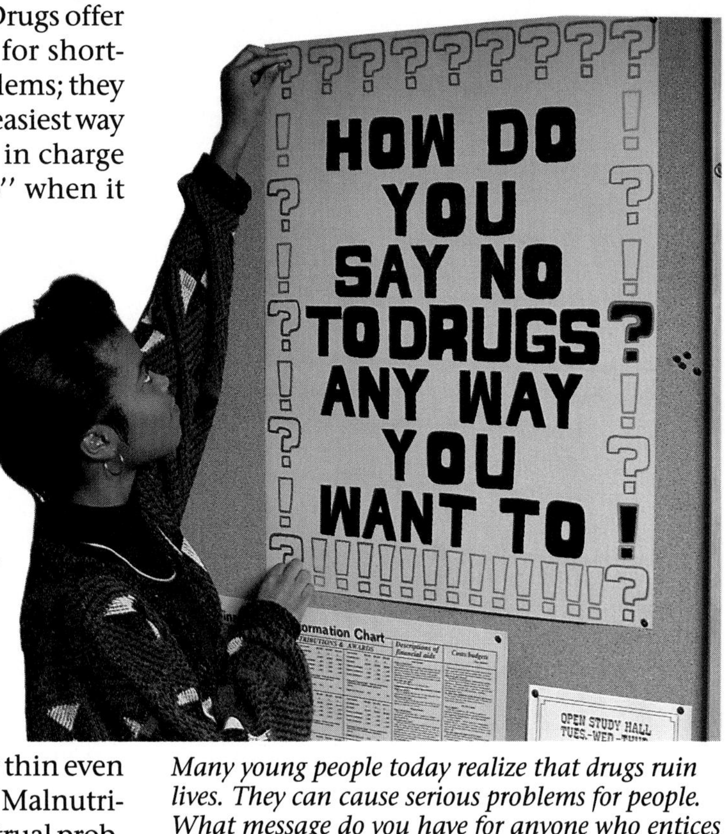

Many young people today realize that drugs ruin lives. They can cause serious problems for people. What message do you have for anyone who entices you to try a drug?

More About Eating Disorders. Many teen eating disorders are a way of dealing with other psychological problems. The disorder is a way for the teen to shut out painful feelings. Have students share possible causes and problems that might spur eating disorders.

Activity. Invite a counselor who specializes in eating disorders to talk with the class. Have students ask questions to find out more information. Who is most affected with eating disorders? How do people around an anorexic or bulimic react to the person's mood change and eating habits? How do people come to seek help?

CHAPTER 4

Review

Summarizing the Chapter

- Wellness includes emotional as well as physical health.
- Hygiene, nutrition, rest, and exercise are all parts of physical wellness.
- Good nutrition means eating the right number of servings from the five basic food groups.
- Exercise should be done regularly.
- People react to stress in many different ways.
- Defense mechanisms are used in response to stress.
- Stress can be managed by following several tips and techniques.
- Tobacco, alcohol, other drugs, and eating disorders threaten total wellness.

Testing Your Memory

1. Why are people more concerned about wellness today than they used to be?
2. List five factors that contribute to wellness.
3. Are the rules of good hygiene identical for all people? Explain your answer.
4. What is the significance of the arrangement of foods on the Food Guide Pyramid?
5. How much sleep do most people require a night?
6. What are the benefits of regular exercise?
7. List five signs of stress.
8. Explain three defense mechanisms and tell whether they are negative or positive.
9. List five suggestions for managing stress.
10. What are two good reasons for not drinking alcohol?

Answers
Testing Your Memory

1. People did not have the time or the knowledge to deal with wellness. Today people know more about health and realize that good health practices can often prevent or postpone many illnesses or decrease their severity.
2. Good hygiene, proper nutrition, plenty of rest, regular exercise, and emotional health.
3. The rules of hygiene are not the same in every society and culture. Also not every skin type requires the same care.
4. You need the most servings of the foods at the bottom. The number of servings you need goes down as you move up the pyramid.
5. Most people require eight-ten hours of sleep per night. Women require more than men, and teens require more than adults.
6. The habit of exercising at a young age is more likely to carry over to adulthood. Exercise helps your body run more smoothly, burns excess calories, releases stress, improves posture and appearance, and improves your attitude and mental agility. It feels good too.

Thinking Critically

1. At which age do you think people are most concerned about wellness: childhood, adolescence, young adulthood, middle-age, or elderly? Why?
2. Is there a relationship between stress and any of these: smoking; alcohol and other drug use; eating disorders? Explain your answer.
3. Can you tell whether or not someone is under stress? Explain your answer.
4. If you walked into a party where teens were drinking alcohol, what would you do?

Taking Action

1. Keep track of your eating habits for a week. Make a list of ways that you could improve.
2. For a week practice deep breathing and muscle relaxing exercises in response to stressful situations. (Do some research to find other relaxation techniques.) Write a paragraph explaining how these worked.
3. Plan and perform a skit that demonstrates a defense mechanism. If negative, show also how the situation could have been handled better.

Making Life Choices

Ashley is about 10 pounds overweight, according to the charts. Every time she picks up a magazine, she sees pictures of the thin, attractive models. In her heart she longs to look like them. She feels that thinness would be an accomplishment and bring her self-satisfaction and perhaps love. Ashley is an excellent student. She knows how to tackle projects with intensity. The thought of losing weight is on her mind much of the time.

How would you evaluate Ashley's feelings about weight? If you were her, what would you do?

Using Your Journal

In this chapter you learned about wellness and some of the threats to wellness. Think about your own state of health. Is it as good as it could be? Can you see room for improvement? Use your journal to analyze your physical and emotional health. List any threats to your health that you need to deal with. Then prepare a plan for dealing with each threat in turn.

7. **Any five** of the signs listed on page 59.
8. **Any three** defense mechanisms listed on pages 60-62.
9. **Any five** of the skills listed on pages 62 and 63.
10. Alcohol is a harmful drug and it is illegal for those who are underage.

Thinking Critically

1. Answers will vary. Students may choose older age categories because this is when people are more likely to be ill. Point out, however, that a concern for wellness at a young age can affect the quality of life later on.
2. Yes. Explanations will vary.
3. Often you can tell by watching for the signs of stress.
4. Leaving is the most responsible decision.

CHAPTER 5

Your Future

Chapter Challenge

Resources. Refer to the Teacher's Classroom Resources box and Student Workbook for materials related to this chapter.

Look for These Answers . . .

- What philosophies of life show attitudes about the future?
- Describe the trends that are likely to affect your future.
- What are the five basic human needs that were identified by Maslow?
- What are goals and how are they determined?
- How can you take control of your life?

Look for These Terms . . .

- coping skills
- goal
- hierarchy
- mobility
- needs
- self-actualization
- trends
- wants

"Class is just more interesting on some days than it is on others," Phil thought.

"What worries you most about the future?" Ms. Garrison had asked. Phil listened to what Jamaal had to say.

"I just hope I'll be able to find a good job," Jamaal said. Some of my friends haven't been able to find anything. They spend all their time just hanging out." Phil wondered if Jamaal's friends had stayed in school. He knew it was hard if you didn't.

"Money — that's my concern," said Eileen. "I'd like to be able to live the way my parents do — or better. It's going to be harder for me than it is for them. I guess that means getting a decent job too."

"None of that matters if we ruin the environment," said Dwight. "That's what worries me most."

The exchange went on. Some had concerns about family, some about health. Some were anxious about possible war. They all had important things to say, but it was Audrey's comments toward the end of class that most affected Phil. He would remember Audrey's words for a long time.

Audrey said, "I try not to worry about things. I am in control of my own life, and I'll do my best to make my own future secure. As far as the world is concerned, some things are out of my control. I can't worry about those things. What I can do, though, is try to make the world a little better place in my own way. At least that will make me feel like I'm part of the solution rather than the problem. If everyone would do that, we'd all have less to worry about."

Chapter Opener. Ask students to read the opening scenario to the chapter. Ask these questions: What concerns do you have about the future? How would you describe Audrey's self-esteem? Why do some people contribute to the world's problems and others contribute to the solutions? If you do not control your life and future, who will?

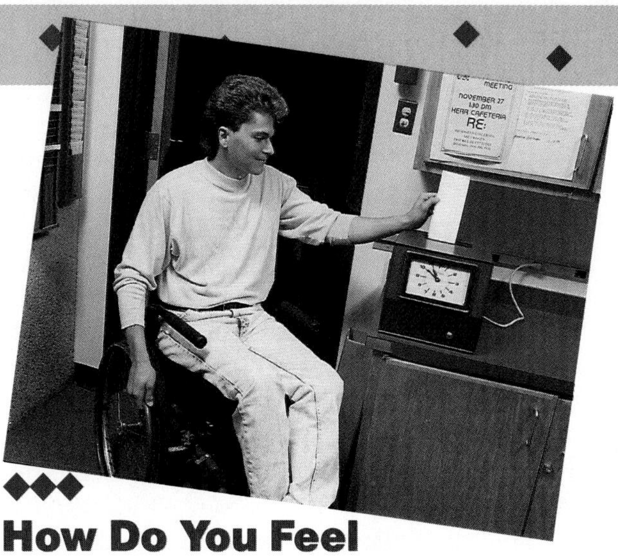

How Do You Feel About the Future?

All the world's a stage. And all the men and women merely players:
They have their exits and their entrances,
And one man in his time plays many parts.
Shakespeare, *As You Like It*

Nothing stays the same. The world is an ever-moving, ever-changing stage for the drama of "Life." When you think about the future, what do you picture? What will the world be like? What does life have in store for you? Are you ready to reap the rewards and conquer the challenges?

Thoughts of the future bring forth a wide range of responses. How people feel is often rooted in one of these basic philosophies. Which one comes closest to your way of thinking?

- **Fate.** "Whatever will be will be." This attitude reflects a fatalistic philosophy. It assumes that you have no control over what happens.
- **Present Focus.** Some say: "Live for the moment" and "Worry about it when the time comes." These feelings deny the need for concern or planning for the future.
- **Work Ethic.** "Life is what you make it." This stresses the value of hard work and makes the individual the master of his or her own fate.

For some, the future represents the unknown and causes a natural feeling of fear. After all, there are many uncertainties, many question marks. When seven-year-old Brandon went to the hospital for surgery, his parents and the hospital staff explained to him much of what would happen. They showed him the equipment that would be used and the garments that would be worn. They also planned what to bring to make the experience more comfortable. This helped eliminate some of Brandon's fear before and during the hospital stay.

The same principle can be applied to the future. When you think about what to expect and you plan for it, doubts and fears can give way to clarity and confidence. You can move forward with a positive outlook.

Americans move often. Where do you think you will live during your lifetime?

◆◆◆

What Trends May Affect You?

Change is a sure thing. Ironically, change is the only absolute constant in life. People change, circumstances change, and the world changes.

Changes will occur within you. Some inner changes are part of your progress through the ages and stages of development. Other inner changes are reactions to life experiences and responses to people in your environment. Inner changes are largely within the limits of your self-control.

Changes will also occur around you. Changes will be seen in all aspects of life, from individual to family to work. The fields of health, communication, and transportation will continue to undergo rapid change, along with government, international relations, and the economy.

As changes are noted, observers recognize **trends**, or general directions of change. What trends are likely to have an effect on your future?

- **Mobility.** The **mobility** of Americans, meaning their tendency to move often, has increased. In fact, half of all families change dwellings every five years. Young, single people move far more often.
- **Changing Family Patterns.** The traditional family of breadwinner dad, stay-at-home mom, and children accounts for a smaller number of American families today than it did in the past. Families with several generations of relatives in the same home are increasing. Family patterns now include increasing numbers of single-parent families, step relationships, and singles living alone.
- **Two-Income Families.** Economic conditions as well as career interest have brought about an increase in the number of two-income families. This, in turn, has increased the demand for quality child care.

Problem Solving. Ask students to write a brief paragraph that describes an ideal future for themselves. Where would they live? What would they do? What lifestyle would they have? Ask them to list at least three ideal goals. Then have them evaluate their imaginary plans. What aspects are fatalistic, lying beyond their control? What aspects do they have the ability to achieve through hard work? What concrete steps can anyone take to realize future goals?

• **Shifting Gender Roles.** A move toward gender equality has changed the way men and women are treated in many arenas. In the world of work, women are gradually advancing to levels of responsibility once reserved for men. Men are doing jobs once done mainly by women and vice versa. In the home, attitudes about what males and females "should" do are giving way to dividing responsibilities according to skills and interests.

• **Aging of America.** Americans are living longer, and the percentage of older people in the population is growing significantly. Many older people rely on social security payments for support in their retirement. Some people are concerned about the ability of younger people in the work force to support this growing population of older people. There are also concerns about health care, transportation, and housing for the elderly. Many older people have financial problems.

• **Changing Employment Conditions.** In this age of corporate takeovers and "downsizings," employees have less job security than they used to have. People need greater flexibility than ever before to learn new skills and switch fields of employment as conditions change.

• **Changing Work Patterns.** Many companies are allowing employees more flexibility in the way they work. Some employees telecommute — they work at home and send their work to their office electronically. Others choose the hours they work under a system called *flextime.* More companies are also offering part-time work or are allowing workers to share a job. Such changes have been particularly welcome to parents with small children.

• **Home-Based Businesses.** More and more people deal in information. Computers and communications technology make it possible for people to obtain and transmit information from their home. The last few years have seen a significant growth in the number of people who have moved out of the corporate world and who now operate a small business from home.

• **Technology.** The computer has brought about profound changes in almost all aspects of our lives. In the home, in business and industry, in education, recreation, communication, and government, computers have changed the way people operate. Routine tasks can now be done much more quickly and efficiently, freeing up time for more challenging work. Information technology has increased our awareness of the world. Today, thanks to satellite television, you can witness events in other parts of the world at the time that they are occurring.

Advanced technology makes it possible for people to telecommute — to work at home and transmit their work to their office electronically.

Photo Focus. Have students look at the photo on this page. In what ways has technology enabled more people to work from home? What effects is modern technology likely to have on the way people organize their homes?

Work and Family. Ask students to report on one nontraditional, two-income, multigenerational or single-parent family. Have them choose one they know or one from a TV program. Ask them to show how members share household tasks and responsibilities and manage efficiently.

• **Information Economy.** Automation carried the American economy in the first half of the twentieth century from an agricultural focus to an industrialized one. Now the computer is producing an age of information. This affects job opportunities and the skills needed to work in the information economy. Many jobs will require computer literacy — an ability to use computers to gather, manipulate, and exchange information.

• **Service Economy.** As manufacturing becomes more automated, fewer workers are needed to produce goods. At the same time, more workers are needed to provide services for busy families. People eat out more. They need child care. They want assistance with everyday tasks that they don't have the time or the ability to do themselves. Older people need care and help with daily chores. For these and other reasons the number of service jobs has increased and is likely to continue to grow.

Jobs of the future will include many in the service area. Can you think of services provided today that were not available in the recent past?

◆◆◆

Your Needs and Wants

You have read about what the future world may be like. Now put yourself in the picture. What will your future be like? What do you need and want for a successful and satisfying life?

Needs are required for your survival. **Wants** are things you would like to have or do, but they are not essential. Needs can be looked at on a theoretical, as well as a specific, level. According to the theory of psychologist Abraham Maslow, there are five basic human needs: physical, safety, social, self-esteem, and self-actualization (self-ak-chuh-wuh-luh-ZAY-shun). Maslow presented these needs in the form of a **hierarchy** (HY-uh-rahr-kee), or ranking, from most essential to least. The ranking indicates which needs must be met before others can be addressed. For example, physical needs for food, clothing, shelter, exercise, and rest must be met before the fulfillment of safety needs is possible.

Safety needs are both emotional and physical. These include feeling safe from threats, free from danger, and out of harm's way. Feeling financially secure is another safety need.

Social needs show that humans are social beings. The quote, "Man cannot live by bread alone," points to the need for social interaction. Social needs include companionship, acceptance, recognition, and love.

The fulfillment of social needs contributes to a feeling of self-esteem. When you sense that others are pleased with you, you are more likely to feel satisfaction within yourself. Self-esteem may be seen in a self-confident attitude and assertive behavior.

Activity. Have students choose and report on one specific product or process of high technology that has an impact on the way people live. How does their choice work? How does it help people? How does it save time?

Discussion. Many people have their basic needs provided for them; however, some people aren't as fortunate. Have students explain what happens to people when their basic needs are not met. Ask students about their wants. What do they want in the future? Do they tend to list material things or do they have other wants?

At the peak of Maslow's hierarchy of human needs is the need for **self-actualization**, or reaching one's highest potential. Being the best that you can be is certainly a lofty aim and is possible only for those who have first fulfilled self-esteem, social, and safety needs, as well as needs of the body.

Maslow went on to identify two needs that reach beyond the basic needs found in the hierarchy. These are the search for meaning in life and the need for spiritual harmony and truth.

As you plan your future and live your life, you will strive to meet the needs described by Maslow in specific ways. For example, one physical need will be shelter. You will need housing of some kind. What will it be? Notice that now you are starting to think about wants. What you need in housing is not necessarily what you want. Do you see the difference? As you think about the rest of Maslow's needs, determine what specific things you need to fulfill them. At what point do you begin to turn your list into wants?

◆◆◆

Your Goals

Once you know what you need and want in life, you can turn these into goals. A **goal** is something you plan to be, do, or have, and you are willing to work for it.

Goals that are consistent with values help pave the way for a happy future. What is important to you? Base your goals on the answer to this question.

Goals should be realistic, specific, and measurable. Your best answers to major life questions will lead you to goals that are "good" for you:

- Will I be an informed consumer?
- How will I earn a living?
- How much education will I need?
- Will I remain single and, if so, for how long?

Maslow's Hierarchy of Needs

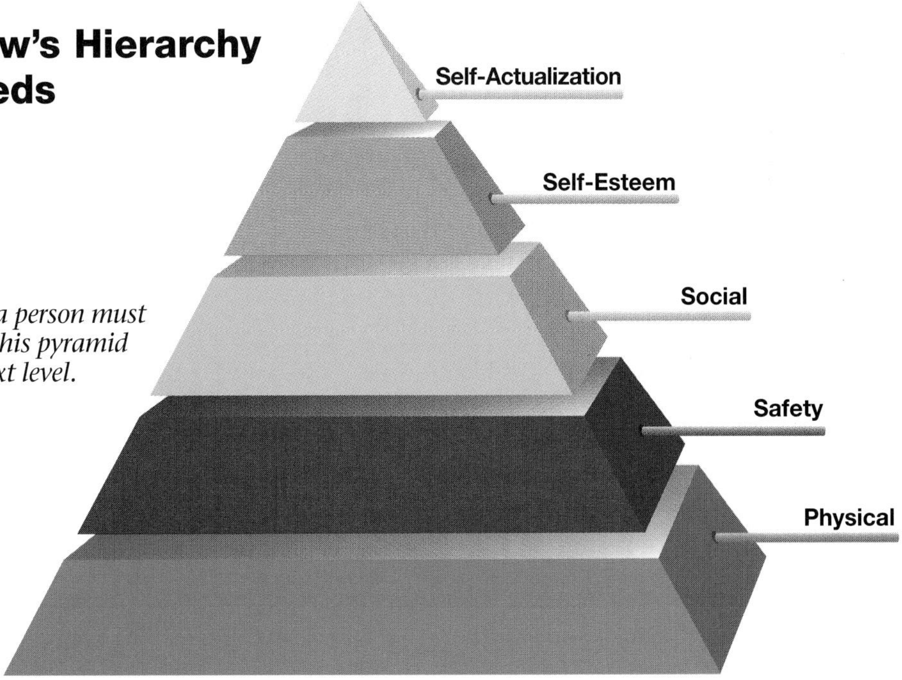

Maslow's theory says that a person must meet each need shown on this pyramid before moving up to the next level.

Activity. Have students write a paragraph on someone they know who seems to have achieved Maslow's concept of *self-actualization.* What makes them think the person has reached his or her highest potential? What personal qualities does the person possess that contributed to his or her achievement?

Problem Solving. Have students come up with some options that might enable these teens to reach their goals: Kelly wants to be a teacher but her parents can't afford to put her through college; Joey wants to get a role in the next school play.

- Will I marry and, if so, when?
- If I marry, will I work to build a strong, lasting partnership?
- Will I have children and, if so, how many?
- If I have children, will I be an effective, responsible parent?
- Will I learn ways to cope with crisis and conflict?
- Will I be a responsible family member, friend, and citizen?
- Will I make the world a better place to live in?

Most young people offer positive responses to such questions. They look forward to the future. They want to have a happy family and a rewarding career. For some, these goals will almost certainly be realized. How can you ensure that your goals will become reality?

◆◆◆

Your Future

Personal success and satisfaction depend on you. By now you should have an understanding of who you are. You have studied personality and examined your own. You know about development, and you have thought about your own progress. You know what character is and how close you are to being a mature person. You have learned what it takes to be healthy and related that to your own well being. When you make the best of yourself, you take the first steps toward a bright future.

SIDELIGHT

Choosing a Lifestyle

Lifestyle is the way you choose to live. What works for someone else is not necessarily the right choice for you. Since contentment is directly linked to lifestyle, it makes sense to ponder and prepare in order to make appropriate lifestyle choices. Can you turn your thoughts into goals? These questions will guide your thinking:

- Where would you like to live? Do you prefer a rural, urban, or suburban setting? Would you like a house or an apartment?
- What type of work do you enjoy? Do you want to work with people, with things, or with ideas? Do you want to be outdoors or indoors?
- What kind of family and personal life do you want? Will you marry or stay single? Do you want children?
- What does money mean to you? Does it represent security, power, material desires, or an opportunity to help others?
- What pace would you like to keep? Are you always on the go or do you like peace and quiet?
- What do you like to do with your time? Are there leisure-time activities and organizations that appeal to you?

◆◆◆

More About Your Future. Goal setting is a crucial activity if students are to take control of their futures. Without goals, they will be at the mercy of others or external events that make future decisions for them. Have students respond to the following in writing: What specific steps can you take to be an informed consumer? How will you pay for future education you need? What are ways to build strong relationships? What are ways to cope with conflict and crisis? How can you make the world a better place?

Discussion. Discuss with students why people choose different lifestyles. Ask them to look at some of the people around them (relatives, friends, etc.). What are some of their lifestyles and why did they choose them? What about their best friends? Do students want the same lifestyle that their best friends want? Why or why not?

A Slice of Life

"I'll see you later. I have to go by the Guidance Office before the bell rings. Have you turned in your registration form to take the SAT in November?"

Mindy shook her head. "No, Mrs. Shubert never gave me the form. I guess I forgot about it. I don't know why nobody reminded me."

Donnell responded with a suitably sympathetic look as he turned to enter the Guidance Office. He wondered if Mindy realized that tomorrow was the deadline to register for the test.

Mindy walked on to the cafeteria to get a quick snack before break was over. She put thoughts of the SAT to the back of her mind. Her break was almost over anyway.

"Oh, no," she thought, as the bell sounded. "Well, I'll finish my doughnut first. Mrs. Wortham will just have to understand."

Managing to enter the lab seconds before the last bell rang, Mindy took the only empty seat. She noticed that Donnell and the others were getting out blank sheets of paper and clearing their desktops.

"What's going on?" she whispered to Donnell.

"The test," Donnell said in disbelief. "You mean you didn't hear Mrs. W. announce it on Monday?"

"I guess my mind must have been someplace else. I don't remember anything about it. Are you sure she announced it?"

"Yes, we all heard her."

"Well, I should have never gotten out of bed this morning! The whole world is against me! What else can go wrong?"

Thinking It Through

- Would you say that Mindy has control of her life? Cite examples of behavior to support your answer.
- What advice would you offer Mindy?

◆ Taking Control of Your Life

Goals are most often reached by people who take control of their lives. The difference between in-control and out-of-control may be compared with the difference between swimming and floating. When you float in the ocean waters, you let go of your control and submit yourself to the whims of the waves. These are unpredictable influences that carry you forward and backward. You feel the ebb and flow of life around you, but you have no control. When you start to swim, you bring your own will and effort to bear against forces that would move you away from your goal. You also work to make best use of the tides when they work in your favor.

You can take control of your future by following the suggestions below.

- Believe in yourself, and in your own personal power to affect your future.
- Develop the personal skills you need to function in the world. This includes **coping skills**, all the techniques that enable you to handle the stress and conflicts in life. You have already read about managing stress. You will learn other coping skills in chapters to come.
- Become an effective communicator.
- Make informed decisions.
- Accept the results of your own decisions. Refrain from blaming others.
- Learn to love learning, so that you can enjoy keeping up with the changes that are sure to occur during your lifetime.
- Develop a positive outlook on life. See problems as opportunities. View changes as challenges. Think of choices as chances to succeed.

Take control of your life, and you will have every hope for happiness, every expectation of success.

Life Management Skills. Have students list five coping skills they use to deal with stress and conflict. If they feel the lack of such resources, ask them to list five skills they would like to develop in the future. How can they go about developing them?

CHAPTER 5

Review

Summarizing the Chapter

- The world is constantly changing. Changes produce a wide variety of reactions, ranging from fear to challenge.
- Changes come from within and from without. Human beings experience inner changes as they grow, develop, and experience. Outer changes are those that occur in the environment.
- Many trends in America are likely to affect your future.
- Maslow identified five basic human needs: physical, safety, social, self-esteem, and self-actualization needs.
- Goals are based on what you need and want in life.
- Goals should be consistent with values.
- Goals are more likely to be achieved by those who take control of their lives.

Testing Your Memory

1. How does a fatalistic philosophy differ from a belief in the work ethic?
2. Explain how families have changed over the years.
3. In what ways have gender roles changed in recent years?
4. Give three examples of ways companies are allowing employees more flexibility in the way they work.
5. Why is the current economy referred to as an "information economy"?
6. Why is a growth in service jobs anticipated?
7. Give one example of each of the five basic needs described by Maslow.
8. How do wants differ from needs?
9. What are goals?

Answers
Testing Your Memory

1. A person with a fatalistic viewpoint feels that little can be done to control the future, whereas someone with a belief in the work ethic will strive to create a bright future.
2. There are not as many traditional families of breadwinner dad, stay-at-home mom, and children. Families with several generations are increasing. So are single-parent families, stepfamilies, and singles.
3. There has been a move toward greater equality in the workplace and in the home.
4. **Any three:** telecommuting; flextime; part-time work; job sharing.
5. Because more and more people deal in information.
6. Working families are likely to want to use more services; older people need care and help in the home.
7. **Any one for each need**: *physical* — food, clothing, shelter, exercise, rest; *safety* — safe from threats, free from danger, out of harm's way, financially secure; *social* — companionship, acceptance, recognition, love; *self-esteem* — a sense that others are pleased with you, self-confidence, assertive behavior; *self-actualization* — being the best you can be.

Thinking Critically

1. You have read about current trends that may affect your future. Which trends do you think will work to your advantage? Which are likely to be disadvantages? Give reasons for your answers.
2. What are some examples of unrealistic goals? If goals are unrealistic, what might happen? How can you tell the difference between a goal that is unrealistic and one that is a challenge?
3. Do you think people find happiness or make it?

Taking Action

1. Conduct interviews of males and females in different age ranges to determine views on appropriate sex role expectations. Begin by writing specific survey questions. Assign each student an equal number of interviews. Summarize findings in chart form and discuss.
2. Write a goal for your future that is realistic, specific, and measurable.
3. You have read an analogy between swimming and taking control of your life. Create your own analogy for taking control of your life. Substitute a different activity for swimming. Rewrite the paragraph using your analogy.

Making Life Choices

Tara has always liked living in the country. She finds the city noisy, crowded, and somewhat frightening. She is very interested in a career in fashion merchandising. Tara knows that the only way to become successful in this field is to move to a city after college to establish her career. As a high school senior, Tara wants to decide on her major before starting college in the fall.

What is Tara's problem? What options does she have? If you were Tara, what would you decide?

Using Your Journal

Reread the last section of this chapter, titled *Taking Control of Your Life*. What effect does it have on you? Do you feel that you're moving toward taking control of your life? Do you feel apprehensive about some things? Use your journal to identify skills you need to build in order to take greater control. Write down some ideas for building those skills. Then start practicing them.

8. Needs are required for survival. Wants are not.
9. A goal is something you plan to be, do, or have, and you are willing to work for it.

Thinking Critically

1. Answers will vary.
2. Answers will vary. People become frustrated and discouraged when they set unrealistic goals. They may also waste time and energy working for them. Examine goals carefully and evaluate your own abilities.
3. Answers will vary. Suggest that continually searching for happiness makes it seem elusive. Creating happiness is a more positive approach.

Ian reaches out to a peer in need.

Ian "Last year a teacher asked if I'd act as a kind of friendly 'counselor' to two new students who were at risk of quitting school; they'd had a lot of problems at their old school. The teacher asked if I'd tutor them in math and maybe rap and shoot basketball with them once in awhile. It didn't sound like a big deal to me, so I agreed to try, but it *was* a big deal to some of my friends. They called me a 'do gooder.' I went through my own hard time over the issue. I almost told the teacher to forget it. In the end, I decided to stand up for what I believe is right. That was a decision I've never regretted."

Kevin "I was the first person to put Ian down for trying to help the new guys in school. I think it bothered me that he decided to be different than the rest of our crowd. Besides, who was he to think he could help those guys. He must have done something right, though, because he spent two nights a week tutoring them in math, and both their grades went up. Ian says if he can help them stay in school, he's doing something valuable. Maybe he's right after all."

Muriel Tree "I merely gave my student Ian a friendly push to get involved with two new students at school. I believe that if given the chance, many teens possess some ready-to-use leadership qualities inside — that need practice. I didn't realize his friends would give him a hard time about reaching out to people outside their crowd, but I was really pleased to see Ian stand up for the positive choice he made. I know that teens who are willing to take risks can change rules and break negative stereotypes. Ian did that by lending a hand to two teens in trouble."

Ray "I had pretty much decided school wasn't going to work out for me, and I was ready to quit. When Ian introduced himself, he said that Mrs. Tree wanted him to help me out in math. I knew this might be my last shot. I wasn't thrilled about the idea, but I went along with it anyway. Ian really seemed to want to help, and besides that, he knows his math. We hit it off right away. Ian just may be the reason I'm still in school today."

You can make a difference too.

- Do you think taking on responsibility to help others builds character and self-esteem? Why or why not?
- Are you quick to form stereotypes about others that may be untrue? If so, why?
- Would you have a hard time going against the crowd? Why or why not?

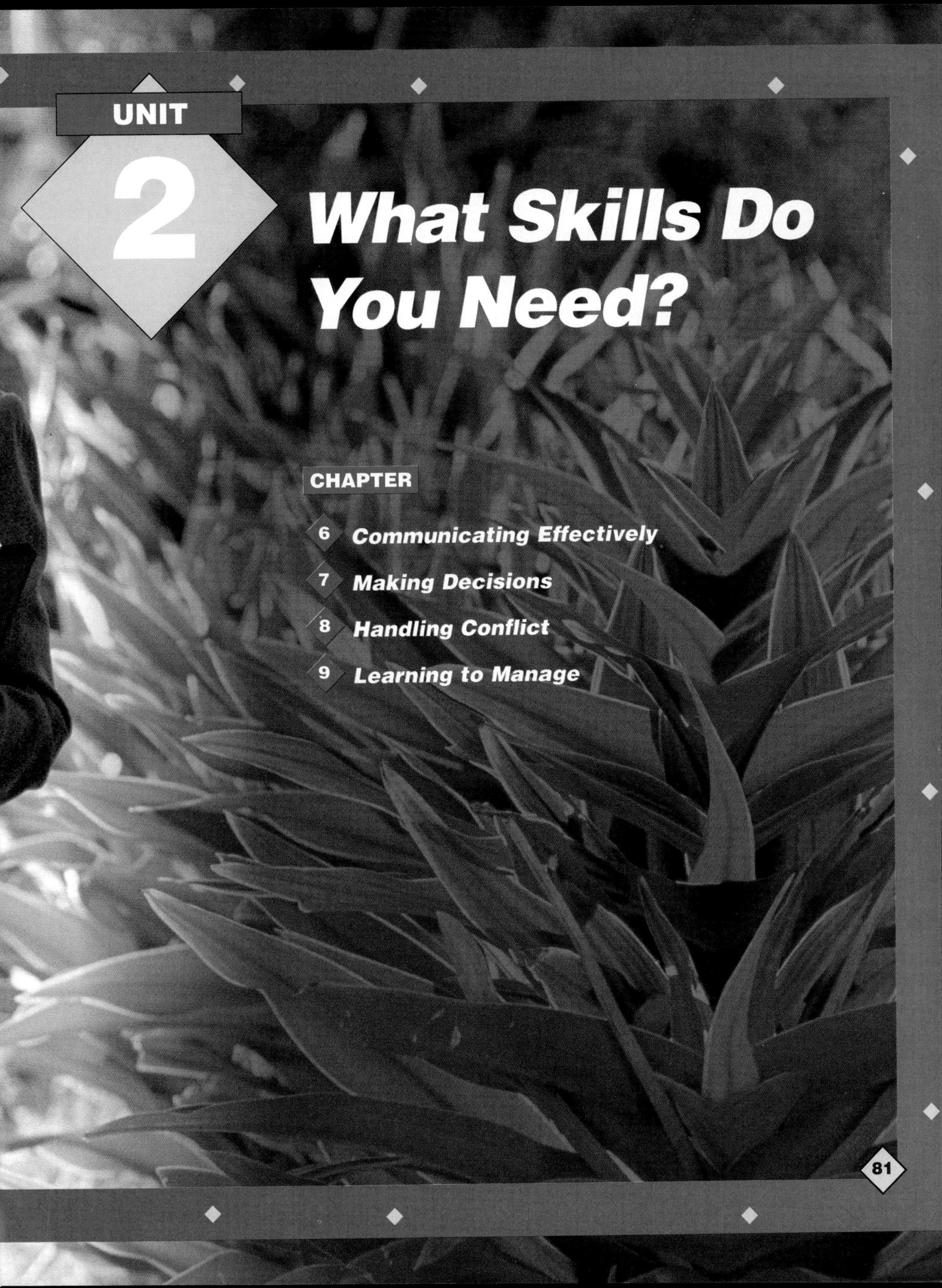

UNIT 2

What Skills Do You Need?

CHAPTER

CHAPTER 6

Communicating Effectively

Chapter Challenge

Resources. Refer to the Teacher's Classroom Resources box and Student Workbook for materials related to this chapter.

Look for These Answers . . .

- How do people communicate?
- What are the barriers that interfere with communication?
- What techniques will help you communicate more effectively?

Look for These Terms . . .

- active listening
- body language
- communication
- distractions
- feedback
- nonverbal communication
- paraphrasing
- selective attention
- verbal communication

"How was your day, Conchita?"

"Okay, I guess," Conchita replied to her father.

"How did your classes go?"

"Oh, just the same old thing," she said as she shrugged her shoulders.

"Conchita, is there something wrong?" Mr. Santiago looked intently at his daughter.

"No, not really. I just had a rotten day. Okay?"

"Why? What happened?"

"I don't really want to talk about it." Conchita turned to walk away.

"I'm only trying to help," Mr. Santiago said. "Did you have another run-in with Mr. Pageant?"

"I wish you'd just leave me alone. You're always giving me the third degree."

Conchita whirled around and walked briskly from the room. It had happened again. Why was her father always picking on her? One minute everything was fine and the next there was tension in the air. Conchita hurried into her bedroom and closed the door firmly behind her. She hoped the knot in her stomach would go away soon.

Meanwhile, Mr. Santiago had not moved from the chair in the living room. His shoulders were slumped and his head was lowered to a supporting hand. He sighed as he stared at the floor and saw nothing.

Chapter Opener. Have students read the opening scenario to the chapter. Ask students the following questions: How did Conchita misinterpret her father's intent when he asked her about her day? How could Mr. Santiago have helped Conchita if she hadn't walked away? How did Conchita and her father feel as a result of this confrontation? In what ways may the conversation have been different if both Conchita and her father were more open with their feelings and more specific in the way they expressed their thoughts? When you've had a bad day, how do you react to someone offering to help you? Does it help you to talk to someone?

What Is Communication?

By definition, **communication** is the exchange of information, thoughts, and feelings. Three elements are needed for communication, a message sender, a message receiver, and an understandable message.

The *message sender* provides the information. The *message receiver* observes or listens to the information, forms an impression, and may offer a response or reaction. The third requirement, the *understandable message*, is essential, because communication does not always occur when a message is sent and received.

Photo Focus. Have students look at the photo on page 82. Ask students to decribe ways in which the couple appear to be communicating effectively. What qualities give the impression that communication is occurring?

How Do People Communicate?

In general, messages are sent in two ways. They may be verbal or nonverbal.

◆ Verbal Communication

Communication that uses spoken or written words is known as **verbal communication**. With words you can communicate facts, points of view, feelings, and explanations. How well are you able to do this? Several techniques may help you — or hinder you if you are not careful.

Word Choice

Words do not always convey the same meaning. You may have heard children recite the pledge of allegiance with results like this: "I pledge a legion . . ." or "I led the pigeons to the flag of the United States." Obviously, words can be misinterpreted.

Words may also trigger emotional reactions. For example, suppose Denise knows nothing about making pottery. Would you call her ignorant, inexperienced, or uninformed? Since Webster defines "ignorant" as lacking knowledge or experience, this term fits. Still, the word "ignorant" is unappealing. Why is this true?

I CAN ◆◆◆ Handle a Compliment!

How do you respond when someone gives you a compliment? Do you reject, rebound, or accept the kind words? Mary Beth learned to make some improvements in this area.

"Someone told me once that I never handled compliments very well. I started to listen to myself and discovered that this was right. If someone said to me, 'You sure look nice today, Mary Beth. I love that blouse,' I would respond with something like, 'Oh, this old rag? I hate it, but it was all I could find to wear!' In a way I was rejecting the compliment. Sometimes I felt the need to turn the compliment around. At times like this, my reply would have been more like, 'I like your blouse better.' With practice, I have found a better way to respond to compliments. Now I am more likely to say, 'Thanks. My grandmother gave it to me. It's one of my favorites.' I realize now that this makes the other person feel good about giving me a compliment. We both go away with a better feeling when I accept a compliment."

- How would you describe Mary Beth's self-image based on each of her responses?
- What reaction do you expect when you give someone a compliment? Why?
- Which of Mary Beth's responses sounds most like your reaction to a compliment? Do you need any improvement in this area?

More About Communication. The *denotation* of a word refers to its direct meaning. The *connotation* of a word refers to its implied meaning. In the example above, "ignorant," "inexperienced," and "uninformed" have both specific denotations and negative connotations. Make students aware of the two different ways words are used. Have students offer examples showing both ways the words ignorant, inexperienced, and uninformed may be used in Denise's case.

Sometimes words imply expectations. Consider your reaction if someone said to you, "If I've told you once, I've told you a thousand times..." or "Don't take this personally, but . . ." Such comments clearly encourage a negative response.

Tone of Voice

The way you present a message is just as important as the words themselves. What tone of voice did you imagine in the conversation between Conchita and her father? Messages stated in a bright and sincere voice aid communication. On the other hand, statements said in a downbeat way can distort the meaning of the words. Test it yourself. Try saying an upbeat phrase, such as "I like you" or "You're a good friend," with an angry or sarcastic tone. Suddenly the words have new meaning. Voice tone can be an effective tool. Be careful, however, that the tone you use conveys the message you want to send.

Silence

Even saying nothing conveys a message. A comfortable silence between two good friends does not demand an exchange of words. At a time of bereavement, no words may be best. Sometimes too much excitement makes a person speechless. A very angry person may sulk, indicating, "I am too angry to even speak to you!"

Written Messages

When you prepare a written message, think about how the appearance will affect the reader. A neat, hand-written message on fine stationery conveys more sincere caring than a penciled note on a page from a yellow legal pad. A love letter typed on business stationery appears cold and impersonal, even though the words themselves may be loving.

Activity. Have students write down the lyrics of a favorite song. Have them recite the songs in class, using different tones of voice (for example, a sincere, sarcastic, or an angry tone). How do the various tones of voice affect the meaning of the words? Depending upon what the song is about and what the tempo is, how should it really be recited?

◆ Nonverbal Communication

Communication is more than just an exchange of words. In **nonverbal communication** messages are sent in visible ways.

Body Language

Using facial expressions and movements of the head, arms, hands, and body to convey messages is called communicating with **body language**. Many successful students have learned that sitting up straight in class shows interest. Slumping down in the seat says the opposite. A smile extends cheer and good will, yet a frown says, "Keep away," or shows disapproval or disappointment. Sometimes facial expressions do not match the words. For example, someone might say, "I'm so glad to see you," but the eyes say something quite different. The librarian who puts her finger

Body language says a lot about how you feel. What messages are conveyed to the teacher by the students in this classroom?

to her lips knows how to bring silence to the reading room with a gesture. Looking at people as you talk with them gives the impression that you are direct, self-assured, and concerned. Turning your eyes to look elsewhere can make you seem insecure, disinterested, or even dishonest. Touching can be positive or negative. A pat on the back gives encouragement, but a tap on the back of the hand tells a child "no-no." Body language is a powerful means of expression.

Think about these examples of body language. What messages do you think they convey?

- Thumping fingers on the table.
- Folded arms across the chest.
- Swinging legs while seated.
- Leaning forward.

◆ Dress

Clothing communicates a message about the wearer. Think of a police officer's uniform, with its message of authority. Picture the professional dress of a lawyer in contrast with the practical dress of a construction worker in hard hat. What messages do you communicate with the clothing you wear?

◆ Grooming

Even the right clothes cannnot make up for poor grooming. Physical appearance and personal hygiene contribute much to the impression you make. A neat, tidy appearance shows you care and have self-respect. A well-groomed person has clean, shiny hair, neatly manicured nails, and dust-free shoes. What are some other indicators of good grooming?

Some people almost talk with their hands. Gestures can be helpful or annoying. Can you think of some examples?

Life Management Skills. Instruct students to report on the proper appearance of a: resume, term paper, wedding invitation, consumer complaint letter, and condolence card. What kinds of paper are appropriate for each? Which should be handwritten and which typewritten? What messages may be sent if the above items appear in an inappropriate form?

Your appearance sends a message. If you really want to get the job, make sure your clothes and grooming will help you.

◆◆◆

Barriers to Communication

Communication can break down so easily. Think about it. The process depends on a message, a sender, and a receiver. This provides three opportunities for problems.

◆ The Message Sender

Suppose someone begins a conversation with you in one of these ways:

- "You're wrong about . . ."
- "You should . . ."
- "You know better than . . ."

Do any of these seem judgmental? Which have a preaching attitude? These you-messages blame and accuse, which greatly diminish communication.

Sometimes a message sender tries to avoid an issue in order to keep the peace. For example, an employee who is unhappy with something on the job may decide not to say anything in order to prevent trouble. If the complaint is legitimate, however, nothing is accomplished.

Others may hide behind walls of silence because they fear being hurt. Children who have been teased or punished when they say what they feel may choose silence to avoid the risk of pain. People in love may be slow to share their true feelings, knowing they run the risk of rejection. No one wants to be turned down. When the fear of losing someone overrides the strong desire to set things straight in a relationship, invisible barriers are erected. These barriers can be damaging.

◆ The Message Receiver

Have you ever tried to talk to someone who was not listening? The person's eyes wandered as you talked. When a response was made, you could tell the person didn't hear you. Your message was not received.

Message receivers can hinder communication in several ways. Giving no response to the speaker, either verbally or nonverbally, is one. Interrupting when the speaker is talking is another. A wandering mind also blocks communication. Hearing only what you want to hear can also be a problem. Sometimes fatigue, either physical or mental, can cause the listener to be inattentive and unresponsive.

At times a message receiver uses negative body language to discourage communication. A frown, a yawn, or turning away says, "I don't want to hear this."

Sometimes attitudes get in the way even before the sender speaks. For example, if you don't like the way a speaker looks, you may not like what is said either. Is this fair? Some valuable messages can be lost this way.

All of these attitudes show the receiver's lack of consideration for the other person. Of course, not all messages are important, but people are. If you show others the courtesy of good listening, the same will be returned to you.

Activity. Show students photos of four different people, each dressed very differently. Have students write down at least two messages that each person's clothing sends. Are the messages desired or unintentional? How should people dress to send the messages they desire?

When a message receiver uses negative body language like this, the message sender needs to find a better way of communicating.

◆ The Message

Sometimes the message itself causes problems. It may be unclear for some reason.

People's perceptions are not always the same. After a walk in the park, two boys were asked what they noticed. The first talked about the flowers in bloom. The second described cloud formations and the jet contrails he saw. Based on their interests and experiences, they saw different things. Psychologists call this tendency to see things in terms of previous experience **selective attention**. Confusion can result when people take from a message only that which catches their attention.

When several messages are present at one time and place, the listener may have difficulty concentrating on only one. The extra messages are known as **distractions**. What is a distraction for one person may not be for another. For example, some students like to study with the radio on, yet others find it distracting.

Distractions can get in the way of messages. This teen has learned to block out the distractions caused by his younger sibling when doing his homework.

Balancing Work & Family

Communicating with Family Members

"Selena invited me to the movies tomorrow night," announced Jake excitedly.

"Don't you remember?," asked his mother. "I need you to babysit. I have to work late tomorrow. We talked about it last week." She saw the disappointment on Jake's face. "Why don't you ask Selena if she could go with you this weekend instead?"

Like many parents who are balancing work and family, Jake's mother made a choice. She offered to work late so that she could make some extra money. Last week, she took the time to explain it to Jake. Her basic salary is enough to pay for essentials. But by working late once in a while she gets to make some extra money that pays for the movies and other things that Jake enjoys. Jake made a commitment to his mother to support her choice, by babysitting his sister.

When choices need to be made, communication is essential. Teens need to understand choices their parents make, and what they mean for the family. For example, they may not like their parents working long hours, but they may love the extras it finances. Similarly, teens have needs their parents must meet, regardless of a job.

One way to communicate is with regular family meetings. Such meetings are a great time to discuss choices and concerns, or to praise family efforts. In addition, parents and teens need to talk regularly on a one-to-one basis.

Good communication skills encourage understanding. Then everyone in the family can work together toward solutions.

Think About It

1. What are some ways busy families can communicate daily and weekly?
2. What times and places may be best suited to this type of communication?

Discussion. Have students discuss specific situations in which avoiding an issue makes it worse. What are situations in which silence is more effective than honest verbal communication, and vice versa? How should people approach sensitive or painful situations?

Discussion. Have students share past experiences in which a sender's physical appearance affected the way they reacted to a verbal message — either positively or negatively. If negative, how could the situation have been handled differently?

Messages may also be unclear when signals conflict. When Will met Randall, he said out loud, "It's nice to meet you," but the limp handshake and bored voice said, "Meeting you is not at all important to me." Consider the mixed messages in, "I'm so happy I could cry," and "You're just *too* good to be real!"

When speakers talk too long or ramble from one topic to another, messages get lost. The words they use can also be confusing. If the vocabulary level is too high, the message might not be understood. When you don't understand the words, the speaker may as well be talking in a foreign language.

Small talk is a necessary form of communication in our society.

Photo Focus. Ask students to look at the photo to the left. Small talk is common. If we ask someone how he or she is doing, do we really care what the answer is? Sometimes we take for granted that the person will say, "I'm fine." Should we listen for a more genuine answer? Why or why not?

◆◆◆

Learning to Communicate Effectively

Think about how parents would raise children if they could not communicate with them. Consider what friendships would be like if friends did not open up with each other. Communicating effectively helps make lives and relationships run smoothly.

◆ Levels of Communication

People communicate on different levels. From lowest to highest, the levels are: small talk, sharing facts, sharing ideas, sharing emotions, and peak communication.

Small talk refers to the greetings and cliches used in routine, everyday dialogue: "How's it going?" "The weather sure is nice today." You *share facts* when describing or telling what your day was like. When you *share ideas,* you may offer a suggestion or a new way of doing something. *Sharing emotions* means voicing your feelings in a frank and open way. The highest level of communication, however, is *peak communication.* With this, relationships reach a high point of understanding when communication is honest and mutually fulfilling.

Peak communication is relatively rare. Such moments are usually remembered as special. A heart-to-heart talk between mother and daughter on the daughter's wedding day is one example. The look of wonder exchanged between husband and wife as they share the miracle of birth is another.

All of these levels are used in communicating. All are needed. To find the most satisfaction in your communication with others, however, you will want some of your relationships to include the levels that are high on the scale. This may require some effort, but it is worthwhile in the long run. Who would you like to communicate with in this way? How can you make this happen? The rest of this chapter will give you some ideas.

A Slice of Life

"Ten years! It's hard to believe! It's actually been ten years since we graduated from high school!"

"I know! Time has gone by so fast; it seems like only yesterday we were cheering the Eagles on to another win and passing notes in Mrs. Beckham's biology class."

Such was the nature of conversations all around the gym as the Charity High School graduates enjoyed their ten-year reunion. Old acquaintances were renewed with greetings like "How have you been?" and "I'm doing just fine." Compliments like "You haven't changed at all!" and "I believe you've lost weight!" were in abundance, though believed by few.

In some conversations friends caught up on what had happened since graduation. They talked about school, work, family, and personal situations. One businessman shared with another his plan for streamlining his office management system. Two mothers explained how they were dealing with potty-training.

One pair of best friends, who had kept in touch over the years with occasional letters and phone calls, talked about their feelings. One feared that the man she loved was thinking of ending the relationship. The other offered comfort and understanding, remembering a similar time in her own life. For awhile the two sat in silence side by side on the bleachers, each drawing comfort from the other and feeling better for the shared moment.

Thinking It Through

- What levels of communication took place at the class reunion? Give examples.
- Why did some people at the class reunion share small talk and others peak communication?
- On what levels do you communicate with the members of your class right now? Do you think this will change in the ten years after high school? Ask some adults what happens when they are reunited with high school friends after several years apart.

Work and Family. Have students work in pairs to act out the five levels of communication positively. Have them use the following situations: friendly small talk with a foreign co-worker and stepparent; job facts with a new co-worker; a school day with a grandparent; a new job procedure with a trainee; a newsworthy issue with a parent; mixed feelings about a job to an employer; feelings about wanting to improve a sibling relationship; a peak exchange with an employer when being hired in a sought-after job; announcing one's marriage to family.

◆ Attitudes for Effective Communication

Two basic attitudes are essential for successful communication: a sense of responsibility and empathy. In order to learn to be a good communicator, you must accept responsibility for your own ideas and feelings. You can do this with I-messages. I-messages are free of assumptions, criticisms, and speculations. They invite the listener to understand your point of view and are much more effective than the you-messages you read about earlier.

Suppose you arrived home an hour after curfew, and your parent or guardian said:

> "You have no regard for anyone's feelings but your own! You come in an hour late— no phone call, no explanation. Do you expect us just to look the other way?"

Does this make you want to explain what happened, or does it put you on the defensive? Compare this with a similar scenario that uses I-messages:

> "I have been so worried about you. I expected you home an hour ago. When you still weren't here at 12:30, I was sure you had been in an automobile accident. I was just about to call the hospital when I saw your lights. What happened?"

Here the adult shares honest, true feelings, rather than lashing out without all the facts.

Empathy also helps communication. With it, a person can set aside personal concerns and assume another's point of view. You may have heard this well-known Indian prayer: "Great Spirit, grant that I may not criticize my neighbor until I have walked a mile in his mocassins."

Problem Solving. Have students work in small groups to resolve the following dilemmas using "I-messages:" Tracy and Leslie plan to go to a movie, and Leslie invites Charlene, whom Tracy dislikes; Jeff wants to confront Mason about his drinking problem; Shirley feels Barbara calls her only when she needs a favor; the basketball Terry loaned to Gil is returned deflated and destroyed; Susan agrees to babysit for her little sister but then decides to go out, so she talks her sister Sarah into babysitting. After the dilemmas have been resolved, have students act out their solutions.

People can choose to use I-messages or you-messages when communicating. Which type do you think this parent is using with her son?

Suppose a friend calls to tell you that she has had a fight with her boyfriend and cannot sleep. A typical response would be, "There are lots of other guys around." This response, however, tells your friend that she should not feel the way she does. It denies feelings that she cannot change at that moment. Using empathy, you could say, "You must feel awful." With this remark you show your friend that you understand. She will be relieved by your concern rather than frustrated by any attempt to change her feelings. In time she may decide that another boyfriend is the answer for her, but right now she is not ready for this thought.

Discussion. Have students discuss ways they might communicate empathy in the following situations: Tina is devastated by the breakup of a relationship; Todd's dad recently lost his job; Janet wants to talk about her mother, who is very ill.

SIDELIGHT

Communication Etiquette

Knowing what to do in social situations helps you feel confident. The rules that describe proper behavior are called etiquette. The rules of etiquette are useful when you face new situations.

- A *firm,* but not crushing, handshake shows confidence and friendship and can be extended by both males and females. A handshake is an appropriate end to a job interview. It is also often used during introductions.
- When making introductions, give the names of both people. Mention the key person first, the one you wish to honor. An introduction can be stated like this: Miss Davis, I would like you to meet my stepfather, Mr. Warden. Dad, this is Miss Davis, my soccer coach.
- When using the telephone, remember to time your use so that others have a chance to use the phone too. When you take a message for someone, write it down and make it complete. You can say: "Bob is not here right now. May I take a message?" Include a phone number if possible. If you reach a wrong number, apologize rather than hang up in someone's ear.
- In any social situation, if you are not sure about what to do, follow the cues of someone whose knowledge you respect.

◆◆◆

Discussion. Discuss with students the importance of really listening when people are talking. How can people benefit from listening? Should families develop a regular system for communicating? Are some times of the day better than others for communicating in families? Why or why not?

◆◆◆

Skills for Effective Communication

Good communicators know the importance of choosing an appropriate time and place for important conversations. No wise employee asks for a raise when the boss complains of a splitting headache. No smart student asks the science teacher for extra time on an assignment immediately after another student breaks six beakers in the chemistry lab. Although you cannot always control time and place, some messages will be much more effective when you do.

When the time and place are right for meaningful conversation, do so with straight talk. Say how you feel simply and honestly. If you are discussing a sensitive issue, open by saying, "I feel uneasy." This reduces tension and invites the other person to understand.

As you have read, communication involves listening too. Many people have learned not to listen to others. They may want to do all the talking or simply spend time thinking of what to say next. This is talking *to,* rather than *with,* the other person. Learning to talk *with* someone means learning to respond to another's remarks. This is the give and take that makes conversation flow. You won't have to worry about what to say next if you listen and respond to what you hear.

How should a person respond? The answer is through active listening. With **active listening,** the message receiver hears what is said and supplies nonverbal or verbal reactions.

Nonverbal responses signal the speaker to continue talking. They say, "I'm interested in hearing more. Please continue." A nod of the head can convey this. A look of interest does too. Maintaining eye contact is also effective.

Verbal listener responses are known as **feedback.** You might respond with a simple

With active listening, a person shows interest by maintaining eye contact and by giving feedback.

"Mmhmm," "Yes," or "Okay." Other forms of feedback include questions or statements, such as "Tell me about it. . . "or "How did that make you feel?" The highest level of feedback is that of summarizing what was heard. This is called **paraphrasing.** By restating the main message, the listener can determine whether or not the message received was accurate. When paraphrasing, the listener might say, "Let me be sure I am understanding what you are saying . . . " or "What I am hearing you say is . . . "

Active listening pays off. Here Dean recalls how it helped him:

> "One night Tonya and I sat in the car and talked. She told me about herself and her past romances. Then I did the same. We opened up to each other and shared some very special thoughts. Neither of us asked anything in return. It was wonderful.
>
> "So much of what Tonya said described my own feelings. She helped me realize that I wasn't the only one uneasy with the opposite gender. I told her how I had been hurt when I was more in love with a girl than she was with me. Tonya had been through the same thing.
>
> "We both listened that night as we poured out our hopes and fears. I found myself saying things I had never told anyone else before. For the first time in my life, I was totally honest. It felt good to talk so freely. I learned that Tonya shared many of my concerns. She also helped me discover that I could be a friend with someone of the opposite gender."

◆◆◆

The Power of Communication

Communication is the key to getting along in life. Every relationship you have will be affected by your ability to communicate. Anyone can communicate, but not everyone can communicate well. As you can see, much more is involved than just talking clearly or writing neatly. Good communication is a skill. If you are open-minded and willing to try, you can find ways to improve. Like Dean and Tonya, you will find the rewards are well worth the effort.

Activity. Divide students into small groups and have one student in each group write down a paragraph about a recent experience. The student should verbally communicate the experience to one person in the group. Have the receiver respond by using active listening and paraphrasing, until he or she is able to send the message on to another receiver. Repeat the process until everyone in the group has received the message. Have the last receiver recite the message back to the group. Have the original sender read the written paragraph to the whole group. Have students compare messages. How effectively were messages sent and received?

CHAPTER 6

Review

Answers
Testing Your Memory

1. Communication requires a message sender, a message receiver, and an understandable message.
2. The tone of voice you use can change the meaning of your message.
3. **Any three** of the examples given on pages 85 and 86.
4. **Any two:** judgmental; preaching; trying to avoid an issue in order to keep the peace; maintaining silence for fear of being hurt.
5. **Any four** of the behaviors listed on page 87.
6. Messages that are free of assumptions, criticisms, and speculations. The communicator takes responsibility for ideas and feelings expressed. I-messages invite the listener to understand your point of view.
7. Empathy allows a person to set aside personal concerns and assume another's point of view.
8. With active listening, the message receiver hears what is said and supplies nonverbal or verbal reactions. Nonverbal responses include maintaining eye contact, looking interested, and nodding of the head. Verbal feedback is given by paraphrasing.
9. Verbal responses by the listener.

Summarizing the Chapter

- Verbal communication is both spoken and written.
- Nonverbal communication is visible and includes posture, facial expression, eye contact, gestures, touch, dress, and grooming.
- The process of communication consists of a two-way exchange of messages.
- Individual perceptions of events differ from person to person because of past learnings and current interests.
- Barriers to communication exist because of negative attitudes of the message sender, ineffective behaviors of the message receiver, and messages which are not clear.
- Five levels of communication, from lowest to highest, are small talk, sharing facts, sharing ideas, sharing emotions, and peak communication.
- Skills in straight talk, timing, and active listening promote good communication.

Testing Your Memory

1. Name three requirements for the process of communication.
2. Describe how tone of voice can affect communication.
3. Give three examples of communication with body language.
4. List and discuss two attitudes which may present barriers to communication.
5. Describe four behaviors which may be observed in people with poor listening skills.
6. What are I-messages?
7. Explain why empathy is important for effective communication.
8. What is active listening?

9. What is feedback?
10. Discuss the value of communication skills in successful living.

Thinking Critically

1. What does the following statement mean? It's not *what* you say, but *how* you say it, that matters.
2. Give an example of an I-message and an example of a you-message on the subject of schoolwork. The teen is the speaker, and the parent is the listener. Compare the effectiveness of the two messages.
3. Explain what might happen when two people have a disagreement and one refuses to talk about the problem.
4. Think about the last time you met someone for the first time. Without giving the name of the person, describe your first impression of him or her. Are first impressions always accurate?

Taking Action

1. Write a brief half-page essay to interpret the meaning of the Indian Prayer on page 91.
2. Good listeners are active listeners. List the actions that good listeners display. Illustrate each action with a clipped picture, cartoon, or original drawing. Display or prepare a bulletin board.

Making Life Choices

As a sophomore, Cleve entered Travis High School in the middle of the year. He came from a school where he had few friends and felt that he did not belong. Always a very shy person, Cleve was ready to do something different to make his days at Travis better than those of his past. Here was an opportunity to start fresh. What could he do to accomplish this, he wondered.

Cleve must make some decisions about the way he communicates with the people in his new school. If you were Cleve, what would you do?

Using Your Journal

Now that you have read about the skills for effective communication consider your own skills. Think back to some recent important conversations, then use your journal to analyze your effectiveness as a communicator. What did you communicate well? What badly? How could you have been a better communicator? A better listener? Write down the communication skills that you need work on. Use your journal regularly to record your progress.

10. Communication is the key to getting along in life. Having good communication skills will help you in all your relationships.

Thinking Critically

1. The tone you use can change the meaning of what you say. If you mean to be sincere, your voice should reflect sincerity.
2. Answers will vary.
3. The problem will continue to exist until both parties decide to talk about it and clear things up.
4. Answers will vary. First impressions are not always accurate. For example, the person you meet for the first time may not be at his or her best.

CHAPTER 7

Making Decisions

Chapter Challenge

Resources. Refer to the Teacher's Classroom Resources box and Student Workbook for materials related to this chapter.

Look for These Answers . . .

- How do decisions affect you and others?
- What influences the decisions you make?
- What are the steps in decision making?
- What are some frequently used, but ineffective, approaches to decision making?
- How can you become a more responsible decision maker?
- What is the key to successful problem solving?

Look for These Terms . . .

- alternatives
- consequences
- impulse decisions
- prioritizing

"I just can't figure out what happened to it," Mrs. Parsons said. "That was my mother's ring, and I haven't even worn it for weeks. I was sure I put it back in the jewelry box the last time. Where in the world can it be?"

"Ask the girls," Mr. Parsons suggested. "Maybe one of them saw it somewhere. In fact, if I had my guess, Marie probably took it and lost it. It wouldn't be the first time," he said with disgust.

Ardeen stepped away from the kitchen doorway, from where she had heard the last part of her parents' conversation. Suddenly she wished she had never walked by her parents' bedroom door that night last week. Marie had been standing in the bedroom alone. Her back was to Ardeen, and she was right in front of the dresser where her mother's jewelry box was kept. At the time Ardeen thought nothing of it—but now? Why did Marie always have to do things to get herself in trouble? Ardeen loved her older sister. Marie was always there for her when she needed her.

Mrs. Parsons looked into the room. "Oh, Ardeen," she said, "come here a minute. I have something I want to ask you." Ardeen swallowed hard as she waited for the question.

Chapter Opener. Have students read the opening scenario. Ask the following questions: What should Ardeen tell her parents? Is Ardeen making any assumptions? In what ways may this situation seem unfair to Ardeen? Why did Ardeen's parents come to her first to ask about the missing ring? In what ways did Marie make poor decisions? Should Ardeen cover up for her? Why or why not? What consequences may be faced by both girls as a result of Marie's decision?

More About Making Decisions. Making choices often involves trade-offs, or choosing one option over another option according to priorities. Have students share examples of trade-offs they have recently made. Were they satisfied with their choices? Why or why not?

How Decisions Affect You

Life is filled with decisions. Each day you choose what to eat, what to wear, and what to do; countless other routine decisions are made. These types of options pop up often. Many routine decisions are made without much thought.

Large or small, decisions produce results. The results that come from a decision, or **consequences** (KAHN-suh-kwen-sez), can affect your life and the lives of others. Ardeen was facing a decision that could cause some things to happen. This is why Ardeen's decision was not easy. In an instant, the possible consequences of her decision flashed through her mind.

When important questions must be answered, looking at consequences can be vital. The decisions you make affect your relationships and your happiness. Some decisions you make will set the direction of your entire life. For example, the decisions you make about tobacco, alcohol, and other drugs will have a major impact on your life. So will your education and career choices. Choosing single life or marriage is another high-impact decision. At times you may reverse decisions you have made. It is always your choice to change your mind.

Often the effects of a decision are like a chain reaction. Chad has a habit of turning off the alarm clock and sleeping later than he should. Because he is usually in a hurry for school, he often skips breakfast. This affects his energy level and his ability to concentrate. In turn, his schoolwork suffers. In ways like this, even so-called small decisions can have big effects on your life.

◆◆◆

How Your Decisions Affect Others

Many of the decisions you make are personal ones that affect no one but yourself. Some decisions, however, can directly affect others. Think about what will happen to others because of your actions. You may be sorry if you don't.

Roger loves racing cars. The highlight of his week is getting his stock car ready to race on Saturday night. On his way to work at the garage one afternoon after school, Roger was stopped at a traffic light. The fellow in the car next to him started gunning his engine in anticipation of the light change. Roger answered back by revving up the engine on his car. He wanted to accept the challenge to race, but then he thought for a moment. Traffic was heavy. It was too dangerous, for others as well as himself. He would save racing for the track, where it was legal and safe.

Many decisions have powerful consequences. Thinking about these ahead of time can have great benefits in the long run.

◆◆◆

Influences on Decision Making

Learning to make decisions is an exciting experience. Along with each important decision a person learns to make in life comes a feeling of satisfaction and independence. This is the way five-year-old Jessica felt when she was first allowed to cross the street by herself. Her parents helped her learn how to make this decision safely. As Jessica grew, her family helped prepare her to make other decisions.

A family has a strong influence on decision making, especially during the early years. Families begin by making all decisions for you. Gradually, they allow you to make little decisions for yourself. As you grow older, your family keeps letting go a little, enabling you

Many decision-making skills are learned from your family. Early decisions are basic ones, such as deciding when to cross the street safely. Later, decisions are more complex.

Problem Solving. The plots of many TV sitcoms and dramas revolve around tough decisions the leading characters face. Have students view a favorite TV show. Have them analyze a single decision and its consequence in the plot. Students should write a brief summary regarding the decision the character had to make. Have them list at least three options the character may have chosen. Did the consequence of the decision please or disappoint the character? Why?

The decisions you make are influenced by your beliefs and values. Many people use their religious training to help them make decisions.

to make more decisions, including harder ones. They allow you to take over when you show readiness and ability. When you are an adult, if you have learned well, you will be ready to make complex decisions. This is all part of the maturing process.

In addition to families, there are other influences on decision making. Religious training and education also play a role. They lay a foundation for values and beliefs that become part of the framework for making good decisions.

◆◆◆

Steps in Decision Making

Decision making is a step-by-step process that can be learned and applied to any of life's choices. Once the process is understood, it can be used on any decision, large or small. Becoming aware of the steps in decision making will pave the way for smarter decisions and greater satisfaction with the results.

◆ Step One: Identify the Decision To Be Made

What is the decision you need to make? First you need to put it into words. If the decision is very minor, you might just think about it and complete the decision-making process immediately. A major decision may need to be written down and explored for days — even weeks or months. Whether the decision is major or minor, a clear statement will direct your thoughts along the right channels.

Discussion. Have students discuss the way others, including family, peers, school, and church, influence decision making. Ask them to share some decisions they have made lately. How were those decisions influenced by others? Were the influences positive or negative?

◆ Step Two: List the Alternatives

Think of all the choices that are possible for the decision you must make. These are called **alternatives**. For major issues especially, let your mind run wild. Give some thought to each alternative, no matter how silly or impossible it may seem at first. Some alternatives may seem like dreams. With good planning and hard work, even dreams can come true. Ruling these out with little thought may cause you to settle for less unnecessarily. Keep an open mind during this step.

Discussion. Ask students to discuss the benefits of thinking through major decisions in a logical way. Does decision making need to be a time-consuming process? Why or why not?

A Slice of Life

As a high school senior, Shannon is about to decide what college she wants to attend. She began the decision-making process over a year ago by going to college open houses, poring over catalogs, and talking to older friends who were already in college. Shannon has decided that she wants to major in early childhood education. Deciding which school to attend, however, is a tough decision.

In September Shannon narrowed her choices down to three colleges. One was a small, four-year, private college located two hundred miles from home. A second choice was the state-supported university sixty miles away. A third option was the community college in her home town, from which she could transfer to a four-year school at the end of two years.

Shannon checked out the instructional programs and found that the state-supported university ranks among the top ten in the country in her field of study. The private college is a very good school. Although small, it is known for the individual interest taken in students and the comfortable, small-campus atmosphere. The two-year community college has a positive image in her home town, though it has limited course offerings and extra-curricular opportunities.

Shannon checked on the expenses for attending each school. Tuition, living, and travel expenses for the private college are the highest. The least expensive option is the community college, especially since she would be able to live at home. Mid-range is the cost of attending the state-supported university. Loans are an option at the university, and part-time work is an option at all three schools.

Having narrowed down her choices, Shannon sent in applications for admission to all three colleges, along with applications for financial aid. Fortunately, both her grade point average and SAT scores were above average. She was accepted by all three schools on early admission programs.

Results of financial aid requests were disappointing. Her family's income is large enough to rule out scholarships based on financial need. Due to medical and other expenses, however, Shannon's family cannot pay her expenses in full. Neither can they afford to buy her a used car for traveling to and from school.

As you can see, Shannon has worked hard to collect the facts she needs to make a wise decision. She knows that her whole future is at stake. Now she must weigh the pros and cons of each option. She must scale her values to determine which are most important to her. She wants to make the decision that is best for her, a decision that she can live with.

Thinking It Through

- What alternatives has Shannon identified?
- What are the pros and cons of each alternative?
- If you were Shannon, what would your decision be? Why?

Life Management Skills. After students read through the six-step, decision-making process, have them keep a *Decision Log* for a week. Instruct them to record the six steps for at least three choices that they make. These choices should vary from personal issues, such as making changes in friendships, to consumer issues, such as shopping for food or clothes. Share results as a springboard to discuss the following questions: What are the benefits of step-by-step decision making? How does making a positive choice affect self-esteem? What may be the result if the decision-making process is not used?

◆ Step Three: Consider Advantages and Disadvantages

Write down all the pros and cons of each alternative. Think about the worst and best results if you followed through in each possible way. Ask questions like these: How might a certain action affect your future? What about tomorrow, a year from now, and in five years? What's good and bad about this alternative? How can it help or hurt you now? In the long run?

Try to test your decision step by step. Imagine that you have already made a choice. Then live it through like a movie in your mind. This preview method may reveal unexpected traps.

As you list advantages and disadvantages for each option, be thorough and resourceful. Get the facts and advice when needed. Listen to ideas of friends, relatives, and others. If you need to be more objective, switch your viewpoint. To get a totally new slant, try this question: If your younger brother or sister were facing this decision, what would you say?

◆ Step Four: Choose the Best Alternative

Making a choice means deciding what is best for you and perhaps those around you. Take into consideration all facts and options as well as your values. Your decision should reflect the measure of importance you assign to each factor.

Think about the values that affect Carol's decision in this situation. Carol agreed to babysit for her sister Brooke so that Brooke could attend a weekend conference out of town. On Friday Brad asked Carol to go out on Saturday night. Carol wanted to go, but she knew that her sister would not want anyone else to look after her six-week-old baby. What responsibilities does Carol have in making this decision?

She must weigh her values. How important is family to her? How important is a date with Brad? Is keeping her word important? In the long run, what does society say about keeping your word? What alternatives may be possible for Carol's situation? If Carol makes a choice that agrees with her values, she will be happy with her decision.

Before making a decision, it helps to get advice from others who have some knowledge or experience that may be useful.

Work and Family. Have students work in small groups, responding to the following dilemma: Nina is excited because she has been offered a part-time job as a library clerk; however, her work schedule will conflict with helping out her grandmother after school while her mother is at work. She would like to have the extra money, but at the same time, she knows there is no one else to help care for her grandmother. What decisions can Nina make to help her resolve this conflict of interests? Use the six steps to evaluate each decision.

◆ Step Five: Put the Decision Into Action

Once you have made a decision, you should put it into action. Too often, carefully made decisions are never carried out. Following through on a decision once it is made is a sign of commitment and determination.

◆ Step Six: Analyze the Results

Perhaps the most important step in decision making, and the one most often ignored, is evaluating the outcome of the decision. After you have put your decision into action, you can determine whether you made the best choice. How did everything turn out? Were the results satisfactory? Did you realize the advantages you predicted? How did you deal with the disadvantages? Given a similar situation in the future, what would you decide to do? Analyzing the results of your decisions will help you learn to make better ones in the future.

Approaches to Decision Making

Have you ever regretted a decision that you made? Most people do at one time or another. This is often because they fail to use good decision-making skills. Instead they use some other approach that does not work. There are several of these. Are any of them familiar to you?

◆ Pass-the-Buck Decisions

At times, decisions are passed along to another person to be made. Some reasons for this approach may be lack of self-confidence, fear of consequences, or lack of experience. For some, passing the decision may be an attempt to escape responsibility.

This approach has both a positive and a negative side. Turning to others for advice can be a very positive step. This is especially true when you do not have the knowledge or experience needed to make a wise choice. It also helps to talk through a decision to clarify the alternatives and to anticipate the possible outcomes. Sharing a decision can be a smart move.

On the negative side, allowing someone else to make decisions for you means putting your future into their hands. Not only have you given up responsibility for yourself, but you have also put yourself in a risky situation. Other people will not always make the decision that is best for you. Their perspective will be based on their knowledge and experiences, not yours. They may also have hidden motives which may not be in your favor.

Just making a decision about what to order in a restaurant is difficult for some people. Have you ever selected what someone else was having just to avoid the decision? This is a passing-the-buck decision.

Activity. Divide students into two groups. Using a fictional name, each person in one group should write an imaginary letter to an advice columnist. The letter should describe a regretted decision, either real or fictional. Gather the letters, and have each person in the second group pick a letter out of a basket. Have students in the second group assume they are the columnist. Have them respond to the letter with positive decision-making advice. Share the results with the class, and have students select the most interesting, helpful examples.

As a high school senior, Yokita was thinking about going to college. She liked math and was good at it. Her math teacher said that there were many opportunities for someone with math skills out in the working world. Yokita's best friend was planning to become a dental hygienist. She wanted Yokita to train with her. In a relatively short time, they could have jobs and an apartment together. Yokita decided to go along with her friend. What do you think about this decision?

◆ Following-the-Crowd Decisions

Some decisions are made and justified by thinking, "Others are doing this, so why shouldn't I?" Many assume that because others do something, it must be okay. This feels reassuring, especially to those who are uncertain of themselves.

Is it wise to base decisions on what others do? Stop and think about a specific situation. If the friends ahead of him in the cafeteria line choose pizza, does that mean that Neal should ask for pizza too? If he is allergic to cheese, he shouldn't. If he doesn't care for pizza, he shouldn't. If he had pizza for dinner last night, he probably would prefer something different. Obviously, the fact that everybody else is getting pizza is not a valid reason for going along with the crowd.

This conclusion applies to more significant decisions as well. What others do concerns them, not you. They may have consequences to pay for their actions. Do you want to pay them too? The price you pay may be high, depending on the decision. Think about it. What price might you pay for getting involved with a gang, drinking alcohol, or becoming sexually active?

Francesca discovered that many of her decisions were based on her feelings about others rather than her own good judgment. For example, when driving alone, she concentrated on what she was doing. She was careful. She wore her seatbelt and drove a bit under the speed limit. When her friends were with her, however, she was easily distracted. She wanted to show her confidence and ability by driving more aggressively. If her friends didn't wear seatbelts, she didn't either.

Discussion. Have students review the decision-making process and apply it to Yokita's situation above. What are her alternatives? What are the advantages and disadvantages of each option? Which seems to be the best alternative? How can she analyze the results of her choice?

Why do some people act differently when they are with others? Francesca can make the right decisions when she is alone, but something gets in the way when she is in a group. You may have heard of incidents where people in a group do nothing while someone is beaten and robbed nearby. If alone, would any one of them have taken some action to help? The ways people react in a group are sometimes puzzling. When you realize this, you can be prepared to do the right thing wherever you are. It may take courage, conviction, practice, and confidence, but you can do it.

Decisions about appearance are often made with other people in mind. This teen wants to cut her hair short because her friends wear their hair that way. Whether or not the style will look right is not important to her. What do you think about this?

Activity. Divide students into teams and have them act out situations in which one person pressures another to become a gang member, use alcohol or drugs, or become sexually active. Have the other team member resist the peer pressure without becoming angry. Have students select those teams that best defended their choice.

This may seem like a silly question, but would you stick your head into a fire because everyone else does? Of course, you wouldn't, because the consequences are immediately obvious and hazardous. All answers are not as clearcut, but they are there if you will look for them. Even when the crowd is not thinking clearly, you can. Your best option is to think for yourself. Make informed choices that reflect your factual knowledge as well as your values and beliefs.

◆ Impulse Decisions

An impulse is a sudden urge to act. Craig and his friend decided to skip school just before first hour. They had planned to do one thing and suddenly ended up doing something else. This is acting on impulse.

Decisions about food are often impulsive. Who has not regretted eating too much or the wrong thing at one time or another?

Impulse decisions are made without thought and planning. They occur as a response to a sudden, very appealing stimulus. The stimulus may be something tangible like the tempting chocolate fudge cake in the buffet line. It may also be a feeling, such as the thought of having great fun, making lots of money, or finding the love of your life.

Because little thought goes into impulse decisions, they often lead to disappointment. When the surface appeal wears off, other less-appealing facts become clear. The chocolate cake that looked so good in the buffet line is gone in minutes. Moreover, it was loaded with calories and fat, both diet hazards. What might result from the impulse decision to skip school? Impulse decisions, which are made in haste, are often regretted in leisure.

◆ No Decision

Faced with options, some people simply do nothing. They may not even realize they have a choice. In other instances, they hesitate to take a stand, fearing the consequences or what others may say.

In a sense, not making a decision is a decision. It is a decision to let other people or circumstances determine what happens to you. This is decision by default. Refusing to think for yourself means losing control over your own life and future. The no-decision approach is a risky way of handling choices.

Richard heard that applications for jobs at the new theater in the mall were to be taken on Saturday only. He needed a job, but he didn't know whether or not he wanted to work there. Once Saturday came and went the decision was made for Richard. It was too late to put in an application. This is an example of a decision made by default. No decision was made by Richard, so the decision was eventually made for him.

More About Impulse Decisions. In some cases, impulse decisions are positive choices. For example, when browsing in the mall, Allen discovers that blue jeans and a sweater he's been wanting are half-price for one day only. He could really use the jeans. After quickly going through the decision-making process, he decides to purchase two pairs. Ask students: What steps does Allen need to consider before acting on his decision? Should he buy the sweater too? Give some examples of other positive impulse decisions. What are some negative impulse decisions?

◆◆◆

Responsible Decision Making

Brian had to be at work at five o'clock on Saturday evening. Some friends of his were going to the lake to swim and fish for the afternoon, and they asked Brian to come along. Brian knew he might have trouble getting to work on time, but he decided to go anyway. When he arrived late, his boss was not pleased. Brian quickly explained how his friends had kept him out too long.

How do you feel about Brian's response to his boss? Most people would agree that Brian did not act responsibly. First, he made his own decision to go, knowing that he might have a problem. Second, when the consequences of his decision came true, he tried to shift the responsibility to someone else. This method of operating does not work. Sooner or later, people lose respect for people like Brian. They see through his excuses. They peg him as irresponsible.

SIDELIGHT

In the Driver's Seat

Learning to make decisions puts you in control of your own life. It's a matter of passive versus active. You can sit back and watch what happens around you, or you can sit up, decide where you are going, and plan ways to get there.

Beware of the passive pose. When you do not have control of your life, you are more vulnerable to the pitfalls around you. You are subject to negative reactions, such as anxiety and stress. Feeling out of control can add worry and strain to anyone's list of troubles. This leaves a feeling of helplessness. Lacking a goal and direction in life will also cause feelings of boredom because there is no sense of purpose in school, in work, or in relationships.

The active stance, on the other hand, puts you in control, as you make decisions and work through them. This makes you more capable and more confident. You learn to recognize the results of your own efforts. You learn to be creative in problem solving and to venture bravely into unknown territory.

Life is what you make of it. You can be in the driver's seat. Practice making decisions, and take control of your life!

◆◆◆

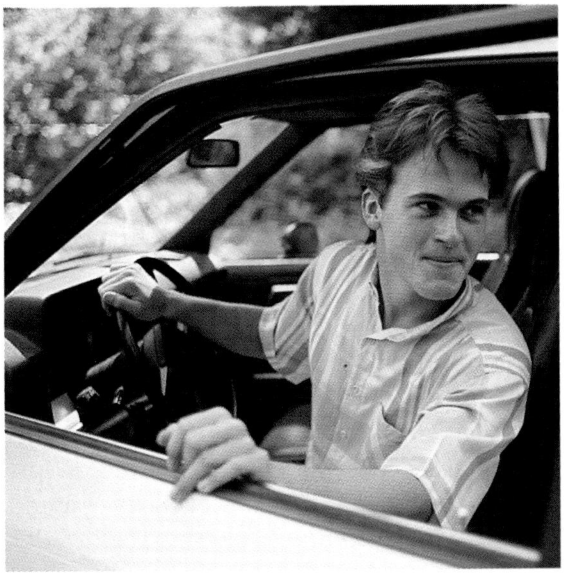

Responsible decision making involves thinking of other's needs as well as of your own. If you decide that you want to use the family car on Saturday night, talk to your parents early enough so that plans can be made.

Photo Focus. Ask students to look at the photo above and read the caption. Then ask them to give examples of other decisions they might make that would affect family members.

Discussion. Ask students to think of a situation in which peers influenced them to do something they knew was not right. What were the consequences? Why is it important to make decisions based on personal values and beliefs rather than by following the crowd?

Responsible decision making means distinguishing between wants and needs. Do you really need those new sneakers or could the money be better spent?

Responsible decision making means accepting responsibility for whatever you decide. This includes ownership of credit for good decisions and blame for bad ones. In Brian's case his boss might not have been happy but she probably would have had more respect for Brian if he had said something like: "I'm sorry I'm late, Mrs. Nelson. I shouldn't have gone to the lake this afternoon, but it seemed like a good idea at the time. I knew I would be cutting it short, and that was my mistake. I won't let it happen again."

Making responsible decisions is not always easy. The following pointers should help:

- Beware of distracting emotions that may keep you from viewing a situation honestly. These include anger, jealousy, and pride.
- Learn to distinguish between *wants* and *needs*. These two do not always go hand in hand. Needs should be given priority over wants in most cases.
- When you face tough choices, attempt to rank the relevant values in order of importance. This is called **prioritizing** (pry-OR-ut-eye-zing). Select the alternative which best meets the highest priority value.
- When appropriate, consider the effects of your decision on others. Looking at the decision from a broad perspective may eliminate some unfortunate consequences for yourself and others. It may also indicate your respect for the welfare of others.
- Remember that action is the best revealer of true values. Actions *do* speak louder than words.

◆◆◆

Problem Solving

Once you learn to make decisions skillfully, you can use the following techniques to help you solve problems. Life is full of problems that need solving. They may concern everyday situations, relationships, and even crises.

Sandra lives in a small house and all her relatives are coming for a weekend over the Christmas holidays. She is thrilled that they will all be together, but she has a problem to solve. How can she accommodate them all?

When faced with a problem, some people are overwhelmed. They may even try to avoid dealing with it. Sandra could skip the holiday

Activity. Have students report on examples of real or fictional characters in books, movies, or television, who make decisions out of anger, jealousy, or pride. How do such emotions affect the character's choices and the consequences of their decisions? How could they act differently to affect the end result in a positive way?

Activity. Have students list five *wants* and five *needs.* Then have them *prioritize* the wants and needs according to order of importance. Have students write a step-by-step action plan to make the top choices become reality.

gathering, but that would mean missing out on something special. Instead she will tackle the problem logically, by breaking it down into bite-size pieces.

Breaking a problem down into parts that you can handle makes it much easier to solve. After some thought, Sandra realizes that her problem involves several decisions. She lists them. Where will people sleep? How can eating be managed? What will the schedule for the weekend be? Once broken down, Sandra can tackle each decision individually, using her decision-making skills. Once each decision is reached, Sandra's problem is solved.

Of course, some problems are more difficult to solve than others. A family faced with a crisis may have to deal with emotions. Communication skills will be important. Identifying the decisions to make may even be a challenge. Whatever the problem, however, remember that breaking it down into parts you can handle is the key. With this ability, you can become a skillful problem solver in life.

Problems are not so difficult to solve if you break them down into small parts that you can handle. Solving a complex problem may mean making many decisions. This chart shows how one person approached the need to lose weight. Not everyone will break a problem down in exactly the same way.

Problem-Solving Strategy

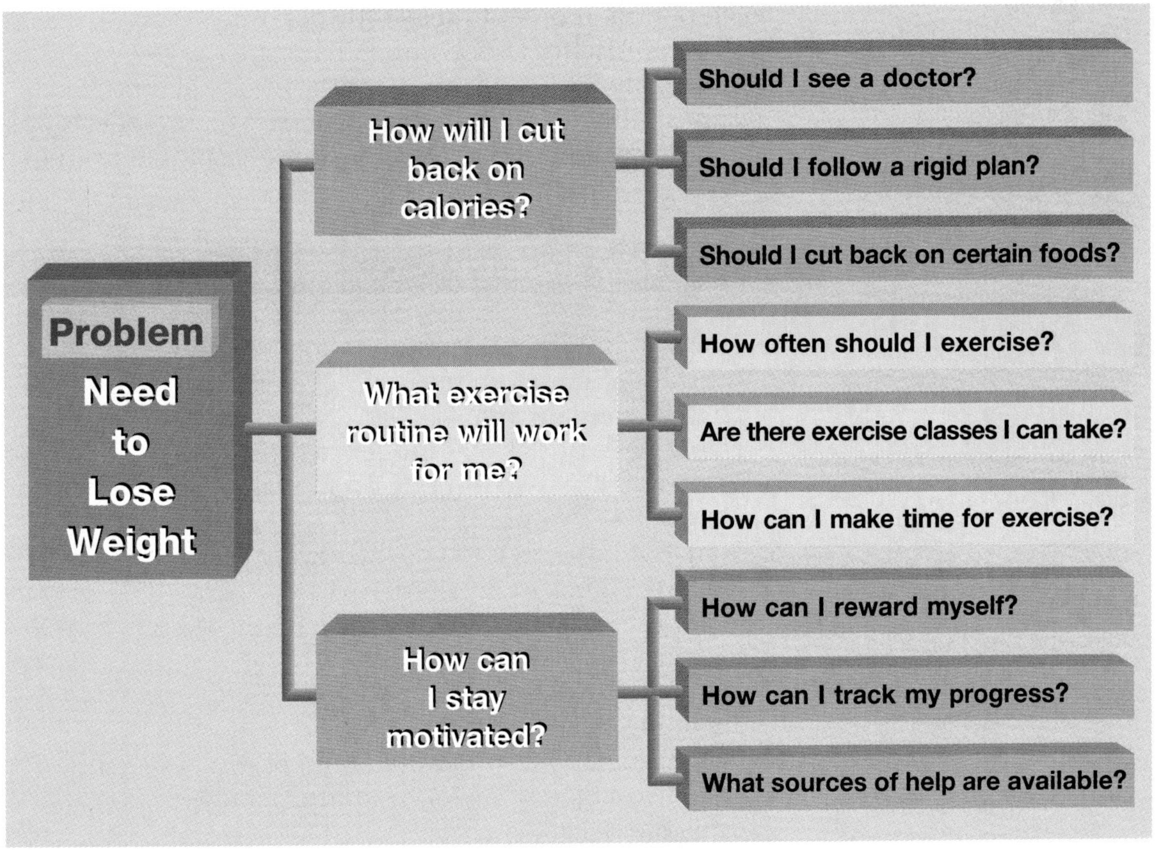

Life Management Skills. Have students select one or more of the following problems to solve: Jim's family is moving to another state before the end of the school year, and he would like to finish the year at his current school; Parker's best friend has a serious drinking problem that is affecting his health and school work; Ruellen is crippled by low self-esteem that is affecting all of her relationships; Celia has been given $500 for a trip and needs to decide where to go; Darwin has narrowed his choice of colleges down to two and is struggling with the final decision. Have students break the problem down into smaller pieces (as in the chart above) to find a solution.

CHAPTER 7

Review

Summarizing the Chapter

- Everyone must make minor and major decisions.
- The decisions you make will affect your daily routine, your relationships, your accomplishments, and your happiness.
- Making good decisions is a skill that may be learned.
- The best decisions result from pinpointing the issue, thinking of all alternatives, and weighing the pros and cons of each option in order to select the best one.
- Many approaches to decision making are risky.
- Responsible decision makers are those who accept the responsibility for, and the consequences of, their decisions.
- Decision-making skills can help you solve problems in life.

Testing Your Memory

1. How can important decisions affect your life?
2. Do the decisions you make affect anyone besides you? Explain your answer.
3. Name three things that influence the decisions you make?
4. What are the six steps in decision making? Explain each in your own words.
5. Why is it important to consider every possible option when thinking about alternatives?
6. What is the danger in using the pass-the-buck approach to decision making?
7. Why is it unwise to make decisions based on what others are doing?
8. What causes a person to make an impulse decision?
9. State two suggestions for becoming a more responsible decision maker.
10. What is the key to solving problems in life?

Answers
Testing Your Memory

1. Decisions produce results, or consequences. Results, whether good or bad, affect your life.
2. Some decisions are personal; they only affect you. Some decisions, however, have an impact on others.
3. Family, religious training, and education.
4. Identify the decision to be made; list the alternatives, considering all possible choices; consider advantages and disadvantages and the consequences of each choice; choose the best alternative — take into consideration all facts and options to determine which is best; put decision into action — follow through on decision; analyze results — evaluate the outcome.
5. If you don't, you may settle for less. Some alternatives may be like dreams but achievable with work and effort.
6. The danger is in putting your future into someone else's hands. You give up responsibility for yourself and may put yourself in a risky situation.
7. You may have to face undesirable consequences. What seems right for others may not be for you.

Thinking Critically

1. Give an example to illustrate how your decisions can affect your life.
2. Why do you think people sometimes act differently in a group than they would if they were alone?
3. At age seventeen Julian has a drinking problem that began with his decision to drink with friends over a year ago. Describe who might be affected by Julian's decision and how.

Taking Action

1. Interview three people whom you consider to be successful. Ask them what approaches they use in making decisions. Compare and contrast responses.
2. Think of a major decision you made within the past year. List the reasons for the decision. Do you feel that you made the best choice? Why or why not? Would you change your decision in any way if faced with a similar second situation?
3. Write a paragraph that summarizes your personal philosophy of decision making.

Making Life Choices

Anthony is a high school junior who has a decision to make. He has been offered a part-time job. Recently his father was laid off from work, and his mother's salary is not enough to make ends meet. Anthony wants to buy a class ring, and he needs gas money when he takes the car. Anthony's grades have never been good; however, he has managed to get by. Right now his grades are borderline in two of six subjects. School lets out at three o'clock. The part-time job is within walking distance of school and home. The employer would like Anthony to work from three to nine o'clock three afternoons a week and eight hours on Saturday.

Using the decision-making process, decide what you would do if you were in Anthony's situation.

Using Your Journal

Now that you've learned about the decision-making process, think back to some of the important decisions you made in the past few weeks. In your journal write down each decision and explain how you reached that decision. Were some decisions made because of peer pressure? Did you let others make decisions for you? Analyze what you have written. Then write a summary of any changes you need to make in the way you make decisions.

8. They occur as a response to a sudden, very appealing stimulus.
9. **Any two** of the suggestions listed on page 106.
10. Break the problem down into parts. Once broken down, tackle each decision individually. When each decision is reached, the problem is solved.

Thinking Critically

1. Answers will vary.
2. Answers will vary. Point out that insecurity may cause people to act differently in a group.
3. Answers will vary. Point out that Julian is the first one affected, but his family and friends will be too.

CHAPTER 8

Handling Conflict

Chapter Challenge

Resources. Refer to the Teacher's Classroom Resources box and Student Workbook for materials related to this chapter.

Look for These Answers . . .

- What are the basic causes of conflict?
- How can conflict situations be prevented?
- What are the negative and positive approaches to handling conflict?

Look for These Terms . . .

- compromise
- conflict
- role expectations
- suppression
- tantrum
- tolerance

"There's no doubt about it," Towanda thought. "This one is going in the jar." Her sister Cicily had borrowed a sweater again and not returned it. Both girls borrow from each other, but Towanda always returns everything—and in good condition. Cicily seldom does. Towanda took a little slip of paper and wrote down her complaint. Then she dropped it in the jar.

That evening the girls' mother also dropped a slip of paper in the jar. There was mud on the floor again where seven-year-old Lamont had come running in the front door. In fact, the whole family was careless about tracking in dirt from outdoors. It was time that they all had a talk about it.

The jar already contained several slips of paper. "The family conference this weekend should be a lively one," Mrs. Lewis thought to herself as she chuckled out loud. She welcomed the conversations they had together every week. Not only did they settle their differences, but they also became closer as a family. She thought about how well the telephone schedule they had set up was working. "Cicily and Towanda never fight about someone being on the phone too long anymore. They are even polite about it," Mrs. Lewis thought. "I think I'll put a note about that in the jar too. It's a big jar. There's room for something positive in there too."

Chapter Opener. Ask students to read the opening scenario to the chapter. Point out that family discussions can be a time to talk about conflicts as well as positive happenings. Ask students to discuss the benefits of placing positive notes as well as complaints in the conference jar. What other items could be put into the jar? How may handling conflict in this manner eliminate hurt feelings and boost the self-esteem of family members? Do you think a conference jar would be a positive way to handle conflict in your family? Why or why not? What are some other ways that families can cope with conflict in a positive way?

What Is Conflict?

Conflict is nothing new. As you think back on history, you will see that human beings have always come into conflict.

Conflicts come in all sizes. They range from the small skirmishes of young children over who gets to play with a favorite toy to the bloody battle scenes of major world powers fighting for control. In between, fall the arguments of married couples, feuds between families, and media contests between political candidates.

A glance at the daily newspaper shows the scope of conflict in the world today. Front page headlines tell of conflicts around the globe. The news provides reports on lawsuits, political controversy, and crime on the streets. Advice columns offer help for those with rocky relationships. Even the comic strips tell of characters in conflict, each trying to have his or her own way.

A **conflict** is a disagreement or struggle between two people or groups with opposing points of view. Conflicts occur in friendships, families, the workplace, society, and among nations. Unless handled properly, disagreements can expand into destructive battles.

Too often, opponents leave a conflict both exhausted and angry. Relationships can be damaged or destroyed as people take sides. Each side refuses to do what the other wants, and a deadlock results. Many people, regardless of age or life experience, are not good at settling their differences.

This does not mean that disagreement is altogether bad. It is only natural for different people to have different views and values. To expect any two people to always agree is to expect the impossible. Each brings past experiences to the current situation. Also, individuals will always have different beliefs and personal reasons for acting as they do.

On the bright side, disagreements help to bring issues out into the open. Through sharing viewpoints and feelings, two people can reach a better understanding. Open communication helps to clear the air, increasing visibility for everyone. It has also been said that life without any disagreement would be dull indeed!

When two people claim rights that conflict, they need to find a solution to the problem.

Activity. In order to develop a more realistic understanding about rights, have students examine the first ten amendments to the Constitution, known as the Bill of Rights. Ask students to identify what rights are guaranteed to citizens of the United States. How do rights that are designated by law often conflict with what some people claim as "their rights"? Have students examine how privileges they claim are subject to how they affect others. To expand this experience, have students clip news articles related to individual and family issues the government is addressing today. How may these issues be affected by the Bill of Rights?

◆◆◆

Understanding Causes of Conflict

Sources of conflict revolve around differences. These differences are usually related to one of four basic causes: rights issues, role expectations, value violations, and personality clashes. You will see that these causes are often closely related, even overlapping.

◆ Rights Issues

What are your rights? Simply trying to answer this question could cause conflict. Most people claim many rights but often have no real basis for their claims. For example, do you have the right to listen to a CD player in your home? What if the music disturbs the neighbors? What has happened to your right?

In general, rights are defined by laws and rules. Beyond that, the privileges that you claim are subject to their effect on others. In other words, you may feel you have certain rights, but at the same time someone else may claim a right that disagrees with yours. This creates a conflict. Here is an example. Mr. O'Toole grows a tree at the edge of his yard. He feels he has the right to do so because it is his property. Mr. Clancy has no trees in the yard he owns next door because he doesn't want to rake leaves. Mr. O'Toole's tree has branches that extend over Mr. Clancy's yard, where the leaves fall and blow all over. Since Mr. Clancy feels he has the right to have a clean yard, he is unhappy. Like so many situations, who has what right is no longer clear.

Be careful about claiming rights. When you say, "I have the right to . . . ," it sounds like no one can tamper with that right, that it cannot be taken away from you. Unless your so-called right is covered by laws or rules, however, this may not be true.

Many disputes over rights are settled by laws or rules that are designed for this purpose. When laws and rules do not cover a situation, however, people must look for other ways to settle their conflicts. That's what this chapter is all about.

What is the role of a student? When a teacher and a student disagree over the student's role, what happens?

◆ Role Expectations

As you know, people take on different roles in life. For each role you have, people will look for certain behavior from you. These are **role expectations**. Do all people agree on what the behavior for a certain role is? No, and that can lead to conflict.

College roommates may see the role of a dorm roommate in different ways. One may expect the other to let her know where she is going and when she will be back. The other may see this as unnecessary. One may assume they will go everywhere and do everything together, while the other may resent being tied to a constant companion. These differences can lead to conflict and incompatibility.

Take a moment to think about the expectations you have concerning people in different roles. What about teachers, salesclerks, strangers, and parents? Which ones can hug you, ignore you, talk to you, or advise you? What happens if they do not act as you expect? If a salesclerk ignores you and a stranger hugs you, for example, conflicts may be in the making.

For people who have close relationships, differing role expectations can be especially troublesome. Explore this thought as you identify the conflicts that could occur in the following relationships:

- A father who thinks his son should be an athlete and a son who wants to be a musician.
- A wife who does not like to cook and a husband who thinks cooking is a woman's job.
- A boyfriend who feels he should make all decisions and a girlfriend who is independent and assertive.

◆ Value Violations

You can easily see why values would be a source of conflict for people. When you value something, it is important to you. Anyone who challenges your values is likely to encounter some resistance. The degree of conflict will depend on just how important the issue is to you.

Conflicts over values can occur in many types of relationships. An English teacher may feel strongly about neatness on a theme, yet a student thinks only content should be graded. A boss may value schedules, but an employee feels flexibility is more important. A football coach may value regular football practice above all else, yet a key team player values his academic standing above sports. A parent may value peace and quiet, yet the son likes to practice playing the drums in his room. With a little thought, you could come up with many examples of value conflicts.

Activity. Have students act out positive solutions to role-expectation conflicts listed in the text above. Include: two college roommates who need to work out different expectations of each other; a frustrated customer who is ignored by a salesclerk; a teen coping with a seldom-seen aunt who always gives excessive, but well-intended, hugs; a young woman, who wants to be a military officer, attempting to enlist the support of her mother, who wants her to marry and have children. Emphasize the communication skills needed to attain positive solutions.

People from different cultures often have different values. How could this lead to conflict? How does this pertain to relationships between nations?

People who work together must strive for compatibility even though their personalities may be quite different.

◆ Personality Clashes

Personality studies are fascinating. Similarities can make two people highly compatible or prone to conflict. Differences between people can have a bonding effect or a clashing impact. The examples that follow show this.

Two friends who are both outgoing can enjoy going places with others. This similarity makes them compatible. Two friends who both like to be in charge can come into conflict when trying to make joint plans. This similarity causes conflict.

In the work setting, a boss who cannot handle details will appreciate a secretary who pays careful attention to the appointment book. Here, the difference produces compatibility. A secretary who is even-tempered and likes a calm work atmosphere will clash with an unpredictable boss who blows up frequently. Here, the difference brings about conflict.

Problem Solving. Have students respond to the following: Josh and Elaina meet and instantly like each other. While talking, it becomes evident that their values differ on certain issues. Can their individual differences in values be resolved? Why or why not?

As you can see, the relationship between personality and conflict is complex. Since every personality is a unique mixture of qualities, conflicts can easily occur.

◆◆◆

Preventing Conflict

The best way to prevent conflict is to deal with the cause. This means being open-minded and observant enough to recognize causes before conflicts develop.

If you wish to claim certain rights, it helps to consider the attached responsibilities. For example, if you want respect, you must show

Work and Family. Point out to students that many teens and adults have conflicting expectations of each other. How can people learn to handle these differences? How can people learn to deal successfully with others at home, work, and school? Have students suggest possible solutions?

A Slice of Life

Grandma sinks the golden knife into the base layer of the beautiful tiered cake, as Grandpa looks on. The room is filled with smiling well-wishers while the happy couple enjoys the limelight of their golden wedding anniversary. As the organ notes of "I Love You Truly" float across the room, Grandpa reminds Grandma to hold the knife straight, and Grandma replies with a big smile, "Of course, dear."

Then they move on to the living room for gift opening, where Grandma and Grandpa take turns opening the packages. Grandma tears into the packages with glee, while Grandpa uses his pocket knife to cut the ribbons and tape. He then neatly folds the wrapping paper and carefully opens the boxes to reveal their contents. Exclamations of "Ooh!" and "Ah!" and "How nice!" show appreciation for the seemingly endless stream of gold towels and sheets, gold albums, picture frames, and gold flatware. Grandpa smiles to himself as Grandma tells everyone what a beautiful day it has been.

"A beautiful day to celebrate a beautiful fifty years!" comes the comment from one outspoken cousin. Grandma smiles and says, "Oh, yes — fifty wonderful years!" Grandpa grins sheepishly and replies, "Well, at least forty-eight or forty-nine!" Grandma laughs and decides to let that one pass.

At the close of the reception, a few grandchildren remain to help Grandma and Grandpa clean up. Married grandson Corbin helps Grandpa pick up bits of paper and ribbon. He shares with Grandpa his problems in understanding his young wife. "She's so unpredictable. I never know what to expect next, and she always wants to talk over every little thing! Sometimes I just need a little space."

Grandpa replies, "Son, you just need to be patient. You'll understand one another better in time."

"But, Grandpa, tell me how you learned to get along so well with Grandma. You two *never* fight!"

Grandpa chuckles at the thought. "Corbin, you have to realize that Grandma and I have been working at getting along for fifty years now. Sure, we've had our differences."

"How do you handle them?"

"Well, some things you just learn to accept. Grandma puts up with me and I put up with her. Then when a serious difference comes up, we sit down and talk it through. Usually we can work something out."

Corbin and Grandpa continue to talk as punch cups are cleared and vacuuming done.

Some advice is really worth its weight in gold!

Thinking It Through

- What differences did you notice between Grandma and Grandpa?
- How did Grandma handle their differences?
- How did Grandpa handle them?
- Did you see any examples of tolerance in the scenario? What were they?
- How has Grandpa's sense of humor contributed to their lack of conflict?

Activity. Ask students to ask couples they know who have been married a long time how they have handled conflict. Set aside classroom time for students to report their findings.

Discussion. Have students discuss the following: How may developing long-term relationships over months or years be a benefit in dealing with conflict? Sometimes the better people know each other, the easier it is to resolve a conflict. Is this a true statement? Why or why not?

done as this "last straw breaks the camel's back" usually sends shock waves that rock the relationship to the roots. Suppressing differences only leads to increased conflict in the long run.

Refusing to face conflict is an escape approach. Of course, avoiding an argument or turning away from a fight can be a very positive step. Postponing a confrontation until tempers have cooled is a smart move. The negative side of refusing to face conflict comes when it is part of an attempt to hurt the other person. Walking out on an argument can bring about fears and worry. Using the silent treatment prevents differences from being aired and settled.

The **tantrum** approach to conflict is used by people who lose their tempers easily. When they become angry or upset, they explode with fast and furious word attacks. In the heat of the moment, they sometimes say things that they do not always mean. They are often as quick to apologize as they were to explode. The danger lies in the reaction of the other person, who may find it difficult to forgive and forget the hurtful things that were said.

Violence is the most destructive approach to conflict, both physically and emotionally. Causing injury to another person is inexcusable. Only if your own safety is threatened is there cause for a physical reaction. When angry people lose control, the damage is often lasting. Physical and emotional injuries are not easily forgotten. Patterns of hitting back are often learned in childhood and carried into adult relationships. In people with psychological problems, these may lead to abuse of all types including child abuse, spouse abuse, and elder abuse. When these problems exist, healthy relationships became impossible to achieve.

◆ Positive Approaches

On the flip side, positive approaches to conflict can promote healthy relationships. The following tips will help you handle conflicts constructively:

- **Target the issue.** Identify the real issue in any conflict. Try these leads: What do you mean? What's really bothering you? After the other person explains, repeat what you think you heard to be sure you got the intended

If you need to resolve a conflict, try to find a quiet place where you talk calmly and carefully.

Activity. Have students write a scenario, real or imagined, about someone who suppresses, shuns, or has tantrums in dealing with conflict. The composition should describe a person (unnamed if a real person), a specific conflict, his or her behavior, and offer an alternative solution.

message. Use your own words. What you thought was a sarcastic comment may not have been intended that way at all.

• **Tackle the issue.** Once you have identified the real issue, stick with it. Do not get sidetracked by past hurts or problems. Avoid sending up smokescreens that cloud the issue, such as insults and sarcastic remarks. Personal attacks interfere with the discovery of solutions. Which statement would be less likely to begin a confrontation with your locker mate: "If you weren't such a slob, we could find things in our locker," or "Do you think there is anything we can do to get control of this locker?"

• **Time discussions of the issue carefully.** Choose the best time and place to confront a conflict. Keeping private differences private is essential to preserving trust in a relationship.

• **Talk things over.** Be straightforward, direct, and calm. Share real feelings, using I-messages. Listen closely to the other person's feelings and ideas. Work together to find a solution.

Make sure the message you send is the one received. So often people speak without thinking how their words sound to others. Which comment would be clearer to you: "Your hair sure looks different today," or "I like your new hairstyle." Both statements may be intended to say the same thing, but one might be misunderstood.

• **Trade places.** Switch roles. Be willing to see the other person's point of view. This can lead to the most ideal resolution of any conflict — compromise.

Choose the right time and place to have a serious discussion over a disagreement. You are more likely to reach a satisfactory conclusion if you do.

I CAN ◆◆ Be a Mediator

Some people are good at helping others resolve conflicts. Leon discovered this about himself.

"I never realized I was good at helping people mend their differences until someone told me. Actually, it was my boss at the fast food restaurant where I work part-time. One of the guys I work with said some things that somebody else didn't like. I could tell they were about to start with the punches. I just said to Dell, 'Hey, man, I think you've got the wrong idea about what Walt said.' This got us all talking. I threw in a little humor and pretty soon, the whole thing blew over. My boss said I was a good mediator. You know, I think he's right!"

- What skills do you think a person needs to be a mediator?
- Are there any dangers involved in being a mediator?
- Have you ever acted as a mediator?

Activity. On a chalkboard write: *sarcasm, sidetracked,* and *smokescreen*. Select pairs of students to act out conflicts (perhaps have conflicts listed individually on index cards, using situations common to teens). Have each student defend his or her position while the remaining students judge the process. They should call out any of the three words above if the tactic is used, explaining how it hindered conflict resolution. Have the class identify situations that may be resolved more quickly if a mediator is involved. Ask for student volunteers to act as mediators in resolving some of the conflicts. Were the conflicts resolved more easily? Why or why not?

◆ Learning to Compromise

A **compromise** is a solution that requires both parties to give in on certain points and allows them to have their way on other points. Through reaching a compromise, each person leaves feeling that the solution to the conflict is acceptable. Everyone wins!

Try your hand at compromise. What are the possibilities for compromise in these situations:

- Dawn and Courtney usually eat lunch together in the school cafeteria. Dawn enjoys it more when the two of them sit alone together and talk. Courtney likes to join a group of friends. This becomes an issue every day at lunchtime.
- Juan wants to use the family car for his activities on weekends. His family wants it available for their use. Every time Juan asks to take the car, they argue about how often he uses it.
- Mr. and Mrs. Diaz are both employed. Mr. Diaz is meticulous. Mrs. Diaz is not. It really bothers him when she leaves things lying around and ignores the mess. She tells him that neatness is not really important to her.
- The Petrosky family is planning a summer vacation. Mr. Petrosky likes to camp and fish, but Mrs. Petrosky does not. She doesn't want to cook and likes to be where she can have a soft bed. Patty, who is twelve, loves amusement parks and doesn't want to do anything boring, like fishing. Tim is sixteen. He wants to stay home so he won't have to leave his friends. Finalizing the family vacation plans has not been easy so far.

◆◆◆

Taking Charge of Your Life

For most people conflict is not enjoyable. The stress alone is enough to make it unpleasant. Now take a close look at you. How much conflict do you have in your life? Would you like to take charge — to reduce the amount? If so, there are some things you can do. First, try to have a more positive outlook. When you are busy looking for the good in yourself and others, your focus will move away from the negative. There will be less chance for conflict. In addition, try not to let others irritate you. Why let their problems become yours? Ask yourself if an issue is really worth the hassle. If not, say nothing, smile, change the subject, or simply walk away. You have the power to defuse a situation with your own reaction. Try it. You may like it.

When a compromise is reached, both sides can walk away from an argument with good feelings.

Discussion. Have students share personal examples of resolving conflict through compromise. What did they think about how the conflict was resolved? How did it affect their relationship with the other person? Can learning to compromise boost self-esteem? Why or why not?

Activity. Ask students to write down five changes they would like to make in their lives or in themselves that would eliminate some of the conflict in their lives. Emphasize confidentiality.

CHAPTER 8

Review

Answers
Testing Your Memory

1. A disagreement or struggle between two people or groups with opposing points of view.
2. Conflict results when people claim rights that are not generally covered by rules or laws. Often these rights are claimed without regarding the effects on others.
3. All people do not agree on what the behavior for certain roles should be. This causes conflict.
4. When you value something, it is important to you. The degree of conflict will depend on how important the issue is to you and the other person, whose opinion differs from yours.
5. *Suppression:* holding feelings inside to avoid conflict; *escape:* refusing to face conflict; *tantrums:* exploding with fast and furious word attacks; *violence:* attacking someone physically or emotionally, causing injury.
6. Target the issue; tackle the issue; time discussions of the issue carefully; talk things over; trade places.
7. It allows each person to feel that the solution to the conflict is acceptable.

Summarizing the Chapter

- Conflict is a necessary part of life because of differences that exist among people.
- Conflicts can have constructive or destructive effects on relationships, depending upon how they are handled.
- Conflicts are caused by differences related to rights issues, role expectations, value violations, and personality clashes.
- Identifying specific causes of conflict in a given situation is the first step in preventing conflict.
- Certain approaches to handling conflict are destructive to relationships, namely, suppression, escape, tantrums, and violence.
- Positive approaches to handling conflict include identifying and addressing the main issue, choosing the best time, and talking things over.
- Compromise is the most ideal way to solve a conflict because nobody has to lose.

Testing Your Memory

1. What is conflict?
2. Describe how rights issues can lead to conflicts.
3. Why do differences in role expectations cause conflict?
4. How can value differences cause conflict?
5. Describe each of the following negative approaches to handling conflict: suppression, escape, tantrums, and violence.
6. List five suggestions for handling conflicts constructively.
7. Why is compromise useful in handling conflicts?

Thinking Critically

1. Why do you think clubs and organizations set up rules for people to follow?
2. How can too many expectations cause conflict?
3. When people debate an issue, is this the same thing as a conflict? Explain your answer.
4. Do you think some people enjoy conflict? Why or why not?

Taking Action

1. Plan and perform a skit depicting one of the following conflict situations, or think of your own. Then trade roles and re-play the situation.
   - Parents and teen disagree on the teen's choice of friends.
   - Engaged couple disagree on where they will live after marriage.
   - A brother and sister disagree on what television program they want to watch.
2. Use the newspaper to find one example of a positive approach to conflict and one example of a negative approach.
3. List the roles you play at the present time. For each role, state one role expectation and tell whose expectation it is.

Making Life Choices

Melody and her mother have frequent arguments over Melody's messy room. It seems that the more Mom reminds Melody of the need to keep her room clean, the worse the room becomes. Mom likes to keep a neat, clean home and feels that Melody's messiness is an act of rebellion and laziness. Melody, on the other hand, does not really mind leaving a "few" things out in the room. She likes the "lived-in" look and has better things to do than make her bed and hang up her clothes every day. She feels that her mother is wrong to nag her all the time about the room. After all, it is her room!

What is the cause of the conflict between Mom and Melody? What are Mom's rights in this situation? What are Melody's rights? Can you think of a compromise solution to this conflict?

Using Your Journal

Do you feel better equipped to handle conflict after reading this chapter? Use your journal to describe two or three conflicts you experienced recently. Explain what skills you used to deal with them. If necessary, explain how you could have handled the conflicts more effectively. Which of the approaches to conflict resolution described on pages 117 and 118 do you need to work on?

Thinking Critically

1. Answers will vary. Point out that clubs and organizations want to avoid as much conflict as possible.
2. Answers will vary. Having too many expectations places unrealistic demands on everyone involved. It may be difficult to sort out items of real importance.
3. Most people consider a debate a good way to exchange differing ideas about an issue. Only if tempers and other emotions get in the way does it become a true conflict.
4. Answers will vary.

CHAPTER 9

Learning to Manage

Chapter Challenge

Resources. Refer to the Teacher's Classroom Resources box and Student Workbook for materials related to this chapter.

Look for These Answers . . .

- What is management?
- Explain what is meant by goal setting.
- What are some examples of human and material resources?
- What are the steps in the planning process?
- What are the benefits of good management?

Look for These Terms . . .

- aptitudes
- goal setting
- human resources
- long-range goals
- management
- material resources
- mentor
- resources
- resourceful
- short-range goals

"First place," she had said. "First place goes to Hung Nguyen."

Hung was humbled as he saw the people in the audience jump to their feet. The applause pushed aside the silence that had encompassed the room only seconds ago, yet for a moment Hung heard nothing but the splashing of water against the boat adrift on the ocean. The applause brought him back to the room, where his eyes met those of his American family.

"What America means to me," he thought. "I can write the essay and read it, but can they really know?" Vietnam was no longer home. This was home. The image of his uncle waving goodbye to him as the boat pulled slowly away flashed through his mind. "There is hope for you, my son. Make the best of what you find. My spirit will aways be at your side," his uncle had said.

"I promise, Uncle," Hung replied, and he kept his word. While others played, Hung used his time to study. He learned a whole new language. While others complained, Hung struggled to master every challenge presented in a new culture. While others rested, Hung put forth extra effort to achieve his goals. His new friends and family were always there for him. He turned to them often.

Hung stepped forward to receive his plaque. "Thank you, my uncle," he said. Few in the audience that night fully understood the meaning of his words.

Chapter Opener. Have students read the scenario at the beginning of the chapter. Ask the following questions: What did Hung mean when he said, "Thank you, my uncle," as he accepted his award? Why do you think Hung was such a high achiever? Why are some people motivated to do well despite hardship and others are not? How is good management related to achievement?

About Management

Did you ever wonder why people manage their lives in such different ways? What some people do in a day takes someone else a week to do. What some people accomplish in a year may never be achieved by others. How do you account for this? Is it motivation? Attitude? Ability? Does it take experiences like Hung's to create the will to take charge of your life?

There is no simple answer to these questions. The bottom line, however, is this: Only you can make things happen in your life. You may have some inborn qualities that will help you along the way. On the other hand, you may have to develop some abilities. The ability to manage life comes more easily to some than others; however, the skill can be learned — and improved — if you want to.

Managing is not just an instinctive ability that everyone automatically develops, nor is it only common sense. It is a skill that can be learned through practice.

Management may be defined as the planned use of resources in order to reach goals. Good managers have clearly defined goals and know how to use the resources available to reach these goals.

◆◆◆

Goal Setting

The foundation of good management is laid when goals are carefully selected and clearly stated. This process is known as **goal setting. Long-range goals** usually have a time span of one year or more. **Short-range goals** are generally set for a time period of days, weeks, or months. Good managers know the advantages of having both long- and short-range goals.

Long-range goals give a sense of direction to your life. With a goal in sight, you can look forward to its fulfillment as you are making decisions and taking action to reach the goal. This can help to keep you on track as you face obstacles along the way,

Kelly's goal was to become an interior designer. She wanted to earn her bachelor's and master's degrees in interior design. Her first three years of college were a success story in every way, but her senior year was another story. Kelly's parents ran into unexpected financial problems, which left her without tuition, board, and other living expenses. With her goal still in sight, Kelly secured a student loan for two-thirds of the total cost. She then began the search for part-time work, plowing through want ads, phone calls, and a series of job interviews before finding suitable work. Had she not kept her goal in sight, she might have quit when things looked hopeless. Kelly's goal was like a voice calling her to keep trying and not give up.

Short-range goals serve as stepping stones to larger, long-range goals. In Kelly's case, obtaining the loan and locating a part-time job were both short-range steps necessary to her larger purpose. Kelly could have chosen other short-range goals as well. She might have approached another family member for a loan or taken a semester off to work full time. If one short-range goal had not worked out, she would have tried another, assuming her long-range goals remained important to her.

Kelly's goal worked for her because it was a realistic one. Selecting goals that are attainable paves the way for success, while dreaming of things that are highly unlikely to happen only leads to frustration and disillusionment.

Some goals are more realistic than others. How many athletes make it as professionals? Is such a goal realistic for most people?

Activity. Ask students to interview someone they consider to be a high achiever. Ask the person to share insights into motivation, a positive attitude, and ability. How do these qualities help someone achieve one's goals?

Activity. Have students list any five goals they hope to meet. Collect the lists and read examples. Ask students: Are the goals short-range or long-range? Do they sound realistic? What are ways to meet such goals?

Luke's goal was to become a successful rock singer. Luke was talented and he enjoyed music more than anything else. He decided not to go to college but instead moved to the city where his music career could get off the ground. He poured all his money, time, and energy into his music. He was able to get a weekend job singing in a local restaurant. He tried all the other likely steps that sometimes lead to success for other singers, from demo tapes to charity performances. It seemed that every door of opportunity remained closed. Luke remained undiscovered as a major music talent. Finally, he realized that he would have to find another direction to take. He could keep his music as recreation, but it was not to be his major occupation.

Recognizing the difference between a realistic goal and an unrealistic dream is not always easy. Trying to visualize the steps necessary to reach a goal will help. Seeking the advice of knowledgeable people can also be beneficial. Being able to recognize resources also leads to more realistic goal setting.

How realistic is education as a goal? What resources are available for achieving such a goal?

◆◆◆

Recognizing Your Resources

Resources are those assets which are available for use in reaching goals. They include everything you have going for you. Everyone has resources, though the nature and quantity of resources differ from one person to another.

Resources may be classified in a variety of ways. One system identifies them as either human or material. Human resources, of course, are those related to people; material resources are related to the physical environment.

Discussion. Have students discuss the examples of Kelly and Luke, who try hard to reach their career goals. Why does Kelly clearly succeed? Does Luke's decision to redefine his goals make him a failure? Why or why not?

◆ Human Resources

Human resources include five major elements. These are time, energy, ability, attitude, and people.

- **Time.** Since everyone has twenty-four hours a day, seven days a week, and fifty-two weeks a year, time has been called the universal resource. People who are very busy, either by choice or necessity, find limits on their time. As you grow older, time changes as a resource. The time available to accomplish goals is obviously less for an eighty-year-old man than it is for an eighteen-year-old youth. Factors, then, that affect the resource of time are age and involvement.
- **Energy.** This is clearly a variable resource. Many factors affect the amount of energy a person has at any given moment. These include health, age, diet, work load, and general physical condition.

Activity. Have students write a list of "My Ten Most Valuable Resources." These can include personal qualities, skills, other people, and material resources. The list should emphasize those assets the students value most.

The resource of time is not the same for everyone. The same can be said of energy. How does this relate to the individuals pictured here?

• **Ability.** Abilities may be inherited or learned. You have inherited certain **aptitudes** (AP-tuh-toods), or natural talents, some of which you have discovered and others that remain undiscovered. You may be good with numbers or have an ear for music. You may find it easy to understand people or to relate to small children. Sketching or painting shows signs of artistic talent, while ease in taking things apart and putting them together shows a mechanical aptitude.

Some abilities are learned. Knowledge is gained from study and experience. Skills develop through practice.

Of course, natural aptitude is part of ability, but it is by no means the sole factor. Many people with little natural talent have developed skills. Even some with supposedly low learning potential have defied predictions of IQ tests by doing well in school. What explanation is there for these contradictions? How can people defy the odds and achieve beyond their expected potential? The next two resources may provide an answer.

The ability to relate well with children is a natural aptitude that may be enhanced by study and experience.

• **Attitude.** Your attitude is a very important resource as you work toward a goal. A positive point of view serves as a resource, yet a negative point of view acts as a liability. Does your attitude work for you or against you?

Jeff worked hard to reach his goal, which was to bring up his C and D grades to As and Bs. When his report card arrived with Bs and Cs, his reaction was positive. He was happy to have brought up his grades and felt confident that if he kept trying, he could reach his goal — all As and Bs — during the next term. A person with a negative attitude would probably have reacted differently. He might have felt like a failure and been ready to give up his goal. Attitude makes a big difference in the pursuit of a goal.

• **People.** Other people can have great impact as a resource for you. Having someone to turn to for support and encouragement helps you deal with problems. You would probably classify such a person as a friend. Another term for a loyal, wise adviser is **mentor.** Mentors offer not only the support and understanding of a friend but also the advice of one who has wisdom in a field that concerns or interests you. Using other people as resources means tapping into *their* time, energy, ability, and attitude. Successful people know the value of forming a network of resource people to call upon when needed. In return, they serve as human resources for other people.

◆ Material Resources

Material resources are those that generally have physical form. These include money, property, supplies, tools, and information.

• **Money.** As a resource, money may take the form of cash currency, a checkbook, or a credit card. There are many goals that may be readily accomplished when sufficient funds are available, but money is not the only significant material resource.

Life Management Skills. Ask students to share examples of an adult other than a parent whom they consider to be a *mentor.* How does the person help or advise them? Ask students without mentors if there is an adult whom they might ask to help or advise them.

Even when natural aptitude is limited, attitude can make the difference.

• **Property.** Not only is property a resource in and of itself, but it is also a means of obtaining other resources. Property-owners can obtain credit; people tend to have confidence in those who have managed to acquire property.

• **Supplies and Tools.** Supplies serve as raw materials from which end products can be created. Tools and equipment make possible the transformation from raw material to finished product. Imagine how difficult it would be to make a jacket without the use of a sewing machine. All stitches would have to be made by hand, which would require a much greater amount of time, energy, and special ability. Note that it *could* be done, however, by a person who is willing to make the effort. Many of life's challenges center around using human resources to make up for a lack of material resources.

Problem Solving. Ask students to report on a notable person who started a company. What material resources did the person need to start the business? What material resources changed over time? What personal qualities made the person a success?

- **Information.** This is an increasingly important resource in today's world. Part of learning to manage is learning to find the information you need. Successful people take advantage of new sources of information made available by modern technology. They have learned how to use computers to access up-to-date information quickly from a variety of sources. Equally important, they have learned how to manage the information they obtain. In this rapidly changing world nobody expects you to have all the answers, but they expect you to be able to find them. With adequate information sources, many goals are possible.

◆ Resourcefulness

People who are good at recognizing and making the best use of their resources are said to be **resourceful.** How resourceful are you?

With so much information available today it's important to know where and how to access it.

Life Management Skills. Discuss with students the need to use modern technology to access information. Have volunteers give examples of ways they have used library computers, and perhaps home computers, to obtain information. What advantages does this method offer?

Jerry complains that he never has any spending money. He stays home and watches TV almost every weekend. Though he is often bored with this routine, he does not have the money to go out. Do you recognize a resource Jerry could use better?

Marian likes to be self-sufficient. While she makes good grades in most subjects, she is on the verge of failing geometry. Math does not come easily for her, but she feels uncomfortable about asking her friend Susan for help. What is the unused resource here?

Jake wants to invite Marcie out to dinner, but he cannot afford the prices in nearby restaurants. What other resources could Jake use so that he and Marcie could have dinner together?

Resourceful people realize that when one resource is limited, you must recognize and make better use of other resources. This involves creative thinking.

The greatest roadblock to resourcefulness is a closed mind. Some people take a defeatist's attitude. They refuse to look at ways of getting around obstacles. Perhaps they find it safer to admit defeat than to try again and risk a second failure. Perhaps they lack motivation. For whatever reasons, some people have a high level of drive, yet others are satisfied with whatever life hands them.

Resources may be converted into, or traded for, other resources. Jerry could convert his resource of free time into money by getting a part-time job. Marian could trade off with Susan for help with geometry. Perhaps Susan needs Marian's help with another subject in return. Jake's dinner date with Marcie could become reality if he opened his mind to other options. He could invite Marcie to his house for a family dinner or offer to do the cooking himself. He could pick up an odd job or two to earn the money or save his allowance for a few weeks. In each case, whether Jerry, Marian, and Jake achieve their goals depends upon how much they want them and on how resourceful they can be.

A Slice of Life

Lucinda Warner was known as "Miss Efficiency" in the real estate office where she worked as a secretary. She was a hard working, high achiever with a heart as big as the state of Texas, but Lucinda suffered from one infirmity. She had a speech problem. She was unable to say the word "no."

Whenever any of the agents wanted typing done just right, they brought it to Lucinda. When time was short and someone needed a fast letter or lease agreement, Lucinda was their best bet. She would cheerfully give up her lunch hour or work as late as needed to meet a deadline.

There were other competent secretaries in the office. Their typing speeds were good, their work reasonably neat, but they were not always as agreeable as Lucinda about rush jobs, particularly when they felt that the rush was the result of poor planning on the part of the agent. They definitely knew how to say "no" and did so frequently.

It was not unusual for Lucinda to work as late as seven or eight o'clock on must-have work for the agents. She would say good night to the cleaning staff as she dragged herself home exhausted.

Lucinda lived at home with her widowed mother. After working late, she would find her dinner on the counter covered with a paper napkin and ready for the microwave. Dinner was followed by a nice hot bath and a good night's sleep. Then Lucinda was ready for another day at work.

Her mother's accident changed Lucinda's routine. Mrs. Warner fell and broke her arm. She would need to keep it in a cast for at least six weeks. She could no longer do all the things around the house that she had done before.

At first, Lucinda tried to keep up with the old routine at the office. She took work home on days when she could not stay late at the office. Soon she realized, however, that the long workday was no longer practical. She needed time to be with her mother, to fix dinner, and to take care of the home.

It was three weeks after the accident that Lucinda reached the end of her rope. When one of the agents came to her desk at five-twenty with an urgent letter that he "simply had to have today," Lucinda's rope of willingness snapped. She said her first "no" and patiently explained why she just could not work late. The agent's reaction of surprise was followed by a promise that he would remember to give her more notice from now on if she would just help him out this once.

Lucinda thought it over for a moment before making her reply.

Thinking It Through

- What reply do you think Lucinda gave to the agent?
- How would you evaluate Lucinda's management strengths and weaknesses?

Photo Focus. Have students look at the photo on the previous page. Ask them to describe the resource tools that are available in a library. List ways in which the library can provide them with help. How could they be helped with ideas for hobbies, travel plans, music interests, legal information, schoolwork, learning about family history, reading for pleasure, community activities, medical information, and statistics? If your students are not familiar with library resources, you may want to explain such tools as the *Reader's Guide to Periodical Literature,* microfiche, and computerized cataloguing. A library tour with explanations of these and other tools may also be helpful.

◆◆◆

The Process of Planning

So far you have read about goal setting and recognizing resources. To be a good manager, you need to know more. If you want to accomplish things, either as an individual or in a group, you need to know how to plan. Planning is essential for success in reaching a goal. Failure to plan is often the same as planning to fail. A goal is important because it makes you aware of where you are headed. A plan is equally important because it shows you how to achieve your goal.

A plan is more than a single good idea. It is a detailed program of action. "The Planning Process for Individual and Group Action" (Future Homemakers of America, Inc.) is a useful tool in planning. If you master this five-step process, you can become a good manager. You will have the ability to accomplish what you want to in life. You will see that this method is similar to the decision-making process. The difference is that here you are setting a goal and working to achieve it. You may make many decisions along the way. The decision-making process deals only with making individual decisions.

◆ Step One: Brainstorm Concerns

First you must decide what you want to accomplish. This is the brainstorming step. As an individual, you may be thinking about what you need to do today as well as in the future. If you are part of a group, you may be formulating an agenda. The brainstorming step in planning is well-named because it can be compared to a thunderstorm. Just as weather conditions go wild during a storm, you should allow your mind to run wild when brainstorming. List every idea that comes to mind, without judgment or analysis. Only after you have listed every possible idea, consider which ones are workable. Narrow down the list to those that are realistic and will address your purposes.

When people work in groups, they must plan in order to accomplish goals.

Activity. Divide the class into small groups and have them list ideas for a class project. Encourage students to let their minds run wild. Have one person in each group record everyone's ideas. Choose the best idea for a project.

Problem Solving. Have the class determine ways to carry out a class project, and ask students to write down a clear plan to carry out the project. How does a written plan make a project easier to carry out?

SIDELIGHT

Working in a Group

If you have ever worked in groups before, you know that some function more efficiently than others. When people know how to manage within a group, the group as a whole can accomplish more. Here are some pointers:

- Someone must act as the *leader/manager.* This person guides the group and makes sure that the goals are accomplished. As you know, he or she must be diplomatic, well organized, a good communicator, energetic, and dedicated.
- In some groups a *moderator* may be assigned to coordinate activity. This person gets along well with others and can keep the peace.
- A *recorder* is assigned to keep the written records of what is going on.
- *Team members* cooperate to accomplish the work of the group. These people should respect the leader and other members. They should also be willing and dedicated workers. Group members who distract others from the goals of the group or who do not carry their load of responsibility lose the respect of other team members.
- Groups set *goals*. Then they use the planning process to accomplish them.
- Rules of order, or *parliamentary procedures*, are used in many groups. To what extent depends on the nature of the group. Books, such as *Robert's Rules of Order*, can be found that describe these rules in detail.
- A group may also set up its own rules of operation. Sometimes called *bylaws*, these rules govern the long-term action of the group.

◆◆◆

◆ Step Two: Set a Goal

The goal statement gives a clear vision of what you wish to accomplish. It should be stated in specific terms, so that you can tell when you have achieved it. Compare these two goal statements:

Goal Statement 1: To earn extra spending money.

Goal Statement 2: To obtain a part-time job, working twenty hours a week at minimum wage.

Which goal statement is more specific?

◆ Step Three: Form a Plan

Forming the plan means deciding what needs to be done. Who will do it? When and where will it be done? What resources will be used? How will you tell when everything is complete?

A written plan has several advantages. In group endeavors, the written plan lessens confusion. There is less chance that an important task will be left undone. Everyone is better informed, which contributes to a more positive attitude toward the project. In some cases, the written plan will also uncover potential roadblocks. By anticipating these, good planners can develop ways to get around roadblocks.

The written plan may take several forms. Examples include a list of things to do, a checklist of tasks, or even the hurriedly scribbled memo on the refrigerator door. Many good planners use desktop or pocket calendars. Others like to use tape recorders or personal computers for planning.

Activity. Have students assume that they are forming a club within the class. The club will have officers and committees. Using correct parliamentary procedures, students should conduct a meeting to elect officers and select committees. Have them study and discuss parliamentary procedure according to *Robert's Rules of Order* before conducting the meeting.

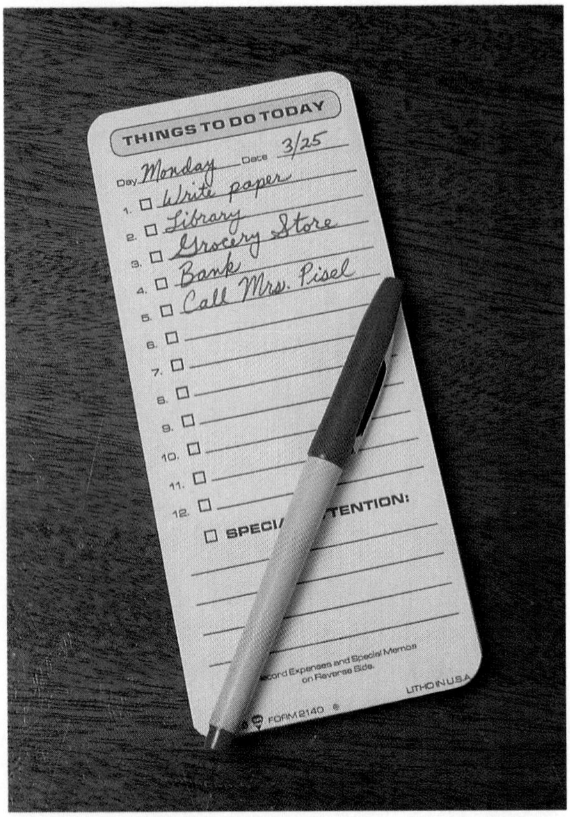

Plans come in many forms.

◆ Step Four: Act

The best-laid plans accomplish nothing without action. Attempt to carry out the plan. Use available resources wisely. If the plan does not work, stand by to revise. Never feel that the plan is sacred. If Plan A does not work, try Plan B and continue to pursue your goal.

◆ Step Five: Follow Up

Evaluation is the key to improved planning skills. Ask yourself what worked and what did not work. Were resources used effectively? What should be done differently next time? Many of life's best lessons are learned from plans which failed.

Photo Focus. Have students look at the photo at the top of the page. Ask how many keep lists that help them manage their activities. Do some use lists for homework assignments? What suggestions do they have for each other that will help them be better organized?

◆◆◆

Benefits of Good Management

Have you ever been told that "you can't have everything"? Perhaps you have heard this observation: "You can't be all things to all people." There is truth to be found in both of these, but the questions remain: What *can* you be, and what *can* you have? Your life goals reflect your search for answers to these questions. Your priorities reveal the importance you give to each goal. The challenge lies in keeping your life in balance.

With good management, you can balance your time, money, and energy against the personal goals you set and the demands of others. You can attend to major needs in all important areas of your life — personal, family, and career. While no one can "have everything," you can *manage* to have many of your goals realized. Life can be satisfying and rewarding.

With good management skills, you can get more out of life.

More About Management. The thought of applying management principles may be overwhelming to some students, especially if this is new to them. Encourage students to practice management skills in one aspect of life before moving on to others. For example, they might tackle managing health, schoolwork, leisure time, or career plans as a starter.

Balancing *Work & Family*

The Home Team

It may be the most unusual team you know. You don't need to excel in anything to join it. You don't even need to try out. You're automatically recruited. What team is it? It's your family—a team that can pull together to meet family needs.

Teamwork is the most efficient way to complete the household chores. Imagine being in charge of making meals, doing laundry, cleaning the house, going food shopping and much more. In most homes with working parents one person just can't do all that. However, if the whole family works together, these tasks become much more manageable.

Teams work best when a leader provides guidance. That keeps members on track and mindful of their responsibilities. Parents make good managers. They know what needs to be accomplished and they know what each family member is capable of doing.

As a team manager, a parent's job is to devise a game plan and help the team to complete it. The five-step planning process works well.

- **Brainstorm concerns.** A family gets together to talk about things they'd like to accomplish. Every idea is accepted at this early planning stage.
- **Set a goal.** The family reviews the ideas and decides what they can accomplish. There may be more than one goal.
- **Form a plan.** A written checklist works well for many families. Each person can consult it to see who is responsible to each daily or weekly task.
- **Act.** Family members complete their tasks. Parent managers can remind team members about jobs and provide guidance if problems arise.
- **Follow up.** The family meets again to talk about what worked and what didn't, making revisions for next time.

To help remind team members of tasks that need to be done regularly, some families post a central calendar. The calendar may note, for example, trash collection days or it may establish a room-by-room schedule for cleaning. This calendar becomes the main reference for the family. All chores are listed on it, on the day the chore needs to be done. The calendar is kept in a noticeable place, such as the refrigerator door, so that family members are regularly reminded of what is expected.

Some household tasks are made easier by dividing responsibilities. For example, one person may clear the table, another may wash the dishes (or load the dishwasher) and a third person may dry the dishes (or unload the dishwasher). Or two people may share the responsibility for preparing a meal, with one doing all the chopping, mixing, and preparation and the other doing the actual cooking. Dividing tasks in this way helps to lighten the load on family members with busy schedules and other commitments.

No matter how the tasks are assigned, families soon see the value of teamwork. Not only can its success be measured by the work accomplished, it can be shown in family pride at working together to reach their goals.

Think About It

1. What are some other examples of household tasks that can be shared or divided?
2. What are the benefits of a family working together as a team?
3. Give examples of what a family might discuss during the follow-up stage.

Life Management Skills. Have students identify the management problems in the following situations: 1. At a meeting of an ecology group, they were making plans for recycling in the community. Andy spent much of the time explaining how they had worked for clean air in the city where he had previously lived. 2. Kathleen always makes New Year's resolutions and forgets about them in a couple weeks. 3. When Jackie was forty years old, she had no money in savings, no property of value, and a dead-end job. She wondered why she wasn't better off after 20 years of working. 4. When Harlan lost the election for class president, he decided never to run for an office again. 5. Aisha had a report due on Friday. She stayed up until 1 a.m. to get it done in time. 6. Devon keeps important papers at home in different places. When he needs to find something, it takes him a long time. Sometimes he doesn't find what he needs at all. 7. Often people give Randy suggestions that might be helpful to him in life. He rejects their help because he feels he knows what is best.

Have students offer suggestions for improved management in each of the situations above.

CHAPTER

9

Review

Answers

Testing Your Memory

1. Some people may have some instinctive ability to manage, yet the skills can also be learned.
2. Long-range goals usually have a time span of one year or more, and short-range goals are usually measured in terms of days, weeks, or months. The three examples of each type will vary.
3. **Any two:** visualize the steps needed to reach a goal; seek advice; recognize resources.
4. Time is called the universal resource because everyone has it.
5. Yes. They may have to work hard to develop skills, but it can be done.
6. Attitude is a resource because when your attitude is positive, you will be able to accomplish more.
7. A mentor is a loyal, wise adviser.
8. Money, property, supplies and tools, and information.
9. A plan shows you how to achieve your goal.
10. The five steps in planning are: 1. Brainstorm concerns; 2. Set a goal; 3. Form a plan; 4. Act; 5. Follow up. (Explanations will come from the text on pages 130-132.)

Summarizing the Chapter

- Management skills include goal setting and recognition of resources.
- Good managers set both long-range and short-range goals.
- Workable goals are clearly stated and realistic.
- Human resources include time, energy, ability, attitude, and people.
- Material resources usually have physical form.
- Resourceful people know how to recognize and make the best use of resources.
- The planning process is a step-by-step approach to management: (1) Brainstorm concerns; (2) Set a goal; (3) Form a plan; (4) Act; and (5) Follow up.
- Good managers enjoy the benefits of a balanced, satisfying life.

Testing Your Memory

1. Is the ability to manage instinctive? Explain your answer.
2. What is the difference between long-range and short-range goals? List three examples of each.
3. What are two suggestions that may help to distinguish a realistic goal from wishful thinking?
4. Which human resource is often called the universal resource and why?
5. Can people without natural ability still develop skills? Explain your answer.
6. Why is attitude considered a resource?
7. What is a mentor?
8. List four categories of material resources.
9. What is the purpose of a plan?
10. List and explain the five steps in planning.

Thinking Critically

1. In your opinion, which of the human or material resources is the most valuable, and why?
2. Make a list of five or more people whom you feel are qualified to serve as mentors for you. Beside each name, state the area in which their wisdom or expertise is found.
3. It has been said that "love of money is the root of all evil." Do you agree? Why or why not?

Taking Action

1. Research to find a real-life story to illustrate that attitude can be a major resource in overcoming obstacles.
2. Watch a television situation comedy. Identify a goal that was set by one of the characters. Analyze the character's use of resources in pursuit of the goal.
3. Devise a written plan for a project or activity that you need to do.

Making Life Choices

Nineteen-year-old Joel is the only son of Mr. and Mrs. Joseph Bowers. Joel is a freshman at the state university located ninety miles from home. Joel's Christmas vacation begins December the sixth and ends January the fourth. The Bowers will celebrate their twenty-fifth wedding anniversary on Thursday, the fifth of December. Joel would like to honor his parents with an anniversary celebration of some kind.

Brainstorm to develop a list of ideas that Joel could consider. Narrow down the list by starring those ideas that seem workable. Select one idea and form a written plan to include information on who, what, when, where, and how.

Using Your Journal

Use what you have just learned about the process of planning to figure out a plan for reaching one of your goals. First you need to set a goal. Write the goal in your journal (it can be a short-term or a long-term goal). Then prepare a written plan, listing the steps you need to take in order to reach your goal. At an appropriate time, put your plan into action and then continue to use your journal to evaluate it.

Thinking Critically
1. Answers will vary.
2. Answers will vary.
3. Answers will vary.

Alex reaches out to mediate a conflict.

Alex

"Saturday at the Spanish Club's Car Wash, I was sure Juan and Annie were going to have a fist fight. I couldn't believe it because they'd been such close friends. They argued over everything — who would clean the windows and who would spray the cars. When Juan said he and his friend from the basketball team would take care of the money box, I was sure Annie was going to hit somebody. I knew I had to step in before things got any worse. Being on the conflict resolution team at school has certainly made me more aware of the need to get involved before things get out of hand. Fortunately Juan and Annie were willing to separate and cool down a bit. When we got back together it was easier for them to talk about their problem. As it turned out, they really weren't angry about the car wash. Annie resented Juan's commitment to the basketball team, which left little time for them to spend together. Juan was upset that Annie never called him anymore."

Ms. Coronado

"I was surprised to see Juan and Annie bickering at the car wash. As faculty advisor to the Spanish Club, I had always seen them talking and laughing together. They seemed like great friends. I was just about to step in when Alex made his move. I watched him calm the students down using the conflict resolution techniques we teach to members of the school's conflict mediation team. Seeing him put those skills to use gave me a real boost. Being able to help two friends probably made Alex feel pretty good, too."

Annie

"Juan and I used to be such good friends, but in the last month, it seems that all he's done is play basketball. He even stopped returning my calls, so I just quit calling. I knew he would be at the car wash and I planned to have a talk with him about our friendship. Well, there he was, but he purposely ignored me. I got angry and started to argue with him. I guess I just wanted his attention. Of course, he got angry too. I'm glad Alex was there. By getting involved he probably kept us from doing and saying things that might have split us up permanently. Instead we were finally able to talk about the real problem."

Juan

"I couldn't figure out what was the matter with Annie. She hadn't called me for a while, but I thought she was probably busy. Then, when I saw her at the car wash, all she did was criticize me and pick fights. Alex helped me see the problem from Annie's perspective. I guess I didn't realize how much time I'd been spending playing basketball. I had been ignoring Annie as a friend. Now that we talked things out, I feel much better. Annie's even coming to next Saturday's game, and we're going out afterward for pizza."

You can make a difference too.

- How could Annie's and Juan's conflict have been avoided in the first place?
- What skills do students need when they reach out to friends in conflict?
- Have you reached out to friends in conflict? Why or why not?
- What are the benefits of having a third person help two others resolve a conflict?

UNIT 3

What Are Families Like?

CHAPTER

CHAPTER 10

Patterns of Family Living

Chapter Challenge

Resources. Refer to the Teacher's Classroom Resources box and Student Workbook for materials related to this chapter.

Look for These Answers . . .

- What is a family?
- Describe the different types of families.
- Describe the family life cycle.
- What are some things that affect families?
- Why are strong families needed?

Look for These Terms . . .

- blended family
- extended family
- family life cycle
- nuclear family
- role
- siblings
- single-parent family
- stepfamily

Dru peered into the silent room. There she was in her chair. At eighty-nine she looked so frail.

"Grams, are you asleep?" Dru quietly asked.

Dru's great grandmother opened her eyes and looked at her. "Is that you, Edwina?" she inquired.

"No, Grams, it's me, Dru. How are you feeling today?" she asked as she kissed her on the cheek.

"Oh, Dru — Dru, of course. For a moment I thought you were your mother. Is she coming today?"

"She can't. Grandpa Ev has a doctor's appointment today, so mother took him there."

"Oh, that boy of mine. Why doesn't Everett ever come to see me?"

"Grams, he was here yesterday. You must have forgotten," Dru said patiently.

"Oh," Great Grandmother Reed sighed in disappointment. Dru couldn't tell whether she was saddened because Grandpa Ev was not coming today or because she had simply forgotten something else.

"Grams, guess what? I have something to tell you. Carlin and I are going to be married — this summer. Just think. One of these days when we have a child, you'll be a great great grandmother. Isn't that exciting?"

The eighty-nine-year-old eyes focused intently on Dru. A hand moved slowly to rest on Dru's arm. "How wonderful," she whispered. "You've grown up so fast, Dru. This is just the beginning for you, dear, just the beginning." Then the eyes seemed far away — very far away.

Chapter Opener. Have students read the opening scenario to the chapter. Ask students to describe the relationship between Dru and her great grandmother. What do you think Dru's great grandmother is thinking at the end of the scenario? How does this scene depict an ending and a beginning?

What Is a Family?

When you ask children to describe a family, they will tell you that it consists of a mother, a father, and their children. Ask the children to describe their own families, and their answers may be quite different. They may tell you that they live with mother and see daddy on weekends. They may talk about having stepfathers and stepmothers as well as fathers and mothers. They may point out that they are adopted or are foster children.

Most people have some idea of what a family is. Defining it, however, is not easy. This is because there are so many patterns of family living.

The word "family" is often used in connection with a person's ancestry. Most families are based on kinship. Members belong to the family through birth, marriage, or adoption.

Activity. Ask each student to write a definition of family. Then have them work in pairs to create a common definition. Finally, have two pairs work together to write a group definition of family on a large sheet of paper. Students should post the definitions around the room. Ask students to: Compare and contrast the group definitions. How does the dictionary define family? Where in society, government, or law is it important to have a definition of family? Why? How important is it that all people have the same definition of family? Why or why not?

Some groups are considered to be families because they share or feel ties of affection. Joel is a foster child. He and his foster parents are not related by adoption, birth, or marriage, but they are a family nevertheless.

When family attributes, the characteristics of a family, are taken on by a group of people, they may think of themselves as a family. Susan and Erica were best friends during their college years. They liked to call their close-knit circle of dorm friends a family.

Families vary in size. John and Sarah are a couple with no children. Monica is a single parent with one child. Ashton and Kara are a couple who adopted two Romanian children. BJ lives with his parents and seven brothers and sisters. BJ's brothers and sisters are called his siblings. **Siblings** are people who have a common parent. In general, families tend to be smaller than they were in the past.

Family Roles

The people within a family all have different roles to fill. A **role** is the socially expected behavior pattern determined by a person's status in society. Some roles are based on gender. What activities and behavior do you associate with the males and females in a family? Other roles are associated with the positions of family members. What comes to mind when you think of husband, wife, father, mother, son, daughter, sister, and brother? You will read more about family roles in the next chapter.

You have other roles besides those within your family. Friend and student are two. Can you think of others? Obviously, people can have more than one role in life. These roles will change as they grow older.

At times roles can be confusing. People don't always agree on what the behavior should be for a specific role. As society changes, attitudes about roles do too.

People need families. Sometimes a substitute family temporarily supplies what a person needs. A "family" of college dorm friends is an example.

Photo Focus. Ask students to examine the above photo. In what ways may these young men represent a family? Are other groups in society able to meet family-type needs? Why or why not?

Work and Family. Have students brainstorm ways in which family roles change when parents work outside the home. How may the roles of children change? Ask students to discuss other roles they fulfill in their lives. How do these roles affect family life? If students work outside the home, how may this affect their roles in the family?

◆◆◆

Types of Families

Families vary in composition, as you can see from these descriptions:

- **Nuclear Family.** A **nuclear family** (NOO-klee-ur) consists of members of two generations: parents and children. Brandon's family includes his mother and father and his sister Laura.
- **Extended Family.** A family that includes relatives other than parents and children, such as grandparents or cousins, is an **extended family.** Raul's family is a large group that includes his grandparents, a sister and her two children, and two cousins. Tom's nuclear family temporarily became an extended family when his sister and her two children moved in following her divorce.

Different combinations of people can make up a family. What type of family is this?

Discussion. Ask the students why extended families were more common in past generations than they are today. What benefits may there be in living in an extended family today? What are the positive aspects for parents, children, and other relatives living in the household? Are there negative aspects of living in an extended family? If so, what?

- **Single-Parent Family.** A **single-parent family** is headed by one parent who has never married or who is left alone after a death, divorce, or desertion. LaWanda and her two children became a single-parent family after her husband's death. This type of family is increasingly common in the United States.
- **Stepfamily.** When at least one spouse has children from a previous relationship, a **stepfamily** has formed. The non-biological parents in such families are called stepparents. The children who are not related to them biologically become stepchildren. Stepfamilies are also on the rise. In the future, increasing numbers of children under age eighteen will not be living with both biological parents.

In one type of stepfamily one spouse has children from a previous relationship and the other does not. When Dominick, who had no children, married Danette, he became a stepfather to her two children.

Some stepfamilies are called blended families. A **blended family** is formed when both spouses have children from a previous relationship. George became part of a blended family when his mother remarried. George now has a stepbrother who lives with the family and a stepsister who visits regularly.

Stepfamilies face many challenges. Unlike traditional newlyweds, spouses may find it difficult to find time just for themselves. Relationships with former spouses may add to the tensions. Children may still be mourning the family they lost. Some may even resent their new stepparent, dislike their new stepbrothers and stepsisters, or miss their old family, home, friends, and neighborhood. They may feel torn between their biological parents and their stepparents. Every aspect of family life — discipline, chores, finances, traditions, mealtimes, and vacations — may have to be negotiated. With some effort, stepfamilies do adjust to living together. You will read more about this in Chapter 22.

The Family Life Cycle

Just as individuals go through stages of life, families are also continually changing. This predictable pattern of change throughout the adult years is called the **family life cycle**. In the beginning couples marry and establish a home together. As children enter the picture, the family expands. The family develops as children grow and become adolescents. Once children become young adults, they move out on their own. With children gone, parents move into their middle years and eventually into the retirement and aging years. As the cycle is completed for one generation, it begins again for another.

Each phase of family development brings new challenges, new tasks, and new rewards. Remember that even though a pattern exists, families are so different that you will find many variations. Interruptions in the cycle can be caused by separation, divorce, and death. Not everyone experiences the family life cycle in quite the same way.

◆ Young Adult Years

As you grow out of your teens, you will learn to become emotionally and economically independent. You will begin to establish your adult identity. Already you probably look more to your friends than to family for companionship. As a young adult, you will complete your schooling, launch a career, and

The Family Life Cycle

(The Blake Family)

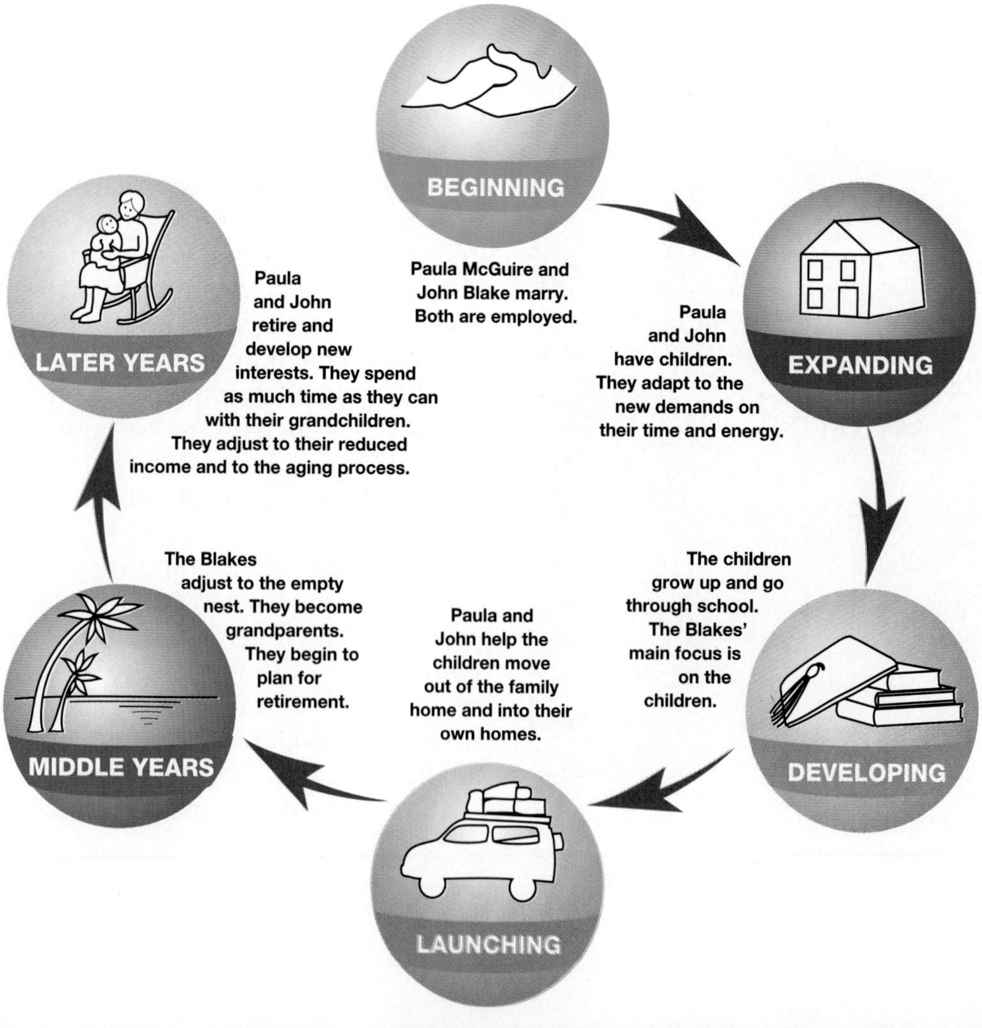

establish a home of your own. You will also make decisions about the type of lifestyle you want to have. All of this marks the beginning of the family life cycle.

During the early years of adulthood, those who have chosen marriage adjust to married life. Deacon and Dedra are learning to live together harmoniously. They find that they must switch from individual to team thinking. They are beginning to feel united by bonds of trust. They are working out comfortable routines for their life together. They are making decisions about careers, money management, lifestyle, and children. Each has had to adjust to the other's family. Deacon and Dedra are learning that it takes cooperation and communication to build a successful partnership. An important outcome of their early years of marriage will be establishing a feeling of interdependence.

Of course, not every family operates the same way during this stage. Some couples have children right away. Some postpone parenthood, often to establish careers. Some prefer not to have children at all.

A couple without children may be considered a family. What happens to the family life cycle in this case?

When children are part of a family, adjustments must be made. Manuel and Carlita found that their focus quickly shifted to include the needs of their infant son Javier. As parents, they have new responsibilities and new demands on their time and energy. Manuel and Carlita admit that parenthood limits their freedom and has created new expenses. They are working to balance their roles of spouse and parent. If they have additional children, the pressures and responsibilities of parenthood will increase.

As children grow, their individual needs become increasingly important. ShiMin and Lee are preparing their children for school, church, sports, and other activities. They are teaching their children what to expect in their new activities, working to assure their safety, and learning to work with teachers, coaches, and counselors. At home, ShiMin and Lee give their children increasing responsibility: making beds, setting the table, caring for pets. The pace of their family life has become more hectic. Already, the tug between their children's dependence and their need to become independent has begun.

As children grow toward adolescence, they need increasing responsibility and freedom to prepare them for adulthood. Once children are grown, they begin to leave home. Some call this the launching stage, as parents send their children out into the world to live on their own. Many young adults today live with their families longer than they did in the past, thus postponing the launching stage. Often the reasons for this are economic.

Work and Family. More often, both parents in a two-parent family must work full-time to support the family financially. Have students interview working parents of school-age children to find out how these families meet the demands of work and family. Do employers offer assistance? Are parents able to adjust work schedules in order to attend school functions? How available and affordable is child care for preschool and school-age children in your community? Is sick child care available for families who need it?

SIDELIGHT

The Family Life Cycle

During the stages of the family life cycle, families have different concerns. Think about the list below. At which point in the family life cycle do you think each item is of most concern to a family?

- Education
- Medical needs
- Career
- Finances
- Retirement plans
- Relationship with spouse
- Relationship with children
- Relationships with others
- Personal interests

◆◆◆

◆ Middle Years

During the middle years, many changes occur in the family. Ernest and Yvonne's children have grown up and left home to pursue education and career goals and to establish families of their own. As their active parenting role ends, Ernest's career is peaking, leaving him less to look forward to. Yvonne is taking a close look at what she wants for the rest of her life now that her children are grown and gone. For those families that have had children, this period is often called the empty nest stage. In other words, the children are all gone from the family home. Sometimes individuals go through a period of serious self-examination at this time, often called a midlife crisis.

Couples react to the middle years in different ways. When they hit midlife, Joe and Becky decided to change their lifestyle by moving to a small town. Jim left a job with a large company to start his own business. Dennis and Melissa divorced at midlife. When Paul and Nancy's children left home, they focused on renewing their relationship as a couple.

Most couples can look forward to living childlessly for 15 to 20 years. For a couple who have neglected their own relationship while raising children, this can be a difficult period. They need to redefine themselves as partners, not parents. They must also think about saving for retirement if they have not begun to do so already.

More middle-aged parents today find themselves responsible for both older and younger relatives. This responsibility has usually fallen upon women. Since so many women are employed now, the need for community services for the elderly has increased.

After children leave the family nest, many couples have more time to spend together than they have for years. This often requires adjustments and new focuses.

Activity. Invite several families in the launching stage of the family life cycle to share their experiences with the class. What are the most difficult aspects about this stage? What are the nicest aspects? Of those who have completed the launching stage, what advice can they give to families who are about to begin the launching stage in the family life cycle? What qualities are possessed by families who appear to have an easier time during this stage? What qualities would seem to make this stage more challenging?

Doyle and Clara's elderly parents are in their eighties. They have become more dependent and require more attention because of illness and age. When their parents die, Doyle and Clara will have to cope with their grief and with the reality that they are aging themselves. Glen and Donna's adult daughter, Lurine, has returned home with her three children. Lurine has moved home before for periods ranging from a few weeks to several years, due to financial problems, separation, and this time, divorce. Although they want to help, Lurine's middle-aged parents feel increased pressure from her return home.

◆ The Later Years

Retirement often marks the beginning of the later years. The age of retirement varies. Some people take early retirement. Others continue working as long as they are physically able. Some people fear retirement. Ed feels that his usefulness will end when he leaves his job as a high-salaried executive. Erma does not look forward to retiring because she faces economic hardship.

On the positive side, the leisure time offered by retirement is welcomed by many. At last they are able to do those things they always wanted to but never had time for. They can focus on hobbies and interests, including travel, friends, and volunteer work. Retirement gives them a second chance to enjoy parenthood through their relationships with grandchildren. Doris cares for her grandchildren while their parents work. Although she enjoys it, she has some friends who do the same only because they feel pressured to do so. What do you think about this?

As the later years roll on, people must deal with aging, which is a normal part of life. It is accompanied by inevitable physical changes. Eyesight and hearing often decline. Food may not taste as good as it once did. Falls can cause serious injury, such as a broken hip.

Retirement means an opportunity to try new interests and do the things you never had time for.

All the unavoidable signs of aging appear — gray hair, wrinkles, and bodies that aren't what they used to be. Physical problems can limit the abilities of elderly people. This makes something as simple as running errands difficult. In some areas trained people shop, clean, and provide companionship for those who still live at home.

As people grow older, they face new decisions. These concern health and safety, finances, and housing.

◆ Health and Safety

Attitudes toward aging vary. Emma considers herself active, alert, and open-minded; however, she believes that many elderly people lack these characteristics. Jim enjoys the respect of family and friends because he owns a successful family farm. Alice feels that she lost status when she quit working to live on a small retirement income. Attitudes toward aging can be either positive or negative. They are often influenced by the person's health and income.

Life Management Skills. Preparing for retirement is one of the tasks in the middle years. Have students research suggestions for families facing retirement in the next five to fifteen years. What issues should be addressed? How can money be saved for retirement? How much money will it take to retire comfortably? What factors, other than financial, should couples consider about retirement?

Aging people look and feel better when they pay special attention to their diets. Good nutrition improves mental attitude and physical health. Older people usually need fewer calories. They need a well-balanced diet that includes a variety of foods, including plenty of fresh fruits and vegetables and whole grain cereals.

Medical care is an important concern of the elderly. Elizabeth receives benefits from Medicare, the federal government's medical insurance program for senior citizens. It pays part of her expenses for physicians, drugs, and hospital care. It will also pay a portion of the cost of medical services at home or in a nursing home after she is discharged from the hospital. Elizabeth finds it difficult, however, to pay her part of these costs from her small retirement income.

Some of the problems older people have are caused by loneliness. The death of a spouse leaves the widow or widower without companionship and assistance. A person who does not like eating alone may start to skip meals. Many community organizations offer meals for senior citizens. Some even provide home delivery. For those who feel isolated, an effort must be made to stay involved. Where community centers are available, seniors can visit, play games, or try hobbies. Sampson was depressed following retirement until he got involved with a church group that refurbishes homes of low-income families. This put meaning back into his life.

Crime has a strong impact on the elderly. Ellis and Fran watched sadly as their neighborhood deteriorated. A neighbor's house was burglarized recently. A friend was robbed on his way home after cashing his social security check. Another was swindled out of her life savings. Ellis and Fran are considering selling their family home and moving to another area.

Discussion. Ask students to assume they are retired workers. Then have them answer the following questions: What have they done for work? What are they doing now? What is life like at this stage? What is their health like? Where do they live? What do other people say about them? What could young people do to make their retirement more enjoyable?

Many senior citizens need services provided by communities and volunteers. Providing nutritious meals is one example.

◆ Finances

Finances can also be a problem. Frank and Shirley's monthly income is now less than half what they earned while working. Frank stopped working as a plumber following a heart attack. Shirley wanted to increase their income by working. Until she is 72, however, the government will allow her to earn only a small amount without losing part of her social security benefits. Even if she decides to look for a job, she wonders if she will be able to find one. Shirley knows that older workers can be as productive and efficient as other workers. They also miss fewer days of work and have fewer accidents on the job. Still, finding a job isn't always easy. At this point in their lives, Frank and Shirley rely on careful money management for security instead of work.

Activity. Have students explore opportunities for volunteer service in the community with senior citizens. Perhaps some volunteer time could be part of the school curriculum. Ask students to examine the ways in which young people and senior citizens can benefit from volunteer programs.

◆ Housing

Elderly people need housing that is convenient, safe, comfortable, and easy to maintain. Consider the choices these elderly people have made:

- **Maintaining Own Home.** Mike and Lora met their needs by making minor changes to the house they have shared for forty years. Like more than half of Americans over 65, Mike and Lora live near one of their children.
- **Living with Adult Child.** Alma and Ray moved in with their daughter's family when they could no longer maintain their own home. Before moving in, they talked with their adult children about their roles. Alma and Ray feel that they are a useful and active part of the family even though their adult children make the major family decisions.
- **Moving to Retirement Community.** Richard and Stella are among the less than ten percent of the nation's senior citizens who live in special housing called retirement communities. These communities may consist of apartment buildings, neighborhoods of individual houses, or groups of mobile homes. Richard and Stella's retirement community provides recreational and social activities and offers medical care.
- **Receiving Institutional Care.** Dorothy is one of the five percent of the elderly who live in a nursing home or institution. She receives the specialized nursing care she could not get at home.
- **Living with Friends.** More and more, small groups of senior citizens who do not need nursing care are joining forces. By sharing housing costs, they satisfy their desire for independent living.

Retirement homes can be very expensive. Can you think of some advantages and disadvantages of this type of housing for senior citizens?

◆◆◆

What Affects Families?

As families move through the family life cycle, they are affected by what goes on around them. Both negative and positive results occur.

◆ Technology

Technology affects the way families live. Think about all the devices that families use today. In the kitchen, for example, the microwave oven makes food preparation speedy. Even young family members can fix a quick meal by heating something in the microwave. When busy families are on the go and keeping different schedules, this can be helpful. Do you see any negatives to this?

Today many families have an automobile, some more than one. At one time high school parking lots were small. Today large lots often hold automobiles that students use for transportation to and from school as well as to jobs and social events. Young people often need this transportation to get themselves where they need to go when employed parents are not available. They are also able to help run errands for the same reason. On the other hand, easy mobility can keep them away from the home more than some families would like.

Life Management Skills. Have students find out how much the average retired person receives from Social Security. Plan a budget for a person living only on that amount. What would this person's lifestyle be like? In what ways could this person enhance his or her lifestyle without over-extending the budget? How can a limited income affect housing choices for the elderly? Should elderly people with limited income live in a retirement community, live alone, or live with adult children? What options would students like to see their parents have?

A Slice of Life

It was a typical evening in the Thomas family. Mr. Thomas had to work late, so he would not be home for dinner. Mrs. Thomas had to run a few errands after work, so she was running late. Four-year-old Davey had to wait a little longer at the child care center until she could pick him up.

At age nine Shelly was home from school. She had a key so she could let herself in the house. She found a snack and turned on the television for company. Her older brother Russ came in a little after her. He heated a microwave dinner since he had to go back to school for an evening basketball practice.

When Davey and Mrs. Thomas got home, they ate a quick supper. Davey sat down to watch television while Mrs. Thomas did some laundry and cleaned up the kitchen. Then she joined Davey in front of the television. Shelly put on her earphones so she could listen to music. When Mr. Thomas arrived home late, he sat down to try out a new computer program. The evening was gone before they knew it.

Thinking It Through

- How do you think technology and the economy have affected this family?
- What are the positive and negative aspects of this family scene?
- What suggestions would you offer to the Thomas family?

Today families and friends are often scattered about, living in different parts of the state, nation, or world. It requires more work to retain close ties with those far away. On the other hand, people can travel more easily to visit and maintain contact.

In the entertainment area, families have access to television, music equipment, and computers. Although these are enjoyable, they can cut into the communication that families need. Can you think of ways that families could combine communication with the use of such equipment?

Through television, radio, magazines, newspaper, and other media, mass communications reach nearly everyone. There is no doubt that this influences attitudes and expectations.

Technology has an effect on families. How would you describe the effect that the computer has had?

Work and Family. Technology can make the job of taking care of a household easier. Ask students to answer the following questions: In what ways has technology helped make household tasks easier for family members? In what ways may families divide work and household duties to insure that tasks get done? In small groups, have students devise a system for managing household tasks for a family of three (parent, step-parent, and teen) in which all three work outside the home. What tasks need to be done? How often? By whom? Is there an incentive or reward for the job? What happens when tasks are not completed?

Photo Focus. Have students examine the above photo. How may these people effectively use a computer in the home?

◆ Economic Factors

The economy affects family lifestyles. In many families both parents are employed because they need two incomes in order to meet basic needs. This is very common today, and few would argue about this necessity. There is some concern, however, about how children's needs are met when both parents are employed. The debate usually centers around those who work by choice rather than need. Still, raising the question at all is enough to make parents who need two incomes feel guilty. What do you think about this issue?

Employment options are increasing in response to the problems of families with two workers. In the years ahead an increasing number of Americans will be doing part or all of their work at home via computer. In some families, the husband stays home while the wife works.

◆ Social Factors

Social trends affect the makeup of families as well as the way they live. People have more freedom to make decisions about marriage and children. This affects the size and composition of families. Divorce, which you will read more about in another chapter, also affects families.

One disturbing social trend in the United States is the increase in domestic violence. One-third of all murders in the United States occur within the family. Domestic violence is the leading cause of injury of women between the ages of 15 and 44. About 1,400,000 children are abused each year, resulting in 160,000 serious injuries and as many as 2,000 deaths. Drinking is a factor in a significant number of the child abuse cases. Alcoholism and drug use shatter families in other ways too. These are very serious situations that have far reaching effects on families.

More About Employment. More families are making use of employment options that allow couples to work and share care of their children. Some work at home using a computer, others share a full-time job with someone else (each person working part-time). Some jobs have flexible hours that allow employees to adapt work hours to family needs.

◆◆◆

The Foundation of Society

Many people today worry about the condition of the American family. It is changing rapidly in response to all the factors you just read about. When changes occur, people need to learn how to adjust, to make things work right. This is what families are trying to do, and they need to succeed. Why? Because the family is the foundation of society.

Each family raises a new generation that is responsible for raising the next. A troubled family breeds a new generation with problems, and the cycle continues. To have a strong society, strong families are needed. This is where you come in. When you build a family of your own, it must be a strong one. How will you do that? The next chapter will give you some ideas.

A strong family today means strong families in the future.

Activity. Have students begin a file for newspaper articles related to the family. Use these articles for class discussion, reaction and opinion papers, bulletin board displays, as well as ideas for reports and term papers.

CHAPTER 10

Review

Answers
Testing Your Memory

1. No. With so many patterns of family living, one definition may be impossible. Generally, members belong to the family through birth, marriage, or adoption.
2. A socially expected behavior pattern determined by a person's status in society.
3. For descriptions of the four family types, refer to page 143.
4. No. Because families are different, there will be many variations. Interruptions, such as separations, death, or divorce, may cause families to experience the family life cycle in different ways.
5. **Any three:** adjusting to married life; establishing a feeling of interdependence; establishing careers; if children, adjusting to their needs; preparing children to leave home.
6. **Any three:** children leave home; active parenting role ends; careers peak, leaving less to look forward to; self-examination about goals for the future may occur (midlife crisis); lifestyle may change due to more freedom; focus on renewing relationship as a couple; may need to care for elderly relatives.

Summarizing the Chapter

- People fulfill different roles within the family and in other aspects of life too.
- Families differ in composition. They include the nuclear family, extended family, single-parent family, and stepfamily.
- A blended family is a form of stepfamily.
- The predictable pattern of changes throughout the adult years is called the family life cycle.
- The family life cycle begins when couples marry. Children are raised and launched, after which couples move into the middle and later years.
- Technology, the economy, and social trends all have an effect on families.

Testing Your Memory

1. Do all people define family in exactly the same way? Explain your answer.
2. What is a role?
3. Describe each of these family types: nuclear family; extended family; single-parent family; and stepfamily.
4. Do all families go through the family life cycle in the same way? Explain your answer.
5. Describe three changes that can occur during the young adult years.
6. Describe three changes that can occur during the middle years.
7. Describe three concerns of the aging.
8. Explain one way that families are affected by each of these: technology, the economy, and social trends.

Thinking Critically

1. Would you consider a group of unrelated adults who share a home a family? Defend your answer.
2. The number of retired people is expected to put a strain on our economy in the 21st century. What solutions would you propose?
3. What advantages and disadvantages do you associate with the different types of families?
4. What preparations can you make now to smooth your transition from one stage of the family life cycle to the next?

Taking Action

1. Plan and prepare a poster that depicts the different types of families.
2. Research the types of housing that are available for elderly people in your community. Visit one or two if possible. Present your findings to the class. Which would you prefer for one of your relatives?
3. Browse through magazines to find pictures that show how technology affects families. Design a bulletin board to display this theme.

Making Life Choices

Cassie used to live with her mother. She has never known her father. When Cassie was eight, her mother moved to another state. Cassie moved in with her aunt and her two children. At age twelve Cassie feels secure and loved in her aunt's care. Sometimes she compares her family situation with others and she feels different.

Why does Cassie feel the way she does? Does she have a family? What might make Cassie feel more comfortable?

Using Your Journal

You have just read that families are constantly changing. What kinds of changes are happening in your family? What changes do you expect over the next few years? Use your journal to explore current and anticipated changes, and your feelings about those changes. You may want to share your thoughts with a family member or with somebody else you trust.

7. Health and safety, finances, and housing. Refer to pages 147-148 for descriptions.
8. Any one for each topic: *Technology* — food preparation, automobiles, travel, entertainment, mass communications. *The Economy* — family lifestyle, meeting children's needs, increasing employment options. *Social trends* — affect makeup of families and how they live, size and composition of families, trend toward domestic violence and child abuse, alcoholism and drug use.

Thinking Critically

1. Answers will vary.
2. Answers will vary. Point out that students should examine economic, social, housing, and safety implications.
3. Answers will vary.
4. Answers will vary. Emphasize that students should think about parenthood expectations, career plans, and possible plans for retirement.

CHAPTER 11

Living in a Family

Chapter Challenge

Resources. Refer to the Teacher's Classroom Resource box and Student Workbook for materials related to this chapter.

Look for These Answers . . .

- How do families of the past compare to those of today?
- What are the functions of a family?
- How can you make a family strong?

Look for These Terms . . .

- commitment to family
- cottage industries
- dysfunctional family
- egalitarian family
- functional family
- matriarchal family
- patriarchal family
- role anticipation
- role strain
- traditional family

"I think I found one, Dad! Look! Is this one?" Jeremy had reached down quickly into the stream where he was wading. In his hand was a small, rough, and rather ugly stone. It was round and resembled concrete on the outside.

Mr. Cline waded over to his son. "I think it is, Jeremy," he said with enthusiasm. "Is it a light weight for its size?"

Nine-year-old Jeremy pondered the possible geode carefully and decided it was light in weight.

"It might be a good one then, Jeremy," his father said. "We'll know for sure when we open it up. If it's hollow, it could have some beautiful crystals inside."

Jeremy hoped it would. He loved this form of treasure hunting with his father. They had looked for fossils the last time.

Just then Mr. Cline looked off to his right and gasped. "I don't believe this, Jeremy. I think this may be a geode too." His hands reached down to grasp a huge stone. "It must be over a foot in diameter. I'll see if I can lift it. If I can, we'll take it home and open it up too."

That evening Jeremy and his father set about trying to split their geodes in half. It took careful scoring around the diameter of the stones until each one split to reveal the insides. It took them a long time to get the giant geode open, but when they did, Jeremy stared in awe.

"Just look at those crystals, Dad. That's the most beautiful geode I've ever seen, and we found it ourselves."

Mr. Cline put his arm across Jeremy's shoulders. It was a day they would never forget.

Early Families

How do you think living in a family today compares to the past? Take a step back in time to see.

In early families, everyone worked for the survival of the family by searching for food. Eventually, people developed the means to kill or capture large animals. This probably led to the first divisions of labor between men and women. Women probably found hunting difficult during pregnancy. After giving birth, they may have stayed near home to nurse and care for their young. The women probably gathered plants and hunted near camp while the men went off for hours or days to hunt large game.

Chapter Opener. Have students read the opening scenario to the chapter. Ask students the following questions: What healthful characteristics are demonstrated in the relationship between Jeremy and his father? In what ways do Jeremy and his father show emotion?

Discussion. In a matriarchal family, the lineage is traced through the mother's family. The children may also take the mother's name, rather than the father's as is common in the United States. Have the students brainstorm ways our society would be different if matriarchal families were the norm.

Over time, people learned to raise plants and animals for food. In many cultures, women raised crops while men tended herds of sheep, goats, and other animals. Together they provided food for the family. The family's wealth, however, depended on its herd, because the animals could be traded for other goods. Control of the herd gave the husband economic power within his family. In time, he became known as the head of the family. A family in which the father has the most power is called a **patriarchal family** (PAY-tree-AHR-kul). A **matriarchal family** (MAY-tree-AHR-kul) is one in which the mother is the head of the family.

Until the Industrial Revolution in the 1700s, families produced their own food and made most of their clothing, furniture, and tools. Some families worked together at home to make clothing, textiles, or other products for market. These were called **cottage industries.**

American pioneer families worked together to clear the land. Together, they planted, cultivated, and harvested crops. Settlers needed large families to help with the family's work. Children began doing chores at about age six. Girls learned to spin, weave, and sew from their mother. Boys learned farming or a trade from their father or were apprenticed to a skilled worker. Children also received religious training from their parents. Young children, the sick, and the aged were cared for in the home. Much of the family's social life also took place at home.

As industrialization continued, many rural people moved to cities to seek factory work. Often, everyone who could — father, mother, and children — held jobs. The home became less central to family life. Hospitals, schools, and other social institutions took over many family functions. Police and fire departments were created to help protect the lives and property of families.

By the late nineteenth century, industries that had employed large numbers of women and older children gradually disappeared. Men became the primary breadwinners for their families. Women began to concentrate on motherhood and household management. This became known as the **traditional family**. Since children's work was no longer needed, families became smaller. Children spent more time in school and in leisure activities.

Less than one hundred years ago it was not uncommon for women and children to work 12 hours a day in factories and sweatshops. What effect do you think this had on family life?

Discussion. Have students compare the ideas in the text with stories they have read about pioneer families. The Laura Ingalls Wilder books have some good examples. How was family life different during pioneer years? Investigate child labor laws in regard to the effects on earlier families. How do they affect families today?

◆◆◆

Modern Families

Now that you've thought about the past, relate that to the present. Starting in World War II, women's roles began to change again. Wives and mothers moved into the work force in increasing numbers. Today, more women of working age have jobs outside the home than stay at home.

This situation has given women more independence. Wives are less financially dependent on their husbands. Many also experience stress as they try to balance the demands of work and family. The situation has caused many couples to question the roles of men and women.

As a result, many families have modified traditional family roles. They have created relationships based on the equality of family members. This is called an **egalitarian family** (ih-GAL-uh-TER-ee-un). It aims to distribute power and responsibility more evenly between husbands and wives. Parents in egalitarian families make family decisions together. They usually also give greater consideration to their children's opinions.

If both parents work outside the home, young children are likely to spend time in child care. Fathers are more likely to function as equal partners in home and child care than in the past. Older children are expected to help with chores that were once performed by the mother alone.

These changes in gender roles and expectations give people more options than they used to have. It is no longer a given that when a couple has a baby the mother will stay home to care for it. In many families, two incomes are needed just to cover necessities. Even if that is not the case, a mother may decide to continue her career. By the same token, the father may choose to stay home with the child instead. Sometimes the mother and father work different schedules and share child care responsibilities. In general, fathers tend to be more involved in family life than they used to be.

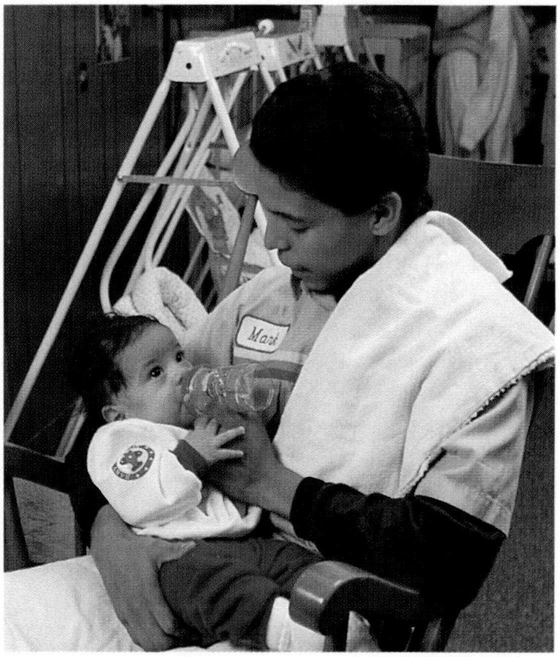

Fathers today play a more active role in the raising of their children.

◆◆◆

The Functions of Families

Having looked at the past and the present, what is your conclusion? Are families quite different today? In the way they live, they probably are, but in the way they function, the differences are not as apparent. Even today families fulfill many of the same functions that they have for hundreds of years.

One of these functions is protection for their members. This includes a sense of safety and security. Families have always sought to provide the physical needs of family members.

Work and Family. Have students discuss the benefits of an egalitarian family. Why may this type of family be a positive alternative for families today? What process may an egalitarian family use to make decisions regarding household management, use of family resources, and allocation of family members' time, especially when several members work outside the home?

Activity. Have students make a chart comparing ways a family in 1850 and a family today would accomplish the family functions. How are the families similar? How are they different? Also, ask students to hypothesize what families may be like 50 years in the future. How may family functions be fulfilled in the future?

Families provide economic support for their members at whatever level is right for the time and the family. Some families work together in a family business to make a living. If a family is able to, they may pass on money or property to the next generation through inheritance.

Families provide a member with an identity. People are known by their families. Families help children shape viewpoints and attitudes. They also help shape personalities.

Strong families provide a sense of acceptance and belonging. Within the family, members can be themselves and feel free from outside pressures. They support each other in times of crisis.

As you know, families are responsible for the socialization of children. They teach children what is acceptable behavior, both within the family and in society. They also help children learn the culture of their society.

Emotional needs are met through companionship and affection. Many people find emotional fulfillment in family gatherings, celebrations, rituals, and traditions. A family's love and affection help children become healthy, well-adjusted adults.

Families provide the setting for personal development. When a positive environment nurtures personal development, a **functional family** exists. If the environment is negative, contributing little to the personal development of family members, this is a **dysfunctional family** (dis-FUNK-shun-ul).

As you can see, even families of the past fulfilled the same functions that they do today. Because circumstances are different, however, fulfilling some of these functions may not be as easy as it once was. It doesn't matter what type of family a person lives in. It doesn't matter where people live or what their lifestyle is. What does matter is how well families provide for the needs of family members. A strong family does this well. As you read on, you will see how.

A family provides people with an identity. Some people can trace their heritage back many years.

Activity. Draw an outline of a family crest and divide it into six sections. Make enough copies for every class member. Have every student fill in each section of the crest with a drawing or written statement indicating how his or her family has met six functions of the family. Emphasize confidentiality.

Problem Solving. In small groups, have students identify some solutions to the following situation: Katlyn lives in a single-parent family with her father. Her father is an alcoholic. What dysfunctional characteristics may this family display? What are some ways this family may work its way back to health?

SIDELIGHT

Starting a Family Tradition

Many family traditions arise spontaneously. The McDade family took a drive through the mountains one autumn to view the changing colors of the trees. They decided to repeat the trip the next year. A tradition was born.

Other traditions are started by design. One family celebrates Thanksgiving in a special way. They set the table with special decorations, bring out Grandmother's fine china, hold hands while saying grace, and always take a formal Thanksgiving Day photo.

When establishing traditions for your family, begin by thinking about your past. If you have warm childhood memories of picking up leaves with your grandfather, you might renew the tradition with your younger brothers and sisters. If a friend's weekly Sunday afternoon family sing-along seems like fun, why not try it in your own family? If you have read about an interesting family tradition in another culture, would it be one your own family would enjoy?

Traditions strengthen the links among family members, build a bank of common memories, and provide a structure to family life that everyone can understand. Why not start one?

◆◆◆

◆◆◆

Making Families Strong

Families can do many things to strengthen the bonds among family members. Researchers have studied strong, close-knit families to identify the qualities they share. There is no one formula for successful families. In general, however, people have found that family strength is based on the principles described below. You need to think about these both in terms of your family position now and the family you will have in the future.

◆ Commitment

Ensuring family happiness requires commitment. **Commitment to family** means that each family member is willing to work together and sacrifice for the benefit of the whole family. Members of strong families put the family first. They are dedicated to each other's welfare and happiness.

Parents of successful families work as a team to see that careers, hobbies, and other interests do not get in the way of meeting family needs. Marge turned down a job promotion because it would mean traveling — and more time away from her family. Don dropped out of his bowling league for the summer so he could spend more evenings playing ball with his five-year-old son Todd. These parents do not devote themselves exclusively to their children, yet they clearly give high priority to their families.

Discussion. Before reading the section "Making Families Strong," divide students into small groups and have them brainstorm qualities they think make families strong and healthy. Post the lists around the room and discuss the differences and similarities. After reading the text, have students compare the text with ideas developed by the class. How were student ideas similar to the text? How were they different? What conclusions can be drawn from this experience?

Activity. Ask students to write paragraphs about families they know that display definite qualities of commitment. Students should give several examples indicating how the families show they are committed to each other. Students should not use the family name in the paragraph.

Being committed means more than just being a member of a family. Each person must take an active role. As a teen, that may be hard for you at a time when you have a strong need for independence. When you have a hard time choosing, try looking for a middle ground. Rubin's family objected to the amount of time he spent with his friends. They compromised by working together to establish family rules. Now Rubin spends time with his family as well as his friends. Just as his parents had made sacrifices for him, now it was his turn to sacrifice a little something too.

Families that spend time together become closer and stronger.

◆ Time Together

Strong families spend time together. They play, go on trips, or just enjoy being together. Greg's family enjoys after-dinner walks to the park on nice evenings. Kelsey's family takes an annual camping trip. Lemar's family enjoys working on home improvement projects. Abby's family sets aside a family night each week. They enjoy working on jigsaw puzzles, viewing home videos, or making cookies together. The important thing is that all members of the family share the experience and build memories together.

Look for ways your family can spend time together. What are some things you can do to make this time special? What activities did you enjoy with your family when you were younger? Perhaps you can revive some of those special moments by looking at photographs together, or you might try some of the activities again.

◆ Communication

Close-knit families spend time talking — and listening — to one another. Raymond listens attentively to his four-year-old's story about an outing at the child care center. Margaret shares her anxieties with her teenage daughter about her own first date. A good place to visit and to share the day's events is at mealtime. Many families try to have some meals together regularly. Some families schedule family conferences to discuss important matters.

Problem Solving. How do families make time for each other? Have students solve this problem: Greg's family takes a two-week vacation together each summer. Greg has a summer job and may not be able to take time off for the family vacation this year. What alternatives do Greg and his family have? What consequences may there be for each alternative? What alternatives are there to a two-week vacation? Select two or three alternatives and prioritize them. Students should defend each response with logical reasoning.

More About Communication. Some families enhance communication by scheduling regular family meetings. Everyone takes a turn chairing the meeting on a rotating basis. Notes are recorded so that follow-up occurs on decisions. Topics of discussion may concern everyday matters, such as taking out the garbage or what a family should do about holiday plans. Even the youngest family members participate. Family meetings can take place anytime but generally not at mealtime.

Disagreements are openly discussed in strong families. When you don't talk things out, feelings tend to build up inside. Eventually, you will explode. When family members disagree, they should fight fairly, with the goal of solving the problem. Avoid bullying, dominating, blaming, or controlling others.

Talking allows you to deal with differences honestly. Lincoln and his parents have different opinions on the number of hours he should spend on his part-time job. Talking helped them get their feelings out. Lincoln did not change his parents' minds, but he let them know where he stood.

A Slice of Life

Allen gained a new understanding of his family through a genealogy project he did for his family living class. Allen and his family worked together to collect and assemble family information. Their activities included recording family legends, filling out family trees, identifying family photos, and visiting places where their ancestors once lived. Allen got a history lesson and learned the value of family records while interacting with family members.

The activity Allen enjoyed most was interviewing older relatives and recording their experiences and memories so that they can be enjoyed in the future. Allen felt that recording an oral history of his family gave him a better understanding of himself and of older family members.

Allen got more than just a roll call of his ancestors from his grandparents. He got a feeling about his family. He learned what his ancestors did, how they lived and coped, and what they left behind. He saw the passports that brought his great-grandparents to this country. He read the old letters and yellowed diaries his grandmother brought down from the attic trunk.

Allen's tapes are filled with stories. One tells how immigration officials misspelled the original family name, thereby starting a new family name. Another tells how Uncle Gene tricked Aunt Ida into marrying him. Still another describes how Aunt Maggie's false teeth were found in an oatmeal box long after her funeral. Allen's favorite stories are the ones about what his parents were like as children.

All of the stories have been told and retold at family gatherings and now Allen has them on tape. They give him an important sense of family, one that he can preserve for future generations. The stories help Allen place his parents on the continuum of family history — as children of an earlier age, as parents of today, and as grandparents of tomorrow.

Thinking It Through

- What might happen if a person put off doing a project like Allen's?
- How can a project like this promote family strength?
- Do you have the resources to do a project like Allen's? Why not try it?

Activity. As an optional activity, have each student trace his or her genealogy as far back as possible. Students may want to interview relatives and look at old family photos. Have each student draw conclusions about characteristics that indicate family strength in his or her ancestry.

◆ Appreciation

Showing mutual affection and appreciation contributes to family stability. You can show affection for your family through hugs, kisses, smiles, and words of praise. You can create good feelings by showing respect, concern, caring, and love for others. A simple way to do this is by using such phrases as "Thank you," "I'll help you," "Let's do it together," "You did a great job," and — most important — "I love you." Such expressions contribute to each family member's self-esteem. Shared affection will create a positive atmosphere in your home.

Be sure you give sincere compliments more often than criticism, especially in trying times. Don't wait for someone to do something wonderful before you acknowledge them. Look for the little things they do. Think about what statements like these might mean to the people involved:

- "This spaghetti tastes great, Dad. I even like it better than Uncle Harry's."
- "Thanks for calling home, Sal. We'll just go ahead and eat without you."
- "You built that block tower all by yourself. You did a great job!"
- "You look nice tonight, Mom. Have a good time."
- "It's nice to just sit down and talk with you. We should do it more often."

Do you usually remember the birthdays or important dates of other family members? If so, you are showing appreciation for them. Greeting card companies have a seemingly endless supply of cards that show feelings. You can even make your own. You don't need an occasion to send one. Sometimes the surprise element on a day that has no significance is very special.

You could even start your own tradition to show appreciation. How about cooking breakfast on Mother's Day, Father's Day, birthdays, or anniversaries. Fixing a regular Friday night dinner for a parent who has worked all day is another idea. These are easy ways to give family members a special pat on the back.

One creative mother told her children that they were having very special company for dinner. She kept their identities a secret as they prepared a nice dinner and set the table for company. When the time of arrival came, the mother took the two children to the door and had them step outside. She then invited them in for dinner. *They* were the special guests.

How do you feel when people do something special for you? They feel just as good when you do something for them.

Photo Focus. Have students examine the above photo. Ask them to identify ways in which these two people are demonstrating appreciation.

Discussion. Expressing appreciation is a sure way to boost self-esteem in others. Ask students to identify ways they show appreciation to family members. Have them brainstorm additional ways that family members can be more appreciative. What traditions do students have in their families that demonstrate appreciation?

Balancing Work & Family

Support Systems

"I'll be working late tonight," Mrs. Reynolds reminded her daughter as she kissed her good-bye.

"So we can expect Debbie to check up on us, right?," asked Tiffany.

"Right," said Mrs. Reynolds with a smile. "She'll be here around 6 o'clock, along with her famous spaghetti. Have fun, and call me at work if you need me."

Debbie is part of Mrs. Reynolds' support system — people she can call on to care for the children when she has to work. Many families today need a support system. When both parents go out to work, the children often go to a child care facility, or else to school. But what happens if a child is sick and the parents can't take time off work? Who takes care of school-age children when school is out? Who can help out if parents need to go away on business?

Single parents, in particular, need a support system. Without a partner to share child-care responsibilities, they need to know there are people they can turn to in times of need.

In earlier times, most parents could turn to their extended family for support. Today, however, with so many families on the move, that is less likely to be an option.

Many communities have responded to this need by providing after-school programs and summer programs. For at-home care, parents often reach out to friends and neighbors. They may keep lists of available babysitters. They may also pay someone to come to their home for a few hours each day. As with other social changes, people are finding solutions to this new problem.

Think About It

1. What happens if a parent doesn't have a support system and a child gets sick?
2. What are the advantages to having as many people as possible in a support system?

Sometimes people of different generations have differences to work out. Understanding the other's point of view at times like this can help a great deal.

◆ Shared Beliefs

Family strength is often based on shared beliefs. Shared beliefs give the family a sense of purpose. Beliefs may be expressed through religious activities. They can be shared through family rituals and holiday traditions. They can also be communicated to children through family participation in volunteer activities that benefit the community. For example, Joanna's family sponsors a foster child, visits nursing home patients, and participates actively in politics. Their beliefs give the family a frame of reference for making decisions and coping with life's ups and downs.

◆ Adjusting to Changing Roles

As you have read, roles in a family change as people grow older. Changing from the role of child to the role of adult may create **role strain**, a pull between familiar behaviors of the past and the unknown challenges of the future. Role strain is accompanied by varying degrees of stress. Strong families learn to deal with this.

Activity. Ask students to survey newspapers and talk with people about ideas for volunteer service in the community. What could they do as individuals, as a class, or as a family to help someone else? Perhaps initiate a class project that allows students to help at a local food shelf, a child care center, a nursing home, etc.

As a teen, you have your own point of view. Others, however, see things in a different way because of their roles and experience. Some may be responsible for everyone else. Some may feel little and insignificant compared to the rest. Some may be dealing with concerns about age, health, or finances.

As you move toward independence, you and your parents may not always agree. They need to realize that you are preparing for your new adult roles. Thinking about your future roles is called **role anticipation**. This advance preparation will help you make the transition from child to adult more easily. You need to realize that your parents are watching you change and trying to let go of you a little bit at a time. This is not easy for a parent. A little understanding on both sides will go a long way.

◆ Understanding Others

So often family differences are based on a lack of understanding. Think about these situations:

- Heidi gets disgusted when her little sister Kate always hangs around when Heidi has company.
- Dewayne feels like his grandmother is prying when she asks him so many questions all the time.
- Ian wants his parents to ease up on the rules he is supposed to follow.
- Lori's parents wish she would do more voluntarily around the house.

In each of these situations the key to understanding is to get a handle on the other person's point of view. Remember the term "empathy"? Try it out here. Why does Kate always hang around Heidi? Maybe she isn't really trying to be a pest. Maybe she just wants to feel big. She may idolize her older sister and want to be like her. She may simply feel left out.

Is there a solution for Heidi? Actually, there are many. The best approach is a consistent pattern of understanding that shows respect and love for Kate. Spending some time with her will help. Including her once in awhile will too. Talking to her calmly about the situation is a good idea. Diverting her interest may work. Heidi found some old scarves, jewelry, and other accessories that Kate could use for playing dress-up. She gave them to her on the day her friends were coming over. Can you think of other ideas for Heidi? Now try your hand at understanding and solving each of the other situations described above.

◆ Coping Skills

Strong families are well-equipped to cope with the problems they encounter. When sickness, money problems, death, or other stressful events occur, the family pulls together to face the crisis. When John's father lost his job, the family called a meeting to decide ways for everyone to help cut expenses. When Su Ling's grandmother became seriously ill, the family reached out to relatives and neighbors for help. Strong families accept their problems and keep them in perspective. They know that whatever happens, the family will hold together.

If you had a problem with a friend or got into trouble, would you turn to your parents for help and advice? Trying to solve the problem yourself leaves you feeling isolated. By confiding in your parents, you're showing your trust in them. Working through the crisis together may actually improve the relationship between you and your parents.

Life Management Skills. Ask students to imagine they are the parent of a teen. In what ways would they allow a teen to experience some adult roles? What rules and expectations would they have that would allow a teen to experience some adult responsibilities without actually leaving home? In what ways could a parent allow a teen some financial freedom?

More About Coping Skills. Often the attitude family members have toward a stressor is as important as the action they take to cope with the stressor. When family members have the desire to cope and work through a problem, they are more likely to weather a crisis positively. If a family has a negative attitude and sees disaster at every turn, it is more likely that they will have difficulty resolving a crisis positively.

SIDELIGHT

Strengthening Your Family

In their book, *Secrets of Strong Families*, family researchers, Nick Stinnett and John DeFrain, suggest five ways you can play a more positive role in your family:

- Examine the way you spend your time. Schedule your time so that you can spend more time with your family. Perhaps you can spend more time with a sibling. You can also plan activities your family can do together.
- Make a list of things you like about family members; then show it to them. Remember to compliment other family members.
- Set aside time to communicate. You may want to plan a certain time for conversation each day, such as breakfast.
- Tape record memories of older family members. Find out where they were born and where they have lived. Ask what their lives were like.
- Seek outside help when needed. Even the strongest families sometimes need outside help. If your family is overwhelmed by family problems, get help from a professional counselor. Turn to someone you trust, like a favorite teacher, to find the right source of help.

◆◆◆

Activity. Have each student complete some personal brainstorming on a sheet of paper. Have students write down some ideas about the following, emphasizing confidentiality:

- What are some specific ways you can take a more positive role in your family?
- In what ways can you encourage others in your family to help strengthen the family bond?
- What ideas do you have about building family strength for your own family in the future?
- How may qualities that build family strength affect other relationships you have?

◆◆◆

Your Family — Today and Tomorrow

Families don't get strong by themselves. Family members must work to make the family strong and keep it strong. They can't afford to leave family strength to chance. You can do your part to strengthen your own family. Make a list of things you can do. Then make a commitment to discuss your ideas with your family and then put them into action.

What you practice and learn today can be carried over into your future. The role you have in your future family will be different than the one you have now. Are you prepared to bring strength to the family of your future too?

Spending some time with a younger brother (sister) shows you care. By doing this, you are more likely to get cooperation when you want to be alone.

CHAPTER 11

Review

Answers
Testing Your Memory

1. The home became less central to family life. Families went from working together to produce everything they needed to seeking factory work in cities to meet their basic needs. Often every family member held a job outside the home.
2. In patriarchal families, the father holds most of the power. In egalitarian families, the power is equally distributed between husband and wife. Children are often included in decisions within egalitarian families.
3. **Any four:** provide protection by meeting physical needs, safety needs, and security needs; provide economic support; provide a sense of identity by shaping viewpoints, attitudes, and personalities; provide a sense of acceptance and belonging; provide support for each other in times of crisis; provide for socialization of children; meet emotional needs; provide a setting for personal development.
4. Dysfunctional families do little to promote personal development of their members. The environment is negative.
5. Making sacrifices for the common good of the family indicates dedication or commitment to the family.

Summarizing the Chapter

- The roles of family members have changed over time. Some roles are associated with gender. Others are based on position within the family.
- Today many families are turning away from traditional family roles. These changes are giving family members more options than in the past.
- Although families have lived differently over the years, they have always fulfilled the same basic functions.
- A family meets the needs of its members. These needs range from physical to social and emotional.
- Strong families share certain characteristics that have been identified by researchers. However, family members must work to make the family strong and keep it strong.
- Strong families are created when people are committed, they spend time together and communicate, they show appreciation and understanding, and they share beliefs.

Testing Your Memory

1. How did industrialization change the American family?
2. How do patriarchal and egalitarian family forms differ?
3. Explain four functions of a family.
4. What causes families to be dysfunctional?
5. How is sacrifice related to commitment?
6. How does communication help families stay strong?
7. List three ways you can show appreciation for family members.
8. When people in families have different points of view, what is the key to dealing with this?

Thinking Critically

1. Give three examples of sacrifices you have made to meet the needs of your family or of other family members.
2. What options are available to you as a result of changes in gender roles over the years?
3. Do you think males and females show affection in the same ways? Explain your answer.
4. Describe the "ideal" family. How closely do you expect your future family to resemble this ideal?

Taking Action

1. Make a list of TV shows that depict different family types. Watch three different family shows; then write a summary of each. Identify the TV show, the type of family, the family members, the family roles portrayed, and the family strengths. How realistic is the portrayal of family life in each show?
2. Work with several classmates to write a play depicting a strong family or a weak family. Present the play to your class.
3. Analyze how childhood experiences prepare people for certain gender roles. Consider the following: household tasks, roles of a spouse, parenthood, career.

Making Life Choices

Lela and Denise are good friends. Denise has difficulty getting along with her family. Lela has noticed that whenever Denise talks to people in her family, her voice is filled with impatience, sarcasm, and negativism. It makes Lela uncomfortable. Denise blames her family troubles on the rest of her family.

Is Denise seeing her situation accurately? If you were Lela, what would you do?

Using Your Journal

In this chapter you learned about the things that make families strong. Now think about your own family. Is it a strong family? Could you do things to make it stronger? Use your journal to write about your family. Describe its strengths and its weaknesses. Then write about your own role within the family. Do you make an effort to communicate? To show your appreciation? Make a list of some actions you could take to help your family stay strong or be stronger.

6. Communication helps families solve problems in a positive way. Family members feel valued when they are able to share openly.
7. **Any three** of the ways listed on page 162.
8. Use empathy in trying to understand how the other person thinks and feels.

Thinking Critically

1. Answers will vary.
2. Answers will vary. Point out that women and men have more career opportunities than in the past. Roles within the family are more flexible.
3. Answers will vary.
4. Answers will vary.

CHAPTER 12

Facing Family Challenges

Chapter Challenge

Resources. Refer to the Teacher's Classroom Resources box and Student Workbook for materials related to this chapter.

Look for These Answers . . .

- What kinds of challenges do families face?
- How do people react to difficult situations?
- What resources do people have in times of difficulty?
- How can people cope with these challenges: balancing work and family life; unemployment; moving; illness and disabilities; addictions; family violence; suicide; and death?

Look for These Terms . . .

- abuse
- addiction
- alcoholic
- co-dependency
- dual-earner families
- incest
- intervention
- neglect
- unemployment

Jay was numb with fear as he drove his parents to the hospital. His father had always been healthy. The idea that something might be wrong with him was shocking.

"I think I have a bad case of indigestion," Mr. Fillmore had said as he got up from the dinner table. He put his hand to his chest and walked slowly away. A few minutes later he said, "The pain has moved to my arms. You'd better get me to a hospital."

The wait in the hospital seemed endless. At last the doctor came out. "It was a heart attack," he said, "and we're doing our best." A couple hours later Jay's sister arrived. Her boyfriend drove her down from the university. Uncle Mac arrived at the same time.

It was a long night of waiting for Jay and his family. They hugged each other and held hands, each one trying to make sure the others were comfortable.

At first Jay felt weak with fright. "How could this happen," he said angrily. Tears followed and then a feeling of sadness. Then he thought to himself, "I've got to keep up the morale. We've all got to think positive." It had been a long time since he had thought about it, but Jay was suddenly overwhelmed by the realization of how much he loved his father — and the rest of his family. "Dad," he thought, "I'm going to tell you — when I get the chance."

It was many hours later when Jay was allowed to slip quietly to the side of his father's bed. As he did, his father's eyes opened slowly to focus on Jay. It was a slow wink, but a wink nevertheless. Jay knew then that all would be well.

Chapter Opener. Have students read the opening scenario to the chapter. Ask the following questions: How did Jay and his family cope while waiting for news about his father's condition? What characteristics of family strength are evident in Jay's family? What are some positive ways that families can express what they are feeling? In what ways can working through a crisis draw a family closer together?

The Challenges of Life

Life would not be life without challenges. The more routine ones occur every day. For example, keeping up with an active toddler can leave parents exhausted. Managing busy schedules can also be challenging. Other challenges are more serious, such as disability, death, desertion, divorce, and prolonged unemployment. Some challenges can occur without warning, such as a fire or tragic accident. Others may build slowly the way many illnesses do. As you read about the challenges families sometimes have to face, think about how you would handle them.

Photo Focus. Have students examine the photo on page 168. In what ways may this argument affect the young child? How is this child learning to cope with conflict? What are some positive ways this couple could settle their differences without having any negative effects on their child?

Photo Focus. Have students examine the above photo. Home fires can be devastating for families. Have students discuss ways that families can cope with a crisis such as this. How can other family members and friends be supportive during a crisis?

◆ Balancing Work and Family Life

In many families today, both parents of school-age children work. These are called **dual-earner families**. Maintaining the balance between work and family is an ongoing challenge for them. If you ever face this challenge, remember these tips:

- Be supportive of your partner in attitude. If one spouse disapproves of the other's job, that person may get the blame for everything that goes wrong at home.
- Be supportive of your partner in actions. Sharing household responsibilities and child care is a necessity. Employed women today still carry a larger burden in this area.
- Delegate responsibilities. Other household members should be involved in home duties.
- Set priorities. That is, which is more important, reading a story to a child or scrubbing the floor?
- Use management skills to your advantage. Setting goals and planning, for example, can help control your time. It will also help you accomplish things that you think will never get done. Use lists and schedules. Even a chart, calendar, or bulletin board can help. One family keeps a calendar upon which all activities are noted.
- Talk about your needs, schedules, and problems. That way you can work toward solutions. Sometimes others don't know you are overburdened until you tell them.
- Include some time for fun in your life. Happiness and a low-stress lifestyle depend on this.

Balancing work and family life is easier for everyone when every family member handles some of the responsibility.

Work and Family. Ask how many students live in dual-earner families. Have students discuss differing ways that families meet the combined challenges of work and family life. What can families learn from each other? What role does communication play in effectively balancing work and family life?

Work and Family. Have students evaluate this situation: Megan and Stan are both engineers for a corporation. Megan has full responsibility for their two small sons, one of whom has chronic asthma. She often stays up late getting household work done and must be up at night with a sick child. She has lost weight and is very tired.

- Develop a support system. If you can't run one leg of a carpool, maybe a neighbor can. Often friends, family, and community programs can help. You will not want to take advantage of people, but cooperation will work.
- Look for job arrangements that suit you. Employers are beginning to offer options that help ease the stress felt by dual-earner families. Part-time employment, job sharing, and flexible work schedules help some families. Some employers provide parental leaves, child care, flexible benefits, and employee counseling. Career ladders are becoming less rigid. Working at home is another possibility.

◆ Unemployment

Unemployment occurs when a person who wants to work does not have a job. Men and women are most likely to be out of work through no fault of their own; however, the person without a job is likely to experience a loss of self-respect. As with other serious losses, the person may go through stages of shock, disbelief, anger, and depression. Job loss damages the ego so badly that many people make up face-saving excuses. They may keep the news from the family for awhile by keeping work hours or by claiming that they quit.

Adam, an unemployed carpenter, says he feels like a failure when his children ask him for money. Since losing his job, he has often had to say, "Sorry, I don't have it." Adam's teenage son describes his father's job loss like this. "It was like he wasn't a good person any more. He just felt like he flunked or something."

Occasionally, unemployed people make the mistake of choosing destructive ways of dealing with the problem, alcohol or abusive behavior, for example. They need to find constructive approaches. Job retraining is one. Supportive families can help.

Unemployment can cause serious problems in a family. When this happens, members must work together to decide how to cut their spending and use their resources. You will read more about this in Chapter 29.

If unemployment is prolonged and no other resources are available, some families lose their homes. Homelessness is very difficult — for adults and children. Many communities provide shelters for people who need a place to stay.

◆ Moving

A job promotion is a common reason for a family to move. A desire for a change and the wish to be closer to certain friends and family members are other reasons. Moving affects families in different ways. Some people adjust easily and get on with their lives. Others may need to work at the adjustment.

Even before moving, families can help themselves. Including everyone, especially children, in the plans helps. A visit to the new community is a good idea too. Ellen saw her new school and neighborhood before her family moved. Knowing what to expect made the move easier.

After moving, a new place just doesn't feel like home right away. This is a normal feeling, and it goes away after awhile.

Life Management Skills. Have students keep track of how they currently use their time. Have them write down their activities in 30-minute increments for two days. They should analyze when and where they waste time. Have students develop a plan for effectively managing their time. After students have used their time management plan for one week, have them evaluate the plan for effectiveness.

Activity. Ask students to identify resources in the community that offer services for homeless people. Have students contact social service agencies, churches, and any other supportive agencies to find out more about their services. What additional services are needed in the community? What can students do to help raise awareness of the problem? In what ways can students help their peers who may be homeless or living in severe poverty?

Problem Solving. Ask students to investigate all the alternatives available to help families move to a new city. What are the pros and cons of each alternative? What costs are involved? What alternative would you recommend for a family with a limited budget? A moderate budget? What alternative would be best for a family that needs to move quickly?

Making social connections after a move is important. Parents may need to help children meet new friends. Many communities have newcomer organizations that help adults get acquainted.

If moves are frequent, children can have problems with schooling. When school districts teach subjects at different times, a child can easily fall behind by missing out on important topics. Parents need to pay close attention to the educational needs of their children.

The right attitude can make a move successful. Family members who view the move as an adventure and an opportunity to have new experiences will adjust more easily.

Moving is more likely to be a positive experience for those who make the effort to meet others and make new friends.

◆ Illness and Disabilities

At some time in their lives, serious health problems strike most families. At least one in ten people suffers from some serious physical or mental disorder.

A prolonged illness or an unexpected disability can cause tremendous stress on the family. This is especially true when a major breadwinner is unable to continue working. It is natural for other family members to feel some resentment toward the stricken person. This is just part of the way people deal with the pressures.

Children may feel that the illness or disability is somehow their fault. They may feel especially vulnerable. Some children become more demanding than usual. Others try to work some magic cure on the patient by being on their best behavior.

The impact of any serious illness or disability often depends on the attitudes of the family. If someone close to you suffers a serious illness or a crippling disability, learn all you can about it. You can get accurate information from a physician or library sources. Look for those who have lived through similar situations. Try to learn how they coped.

A serious illness or disability can disrupt the strongest of families. The condition can also encourage a responsible and mature attitude. When her older sister Christina developed a severe case of scoliosis, Kim learned to think about life differently. Christina had to have a six-hour operation to straighten her badly curved spine. Afterwards, Kim made this comment. "Christina's illness had a great effect on me. It made me realize that others must come first and that I'm not always the most important one. I learned the meaning of humility and how we all can suffer. It's easier for me to feel empathy for the sick now. I've even thought of becoming a doctor."

Activity. Have students find out about organizations in their community that welcome newcomers and about the kinds of activities and services that they provide. Selected students might then compile an information sheet that can be copied and given to parents of new students.

Discussion. Have students discuss ways that strong families cope with illness and disabilities. In what ways may a dysfunctional family cope with these problems?

◆ Addictions

An **addiction** is a physical and/or psychological dependence on a substance or behavior. The addiction may be to nicotine, alcohol, other drugs, or a compulsive action, such as gambling or overeating. When one family member develops an addiction, others suffer. Addictions can ruin careers and finances. They can be devastating to families.

◆ Alcoholism

Someone who is addicted to alcohol is an **alcoholic.** Families have a tough time facing this problem. The behavior of an alcoholic may be embarrassing, unpredictable, and even endangering to others in the family.

Co-dependency is a common reaction to alcoholism in families, although it can occur in other situations as well. The dependent person is the alcoholic. The co-dependents are those who are close to the alcoholic and feeling powerless. They want things to be different but they feel helpless. They may even enable the alcoholic to continue by hiding the problem from others.

Children of alcoholics may react by blaming themselves. Their grades often suffer and they may feel resentment toward the parent who is no longer there for them.

People who are close to alcoholics need to learn about this disease. They need to talk to others and get support. They should seek help even if the alcoholic will not. The problem cannot be cured at home. Lectures, nagging, begging, deals, promises, and threats do not work. Alcoholics will not stop drinking until they are ready to make that decision for themselves. A thoughtful, caring approach with an alcoholic works best. This should be combined with directness. Call the problem by its name, alcoholism, and tell the alcoholic what is happening to the family because of the drinking problem. Then let the alcoholic work toward a decision. If he or she does seek help, remember that the road to recovery takes time and effort. Many people and families can and do make it.

When someone in a family is an alcoholic, the whole family needs professional help in handling the problem.

More About Alcoholism. Alcoholism is a family disease. No matter which person in the family is dependent, the entire family is affected. Alcoholism is a progressive disease; unless it is treated, the alcoholic will die. Sometimes alcoholics die from liver damage or malnutrition, but more often death occurs due to an accident during a drinking episode. Alcoholism contributes to lost work time, dysfunctional families, and higher insurance rates. The good news is that alcoholism is treatable. Many treatment programs are available to help alcoholics and their families recover.

I CAN ◆◆ Get Help

Alcoholism can be devastating to a family. For Marci it meant experiencing a wide range of emotions, everything from fear to anger to hate before she and her family found a way to make things better.

"My father is an alcoholic. His drinking tore our family apart. My parents argued a lot and blamed each other for their problems. When my father came home roaring drunk, Mom would never say anything for fear of making things worse. The next morning she would fight back by pulling all three girls into her act. We weren't allowed to talk to Dad unless it was absolutely necessary.

"My sister Jodi tried to help by doing extra things around the house. She would take out the trash, fix leaky faucets, wash the car — anything that needed doing. My little sister Sarah usually pouted and stayed in her room. I hated what he was doing and spent as much time as I could off with friends. That really made Dad angry.

"Finally he joined Alcoholics Anonymous. Soon after, the whole family went for counseling. My parents learned how to communicate for the first time. My sisters and I also discovered the importance of talking honestly with each other. I learned that I had built up a lot of resentment, anger, and even some hate. I felt ashamed of my parents. Gradually I began to admire their willingness to change. I even learned to forgive them."

- How do you think Marci's family suffered because of her dad's dependence on alcohol?
- Experts have identified three main roles an abuser's family may play that help the substance abuse continue. The roles are the enabler, the victim, and the provoker. The enabler comes to the abuser's rescue. The victim takes over the abuser's responsibilities. The provoker takes revenge through anger and resentment. Which of these roles did members of Marci's family play?
- If you were faced with a problem like Marci's, where in your community would you go for help?

◆ Compulsive Gambling

Compulsive gambling, in which a person becomes addicted to gambling, is a growing problem in the United States. Until recently, gambling was banned in most states. However, many states have now legalized gambling and have introduced lotteries, casinos, and racetrack betting. People who become addicted to gambling cannot stop gambling, even when they have lost large sums of money. Sometimes, after spending all the family money, they borrow from friends, and continue to lose. Compulsive gamblers need professional help to break their addiction. Many communities, especially those located near gambling centers, have hotlines to help compulsive gamblers.

Activity. Have students investigate how groups such as Alcoholics Anonymous, Alateen, and Families Anonymous help families get on the road to recovery from alcoholism. How do families benefit from these organizations?

Discussion. Have students respond to the following: Should close relatives of an alcoholic seek counseling even if the alcoholic refuses to seek treatment? Why or why not? In what ways may family members seeking treatment encourage the alcoholic to get help as well?

◆ Family Violence

Abusive situations exist in far too many homes today. **Abuse** occurs when one family member harms or threatens another's physical or mental health. It can be directed at a child, a spouse, a disabled person, or an elderly person.

In some families, violence is a way of life. As a result, many families become dysfunctional. The pattern is predictable. Parents strike children who, in turn, attack others. When they grow up, the pattern is repeated in their own families. Abusers grow up believing that hitting is the only way to settle family problems. This is not true at all.

Those who marry into a family with an abuse history can expect to face the problem themselves. Counseling before marriage is wise to avoid this.

Although abuse is inexcusable, people point to many reasons why it occurs. They include ignorance and contempt for self. Problems with a job and money are also cited. People who are troubled by an unhappy home life or marriage may resort to violence. Illness and chemical addictions can also play a role.

◆ Spouse Abuse

Violent behavior between spouses frequently goes unchecked and unreported, even though domestic violence is the leading cause of injury among women ages 15 to 44. Police officers have tended to be cautious in dealing with domestic disturbances. In some cities, though, they are now acting more quickly and decisively when they receive reports of spouse abuse.

Abused wives often have mixed feelings about how to handle their problems. If their self-esteem is low, they may think that they brought on the trouble themselves. The abusive husband may make them feel worthless. Going to the police can mean losing the family breadwinner. For this reason, many wives drop charges that they filed earlier. In an attempt to escape continued abuse, some women resort to violence themselves.

Domestic problems make up a large percentage of the calls that police officers must handle.

More About Family Violence. There is more to family violence than the physical act of hitting. Violence has to do with power and control. There are many ways an abuser seeks to gain control over a victim. One way is to control the family budget and checkbook, leaving the victim with little or no money. Another is to threaten to take away the children if a victim reports the abuse. Sometimes the abuser (often a male) uses privileges as a way to keep the victim in line (i.e., because he's a man, he can do what he likes). Victims of abuse feel powerless in situations such as this. Low self-esteem often keeps a victim from reaching out for help.

Shelters provide victims of abuse with a place to stay while they decide what to do next.

People who are living in abusive situations must realize that there is a way out. Many communities provide shelters for battered women and their children. In a protected and supportive setting, counselors help abused victims make plans for the future. Staff members at these shelters help cool tempers and provide lodging for a few days; however, they cannot eliminate the causes for physical attacks.

◆ Child Abuse

All states have laws protecting minor children. Child abuse and neglect take several forms. **Neglect** occurs when the youngster does not receive enough food, clothing, or supervision. It may mean that the child is left alone for long periods of time. Physical abuse often occurs in the name of punishment. Physical abuse is any extreme, severe, or excessive treatment. Anything that leaves a mark — a bruise, a cut, a scar — is physical abuse. Emotional abuse includes insulting, ridiculing, or otherwise verbally "beating up" a child.

Sexual abuse is the most secret kind of abuse. Sexual abuse takes place when adults subject children to fondling, incest, or rape, or they lure them to be part of sexual activity. **Incest** is sexual activity between persons who are closely related. In most abuse cases, the child knows the molester. The abuser may be a parent, a stepparent, a sibling, or some other person living in or visiting the home.

◆ Finding Help

Any citizen should report child abuse of any type to welfare authorities. Many public officials, such as teachers, are mandated by law to report suspected child abuse. When people step in and take action in order to stop abuse, this is called **intervention**. In serious cases the legal action taken may cause the youngster to be removed from the home for a brief or extended period of time. Some abusive parents must attend counseling sessions before they can regain custody of their children.

Professional services are available for people who abuse a spouse and children. Counselors try to help them develop self-control and a sense of responsibility. The treatment process stresses that abusers always have choices of action available to them. Given a chance to understand and deal with the causes for their behavior, many abusers do change. They develop new ways to hold back when they feel the urge to strike out.

Activity. Invite a trained crisis counselor to speak with the class about family violence. The counselor should address such issues as why violence occurs, the effects of family violence on society, help that's available for victims of violence, how the cycle of violence can be broken, and ways that families can recover from violence.

Activity. Have students research state laws regarding family violence. What legal help is available for victims of abuse? If a person can't afford a lawyer, what help is available? If possible, invite a lawyer or advocate for abused persons to speak with the class.

◆ Runaways

Some teens who have been abused at home run away. Other runaways have not been abused, but may have had serious disagreements with their parents. Running away from home does not usually solve any problems — it simply creates new ones. Teens who are thinking of running away need to talk through their problems with an adult they trust.

◆ Suicide

Suicide is not a solution to problems. It is permanent, and problems are not. Sometimes people cannot see that low feelings will be gone in time and problems can be overcome. Even when the feelings seem overwhelming, there are ways to ease them. Time is the first healer. If that doesn't work, friends, adults, and trained counselors can help find solutions.

◆ Prevention

You can help prevent suicide by first recognizing the signals that people give when it is on their minds. The person may express a loss of interest in living or a wish to die. Other signs include eating or sleeping problems, withdrawal, decrease in self-care, abuse of alcohol or other drugs, or a sudden change in behavior. Sometimes the person will exhibit sudden dramatic improvement for no apparent reason after a period of depression. The person may make final arrangements. For example, he or she may give away possessions, pay off old debts, or apologize for past arguments. Poems or songs that deal with death may be circled or written down. The purchase of pills, rope, or weapons may be another signal.

If someone you know talks about committing suicide, you can help. Don't be afraid to ask a direct question if you wonder. Listen quietly, and let the person talk about the problem. Express your concerns clearly and honestly. Take a firm stand against suicide. Suggest that the person see a professional counselor. Tell someone responsible even though you may have promised secrecy.

Many communities have established suicide prevention centers. People can telephone these centers and discuss their problems. Family physicians can make referrals to a professional counselor or hospital.

◆ Death

Dealing with death is not easy. The closer you were to the person, the greater your loss. The age of the person and the circumstances of the death may affect the way you feel too.

It takes time to recover from a death in a family. People must work through their feelings. A person who does will eventually resume normal living.

Activity. Use this activity as a way to boost self-esteem among students. *Use this activity only when class members have developed a rapport and trust with each other.* Each person, including the teacher, receives a blank sheet of paper and a safety pin. Each person should pin the paper to another person's back (everyone should have a piece of paper pinned to his or her back). Each person is to write one affirmation or positive comment on every person's paper. When everyone has finished writing, each student should be able to read a number of affirmations about himself or herself. Encourage students to keep the paper to read when they are feeling down.

Sometimes people feel guilty about not saying things they wish they had said. A spouse or child may feel resentment for being left behind. Mixed feelings are common. For example, sorrow may be felt at the death of a much-loved but elderly grandparent. At the same time a feeling of relief may come when the ordeal has ended.

Methods of coping with death vary with individuals. Expressions of sorrow are normal, necessary, and healthy. For many, acute grief lasts a month or two and then gradually begins to fade. Feelings of anguish may flood back on occasion but less and less often.

If you must deal with death, the best way to regain balance is to face up to the loss and mourn it. Talking and crying both release pent-up emotions. Viewing the body and discussing the death with friends help you accept the permanency of the loss. Remember the good times you had with the deceased. Avoid making any major decisions until you can think clearly and have time to seek proper advice.

Holding back your sorrow denies the value of the loss and what it really means to you. Survivors need to work through the pain. The use of alcohol, tranquilizers, or other drugs can interfere with the mourning process. As stress subsides and support from others becomes less necessary, most mourners return to a normal schedule.

The survival process is more difficult for a violent or unexpected death. In such cases, guilt and anger sharpen. With a chance to prepare for death, you can usually explore and express strong emotions. When death happens suddenly or violently, however, the survivor's brain acts automatically. It protects you with numbness. When emotions are in neutral, the thinking system seems frozen. In time, you can face the reality of the loss.

A Slice of Life

Benjamin carefully patted the dirt down over the makeshift grave. Shuffles had been a good dog, but he was very old. At age five Benjamin had grown up with Shuffles. The rest of the family had known him for much longer.

Benjamin's older brother Barry handed him the little stick cross they had made. Ben put it in place.

"We're sure going to miss old Shuffles," the boys' father said. "It's not easy when a good friend dies. I loved him. You know what I'll always remember best? The way he sat on my feet while I read the paper each night."

Benjamin had a funny feeling in his stomach. "I'll miss him in the morning. No more wet nose on my face. That's how he tried to get me out of bed."

All three lingered for awhile as the tears fell. They exchanged memories about their beloved pet and shared their feelings. They would always remember Shuffles.

Thinking It Through

- In what ways will this event be beneficial for Benjamin?
- How can a clear and honest approach to death help children?
- Most authorities feel children should be included in the mourning process when a loved one dies. What do you think?

Discussion. Ask students to discuss the kinds of traditions families have when death occurs in the family. In what way do rituals and ceremonies help family members cope with loss? How does society view death? What words (euphemisms) do we use to describe death? How do euphemisms help or hinder the grief process?

More About Grief. Often events that happen the first year after a loved one dies are the most difficult for family members. Every holiday, anniversary, and birthday are reminders of the loss. At times such as these, a good friend can help a grieving person by being available to talk and listen. Acknowledging that a day might be difficult is a way to begin a conversation or encourage a grieving person to talk about the loss.

Helping Others with Grief

When you know someone who is grieving, how should you handle it? Many people do not know what to say or do, so they make the mistake of doing nothing. People who are grieving need to know that people care. Many people send cards or bring food to the family during the difficult time. Words should be kept simple. Saying that the deceased is better off now is not usually helpful to a grieving person. When words cannot be found, a hug will do.

Don't forget the deceased person or the one who grieves. Later, when the time is right, you may want to say, "I was thinking about Don the other day." This lets the grieving person know that the deceased has not been forgotten. It also gives him or her a chance to talk if desired. This may be welcomed if others have been avoiding such conversations.

Some people need professional help to come to grips with the death of a loved one. If the grieving person seems especially depressed, suggest talking to a trusted adult or call a local community mental health center for help.

People need the support of others when a death occurs. What ways can you think of to serve this need?

Handling Challenges

As you can see, life can present some moments that will test your ability to cope. People tend to experience similar reactions whenever a severe and unexpected challenge occurs. Reactions to major challenges commonly follow a pattern of denial, anger, bargaining, depression, and acceptance. These stages are often linked to dealing with death, but they can be seen when people handle other crises as well.

At first Cynthia denied that her father's job transfer was really true. She felt anger that she directed at her parents. She tried to delay the event by bargaining to stay with friends until school was out. She promised good behavior in the future if her parents agreed not to move. Finally, Cynthia became willing to face the truth. She felt sad about leaving her home and friends, but she began to plan for the move.

Problem Solving. Have students respond to the following situation: Troy and Dianna both work and have two children, ages 14 and 16. Dianna's mother needs a serious operation and a long period of convalescence. Dianna, as an only child, feels an obligation to care for her mother. The family needs two incomes to meet their financial needs. What can Troy and Dianna do to solve this dilemma? Students should list the alternatives, identify the consequences of each alternative, and propose a reasonable solution. Students should defend their responses.

Stress is another common reaction to difficulties. All of the stress management techniques you learned earlier will become particularly important to you when you are faced with problems.

Each family challenge requires a response. Some reactions make more sense than others. Families that cope well have the best chance to maintain closeness and stability. For this reason, it's good to learn some coping methods before you face a major challenge.

SIDELIGHT

Coping Skills

Everyone needs to develop skills for coping with the challenges they face. Consider how you might use the suggestions that follow.

- Describe the challenge in simple terms. "My sister broke her arm." "My folks are getting a divorce." "My boyfriend says it's all over."
- Face the facts. "The situation is pretty bad. The doctor says Dad may not work again." Admitting the reality of the situation can make the challenge easier to handle.
- List your present emotions. Remember that it's all right to be worried, scared, angry, or resentful. Saying so out loud will help you to keep your balance and clear your head for needed thinking.
- Review your inner resources. You may look to your moral and ethical standards for stability. If you have a religious faith, prayer can be your source of strength and a way to see current events as part of a bigger picture. Recognizing that you must accept what you cannot change makes it easier to make the best of the situation.
- Consider possible options: "I can keep a near-normal life by making some changes in my daily routine. I may have to quit basketball, get a job, or study more."
- Take effective action. Doing nothing paralyzes thinking and keeps stress levels high. After checking resources and possible solutions, try the most promising. For example, after failing a required course, you may be able to take a makeup test or go to summer school.
- Plan ahead. After you have faced the challenge, consider how you can avoid the situation in the future or what you would do if it were repeated. Obviously, you can't prevent natural disasters like tornadoes or earthquakes no matter how well you plan. However, knowing how you will respond can save spending time in indecision.

◆◆◆

Discussion. Have students discuss the following situation: When family finances are tight, should teens be required to add a certain amount of income to the family budget in order to provide housing, food, etc., for the family? Why or why not? How might a strong family cope with this situation?

Problem Solving. Have students work in small groups to identify how the above coping skills may be used in the following situation: The Cline family is under a great deal of stress as they attempt to pay off medical bills from a car accident. Students should address each coping skill and offer suggestions for the Clines.

◆ Resources

Families need not face challenges alone. Relatives, neighbors, and friends can help in time of need. People who know and care for you are good sources of emotional support. They can provide needed help and sometimes financial support.

Communities provide many services for families. Libraries are a good source of information about problems families face. Police and fire departments provide assistance in emergencies. Medical services and support groups are available in most communities. Welfare assistance is available to families that cannot meet their basic needs. Religious and community organizations provide families with a variety of services. Professionals also help families deal with many problems.

People do not need to face difficulties alone. Relatives, neighbors, and friends can help when you have a need.

Photo Focus. Have students examine the above photo. Ask students to describe the benefits of comforting another person. Why is support from others important during a time of crisis?

◆◆◆

Family Law

Some challenges that families face are controlled and settled by laws. Family law deals with issues on marriage and divorce, protection of children, juveniles, and life and death. Many of the laws deal with difficult questions like these: What are a parent's legal responsibilities to a child? Who is entitled to child support after divorce? What should happen to youths who commit crimes? How can spouses and children be protected from abuse? What are the rights of a newborn?

Issues surrounding family law are not easy to decide. Nevertheless, the courts and legislators deal with them, always mindful of public input. Not every state handles laws in exactly the same way. When you need legal assistance, check with an attorney for help. Some communities provide free legal assistance for those who cannot afford it.

◆◆◆

Be Prepared

No one wants to face difficult challenges like many described in this chapter. Still, they happen. At these times, knowledge is your ally. When you know what can happen and you are prepared, you can handle what life sends your way.

Activity. As a class project, have students investigate what community services are available to families that face difficult challenges. Have students create a directory that provides a list of services available in the community. Students may want to categorize the directory according to specific services offered for each family challenge. Students may also want to list services available to assist families in developing family strength. Make the directory available to other students in the school.

CHAPTER 12

Review

Summarizing the Chapter

- Families face many challenges which may occur without warning or build over months.
- Balancing work and family life is an on-going challenge for dual-earner families.
- Families face a variety of other challenges, including unemployment and moving. They may have to deal with illness, disabilities, and addictions. Family violence is a serious problem for some. Suicide prevention and dealing with death are still other challenges.
- Families tend to experience similar reactions to any sudden or severe challenge.
- The challenges families face require a response, but they need not be faced alone. Relatives, neighbors, friends, and community services are possible sources of help.

Testing Your Memory

1. List three management techniques that could help with balancing work and family life.
2. Why are frequent moves especially difficult for children?
3. What is a co-dependent?
4. What do people who live in abusive situations need to do?
5. How can you help someone deal with the death of a loved one?
6. What five stages do people often go through when dealing with a major life challenge?
7. List three possible resources for meeting a challenge.

Answers
Testing Your Memory

1. **Any three:** have a supportive attitude; show support through action; delegate responsibilities; set priorities; use management skills to your advantage; talk about needs, schedules, and problems; include some fun in your life; develop a support system; look for employment arrangements that suit you.
2. Children may have difficulty making friends. Children may miss important topics in school when moves are frequent. Parents need to pay close attention to the education needs of their children.
3. A co-dependent is someone close to the dependent person. Co-dependent people feel powerless.
4. People who live in abusive situations must realize that there is a way out. They may seek help through community shelters that provide a supportive setting with counselors who help abuse victims make plans for the future.
5. The best way to cope with death is to face up to the loss and mourn it. Talking, crying, viewing the body, and discussing the death with family and friends helps you accept the permanency of the loss.

Thinking Critically

1. Why do you think some people cope with challenges better than others?
2. Sometimes people avoid someone who is very seriously ill. Why do you think this happens? How does this affect the ill person?
3. If a family has a pattern of violence that moves from generation to generation, how can this cycle be stopped?
4. Intervention can mean the difference between life and death to an abused child. Why do you think some people avoid stepping in to help?

Taking Action

1. Assume that you are a young parent in a dual-earner family. Make a list of specific things you would do to balance work and family life.
2. Assume that your grandmother will be moving in with your family. Write a diary entry, expressing your feelings about this change in your family.
3. A friend has seemed depressed for some time. He has made you feel uneasy with talk of ways people commit suicide. Today, he seemed unusually happy. He insisted on giving you one of his favorite compact discs, saying he wouldn't be needing it. Write a dialogue of the conversation you would have with your friend.

Making Life Choices

Maurice babysits for a family in his neighborhood. On several occasions he has noticed bruises on little Timothy's back and legs. The child seems withdrawn and frightened by sudden movements.

Should Maurice confront Timothy's parents with his observations, tell his own parents, contact the child welfare office, or just keep quiet?

Using Your Journal

Are you having to deal with any of the challenges described in this chapter? If so, use your journal to explore how you can best cope with the challenge. Who can you talk to? What actions can you take? If someone you know is dealing with one or more of the challenges described, use your journal to write about what you can do to help the person.

6. Denial, anger, bargaining, depression, and acceptance.
7. **Any three** of the resources listed on page 181.

Thinking Critically

1. Answers will vary. Point out that some people have had more opportunity to learn about coping with challenges by observing family and friends as they cope.
2. Answers will vary. Often people avoid those who are ill because they don't know what to say.
3. Answers will vary. Family members or other caring persons can intervene and get help for families that are prone to violence.
4. Answers will vary. Some people may fear getting hurt themselves. They may be afraid of accusing someone falsely. (Point out that there should not be fear as long as a person reports abuse in good faith.)

Robby reaches out to an unemployed parent.

Robby

"Recently my dad was laid off from his job at a finance company. This left him pretty depressed. His moods were hard on the family. Mom has her own job as a paralegal, and she became more tired and tense. My brother Daniel reacted to the tension by fighting with *me.* One night we got into a huge argument. After clearing the air, we realized that the real problem was the tension in our house. We put our heads together and made a game plan to help Dad through the bad times. We knew we had to be supportive but let him alone when he needed space. We made a list of ways we could help to cut expenses. We even thought of a couple places where we might find part-time work. The next day we sat down and talked to Dad about our plan. He really appreciated our concern. Things were better after that."

Sam Lee "I've always been proud of my sons, but they really came through in a pinch when I lost my job. I wasn't easy to put up with, and I lost my temper unfairly more than once. Robby and Daniel both kept their cool, and they expressed their thoughts and feelings with common sense. We learned how to talk to each other more openly and sensitively because of my personal crisis. A lot of issues and conflicts came up, and we had no other option but to learn to deal with them. My wife and sons stood by me. I'll never forget that."

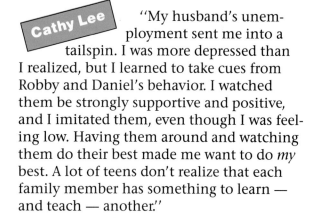

Cathy Lee "My husband's unemployment sent me into a tailspin. I was more depressed than I realized, but I learned to take cues from Robby and Daniel's behavior. I watched them be strongly supportive and positive, and I imitated them, even though I was feeling low. Having them around and watching them do their best made me want to do *my* best. A lot of teens don't realize that each family member has something to learn — and teach — another."

Daniel Lee "Robby really pulled the family together in a moment of crisis. He showed us all how a support system of people around you is a great comfort and self-esteem booster. We've gotten closer because of the hard times. That doesn't mean we want it to happen again, but we have learned that sometimes you have to make the best out of a bad situation. Pulling together has made us stronger as individuals, and that feels good."

You can make a difference too.

- What is your definition of a family?
- What can a family do to lend support to a member in trouble?
- What are some traits and qualities that make up a strong family? What are the traits and qualities that make up a weak family? Which of these did you see in Robby's family?
- Have you ever reached out to a family member to provide support?

UNIT

4 How Can You Handle Relationships?

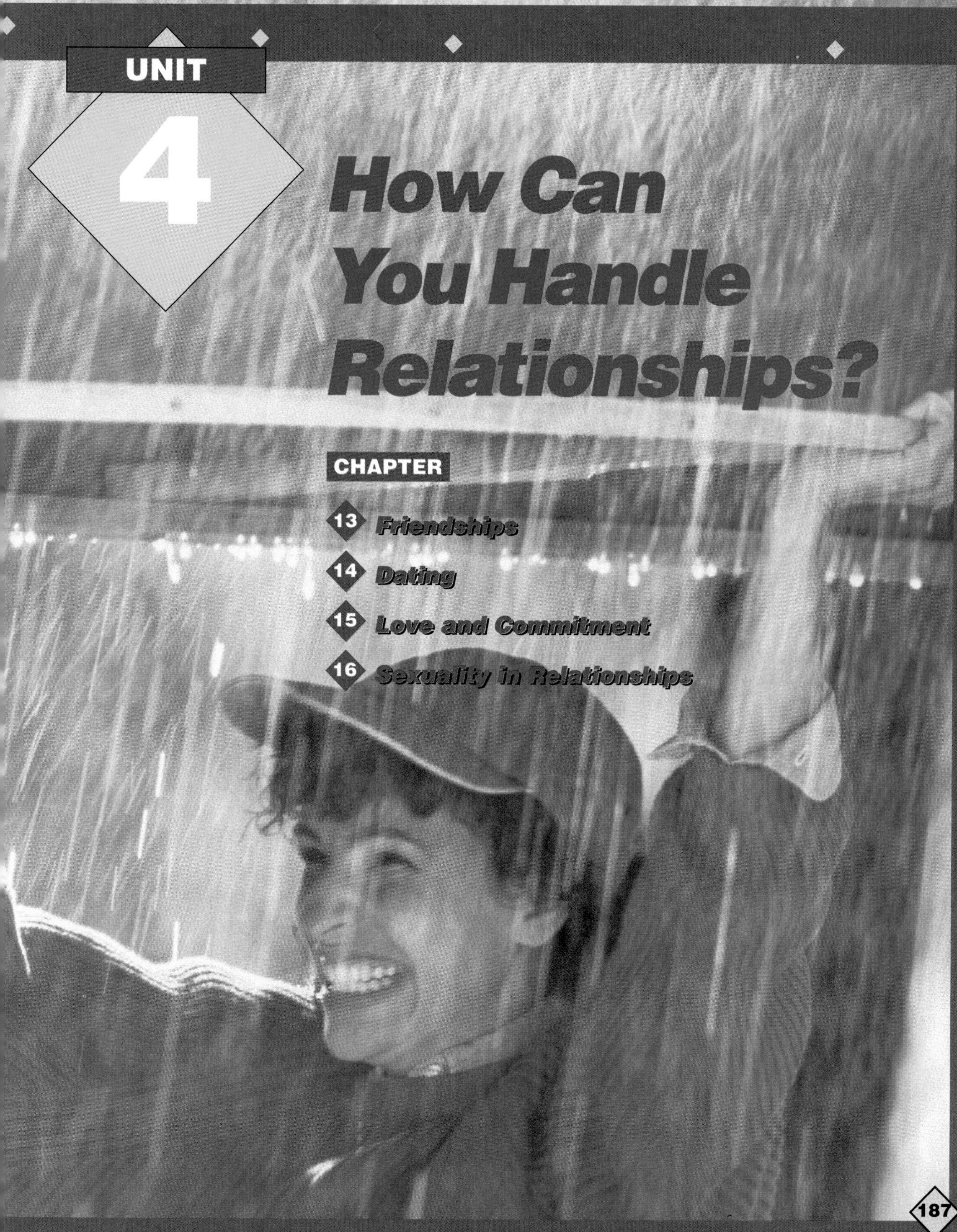

CHAPTER

CHAPTER 13

Friendships

Chapter Challenge

Resources. Refer to the Teacher's Classroom Resources box and Student Workbook for materials related to this chapter.

Look for These Answers . . .

- What are the qualities of a true friend?
- What are the three main types of friendships?
- How can a person build friendships?
- How are friendships maintained?
- How does peer pressure affect relationships with friends?

Look for These Terms . . .

- casual acquaintances
- close friends
- conformity
- lifelong friends
- manipulators
- peer pressure
- peers

"Hey, have I ever done anything for you?" Dirk asked. He peered directly into Jimmy's eyes as he put a hand on his shoulder. Then he looked quickly to both sides of where they stood.

"Of course you have, Dirk."

"Then what's the problem?"

"I don't know. I just don't know," Jimmy replied.

"Look — buddy — you're my friend, aren't you? What are friends for anyway? They help each other, right? That's all I'm asking. I just want a little help."

Jimmy stared at the ground. He shifted his weight from one foot to the other. Dirk was right. They were friends and had been for a long time. You were supposed to be loyal to your friends. You were supposed to stand by them.

"Okay, Jimmy, what do you say? Are we together in this, or what?" Dirk rubbed his hands together nervously as he looked intently at Jimmy and waited for an answer.

What Is a Friend?

- "I can talk to you about anything. I don't worry that you'll judge me or give up on me. I can depend on you to listen with an open mind."
- "When everyone else believed the rumors that were going around and talked about me behind my back, you stood up for me. You gave me the benefit of the doubt."
- "I can always count on you to keep a secret."

Remarks like these describe how some people feel about their friends. Think about your friends for a moment. What is it that makes you count them as friends?

Families are usually assigned to people through heredity. Friends, however, are the people with whom you *choose* to associate. The ability to recognize the qualities of a true friend, one who has your best interests at heart, is a valuable skill.

Chapter Opener. Ask students to read the opening scenario to the chapter. Ask the following questions: What do you think Dirk wants from Jimmy? Describe the emotions that Dirk and Jimmy are feeling. How would you describe their friendship?

Activity. Divide students into groups. Have them make lists of the ten most important qualities in a friend. When done, compare group lists to see similarities and differences.

◆ Characteristics of a True Friend

A true friend understands your needs. He or she sincerely wants to be part of your life.

As she was making the final preparations for Mandy's surprise birthday party, Danae thought about their friendship. "Mandy is such a giver, always thinking of others before herself. When I'm feeling down, I can always count on Mandy to encourage me. I can trust her with anything," thought Danae. "Mandy is one of the most generous people I know. I can hardly wait for the party to begin. It will feel good to be able to do something for her for a change."

Mick really appreciated his friend Carlo. When Mick's father died, Carlo was there for him. Most of Mick's other friends avoided him, unsure of what to do. Carlo was generous with his time and listened as Mick talked about the way he felt after his father's death. Carlo gave advice only when Mick asked for it.

Showing the qualities of a true friend is easy enough when things are going well. The real test comes when problems arise, as in Mick's case. The term "fair-weather friend" is often used to describe the type of friend who is by your side as long as the sun is shining but disappears when storm clouds gather. Fair-weather friends are on the scene to enjoy successes and share good times. True friends are still there to face life's challenges and help you through difficult times.

Being a good friend does not mean that you agree all the time. Good friends owe it to one another to be honest about their feelings. Good friends may agree to disagree. Maintaining your own individuality, views, and values is no problem with real friends.

As friendships develop, true friends find ways to esteem others, or make each other feel important. Martha and Jenna Beth are best friends. Martha is a worrier, especially just before a gymnastics meet. Jenna Beth is always there for Martha, encouraging her and building her up just when she needs it. Martha finds ways to help Jenna Beth as well. They both wind up as winners by building self-esteem in each other.

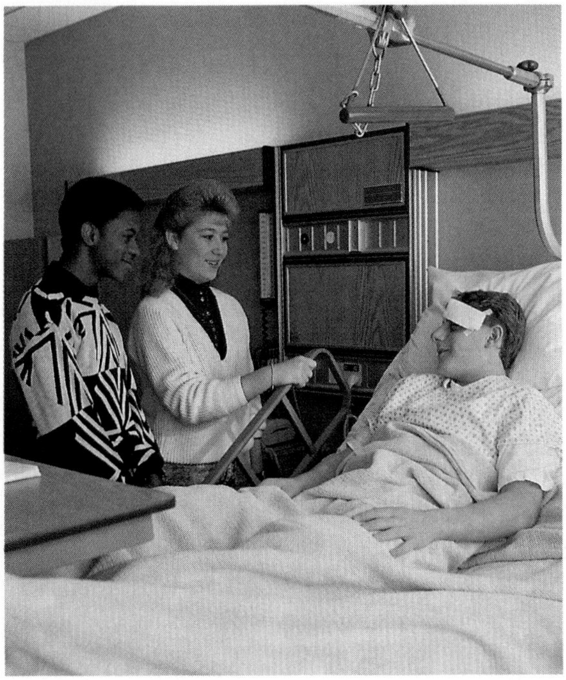

True friends are there for each other even when the times are tough.

As you can see in these examples, people appreciate certain qualities in their friends. Not everyone needs or wants exactly the same things. What qualities do you value in a true friend?

Discussion. Ask students to list the qualities they like least in a friend. Do they ever tolerate some of these in friends? What qualities are never tolerable?

◆◆◆

Who Are Your Friends?

When answering this question, most people think first of their **peers**. These are the people you associate with who are a similar age to you. You are drawn together by shared interests and experiences.

Activity. Ask students to identify people (not peers) who are potential friends for them. Have them suggest ways to begin a friendship. If you wish, ask them to try starting a new friendship and report back the results.

A Slice of Life

Seventeen-year-old Karl had been running with a gang since the age of twelve. The anger, the fighting, the violence — it had all become easier with time. What he did as a member of the gang, however, he could never have done alone.

Outwardly Karl was tough. Inwardly he often felt empty, scared, and alone. Sometimes he thought that the gang went too far, but how could he say so? That would show he was weak. He didn't want the others to know.

Buddy was also a gang member. Ironically, he too had feelings like Karl's. He had to keep them inside, though, because Karl and the rest would lose respect for him. He also feared what they might do to him if they knew how he felt.

As they stood united, the members of the gang let their anger run wild. No one could challenge them without a battle. They began to carry knives, and the threat to their own lives became stronger.

After school one day, fifteen-year-old Andre made the mistake of bumping into a gang member in a nearby parking lot. A fight developed. Andre was shoved, fell, and hit his head against a concrete step. He died shortly after. "It's getting out of hand," Karl thought. Buddy's thoughts were the same. They said nothing.

Thinking It Through

- Why did Buddy and Karl keep their feelings to themselves?
- Would anything be different for them if they knew how the other felt?
- What are the short- and long-term effects of gang violence?
- Why do people in gangs deal with anger in violent ways? What alternatives do they have?

The people in your peer group are both male and female. You may have friends of both genders. During childhood, people tend to focus more on friendships with those of the same gender. With puberty, friends of the opposite gender become more important.

Who else can you count as a friend? As a matter of fact, your life will be enriched if you look for friendship in many places. People of all ages, races, income levels, and nationalities can contribute so much to your life. They will make you more knowledgeable, more understanding, and more well rounded as a person.

Joshua met Esther when he went to the nursing home with his family living class. Joshua now visits regularly with Esther. He has learned a great deal about history and what life is like from an older person's perspective. Esther feels energized after visiting with Joshua. They have lively conversations

Your peers, the people that you associate with and who are close to you in age, have a strong effect on you.

Discussion. Ask students why teens might tend to choose friends who are only like them. In what ways is this limiting?

All types of friends can enrich your life. What benefits are derived from knowing people who have different backgrounds and experiences?

about world events and what's going on with the younger generation. Joshua and Esther value each other's friendship. Joshua appreciates the humor and wisdom Esther has, and she relishes the excitement, energy, and idealism of Joshua's youth.

While working on a term paper at the library, Trent met Stephan. They struck up a conversation while sitting at a table together. Trent listened carefully to understand what Stephan was saying. It took Stephan some time to get the words out. Trent learned that Stephan, who was bright and had a sharp wit, had cerebral palsy; you just had to give him some time to speak. Trent did that and discovered a special friendship.

◆◆◆

Types of Friendships

In thinking about friendships, people often classify them according to degree of closeness and length of relationship:

Discussion. Ask students if they can tell when they first meet someone whether or not they would like the person for a friend. For those who can, have them analyze why this happens. Is this positive or negative? Why?

- **Casual acquaintances** are sometimes called speaking friends. They exchange greetings and a few words whenever they happen to be together. Their shared experiences are usually routine, and conversations are about everyday happenings.
- **Close friends** have come to know and trust one another. They have shared a variety of experiences and have common interests. Sonya and Ellie became friends a year ago. They met the first day of play practice and have been inseparable ever since. They share their deepest secrets and have heart-to-heart talks about their feelings.
- **Lifelong friends** are close friends for whom the ties have lasted over time. Lifelong friendships sometimes begin in childhood. The bonds strengthen as they share the highs and lows of adolescence. Throughout the changes brought about by stages of life, these friends manage to maintain their relationship. Martin and Clyde met in grade school and have maintained their friendship for nearly thirty years. Even though they are separated by great distances, they nurture their friendship through phone calls and occasional visits. Their sincere interest and concern for one another remain a constant part of life. No matter what, they can depend upon each other.

Life will bring you many casual acquaintances. You are likely to forget the names of many of these people. You will probably have several close friends in your lifetime, although few people enjoy more than two or three close friendships at a time. Lifelong friends are much less common. One lifelong friend may be a rare treasure indeed. How do the friends you have fit into these categories at this point in your life?

Lifelong friendships are rare but very special. Do you have a friend with whom you might like to keep in touch throughout life?

◆◆◆

Building Friendships

Finding friendship seems to be easier for some than it is for others. Some people have plenty of friends in the casual acquaintance category, but getting beyond that is the hard part. How do you build friendships? Try these steps:

1. Look around for someone else who might need a friend. Get involved in groups outside of school. Lauren joined a biking club and found new friends. Tad noticed someone in his class who was often alone and soon got to know him.
2. Start a conversation. Even the simplest openers can begin a friendship. A simple greeting and a comment about the weather have begun many conversations that eventually lead to friendship.
3. Reach out. Once you are on speaking terms with someone, take things one step further. Offer a favor or a simple invitation. You may never develop a friendship with someone you like if you don't take that first step.
4. Hold up your end of the friendship. As the old saying goes, "To have a friend, be one." Don't wait for the other person to do all the inviting or suggesting of activities. Take the initiative yourself part of the time.
5. Share your feelings. A deeper friendship comes when you exchange ideas and attitudes. Be willing to open up and listen.

Life Management Skills. Ask students to explain what might prevent people from easily maintaining a lifelong friendship. What suggestions do they have for keeping such a friendship going?

Activity. Have students write paragraphs describing how one of their current friendships developed. Have volunteers share their paragraphs with the class. Make a list of techniques people use to begin friendships.

Friendships are built and maintained when people go out of their way to do things for each other. Sometimes a special surprise or favor can mean a lot.

◆◆◆

Maintaining Friendships

Once you have friendships, how can you keep them healthy? There are three qualities that are especially important in friendships. These are communication, caring, and trust.

◆ Communication

As you know, communication is the key to sustaining any relationship. By using the communication and conflict resolution skills you have learned, you can put strength and longevity into your friendships. Communication can keep a friendship going and even retrieve one that is threatened.

Hope and Keena had been friends since elementary school but lately felt distanced from each other. Hope was disturbed by the change in their friendship and approached Keena one day after school.

"I'm really concerned about our friendship. It's important to me, and I don't want to see it fall apart," Hope said.

"I feel the same way too," Keena replied. "Things have changed between us."

"I know you have some new interests in your life right now," Hope continued, "but do you have some time to get together? Maybe we could do a little catching up."

Keena and Hope were making a conscious effort to keep their friendship strong by talking and sharing together.

◆ Caring

What relationship can survive without caring? People need to know that you like them and are concerned about their welfare. You can either say it or show it, but you need to find a way. If you don't, the friendship is likely to fall by the wayside.

There are many levels of caring. You may use different levels for different friends. You could smile. You could give a hug or a gift. You could do a favor. You could give your time. People have even been known to put their lives on the line for friendship. How much would you give and for whom?

Work and Family. When parents in a family work, teens often have to share in the responsibility. Ask students how this can affect their relationships with friends. Could it sometimes be more difficult to maintain a friendship? What suggestions do they have for people in such situations?

Problem Solving. Ask students if they have ever had friends who did not get along with each other. How did they handle such situations? What can a person do when this happens?

Discussion. Ask students to explain what a grudge is. Why are grudges hazardous to friendships?

◆ Trust

True friendship does not survive very well without trust. In a close friendship people confide in each other. You cannot confide in people very easily if you don't trust them. Trust is earned through keeping private talks private. A secret is no longer a secret when shared with a third person. Trust is also earned when you say what you mean and mean what you say. You can also prove yourself to be trustworthy by being honest, sincere, and sensitive.

◆◆◆

When Friendships End

Not every friendship will last. Not every friendship should last. Sometimes things get in the way to bring friendships to an end.

Some friendships end. Although it isn't always easy to let them go, it may be necessary. Can you think of reasons why?

As you mature and change, you may not want exactly the same things from a friendship. Interests, attitudes, and goals all change, bringing about new ones that may fit better with new friends. In order for friendships to endure change, there must be a conscious effort and desire to keep the friendship strong.

Separation poses a threat to many friendships. When friends are miles apart, physically speaking, they may become worlds apart in an emotional sense. Communication becomes more difficult; opportunities for caring and confidence-building become few. Only deep friendships that are of prime importance to both individuals usually endure prolonged separations.

If a friendship ends against your wishes, realize that sometimes this just happens. No one can ever take away from you the special memories and feelings that you have. These are yours forever. They will help as you build new friendships in the future.

◆◆◆

Peer Pressure

One of the interesting things about friends is the effect that they have on each other. Friends can influence one another, both by example and word. Have you ever imitated a friend's hairstyle or choice of clothes? Perhaps you find yourself using a friend's favorite expression. This can happen without either person even realizing it.

Sometimes people purposely try to influence one another. This may take the form of advice, persuasion, or pressure. An attempt to influence a contemporary is known as **peer pressure**. When cliques form, pressures to go along with the crowd may be especially strong. Peer pressure is positive or negative, depending on the nature of, and reason for, the pressure.

Discussion. Have students explain what effects these types of people have on others: bullies, intimidators, and critics. How can people handle them?

◆ Cons

The bad news about peer pressure concerns personal power versus peer pressure. You have a certain degree of control over your life, or personal power. This power is based on your personal code of ethics. When you choose to give in to peer pressure, you give up this power. Power then belongs to those who represent the group. Control of your life is lost as you allow others to manipulate your actions.

A close look at manipulators (muh-NIP-yuh-layt-urs) shows that they are not real friends in any sense of the word. **Manipulators** take advantage of the weaknesses of others. Jackson is a good example of a manipulator. When convincing someone to do something questionable, his favorite line is: "I'm only thinking of you. You don't want to be different, do you?" Manipulators prey on people with low self-esteem. Manipulators like Jackson pretend to be concerned; however, their only real concern is having their own way.

Most teens want to be in control. You may remember a time when you have thought or said, "I wish everyone would realize that I'm old enough to make my own decisions" or "I won't allow anyone to pressure me into doing something that I think is wrong." If you have thought these thoughts, you surely value your sense of personal power.

The real threat of peer pressure is the possibility that, although convinced of your own self-control, you fail to see the subtle ways that peer pressure can be exerted.

Why does peer pressure affect so many people? Why do people allow themselves to be manipulated? The answer is as simple as the basic need for acceptance. It is natural for everyone to want to feel liked and accepted. Feeling the approval of the group satisfies a basic social need. The need for acceptance, in balance with other needs and values, is not a weakness. When it becomes such a tremendous need that it overshadows all other values, however, personal power is threatened.

Peer pressure can be difficult to resist. What skills do you need to know in order to be able to do what is best for you?

Peer pressure often leads to immature behavior, not only for teens but for adults as well. Peer pressure is to blame for many forms of destructive behavior — smoking, drinking, drug use, and irresponsible sexual activity. Peer pressure may cause people to behave in dishonest, unfair, and even criminal ways.

Changing in order to be like a group is called **conformity** (kun-FOR-mut-ee). When the change is negative, peer pressure is a negative force. If change is positive, peer pressure is a positive influence.

◆ Pros

The good news about peer pressure is that it can be a positive force that helps you grow. When people influence you to learn new skills or improve personal qualities, peer pressure is a definite advantage.

More About Positive Peer Pressure. In some cities programs have been devised to enable peers to help each other. In groups teens work on a regular basis with those who are potential drop-outs, have trouble with grades, have become involved with gangs, or have other problems. These support groups are making a difference in the lives of many teens.

I CAN ◆◆◆ Resist Pressure

Angeline felt that she had lost control of her own will until she learned some techniques that helped her do what she wanted to do instead of going along with others.

"At first I thought it would never work. I learned how to say 'no' in my independent living class, but it didn't sound easy. I guess I was too used to just giving in all the time.

"I decided to start with Clark. When he asked me for my homework for the umpteenth time, I stood firm, looked him straight in the eye, and said, 'Not anymore, Clark. I don't feel right about it. I hope we can still be friends anyway.' I said it calmly and without smiling. I wanted him to get the message straight.

"Clark was taken back by my answer. He even pushed me a little more. I just told him I had to meet Dee, and I left. He never asked me for my homework again. He has been a little distant since then. I don't know whether we'll ever be good friends again or not, but if he was just using me, I guess I don't need that kind of friendship."

- What techniques did Angeline use that were helpful to her?
- How can you say "no" and attempt to keep a friendship at the same time?
- Describe some other situations in which these techniques might be useful.
- Do you need to learn to be more assertive about saying "no"? Think of some times when you should have said "no" in the past. How would you handle similar situations differently in the future?

Friends may at times exert positive peer pressure. Alexis was very shy and had a difficult time developing relationships until she became part of a child development class. Her classmates were very concerned about her and made an extra special effort to include her in everything. In class discussions, a common response was, "We want to know what you think about this, Alexis." They were a group of encouragers exerting a positive influence on Alexis's social development.

Friends may step in, exert pressure, and prevent major crises as well. Friends don't let friends get involved in things that may be immoral, dangerous, or illegal. How can you and your friends be a positive influence on others?

Photo Focus. Have students compare the photos on these two pages. Ask which one depicts positive peer pressure and which one negative. Have them explain what might be going on in each photo.

Peer pressure can be positive. Have you ever encouraged a friend to learn a new skill? This kind of pressure is helpful to people.

CHAPTER

13

Review

Summarizing the Chapter

- Friends are people you choose to associate with because they have qualities you value.
- People of all ages, races, income levels, and nationalities can be your friends.
- Three main types of friends are casual acquaintances, close friends, and lifelong friends.
- Building and maintaining friendships requires much effort from both parties.
- Peer pressure is positive when an individual is influenced to make a mature decision or change. It is negative when it manipulates individuals to take part in harmful, immoral, or illegal actions.

Testing Your Memory

1. Name four qualities of a true friend.
2. What is a ''fair-weather friend''?
3. What is meant by the term ''peers''?
4. Name three benefits that come from having friends of many types.
5. What is the difference between a close friend and a life-long friend?
6. List the five steps to building a friendship.
7. Describe three qualities that are important in friendships.
8. How should people view the ending of a friendship?
9. Why do people allow themselves to be influenced by peer pressure?

Answers
Testing Your Memory

1. **Any four:** understands your needs; wants to be part of your life; giving; thoughtful; someone you can count on; trustworthy; generous; there when needed; there when times are difficult; honest; someone who esteems others. (Students may list other qualities as well.)
2. Someone who is only your friend when all is well.
3. The people you associate with who are a similar age to you.
4. You will be more knowledge-able, more understanding, and more well rounded as a person.
5. Close friends and lifelong friends are the same except that with the latter the ties have lasted over time.
6. The five steps are: (1) Look for someone who might be interested in a friendship; (2) Start a conversation; (3) Reach out; (4) Hold up your end of the friendship; (5) Share your feelings.
7. Communication; caring; trust.
8. Friendships often end for good reasons. This should be accepted and viewed as an experience that can help you with future friendships.
9. They have a strong need for acceptance.

Thinking Critically

1. In thinking about the qualities of good friends, what characteristics do you value most? Why?
2. What criteria do you use to eliminate people as possible friends? Does your list need any revision? Explain.
3. Describe a time when you have been positively influenced by a friend. Describe when you were negatively influenced.
4. Which do you think is more difficult, starting a friendship or ending one? Why?

Taking Action

1. Develop a "Help Wanted" ad to advertise for a friend. Include the qualifications needed and the compensation to be offered in return.
2. Write a poem, song, or essay on one of these topics, or on another friendship-related topic of your choice: "To have a friend, you must be one." "A friend in need is a friend indeed."
3. Develop a list of news story headlines to suggest possible results of peer pressure, both good and bad.

Making Life Choices

Claudia and Ricardo have been friends since childhood. As teens, they still spend time together. Now that Claudia is dating Rudy, some complications have arisen. Rudy says, "You can have all the girlfriends you want, but I don't like your spending so much time with Ricardo."

Do you think it is possible for male-female friendships to survive with no romantic feelings? What do you think about Rudy's attitude? If you were Claudia, what would you do?

Using Your Journal

What are your main thoughts about your friendships? Are you happy with the friends you have? Do you wish you had more friends? Do you wish you could start, or break off, a friendship but you don't know how? Use your journal to explore your feelings about your friendships. If you feel that you need to make changes, list the changes you want to make. Then write down a plan for implementing them. Keep track of your progress and write new plans when they become necessary.

Thinking Critically

1. Answers will vary.
2. Answers will vary. Encourage students to examine their prejudices and attitudes about people.
3. Answers will vary.
4. Answers will vary.

CHAPTER 14

Dating

Chapter Challenge

Resources. Refer to the Teacher's Classroom Resources box and Student Workbook for materials related to this chapter.

Look for These Answers . . .

- What are reasons for dating?
- What determines a person's readiness for dating?
- What is the typical dating pattern and the advantages and disadvantages along the way?
- What can you do to make your dating relationships successful?
- Describe some challenges that must be handled in dating and explain how to deal with them.

Look for These Terms . . .

- blind dates
- date rape
- exclusive dating
- rape
- responsible freedom

"Why does it have to be so difficult? After all, I have nothing to lose. So what if I get rejected. It happens to the best of us." Terry's hand lifted the telephone receiver from the hook. In seconds the phone was back in place.

"I just can't do it," Terry thought. "I'll do something else this weekend — maybe rent a movie with a friend or something. Who needs a date anyway?"

Asking for a date, especially with someone you don't know well, is not easy. Terry walked a few feet away from the phone and then slowly moved back.

"Maybe I should think about it for awhile," Terry thought. "Next week might be a better time anyway. No, this is silly. I can do it. If the answer is no, I'll live with it."

Terry picked up the phone a second time and carefully pressed the numbers. The phone rang for several very long seconds before someone answered.

"Hello," Terry said. "Is Scott home? May I talk to him please?"

Reasons for Dating

Ask a room full of teens what dating means to them and you are likely to get a wide range of responses. Young people who live in different areas do not all approach dating in the same way.

Most teens who do date agree that dating gives them a chance to share good times with others. Friendships have already allowed them to begin learning how to get along with others, but dating goes beyond this. Through dating, young men and women explore what it takes to get along with someone of the opposite gender. Perhaps without even realizing it, they examine dating partners to see what qualities they might want in a permanent relationship later on. At some point, romance enters the picture. This brings a new dimension to friendship and new needs for responsibility.

Through dating, teens practice responsible freedom. **Responsible freedom** means making decisions independently and taking responsibility for the consequences. Many choices arise that call for value judgments.

Chapter Opener. Ask students to read the opening scenario to the chapter. Ask the following questions: As you were reading, did you expect Terry to be a male? Why? Do females ever ask for dates? What are the advantages and disadvantages of this?

More About Dating. The dating stage is longer than it used to be. This is because people are marrying at a later age and starting to date earlier.

Problems of finances, transportation, and time limitations call for solutions and compromises. Moral dilemmas may develop over such things as movie ratings, sexual activity, alcohol, and drugs. Teens learn to make responsible choices and to live with the results.

◆◆◆

Readiness for Dating

Just as people develop at different rates, their readiness for dating is not the same either. Clay went all the way through high school without dating. In his senior year, he did ask someone to the prom, but it just seemed like the thing to do. It wasn't until Clay was out of high school that he developed a genuine interest in dating. At that time it worked fine for him.

Not everyone is ready for dating at the same age. Until the interest and opportunities are there, most teens continue to spend time with friends.

Cherie started dating seriously in high school. She felt ready and was interested when she was fourteen, but family rules said she had to be sixteen. She dates often now.

As you can see, readiness for dating is more than just an age question. Maturity level is a prime factor. Since males generally mature a little later than females, they may not be ready as early as many females of the same age. Personal preferences and interests of either gender can make other activities more important. Some are just not ready for the challenges that come with dating. This is all okay. Although it may not seem like it, teens have plenty of time to enter into dating relationships. There is no rush.

On the other hand, many teens are ready and do date in high school. They must learn to deal with the challenges and accept the responsibilities.

◆◆◆

Who Do You Date?

Once you are ready to date, who will it be? Some young people make the mistake of looking only at appearances and status.

Delia wanted to go out with a football player. Kevin thought the girls on the pom pon squad were appealing. Although football players and cheerleaders may be fine people, narrowing your choices this way can eliminate some even better ones. Quality people don't always stand out in a crowd. You may have to look for them. You may also have to want to find them.

What is a quality person like? The answer to this question may not be the same for everyone. In general, such people treat you with respect and consideration. They have the same qualities that you look for in any friendship. Sure, they can be nice looking and

Life Management Skills. One of the most expensive dates for teens today is the prom. Have students research the cost of proms for both males and females in your area. Ask them to determine some ideas for saving and/or sharing prom expenses.

More About Readiness. Even though some teens feel ready to date, the opportunities are not always there. This was true for Holly. She really never worried about it. Instead she spent time with her girlfriends and became involved in school activities. In college she found that more young men were interested in dating, so her opportunities increased. This is a typical experience for many teens.

talented too, but only you can decide how high to put these factors on your list of priorities.

◆◆◆

Dating Patterns

Dating often leads to a serious relationship. When it does, it goes through a typical pattern. A person dates different people and eventually settles on one. As that partnership grows, an understanding develops. If it becomes serious enough, an engagement and then marriage take place. The early stages of this pattern bring their own opportunities and problems.

◆ Dating Different People

At this stage each dating partner is free to date whomever he or she wishes. This means that you can get to know different people. You can shop around for the qualities you admire in a partner and see how you get along with many personality types. Through this experience, you can clarify your own views. When you meet someone you would like to know better, you are free to become closer friends.

Dating of this type is often done in groups. There is comfort in numbers. You don't feel the pressure of keeping up the conversation, for one thing.

When dating different people, you always run the risk of going out with someone you don't care for. This is especially true on **blind dates**. These dates are usually arranged by others with someone you have never met. Some people enjoy the adventure of meeting new people. Not all blind dates go well, yet some do.

◆ Dating One Person Frequently

Seeing one person more frequently is a natural outgrowth of dating many. When two people feel a growing attraction and interest in one another, they spend more time together.

Dating one person frequently has its own problems. Each may be wondering just how the other really feels. "Do we have a date tonight, or don't we? Should I wait for a call or make other plans?" Uncertainty is inevitable when no understanding exists. In time this confusion settles as the relationship either ends or moves into the exclusive category.

◆ Exclusive Dating

With **exclusive dating**, partners stop dating other people. This gives the relationship every possible chance to grow, without the complications of competition. Feelings of friendship deepen to a real sense of caring.

Couples often go out with others in a group when they date. Can you think of some advantages to this?

More About Who You Date. One of the most common places that people meet dating partners is in the workplace. Obviously, some work environments offer better opportunities to meet people than others.

Work and Family. Ask students how the dating routine of a teen is affected in a home where both parents are employed. Is the teen's social time limited due to household responsibilities and the need to care for siblings? How can families manage this fairly?

Feelings of trust and loyalty also begin to develop as partners learn to confide in one another. They have an understanding but no commitment for the future.

There are advantages to this arrangement. Exclusive dating:

- **Feels Comfortable.** Partners get used to each other. They don't have to worry about the awkward moments that people go through when getting to know someone better.
- **Builds Security.** Having someone always available offers protection against loneliness and possible rejection.
- **Reduces Competition.** Since the partners are not involved with others, there is less anxiety about competing.
- **Increases Familiarity.** Regular contact enables the partners to learn more about each other.
- **Meets Emotional Needs.** Someone is always there when you need him or her.

When two people date each other exclusively, they have the benefits of feeling comfortable and secure with each other. Are there any disadvantages?

Activity. Have students make a list of what males and females may expect from a dating partner. What should they not expect?

There are disadvantages too. Exclusive dating:

- **Limits Contacts.** You are prevented from learning more about other types of people. If exclusive dating starts very early and leads to marriage, you may never know what you missed. You may also choose the wrong person for you. What you like in a person in your middle teens may not be at all what you like when you are in your early twenties. People change a great deal between the ages of fifteen and twenty-five.
- **Encourages Sex Too Soon.** Too much closeness can lead to sexual expectations.
- **Pushes Marriage.** Some research suggests that females who date early and go steady early tend to marry early.

◆◆◆

Successful Dating

Whether a single date or a series, successful dating hinges on a few important principles:

- **Be courteous.** Treat others the way you would want to be treated. Accept a date with enthusiasm. See it through with courtesy even if it doesn't turn out quite right. Turn a date down without hurting the asker. Say "thanks" after a date.
- **Follow the rules.** Meet your date's family if possible and be friendly. Adhere to the curfew. If your date's family has other rules, honor them.
- **Be yourself.** You both want to get to know each other. This won't work if you try to be something you are not. People can relax more easily if they are not trying to impress or be phony.
- **Tune in to your date.** Communicate your feelings and listen to your date's. What activities do you enjoy together? Is there trust between you? What about honesty? Do you get along? How do you both feel about the

Problem Solving. Shyness is a common problem for teens on a date. Have students suggest techniques they have used or know of that can help with this. List questions that would make good conversation starters. Also list topics that promote conversation.

SIDELIGHT

Dating Situations

Dating can be difficult, especially when people show a lack of consideration for each other. What do you think about these situations?

- When Yoko and Ti go out, Ti always pays. Costs are high and Yoko likes to spend money.
- Trevor and Sharon had a date lined up for the weekend. When Emil called Sharon and asked her out, she accepted and then called Trevor to cancel their date.
- Reba and Sid have been dating steadily for six months. Just before the prom, Sid dropped Reba in order to go with one of the young women on the prom court.

♦♦♦

amount of time you spend together? If you have serious problems in any of these areas, you may need to end the relationship.

♦♦♦

Dating Challenges

Dating is not without its difficulties. Explore these dating challenges and think about how you would handle them.

♦ Shyness

Shyness affects almost everyone at one time or another. It's a particular problem during adolescence when dating pressures build, although it can be experienced in many other situations as well. People don't want to be evaluated and rejected.

Discussion. Have students react to this situation: Antonio did not care for his blind date. He showed it by not talking to her for most of the evening while they were out on a double date.

If shyness is a concern for you, try these practical suggestions:

- Practice social talk. Ask a friend or parent to help you. Experiment with unfamiliar topics. You'll discover that you have more to say than you think. Practice giving and receiving compliments. Make them sincere when you give them.
- Plan a date that won't demand all talk. If you are worried about making conversation, which would be better, renting a video or going on a picnic?
- Accept your personal worth. Take credit in your own mind for the things you do well. Thinking positively about yourself will help give you the confidence you need in social situations. You may make mistakes along the way, but so does everyone else. Try remembering that even the most popular people have moments of shyness and self-doubt.
- Focus on others. Concentrate on putting others at ease. This will help you forget to be self-conscious.

When you date someone, you should make it a point to get to know the family. Putting your best foot forward will make them feel more comfortable with the dating relationship.

- Be patient. With time and practice, you can overcome shyness. Many teens notice that they become more confident as the years pass by. Remember, though, that you can help things along if you are willing to try.

◆ Who Asks For a Date?

At one time this was not a question. In some circles it still is not. Times have changed, however. More and more young women are doing the asking for a date today. They are finding that it isn't always easy. On the other hand, the privilege of being able to ask means not having to sit around and wait to be asked. Many young men welcome the sharing of this responsibility.

◆ Finances

Dating today is costly. Think about what going to a movie in your community can cost, especially if you add refreshments to the bill. Even so, this is nothing compared to the costs involved in a big event, such as a prom.

Shyness is more of a problem when you spend time alone together on a date. Combat this by choosing an activity that does not require much conversation or that gives you something to talk about.

With costs so high, logic says that perhaps one person should not always carry the burden. Although some males still prefer to do the paying, many females are willing to share this burden. Couples can talk it over to see what each wants. One may have more finances available, which helps settle the question. The person who is not paying should always be thoughtful about selecting activities and ordering food.

When money is a factor, couples need to look for inexpensive ways to enjoy dates. What types of dates can you think of that would not be costly?

◆ Parental Concerns

Many parents make rules about dating. They may set an age at which dating can begin, limit the frequency of dates, or set curfews. They may also restrict who you go out with. Although teens don't always agree, such rules are expressions of parental concern. Some understanding on both sides can often lead to compromises.

Sometimes rules can provide a convenient excuse for withstanding peer pressure. As Vanessa points out, "Sometimes I don't really want to go to a particular party, but I'm not sure how to say so. That's when I just pull out one of my parents' rules to use as an excuse."

◆ Abuse

One would not think that abuse could occur in a dating relationship, but it happens. Partnerships that include this are destined for trouble. If you experience physical or verbal abuse from a date, you are smart to end the relationship before you get emotionally involved with the person. The longer you wait, the more difficult it becomes to get out. Moreover, you run the risk of injury.

Activity. Survey the class, perhaps with a secret ballot, to see how many think that females as well as males should ask for dates. Discuss the results of your survey in class.

Discussion. Ask students what types of statements indicate verbal abuse. Have them explain what can happen to the self-esteem of a person who is continually subjected to this type of abuse.

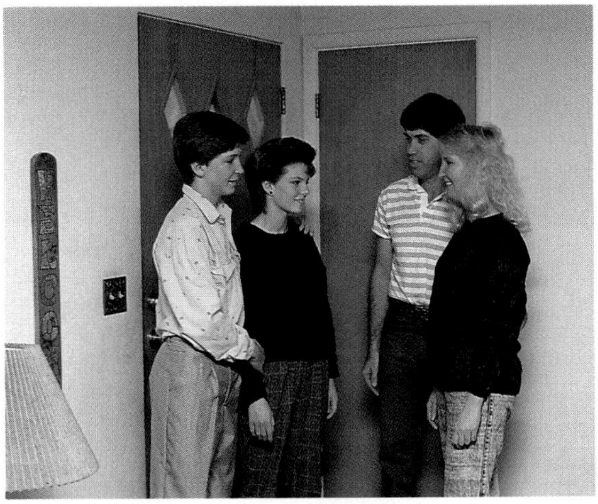

Most families have rules about dating. When you honor these, you are more likely to get along better at home. Proving your responsibility may also lead to more liberal rules in the future.

◆ Ending Relationships

Many relationships end along the way at various stages of the dating pattern. The more serious the relationship, the harder it is to deal with its ending. When a relationship ends, here are some things to think about:

- If you want to end a relationship, tell the other person with gentleness.
- If a relationship is about to end, you need to accept it. Emotional scenes do not change the inevitable.
- Look forward. Although you may feel some pain, you will soon be ready to move on with your life. Whatever you have learned or gained from the relationship will help you in the future.

◆ Date Rape

Rape is unlawful sexual intercourse by force or threat. When it takes place in a dating situation, it is called **date rape**. In either case, the act is one of violence and is inexcusable. The majority of rapes are date rapes, and many go unreported. Alcohol and drugs are sometimes related influences in these situations.

Whether you are male or female, you must take responsibility for your own actions. Be careful about the messages you send to others. They can get you into tough situations. Remember that whatever messages you think you have sent or received, rape is still not permitted.

If you ever feel threatened, be firm about saying "no." Call for help if possible. Leave immediately if you can do so safely. If rape occurs, report it. Only when people begin to realize that rape is a punishable crime will the incidence rate go down.

More About Rape. Rape is an act of violence, whether committed on a date or in any other circumstance. Point out to students that violence in this case does not necessarily mean beating. Even without beating, rape is still considered violent. Females need to know that they do not cause rape. If it occurs, they should realize that they are not responsible and should report the rape to authorities.

A Slice of Life

Pam and Isaac had been dating for several months. In time she discovered that the relationship had become more than she wanted. She knew that Isaac cared more for her than she did for him. She wanted it to be over but could not decide what action to take.

Pam began to act cold and distant. She just hoped that Isaac would get the message somehow. She spoke to him less and even tried to avoid him at school. She made up excuses so that she would not have to talk to him on the phone or meet him after school.

Isaac was confused. He tried to apologize for what he thought he was doing wrong. He became more attentive, which upset Pam. They began to argue and finally ended the relationship bitterly.

Thinking It Through

- What do you think about the way Pam handled this situation?
- How might she have ended the relationship less painfully?

CHAPTER 14

Summarizing the Chapter

- Reasons for dating include having fun, learning to relate with members of the opposite gender, and practicing responsible freedom.
- Dating readiness is largely determined by maturity.
- The typical dating pattern begins with dating different people and moves to dating one person frequently before settling on one person for exclusive dating.
- Courtesy, following family rules, being yourself, and tuning in to your date can all help make your dating days go well.
- Shyness can be overcome if you work at it.
- Some challenges in dating include deciding who should ask for a date, settling financial questions, respecting parental rules, and ending relationships. Since abuse and date rape can occur, people need to be prepared to handle these too.

Testing Your Memory

1. What is meant by the term "responsible freedom"?
2. Does readiness for dating depend on age? Explain your answer.
3. What is the disadvantage in choosing a date on the basis of appearance only?
4. List two benefits that come from dating different people.
5. List two advantages and two disadvantages of exclusive dating.
6. What should you do when turning down someone who asks you for a date?
7. Give four suggestions that can help you deal with shyness in dating relationships.

Answers
Testing Your Memory

1. Responsible freedom means making decisions independently and taking responsibility for the consequences.
2. No. Maturity level is more important than age. Because people mature at different rates, some will be ready to date at a different age than others.
3. You may miss out on finding a quality person.
4. You can get to know different people and also discover how you get along with different types of people in preparation for a closer relationship.
5. **Any two advantages:** feels comfortable; builds security; reduces competition; increases familiarity; meets emotional needs. **Any two disadvantages:** limits contacts; encourages sex too soon; pushes marriage.
6. When turning down a date, do so without hurting the asker.
7. **Any four:** practice social talk; plan a date that doesn't demand all talk; accept your personal worth; focus on others; be patient.
8. End the relationship before it becomes more difficult to do so.
9. You should tell the other person gently, accept it, and look forward even though it may be painful at first.

8. If you experience abuse in a dating relationship, what should you do?
9. List three suggestions to follow when a dating relationship ends.

Thinking Critically

1. In what ways can dating prepare a person for marriage?
2. Chart the advantages of dating different people alongside the advantages of exclusive dating. Write a conclusion statement to express your interpretation of the comparison.
3. Explain the following statement: "It usually takes more courage to end a relationship than to continue it."

Taking Action

1. Imagine that a date interviewing process is to be used in selecting a date for a specific occasion of your choice. Draft a list of questions to be asked of each date candidate during the interview. Conduct mock interviews in class.
2. Interview adults from different generations to determine changes in dating practices over the years.
3. Write a letter to "Daters Anonymous," describing a dating problem or concern, either real or fictitious. Do not sign your real name. Seal letters and place in class "mailbox" for sharing and discussion.

Making Life Choices

Craig and Linnea have been dating for nearly a year. They do not date others. Craig is headed for military service. He will go through basic training and then at least six months in overseas duty. Craig wants an agreement to not date others while he is away. Linnea is not sure about this.

What are the advantages and disadvantages of what Craig is asking? Is such a request ever reasonable? What would you do if you were Craig and Linnea?

Using Your Journal

Whether or not you are dating, you probably have some thoughts on the subject. Use your journal to write about dating. What do you think are important qualities in a dating partner? What kinds of activities would you like to share with a date? What are some of your main concerns about dating? What can you do to deal with those concerns? When you have identified your concerns you may want to talk them over with a close friend or a trusted adult.

Thinking Critically

1. Answers will vary but may include the idea that you can get to know what kind of person you enjoy being with and would like for a permanent partner.
2. Answers will vary.
3. Answers will vary but may include the idea that it is not easy to tell someone you wish to end a relationship.

CHAPTER 15

Love and Commitment

Chapter Challenge

Resources. Refer to the Teacher's Classroom Resources box and Student Workbook for materials related to this chapter.

Look for These Answers...

- Describe the different types of love.
- Explain the difference between infatuation and love that lasts.
- What are the components of lasting love?
- Describe factors that affect partner selection.
- How do you determine readiness for commitment?

Look for These Terms...

- commitment to a relationship
- infatuation
- intellectual love
- mature love
- physical love
- proximity
- romantic love

Wilson watched his friend with interest. As he spoke, Lon's eyes flashed with excitement. There was emotion in his voice. At age seventeen the two young men were friends though they went to different schools.

"I'm crazy about her," Lon said. "She's fantastic. If you went to Central, you'd know what I mean. I'm in love without a doubt."

"How do you know?" Wilson asked. "The last time you were in love, it was over in three weeks. As I recall, you ended up in the battle of the century."

"Oh, but that was different. This time it's real. I feel it. Wait till you see her, Wil. Then you'll understand what I mean."

"Well, have you told her you love her?" Wilson asked. "How does she feel?"

"I . . . I will — eventually," Lon stammered, "but I have to get someone to introduce us first."

What Is Love?

Love is such a little word, but those four letters together have so many meanings. Love is the subject of songs, poetry, and movies. It has been called a "miracle" and credited with "making the world go round." Love helps to sell everything from perfume to pantyhose to pizza. Love appears on T-shirts, bumper stickers, and greeting cards. People claim to love restaurants, television shows, and even football teams. Is it any wonder that people sometimes get confused about what others mean when they talk about love?

Chapter Opener. Ask students to read the opening scenario to the chapter. Ask the following questions: Do you think Lon is really in love? Defend your answer. If Lon is not in love, then what is he actually feeling? How well does Wilson know his friend? Cite some examples to support your viewpoint.

Activity. Have students list titles of songs, books, movies, and television programs that have the word "love" in them. Does their list reflect people's interest in love? Does it show any inconsistencies or confusion over the term?

◆ Types of Love

There are many different types of love. The love you feel for your family, for example, differs from the love you feel for your friends. The affection of a big brother for a little sister is not the same as his love for his girlfriend. Love comes in many other forms, from a child's love for a puppy to an adult's love of country, from love of a favorite toy to love of ideals and causes. Learning about love is part of becoming a mature person.

Love goes through stages. A baby's first love is love of self. Babies cry when they need something and smile when their needs are met. Gradually, young children come to love their parents for taking care of them. Children develop love for their friends. Next comes love of a role model, often called "hero worship," as older children develop loving admiration for an adult who is thought to be ideal. When young teens are excited about being in love, they develop a "love of love." Many young people experience romantic love several times before they discover the kind that lasts.

◆◆◆

Defining Love

Since there are so many types of love, how do you define it? If you check the dictionary, you will find many definitions for the word "love." Each depends on what it is you are loving, the sea, basketball, your family, a friend, or that special person in your heart. If you talk about loving ice cream or apple pie, people understand what you mean. It is usually love for someone of the opposite gender that causes the most confusion, and this is the focus here.

Love is accompanied by a very complex set of emotions. Scientists have found a chemical in part of the brain that triggers a response to feelings of love. This means a giddy reaction to a special person in your life may be automatic, like a sudden flinch on hearing a loud noise.

It's hard to miss the signals of love. For Rochelle love was accompanied by feelings of lightheartedness. She also felt tenderness for Jack. She found herself singing in the shower and smiling for no apparent reason. When she was near Jack, she felt her heart racing. When she was not near him, he was often in her thoughts. If Jack was in high spirits, so was Rochelle. When he was troubled about something, she was bothered too.

People use the word "love" in many ways. Some speak of loving food or a special pet. How do you use this word?

Discussion. Most of this chapter is about love between people of opposite genders. Have students think about other kinds of love too. Ask them to compare the different kinds of love — between a parent and child, between siblings, and between friends.

Discussion. Ask students if they are familiar with the term "puppy love." Have them describe what this means.

The feelings associated with love are easy to recognize. Knowing whether or not the love will last is not so easy.

You may have all of the feelings described and still wonder, "Am I *really* in love?" The answer to this question probably doesn't matter unless you are entering a permanent relationship. Then it becomes critical. You need to know if what you feel is true love. You need to know whether or not it will last or just disappear in time.

◆◆◆

Infatuation

Infatuation (in-fach-uh-WAY-shun) is a love experience that is based on a sudden, intense attraction. The feelings are very real and very powerful. This is the kind of love that disappears in time. Infatuation can be pleasant or painful, depending on the attitude of the second person involved. Infatuated partners often make the mistake of playing up good qualities and ignoring the bad. They also focus on unimportant features, such as big brown eyes or cute dimples.

You've probably heard it said that "love is blind." Actually, infatuation is blind. While infatuated, people are in love with a dream they each hope the other will prove to be. Infatuation fades, along with the shine on the halo, as they begin to focus on shortcomings, such as insensitivity, selfishness, or a bad temper. When the gap between the dream and the real person becomes too wide, love is gone, and the relationship becomes merely a habit or a burden to unload.

Infatuation experiences may reach an even quicker end when couples face separation. The "absence makes the heart grow fonder" maxim yields to "out of sight, out of mind." Infatuation is not strong enough or deep enough to last when distance divides.

◆◆◆

Love That Lasts

True love is lasting love. Identifying it isn't always easy. Often people confuse it with infatuation. How can you tell whether the love you feel is the lasting kind? Although there are no guarantees, you can learn to recognize the components of lasting love.

Real love is more than just an emotion. It is a relationship that puts feelings into action.

Life Management Skills. Sometimes people experience intense crushes that are unrealistic, a student's feelings about a special teacher, for example. Ask students to offer suggestions on how a person might deal with such feelings so that they are not disruptive to his or her life.

Discussion. Ask students if they have ever watched a television soap opera for any period of time. Do they think the handling of love on the program resembled real life at all? Have them support their opinions with examples.

A Slice of Life

Nothing that Gail had ever experienced had hurt so much. At her lowest point, she felt that she would never get over it.

Gail had dated Luke for nearly a year. They were very close, and she thought they were in love. When he began to back away from their relationship, she tried to ignore the signs at first. Finally, he told her straight out that it was over. Gail remembered the cold feeling that overwhelmed her. She had cried. She wanted to plead with him to reconsider, but her pride kept her from it. If he didn't love her, there was little she could do to change that.

The first week without Luke was the hardest. Gail had trouble focusing on what she was supposed to do. Her thoughts were always on him. First she felt angry, wondering why he had done this to her. Then she just hurt. Each day, however, became a little easier. She put away the pictures and the mementos. Someday she might want to look at them again.

Then Gail started doing things with her friends. Thoughts of Luke were no longer painful. In fact, she began to see that she had learned a little about relationships and love. She would remember and use what she had learned.

As Luke slowly faded from her thoughts, Gail began to notice others. One young man at the community center always seemed to be nearby. "He's kind of nice," Gail thought.

Thinking It Through

- You probably recall that people often react to challenges in life with denial, anger, bargaining, depression, and acceptance. Where do you see evidence of these in Gail's reactions to losing Luke?
- Do you think experiences like Gail's are a necessary part of life? Defend your answer.
- Would you say that Gail and Luke were in love? Why or why not?

It means caring about another person so much that his or her health, happiness, and well-being are as important to you as your own, sometimes even more important. Real love also means:

- Give and take
- Sharing
- Understanding
- Strong affection
- Deep devotion
- Togetherness
- Respect
- Like
- Trust

Here is how one writer summarized the meaning of ideal love: "Love is patient and kind. It is never jealous, boastful, conceited, rude, or selfish. Love takes no offense and does not resent. Love finds no pleasure in the failings of others, but delights in the truth. Love is always ready to excuse, to trust, to hope, and to endure whatever happens." The apostle Paul recorded this version of love almost two thousand years ago.

Discussion. Ask students whether or not they think true love can happen only once in a lifetime.

Activity. Have students suggest additions to the above list of qualities that make up real love. Have them write their own definition of love.

Romantic love is one dimension of lasting love. It is displayed in many ways, such as enjoying simple pleasures together.

◆ Dimensions of Lasting Love

Love that lasts, sometimes known as **mature love**, has three dimensions. These are romantic, intellectual, and physical love.

Usually the first dimension to appear, **romantic love** involves getting to know and cherish all the wonderful things about a person. Love feelings are based on knowing the total person as well as loving the many good qualities and accepting those that are not so good.

Romantic love is the thoughtful and spontaneous side of love. It is the wildflower picked to go in her hair or the batch of brownies baked just for him. Romance is the ingredient that makes a love relationship unique. It is the feeling that can make raking leaves or washing dishes together a special moment. Romance is hand-holding, sweet nothings whispered, and flowers pressed between pages. Romantic love may be kept alive through thoughtful gestures and sharing time alone together.

It is important to remember that the feelings in a lasting love relationship may become less intense over time. If the love is real, this does not matter.

Intellectual love involves mutual respect, that is, valuing the beliefs, opinions, and life goals of the loved one. This is achieved through getting to know one another. Having long talks about subjects is important. Seeing each other in different real life experiences is also helpful. This means that couples need to see how the loved one reacts to boredom, crisis, and stress. Too often, limited dating experiences only show what a person is like in the most favorable of situations.

Intellectual love is the friendship side of love. It grows through companionship and communication. It is the basis of trust in the relationship. It is the long talks about everything, the daily letters written when one is away, and the shared laughter of inside jokes.

Discussion. Ask students if they think people can talk themselves into love.

Discussion. Ask students if they think males and females handle love relationships differently. Why or why not?

Physical love refers to the intimacies expressed by two people in love. It is based on an initial attraction, which is made stronger by romantic and intellectual love feelings. It is touching, kissing, and holding. It is the warm, secure feeling of being close, along with the excitement and passion of sexual intimacy. Physical love is based on a desire to make the loved one feel loved and needed, rather than on a desire for personal gratification.

◆◆◆

Telling the Difference

How can you tell the difference between infatuation and love that will last? Both seem very real when they happen. Remember that infatuation is based on only a few desirable traits, but lasting love knows and cares for a person as is.

SIDELIGHT

Is It Love?

It is not love when . . .

- It happens suddenly.
- You want or plan to change the person.
- Separation causes you to forget him or her.
- Thoughts are of your own needs and feelings.
- Feelings are based on one or two qualities of a person.
- You are too much in love to eat or work.
- Differences are ignored.
- You can't wait.
- It fades fast.

It is love when . . .

- It grows as two people get to know one another.
- You accept the person's faults.
- Feelings endure separation.
- You put the loved one's needs ahead of your own.
- Feelings are based on the total personality of the loved one.
- You work for your loved one, yourself, and your relationship.
- Problems are faced together.
- You are patient.
- It lasts!

◆◆◆

Physical love in a relationship is expressed in intimate ways.

Problem Solving. Sometimes people feel love for someone and the feelings are not returned. Ask students how such situations should be handled.

Infatuation is self-centered, but love is focused on the loved one. Infatuation leads to daydreams and lack of interest in real-life concerns, but love fosters ambition, hard work, and planning for the future. Infatuated people try to ignore problems, while people in love work to solve their problems together. Infatuation places major importance on the physical side of a relationship; love sees physical intimacy as a meaningful expression of feelings, not just a source of pleasure.

It takes time for differences between infatuation and lasting love to become apparent. Enduring love deepens as you get to know the person, while the infatuation of love-at-first-sight simply disappears upon closer inspection. This is why time is the only valid test of love.

The theory of proximity says partner choices are limited by your environment. Is there anything a person can do to widen his or her opportunities?

◆◆◆

How Love Develops

Love relationships tend to move through a series of stages:

1. An intense, sometimes unexpected attraction to a particular person develops.
2. A willingness to share deepest secrets surfaces.
3. Each partner looks to the other for support and encouragement in everyday living.
4. Each partner attempts to meet the emotional needs of the other.

When you think about stages, it is difficult to understand the widely used phrase, "falling in love." You may fall down the stairs, fall in the deep snow, or even fall into a trap, but love is not something you truly "fall" into. Love requires a sense of purpose in order to develop. Love needs to be built through self-control and sacrifice. Love must be nurtured and nourished in order to last.

Discussion. Ask students how this expression might relate to falling in love: "Time will tell."

◆◆◆

Partner Selection

"Don't they make an odd couple?"

"I wonder what she sees in him."

"I don't think they were made for each other."

All of these remarks show that the reasons for choosing a particular person to love are not always apparent to others. Why do people pick certain partners? There are several theories about what affects their choices.

◆ Proximity

The theory of **proximity** (prahk-SIM-ut-ee), or nearness, explains why people do not marry just anyone. Your place of residence, social setting, workplace, and other environment factors largely determine the people with whom you associate. This closeness to specific people filters out great numbers of potential partners, leaving you with relatively few choices.

◆ Opposites Attract

The theory that opposites attract is based on the idea that people look for partners whose qualities make up for gaps in their own personalities. The result is that people with different personalities may prove to be very compatible. Here are some examples:

- A high achiever may be compatible with a highly supportive person.
- A talkative person may be happy with a good listener.
- A dominant person may choose a partner who is easygoing and directable.
- A person who has trouble making up his or her mind may seek out someone who is a good decision-maker.
- A shy, uncertain person may look for a secure, assertive person.

Usually people are unaware that they are making a selection on this basis. At some point they may notice that they are attracted to people who complement them in this way. The advantage, of course, is that each person fulfills the unmet needs of the other. The disadvantage is that the differences could possibly lead to incompatibility.

◆ Similarities

Another theory says that you are most likely to match up with someone who is much like yourself in terms of age, race, religion, social group, education, and interests. This is because you will have more in common with people who have a similar background and experiences.

◆◆◆

Readiness for Commitment

A **commitment to a relationship** is a promise or pledge of loyalty to another person. Being ready for such a commitment requires the individual readiness of both partners as well as the readiness of the couple.

When individuals are ready for commitment, their personal life goals and priorities are not in serious jeopardy. These life goals include career plans, education goals, and family obligations.

Problems often arise when these areas are overlooked under the influence of overpowering feelings of love. The claim that "love conquers all" is actually a form of rationalization, an attempt to justify decisions made without sound reasons. The fact that so many relationships end unhappily may suggest that love is not the only requirement for a successful, lasting relationship. Individuals who sacrifice their careers or educational goals may later regret the marriage. Those who put other family obligations on hold in order to make a commitment to a loved one may find that resulting conflicts are not easily resolved.

People are more likely to pair up with someone who has similarities to them. For example, an educated person will probably choose someone who has a similar educational background.

Activity. Have students interpret in writing the following quotations: Shakespeare — "Love looks not with the eyes, but with the mind." Emerson — "Love is strongest in pursuit; friendship in possession."

The couple's readiness for commitment also depends upon the level of understanding reached in the relationship. This is based on time spent talking about important issues and sharing routine daily experiences. Asking yourself questions like these will help you determine if you are ready for a commitment:

- How does your loved one handle unpleasant situations?
- How does he or she react in an emergency?
- Can he or she handle a problem with patience and determination?
- How does she or he react to boredom, frustration, and hard work?
- Has your loved one seen you looking less than your best?
- Have you been together when one of you was sick, tired, or discouraged?

SIDELIGHT

Jealousy

Love is easily threatened when certain attitudes get in the way. Jealousy is one of these. When love is lasting and strong, jealous feelings subside. Both partners become confident that the love is real and will not end the minute another person walks on the scene.

When people feel insecure in a love relationship, they may show signs of jealousy. Louisa could not even speak to another young man without Alfredo getting upset. This was a constant problem for them and soon led to the end of their relationship. Living with jealousy in a committed relationship is very difficult. An insecure person may have some maturing to do in order to overcome this problem.

◆◆◆

Photo Focus. Have students look at the photo on this page. Ask them why couples should spend time together in ordinary activities before they take on a commitment.

There is a familiar saying that "when hardship comes in the door, love goes out the window." While this may sound like a cold and heartless view, it does stress the fact that love is not the only requirement for a lasting relationship. Love is important, but relationship readiness is also essential in order for a commitment to endure when troubles arise.

◆◆◆

Careful Commitment

As you can see, the road from love to commitment is affected by many factors, some of which you cannot easily control. There is much, however, that you can control. When you love someone and you are thinking about making a commitment, you need to take a close look at your potential partner. You will read more about what to look for later in this text.

Before people commit to each other, they should share some ordinary experiences together.

CHAPTER

15

Answers

Testing Your Memory

1. People use the word "love" in so many different ways that it is sometimes not clear what is actually meant, especially when talking about love between two people who are romantically linked.
2. **Any four:** family, friends, pets, country, possessions, ideals and causes, admiration for an ideal person, opposite gender.
3. Infatuation is a love experience that is based on a sudden, intense attraction. Although the feelings are real, they do not last.
4. The other person's health, happiness, and well-being are as important to you as your own, sometimes even more important.
5. Romantic love; intellectual love; physical love.
6. Infatuation is based on only a few desirable traits, but lasting love knows and cares for a person as is. Infatuation is self-centered, but love is focused on the loved one. Infatuation leads to daydreams, lack of interest in real life, but love fosters ambition, hard work and planning for the future. Infatuation is more physical. Time is the best test for distinguishing between infatuation and real love.

Summarizing the Chapter

- The word "love" is used in many different ways.
- There are many kinds of love, everything from love of food to the love for a special person in your heart.
- Infatuation and love are not the same thing.
- Determining whether or not love will last is not easy. You must look at the relationship carefully and give it the test of time.
- People choose partners from those they associate with. Often they choose people who complement them in personality or who have similar backgrounds and experiences.
- Careful thought must go into making a commitment to a relationship.

Testing Your Memory

1. Why is the word "love" confusing to people?
2. List four examples of different types of love.
3. What is infatuation?
4. When you love someone, how do you feel about that person's health, happiness, and well-being?
5. What are the three dimensions of lasting love?
6. How can you tell the difference between infatuation and lasting love?
7. Explain how love develops.
8. Why do opposites often attract?
9. What is a commitment to a relationship?

Thinking Critically

1. How long do you think it takes to determine whether or not love is the lasting kind?
2. Rank the three dimensions of lasting love in order of importance as you see it. Defend your answer.
3. How do crushes and infatuation help prepare people for real love?

Taking Action

1. Listen to others for one day and observe how often they use the word "love." Write a paragraph that summarizes your observations.
2. Write five questions a person should be able to answer in order to determine whether or not love is real.
3. Look up quotations that deal with love. Explain what they mean in your own words and evaluate their truth.

Making Life Choices

Dominick is obsessed with thoughts of a particular movie star. He cannot get her out of his mind. A year ago he started writing letters to her, explaining his love for her. More and more of Dominick's time and energy seem to be spent on this obsession each day. As Si sees what is happening to his friend, he is becoming very concerned.

What do you think about Dominick's thoughts and actions? Is this situation reaching the point of concern? What would you do if you were Dominick and Si?

Using Your Journal

Have you ever thought you were in love, and then realized that it was a case of infatuation? Use your journal to record your thoughts about love. Think about love relationships you have observed. What kinds of things give pleasure? What causes pain? At the end of your journal entry write the phrase "I'll know I am in love when . . ." Complete the phrase as many times as you wish. Be sure to return to this page in your journal when you think you are in love!

7. Love develops after an initial attraction moves into a sharing of feelings. Each partner looks to the other for support, encouragement, and the meeting of emotional needs.
8. Opposites may attract because they find something in the other that makes up for the gaps in their own personalities.
9. A commitment to a relationship is a promise or pledge of loyalty to another person.

Thinking Critically

1. Answers will vary.
2. Answers will vary.
3. Answers will vary. Point out that learning how you feel when love does not turn out to be real can help you recognize what real love is.

CHAPTER

16

Sexuality in Relationships

Chapter Challenge

Resources. Refer to the Teacher's Classroom Resources box and Student Workbook for materials related to this chapter.

Look for These Answers . . .

- What is the difference between the terms "sex" and "sexuality"?
- Describe how the five areas of development relate to sexuality.
- What are the risks of sexual involvement?
- Describe the sexually transmitted diseases and explain their hazards.
- How can people take responsibility for their sexual behavior?
- How can sexual desire be controlled?

Look for These Terms . . .

- AIDS
- abstinence
- chlamydia
- genital warts
- gonorrhea
- genital herpes
- HIV
- sex
- sexuality
- sexually transmitted disease
- sterility
- syphilis

Ross sat down on the back steps, reluctant to go inside. Head in hands, he sat as the wind whipped through the trees and thunder cracked the silence of the hot summer night. Ross's thoughts were just as unsettled. He was barely aware of the storm brewing around him.

"What are we going to do?" he wondered. "I didn't think Shelly would get pregnant — not after only one time. Actually, I guess I didn't even think. Someday I'd like kids, but at seventeen? What about school? What about my plans for the future?"

As Ross sat there, he thought about his conversation with Shelly. "I guess I could have an abortion," she had said to him with tears in her eyes. Ross shuddered at the thought. Was that what they wanted? Ross pondered their other options. They could get married, but they weren't really ready for that. Although they cared for each other, they were a long way from love and commitment. They could give the baby up. Ross swallowed hard at the realization of how difficult that would be. There was no easy answer.

The minutes ticked by as Ross sat thinking. No answer would come tonight. "We can't make the decision alone anyway," he said to himself. He had to face up to that thought. Ross stood to walk into the house where his family was gathering for dinner.

What Is Sexuality?

This chapter is not about sex; it's about sexuality. There is a difference. The word **"sex"** is often used just to mean intercourse. The word **"sexuality"** has a broader meaning. It is not just an action; it is much more.

When thinking about sexuality, you must consider your self-image and behavior as a male or a female. Sexuality includes more than just the physical aspects of your development. It involves the other areas of development too — intellectual, emotional, social, and moral. Each of these has an effect on how you handle yourself sexually. When you have a mature approach to sexuality, you take all of these into consideration.

Knowledge is your ally in all aspects of life, sexuality included. Learn all you can from reliable sources so that you make informed decisions.

Chapter Opener. Ask students to read the opening scenario to the chapter. Ask the following questions: What did Ross mean when he said, "I guess I didn't even think"? How will the lives of Ross and Shelly change because of what has happened? How do you think Ross and Shelly will go about making the decision they face?

Discussion. Ask students why some people find it difficult to talk about sexuality in a serious manner.

◆ Physical Maturity

Physical maturity begins with the changes brought on by puberty. The production of hormones triggers body changes that transform boys into young men and girls into young women. Male and female reproductive systems begin to activate, to prepare for the functions of fertilization, pregnancy, and childbearing. While changes usually begin during the early teen years, the body often does not achieve a balance in reproductive functions until several years later. For this reason, sexual activity in young teens often leads to infections and early pregnancies with frequent complications.

When you don't make decisions based on values that are important to you, you may have regrets.

◆ Intellectual Maturity

When you are intellectually mature as far as sexuality is concerned, you have the knowledge and understanding you need. Becoming informed about sexual functions and body processes is essential. This includes understanding the male and female reproductive processes and having knowledge of birth control, sexually transmitted diseases, and other risks. Misinformation received from peers and other sources is responsible for many sex-related disasters among teens.

◆ Emotional Maturity

To handle your own sexuality properly, you need a clear self-image and a strong sense of self-esteem. Unfortunately, many teens seek sexual relationships as a way of feeling needed. Because they want to feel that someone really cares and accepts them as they are, they take the risks that are associated with being sexually active. Sadly, many promises of true and undying love are quickly forgotten after sexual intimacy is experienced.

◆ Social Maturity

Sexuality means more than just a concern for yourself. You must think of others as well. This is part of maturing socially. The socially mature person thinks of more than just self-gratification. The well-being of others is also important. Social maturity means asking questions like these: How will my actions affect others? Could pregnancy occur and, if so, can I take responsibility for the child? Am I free of sexually transmitted diseases that might be passed on to another? Will my actions affect any others, such as family and friends, in any way?

Discussion. Ask students if they have ever heard people give incorrect sexual information to others. In what ways was this information wrong? Could it have lead to problems for the people involved?

Problem Solving. Sometimes people become sexually active in order to make up for a lack of loving attention in their personal lives. Ask students what a person might do to satisfy this need without running the risks involved with early sexual involvement.

Discussion. Ask students why sex without love is often damaging to a person's self-esteem.

◆ Moral Maturity

Moral maturity means that you are doing what you know is right. If you are confused about this, you need to get your thoughts clearly together. Remember that even when others choose to be sexually active, that does not make it right for you — or for them. Many people rely on religious training, parental values, and their own sense of personal worth to help them make decisions. Relying on your conscience can help prevent guilt feelings and regrets.

◆◆◆

Understanding Differences

Just as people vary in their physical appearance, they also differ sexually. For example, sex drives are not the same for everyone. For some people the differences go beyond this.

Most people are heterosexual. They desire sexual relationships with the opposite gender. Homosexuals desire same-gender sexual relationships. There is no clearcut explanation for why some people are homosexual. It may be that the reasons are complex and not the same for every individual.

In general, homosexuals differ little from anyone else, except for their sexual preferences. Some do seek support from counselors and physicians if they feel the need. Others are comfortable with themselves and live ordinary lives similar to everyone else.

◆◆◆

Risks of Sexual Involvement

A mature person who understands sexuality knows that risky behaviors are not good for you. Those who choose sexual involvement take risks. Often they pay a heavy price.

◆ Self-Esteem

Many who are sexually active sacrifice self-esteem. Meg had always wanted to save sex for a loving, committed relationship. She did not stick by her plan, however. This made her feel used and disappointed in herself. Lennie had a similar goal that he let go. Afterwards he had low feelings about himself and the way he had taken advantage of others.

◆ Pregnancy

Pregnancy is, of course, an obvious risk for the sexually active. The high teen pregnancy rate points to the fact that many disregard this risk. When they do, they severely reduce their chances to be self-supporting and successful in life. Their actions also affect others, especially the children they bring into the world.

Teens with high self-esteem are able to stick by their convictions. They can communicate their feelings to others.

More About Pregnancy. When pregnancy occurs, the responsibility lies with both partners. Even if a male does not parent the child, he is still responsible for support of that child. How he feels about the mother and child and his financial status are irrelevant. Laws now allow an employer to take child support payments from a paycheck or deduct them from an income tax return when a father is reluctant to pay.

◆ Health Risks

Health risks cannot be overlooked. Sexually transmitted diseases are serious indeed. A **sexually transmitted disease** (STD) is a communicable disease that is spread from one person to another through sexual contact. STDs claim millions of new victims each year. Most of these are adolescents. There are ways to control and prevent the spread of STDs, but the rates are increasing steadily.

Who is at risk? Anyone who is sexually active can contract an STD. Those who are even more at risk include people who begin having sex early, those who have multiple sex partners, those who experiment with alcohol, drugs, or sex, and those who find themselves in social situations that they cannot handle. Perhaps the greatest risk is for teens who believe that they are young and healthy and that none of these diseases will happen to them. Some think they know how to take care of themselves and are tough; they are kidding themselves! Here are the facts about the sexually transmitted diseases that threaten people today.

Anybody who is sexually active can get a sexually transmitted disease. Young healthy teens are particularly at risk because they tend to think they are invulnerable.

More About Teen Pregnancy. For additional information about teen pregnancy, you may wish to refer to Chapter 23.

◆ HIV and AIDS

HIV is an abbreviation for *human immunodeficiency virus*. That is the virus that causes the disease known as AIDS. **AIDS** is an abbreviation for *acquired immunodeficiency syndrome*. AIDS is a deadly disease that interferes with the body's ability to fight infection. There is no vaccine to prevent HIV infection, and there is no cure for AIDS.

People who become infected with HIV may experience no symptoms for many years. (During that time, however, they can infect others with the virus.) Over time, the virus will attack their body's immune system. As the immune system weakens, it becomes unable to fend off diseases that will eventually cause death.

HIV is spread from one person to another in body fluids — blood, semen, and vaginal secretions. Most people contract the virus during intimate sexual contact, or as a result of sharing needles to inject drugs. Some people have also contracted HIV as a result of blood transfusions in which they were given contaminated blood. New screening methods now protect people from this source of infection. Finally, HIV-infected women who become pregnant can pass the virus to their unborn child. HIV is *not* spread through kissing, hugging, or casual contact with an infected person.

It is difficult to know how many teens are infected with HIV. Most often AIDS strikes people in their twenties and above. However, ten years or more can go by between HIV infection and the appearance of AIDS symptoms. That means that many of the adults who have AIDS today contracted it when they were teens.

There are two sure ways of avoiding HIV infection. First, avoid all sexual contact. Second, avoid illegal drugs, especially drugs that involve needles. Remember that you have no way of knowing if a person is infected with HIV. In the early stages of HIV infection there are no visible symptoms; the only way of knowing if a person is infected is through a blood test.

A Slice of Life

At age twenty-eight Ruth was devastated by the report from her physician. She had not been feeling well for a long time. Of everything that could be wrong with her, she had never expected AIDS.

"How?" she asked the doctor. This just did not happen to people like her. As they talked about her sexual history, the answer became clearer. There was one young man when she was seventeen. She had not known him well. In fact, she had trouble even remembering his name. He was older and had been in and out of her life very quickly. Ruth thought that they had only been together once or twice.

Now eleven years later he was returning to her life in a way that she never dreamed would happen. All these years she had lived a normal life, never realizing that a time bomb of sorts was waiting to go off inside her. Eventually it did, and now time was precious to Ruth. She did not know how much she had left.

Thinking It Through

- Could Ruth have determined eleven years ago that the young man had AIDS or was a carrier of the virus?
- What mistake did Ruth make?
- Is it safe to take the attitude, "It won't happen to me"?

More About STDs. STDs are a particular threat to young adults. About 85% of all STD cases involve people in the age range of 15-30. The teenage population has the highest rate of increase.

More About AIDS. People do not actually die of AIDS. They die of infections that would not have had a chance to do any damage to the body if the immune system were healthy.

Chlamydia

Chlamydia (kluh-MID-ee-uh) is a bacterial STD that poses a serious threat to teenagers. Chlamydia may be difficult to diagnose, since its symptoms are typical of several other possible conditions. Females with chlamydia may feel pain in the abdomen, nausea, and have a low fever. Males experience a discharge from the penis or painful urination. Without treatment, chlamydia can spread throughout the reproductive system. In women, it can cause pelvic inflammatory disease (PID) — a painful infection that can lead to **sterility** (stuh-RILL-uh-tee), the inability to have children.

Genital Warts

Genital warts are small growths found on the male and female genitalia. These may cause discomfort and itching. A few small warts are usually not dangerous, but when allowed to keep growing, they may produce blockages of body openings.

Genital Herpes

Genital herpes (HUR-peas) is a painful STD that produces blisters and sores in the genital region. These symptoms go away after two or three weeks. However, the virus that causes the disease remains in the body and the symptoms may recur from time to time.

Genital herpes can be passed from one person to another during sexual contact when the symptoms are present. A person may also be contagious before the symptoms appear and after they have gone. That means that a person can spread the disease to a sex partner without knowing it. A pregnant woman can pass the disease to her baby during birth if the symptoms are present at the time of the birth.

At present there is no cure for genital herpes. Medications are available to relieve some of the symptoms.

More About STDs. A person can have more than one STD at a time. Different pathogens cause the diseases. When a person comes in contact with more than one of these, multiple STDs can develop.

Gonorrhea

Gonorrhea (gahn-uh-REE-uh) is caused by bacteria that live in moist, warm areas of the body, such as the male urethra lining and the female cervix. These bacteria are transmitted during sexual contact. Symptoms are difficult to pinpoint, as they may be slight or intermittent. A lab test is necessary for diagnosis of gonorrhea. Antibiotics are a safe and effective cure in most cases. Left untreated, gonorrhea can cause sterility, both in males and females, along with damage to the heart and other organs. It can also lead to PID.

Syphilis

Less common than gonorrhea, **syphilis** (SIF-uh-lus) is also caused by bacteria. Syphilis develops in three stages. The first symptom of syphilis is a red sore or inflammation found on the genitals. This sore is called a chancre and marks the place where the syphilis germ entered the body.

After the sore disappears in one to five weeks, the disease progresses to the second stage. The untreated syphilis germ travels into the bloodstream and causes a non-itching rash with sores, draining, and swelling. The victim may have a fever, sore throat, and feel sick all over.

In the third stage, usually two or more years after the infection first occurred, the symptoms described above disappear. The victim may feel well. Actually the germ is busy attacking the heart, blood vessels, and central nervous system. Organ tissue is destroyed. Damage proceeds slowly but steadily. The results may be blindness, insanity, or even death. When diagnosed, syphilis is usually best treated with penicillin. Early diagnosis is important, since nothing can be done to repair organ damage that has already occurred.

Other STDs

Several other STDs exist. Some are more serious than others, but they all require medical attention. Note that all the conditions described here can be transmitted through sexual contact, yet this is not the only way they can be acquired. Vaginitis is an inflammation of the female vagina, which causes a discharge and itching. Scabies, also called itch, is caused by tiny mites that burrow into the skin. Pubic lice are parasites that infest pubic hair. Small nits, or eggs, cause severe itching and may be eliminated with a special medicated shampoo and disinfection of clothing.

Couples who are sexually active risk contracting sexually transmitted diseases. Abstinence is the only safe alternative.

More About Syphilis. Syphilis may be passed to an unborn child by the mother. This is known as congenital syphilis because it exists from birth. Syphilis can develop in the unborn child after five months of pregnancy. Symptoms will develop in the child within three to four weeks after birth. If diagnosed early enough in the mother, penicillin treatment will usually protect the unborn fetus.

Avoiding STDs

The only absolute way to avoid STDs is by not having sexual intercourse. This is the only way to practice absolutely safe sex.

Those who are sexually active face additional risks if they fall into certain categories. First, young teens tend to be more prone to infection. Second, having multiple sex partners greatly increases the risk factor. Finally, spontaneous sex is usually unsafe sex, since no protection is available.

STD germs become better able to fight off the antibiotics designed to kill them. When treated early enough, most victims can recover from some STDs. At present there is no absolute cure for genital herpes or AIDS.

Treatment for STDs

It takes both good sense and courage to own up to having an STD. Some people deny the condition even when the signs are obvious. Seeking medical treatment can be embarrassing; however, ignoring an STD or attempting self-treatment is both foolish and dangerous. Anyone who suspects exposure should get an exam as soon as possible. Every county in the United States has a clinic where all residents can be tested and treated free of charge. Services are strictly confidential. To wipe out STDs, infected people must provide the name of the sex partner. In this way, public health officials can trace and treat the carriers of harmful diseases.

◆◆◆

Taking Responsibility

You see it all over — in many movies and magazines, on certain television programs, even in some of the music you hear. The enticement to become sexually active is everywhere. Before you accept their theme, however, ask yourself this: Who is more concerned about my well-being, me or the entertainment industry?

Anyone who has signs of an STD should seek the help of a physician.

Discussion. Ask students why people are often reluctant to seek treatment for an STD, yet they wouldn't hesitate to get help for a lung problem, injury, or stomach disorder.

Discussion. Have students answer the question at the end of the second column of text above. Ask them what motivates the entertainment industry to use the themes that they do. Do they think that real life is simple to portray in a show that lasts for only 30 minutes or an hour?

Pressure may also come from your peers. They may talk — and brag — about their experiences. Often this talk is not based on fact. They may use put-downs to convince you to do as they say they do. If you are secure, they won't be able to talk you into something you don't want to do.

Whether you are male or female, sexual responsibility concerns you. What does a female need to know? For one thing, your clothing and your attitude can be suggestive. Although he has no right to use this as an excuse, you can avoid trouble by watching how you conduct yourself. Remember that you never owe sex to a male. What he says and how much he spent on the date do not matter. You have the right and the responsibility to yourself to say "no."

What does a male need to know? You have no right to expect sex from a female for any reason. Pressuring her is irresponsible and just plain wrong.

◆ Abstinence

Responsible people understand the risks associated with sexual activity. They realize that a mistake made today can cost them heavily in the future. It may even cost them their life.

Responsible people care about themselves and about others. They make their decisions based on facts and careful thought. Many choose **abstinence** (AB-stuh-nuns), which is refraining from sexual intercourse. They recognize that this is the only sure way to protect themselves and others from sexually transmitted diseases and from unplanned pregnancy.

Choosing abstinence means learning to show affection without becoming sexually involved. A reasonable question follows. If abstinence is the answer, how do you handle the desires you feel?

A responsible male will not pressure a female to have sex. If he does, is he showing that he cares about her? How can he show respect for her?

Life Management Skills. Ask students to assume someone is trying to pressure them to become sexually involved. Have them list responses and behavior that would enable them to avoid yielding to the pressure.

Activity. Debate this statement in class: A female asks for sexual pressure from a male when she wears provocative clothing.

Get the Message?

This message . . .	equals . . . this message.
"If you love me, you will make love with me."	"I really want to have sex."
"If I withdraw fast enough, there's no way you can get pregnant."	"I want you to quit worrying so we can have a good time."
"Let me show you how much I love you."	"I'll say anything to get what I want."
"You're the only one for me."	"I want you to trust me so we can get closer."
"Everybody's doing *it*."	"I want you to feel bad about being different so you'll go along with me."
"If you're not ready for this, we can wait."	"I really care about you.
"Let's talk about the situation before we rush into anything."	"I want to be sexually responsible."

◆◆◆

Handling Desires

A basic part of your emerging sexuality is your growing sex drive. The human sex drive, when used safely and responsibly, improves the quality of life. When abused, it can cause personal disaster. Learning to handle it is part of the maturing process. Understanding it is the first step. Here are some facts that will help your understanding:

- The sex drive keeps the human race going. The basic facts about sex were true for your grandparents and will remain so for your grandchildren.
- The sex drive is a normal human function. All people share it no matter what their race, age, intelligence, or social group.

Photo Focus. Have students look at the photo on the previous page. Ask them how the young woman is showing assertiveness.

- Through romantic attractions, friendships, and physical encounters, the sex drive finds expression. It can be responsible for the writing and performance of creative work, such as poetry, music, and dance.
- The sex drive obeys the brain. Each person can control his or her sexual urges.
- Varying hormone levels from person to person determine the level of sex drive. As a result, some people have a greater desire for sexual expression.
- The sex drive develops according to individual experiences. Early training at home affects such factors as interest and direction. Children often follow the example of the adults they live with.
- The sex drive helps decide a person's total personality. As a result, sexual attitudes tend to match other traits. Those who are sensitive and thoughtful will be likely to act that way in their sexual exchanges.

As you know, adolescence is marked by dramatic physical changes, some of which are part of the sexual maturing process. Not only are males and females learning to understand their own feelings, but they must also try to understand those of the opposite gender. This is not always easy.

Emerging sexual feelings in the female tend to center around a desire for affection and warmth. For males the feelings are often stronger, creating a desire for physical expression. Do you see the potential for problems here? If closeness and tenderness are shared by a male and female, this may be satisfying to her while intensifying his feelings. The couple then find themselves in a tough situation. How can he manage the desire to pressure her? How can she handle pressure as well as her own emotions?

Discussion. Ask students if they can add anything to the chart above. Why is it important to be able to understand the true meaning of a person's words?

For Maureen and Leon their moments alone always turned into a struggle. She liked being close to him, but it always led to pressures from him to go all the way. She resisted, although sometimes she didn't really want to. She was confused by her mixed feelings. He said she worried too much, but she thought she had good reasons to. Possible pregnancy was just one. In time Leon and Maureen began to realize that something had to change.

Like many others Maureen and Leon must look for ways to handle their desires. It may not be easy, but there are some things that can help.

- Make an agreement with yourself and each other that your relationship will not include sexual intercourse. Have a plan in mind for what to do if necessary. Write this down and put it in a special place — perhaps a diary or a favorite book.
- Avoid tempting situations. In other words, don't spend time alone in the house or car or anywhere else, for that matter. Go places with other couples and plan activities that keep you busy. You might not have the money to go out, but you can still invite others in and plan a games night or watch a video together. There will be less pressure this way.
- Channel your energy elsewhere. Becoming involved in a sport, hobby, or volunteer activity that interests you can give you a focus that will help balance your life.

I CAN ◆◆◆ Be Responsible

When Miles saw what happened to his friend, he knew that his own approach to sexuality was better.

"My friend always bragged about his conquests. He is older than I am, so I kind of looked up to him, but not anymore.

"Lowell got a girl pregnant. She wanted to marry him, but he wasn't interested. She had the baby anyway and kept it, and now Lowell's paying support until his son grows up. He is trying to finish school and hold down a job in order to earn enough to make the support payments. Sometimes I think I should feel sorry for him, but I don't. I feel worse for his son. Lowell doesn't really care about him — or the girl he hurt.

"I could never do that to anyone. It's not that I don't want to have sex; it's just that I have to think ahead. I don't want to ruin my own future, and I don't want to ruin anyone else's either. I've got something to look forward to, and it will be worth waiting for."

- How does Miles' approach to sexuality differ from Lowell's?
- How did the young woman's life change after her relationship with Lowell?
- Why do people act without thinking about the consequences, both to themselves and others?
- Do you have a responsible attitude toward sexuality? What changes do you need to make in your thinking, if any?

Activity. Have students make a list of activities for couples who are dating but wish to avoid sexually tempting situations. Have them check community resources for possibilities. What activities could be planned that would not be costly?

Work and Family. When both parents (or a single parent) are employed, teens are likely to have more access to an empty house or apartment. Ask students what responsibility teens have in such cases.

When you plan activities with others, you will have fewer opportunities to get involved in sexually tempting situations.

◆◆◆

Looking for Commitment

A responsible approach to sexuality should include commitment. This means taking a mature and long-term view. A casual approach will only lead to disappointment and perhaps disaster. You cannot make someone love you, nor can you prove your own love, through sexual encounters. There must be other dimensions to your relationship.

Remember that a commitment cannot be here today and gone tomorrow. It cannot be one-sided when a relationship is involved. It cannot be reached quickly. It cannot be made without careful thought, communication, and agreement. Your approach to sexuality should include a commitment that is made with all of this in mind.

Activity. Ask students to write letters responding to the feelings of these teens: Kate — "Tad is everything I have ever wanted in a boyfriend. He wants me to prove that I love him by having sex with him. I don't want to lose him." Dave — "I want to feel mature. Some of my friends have had sex already. Maybe if I had sex with someone too, I would feel more like a man." Ivan — "Sometimes I just feel angry, at my family and everyone else. I feel like having sex just to vent some of my frustrations." Michelle — "I want to get pregnant. That way my boyfriend won't be able to leave me."

CHAPTER 16

Review

Summarizing the Chapter

- Sex and sexuality are not the same thing.
- Sexuality includes all areas of development, physical, intellectual, emotional, social, and moral.
- When people ignore the risks associated with sexual activity, they are turning their backs on their own futures.
- Sexually transmitted diseases can be easily avoided by practicing abstinence.
- Taking responsibility for your sexuality means resisting pressures, not applying pressure, and learning to handle desire.
- Commitment is part of a responsible approach to sexuality.

Testing Your Memory

1. Explain the difference between the terms "sex" and "sexuality."
2. List three risks connected with sexual activity.
3. How is HIV passed from one person to another?
4. Why is chlamydia difficult to diagnose?
5. Why is herpes easily spread?
6. Why does syphilis need to be diagnosed early?
7. Why are people with STDs asked to give the name of their sex partner?
8. Describe what responsibilities males and females have concerning sexuality.
9. List three things people can do to help handle their desires.

Answers
Testing Your Memory

1. The word "sex" is often used just to mean intercourse. "Sexuality" has a broader meaning that includes your self-image and behavior as a male or female plus the way you handle yourself sexually in all areas of development.
2. Self-esteem may be sacrificed. Pregnancy may occur. Health risks in the form of STDs are possible.
3. HIV is passed from one person to another in body fluids during intimate sexual contact or as a result of sharing needles used for drugs.
4. The symptoms of chlamydia are similar to other possible conditions.
5. Many infected victims show no symptoms and spread the disease without even knowing it.
6. Nothing can be done to repair damage to organs once it occurs.
7. In order to trace the disease and treat the carriers.
8. Females need to watch the attitude they convey to others through dress and actions. They do not owe sex to a male and have the responsibility to say "no." Males have no right to expect sex from females for any reason. Pressuring is wrong.

Thinking Critically

1. In a relationship, who should make the decision to say "no" to sex, the male or female? Defend your answer.
2. What are the advantages of abstinence?
3. Will giving in to sexual pressure help you keep a relationship going? Defend your answer.
4. What effect do you think the music that young people listen to has on sexual activity?
5. Do you think females ever pressure males to have sex? Why or why not?

Taking Action

1. Do research to find out more about one STD. Present your findings to the class.
2. Look up the word "promiscuous" in the dictionary. Make a list of problems this behavior can cause.
3. Write a pledge for teens that promotes abstinence.

Making Life Choices

On Saturday nights Yvette often has the apartment to herself. Her mother and stepfather are usually out and so is her older brother. Yvette's boyfriend usually comes over, and they watch television together. They have been dating for several months and are becoming closer all the time.

Do you see any possibility for trouble in this situation? What is it? What would you do if you were Yvette?

Using Your Journal

As you have just read, sexual activity carries many risks. Use your journal to list the risks you face if you become sexually active. Then write about the actions you can take to avoid those risks — and to avoid affecting other people negatively. If you have a close relationship with someone, talk about the things you write in your journal. By communicating about these important issues you and your partner can agree on standards of behavior that protect you both.

9. Make an agreement with yourself and partner ahead of time to not include sexual intercourse in your relationship. Avoid tempting situations. Channel your energy elsewhere.

Thinking Critically

1. Answers will vary, but encourage students to see that this should be a shared responsibility.
2. Answers will vary but may include no decisions to make about sex or contraception, no concern about pregnancy or STDs, and satisfaction in making a major life decision.
3. Answers will vary. Point out that a lasting relationship is not based on sex alone.
4. Answers will vary.
5. Answers will vary.

Beverly reaches out to peers about responsible sexuality.

Beverly

"I think teens need to discuss sexuality among themselves in order to make responsible choices. Not long ago I became a member of a hospital's Teen Services Program. I visit schools in our area and talk with students about the basics of human sexuality — and tell them why I believe they should postpone sexual involvement. We talk about the issues, such as the soaring teen pregnancy rate and sexually transmitted diseases. I want people to consider the consequences *before* making their choices. There's too much peer pressure on our age group to be sexually active. I'm just trying to get some of the pressure off."

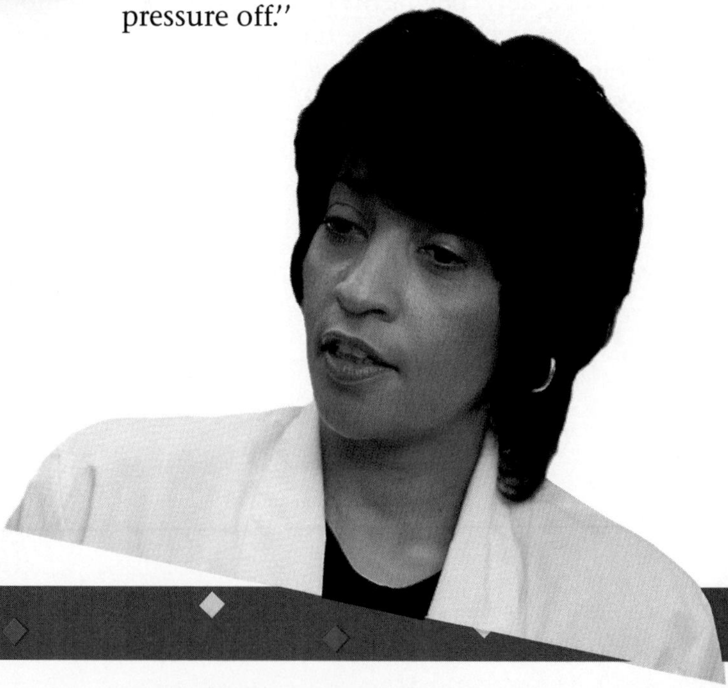

Marion Dunne "When I started the Teen Services Program at our community hospital, I hoped to find teens who'd feel at ease talking to their peers about sexuality. Frankly, I wasn't sure I'd find them, so I was delighted when Beverly volunteered to join the program. Her desire to work hard and her concern for others were very impressive. I knew her warmth and sincerity would help her reach others effectively. In fact, we've asked her to accept a part-time salary and be a leader of our teen staff. By reaching out, she gets others to think before they act. That's a lot to be able to do for people."

Leona Tyson "It didn't surprise me when Beverly told us what she was planning to do. At home my daughter and I had always had open discussions about sexuality. My husband and I have encouraged her to think issues through. Beverly's ability to talk to others comfortably and honestly is pretty special. If she can use this ability to help others, I think that is wonderful."

Zack "Beverly came to talk to our class. At first some of us were reluctant to talk about sexuality, but her knowledge and friendly attitude broke the ice. By the end of class, we were all raising our hands to ask questions and give opinions. Even the ones who didn't seem to care got part of the message. I could see it sinking in. It's really incredible when someone you don't even know makes an impact on your life like that."

You can make a difference too.

- How does peer pressure affect teen dating?
- What are qualities or traits that make for positive interpersonal relationships?
- Are you likely to talk to someone else about sensitive issues? Why or why not?
- Is there anything you could do to help others make responsible decisions about their sexuality?

UNIT 5

What About Single Life?

CHAPTER

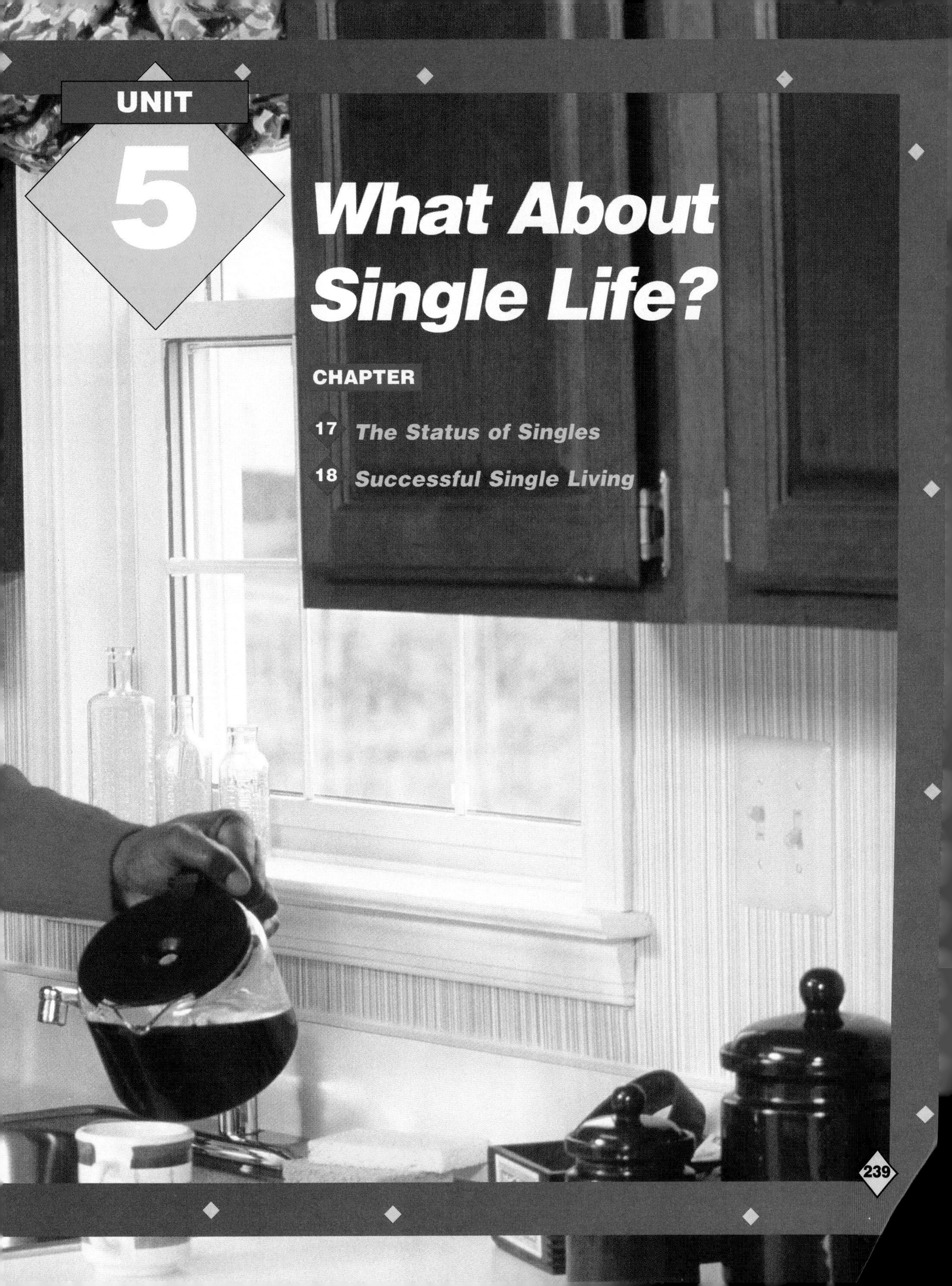

CHAPTER

17

The Status of Singles

Chapter Challenge

Resources. Refer to the Teacher's Classroom Resources box and Student Workbook for materials related to this chapter.

Look for These Answers . . .

- For what reasons do people live the single lifestyle?
- Describe the patterns of single living.
- How has the image of singlehood changed over the years?

Look for These Terms . . .

- delayed marriage
- family nest
- singlehood
- single living patterns

"Miguel, do you want to take this chair with you?" Mrs. Ortega called out. "We never use it, and you're going to need something to sit on."

Miguel was leaving home for the first time. It was hard to believe that graduation was behind him now. The day he had thought about so often was here at last. Then why did he feel so strange inside?

"Are you sure you don't need the chair? I'll only take it if you don't really want it." Miguel looked at his mother, suddenly realizing that she would no longer be close by. He longed to be independent, but part of him was resisting a little.

In a few hours Miguel would be in another town, living in a small apartment. He had taken a job and was enrolled in night classes at a technical school. Miguel tightened the rope over the bed of the truck. Everything was packed and ready to go.

"One last hug, Mama," Miguel said as he put his arms around his mother's shoulders.

"Now you be sure and eat right, do you hear?" she said to him. Miguel was her baby, and he was the last to leave home. When he was gone, she would be alone.

"I will, Mama," Miguel replied. "You know I never miss a meal. I'll call you when I get there."

As Miguel drove away, he took one last glance back at the apartment building where his mother still stood waving. He knew there was adventure ahead for him. He knew he had important decisions to make. He was on his own now and he would make it. Miguel's eyes focused on the road ahead.

Chapter Opener. Have students read the scenario at the beginning of the chapter. Ask the following questions: Do all young people experience feelings similar to Miguel's when leaving home? Why? What feelings do you think parents experience when their children leave? How will Mrs. Ortega's single-living experience compare to Miguel's? What do you think about living on your own in the future?

The Single Lifestyle

Few people go through life without living as a single at one point or another. For some, single living is a choice. For others, living without a marriage partner, or **singlehood**, results for different reasons.

For Miguel the thought of single living is exciting. He does not know how long he will be single. If marriage and a family are in his future, they are far enough ahead that he doesn't even think about them. For now, he must concentrate on building a future for himself.

For Mrs. Ortega single living means two things — a sense of freedom from responsibility but also a feeling of emptiness. She has not been alone for many years. It will be a new experience for her.

Singleness may last for a brief time, a prolonged one, or the total span of adulthood. A person without a partner may be never-married, separated, divorced, or widowed. The percentage of single people in the population has steadily increased over the years. Social changes have resulted in new single situations and new ways of looking at single living.

Many singles enjoy living in their own place and arranging it in their own style.

◆◆◆

Reasons for Single Living

Think about the single people you know. What decisions and circumstances have led them to single living? People live as singles for many different reasons. No matter who you are or what you plan, chances are you will be single for at least some portion of your life. When you think of the many reasons for singlehood, you can see why.

◆ Choosing Independence

Many singles enjoy the freedom of their lifestyle. They want to be independent, some for awhile, some for a lifetime. They can come and go as they wish without having to answer to anyone else. Time is available for personal interests. Single living provides a chance for personal development. For young singles it is a time to learn how to be self-supporting and adjust to leaving home. For some people singlehood is simply a preference.

Discussion. Have students share examples about single siblings or friends they know. How would they describe the single person's lifestyle? Is he or she content being single? What advantages do students see in being single? Disadvantages?

◆ Career Opportunities

As a legislator in his state, Seth has devoted himself to his career. He feels that public service is very rewarding. His single lifestyle gives him the freedom he wants to develop his career.

For some people, a career is all the challenge they need. They have a special dedication to their work. Such people often make important contributions to their communities and to society in general.

Many career-minded singles appreciate flexibility. They can move and change jobs as needed or desired. Without strong ties, relocation is easier.

◆ New Conditions for Women

At one time women were dependent on men for their livelihood. Without a link to a man, economic survival was difficult. Even today many women struggle to make it on their own. Still, improvements have been made. Due to better educational and career opportunities, many women do have the means to support themselves. As a result,

Some careers are very time-consuming and work well with a single lifestyle.

Discussion. Have students explore the changes in women's roles in society. Ask students how new conditions for women benefit both men and women in relationships.

I CAN ◆◆◆ Plan for Singlehood

Some people realize what the future can hold because of what has occurred in their own families. This is what happened to Donna Jean:

"My father died suddenly when I was twelve years old. My brother was six. My mother had been a school teacher before she married, but she had let her certificate lapse. She needed about two years of coursework to teach again. Since we needed money for the basics, my mother took a job as a nurse's aid. The pay was low and we struggled to get by. Today my mother might have been able to get some financial assistance while taking the courses she needed. Back then there weren't any programs like that where we lived. I was always proud of the way my mother kept us going, but I wish she had had some better opportunities.

"Because of that experience, I am determined to be prepared for whatever is ahead for me in life. I plan to get an education and some training that I can always fall back on. Some of my friends don't even worry about the future, but I know better. What happened to my mother taught me a lesson that I'll never forget."

- Why do you think Donna Jean's mother did not prepare for the future?
- Why is Donna Jean determined to be prepared for her future?
- Have you ever learned a lesson in life because of something that happened to a friend or family member? What was that lesson?

women feel less pressure to find a man to take care of them. Marriage can be chosen for reasons other than economic necessity. Thus, women are more likely to remain single, at least for awhile.

Lurleen displays the confidence and independence of such women today. A generation ago she would have been thinking about finding a husband. Today she speaks for many young women with a different perspective. "I don't want to be held back because I'm a woman or because I'm black. People should be free to move ahead and not get stuck with the rules from the past. For me a career is important. I need to know that I can take care of myself no matter what happens. My mother found herself single at age twenty-eight, with three kids to raise, and no job

Activity. Have students make a list of five goals for their future. Ask them how these goals might be affected by a family or personal crisis.

Many women today have incomes that enable them to be self-supporting. This was not always true in the past.

Photo Focus. Ask students to carefully examine the above photo. Have them brainstorm a list of nontraditional careers for women and men. Do singles have more freedom to choose nontraditional careers? Why or why not?

skills. It was tough. That's not going to happen to me."

◆ Delayed Marriage

For the majority of people, singleness is temporary. Marriage is ahead for them, but statistics show that they are waiting longer than they used to before marrying. **Delayed marriage** is evidenced by the rising median age of marriage for individuals. Young people postpone marriage for different reasons.

Some are looking for financial stability first. They are not willing to step into marriage and parenthood without knowing how they are going to support a family. Some feel they need to learn how to handle finances on their own first.

Jay is fresh out of college and starting a new career. "I'm finally on my own and no longer dependent on my parents for financial support. I'm free to spend my money the way I want to. Sure, I have responsibilities, like rent and school loans, but for the most part, I can pick and choose how to save and spend. Saving is real important right now. I would like to own some property in the future. Living on my own has made me realize that I need to examine my spending carefully and establish some priorities in my life."

Many young people prefer to have some time for single living before they marry. This enables them to socialize with others and make better decisions about a marriage partner.

Studies have found that women are less likely to marry as their incomes increase. The better able they are to support themselves financially, the better their options are in choosing a lifestyle.

For men, the higher the pay, the greater the chances of marriage. Because men's salaries have generally decreased over the last decade, men often do not feel they earn enough to support a family. Thus, many males postpone the decision of marriage, hoping for a time when they will be better off financially.

Marriage is also delayed so that people can experience life in ways that are not as easy once you have family responsibilities. Kathleen spent two years in Europe in her early twenties.

"My parents were a little scared when I told them what I was planning. I lived in Europe and found jobs here and there to make my way. It was wonderful. I saw sights and met people that I won't forget for as long as I live. I know this wouldn't be for everyone, but I had to do it when I knew I could. I always planned to marry and have a family, but I'm more ready for that now."

Marriage may be delayed, or even rejected, because a person fears divorce. As Walt says, "I've seen too many of my good friends have unsuccessful marriages. I want to take my time developing a relationship. If and when I marry, I want it to last." Many single people, like Walt, feel the same way. They value close relationships and want to make the right choices.

Discussion. Have students develop a list of reasons why some individuals delay marriage. Then ask them to describe the pros and cons of delayed marriage. Ask students to respond to this statement: "I'd rather be single and happy most of the time than married and miserable." Is this a valid statement made by many singles? Why or why not?

◆ Divorce

Some people are single due to divorce. They handle this in different ways depending on the circumstances. Devon's divorce came as a shock to him. He had to spend some time adjusting to single living. For Cherie divorce came as a relief. Leaving an abusive husband gave her a new lease on life. Mattie's divorce complicated her life. She was left as a single parent with no income. Parting seemed best for Carter and Hillary. They married young because of infatuation, not love. They both welcomed single living.

For all of these individuals divorce was not easy, nor was it anticipated when they first married. Few people plan that they will eventually be single due to divorce. Statistics show, however, that for many this will be the case.

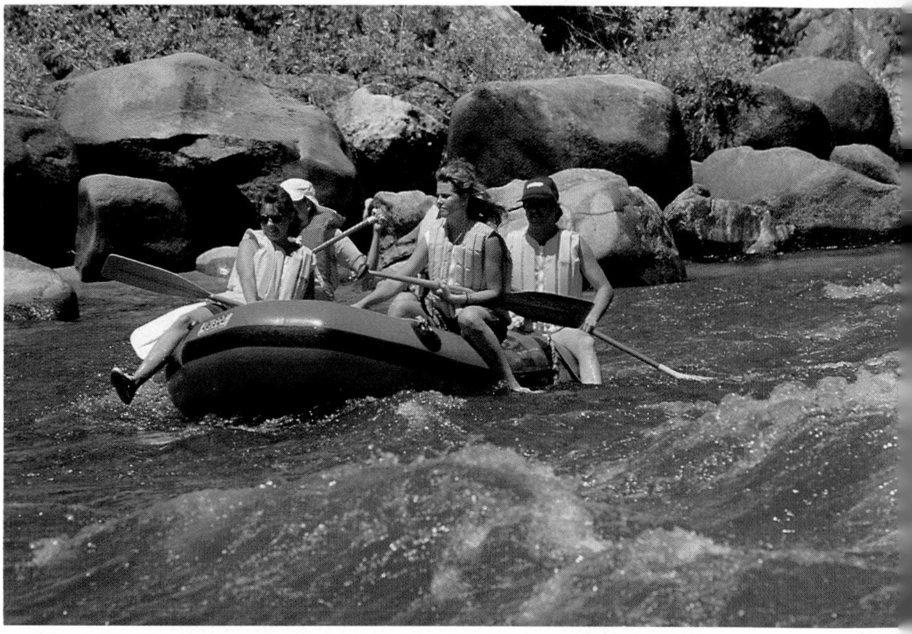

Single living enables a person to do things that are not as easily done when one has family responsibilities. Is there anything you yearn to do while you have the freedom?

◆ Emotional Pain

Even emotions affect a person's attitude about staying single. One who has been hurt in a love relationship may want to avoid similar pain again. Staying single feels safer.

◆ Finding a Partner

Many people remain single because they have not found someone they want to marry. Mr. or Ms. Right simply does not show up. Most are not willing to make sacrifices just for the sake of marriage. A happy, healthy relationship is preferred to settling for the wrong partner. Some, however, set such high standards for a spouse that no one qualifies.

Sometimes people make little effort to find a spouse. In one study of nearly 500 single women, most said they wanted to get married; however, great numbers neither dated nor went out of their way to seek husbands. For women who would like a partner, the opportunities decrease with age. This is because women outnumber men in the population.

The search for a partner can be hampered in other ways — for males and females. Shyness, insecurity, and fear of rejection are a few conditions that can get in the way. People can overcome these if they work at it or seek help if needed.

◆ Family Ties

Some people remain single due to links with the family. If sick or dependent parents need help, a child may stay to take care of them. If a young person feels insecure about

Problem Solving. Using the above examples, have students respond to the following: Because Cherie escaped an abusive husband and Mattie was left a single parent, does this mean they should not become emotionally involved again? If someone is extremely hurt in a marriage, what steps can be taken to overcome fears of a relationship? Have students compile a list of qualities that make for responsible partners in marriage.

leaving home, he or she might not venture out alone. Sometimes children or parents do not want to give up the advantages of the present relationship.

As with every issue, there are positive and negative sides to this. When made willingly and with thought, such choices are fine. If not, other arrangements need to be made before the pattern is too difficult to alter.

◆ Widows and Widowers

When a spouse dies, the partner is thrust into singlehood. This can be a trying time. Adjustments must be made to the death while trying to manage a new lifestyle at the same time. Whether male or female, new skills may need to be learned. Doing the laundry and shoveling snow from the driveway are challenging jobs for people who have never done them before.

Since women tend to live longer than men, a woman is more likely to face widowhood than a man is to be a widower. A widow who loses her husband's income or pension may have economic difficulties.

Something as simple as doing the laundry can be difficult for someone who has never done it before.

Activity. After reviewing the "Reasons for Single Living" section, have students write a response to a letter from someone contemplating singlehood. Students should assume the role of "personal advice" columnist. They should explain the benefits of single life.

◆ Elderly

The number of elderly living on their own has increased dramatically. People are living longer today, which automatically increases that segment of the population. Different generations of a family no longer share a home the way they once did. Moving in with one's children is not always appealing or possible. Some elderly people stay by themselves, often in poverty. Others move into retirement communities or enter into shared housing arrangements with other older people. Such arrangements make it easier for those who can no longer manage on their own. Transportation can be provided for shopping trips, religious services, and trips to the doctor.

◆◆◆

Patterns of Single Living

Singles live in different situations. The most obvious **single living pattern** is living alone. Many singles, however, live with others, in families or in shared living arrangements. Economic, social, and emotional needs usually dictate what living arrangement is chosen.

◆ Living Alone

Singles who are financially able may decide to live alone. They must handle all the responsibilities of home and daily living. Since no one shares their living space, they can go about their routine without having to consider the schedule and activities of others.

More About the Status of Singles. Through community service programs, many singles run errands or read for the elderly. In small groups, have students research such resources available for elderly singles in your community. How can students get involved? What are the benefits to students and others in need?

Increased lifespans mean a larger population of older people. Many live as singles. Besides recreation and health needs, what other needs do you think senior citizens have?

◆ Living with Family

Many singles today live with their families. Some do so because there is a need and others simply because they prefer to stay. Young people often stay home for a time before striking out on their own. It is also common for children to return home after they have been gone for awhile. The **family nest** offers the support and comfort children previously had and, for whatever reason, need again. Economic and emotional hardships are often why. High costs of housing, education, and transportation and a tight job market are some factors. Loss of job, single parenthood, death of a spouse, and divorce add to this occurrence.

◆ Sharing with Roommates

In the face of soaring living costs, singles of every age figure out ways to save money. By splitting costs and responsibilities, two, three, or more people can usually live for less money in a nicer place than would be possible alone. Such situations must be managed carefully to make them work well. You will read more about this in the next chapter.

Many young singles continue to live at home after they have started working or return home after being away at school. Most do so because they can't afford a place of their own.

Work and Family. After reading the section, "Living with Family," ask students to identify some guidelines for singles who choose to live with their families. Should singles pay rent to the family? Contribute to the grocery budget? How should singles contribute to household chores (laundry, cleaning, etc.)?

Photo Focus. Refer students to the photo at the top of the page. Ask them to describe how the senior citizens of today differ from those of previous generations.

A Slice of Life

During his senior year in high school, Jarod's parents moved to another state. They decided that it would be impractical for him to finish his last year in a new school, so they offered to pay half of the rent to his older brother's apartment if he would let Jarod move in with him until graduating. Dylan agreed without hesitation. In Jarod's words, "Without anyone to act as referee, we learned to cooperate and depend on each other. Dylan listened to all my stories about school and friends. Then I'd let him tell me what happened at the company where he works. Learning how to budget money was a real eye-opener. We grew very close in those few months. To this day we are still very good friends."

Things did not work out as well for Dana, Stephanie, and Mindy. They became good friends during their high school years. After graduation, they all got jobs and decided to live together. Dana tells what happened between her and Mindy.

"At first everything in the apartment went okay. Then Mindy started to do things that really got to me. She wasn't fulfilling her responsibilities in cleaning or cooking, nor did she have her share of the money when it was time to pay the bills. She developed a real 'I don't care' attitude. This made me angry.

"Finally, I insisted that we sit down and talk. It turned out to be quite a session. We both had our say. After the talk, I felt let down. I knew that we both said some things that hurt each other. Soon after, she agreed to find another place."

Thinking It Through

- Why did Jarod's shared living arrangement work, yet Dana's did not?
- If you were choosing someone to share living space with, what qualities would you look for in that person?
- Make a list of suggestions for people who plan to share living space.

◆ Cohabiting

In some cases, two individuals decide to live together as a couple without commitment to a marriage contract. Reasons for living together vary from couple to couple, but often include:

- Sharing rising living costs.
- Determining compatibility.
- Avoiding failure in marriage.

Some couples believe it will be easier to end a relationship with a live-in partner than with a marriage partner. In reality, this is not the case. A large percentage of those who choose to live together end up separating. Most find that the separation and readjustment that occur after the breakup are just as painful and complicated as a divorce. Besides having to deal with the emotional aspects of the separation, couples often have accumulated property to divide. When there is no legal contract to protect the partners, this process can be painful and complex.

If a couple who live together do choose to marry, the chance of separation or divorce is much greater than it is for those who did not cohabit before marriage. One reason for this is that couples who live together before marriage have a lower level of commitment when they marry. Also, many couples are pressured into marriage by family and friends who disapprove of their living together. An unplanned pregnancy may also affect a couple's decision to marry.

Deciding to live together is a serious undertaking. Choosing to live separately and to find other ways to get to know a potential partner is a less risky option.

◆◆◆

Inaccurate Labels

The image of singlehood has changed over the years. Although some people may still fit the stereotypes, most do not.

Discussion. Have students read "A Slice of Life." In small groups, ask students to respond to the questions at the end of the scenario. When small group work is complete, process the "Thinking It Through" questions with the entire class. Have the class come to consensus on a list of recommendations for sharing a living space.

One false idea about singles is that they pursue a reckless lifestyle. In truth, few have the time and energy after fulfilling a demanding work and personal schedule. People are more cautious about sexual relationships today because of AIDS and other sexually transmitted diseases. Discussions about sexual history and drug use or transfusions are more common. Because AIDS can exist in the body for years before the symptoms appear, some couples are requiring AIDS testing before involvement. People are dating for longer periods of time and looking for quality in their relationships.

The assumption that single people are lonely is inaccurate. Many singles admit that living alone is not perfect, but then what situation is? When they live alone, some singles miss having someone readily available to share the good times and the bad. They also report, however, that loneliness is not a big problem. By developing strong family and social ties, people can be, and are, comfortable in the single lifestyle.

Occasionally the single lifestyle is perceived as self-centered. People who wish to live independently and pursue their own interests may not be looked upon favorably. A more positive attitude toward singles, however, allows for the fact that the world is full of different kinds of people with different needs and personalities. What is right for one person is not necessarily right for another. Not everyone needs to be married or closely linked to another person. Marriage will be better if entered into by choice, not just because society says it is the thing to do. Singlehood can be chosen because it is right for the individual. This is not a selfish decision. People who choose singlehood can be happy and have just as much of a positive influence on the world as anyone else.

By joining clubs and participating in planned events, many singles enjoy an active and satisfying social life.

Activity. Have students brainstorm stereotypes they may have about young singles, single parents, and elderly singles. Have students interview young singles, single parents, and elderly singles. After the interviews, discuss the accuracy of their assumptions about singles. In what ways can they become more tolerant of others?

CHAPTER 17

Review

Summarizing the Chapter

- Most people will live a single lifestyle at some time in their lives.
- The percentage of single people in the population has steadily increased over the years.
- Some people choose single living. Others are single due to a variety of circumstances.
- Singles may live alone, with families, or in shared living arrangements.
- The majority of singles do not live a wild lifestyle.
- Loneliness need not be a problem for singles.

Testing Your Memory

1. Why are you likely to experience single living?
2. List five reasons why people live as singles.
3. Why is it easier for women to live as singles today than it was in the past?
4. Give two reasons why a person might delay marriage.
5. Explain why a person might continue to live at home as a young adult.
6. List three reasons why children return to the family nest.
7. Does living together before marriage insure that the marriage will last? Explain your answer.
8. List three ways in which the image of the single lifestyle has changed over the years.

Answers
Testing Your Memory

1. There are many reasons for single living, making it likely that a person will experience this lifestyle at some point.
2. **Any five:** independence; freedom in career opportunities; new conditions for women; delayed marriage; divorce; avoid emotional pain; unable to find a partner; obligations to fulfill family needs; death of spouse.
3. Greater career opportunities make it easier for women to support themselves. They can choose marriage for reasons other than economic necessity.
4. **Any two:** want financial stability before marriage; independence; pursuit of a career; experience life through travel; fear of divorce.
5. Many young people continue to live at home as young adults because of close family ties, insecurity, or the need for their help at home. They may also want to hold on to the advantages of living at home.
6. **Any three:** economic hardship; emotional hardship; high costs of housing; cost of education; cost of transportation; tight job market.
7. Answers may vary but generally the answer is "no." There tends to be a lower level of commitment with couples who live together. They may be more receptive to the idea of divorce.

Thinking Critically

1. Which reasons for single living do you think might be the most difficult for people to handle? Explain your answer.
2. Which do you think should be more important to a woman today, finding a husband or establishing a career? Explain your answer.
3. Quinn is thirty years old and not married. This bothers his parents, and they tell him so. What do you think about their attitude?

Taking Action

1. Complete this sentence: "For me, single living . . ." Use additional sentences if needed.
2. With a partner select a television program that portrays single people. Prepare a description of the single lifestyles in the program. Include why the characters are single, how they live, and whether or not you think the portrayal is realistic. Present your analysis to the class.
3. Write a diary entry that might be written by one of the following single people: an elderly widow or widower; a divorced person; a young person who has returned to the family nest; a career-minded individual; or a person who wants to stay single.

Making Life Choices

Lamont and Robyn have dated steadily for two years. After Lamont graduated from high school, he lived at home and went through a two-year technical program. He now has a good job. Robyn, who is two years younger than Lamont, is about to graduate from high school. Lamont is ready for marriage. He wants to marry Robyn right after her graduation and start a family. Robyn is having some second thoughts about this.

What do you think is going on in Robyn's mind? If they marry, will either Lamont or Robyn ever live as singles? What security does Lamont have for the future? What about Robyn? What suggestions do you have for this couple?

Using Your Journal

As you have just read, there's a strong chance that you will experience singlehood at some point in your adult life. How do you feel about it? Use your journal to explore your thoughts about singlehood. Ask yourself what aspects of singlehood appeal to you. Then ask what aspects you fear or feel unprepared for. Think, too, about the single living patterns discussed in this chapter and determine which pattern is most appealing to you. Then, based on your responses, prepare a list of skills you need to build in order to be better prepared for single living.

8. **Answers may include:** most singles don't live a reckless lifestyle; generally singles are not lonely; singlehood is no longer viewed as a selfish choice, but a choice right for the individual.

Think Critically

1. Answers will vary.
2. Answers will vary. Point out that a woman cannot count on a man to support her for life.
3. Answers will vary.

CHAPTER 18

Successful Single Living

Chapter Challenge

Resources. Refer to the Teacher's Classroom Resources box and Student Workbook for materials related to this chapter.

Look for These Answers . . .

- How can single people manage each of these aspects of their lives successfully: finances, housing, safety, a healthful diet, relationships, and a desire for children?
- What are some suggestions for managing as a single person who lives at home and one who lives in a shared living arrangement?
- What special challenges do single parents face and how can they handle these?
- How can single people develop a feeling of contentment?

Look for These Terms . . .

- contentment
- secured building

As Crystal turned the key in her apartment door, that same old cold feeling came over her. She opened the door to greet the silence one more time, but she couldn't go in, not just yet. It had been a busy day at work, and Crystal dreaded the thought of another lonely evening.

"You look like you need a friend." The voice came from over her shoulder. It was Monty, who lived in an apartment on the same floor.

"Maybe I do," Crystal responded. "I'm just beginning to realize that — and some other things too. How do you do it, Monty? You live alone, but you always look so happy, so busy."

"I haven't always been that way," replied Monty. "For a long time the television set was my best friend. Then I realized that things had to change. First I joined a singles club. We've got some activity going every week. Between my job and everything else that keeps me busy now, it feels good to come home to a quiet apartment at night. I'm doing some volunteer work now too, and I love it. Have you got a few minutes? I'd like to tell you about it."

"Come on in," Crystal said. She felt something awakening inside her. She knew that she was about to take charge of her life. That cold feeling that had haunted her for so long was gone.

Chapter Opener. Have students read the opening scenario in the chapter. Some singles may find it difficult to fill the hours spent away from work. Ask students to respond to these questions: What kinds of volunteer work could Crystal do that would fulfill some of her needs as well as allow her to link with others? If she wants to join a singles club, what steps should she take in finding out about membership and the types of activities that are involved? Have students explore activity ideas available to singles in your area. Do these activities meet a variety of needs for singles and others?

Discussion. When people suddenly become single, such as through the death of a spouse or divorce, they must often learn new skills. Ask students for examples of what people might have to learn in these situations.

Managing Single Life

Life as a single person can be challenging. As you saw in the last chapter, the roads to single living are varied. Some situations offer unique challenges of their own. A widow or widower must cope with the loss of a loved one. Even aspects of the daily routine can be challenging for these people. For example, one who has spent little time in the kitchen may, among many other things, wonder where the paring knives are stored. Divorced people have special concerns too. What might some of these be?

Regardless of the route to singlehood, people share some common concerns when living as singles. Awareness of these and some practical tips can bring success to managing single life.

◆ Financial Planning

Because of the increasing number of singles, experts agree that everyone needs to be economically prepared for single living. When thinking about singlehood, financial planning must be viewed in two ways.

The first is from the point of view of a married person. A married person should ask this question: Am I financially prepared for single living if my situation changes? Always remember that death and divorce can result in singlehood. To be prepared, you need to know about your current financial status.

Have you heard of situations like this? Tylette, who is not employed, had never paid the bills or managed a checkbook. She had never seen her husband's paycheck and did not know what they had in savings. When her husband died, Tylette was totally confused and worried about her financial condition. Single living can be thrust upon you without warning. A wise person is prepared for such possibilities.

The second view of financial planning for single living is from the perspective of those who are single. If you are, you must do all the managing yourself. You are responsible for your own financial well-being, and you cannot count on someone else. Assuming that you will marry and be taken care of is unwise. So is assuming that you will marry and have access to a second income. The smart approach is to take charge of your own financial future.

To be a good money manager, follow the advice of Laura Sommerfield, a financial consultant who assists people in planning their finances. In her words, "Most people want to feel financially secure and independent. This takes looking at your situation realistically. First of all, look at your monthly income and expenses. Balancing these is the key to financial success. Meeting monthly needs and saving for the future are both part of successful planning."

Laura suggests accumulating three to six months of your living expenses in a savings account. This provides some financial security in case of emergencies. Knowing how to write checks and balance a checkbook, as well as understanding and obtaining credit in your own name, are important in managing finances. Even simple things like learning how to take care of basic household repairs can save money and lead to a more secure financial future.

Some singles meet their financial goals more easily than others. Income makes a difference. Think about the job skills you plan for your future. If necessary, will you be able to make it on your own as a single person? What can you do to make your financial future secure?

◆ Housing

The housing preferences of single people are slightly different from those of others. Land developers are building homes and apartment complexes that are designed for singles. Many offer fewer bedrooms with larger kitchen and living areas for entertaining. Some have pools and exercise facilities that allow singles to maintain fitness as well as meet other people.

The cost of housing is high. When people live alone, no one shares the rent or house payment and other household expenses. This can be difficult on one income. For some singles home ownership may take years of saving and planning to manage alone.

Managing a home is no small task. Cleaning, repairs, and upkeep take time and energy. When you live alone, all the responsibility is yours. For this reason many singles are cautious about the condition, style, and size of the housing they choose.

Life Skills Management. In groups of two or three, instruct students to compile a step-by-step written plan to help Tylette to take control of her finances. What does Tylette need to do first? In what order should she tackle her expenses? Where could Tylette go for advice in dealing with her finances? Why is it so important to take charge of your own financial future?

Many singles live in apartment complexes. They offer the advantages of little or no maintenance, social contacts, and may be more affordable than other types of housing.

◆ Safety

Safety is a concern of most people, but perhaps even more so to people who live alone. Karin puts it this way: "Safety is a real factor for me, living alone in the city as I do. Living in a secured building makes me feel safe." A **secured building** can bring peace of mind to singles. These often have locked exterior doors and an intercom system. Simpler ways to feel more secure at home are deadbolt locks on the doors and inside locks on windows.

As a single person, you can follow certain safety tips. These are useful for others too:

- Always carry identification.
- Find others to walk with.
- If you must walk alone, walk in lighted areas and face traffic.
- Park your vehicle in well-lighted locations, especially at night.
- Look for secure housing.
- Consider an unlisted telephone number or put only your first initial and last name in the telephone directory.
- Carry a whistle when walking alone.
- Try to let someone know where you are, especially if you are away from home for extended periods of time.
- Avoid giving your address and telephone number to people you do not know well.

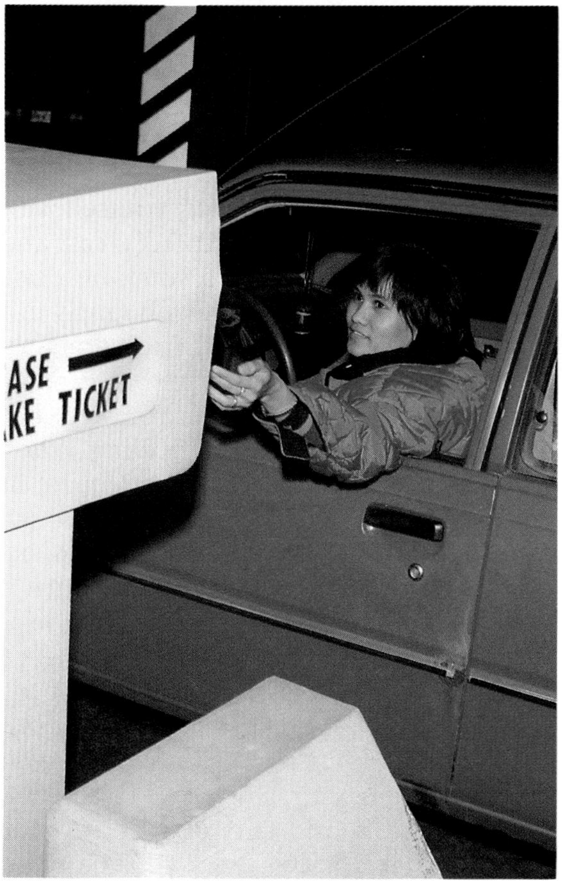

Singles today are very mindful of safety. What precautions should be taken when parking in a facility like this one? Should a woman alone park here at night?

Life Skills Management. Have students check newspapers to report on housing options for singles. Ask students to assume they are tenants. Have them defend their desire for six housing requirements, such as needed space; furnished or unfurnished; number of closets and bathrooms; a view; private yard; health facilities; etc. How will they afford such choices? What tradeoffs would they make to share expenses with a roommate?

Activity. Have students develop a TV commercial dealing with one safety tip listed above. Students should act out the commercials for the class.

◆ A Healthful Diet

When leading a busy life, as many single people do, eating nutritiously becomes a special concern. Cooking small quantities can feel like a waste of time. Since singles do not have to think about meals for anyone else, it is easy to skip the planning and preparation that results in a good diet.

Jon fell into the habit of eating popcorn and cold cereal for his evening meals. Eventually, when he couldn't look at another bowl of popcorn, he decided something had to change. Finding some frozen foods packaged in single-serving containers started him in the right direction. In time he found that buying fresh foods once or twice a week in small quantities worked well. Stir-fried dishes became a favorite for him. A friend gave him a handy cookbook with tasty recipes for one person. By cooking larger quantities once in awhile and freezing the leftovers, he had some good meals ready to go. Inviting a friend over for dinner was a good motivator to eat well too. Once he mastered spaghetti, that became standard fare on company night. Like Jon, anyone can learn to eat well as a single. Good health depends on it.

Jon wants to eat nutritiously even though he often cooks just for himself. Stir-fry dishes are simple to prepare and can be made in small quantities. What other suggestions could a single person use when cooking for one?

Problem Solving. Have students work in small groups to develop a healthful weekly menu for a single person. Students may consult resource materials on healthful food choices as well as cookbooks for foods that are easy to prepare. Ask each group to prepare a dish from the menu for the class. Evaluate the results.

◆ Developing Relationships

Living alone can be lonely, or it can be challenging and rewarding. When you are single, the choice is up to you.

Loneliness and being alone are not the same. Think about the difference. Have you ever settled into a corner all by yourself with a good magazine and a bowl of ice cream and felt really comfortable? If so, you were alone but not lonely. Have you ever felt lonely in a room full of people? Why? This was probably because you were not linked in some significant way with anyone there. You were not alone, but you had that lonely feeling. When relationships are missing or inadequate in your life, you are likely to feel lonely. On the other hand, if you have some strong connections to others, your moments alone will not feel lonely. When you live with others, relationships are automatic. Singles, however, must often make special efforts to develop the relationships they need.

If you stay in the community where you grew up, you may already have a strong network of family and friends who provide support. If you move away, you may not.

More About Successful Single Living. Many mental health experts stress the importance of developing a support system to maintain self-esteem and wellness. Singles need to develop a network of family members, friends, and helpful community connections to help meet their needs. What are ways to develop a support system?

When moving to an unfamiliar area, you can develop a surrogate family or group of friends. Although these people are not blood relatives, they can supply the concern and reliability of a family unit. Such support systems are important to all people.

It's easy to tell someone to develop relationships. The question is how do you do this. There are many opportunities to meet others if you want to. New friendships and relationships take time to develop. Don't expect to be deeply connected to others right away. The same effort must be made to hold a friendship together as is needed for bonding a family and marriage.

Many people find it hard to meet others because of demanding work schedules or limited contacts with others. Singles must be careful not to let a career push relationships aside. Both aspects of life are needed. There are many creative ways of meeting others if you want to. Friendships are waiting via community activities and organizations. Never be reluctant to try them out. Some people are self-conscious and uncomfortable the first time or two in a new setting. This changes with time. A smile and a friendly hello can do much to start a new relationship.

Social and support groups have sprung up all over the country due to the rapid growth in the single population. Groups exist to meet varied interests and needs. Susan is a community-minded person. For her, volunteering at the hospital and museum was a good way to meet people. Tom has found friendship through a support group at his church. He also enjoys playing basketball at the YMCA. Health clubs, vacations of all types, environmental groups, and adult education classes, as well as bookstores and libraries, offer other opportunities to find friendships.

People who get involved in activities have opportunities to meet people. This can lead to worthwhile relationships that prevent loneliness for singles.

These church members are filling boxes with food to take to people who need help. Working with others is a good way to meet people and build relationships. Can you think of other ways?

Discussion. Have students share examples of any singles they know who interact regularly with children. How do both groups benefit from each other? What needs and motives cause adults to want to involve themselves with children?

Activity. Ask representatives from a local YMCA, health club, and organizations such as Big Brothers and Big Sisters to speak with your class about the ways singles can get involved with children in these groups.

Some people use personal ads in newspapers or dating services to meet people. Be cautious about such methods. What type of person will you be meeting in this way? You cannot be sure. Whatever the circumstances, do not give your address or phone number to people you do not know. If you must meet someone you do not know well, meet him or her in a public place and use your own transportation.

◆ The Desire for Children

Some single people want a special kind of relationship in their lives — with children. This need can be fulfilled in a number of ways.

Dorothy, a single career woman in her late twenties, felt she had the time and the need to develop a family. After talking with social workers in her community, she decided that taking in foster children would be fulfilling to her and also provide a home for children who need love, affection, and stability in their lives.

Sherilyn wanted a family but with more permanence. She had an empty space in her life that she wanted to fill. Her job would not allow her to care for a baby, so she decided to adopt two school-age children. Sherilyn felt she had a great deal of love and stability to offer.

Although he is content with his single life, Jamison likes children. He coaches Little League baseball. "I love working with these kids. They really need the attention and caring I have to offer. It's a great feeling to know you've really made a difference in the life of a young person."

Adolph is a widower. He has no grandchildren, so he found a substitute through the Big Brother program. He and Tyrone go fishing and share some wonderful times together.

Single people can be a strong resource for children in a community. The need or desire for family can be met by getting involved with children. For some singles, this helps make life complete.

◆◆◆

Special Single Situations

As you know, many singles do not live alone. These situations present challenges that require special management methods.

Single people often want children in their lives. For those who do, something like taking a neighborhood child fishing can be rewarding. How else might a single person be able to interact with children?

Discussion. Ask students to respond to the concept of singles adopting children. What do they see as the pros and cons of singles adopting? How can single persons and children benefit from adoption?

Activity. If possible, ask students to interview singles who have adopted or provided foster care. How did this experience help the single person meet the need for family? What special challenges might a single person face in a situation such as this?

A Slice of Life

After graduating from high school, Celeste found a job in a plumbing and heating supply store. She did typing and filing and answered the phone. The pay was low, but it was a job. Celeste and two friends shared expenses on an apartment until one got married and the other moved out of town. Celeste could not manage the rent herself, so she returned to her family home.

It seemed strange to be home again. She had been on her own long enough to feel independent, but now she had to answer to her parents again. She wanted to save money for a new car, but they wanted her to pay them rent. She had always lived there for free before. After Celeste left home, the number of laundry loads her folks washed went down. Now the number was up again. Celeste assumed they would wash her clothes as usual. Celeste did not understand the tense atmosphere that was developing in her home. It had never been there before.

Thinking It Through

- Why is home life different for Celeste now?
- How do you think her parents feel about having Celeste home again?
- What suggestions do you have for Celeste and her parents?

◆ Managing as a Single in the Family Home

When singles continue to live in the family home as young adults or they return to the family nest after a time away, new rules may be needed. Parents generally want a young adult to be taking on responsibility. If the young adult is going to school, there will be fewer expectations. If he or she has a job, however, parents are right to expect some sharing of expenses. In both situations household jobs should be shared. The young adult may have some expectations too. More freedom is usually one of these. Since the young person is living at home, parents often feel that they still have some say. To work all of this out, ground rules need to be set up. The following suggestions ought to be included in a written contract between the parents and young adult:

- List responsibilities, such as cleaning, laundry, and food preparation.
- Set a schedule for paying expenses, such as rent, phone bills, electricity, heat, and food.
- Discuss acceptable limits of behavior, such as the handling of privacy and relationships outside of the family unit.
- Set a time limit for living at home, based on the reason for being there.

When young adults live in the family home, a written contract should spell out the rules. What topics should be covered?

Discussion. Have students read "A Slice of Life." Process the "Thinking it Through" questions with the class. In addition, ask the students: How may this situation relate to them? How may talking about expectations help alleviate some tension when singles move back with parents?

◆ Managing Shared Living

When singles share living space, they are smart to understand and agree on the rules of the arrangement. Be sure to know what your legal obligations are in such situations, especially those related to the rent or purchase of your living space. In order to make joint living go smoothly, establish how you will split food and other household costs. Decide in advance who will cook and clean, and when. A schedule may help.

Regardless of age, shared living arrangements work best when all parties cooperate. Respecting the rights of others is important. Some prospective roommates select each other carefully and establish fair ways to share costs and work. Familylike surroundings improve the chances for success.

Employed parents often need quality child care. In what ways will poor child care make things difficult for a parent?

Work and Family. Have students respond to the following: Trent's mom, a single parent, has a hard time balancing work and family. In addition to full-time teaching, she conducts adult education seminars twice a week in the evening. Trent works ten hours a week after school at a bike shop. Create a weekly responsibility chart that divides household chores and duties for the family. What steps can they take to manage their lives smoothly? How can they each have enough leisure time as well as family time together?

◆ Managing as a Single Parent

The single-parent situation commonly results from divorce or death of a spouse. Single parents may be men or women, although the majority of single-parent families are headed by women. Single parents face their own set of challenges.

Most single parents work full time to support themselves and their children, even when child support is provided by a former spouse. Meeting the financial needs of a family can be hard. Generally, single parents are living on less income, yet they have increased expenses. Many must deal with the additional cost of child care. If quality child care is not available, both parent and child may feel the negative effects.

Balancing work, family, and social life is not easy for single parents. Work takes many hours of each day. Still, the parent must find time to supply children with love, affection, and guidance. Some single parents worry that their children will grow up without the positive influence of the opposite gender in their lives. Family and friends may be able to help with this. Support of all kinds can often be found through religious and other groups, such as Parents Without Partners.

Steve, a single parent for several years, said that the most frustrating thing for him was developing a social life. "Other single people have the time to get involved in the community. I spend my time away from work with my daughter. It makes it difficult to meet other adults." Steve is not alone.

Single parents need to establish relationships with other adults. Some feel guilty about going out for social reasons while their children are home alone or with a sitter. Nevertheless, this is important within reason. As one young mother said, "I feel that I am much better with the children when I have an opportunity to get out and have some fun with other adults."

Balancing Work & Family

Single Parent Challenges

Single parents find it particularly hard to balance the demands of work and family. With no partners to share the responsibility of raising the family, single parents shoulder it all. They make all the decisions. They arrange child care. They figure out how to be with family members when needed. Chances are they also have a full-time job. They also need to find time for themselves away from their family.

The increase in single parents has had one good result: more people are aware of their plight. Newspaper articles and television programs have helped raise public awareness of the needs of single parents. Today there are a number of sources of help for single parents:

- Single-parent support groups offer a place where parents can share their problems and find solutions by talking to other parents in similar situations.
- Community recreation programs, along with churches and other places of worship, may offer interesting activities for children at a reasonable cost. With the children safely supervised, a single parent can take some free time.
- Single parents can build a strong support system of relatives, friends, and neighbors to help take care of the children when necessary or to give the parent some time off.
- The family itself can help. Teens can perform many tasks, such as making dinner or doing the laundry, freeing up more time for the parent to spend on other things.

Think About It

1. Why is time off from parenting and work necessary for single parents?
2. What are some other ideas for helping single parents cope?

Developing Contentment

With any lifestyle, **contentment** is a necessary goal. This feeling that you are satisfied with your situation is important to good emotional health. So often people feel that the grass looks greener on the other side of the fence. The married person who is responsible for others envies the single person with more freedom. The single person envies the married friend who has someone there all the time.

Whether single or married, people need to feel they have a purpose in life. Married people often get this by fulfilling the needs of their family. Single people must find their purpose in other ways. Through relationships, surrogate families, and careers, this is possible. Another way is to help others, even something as simple as getting the mail for the elderly woman next door. Tapping into your own interests and creativity helps too. Find something you enjoy doing, and, whether it be skiing, sewing, reading, or one of many other activities, you will put some purpose into your life. Your self-esteem will get a boost, and you will be headed down the road to contentment.

Single people can be content with their lives if they spend time on activities that interest them and learn how to enjoy being alone.

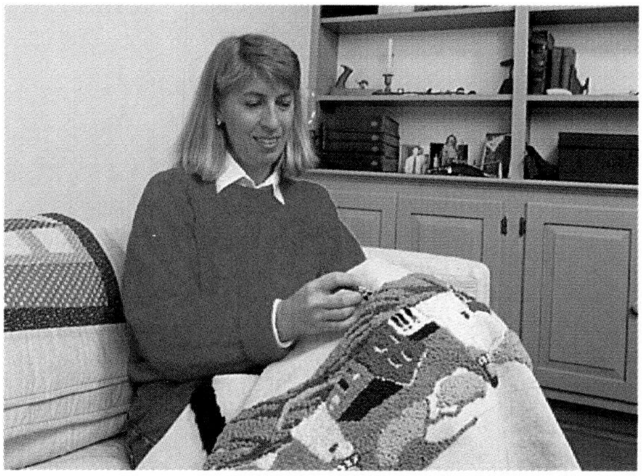

Activity. Ask students to list five activities that offer them contentment, such as playing an instrument or sport, talking to friends, and enjoying a class or hobby. Why are these activities pleasurable? How do these activities help them develop a sense of contentment?

CHAPTER 18

Review

Answers
Testing Your Memory

1. Death of a spouse or divorce may result in singlehood.
2. Developers are providing: housing with fewer bedrooms; larger kitchens and living areas; pools and exercise facilities.
3. **Any four:** carry identification; walk with others; walk in lighted areas and face traffic; park in well-lighted areas; secured housing; possible unlisted phone number; carry a whistle; let someone know where you are when away from home; don't give out your address or phone number to strangers.
4. **Any three:** plan meals ahead that require little preparation; use single-serving frozen foods; buy small quantities of fresh foods frequently; freeze leftovers for later meals. (Other answers are possible.)
5. Loneliness occurs when people are not linked to others in a significant way. Being alone simply means enjoying quiet times by yourself.
6. **Any three:** get involved in community activities and organizations; join a social or support group; say hello and smile at others; vacation with a tour group; meet others with similar interests at bookstores or libraries.

Summarizing the Chapter

- Financial planning is important to the single person and also to the married person, who could become single at any time due to circumstances.
- Singles should choose housing carefully because of the costs and the responsibilities.
- Certain safety procedures can be followed in order to make a single person feel secure.
- Developing relationships is necessary for the well-being of single people.
- Singles can fulfill the desire for children in several ways.
- With good management ideas, singles can live successfully at home or in shared living arrangements.
- Single parents have special challenges that must be met.
- Contentment is important to everyone in life.

Testing Your Memory

1. Why should financial knowledge be important to the married person whose spouse takes care of money management?
2. How do land developers meet the needs of the singles population?
3. List four safety tips for a single person.
4. Give three suggestions that would help a single person eat more nutritiously.
5. What is the difference between loneliness and being alone?
6. List three ideas for building friendships and relationships.
7. How can a single person fulfill a desire for children in his or her life?

8. List two suggestions for managing a shared living arrangement.
9. What special challenges do single parents face?
10. List two ideas that single people could use to help them find contentment.

Thinking Critically

1. Some single people just stay home rather than make an effort to get out and find friends. Why do you think they do this?
2. Why would a single person's safety be more at risk than someone who lives with others?
3. If you experience single living, which of these do you think will be most difficult for you to manage: finances, housing, a healthful diet, safety, or relationships? Why? What could you do to manage this area well?

Taking Action

1. Interview a single adult about the advantages and disadvantages of single life. Report your findings to the class.
2. You and a friend have decided to share an apartment. Develop a plan for living arrangements. Consider sharing expenses, preparing meals, cleaning, and social life. What ground rules would you have? What kind of schedule would you develop?

Making Life Choices

Rod is a college sophomore. He enjoys the companionship of dorm life but is finding that all the noise bothers him when he studies. He would like to live off campus, but finding affordable housing may be a problem. Rod has a part-time job at a department store. He makes about $350 per month. Most apartments for students cost at least $300 per month.

What options does Rod have? How could Rod best use his money to meet his needs? If you were Rod, what would you do?

Using Your Journal

Few singles can afford a place of their own when they first start working. Most continue to live at home or share a place with roommates. Use your journal to explore your feelings about continuing to live with your family, or about sharing with roommates. What qualities would you look for in roommates? How do you rate yourself as a roommate? Are there behaviors that you need to change? Can you start practicing now?

7. They can: adopt; provide foster care; or join community organizations such as Little League and Big Brother and Sister programs.
8. **Any two** of the suggestions given on page 260.
9. Any of the challenges described on page 260.
10. **Any two** of the ideas listed on page 261.

Thinking Critically

1. Answers will vary but may Include fear and shyness.
2. Answers will vary. Point out that someone who intends harm may feel safer in preying upon a household with only one resident.
3. Answers will vary.

Darrell reaches out to his mother, a single parent.

Darrell

"For a while after my parents' divorce, I was confused and angry. I stayed out with friends all the time to shut off problems at home. My mother got a job and was always anxious. Money was very tight. One night I heard her say to a friend on the phone that she felt frustrated and all alone. Then I realized I wasn't helping matters. The next day I asked her if there was anything I could do to help her. Her mouth dropped. When I started taking out the trash and running errands after school, our relationship improved fast. Now we share jobs. I never knew that by helping her I'd get something out of it too. I have to admit that being part of a team at home makes me feel better about myself."

Fran Jackson "I never imagined divorce could be such an emotional trauma. Thanks to my education, I got a job with an electronics corporation as a bookkeeper and assistant officer manager, but my paycheck barely supported Darrell and me. At times I felt I was fighting a losing battle. He wasn't around, and I was too preoccupied to think about sitting down to talk about how we could manage. The morning Darrell asked me if he could help out, I thought, 'At last. I have an ally.' It renewed my hope. That was a year ago, and now I kid him about being our household office manager. Knowing that he's on my side makes things seem less tough. You can get through the hard times when you know someone is there."

Les "Darrell and I met when we were nine, playing basketball on the playground. Not long ago I picked up on a change in him before I knew what it was. Darrell used to say, 'If it's good for me, I do it.' Some kids thought he was selfish. When he told me he had to go to the store for his mom instead of play ball one day, I didn't believe him. I thought it was an excuse to do something else. Now I know better. Since he's more responsible at home, he's different. He's more concerned about others, more grown up. He has made me see how kids and their parents — especially single parents — need each other."

Alice Hart "I was surprised when Darrell signed up for my family life class at school. It wasn't until a month later, during our section on single parenting, that he opened up a little about the ways he helps out his mother at home. I guessed that was why he seemed eager to learn how to get the best values when grocery shopping. He was also very sharp at putting together a household budget. Apparently he's had some practice, and I always say practice makes perfect. I figured that my class would help *him* help his mom better. Seeing a student put schoolwork to practical use is a good feeling."

You can make a difference too.

- What extra challenges did Darrell's mother face when she became a single parent?
- Are you able to talk to a parent or guardian about conflicts that arise? If not, how could you try?
- Are there jobs you could do to help out more at home? How does helping at home make a person feel better about himself or herself?

UNIT 6

Is Married Life for You?

CHAPTER

CHAPTER 19

Marriage Customs and Laws

Chapter Challenge

Resources. Refer to the Teacher's Classroom Resources box and Student Workbook for materials related to this chapter.

Look for These Answers . . .

- How has marriage evolved over the ages?
- What are the legal requirements of marriage?
- What types of marriages are prohibited?
- Why are marriage laws needed?

Look for These Terms . . .

- affinity
- betrothal
- bigamy
- civil
- consanguinity
- monogamy
- polygamy
- prenuptial agreement

Kim first met Asif when they sat next to each other in a college English class. He was struggling with the class because of the language barrier. Having arrived from India only six months earlier, he had trouble understanding certain phrases. Kim took it upon herself to help him.

As they shared study time and friendly conversation over lunches, Asif and Kim became closer. She admired his dedication and determination to succeed. He responded to her warmth and generosity. In time Kim was sure that her feelings had turned to love.

Because the friendship had grown so strong, Kim was puzzled when Asif tried to pull away. He seemed to care for her, yet at the same time he kept some distance between them. At last the time came when she had to face him with her concerns. One afternoon, as they sat beneath a willow tree outside Sherman Hall, Kim said to Asif, "I love you, Asif, and I think you love me, yet you always seem to be holding back. I just don't understand."

"There is something I must tell you, Kim. I should have told you before now. It's something I struggle with every day. My family is in India, as you know, and I have word from them that they have found a bride for me. They want to know when I will return, so the arrangements for marriage can be made."

Kim and Asif sat in silence for the longest time. What was ahead for them? Asif reached out to hold Kim's hand. The only sound was the chirping of robins overhead.

Chapter Opener. Ask students to read the opening scenario. Have students respond to the following questions: How do you think Kim felt when Asif told her that his family had found a bride for him in India? What do you think Asif was feeling knowing his family had found a bride for him whom he had never met? How do conflicting customs provide an extra challenge in developing relationships? Is it realistic for persons from different cultures to attempt to develop a permanent relationship? How might they prepare themselves for future challenges? How would you react if your parents chose a spouse for you?

Marriage Customs

Marriage customs have developed gradually. They are influenced by the social and economic conditions of a time and region. The origin of marriage is difficult to establish. Historians have determined, though, that marriage has evolved through three main stages over the centuries.

◆ Marriage By Capture

The earliest type of union was marriage by capture. Imagine Gar and several fellow tribesmen invading another tribe to kidnap a woman he thinks will be a good slave and worker. Her friends try to save her, but strength alone makes Gar successful. To appease the anger of his "bride's" father, Gar later sends gifts.

By today's standard, this method leaves much to be desired. Still, do you see any links to the present in this scene? Gar's friends would be the groomsmen and ushers we have today. The girlfriends who tried to save the bride were probably the first bridesmaids.

Photo Focus. Ask students what type of marriage is depicted in the photo above.

◆ Marriage By Purchase

The second type of union was marriage by purchase. Girls were under the care and authority of the father or closest male relative. The prospective husband or the elders in his family usually asked the father for the daughter after seeking the father's approval and paying his "demanding price" with gifts and other goods. This was called the **betrothal** (bee-TROTH-uhl). The mother's approval was not necessary since she, too, was under the domination of her husband. The transfer took place in public to let everyone know that the girl belonged to the husband. Following the father's consent, the families of the bride and groom ate together, and the groom took the bride home. Many times these arrangements were made years before the actual marriage took place.

◆ Marriage For Love

The third type of union, marriage for love, evolved during the eighteenth century. While many marriages were still arranged by families, the idea of marrying because of love became popular. The colonists brought this way of thinking to America when they settled here.

Remember Asif and Laura? Even though marriage for love is standard in the United States today, some cultures do not share this custom. In a world where different cultures meet frequently, problems can occur.

American marriage customs have changed much since colonial days. Most colonies in North America, which were mainly English, followed the "old country" customs, which varied quite a bit. These contrast with the customs followed today, as you can see in the chart on page 271.

Marriage Laws

Like customs, marriage laws have also developed slowly. Moreover, they are not the same from one state to another, even today. For this reason, when dealing with any marital question, check the laws in the state where you will marry to be sure you know what is expected.

Trea was living in Hawaii while making her wedding plans. Her marriage, however, was to be in Illinois. To be sure that she would do everything right, she wrote for information to the county clerk's office in the county where she would be married. They sent her the material she needed so that appropriate arrangements could be made.

Most couples in the United States base their decision to marry on love. Why is this different in some other countries?

More About Marriage Customs. In some areas, "stealing" the bride or groom away from the wedding reception is a popular wedding custom. The bridal couple is returned later during the reception. In other areas, a shivaree (a noisy serenade) is provided for the newly married couple.

Activity. Have students research cultures that arrange marriages for young people. What benefits might there be to this kind of arrangement? What drawbacks are there? Invite a foreign exchange student to speak to the class about the marriage and wedding customs in his or her country.

Marriage Customs

Colonial Customs	Current Customs
Parental approval before dating allowed.	Dating begins casually, sometimes before parents are aware of it.
Indiscriminate dating uncommon; serious appraisal of partner.	Young people "play the field," sometimes for years; no serious intentions or commitments.
Dating considered a prelude to marriage.	Dating an enjoyable end in itself.
Mainly group activity; less opportunity for individual couples to be alone.	Choices of activities and companionship entirely up to young people.
Strict regulation of personal behavior.[1]	Individual standards; freedom from parental and social control.
Parental choice of mate.	Individual choice.
Parental choice stressed economic and social considerations.	Individual choice based on romantic attachment.
Courtship carried on within the girl's home.	Seldom in home, mainly outside social activities.
Longer engagement.	Various lengths of engagement — long, short, or none at all.
Marriage considered an arrangement between families, rather than a bond based on emotions.	Marriage considered between individuals, not families.
Parental consent to marriage nearly always mandatory.	Parental consent desired but often not a deterrent when withheld.
Well-to-do gave marriage portions (dowries) with daughters; dowry custom later preserved in "hope chest."	Dowries and hope chests no longer customary.
Transportation poor; availability of young people limited; courtship involved young people living near each other; families well known to each other.	Travel unlimited; college and military service bring together young people from all over world; choice of mate may be from across the nation or from another country.
Marriage considered an obligation as well as privilege.[2]	To marry or not an individual matter.
Widows and widowers expected to remarry.[3]	Individual choice; no pressure to remarry.
Early New England law provided civil control of marriage; clergy forbidden as officiants.	By eighteenth century, nearly all colonies permitted both civil and religious ceremonies; may be either today.
Weddings were small, private ceremonies in the home.	Most weddings are in churches; large, public ceremonies.
No formal invitations sent.	Most couples send invitations.
Music seldom used.	Most weddings have vocal and instrumental music.
No formal attire; most brides in street dress or suit.	Most brides are formally gowned.
No receptions.	Large or small weddings usually followed by receptions.
Simple ceremony, not an occasion for revelry.	Complex ceremony, processions, and merry-making.
Most brides wore no rings.	98 percent of brides have rings.
Very inexpensive ceremony.	Many ceremonies expensive.
Public notice — banns — of intent to wed necessary; marriage had to be recorded to be legal.	Legal requirements — from blood tests to age restrictions — vary from state to state (See chart page 274).
Younger marriage age;[4] larger families.	Later marriage age; smaller families.
Recognition of common-law marriage a functional necessity.	No longer a social need; new states recognize common-law marriages.
Breach-of-promise suits by both sexes recognized because marriage was much more an economic arrangement.	Breach-of-promise suits no longer legal.
Divorce infrequent; stigma attached.	Divorce may be condoned and frequent.

[1]Colonists could be fined for "misconduct." Thomas Wertenbaker, in *The First Americans,* states: "John Lewis and Sarah Chapman were brought before the court in 1670, for sitting together on the Lord's day, under an apple tree, in Goodman Chapman's orchard."

[2]William M. Kephart, in *The Family, Society, and the Individual,* reports that the unmarried were looked upon with disfavor. Bachelors were suspect, and in most of the colonies were heavily taxed and kept under close surveillance.

[3]Queen and Adams, in *The Family in Various Cultures,* cite cases of remarriages within days or weeks, and in one case, "Isaac Winslow proposed to Ben Davis' daughter the same day he buried his wife."

[4]In Colonial America, girls were married by 16.

◆ Monogamy

Under the law a marriage may involve only one wife and one husband. This is called **monogamy** (muh-NAHG-uh-mee). Remarriage may occur but only if a spouse has died or the marriage has been legally ended. When a person who is still legally married enters into another marriage, this is called **bigamy** (BIG-uh-mee). Bigamy is illegal. In the past some religions allowed marriages with more than two partners. Families often consisted of a husband and two or more wives plus all children born of the wives. Called **polygamy** (puh-LIG-uh-mee), this is also illegal in the United States.

◆ Legal Requirements for Marriage

An important element required to make a marriage valid is the mutual consent of both parties. No valid marriage exists if the man or woman is against the idea. There may be no threats forcing the ceremony. Also, if one partner is under the influence of alcohol or drugs or misunderstands the seriousness of the ceremony, the marriage may be pronounced invalid by the court.

Three acts are necessary for a legal marriage:

- A marriage license must be obtained from the person authorized to issue it (usually a county clerk of courts).
- The ceremony must be performed by an authorized official.
- The marriage must be reported to the state department in charge of keeping records. (This is usually the responsibility of the person issuing the license.)

These three regulations are required by all states. They are discussed more fully below, along with other regulations that must be met in many states for a legal marriage to occur. Not all states handle these in the same way.

Problem Solving. Have students discuss the possible consequences of marriage to someone who, at the time of marriage, is under the influence of alcohol or drugs. Are there laws regulating this type of situation? Should a couple consider marriage if one or both partners abuse alcohol or drugs? Why or why not?

◆ Marriage Age

Most states have two age requirements for marriage — one at which young people may marry with parental consent and one without parental consent. Nearly all states permit males and females to marry at age eighteen without consent. With consent, over half the states allow both sexes to marry at sixteen. In the remaining states, the age requirement with parental consent ranges from twelve to eighteen. Specific information on this is shown in the chart on page 274.

Most young people under the age of eighteen need parental consent to marry.

Activity. Have students research age requirements for marriage. Why do age requirements exist? Do students agree or disagree with age requirements for marriage? If parental consent is required, what procedure is followed in obtaining a marriage license? Why do some states require parental consent for teens under eighteen?

A Slice of Life

At age seventeen Julian had experienced plenty. Life hadn't been easy for him, and he felt that he had grown up fast. Ona was only sixteen, but she too had Julian's maturity, or at least what she felt was maturity. Getting married seemed right to them.

It was Ona's parents who got in the way. Julian's would consent to the marriage, but Ona's would not. Ona didn't understand why a law was going to make them wait. It seemed silly to her.

Thinking It Through

- How long will Julian and Ona have to wait to get married?
- Why do you think laws dictate age requirements for marriage?
- If you were Ona's parents, would you give in to her pressure? Why or why not?
- What are the advantages and disadvantages for Julian and Ona in getting married now? In waiting?

◆ Physical Requirements

Some states require a blood test shortly before marriage to show that the partners are free from certain communicable diseases. Sexually transmitted diseases are of particular concern. The examination certificate is good for a specific period of time, usually one week to six months, depending on the state. If the couple does not marry within that time, another blood test must be taken. Specifics are shown in the chart on page 274.

Discussion. Ask students why they think states require blood tests when applying for a marriage license. What problems are states trying to avoid? Do students agree with the laws requiring blood tests? Why or why not?

◆ Documents

Before a couple can be married, they must obtain a license. Legal requirements on applying for and getting the license vary from state to state.

When Julia and Cameron were about to be married, they went to the county courthouse, where they filled out and signed an application for a license. The county clerk gave them two forms to take with them. One was the license, which the clerk partially filled out. The other was a blank form that they could fill in and save as a keepsake. After the marriage ceremony, the minister signed the license and filled in the time and place of marriage. Later he sent the license back to the courthouse. Julia and Cameron filled in their keepsake form and asked the minister to sign it too. In their state no witnesses were required to sign the license.

The license, which was eventually returned for filing with the state, serves as an authorized written record of Julia and Cameron's marriage. Marriage licenses protect property rights, inheritances, and the rights of children. They help the courts make fair decisions whenever necessary.

A license is required in order to get married. This can usually be obtained at the county courthouse.

Life Management Skills. Have students work in pairs to write a sample prenuptial agreement covering financial issues, work and household tasks, social obligations, and other areas they feel are important. This type of agreement may help a couple manage time and energy as well as money.

Marriage Information

State	With Consent		Without Consent		Blood Test Required	Wait for License	Wait after License
	Men	*Women*	*Men*	*Women*			
Alabama	14 a	14 a	18	18	Yes	None	None
Alaska	16 b	16 b	18	18	Yes	3 days	None
Arizona	16 b	16 b	18	18	No	None	None
Arkansas	17 c	16 c	18	18	No	k	None
California	d	d	18	18	Yes	None	None
Colorado	16 b	16 b	18	18	No	None	None
Connecticut	16 b	16 b	18	18	Yes	4 days (l)	None
Delaware	16 a	16 a	18	18	No	None	24 hours
District of Columbia	16 a	16 a	18	18	Yes	3 days	None
Florida	16 a, c	16 a, c	18	18	Yes	3 days	None
Georgia	16 b, c	16 b, c	16	16	Yes	3 days	None
Hawaii	15	15	16	16	Yes	None	None
Idaho	16 b	16 b	18	18	Yes	None	None
Illinois	16	16	18	18	No	1 day	1 day
Indiana	17 c	17 c	18	18	Yes	72 hours	None
Iowa	18 b	18 b	18	18	No	3 days	None
Kansas	18 b	18 b	18	18	No	3 days	None
Kentucky	18 b, c	18 b, c	18	18	No	None	None
Louisiana	18 b	18 b	18	18	Yes	72 hours	None
Maine	16 b	16 b	18	18	No	3 days	None
Maryland	16 c, f	16 c, f	18	18	None	48 hours	None
Massachusetts	14	12	18	18	Yes	3 days	None
Michigan	16 c, e	16 c, e	18	18	Yes	3 days	None
Minnesota	16 b	16 b	18	18	None	5 days	None
Mississippi	17	15	17	15	Yes	3 days	None
Missouri	15 e, 18 b	15 e, 18 b	18	18	No	None	None
Montana	16	16	18	18	Yes	None	None
Nebraska	17	17	19	19	Yes	None	None
Nevada	16 b	16 b	18	18	None	None	None
New Hampshire	14 g	13 g	18	18	Yes	3 days	None
New Jersey	16 b, c	16 b, c	18	18	Yes	72 hours	None
New Mexico	16 e	16 e	18	18	Yes	None	None
New York	16 b	16 b	18	18	Yes	None	24 Hours
North Carolina	16 c, h	16 c, h	18	18	Yes	None	None
North Dakota	16	16	18	18	No	None	None
Ohio	18 b, c	16 b, c	18	18	Yes	5 days	None
Oklahoma	16 c	16 c	18	18	Yes	None	None
Oregon	17	17	18	18	No	3 days	None
Pennsylvania	16 e	16 e	18	18	Yes	3 days	None
Rhode Island	18 e	16 e	18	18	Yes	None	None
South Carolina	16 c	14 c	18	18	None	24 hours	None
South Dakota	16 c	16 c	18	18	No	None	None
Tennessee	16 e	16 e	18	18	No	3 days	None
Texas	14 g, j	14 g, j	18	18	No	None	None
Utah	18 a	18 a	18	18	Yes	None	None
Vermont	16 b	16 b	18	18	Yes	1 day	None
Virginia	16 a, c	16 a, c	18	18	Yes	None	None
Washington	17 e	17 e	18	18	No	3 days	None
West Virginia	18 c	18 c	18	18	Yes	3 days	None
Wisconsin	16	16	18	18	Yes	5 days	None
Wyoming	16 e	16 e	18	18	Yes	None	None
Puerto Rico	18 b, c, e	16 b, c, e	21	21	Yes	None	None

The World Almanac

(a) Parental consent not required if minor was previously married.
(b) Younger parties may marry with parental consent and/or permission of judge.
(c) Younger parties may obtain license in case of pregnancy or birth of child.
(d) No age limits.
(e) Younger parties may obtain license in special circumstances.
(f) If parties are under sixteen years of age, proof of age and the consent of parents in person is required.
(g) Parental consent and/or permission of judge is required.
(h) Unless parties are eighteen years of age or more, or female is pregnant or applicants are parents of a living child born out of wedlock.
(j) Below age of consent parties need parental consent and permission of judge.
(k) Parties must file notice of intention to marry with local clerk.
(l) Waiting period may be avoided.

Marriage licenses do not detail exactly what a couple agrees on or the duties of each as a married pair. Many marital duties and obligations are implied rather than spelled out by law. Still, some couples today do wish to have a formal agreement on certain issues. If they wish, a written contract can be prepared. They may want to clarify their feelings about such concerns as working, children, money management, education, and even where they will live.

When Herschel and Nicole decided to get married, they put their concerns into a contract, called a **prenuptial agreement**. They wanted something in writing about the handling of their property and income should they ever go separate ways. Although this seemed a little negative, they felt that it was a good idea. Writing a contract not only helps a couple work out their marital expectations together, but it can also provide protection on issues that are important to them.

When a couple marries, an oral contract is generally part of the ceremony. This is the "I do" recitation declared by the partners. It may be in the traditional format or be written by the couple themselves. Usually the person who will perform the marriage is consulted when couples wish to write their own vows.

◆ Waiting Period

Many states now require a waiting period between the time two people decide to marry and the time the ceremony is performed. The waiting period takes place either between the application and the receipt of the license or between the receipt of the license and the ceremony. The period varies according to the state, usually one to five days. The chart on page 274 gives more specific information on waiting periods.

◆ Marriage Ceremonies and Officials

Marriages in the United States may be performed in either a civil or religious ceremony. **Civil** refers to the civic or ordinary business of people. A civil ceremony is often performed in a courtroom or some location that has no religious connection. Religious ceremonies vary according to the specific traditions followed in each religion. What traditions have you observed in different wedding ceremonies?

Wedding vows are an oral contract. Some couples use traditional vows and others write their own.

Discussion. Ask students what they think a good age for marriage is. If state law says eighteen, does that make it right for everyone?

Activity. Have students interview couples who have recently married to find out the content of the vows recited at their wedding. Discuss the differences in the vows with the class. Why are vows important?

SIDELIGHT

Civil or Religious?

In colonial America feelings were divided about whether marriage ceremonies should be civil or religious. In the Church of England they were religious. The Virginia colony held with church custom and did not permit civil ceremonies. Still, the ceremonies performed by civil magistrates usually included prayers.

Those colonists who disagreed with the church passed laws in favor of civil ceremonies. In some early American settlements, ministers were not permitted to perform marriages. Time had its effect, however, and by the end of the eighteenth century, both civil and religious ceremonies had become legal in America.

◆◆◆

The person who performs a marriage ceremony may be a member of the clergy or a designated state official. Religious marriages usually are performed by a minister, priest, rabbi, mullah, or bishop. A judge or clerk of courts may perform civil marriage ceremonies. Others who may legally perform the ceremony are higher judges, mayors, recorders, magistrates, notaries public, and ship captains if the ceremony is performed at sea.

Even an ordinary citizen can conduct a legal marriage in some states. In these cases, if the partners solemnly and in good faith declare their marriage vows in the presence of a third party, the ceremony is considered legal.

Some states have specific laws for marriages in the Quaker faith. These require no official, with the two parties simply consenting to the marriage contract in the presence of the congregation.

◆ Prohibited Marriages

All states forbid marriages between blood relatives, or **consanguinity** (kahn-san-GWIN-uh-tee). Thus, a person may not marry his or her parent, grandparent, daughter or son, sibling, aunt or uncle, or niece or nephew. In addition, over half the states prohibit marriage between first cousins and between half-blood brothers and sisters. Some states consider marriages of second cousins illegal.

Objections to the marriages of close blood relatives make sense biologically. You may recall from your studies that blood relatives are likely to inherit the same genes from common ancestors. If so, defective genes have a double chance of being passed on to children who inherit from both parents.

Another objection is the age-old condemnation of incest, sexual relations between two people too closely related to marry legally. The most primitive societies consider incest taboo, or very wrong. All modern cultures maintain that attitude.

Some states also have regulations on marriages between people who are related by marriage only, or **affinity** (uh-FIN-uh-tee), such as a man and his stepdaughter. There is no biological basis for such prohibitions. Objections, however, may be based on the assumption that relationships of this type may not work well under the circumstances.

Activity. Have students research characteristics of civil and religious marriage ceremonies. What qualities make these ceremonies different? Why is there such diversity in marriage ceremonies?

Activity. Have students research the long-term genetic implications for children when any related persons marry. Students should identify groups of people in which intermarriage has occurred (at times unknowingly). What issues are faced in these communities?

◆ Living Together

Some couples choose to live together, or cohabitate, rather than marry. Such arrangements are generally offered few legal considerations under the law. In some states they are even illegal. When unmarried partners break up or one becomes ill or dies, no rights are afforded to the other concerning property or financial support in most states. One partner must sue the other in court to settle any financial disputes.

◆ Common-Law Marriages

In some states, a couple may be recognized as having a common-law marriage. The name common-law comes from the plebians, or common people, who practiced this type of union in years past. In a common-law marriage, the couple consider themselves married even though legal requirements have not been met. The partnership may need to exist for a specified length of time before it is recognized legally. Mutual consent is the key element in common-law marriages. The validity is derived from the consent of both parties. Many states forbid such marriages but recognize them as valid when entered into in states where they are allowed.

◆ Changing Your Name

For many years women have taken the last name of their husbands when they marry. This tradition is no longer followed by everyone. Some women simply keep their own name. Others create a new name by combining last names with a hyphen. Legally, couples may do as they wish on this issue.

◆◆◆

The Need for Marriage Laws

The laws you have read about were written for specific reasons. The partners in a marriage and the children who may be born to them need certain protections. When Urmila's husband left her with two small children to raise and very little income, her marriage license gave her the right to seek child support from him. He was reluctant to comply but was forced by the courts. Without this protection, Urmila would have struggled to meet the children's needs and might have turned to public aid. As you think about each of the legal requirements for marriage, you will see reasons why our legislators have made them part of the marriage process.

Marriage laws help protect people. Even when a legal marriage ends, the parents, whether present or not, are still responsible for providing support for the children.

Activity. Divide the class into two teams. Have students debate the pros and cons of living together before marriage. Students should examine the issue from all points of view. Include research information. Are marriages more successful when couples live together first? Does living together result in more commitment?

Work and Family. Some women decide to keep their maiden names upon marriage. Why? How do female students feel about keeping their name? How do male students feel about women not taking the husband's name upon marriage? What surname should be given to children if a woman keeps her maiden name?

CHAPTER 19

Review

Summarizing the Chapter

- Marriage laws and customs develop from economic and social conditions of different times and different regions.
- The earliest unions were marriages of capture, when the groom kidnapped the prospective bride. This was followed by marriages by purchase and finally marriage for love.
- For a legal marriage to occur, a license must be obtained, a ceremony must be performed by an authorized person, and the marriage must be officially reported.
- State marriage laws vary.
- Marriage laws dictate the age at which people may marry, the physical and mental requirements, the obtaining of a license, the waiting period, and who may conduct the ceremony.
- Marriage laws are designed to protect the couple and their children.

Testing Your Memory

1. How did marriage by capture differ from marriage by purchase?
2. Why was the mother's approval unnecessary in marriage by purchase?
3. List three ways that marriage customs have changed since colonial days.
4. List three reasons for declaring a marriage invalid.
5. On what basis is legal marriage age determined in the states?
6. What is the purpose of a blood test?
7. List five officials who can legally perform a civil marriage.
8. Why are marriages between blood relatives prohibited?
9. What is the major disadvantage of cohabitation?
10. Why are marriage laws important?

Answers
Testing Your Memory

1. Marriage by capture involved kidnapping. Marriage by purchase involved the prospective husband asking a father for permission and approval to marry his daughter.
2. Mothers as well as daughters were under the domination of the husband/father.
3. Refer to the chart on page 271.
4. Marriages may be declared invalid if either party opposes the marriage, if one partner is under the influence of alcohol or drugs, or if threats forcing the marriage were used.
5. Legal marriage age is based on when young people may marry without parental consent. Most states allow marriages at a younger age with parental consent and/or permission of a judge.
6. To make sure partners are free from certain communicable diseases, especially STDs.
7. **Any five:** judge or clerk of courts; mayors; recorders; magistrates; higher judges; notaries public; ship captains if ceremony is performed at sea; an ordinary citizen in some states.

Thinking Critically

1. Why do marriage laws vary from state to state? Do you think marriage laws should be uniform nationally? State your reasons.
2. Why do you think some states require a waiting period between the time a couple decides to marry and the time the ceremony can actually take place?
3. Is a marriage license more than just a piece of paper? Explain your answer.

Taking Action

1. Imagine that you are a bride or groom during the period when marriages occurred by capture. Assuming you could write, record the events of your marriage by capture and your feelings in a diary.
2. Investigate the laws that regulate marriage and prenuptial agreements in your state. Report your findings to the class.
3. Act out a situation that could have occurred during the time when brides were purchased from their fathers. The groom and his family need to arrive at a financial arrangement with the bride's family.
4. Where can a marriage license be obtained in your area? Try to get a copy of the required form or forms to share with the class. What is the cost of applying for a license?

Making Life Choices

Jonathan and Dianne are seriously considering marriage. Jonathan's family is very well off financially, while Dianne's parents have struggled through the years to provide a nice home and good education for their children. Jonathan's brother is urging him to reach a prenuptial financial agreement with Dianne just in case the marriage fails and Dianne demands a large settlement. Dianne feels a prenuptial agreement signifies doubt about the marriage. Her friends tell her not to do it. She feels that she is being pressured from both sides.

If you were Dianne, what would you do?

Using Your Journal

It is no accident that there are so many laws concerning marriage. It is a serious undertaking that requires serious thought. Use your journal to explore your own feelings about marriage. What kinds of marriage traditions does your family have? Would you hope to follow the family traditions if you get married? Would you want to draw up a prenuptial agreement? Why or why not? What kinds of issues do you think should be covered in a prenuptial agreement?

8. There is concern about blood relatives inheriting common defective genes, which may be passed on to children.
9. Very few legal considerations under the law.
10. Marriage laws provide protection to partners and their children, especially in the area of financial support.

Thinking Critically

1. Each state sets its own laws on marriage. Answers will vary.
2. Answers will vary. Point out that sometimes couples may have second thoughts about the marriage.
3. Answers will vary. Emphasize that a marriage license does have some built-in protections for the marriage partners.

CHAPTER 20

The Decision to Marry

Chapter Challenge

Resources. Refer to the Teacher's Classroom Resources box and Student Workbook for materials related to this chapter.

Look for These Answers . . .

- How does your choice of a marriage partner affect your life?
- What factors should be considered before deciding to marry?
- What are the purposes of the engagement period?
- What can make the planning of a wedding go more smoothly?

Look for These Terms . . .

- compatible
- conviction
- engagement
- interfaith marriage
- interracial marriage

Kip watched the doorway as the music began. Megan appeared on her father's arm. "She looks beautiful," Kip thought. His knees were still shaking, but he was starting to feel less nervous.

As Megan moved slowly down the aisle, Kip reassured himself. "We did this right. Father O'Brien knew what we should be thinking about before going through with this marriage. With his help we did a lot of talking. It wouldn't have been easy to go separate ways at this point, but it would have been better than finding out later that we don't belong together. We are right for each other, and I'm sure of that now."

With her wedding train trailing behind her, Megan moved closer to Kip. She was not worried about entering into this marriage. They had spent time getting to know each other well. Megan's eyes met Kip's steady gaze with confidence. Together they stepped before the priest, ready to begin a new life as marriage partners.

Chapter Opener. Ask students to read the opening scenario to the chapter. Discuss with the students some reasons why Megan and Kip thought it was important to know each other well before marrying. Why should major issues, such as children and finances, be discussed prior to marriage? Should the values and goals of a couple contemplating marriage be similar? What may happen if values conflict?

More About Engagements. A marriage counselor once asked a couple considering marriage, "Why do you think you will be among the 50% of marriages that work? What have you got going for you that makes you so sure your marriage will last?" This question encouraged the couple to examine their relationship in depth. The counselor also asked, "What issues could cause you to divorce?" Premarital counseling sessions often focus on resolving areas of conflict.

Look Before You Leap

"Until death do us part" is a promise that has been repeated often in the traditional wedding vows. Nevertheless, many couples enter marriage equipped only with hopes and dreams. The knowledge they need to make this promise come true is often overlooked. They may be convinced that their marriage will endure a lifetime, but have they chosen a partner with whom this will be possible?

Think for a moment. What decisions that you make have a major impact on the direction your life takes? One concerns education, another your career, and one is the marriage partner you may select. That marriage partner will have an effect on your happiness, your standard of living, the way you spend your time, and even what your children are like. Isn't this reason enough to look carefully before you leap? You can say "I do" in a short time, but it commits you for a large portion of your life. When you make the decision to marry, use your head not just your heart. There are many things to think about.

◆ Examining Reasons for Marriage

Sometimes the decision to marry is affected by circumstances and emotions that really have no place in the decision. Rene married at an early age in order to escape family problems at home. She did escape them, but she gained a whole new set of problems and never settled the ones left behind. Holly wanted someone to take care of her. She married an older man who was almost like a father to her. When the marriage ended, she had no way to support herself. Harman married because of pressure from his family and his girlfriend. He knew it was not right, but he gave in and paid the price later. Before you marry, examine the reasons behind your decision. First, the decision should be yours. Second, it should be based on love, commitment, and careful thought.

◆ The Attraction

What is it that brings a couple together in the first place? Often it is something physical — a smile, a way of walking, expressive eyes, an appealing physique. This is fine to get a relationship started, but it is not enough to make one last. People who base a marriage on physical attraction alone often end up with regrets. The qualities that can make a relationship last are much deeper. Think about these when making a decision to marry. They are likely to be much more important to you than physical attractiveness alone.

A Slice of Life

As a senior in high school, Carlos had never been out with a girl. He didn't even bother to ask, because no one ever looked twice at him. Carlos was quiet (around school anyway), his grades were good, and he was a member of the science club. He didn't play sports, although sometimes he wished he did. The girls really seemed to go for athletes.

Andrea was different. She was the first girl who had ever gone out of her way to be friendly to Carlos. He wondered if she could like him as more than a friend. He knew he wasn't good looking, but Andrea didn't seem to care.

Several years later Andrea and Carlos were married. Carlos went to college where he studied aeronautical engineering. In time he took a job with the Space Administration. He received many promotions and had a good income. Andrea and Carlos had two children, whom Carlos loved intensely. He was a fine father and husband. They had a wonderful life together.

Thinking It Through

- Why do you think Carlos never asked anyone for a date?
- What qualities do you think Carlos had that Andrea appreciated?
- Why do people like Carlos often get overlooked as dating partners in high school?
- Which is more important to you, a person's exterior or interior? Why? Is your attitude shown by your actions?

Activity. Have students brainstorm a list of reasons why people marry. The list should include: to escape from family; pregnancy; love; money; status; to be thought of as an adult; pressure from parents and/or friends; to have children; to have companionship, etc. Are some reasons better than others? Is a pregnancy a good reason to get married? Why or why not?

Discussion. Discuss attraction with the students. What role does physical attraction play in a developing relationship? What happens when couples depend only on physical attraction to hold the relationship together?

◆ Maturity Level

"Tyrone wants to get married, but he seems so immature. If he can't handle simple situations like an adult now, what will it be like when we are married?" Erin's observation is a valid one. Immaturity can be a stumbling block in a marriage. Although not a perfect indicator, age is a common gauge of maturity. It may not seem so to you now, but the younger you are, the less likely you are to be ready for the responsibilities of marriage. You may not even realize what you need in a lifetime partner. Moreover, the teens and early twenties are years of rapid change. The person you see at this age may be different when maturity is reached.

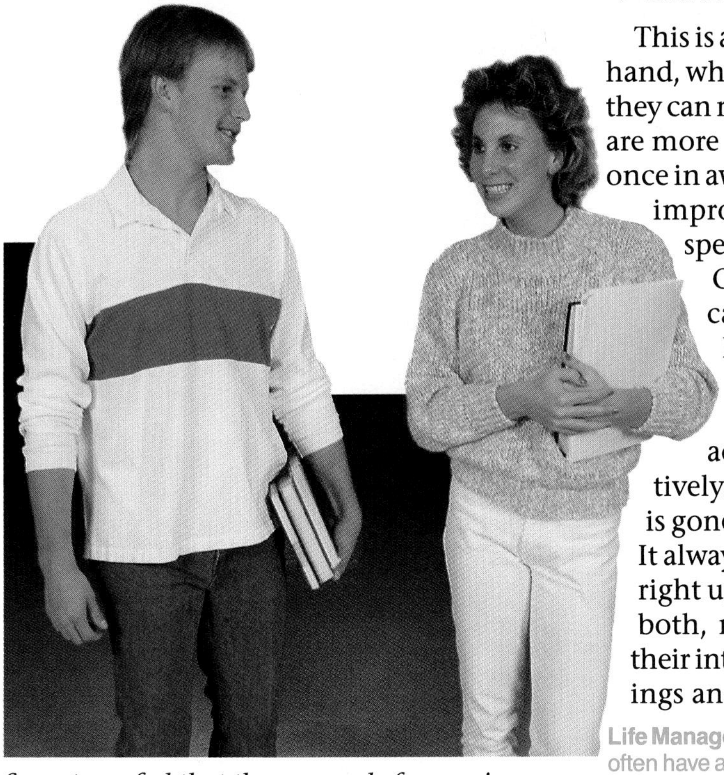

Some teens feel that they are ready for marriage. Statistics show, however, that the younger the couple is, the greater the risk of divorce.

Activity. Invite a couple who have been married 40 or 50 years and a couple married 3 or 4 years to speak with the students. Students should ask questions such as: What attracted the partners to each other? When did they know they were right for each other? How long did they know each other before marriage?

Evidence shows that the loves of adolescence do not last as well as those that begin in later years. The divorce rate is higher for them. Men and women who put off marriage until they are at least in their twenties benefit from emotional maturity and better income. Both factors increase chances for stability and satisfaction.

◆ Education

In general, partners who have the same level of education have a better chance of success in marriage. They are more likely to communicate on the same level. Can you think of other reasons why?

◆ Mutual Interests

This is a difficult area to assess. On the one hand, when couples have different interests, they can retain their separate identities. They are more likely to get away from each other once in awhile for a change of pace. This can improve the quality of the time they spend together.

On the other hand, separate interests can sometimes lead to problems. Denise, for example, loves tennis. She takes lessons, spends countless hours on the courts, and travels across the country to play competitively. Clark likes hunting. In season he is gone from his family for days at a time. It always seems that one season just backs right up to another. For Denise and Clark both, marital conflicts have arisen over their interests. This leads to misunderstandings and resentment.

Life Management Skills. People who marry in their teens often have a difficult time reaching their career goals. Ask students to develop a reasonable budget for a married couple. What kinds of jobs would pay enough to meet this budget? What kind of education is necessary to meet job requirements? What obstacles would teens face in meeting career goals? What would be necessary for teens to meet career goals in addition to education and money?

Discussion. Assign students to small groups. Each group should elect a secretary. Have students discuss and record the role maturity plays in a developing relationship. Ask students to give examples of mature behavior in relationships.

Married couples who share some interests can spend time together in ways that they both enjoy.

Many couples find that sharing at least some interests helps a marriage. They want to spend time together, and this is much easier to do when there are activities they both enjoy.

Before you marry, examine your interests as well as those of your potential partner. Are they different? If so, how much time will you spend apart? Do you share any interests? Do you have any intense interest that you will have to give up for this marriage? Can you give it up permanently?

◆ Qualities and Habits

When the stars get in your eyes, it is far too easy to overlook things that later become important. Depending on your level of tolerance and ability to adjust, many personal qualities and habits can be overlooked. After all, does it really matter how the toothpaste tube is squeezed? Sometimes there are simple solutions. Buy two tubes.

Other characteristics, however, are more important. If you are meticulous and your mate-to-be is sloppy, you may have a problem on your hands. Is your potential partner abusive in any way? If your partner hits you once now, there will be more later. Don't ignore it. How do you feel about marrying a smoker? You may be even more concerned when you have children. Are alcohol or other drugs a problem? These are destructive to a relationship. Whether small or large, look at the personal characteristics that bother you. Know what is important to you and what can have an effect on your life.

When marriage partners are very different in their habits, this can lead to problems. A neat person seldom enjoys cleaning up after someone who is messy.

Discussion. Ask students how important it is for spouses to share interests and hobbies. Is the mate selection theory, "opposites attract," a valid theory? Why or why not? (See Chapter 15) Have students defend their answers logically.

Photo Focus. Ask students to look at the above photo. Then discuss ways in which couples can resolve conflict regarding differences in habits.

SIDELIGHT

Evaluating Qualities

Which of the following qualities would be important to you in a spouse?

Accepts constructive criticism
Affectionate
Attractive
Communicates well
Confident
Considerate
Educated
Faithful
Generous
Has good income
Honest
Intelligent
Mature
Neat
Pleasing personality
Positive in attitude
Religious
Shows sense of humor
Reliable
Trustworthy
Understanding
Wants (or does not want) children

◆◆◆

◆ Compatibility

When people are **compatible** (kum-PAT-uh-bull), they exist together in harmony. The way one couple gets along does not necessarily match the way another does. Some survive with a little friction now and then. Others live a smoother lifestyle. Ask yourself what makes you comfortable. If your spouse-to-be is argumentative and this upsets you, you have a compatibility problem. The way you get along now is an indicator of how you will get along later. Any difficulties you see are likely to get worse, not better.

◆ Goals and Desires

When Todd and Noreen married, they had never talked much about what they wanted for the future. In time Noreen realized that Todd was content with his job in the grocery store. He could stay there forever, as long as he had enough income for a little house in the country close to a lake for fishing. Noreen, however, yearned to live in the city. She wanted access to people and the theatre. Her income would be higher if they moved to the city, and she could have more of what she wanted in life.

When goals and desires for the future clash, couples may have problems. Solutions are not simple. Sometimes compromises work, but often one partner must give up too much. Find out what your spouse-to-be wants in life. If you are far apart in your desires, think twice about marriage. This can pull you further apart later.

◆ Convictions

A **conviction** is something you believe strongly and take very seriously. Your convictions do not easily change. When one spouse feels deeply about an issue and the other disagrees, the chances for conflict and misunderstanding rise sharply. Sharing your thoughts about serious issues with a potential partner helps. You may find that the more differences you discover, the less interest you have in that person as a lifemate.

Activity. Give each student 20 small slips of paper and have them list 20 qualities they would like in a mate. Ask the students to set aside five qualities that are the least important to a good marriage. Then ask them to set aside five more that are not too important to a good marriage. Of the remaining 10 , are there any that they would "give up" for love? Are there any of the final 10 that are very important? Have students discuss their choices and give supporting reasons for their choices. How would these qualities contribute to a successful marriage?

Couples who share the same religious convictions have lower divorce rates than those who do not.

◆ Religion

Many convictions are based on religious training. Partners who worship in the same faith on a regular basis have similar religious convictions and the lowest breakup rates. In an **interfaith marriage** partners come from different religions. These marriages produce more divorces, probably due to the contrasting convictions. Spouses who claim no religious attachment divorce most.

In an interfaith marriage, the sharper the religious differences between a husband and wife, the greater their chances for problems. Many couples do find ways to manage such differences. Sometimes one partner changes to the other's religion, although this is not easy for many people to do. They may decide to follow customs of both religions in the home. They may agree to raise the children in one religion. Although these solutions sound simple on the surface, remember that they are not. Religious convictions are often held very deeply. Challenges to them are felt just as deeply. The source of the challenge can become a focus for resentment. For this reason, consider religion carefully when making a decision to marry.

Activity. Have students interview clergy from several different faiths. What marriage preparation do they offer couples? What problems most often occur? What solutions are offered to couples before marriage? Is contact maintained with couples after marriage? What issues may occur in interchurch or interfaith marriages?

◆ Family

The family of your future spouse is very important. First, it offers clues to what your life may be like. In Wade's family, a typical Sunday afternoon was spent watching football on television. Although she had no interest in football, Candace sat with Wade and the others on many Sunday afternoons while they were dating. After they broke up, Candace realized how much more she enjoyed Sundays when she could get out and do things. Life with Wade would not have been like this.

Another consideration is compatibility with a future partner's family. In general family bonds are tight. Malcolm does not get along with Tamika's father. This always puts Tamika in the middle. The stress she feels in trying to please both her father and Malcolm is likely to cause problems if they marry. Tamika cannot give up her family for Malcolm, nor should she be expected to. If Malcolm is at fault, Tamika would be smart to look elsewhere for a marriage partner.

Spending time with your future mate's family will give you clues about your future. What might you discover?

Problem Solving. Interracial marriages are more common now than in the past. Have students discuss ways in which prejudice against interracial marriage may be eliminated. What challenges may be faced in changing the attitudes of others?

◆ Friends

When you marry someone, you get more than just the individual. You get friends too—your partner's friends. How many and what they are like varies. Your partner may be very closely linked to certain friends. You may be too. Friends need not, even should not, be given up for marriage. Both partners need others for good social and emotional health. Friction can come, however, if you do not like each other's friends or if you resent the amount of time spent with them. This is something to think about before marriage too.

Interracial couples have extra challenges to face. What problems do you think they might have to overcome?

◆ Children

Discussions about children should take place before marriage. Well into their marriage, Cory learned that Anita did not want children. He did. Although the marriage continued, Cory was deeply affected. He buried the resentment he felt as best he could, but it was always a source of heartache for him.

Do you want to have children or not? If so, how many would you like? Strong differences on these questions spell trouble. People do change their minds, but you cannot count on this. Sometimes people are persuaded even though their feelings have not changed. This is unfair to the children born in such a marriage. Talking about children and birth control before marriage helps both partners know where they stand on this issue.

◆ Interracial Marriages

All couples must deal with differences, whether they be age, education, politics, social class, viewpoint, or anything else. Strong differences are obviously harder to handle. Race is one of these.

When people of different races fall in love and marry, theirs is an **interracial marriage.** These couples face extra challenges. In general, society has been slow to accept interracial marriage, particularly the black-white combination. This attitude is based on prejudice. Children in such marriages must deal with feelings about their identities and the negative attitudes of some people. Strong families are able to make interracial marriages work, yet it is not easy. As long as some people continue to use exteriors to judge others, people in interracial marriages will face problems. This realization should be carefully considered when making decisions about interracial marriage.

Problem Solving. Jane's husband Dave is very close to his parents and siblings. Sometimes Jane dislikes Dave's close attachment to his family. Ask students to describe how Jane and Dave could handle this potential problem. What alternatives are there for Jane and Dave? What recommendations would you make? Why?

◆ Different Nationalities

Travel and study in other countries is much more common today than it was in the past. The result is increased opportunities for people of different nationalities to fall in love. These people come from different cultures where traditions, lifestyles, and even food preferences are not the same. People in these marriages must adjust to having families distanced by the miles. Such marriages can work, but the partners must enter them with realistic thought and foresight.

Activity. Have students interview a couple who are of different nationalities. How did they meet? What was it like to meet the partner's family? What adjustments did each have to make to the other's customs and traditions? How did their families react to the marriage? What advice would they give couples considering marriage?

Before marriage it helps to talk about roles. You need to know whether or not your future mate has similar attitudes to yours about who does what household jobs.

◆ Role Expectations

Examine your own thinking for a minute. What should the role of a husband be? What about a wife? If a couple has children, what should parental roles be like? If you and your future spouse do not agree on these roles, there may be trouble ahead.

As you have read, men and women once had specific gender-related responsibilities. Over the years the boundaries have blurred. Today both men and women do jobs that were once clearly divided.

Because of their upbringing and attitudes, people today view roles in different ways. When talking with a future spouse about roles, explore topics like these in order to reach some understandings:

- Who should be employed in the family and when?
- As a couple, how will you handle housework, cooking, and home maintenance?
- How will finances be handled?
- If you have children, who will care for them?

Activity. Divide students into small groups. Provide each group with sheets of paper containing the following questions (one question per sheet): What is a husband's role in marriage? A wife's role? How have role expectations changed over the past twenty years? Discuss small group responses with the entire class.

◆ Parental Input

Sometimes parents have reservations about the partner their child has selected. Although it may not be easy, this is a good time to listen. Parents have your best interests in mind. If you are mature enough, you will be open to their observations. They have the perspective of experience and may see what you have not. Be willing to value their opinions and discuss the situation with them. A marriage that begins with parental approval has one less hurdle to leap.

◆ Counseling

When in doubt, get help. If you are not sure about the partner you have chosen, you may need the unbiased, but trained, input of a third party. Remember Kip and Megan at the beginning of this chapter? They counseled with Father O'Brien, a priest in their church. Religious officials commonly give this kind of help. Professional counseling is another possibility.

Many couples confer with a religious official before marriage. Such individuals are experienced at helping couples evaluate their readiness for marriage.

Activity. Ask students to investigate places in the community where couples considering marriage could get counseling. What are the fees for counseling services? Is there any financial aid for premarital counseling? Have them report their findings to the class.

◆ Putting It All Together

Once people are in a marriage, they will usually do their best to make it work. In the early stages, they may be more willing to give up certain desires. They may tolerate more. In time, however, the differences have a way of surfacing.

An ounce of prevention is worth a pound of cure. You have probably heard this saying before. In this chapter, here is what it means: By making an effort to get to know the other person before you marry, you can find out whether marriage is right for you. If you discover that it is not, you may save yourself many years of regrets.

◆◆◆

The Engagement

Once a couple has decided to marry, they usually become engaged. During the **engagement** period, the partners make wedding plans and continue to take a close look at their relationship. Six months to a year is usually recommended for an engagement. This gives a couple time to make sure they want to be partners for life. If necessary, the relationship can still be ended during the engagement period. Even when wedding plans have been made, it is better to call things off if there is doubt. A lifetime of happiness hangs in the balance.

◆◆◆

The Wedding

Weddings range from simple services in a courtroom to extravagant ceremonies in a church. The wishes of bride and groom, as well as the families of both, are taken into consideration. Getting all to agree on the details is not always easy. To make it work, start making arrangements early. Combine diplomacy with compromise and keep your sense of humor.

Balancing *Work & Family*

Planning for the Future

Debby patted her stomach. "We hope this baby is going to be the first of three," she announced excitedly.

Her husband, Todd, nodded in agreement. "Debby will continue to work, while I stay home with the children," he said.

"But, of course, we'll both be responsible for discipline," they said in unison, laughing when they realized they were thinking the exact same thing.

Debby and Todd share the same vision for the future. It's obvious they discussed what they wanted and came to an agreement. Then, they divided responsibilities between them.

Like Debby and Todd, couples need to agree on how to balance work and family. Here are some issues they may need to discuss:

- Do we want children? Some people don't, while others want several. A couple needs to agree on whether or not they'll have children, and how many they'd prefer.
- Who will pursue a career? Both partners may wish to do so, or one may prefer to stay at home. Still others may change work schedules from full- to part-time, or decide to work at home.
- What about child care? One partner may favor a child care center while the other may prefer a sitter to care for children at home.
- What will be our roles and responsibilities? Will housework be shared? If one parent stays at home, will the other take over child-care responsibilities in the evenings?

Think About It

1. What might happen if couples do not take the time to plan together for the future?
2. What options are open to couples who disagree about having children?

Discussion. Ask students if engagements can be too long. Why? How much of a person's "past life" needs to be revealed during the engagement period? Are there benefits in being totally honest? Are there things the future spouse does not need to know? May lack of honesty during engagement affect the marriage? How?

Many details go into the planning of a wedding. Despite this, calling a wedding off is preferred to going ahead when you have doubts.

Weddings can be very expensive. Costs have a way of adding up without your even realizing it. This is one good reason for setting a budget. List all the expenses ahead of time and decide what is a reasonable budget for covering them. According to tradition, the bride's family pays for the wedding. This is often not followed today. Many families split the costs, and some couples pay for their wedding themselves.

Many details surround the planning of a wedding. There are dates and times to set, a guest list to prepare, invitations to send, and flowers and clothes to select, among many other details. The chart on page 291 will give you an idea about what must be done and when. To make the job easier, books are available that will take you through every step. Bridal shops can be consulted. Magazines have ideas too. If you wish and can handle the expense, wedding services are also available.

After all the planning and preparation, the wedding day finally arrives. If they wish, the couple may follow the ceremony with a reception and a honeymoon trip. This is an exciting time for a young couple. They become a partnership, ready to make a successful new life together. This takes effort, as you will see in the next chapter.

Life Management Skills. Have students gather information from businesses involved in weddings, such as photographers, caterers, florists, musicians, and printers. How much do weddings cost? How can the cost of a wedding be reduced to stay within a budget?

Work and Family. Have students react to the following situation: Garth and Kristina had been out of school and working a number of years when they decided to get married. The major obstacle in their wedding plans revolved around who should pay for the wedding, Garth and Kristina or their parents. How can this be solved?

The Wedding Checklist

Four to Twelve Months Ahead

- ☐ Determine a budget and style of wedding (informal, formal, etc.).
- ☐ Decide where the ceremony will be.
  Visit your clergyperson. Select a service and set the date.
- ☐ Plan the reception.
- ☐ Choose your attendants and ushers.
- ☐ Make a guest list.
- ☐ If desired, register gift preferences at your favorite store.
- ☐ Select a wedding dress, veil, accessories, and bridesmaids' dresses. Consult a men's formal-wear specialist if desired.
- ☐ Make arrangements with the photographer and florist.
- ☐ Select wedding music and make arrangements with organist.

Three Months Ahead

- ☐ Order invitations, personal stationery, and notepaper.
- ☐ Plan the honeymoon.

Two Months Ahead

- ☐ Address wedding invitations.
- ☐ Choose gifts for attendants and ushers.
- ☐ Buy wedding ring(s).
- ☐ Plan to get the marriage license at a time that meets your state's laws for length of validity. Find out whether a blood test is required and when.
- ☐ Plan recording and display of gifts.

One Month Ahead

- ☐ Have your hair styled the way you will wear it for the wedding to be sure you like the style.
- ☐ Have final fitting on wedding gown and bridesmaid's gowns.
- ☐ If necessary, plan the rehearsal dinner.
- ☐ Plan accommodations for out-of-town guests.
- ☐ Mail invitations.
- ☐ Have formal portrait taken.

Two Weeks Ahead

- ☐ Write thank you notes as gifts are received and recorded.
- ☐ Send wedding announcement to paper.
- ☐ If bride's name will change, arrange to do so on social security, driver's license, credit cards, bank accounts, etc.

One Week Ahead

- ☐ Finalize plans with caterer, florist, and photographer.
- ☐ Confirm rehearsal plans with clergyperson and attendants.

Discussion. Ask students to discuss ways in which couples can reduce stress and tension when planning a wedding.

Activity. On index cards, write down situations about couples planning to marry. Provide some information regarding budget, size of wedding, and attendants, etc. Divide students into pairs and provide each pair with a situation card. Using the information on the card, have each pair of students plan a wedding.

CHAPTER

20

Review

Answers
Testing Your Memory
1. No. Physical attraction will not make a marriage last.
2. Lack of maturity and responsibility.
3. Opposing habits, such as smoking, drinking, and neatness; abusiveness; drug related habits. (Students may list other qualities.)
4. Convictions do not easily change. One spouse may feel strongly about an issue that the other disagrees with. This will sometimes cause problems.
5. Marriage to someone of a different faith.
6. It offers clues to what your life with your spouse might be like; compatibility with a future partner's family.
7. You may view this issue differently from your future spouse. It's better to discuss children before marriage than to find out later that your spouse does or doesn't want to have children.
8. **Any three:** Who should work? How will housework, cooking, and home maintenance be handled? How will finances be handled? Who will care for your children if you have them?
9. Make arrangements early. Combine diplomacy with compromise and keep your sense of humor.

Summarizing the Chapter

- Some people marry for reasons other than love.
- A marriage based on physical attraction alone may not survive.
- Examining interests, characteristics, compatibility, and goals and desires can help when thinking about a future marriage partner.
- Convictions are hard to change, including those based on religion. These need to be considered before marriage.
- Family and friends have an impact on a marriage.
- Discussions about children should be made before marriage.
- Differences in partners, such as race, religion, nationality, and education, can complicate relationships.
- Most weddings require much planning and preparation.

Testing Your Memory

1. Should a relationship be based on physical attraction? Explain your answer.
2. Explain why teen marriages are less likely to last than marriages between people in their midtwenties.
3. List three personal qualities that can cause problems for a couple.
4. How can convictions cause marital problems?
5. What is an interfaith marriage?
6. Why should you take a close look at your future partner's family before marrying?
7. Why should the subject of children be discussed by potential marriage partners?
8. List three topics that partners should explore when thinking about roles.
9. What can people do to make planning a wedding go as smoothly as possible?

Thinking Critically

1. Often older couples and those who are marrying for the second time examine their relationship more carefully before marriage than young couples do. Why do you think this is true?
2. Why do you think young people sometimes reject their parents' negative feelings about a future spouse? What might result from such rejection?

Taking Action

1. Have you thought about the qualities you would like in a spouse? Create an advertisement for the type of person you want. Include your expectations and the requirements you feel are necessary for a successful marriage.
2. Working with a partner, make a list of all the considerations discussed in this chapter. Then prioritize them from most important (number 1) to least important. Compare lists with others in the class.
3. Interview three couples, one married fewer than five years, one 20-25 years, and one over 40 years. Compare and contrast the marital roles of these individuals. For those who have been married for many years, have the roles changed at all?

Making Life Choices

Jan and Paul met while she was still a senior in high school. He was a freshman in junior college and still living at home. They liked each other and began to date. In time Jan learned that Paul was keeping their relationship a secret from his family. She was a Protestant and he was a Catholic. Paul's family had never approved of his dating someone outside their religion. Jan was bothered by this secrecy, especially since she and Paul were becoming very close.

How do you feel about the way Jan, Paul, and Paul's family are handling this situation? What would you do if you were in the shoes of each of these people?

Using Your Journal

Reread the section titled "Look Before You Leap" at the beginning of this chapter and think about your plans for education, career, and so on. Then use your diary to record the things you would want to discuss with a future marriage partner. What would you want that person to know about you? What are some of your strongly held convictions? How do you like to spend your spare time? What makes you easy to live with? What makes you difficult to live with? Add any other ideas that occur to you.

Thinking Critically

1. Couples who have been married before know that their previous marriage didn't work out, so they want to examine more closely their current relationship. Older couples know they will probably only marry once and want to be sure it will last.
2. They may think their parents are being overprotective. Parents usually have their children's best interests in mind. The young people may enter into a marriage destined for failure.

CHAPTER 21

Successful Marriages

Chapter Challenge

Resources. Refer to the Teacher's Classroom Resources box and Student Workbook for materials related to this chapter.

Look for These Answers . . .

- Describe ways to make a marriage successful.
- How can you use communication, decision making, and conflict resolution skills to make a successful marriage?
- What role do friends and in-laws have in marriage?

Look for These Terms . . .

- affection
- intimacy

"Fifty years! We salute you, Rosa and Joe, for fifty years of a perfect marriage!"

Rosa smiled. "Well, maybe not so perfect," she thought. "My Joseph is a good man, but perfect he's not. As for me, I haven't been perfect for one day of my life. How did we get this far then?"

It seemed like only yesterday that they were just starting out. Things were not easy for them, but they weathered it all — the good and the bad.

"How did you do it, Grandma Rosa? Grandpa Joe, what has made your marriage last? Tell us all so that we too can be successful."

"I accepted him the way he was," Rosa responded, "silly jokes and all."

"As for me," Joe said, "I loved her, and I still do today." Joe and Rosa exchanged a glance and smiled. They knew it was more — much more.

Chapter Opener. Ask students to read the opening scenario of the chapter. How may this marriage be an inspiration to young couples just starting out? How do you think Rosa and Joe worked through the tough times? What problems may they have encountered in the early years of their marriage? Do couples today face similar issues or have times changed? What advantages do today's couples have that Rosa and Joe might not have had? How can accepting people as they are make working through marriage issues easier?

Activity. Ask students to identify one couple whom they feel has a strong marriage. Have students write a brief paper identifying the reasons why they think this marriage is strong. What qualities do they admire? Why? What qualities would they like to bring to their own marriage some day in the future?

Discussion. Ask each student to identify three things that they could not tolerate in a spouse. Discuss why those habits or qualities would be so bothersome. How could they change in order to be more accepting of people's habits?

Planning for Success

Marriages are much like any of the other friendships people have. They are strengthened and weakened in many of the same ways. For example, look at Isaiah and Roberto's friendship. At first, it was a strong one. When they went places, they always took Isaiah's car. It bothered Isaiah that Roberto never offered to share the cost of gas. Still, they had a good time, so Isaiah let it go. Roberto always decided where they would go on weekends. Isaiah let him choose, because if he didn't, Roberto would be unhappy. Over time Isaiah noticed many things that bothered him about Roberto. He just let them go. After all, they were minor problems, and Roberto was a good friend. Then one day, Roberto was late in meeting Isaiah at the arcade. Isaiah blew up. Roberto was stunned. He couldn't understand why being late would make Isaiah so mad. Soon after, their friendship ended.

What happened in this friendship? The same thing can happen in marriages. Isaiah and Roberto both needed to put more effort into their friendship. Isaiah should have dealt with problems as they came up. When you don't, everything builds until one minor incident becomes the focus for every wrong that has occurred. Roberto should have given something to the friendship. His attitude was self-centered, which put extra pressures on Isaiah.

Like friendships, marriages only work with effort. Everyone wants to be happy in marriage. Saying "I do," however, does not magically ensure that you will have a rich, warm, loving marriage for a lifetime. You must think about what it takes to sustain a marital relationship and plan to address these needs every day — right from the beginning. Successful marriages don't just happen. They are made.

◆◆◆

Accepting Each Other

You have just read that a person should deal with problems as they come up. Now you are going to read that you should be accepting of the other person. Does this seem a bit contradictory? If you think so, you are probably right. How can you know when to take issue with your mate and when to just let things go? It is not easy.

When you accept your mate, you do not plan to change him or her. Entering a marriage with thoughts about change is unwise. People do not become neater, more thoughtful, or more mature because of marriage. Also, troublesome habits, such as smoking, do not disappear after marriage. If anything, the qualities and habits you want to change will become more annoying to you with time. Any attempts you make to force a change will be resented, making things worse. The bottom line is this: If you cannot accept the person as is, think twice before getting married.

Change can occur in marriage as a response to a specific situation. Suppose a couple share household duties, but the outdoor work is always done by the husband. He feels that this should be shared too. A discussion can solve this problem and bring about change. This type of change is healthy.

Whenever something bothers you in a marriage, evaluate its importance. Most couples learn to accept a great deal. In other words, try not to magnify small problems. If the issue is serious to you, however, then find a constructive way to bring about change.

◆◆◆

Communicating

Communication is the key to a successful marriage. Good communication is a constructive tool for bringing about change. It lets you and your spouse know where you stand with each other. Your feelings are clear. Communication is also vital to handling daily routines. If you marry, use the skills you learned in Chapter 6 to help make a better relationship with good communication.

A successful marriage is unlikely without good communication. What are the benefits of talking together about issues and feelings?

Discussion. Discuss with students some ways to cope with the bad habits that marriage partners may have. What happens in a marriage when one or both partners enter into marriage thinking they can change the other?

Photo Focus. Ask students to look at the photo above. What communication skills can students identify in this photo? How do couples benefit from communicating often? How may problems occur when couples fail to communicate? Should couples allow a hectic schedule to interfere with communication? Why or why not?

So often communication in marriage tends to center around concrete issues. You have money to manage, purchases to make, places to go, and children to raise, so you talk about all of this rather than feelings. Shoving your feelings into the background, however, is dangerous in a marriage. Both partners must learn to talk about how they feel. Otherwise problems do not get resolved.

Asking questions can help a reluctant communicator. A simple "What do you mean?" or "Tell me more" clears the air. Similar queries like "What do you think I meant?" encourage helpful feedback.

Speak gently. Watch your tone of voice and the other signals you give. When discussing a sensitive issue, begin by stating your current emotion. Opening with an honest "I feel uneasy" can work wonders. This approach reduces tension and steers you away from accusations. It also alerts the other person to your present mood. Some words can produce a hurt that lasts a lifetime. For any type of truth-telling, a calm approach is always best.

Often Nancy had dinner ready when she expected Kris to get home from work. If he was going to be late, he never called to tell her. Finally, she said to him: "I feel hurt when you don't call to let me know that you will be late." This was a nonthreatening way to open the conversation She got her message across, and they talked about a solution.

Consider timing. The time, the day, or the week you select to talk straight can be just as important as what you say. No sensible spouse would bring up a serious issue as the other is headed out the door for work. Look for a time when you are both relaxed and not distracted. If you need to, set up a time to talk. Then follow through.

Listen to your partner. When issues come up, people naturally want to express their own point of view. Resolution can only come, however, if you listen to the other person too. Understanding follows. Solutions result.

More About Listening. Listening can be a powerful problem-solving tool. Creative listening allows couples to use the best ideas both partners have instead of rejecting ideas right away. Sympathetic listening is nonjudgmental and helps people talk through problems and reach an acceptable solution.

When your spouse wants to communicate, you can help by listening.

People have many techniques for communicating, some good and some bad. Try to identify problems and think of solutions for the following situations:

- Garth is not much of a talker. He spends evenings and weekends reading and watching television. His wife seldom gets more than a mumble in response to her comments and questions.
- Laverne talks constantly. Her husband has learned to block out most of what she says.
- Drake is the life of any party. He has a list of jokes a mile long. He cannot talk about his feelings, however. Any attempts by his wife to talk about sensitive issues are met with silence.
- Whenever Frank brings up an issue, his wife immediately tries to defend herself. She wonders why he always finds fault with her.
- Pauline believes that her husband Darryl loves her, but he never says this to her.

Activity. Have students practice "I" statements with each other in class. Each student should include the word "I," a feeling word, and a "because" statement. For example: "I am feeling annoyed because the breakfast dishes have been left on the counter unwashed."

◆◆◆

Making Decisions Together

Much communication in marriage centers around decisions that must be made. If you are accustomed to making decisions alone, this may be an adjustment in marriage. Most couples find that the self-esteem of both partners is preserved when both participate in making decisions. Excluding one can cause hurt, anger, loss of important knowledge, and resentment.

Sometimes couples learn that one partner is more knowledgeable about a topic than the other. Ray knows more about automobiles than Sybil. When they bought a car, he shared information with her. They made the decision together, even though she relied on his opinion. Not only did Sybil learn something, but she felt good about participating in the decision.

In Chapter 7 you learned about the steps in decision making. Here is a quick review of those steps:

1. State the problem.
2. List all possible alternatives.
3. Consider the advantages and disadvantages of each alternative.
4. Choose the best alternative.
5. Put your decision into action.
6. Analyze the results.

When two people are involved in a decision, following these steps becomes more complicated. First, you must agree on what the problem or issue is. Second, your feelings and opinions will be part of the discussion when listing alternatives and choosing the best. Compromise may be needed in order to reach agreement. Finally, taking action may require a plan that outlines who will do what.

Married couples make all sorts of decisions together. Can you list some major and minor decisions a couple might make? What decisions might they make individually?

Activity. Have students interview several married couples to find out how these couples make decisions. What are the easiest and most difficult aspects of making decisions? What advice do these couples have to offer newly married couples regarding making good decisions in a marriage?

Photo Focus. Ask students to look at the photo above. How can making decisions together benefit a marriage? What happens when partners make independent decisions without talking with each other first? What issues require joint decisions? What issues could be handled independently?

SIDELIGHT

Handling Finances

One area that causes friction in many households is finances. Not having enough money for needs and wants is common. Even when there is enough money, deciding how to spend it can still be a problem. Several decisions must be made for smooth sailing:

- What are the family's financial goals? How will these be reached?
- Who will see that bills are paid? Will one person pay them all, or will they be split?
- Will the couple have joint or separate checking and savings accounts? Should the employment status of a partner be considered when making this decision?
- How will the couple use credit cards?
- How much money can be spent on an individual purchase without consulting the other spouse?

♦♦♦

When couples share responsibilities in a marriage, neither one feels overburdened. This makes for a happier relationship.

♦♦♦

Sharing Responsibilities

In marriage, decisions must be made about responsibilities. You already know that family roles have changed over the years. Not all people, however, change at the same rate. Some people are quicker to see, understand, and accept new ways of operating. A couple may not agree on their roles if they were raised in very different settings or if they simply have different ideas.

If you have not discussed roles prior to marriage, you certainly will need to after. Reaching agreement on who will do what is important in a relationship. When one partner is too heavily loaded with responsibility, resentment can build. Not only is this unfair, it is also hard on the overloaded person. Physical and emotional health is at risk, not to mention the threat to the marriage itself.

Most couples today share responsibilities. Division of jobs can be based on whatever works for the couple. Strength, skill, interest, and time available can all be factored into the decision. Responsibilities to think about include earning an income, cooking, cleaning, laundry, shopping, yardwork, home maintenance and repairs, care of autos and equipment, child care, and financial paperwork. Make a list of specific jobs. Include the time each job requires and how often it must be done. Then decide how to divide the list. Finally, put your agreement in writing so you know you have communicated correctly.

As you carry out your responsibilities, remember to be flexible. One person may handle more for awhile and less later depending on circumstances. This is part of the give-and-take of marriage.

Work and Family. In small groups, ask students to brainstorm the household duties and tasks necessary to keep a home running smoothly. Have them estimate the amount of time needed to accomplish each task. They should construct a plan for maintaining a home while both partners work at full-time jobs outside the home. How should decisions be made regarding who completes each task? Analyze how couples balance the needs of the home with the needs of the job.

◆◆◆

Resolving Conflicts

Is it possible to go through married life without ever having a disagreement? Shaundra and Clete say they have never had an argument, even after 25 years together. Chuck and Leila say they fight about everything, but they still love each other after 15 years of marriage. Because people are different, the way they handle conflict is also different. Then how do you know which techniques are right and which are wrong? If either partner is unhappy or if the marriage is threatened, better ways of handling conflict should be found.

There are some ground rules for handling conflict:

- **Never allow abusive behavior, either physical or emotional.** Belittling someone does not make you a winner. Neither does overpowering anyone with force. Such behavior does not solve problems; it causes them.

Problems should not be ignored in marriage. Sometimes it isn't easy to talk about feelings, but it is necessary.

- **Do not ignore problems.** You can cover them up but they will not go away. Married couples who never talk about issues that divide them are said to have railroad-track marriages. They often share children, friends, and income tax forms, but they keep their real feelings and opinions well hidden. Eventually, the problems surface as major trouble. The list of grievances may be long. Each grievance alone may not seem like such a big deal, but together they could even add up to divorce. How much better it is to solve each problem along the way.

Young couples just starting out may not even realize they have fallen into the trap of letting problems go. Make an agreement right from the start to deal with issues. Perhaps find a technique for doing this. A set time for a discussion once a week might work. Keeping a list and then talking about the most important topic on it could help. Most of all, don't let the day-to-day activities that gradually take over your time prevent you from addressing problems.

- **Count to ten.** When something bothers you, wait before you react. If necessary, get away for awhile. Take a walk or visit a friend. This gives you some time to think about the seriousness of the problem and the best way to handle it. An emotional outburst seldom solves anything.

- **Communicate.** Talking is part of solving conflicts. When your partner has a complaint, listen and react. If you do not respond, you risk not understanding what the other person is trying to say. Some people find it very difficult to talk about feelings and sensitive issues. The closer the bond between people, the harder it may be to have such discussions. You must, however, in order to solve problems.

Discussion. Ask students to respond to the following statement: "Never go to bed angry; stay up and settle the disagreement." Do students agree or disagree with the statement? Why? Is the philosophy behind the statement, "Sleep on it, and discuss it in the morning," more realistic? Why or why not?

More About Solving Problems. Some experts advise couples to have a real or imaginary STOP sign to urge partners to slow down and think through a problem. Holding up the STOP sign may signal that something is not right about what is happening in the problem-solving process. Both partners may need time out to think.

I CAN ◆◆◆ Show My Feelings

Joel grew up in a family with a workaholic father. The time he spent with his father was limited and seemed empty.

"My father never hugged me once in his life that I can remember. When he died, I knew I loved him, but it hurt that we had never gotten beyond the surface with each other. He was my role model, and I guess that's why it has always been difficult for me to show my emotions.

"When Melanie and I married, we did a lot of talking. I was having trouble telling her and showing her how I felt about things. I began to see that the same barriers were coming between us that had been between my father and me. I knew things had to change. I deliberately started to change in simple ways — with a hug every day before breakfast. Then I learned to say 'I love you.' In time I was able to tell Melanie when something made me feel good — or bad. At first it felt forced and awkward. Now it's more natural. Oh, I still hold back sometimes, but it's getting easier. Because of this, Melanie and I are closer than we have ever been. Our relationship will never have the barrier that separated my father and me. I won't let that happen."

- Why do you think Joel's father acted as he did? What about Joel?
- Do you think it is more difficult for males or females to show emotions? Explain your answer.
- How good are you at letting people know how you feel? If you need improvement, what are some specific ways you could do this?

- **Place value on the other's point of view (empathy).** One of the nicest feelings is knowing that someone understands the way you feel. Telling Tom that he should not be upset about his wife's long working hours does no good. This is a true feeling that he has. Accepting his feelings and looking for a way to solve the problem is a better approach.
- **Attack the issue, not the person.** Nothing hurts more than comments directed at you personally. If Marcia spends too much money on clothes, nothing is accomplished by telling her that she is irresponsible. This is upsetting and may make her want to strike back. Such comments can also leave scars that never heal. Talking just about balancing income and expenses helps her see the problem in a nonthreatening way. She too will then want to seek a solution.
- **Discuss one problem at a time.** Many couples have a way of moving from one grievance to another. It is like keeping score. Surely the one with the most complaints will win. Instead of winning, you are more likely to get anger and frustration. Stick to the issue at hand. It will be much easier to remain calm and resolve the conflict.

More About Apologizing. Sometimes saying "I'm sorry" is difficult because it implies a person is weak or wrong. Neither is true. Saying "I'm sorry" is a sign of strength. Sometimes asking how you can make up for the wrong is a way to re-establish a positive relationship.

Activity. Have students act out situations in which a couple is arguing. Instead of focusing on one issue, the couple should bring a past problem up into the discussion about a current problem. What may be wrong with this type of problem solving? In reverse, have students act out situations in which couples solve one issue at a time.

Knowing that someone you love understands how you feel helps to keep the lines of communication open.

- **Learn to compromise.** Does it really matter who is right or wrong? Some people seem compelled to win. In truth winning comes to both of you when you solve a problem. Giving in a little is not a sign of losing. It's a sign of maturity. When you both give a little, you show respect for each other. You can also solve problems more easily.
- **Learn to apologize.** Saying "I'm sorry" or "I was wrong" is not easy for many people. A mature person, however, understands that it is okay to be wrong sometimes. Admitting this clears the air and opens the way for your partner to do the same.
- **Forgive and forget.** Once you settle an issue, forget it. Holding a grudge is not worthwhile. Forgive your partner for the mistakes he or she has made, and forgive yourself too. You will feel better inside when you do.

Discussion. Have students discuss the benefits of forgiveness in a relationship. What may happen in a relationship when one or both partners hold a grudge? How may this affect self-esteem?

◆◆◆

Thoughtfulness

Taking each other for granted is not a typical problem for newlyweds. Like many other problems in marriage, however, it can sneak up on you if you are not careful. How do you take someone for granted? This means that you do not show your appreciation for them and what they do. You may notice, but you fail to act. Right or wrong, your partner may feel that you do not care. The mind may say you do care, but the heart has trouble recognizing this.

Thoughtfulness is the best way to show someone you care. There are many ways to be thoughtful to a spouse. A few sincere efforts now and then strengthen a relationship. Can you think of other ways to show thoughtfulness in addition to those listed here?

- Say thank you.
- Give a compliment.
- Send flowers.
- Give a greeting card with a special message.
- Give a gift.
- Make something for your spouse.
- Plan a special outing.
- Do a job around the house that your spouse normally does.
- Remember birthdays and anniversaries.
- Plan a special surprise for a birthday, a holiday, or whenever.

Photo Focus. Ask students to examine the photo above. Have them describe the attitudes and emotions that this couple is expressing. How are these attitudes and emotions valuable in building a strong relationship?

A thoughtful gesture shows a partner that you care.

◆◆◆

Making Time For Each Other

Spending some time alone together is necessary for married couples. For those without children, this may be simple. As a family grows, it is not so simple. Children quickly consume the time that people have. This is especially true when both parents are employed, as so many are today. Thus, an effort must be made to find time for each other. This need should not be overlooked.

How can busy couples fit togetherness into their lives? Some are able to use the time after children are in bed, as long as fatigue has not set in. You may need to remove more than children from the scene. Other distractions, like the telephone and television, can also get in the way. Some couples arrange a "date" so that they can get away periodically. If expense is a problem, something as simple as a walk in the park or around the neighborhood may do quite well.

Time together is useful to married couples. They can talk about issues, problems, feelings, and just routine things. They can make plans. Such moments can result in the intimacy that is needed in marriage.

Time alone together gives a couple a chance to talk without distraction. This helps them become closer.

Discussion. Ask students how a person's family of origin may influence how a person communicates, solves problems, and gets along in marriage. If a man's father didn't do many household tasks, how easy will it be for him to share household tasks in his marriage? If a woman's family never talked about family problems, will she be more or less likely to be open and share problems in her own marriage? How do families celebrate birthdays and other holidays? How might differences in family traditions affect a couple's relationship?

Intimacy

Intimacy is vital to a marriage. This is not the same as sexual contact. **Intimacy** is the closeness that comes from deep, personal conversation, loving gestures, and displays of affection. Intimacy strengthens the love in a marriage.

Affection is the warm and tender feeling you have for another person. Showing affection is part of intimacy. It should be included in a marital relationship in a way that is separate from sexual contact. Hand-holding, hugs, and touching need not signal sexual desire. They can simply mean "I love you and I care about you."

Affection is part of intimacy. It brings warmth and closeness to a relationship.

When one spouse has a lower level of need for affection than the other, there may be a problem. One partner may have to learn how to show more affection. Talk to your spouse to find out what is important to him or her. Although this is separate from the sexual part of your relationship, it can greatly affect it.

Sexual Compatibility

The sexual side of a relationship is important, although not all-important. When asked, most couples say that a relationship needs much more. Still, sexual compatibility is part of a complete marriage.

Adjustment to sexual relations may take time and effort. Couples who have some biological knowledge have a head start. People come from all sorts of backgrounds, which can affect their thoughts and attitudes about sex. Talking about individual needs and responses helps. Patience and understanding do too. If problems occur, professionals can provide counseling.

Sexual expression is a natural outgrowth of love between two people. Most find that sexual satisfaction comes most easily when a couple is caring and committed. Marriage provides the ideal framework for this.

Making Time for Others

A healthy relationship is not a smothering one. Most people find that they need other people in their lives too, not just a spouse. Angelina has several close friends. Once in awhile she visits them or goes out to a movie with someone. Her husband Bill plays tennis with a friend. Another friend stops in now and then to talk.

More About Intimacy. Recent studies indicate that families are stronger and healthier when appreciation is openly shared. Couples wanting to develop intimacy must learn to show appreciation. Focusing attention on a spouse, saying thank you for small favors, and giving a hug or a kiss are ways to show appreciation. When times are rough, the sense of appreciation is even more important. In order to risk intimacy with others, people need to be loved for who they are, not what they do (or don't do).

A marital relationship stays fresher when a couple includes friendships with others in their routine.

Good emotional health relies on having friendships. Partners should not be resentful. Whenever Ashley spent time with her friends, Noah was jealous. He wanted Ashley to spend all her time with him. His immaturity was showing. Ashley needs her friends. Noah should feel neither threatened nor slighted by this. When people spend time with others, they are refreshed. Togetherness is then more enjoyable.

Many couples seek other pairs for friendship. They may go out together or keep it simple with just visits back and forth. Such friendships can last a lifetime, even across the miles.

Discussion. Ask students to discuss the importance of having friends other than one's spouse. Is jealousy over a spouse's friends a sign of love for the spouse? How much freedom should husbands and wives have in spending time with friends outside the marriage?

◆◆◆

In-Laws

It is often said that when you marry, you marry a whole family, not just an individual. Most couples welcome the new family connections. In time the bonds grow, providing more sources of support, friendship, and love in your life.

Marital commitments are made to last. This means your spouse's family will be part of your life for a long time. Making an effort to get along is worthwhile.

Problem Solving. Ask students to brainstorm ways in which a married couple can build positive relationships with parents and in-laws. Discuss the alternatives, focusing on the benefits and drawbacks of each suggestion. Which suggestions would promote the most positive relationships? In what ways?

A Slice of Life

Shortly after they were married, Stu and Marilyn moved 30 miles away from their hometown. Marilyn wanted to live away from Stu's family if they could. She felt that he was very dependent on them, and she hoped he could learn to be more independent.

Even with 30 miles between them, Stu's family expected regular weekend visits back and forth. They offered advice when Stu and Marilyn bought anything and criticized them when they made mistakes. Stu and Marilyn borrowed some money from his folks when they bought their home. In about 10 years they would have the loan paid back. Every visit seemed more strained than the last. Stu's mother didn't like anything Marilyn did and made that quite clear. Privately Marilyn asked Stu to come to her rescue sometimes. He said he would, but he never did.

As the years went by, the problems multiplied. Marilyn tried to keep the peace, but she finally couldn't stand it any longer. She and her mother-in-law had the worst argument they had ever had. Marilyn told Stu that in the future he could visit them alone. Everyone was upset at what seemed like an impossible situation.

Thinking It Through

- What motivated Marilyn, Stu, and Stu's mother to act in the ways they did?
- Who made mistakes and what were they?
- Is there a solution to this problem? Explain your answer.

The bond between a person and his or her family is strong. It does not matter what a family is like. The ties that bind them are not easily broken, nor should they be. When her son married Hallema, Mrs. Thompson had to fight certain feelings. She felt that she was losing Virgil. She even wondered if Hallema was good enough for her son. "I've got to stop thinking like this," she thought. "I am gaining a daughter, not losing a son." Hallema recognized that Mrs. Thompson and Virgil were closely linked. She did not want to break down that link. She wanted to be part of it. With some effort, she won Mrs. Thompson over. In time Hallema's mother-in-law loved her like a daughter.

In some families in-law relationships are challenging. Understanding what can get in the way can help you prevent problems.

Many couples enjoy sharing time with in-laws. Marriage expands the family circle of each partner.

Problem Solving. Have the students talk with older couples they know about how relationships with in-laws grow and change over time. How may problems with in-laws be resolved in a positive way? How can newly married couples build positive relationships with in-laws?

Photo Focus. Ask students to examine the above photo. Have students describe the relationship between these two couples. What qualities strengthen happiness?

Closeness can be overdone. Even families that get along well need a reasonable amount of separation. A newly married couple needs some distance and privacy in order to learn how to stand on their own feet and share time with each other. Many parents respect this need. As a result, newlyweds are able to take on their new roles as spouses first and as married children second.

Some in-laws expect married children to spend a certain amount of time with them. They may drop in without warning or plan too many activities that include the married couple. If the demands are great, the couple must be clear and firm about their needs. A calm, straightforward statement often works.

Interference can cause resentment. When parents have controlled a child's life for so many years, it may be hard for them to give that up. They may want to offer advice and participate in decisions. This can be either helpful or annoying, depending on the way it is handled. Again, explaining your feelings is probably the best solution.

◆◆◆

Outside Resources

In recent years thousands of husbands and wives have attended religious-sponsored programs for married couples. Known as marriage encounter or enrichment, these sessions are designed to make good marriages even better. Couples learn to talk more openly with each other. Many renew their marriage promises as part of the experience.

More About Outside Resources. Often couples gain a great deal of support and encouragement in their marriage from trusted friends, close relatives, and counselors or clergy. Having someone to confide in and to share joys and frustrations with is important to every relationship. This encouragement is helpful before marriage as well as during. It helps keep the marriage in perspective as well as helping couples appreciate the strengths of a good marriage.

◆◆◆

Making the Commitment

The most important ingredient in a good marriage seems to be a determined commitment to make it succeed. This dedicated desire is an attitude shared by happy and successful couples. It's like wanting your team to win and being willing to play your part to achieve victory.

Even though all marriages go through cycles, the mutual commitment of some couples works as the glue that holds them together during the rough times. Commitment means giving yourself to the partnership with fingers uncrossed. Although it may seem difficult to stay and work for change and improvement when things get rocky, the will to succeed and the positive attitude of "We can do it" keep everything in perspective.

Commitment is vital to a married couple. When two people are willing to give it their all, their marriage will be successful.

Life Management Skills. Ask students to brainstorm examples of how mutual commitment can help keep a marriage together and make it stronger through tough times. List several issues that may cause a marriage to go through troubled times.

CHAPTER 21

Review

Answers
Testing Your Memory

1. Entering marriage with thought of change is unwise since this is likely to cause resentment.
2. **Any three:** talk about feelings; ask questions; speak gently; listen to your partner; consider timing.
3. Making a decision alone doesn't require consulting someone else. Making a decision with a partner requires thinking of the other person's feelings and knowledge. Both must agree on what the issue is. Compromise may be needed to reach agreement.
4. Couples need to divide responsibilities based on the strengths, skills, interest, and time available to do the work.
5. **Any five:** never allow abusive behavior; do not ignore problems; count to ten; communicate; place value on the other's point of view; attack the issue, not the person; discuss one problem at a time; learn to compromise; learn to apologize; forgive and forget.
6. Any five from the list on page 302. Students may suggest other ways.

Summarizing the Chapter

- Marriages are successful because people make an effort.
- Accepting your spouse means not having a plan to change him or her.
- Good communication is vital to a healthy marriage.
- Making decisions together helps self-esteem.
- Sharing responsibilities is common in marriages today. This keeps one partner from being overburdened.
- Conflicts in marriage should be resolved as they come up.
- Time must be allowed in marriage for each other and for friends.
- Intimacy and sexual contact are two different things in marriage, but they affect each other.
- When you marry, your in-laws become your family too.

Testing Your Memory

1. Should you plan to change your spouse's annoying habits? Explain your answer.
2. List three suggestions for communicating in marriage.
3. How does decision making with a partner differ from making a decision by yourself?
4. Describe how a couple might divide responsibilities.
5. List five ground rules for resolving conflicts in marriage.
6. List five ways to be thoughtful in marriage.
7. Explain the difference between intimacy and sexual contact.
8. Why are friends needed by a married couple?
9. How can too much closeness with in-laws be a challenge for some married couples?

Thinking Critically

1. Explain why it is often hard to talk about a sensitive issue with someone you are very close to.
2. Sometimes struggling through hard times makes people stronger. This may even strengthen the bonds in marriage. Why do you think this is often true?
3. Power comes with controlling the money in a marriage. Why is this true? Do you think finances should be handled by one or both partners? Explain your answer.

Taking Action

1. Interview a married couple (or just one partner) who are both employed. Find out how they divide duties, including child care, cooking, cleaning, laundry, yardwork, shopping, household maintenance and repairs, auto care, and bill paying. How did they decide on this?
2. In groups create and perform skits about the following situations. Use good communication techniques to solve the problems.
   a. The husband and wife have set up a list of responsibilities for each of them to do. One of them, however, is not following through, leaving many jobs for the other to do.
   b. One partner spends so much spare time in outside activities that they have little time together as a couple. The other partner is unhappy about this.

Making Life Choices

When Leslie and Torrence were first married, they often went out of the way to do thoughtful things for each other. Sometimes it was just a simple compliment or a loving hug. Other times it was a candlelight dinner or some special surprise. Six years and two children later, the thoughtfulness seems to have been lost along the way. Leslie has the feeling that it doesn't even bother Torrence. It does bother her. She feels the distance growing between them.

What mistakes have Leslie and Torrence made? What do you think is ahead for them? How might this situation be changed?

Using Your Journal

You have just read that commitment in marriage means giving yourself to the partnership "with fingers uncrossed." How will you know when you are ready to make that kind of commitment? What signs would you look for in yourself and your partner? Use your journal to write about the kinds of things you would need to feel sure about in order to make a commitment to marriage.

7. Intimacy is the closeness that comes from deep, personal conversation, loving gestures, and displays of affection.
8. Friendships are necessary for good emotional health.
9. Too much closeness with in-laws can cause resentment among marriage partners. Couples need time to themselves in order to carry on their roles as spouses first and married children second.

Thinking Critically

1. Answers will vary. Point out that fear of hurting someone often makes it difficult to discuss sensitive issues.
2. Answers will vary. Resolving problems in a healthful manner gives couples a sense of accomplishment.
3. Answers will vary. Emphasize that marriages may be strengthened when both partners work through financial matters together.

CHAPTER 22

Divorce and Remarriage

Chapter Challenge

Resources. Refer to the Teacher's Classroom Resources box and Student Workbook for materials related to this chapter.

Look for These Answers . . .

- What should couples do before deciding to end a marriage?
- Describe the ways that marriages are ended.
- How does divorce affect people?
- What challenges do people who remarry and those who form blended families face?

Look for These Terms . . .

- alimony
- annulment
- child support
- custody
- desertion
- grounds
- joint custody
- no-fault divorce
- separation

Andrew covered his ears with his hands. He didn't want to listen anymore. He never wanted to. It frightened him, and he didn't understand.

Shayla slipped quietly into the room. At age nine she was four years older than Andrew, and sometimes she mothered him. She too did not like the arguing, but she worried more for her little brother. He often woke up crying at night. She folded Andrew into her arms to hold him close in the dark.

The next day Shayla's parents talked calmly and quietly to her and Andrew. Shayla knew about divorce, but she couldn't help wondering what was going to happen to her. Where would she live? Who with? Where would Andrew be?

In time everything was settled. Shayla and Andrew were together. Sometimes they were with their father and sometimes their mother. They had a schedule. It wasn't perfect, but it worked. Andrew no longer cried at night. Shayla wished they could all be a family again, but she was beginning to accept the fact that this would not happen. At least the nighttime arguing was over. Her feelings of fear and uncertainty were gone, and that was good.

Chapter Opener. Ask students to read the opening scenario to the chapter. Have them describe the feelings Shayla and Andrew were experiencing as their parents argued. How might Shayla and Andrew have reacted if their parents hadn't talked with them about the divorce? How does divorce eliminate problems in families? Can divorce create more problems in some families? If so, what problems?

Problems in Marriage

Who can say why some marriages end? Each partner brings to marriage a complex combination of personality, background, and desires. The mixture when two people get together can create any number of challenges. What these are affects the quality of the marriage. How the couple is able to handle them does too.

The reasons for a failed marriage are complex. Chapter 20 listed many factors to think about before going into a marriage. The presence of any of these can contribute to problems after a couple is married. The more a couple must handle, the greater the likelihood that the marriage will not survive.

When a couple does not work to make a successful marriage, this is a problem in itself. Everything can fall apart, and yet they may not even have a clear idea of why. Sometimes one person tries but the other does not. It can be very painful and frustrating for one when the other is no longer committed to the relationship.

Looking for Solutions

When a marriage is threatened, most couples look for ways to save it. Rather than give up, they prefer to try to protect their mutual investment in each other.

Some couples who have not worked at having a successful marriage are able to get on track by themselves. Talking is the way to start. First they must identify the problems. Then they work toward solutions.

Remember that children add a special concern to a threatened marriage. They are not to blame, yet they often feel that they are. Children can learn how problems are solved when they hear a discussion that settles a disagreement. On the other hand, hateful arguments wound them. Parents must always keep the needs and self-esteems of children foremost in mind no matter what happens.

When problems threaten a marriage, time is usually on your side. Walking out or reacting in some other emotional way is unwise. Give yourself some time to think it through and talk it through. This will help you make the right decision, one that you will not regret later on.

The exception to this would, of course, be an abusive situation. When a spouse or children are in danger, action should be taken immediately. Friends, relatives, or a shelter home should be sought. Solutions to the problems can be found from a distance.

◆ Counseling

Couples who cannot solve their problems alone may need counseling. In fact, if they seek counseling early enough, improvement is probable. Success is most likely when both are willing to make some changes.

Before giving up on a marriage, many couples try counseling. Sometimes an unbiased and trained third party can help them work through their differences.

Discussion. Ask students what they think about couples having a baby to keep the marriage together. Does this ever work? Identify the disadvantages of having a baby in order to keep the marriage together. Should couples stay together for the sake of the children? Why or why not?

Activity. Ask a marriage and family counselor to speak with the class about common kinds of problems facing families today. What role does the counselor play in helping people solve problems? What advice can the counselor offer to students who desire a strong, healthy marriage in the future?

Marriage and family counselors listen for causes of difficulties and seek ways to relieve them. Professionals don't take sides. They realize that family members are never all right or all wrong.

Most counselors interview the couple together at the first meeting. This way they hear each spouse's story and notice how they get along with each other.

When one partner refuses to talk with a third party, the second may go for help anyway. In such cases, the hesitant spouse often agrees to attend in time. He or she may show up later when the spouse in counseling begins to act in a new and healthier way.

Entire families can use counseling to learn how to get along better. In some cases groups of couples or families meet with a leader. When members are willing to listen and offer moral support to each other, touchy subjects become easier to discuss. It can be a relief to discover that you're not the only one with a particular problem.

◆◆◆

Ending a Marriage

Despite all efforts, some marriages do end. Divorce is the most common method.

◆ Divorce

At one time divorce was a disgrace. Husbands and wives stayed together to avoid the shame. Today divorce is more common. People do not feel compelled to stay in hopeless marriages. They are less likely to stay married for the sake of the children, since children can suffer in a bad marriage too. Many women are better able to support themselves than they used to be, so they can seek a better life if needed. Also, more people now realize that they do not have to endure abuse because they have no way out.

Balancing Work & Family

Marital Problems and Work

Have you ever tried to do a great job when you're feeling depressed? It's not easy, but that's what people going through serious personal problems such as a divorce or separation have to do. They have to go to work and do their job well, even though they're experiencing distressing problems at home.

In such circumstances, it's hard to keep emotions from affecting job performance. However, if emotions keep an employee from doing an adequate job, the individual could be fired — turning a bad situation into a worse one.

People going through marital problems need, therefore, to take some steps to reduce the effect of their situation on work performance. Here are some ways.

- **Confide in your boss.** If you feel comfortable talking to your supervisor, explain, briefly, what is going on. Supervisors can do a better job of managing if they know about stresses on their employees. They may be able to temporarily lighten the workload.
- **Use employee assistance programs.** Some companies offer free, confidential counseling or provide literature that may help.
- **Seek help outside work.** You need to talk about what is going on in your life. Try to do that talking outside of the office. If friends in the workplace are part of your support system, set aside time to talk to them outside working hours. That way you'll be better able to concentrate on your work.
- **Put in an extra effort.** An extra effort shows others you are trying your best, despite the circumstances.

Think About It

1. Why might it be more difficult to deal with marital problems if your boss doesn't know?
2. How might colleagues at work be affected by one employee's marital problems?

More About Divorce. Mediation is a way for a couple to end a marriage in a respectful, businesslike manner. A certified mediator meets with each partner individually. After the initial meeting, the mediator assists both partners in working out the details for division of property, child custody, and other issues relating to the couple. A lawyer is retained for the legal details and usual court appearance. Divorce mediation is common in many states. Consult a divorce mediator for additional information.

Divorces are easier to obtain today. The advantage is that people do not have to suffer through years of unhappiness because of a bad marriage. Although some would say that people choose divorce because it is easy, this is unlikely. Few take it lightly. They know that divorce is complicated and can hurt.

The Divorce Process

A divorce usually begins with the help of an attorney. Each spouse hires a lawyer to help reach an acceptable arrangement for handling property division, alimony, child custody, and support.

Each state has its own laws on divorce. The acceptable **grounds**, or valid reasons, for divorce differ from state to state. Basically, divorces fall into one of two categories — fault or no-fault. When a fault divorce is filed, one spouse is the plaintiff and the other is the defendant. The plaintiff must offer proof, in court, that the defendant broke the marriage contract on stated grounds. In the **no-fault divorce**, there is no defendant or plaintiff. Both spouses agree that the marriage has broken down and is irreconcilable. No blame is placed on either spouse, and no one is found guilty of breaking the marriage contract.

A divorce agreement must address the division of property and income. Some states have community property laws that entitle each spouse to half of all property and other assets that were accumulated during the time of the marriage. A few states allow one spouse to collect **alimony** (al-uh-MOH-nee), a monthly living allowance, from the other spouse.

The care of any minor children is also an issue. The court determines which parent receives **custody** (CUS-tud-ee), or authorized care and control of the children. Although the mother is still most often awarded custody of the children, more fathers are requesting and receiving custody today than they did in the past. Courts often decide that **joint custody** is best. With this arrangement, parents share in the care of any children. A schedule may be set up to establish when the children will live with each parent.

The court also says who must pay any required **child support**, money paid by the noncustodial parent for part of a child's living expenses. The court determines the amount of that support. The incomes of both partners are factored into this decision. Some states have passed laws that prosecute parents who do not make their child support payments.

The divorce process begins with the help of an attorney. The handling of property division, alimony, child custody, and support can be complex, especially when emotions are involved.

Activity. Have students investigate the divorce laws in their state. What are the laws regulating child custody, alimony, and child support? What happens when one parent does not pay required child support? Students may interview a lawyer who works in family law or you may invite a lawyer to speak with the class.

Discussion. Divorce is much more prevalent than it was 50 years ago. Ask students why this change has occurred. Can this trend be turned around? How? How can newly married couples prevent divorce from occurring in their marriage?

Divorce can be difficult for those who feel a deep sense of loss. It is normal to go through a period of mourning.

The recently divorced relieve their stress best by talking. Most seek comfort and support from friends and relatives. Some go to counselors or join self-help groups for divorced people.

Separated mates often think of getting together again. Some get together for brief periods only to drift apart again. Some remarry and make it stick. Others fail at marriage a second time. A surprising number continue as close friends even after marrying someone else.

◆ Adjusting to Divorce

Depending on the reasons for a divorce, the need for adjustment will vary. People who have escaped from a difficult situation may feel relief. Far more, however, do not easily accept the end of a marriage. As with any loss, adjustment may mean going through a mourning period. This can last as long as a year or two. Emotional reactions may range from anger to depression. In time the pain gradually eases; however, it can take years for any deep scars to fade. Denying negative emotions delays the healing process.

Those who recover best from divorce start a new life. They need to regain their balance and self-control. Some return to school, put new energy into their jobs, or dust off neglected hobbies. Building new friendships with both genders boosts self-esteem.

One method of adjusting to divorce is resuming studies or preparing for a new career.

Photo Focus. Ask students to examine the above photo. Students should discuss ways in which this young woman appears to be adjusting to divorce. Ask students to share examples of people they know (without using names) who have successfully adjusted to divorce. How long may the healing process take?

More About Child Support. Point out that the term *delinquent dads* came about as a result of the number of noncustodial fathers who consistently fail to provide child support. Some states have been aggressively pursuing such fathers and looking into more effective ways of ensuring that payments are made.

Coping well means steering clear of traps like the "helpless victim" role. Constant complaints like "See what he (she) did to me" are destructive. In fact, many who go through divorce end up admitting that the former mate had some good qualities. They also realize that each partner must share part of the responsibility for the divorce. They give up hopes for a reunion and ask tough questions like these: "What have I learned about me? What can I do differently next time?"

After a divorce, some people feel compelled to enter into another marriage right away. The idea of being alone may trouble them. They may choose a new partner without much thought or reason. Unresolved feelings connected to the first marriage may surface in the second one. Chances for a second divorce increase greatly when such conditions exist.

A divorce can change the economic condition of the partners. In general a woman's standard of living lowers and a man's goes up. This is because, overall, men have higher incomes than women do. Since most partners must rely on their own incomes after divorce, a woman is likely to have less to live on.

◆ Helping Children Adjust

Adjustment to divorce involves more than just the couple. Children must adjust too. Children commonly feel that they are to blame for the problems in the marriage. They may not fully understand what has happened. Not knowing what will happen to them gives them an insecure feeling. Watching and hearing the troubles in the marriage adds to this. Often the hope that the family will be whole again is in their minds.

Children need calm, clear conversation about divorce. The information should be given at a level they can understand. They also need reassurance that they are loved and will be cared for just like always.

Life Management Skills. Have students investigate how a woman's financial picture changes once she is divorced. How does her income change? What are some resources available to help women with financial problems after divorce? Have students develop a budget for a woman with two young children. Students may develop the budget based on the woman working full-time or part-time outside the home, or not working outside the home. What difficulties may this single-parent family have due to the change in income?

Children need plenty of love and reassurance during such times. They need calm conversation with both parents and explanations that fit their level of understanding. Never should children be used by the parents to get back at each other. A wise parent does not belittle the other parent in front of a child. Children have a strong bond with parents. Tearing down this bond confuses and hurts a child.

When battles over custody are part of a divorce, emotions can run high. In extreme cases, children are kidnapped by angry or frustrated parents even though the courts have not given them custody. They may run away with the child and go into hiding. This is illegal and damaging to the child.

Noncustodial parents have their own set of problems after a divorce. How do you parent a child from a distance? Often the noncustodial parent fills visits with entertainment and does not have to deal with discipline. The child may begin to view the custodial parent in a more negative way. Parents worry about how to handle this.

Many noncustodial parents provide entertainment when the child visits, but have little to do with the child's day-to-day activities.

More About Children of Divorce. Recent studies indicate that the effects of divorce on children are long range and far-reaching. Children of divorce often fear making commitments and sense little control over their lives. Children often feel overburdened, thinking that they must hold their parents together emotionally. As a result, children (often teens) do nothing to meet their own needs during this troubled time. Preschoolers may have trouble initially after divorce but often do better psychologically as time passes.

◆ Desertion

When one partner walks out on the other without notice, the action is called **desertion.** Long known as "poor man's divorce," desertion rates jump during hard times. Unhappy spouses run away to escape conflict, unpaid bills, and other obligations. Spouses left at home can feel everything from shock to anger. Without any word or explanation from the deserter, some wait in hope that the missing partner will return. Others file for divorce.

◆ Annulment

A legal decree of **annulment** (uh-NULL-munt) states that no valid marriage was contracted because the legal requirements of marriage were not met. Therefore, the marriage is declared void or without legal force.

The following two types of marriages can be annulled:

- Marriages that society wishes to dissolve, such as incestuous, bigamous (more than one spouse), and fraudulent (deceptive) unions.
- Marriages that one of the partners wishes to dissolve. The reasons may be fraud or deception (wrong age given; concealed health problems) or the use of force or threat. In some cases one party might be of unsound mind or unable to fulfill the duties and obligations of marriage. The only "duties and obligations" spelled out specifically in the law are the "rights of conjugation" — that is, the sexual consummation of the marriage. Unwillingness or inability of either spouse to have sexual intercourse is a common reason for petitions of annulment.

Each state lists clear grounds for annulment. Some states set a time limit for annulment. Others allow annulment even after years of marriage and several children.

◆ Separation

When one spouse moves out with notice, the action is called **separation.** Both parties remain married to each other though they live apart. The couple can agree to separate and live apart with no legal requirements to meet. A couple can also separate with legal sanctions determined by the court. In a legal separation, a restraining order sets down certain conditions the couple must follow. These conditions may include financial support, custody of children, visiting rights, and division of property.

Separated couples, many times, suffer all the guilt, anger, and depression that divorced couples endure. Sometimes this cooling-off period makes it possible for a couple to resolve their differences and join up again, or reconcile. The longer the separation lasts, however, the more likely it is that a divorce will follow.

Some couples use separation as a means of dealing with marital problems.

◆ Remarriage

Those who divorce do not reject the idea of family life. This is evidenced by the fact that so many people today marry for a second time. As you might guess, they still have many of the same reasons for marrying. Romance, love, and happiness are a few.

After the stress of breaking up, falling in love again can spark new interests, create new friends, and restore lost energy. In fact, the prospect of a second marriage may seem like a new and unexpected chance at life that seemed over just a short time earlier.

People who have been married before are more likely to make a success of their second marriage.

Work and Family. Meeting the obligations of both a full-time job and parenting is often difficult for single parents. Ask students to think of suggestions for helping single parents meet these obligations. Ask several students to tape record conversations with single parents about how they balance their work and family obligations. How could students use some of these techniques to balance school, work, and family obligations currently in their lives?

Many divorced people learn from their first marriage. They claim to have a much better idea of what is really needed in a successful partnership. They are determined to make it work the second time around.

Remarried partners are always older and often wiser. They seem more flexible and willing to compromise. They don't take marriage for granted. The threat of another failure probably makes many try harder. As a result, they learn to spot potential problems. By talking about them early, they avoid repeating the mistakes of the past.

◆◆◆

Blended Families

The family is still the basic unit of society. Today, however, family forms are different. Divorce and remarriage have resulted in what are now called blended families. As you know, blended families may include children that are his, hers, theirs, or any combination of these. The non-biological parents in such families are called stepparents. The youngsters who were not related to them previously become stepchildren.

A Slice of Life

The anger and grief kindled by divorce may flare up when a mother or father finds a new mate. Ginger describes her resentment when her family life changed dramatically for the third time in as many years.

"My parents seemed to have a good marriage. Their arguments weren't too bad until I was a sophomore in high school. We had just moved from the East Coast to Missouri so my dad could take a new job. Suddenly their little spats erupted into a major war, with my sister and me caught in the crossfire. Our best efforts to promote a truce failed.

"After the divorce, my mother and sister moved back to Virginia, while my father and I remained in our Midwest home. More and more I relied on my dad and confided in him. Soon he became my best friend. We worked in the house and yard together. When other girls went out on dates, Dad and I spent evenings playing cards and board games. I thought my 'dates' were as good as theirs.

"Just when I was beginning to feel happy again, my father's future wife came into the picture. I kidded myself into thinking that she was only temporary. I tried to force myself to accept her as a friend. Gradually it dawned on me that I would soon be replaced. She was a sweet lady, but I despised her for ruining my security and stealing my father."

Thinking It Through

- Why was Ginger totally unprepared for her father's remarriage?
- What could her father have done to help Ginger accept the situation?
- What things can the new wife do to ease the hurt Ginger feels and become accepted?

Discussion. Ask students to discuss the benefits of separation for couples having marital difficulties. Should couples contemplating divorce separate first or divorce right away? Why or why not?

Discussion. Ask students to describe their views about how children feel when parents remarry. Why may this be a difficult thing for some children to accept? How could a parent (or a child) make this a more pleasant experience for everyone involved?

As those who live in blended families can tell you, there are often challenges to meet. Resentment may be one of the first barriers to overcome. Children sometimes resent a stepparent who replaces a biological parent. Any attempts by the stepparent to set limits or get close are rejected. Problems are compounded when biological parents side with their natural children in any dispute. Some things just can't be hurried. Good stepparents need to work out their new roles at a cautious pace. If they lack experience with children, they may have some learning to do. Good relationships will not happen overnight. It takes time to earn trust, reduce suspicion, and gain friendship.

At first, children in blended families may also resent the intrusion of stepsisters and stepbrothers into their lives. Schedules change. Space and equipment must be shared. Even parents must be shared. Since new personalities are present, adjustments are needed. The old ways of acting and reacting may not work anymore. Adjusting means trying hard, giving in some of the time, and being willing to take the first step.

Love is expected to be part of family life. In a blended family, however, it does not happen instantaneously. When people who have not even known each other before come together as a family, love takes awhile to grow. Time and patience are your allies in such situations. Start by just getting along. Then move toward friendship. Given a chance, love can follow.

Blended families can have financial concerns. An enlarged household has an increased financial burden. A parent could also be financially responsible for children not living in the home. Understanding helps when money is tight.

On the positive side, good things happen in blended families. Many children and teens gain stepparents who enrich their lives. A stepparent can fill an empty place in a family. Remarriage can create an unexpected bonus, including new aunts, uncles, and cousins, all ready to treat the child as part of the family. The addition of new family members means a bigger source of support and love for all. Victoria explained it this way:

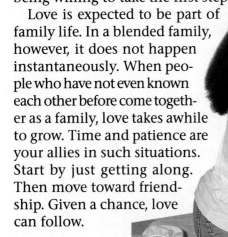

The children in blended families must often share space and possessions in new ways. What other adjustments must they make?

Activity. Ask several parents and children who have blended families to speak to the class about the joys and frustrations of living in a blended family. What advice would they give to others in similar situations? What have they learned from living in a blended family?

Photo Focus. Ask students to look at the photo above. Children who live in blended families often have an adjustment period to go through when they enter a new family. What are some problems they may encounter? How may parents make it easier for them? How do the teens in the above photo appear to be adjusting?

"When my older half brothers married, I became the 'only child.' It wasn't until both my parents died suddenly that I realized what a wonderful family I had joined. One of my half brothers took me into his family immediately. I found myself surrounded by him, a sister-in-law, two nieces, and a nephew. They all treated me like one of the family, never as an unwelcome intruder. My nieces and nephew look up to me and ask all kinds of questions. I love to help them. My new family is great."

Blended families are interesting. All sorts of situations result. One family has two daughters, both named Tracy. Another has two sons, both the same age. People who live in blended families know that it can work. Those that succeed keep a sense of humor and pull together. They are patient, willing to give each other some time for adjustment. They talk about their feelings honestly, openly, and respectfully. They also know that people must learn to accept what they cannot change. The new family is there to stay. Acceptance puts you several giant steps closer to a happy, healthy family life.

Blended families are successful when they communicate well and each member is willing to try to make it work.

Problem Solving. Traditions and ways of doing things are often sources of problems in blended families. Discuss ways in which a family could blend their holiday traditions so everyone feels included and important. Start by listing ways families celebrate a holiday or birthday. How can these differing ideas be meshed or intertwined? Is there value in beginning new family traditions? Why or why not? End the problem solving discussion with statements reflecting the positive aspects of people compromising and beginning to feel a part of a new family group.

CHAPTER 22

Review

Answers
Testing Your Memory

1. No. The reasons for a failed marriage are complex.
2. **Any two:** talk; identify problems; take time to think; or seek counseling.
3. People no longer have to suffer abuse or years of unhappiness.
4. ***Fault divorce:*** plaintiff must offer proof that the defendant broke the marriage contract. ***No-fault divorce:*** both parties agree that the marriage has broken down and no one is found guilty of breaking the marriage contract.
5. A legal decree stating that no valid marriage was contracted because the legal requirements of marriage were not met.
6. Separating with legal sanctions determined by the court. A restraining order sets down certain conditions that the couple must follow.
7. **Any four:** return to school; put new energy into jobs; dust off neglected hobbies; build new friendships; seek comfort and support from friends and relatives; go to a counselor; join a self-help group.

Summarizing the Chapter

- Marriages can end for any combination of complex reasons.
- Before ending a marriage, most couples look for ways to save it.
- Divorces are more common today than they were in the past and more easy to obtain, but they are still difficult to go through.
- In addition to legally ending a marriage, a divorce also establishes custody of minor children, visiting rights, financial support, and division of property and other assets.
- Marriages are also ended through desertion, annulment, and separation.
- Not only must the partners adjust to a divorce but the children must also.
- Blended families are common today. Once family members adjust to the new arrangement, they can benefit from the love and support of an expanded family.

Testing Your Memory

1. Is it easy to determine what causes a marriage to end? Explain your answer.
2. Give two suggestions for a couple who feel that their marriage is in trouble.
3. List two ways in which people are helped by getting a divorce.
4. Name and describe the two types of divorce.
5. What is an annulment?
6. What is a legal separation?
7. List four suggestions for adjusting to divorce.
8. How can parents help children adjust to a divorce?
9. Is divorce a rejection of family life? Explain your answer.
10. What do people gain from blended families?

Thinking Critically

1. If divorces were made harder to get today, would this be good for society or bad? Explain your answer.
2. Why is child custody more complicated today than it was in the past?
3. Which do you think is better, a stable single-parent home or a troubled two-parent home? Explain your answer.

Taking Action

1. Investigate the laws in your state that regulate divorce and annulments. Report your findings to the class.
2. Conduct a survey of at least 25 students. Determine how many live in a traditional family, blended family, or other family type. Calculate the percentages.
3. Create and perform a skit involving a stepparent and stepchild. Choose one of these themes or provide your own:
   a. The stepparent feels the teenager needs to be better groomed.
   b. The stepparent wants the teenager to help with household jobs.
4. Write a fictional letter to an advice columnist about a marital problem. Trade it anonymously with a classmate for a reply.

Making Life Choices

When Stella files for divorce against Mario, she plans to ask the courts for custody of Paul, age four. For Mario the thought of living without his son is agonizing. He wants to fight for custody. Stella wants to work out a schedule for visits instead, saying that Mario doesn't have a chance to win a custody battle anyway. Mario feels that Stella would ignore a visitation agreement. The thought that he might lose his son for good gives him feelings of desperation.

What events do you think might follow in this situation? Who suffers most in cases like this? What would you do if you were Mario and Stella?

Using Your Journal

Chances are that your life has been touched by divorce in some way. Perhaps your parents are divorced, or an aunt and uncle, or parents of a friend. Use your journal to record your thoughts about a divorced couple that you know. Has reading this chapter helped you understand better what the couple has gone through? Has it changed your feelings in any way? Write a general statement summarizing your thoughts about divorce.

8. Provide children with plenty of love and reassurance. Never belittle the other parent in front of a child. Talk about the divorce in terms children understand.
9. No. Many divorced people remarry, desiring a successful partnership.
10. The addition of family members means a bigger source of support and love. Children and teens gain stepparents who may enrich their lives and fill an empty place in a family.

Thinking Critically

1. Answers will vary.
2. Answers will vary. Point out that more fathers request custody than in the past.
3. Answers will vary.

Tracy reaches out to the members of her blended family.

Tracy "It took time to get used to the idea of moving in with a whole new family — a stepfather, stepbrother, and stepsister. My mom and dad had fought a lot, so I expected the same thing to happen with Tim. He's quieter than my father, though, so he didn't yell to make his point. I liked our new house, and Tim, who works in construction, turned the basement into two extra bedrooms. At first everything seemed awkward, but I decided to make a real effort to get along. I shared my music tapes and tried to be open with my new family. Sometimes it didn't feel natural, but it got easier once we all relaxed. Even though it feels a bit crowded at times, we are starting to feel like a real family."

Tim Knight "Marrying Tracy's mom and moving my family into a new house was hectic. None of us knew what to expect. Tracy's mom is stricter than I am, so we all had to get used to new and different rules. I think Tracy was surprised her mom and I got along so well. Her home life hadn't been all that easy. I was a widower, but my first marriage was very happy. Gratefully, I could see Tracy really trying to be friends with my kids. Her sense of humor made all of us more comfortable together. It meant more to me than she knows. She made me see how communication is a key to strong family relationships."

Anne "I never had a stepmother or stepsister, and I didn't think I would like it. I don't think Tracy knew how scared I was when we moved in together. She made it seem easy. Her friendliness made me less nervous. She offered to let me wear a jacket of hers I really liked, and she bought me a bag of my favorite chocolate chip cookies. Little things like that broke down barriers."

Mike "As her older stepbrother, I think Tracy is still a little shy around me, but lately we've spent more time together. I don't think she really knows that by reaching out to Anne and me, she helped unite us as a new family. 'How was your day?' she'll ask now, and even if I'm not in the mood to talk very much, her genuine interest makes me feel good. She's fun to be around, and her caring makes her special."

You can make a difference too.

- Do you know anyone who lives in a blended family? What challenges have they had to face? How were these handled?
- How does a positive marriage between two parents affect the way stepsiblings relate to each other?
- If you found yourself with a new stepsibling, what could you do to make the relationship work as well as possible?

UNIT

7 Will You Become a Parent?

CHAPTER

CHAPTER 23

Parenting Decisions

Chapter Challenge

Resources. Refer to the Teacher's Classroom Resources box and Student Workbook for materials related to this chapter.

Look for These Answers . . .

- What are the rewards of parenthood?
- How are parenting roles different today than they were in the past?
- What readiness factors should be considered before becoming a parent?
- What forms of contraception are most effective for planning parenthood?
- How can people handle the problem of infertility?
- What are the special concerns that teen parents must face?
- What healthful solutions are available for people coping with unplanned pregnancies?

Look for These Terms . . .

- cervix
- conception
- contraceptives
- fallopian tubes
- fertilized
- infertility
- ovum
- penis
- sperm
- uterus
- vagina

"A life without children?" Maria thought. "What would that be like?" As a preschool teacher, she already knew she loved children, and she wanted a couple of her own someday.

"It scares me, Maria," Greg said to her. "I just don't know what kind of father I would make. You know, when my parents divorced, it was tough on me. The one thing I never want to do is put a child through what I went through. Maybe the best way to guarantee that is to just not have children."

Everything had been going smoothly as Greg and Maria made their wedding plans. Then the subject of children came up. Maria had strong feelings one way. Greg was not totally opposed to children. He just had concerns.

Maria knew that this was an issue they needed to work out. It was too important to ignore at this point. "I've made an appointment with Reverend Lindstrom," she said to Greg. "He may be able to help us sort out our feelings about all of this. We can talk to some other people too if you like. I thought maybe Dr. Clayton would have some suggestions too."

Greg felt a sense of relief. He loved Maria and he wanted this marriage to work. On the other hand, he didn't want to be pressured into something that was not right for him — or for them. He put his arms around Maria. "Whatever we discover, it will be right," he said.

Chapter Opener. Have the students read the chapter opener. Discuss the questions within the opener. In addition you may want to ask the following questions: When you hear the word "parenthood," what thoughts come to mind? What benefit is there in discussing whether or not to have children prior to marriage? How could ignoring the discussion about parenthood affect Greg and Maria's relationship in the future?

Understanding Parenthood

Parenting may be one of the most profound experiences known to humankind. At the most basic level, parents create a new life and bring a child into the world. For many years parents must provide the essentials, including food and shelter. At the same time, they must encourage a healthy self-concept, motivate the child to learn, and teach relationship skills and moral values. Raising a child is no simple task! Although it is not easy, parenting can still be a fulfilling and rewarding experience for all involved.

Parenting Roles Today

Attitudes toward marriage, family, and parenting have changed over time. In years past, people were expected to marry young and remain married until death. Families were usually large. Many family members were needed to keep the family farm or business functioning well.

Activity. On index cards, write down various parenting roles. Include current and past trends in parenting roles. Give each student a card and have them respond to the parenting role on the card. Discuss student attitudes and perceptions about parenting roles. Should couples agree on parenting roles? Are any parenting roles ideal?

In families today parenting comes in many forms. Single parents, as well as couples, raise children. Grandparents, foster parents, and adoptive parents provide care and love for children. Some children live with stepparents in blended families. Families tend to be smaller due in part to the cost of raising children. Some couples remain childless by choice, opting instead for a smaller family.

In addition to changes in family form, some families have changed in function. Due to career and economic needs, many families have two working parents. Fathers take a more active part in parenting than they did in the past. Men and women are reorganizing household responsibilities so both parents can spend time with the children. Some families decide to have stay-at-home moms or dads, hoping to save money on child care and have more parental influence on the children.

You don't have to be a parent to fulfill the needs of a child. Why do you think adults other than parents are often in this role today?

Activity. Have students view an episode from an old family television series, such as "Father Knows Best" or "Leave It To Beaver." As they watch the show, have the students write down examples of traditional parenting roles. Following the viewing, lead a discussion examining past and present parenting roles. Changes? Similarities?

◆ Readiness for Parenthood

Deciding to become a parent is probably the biggest decision most people make in a lifetime. Emotional, physical, and financial factors must be weighed when making this decision.

◆ Emotional Factors

Some people are more ready for parenting than others. What makes the difference? Ralph and Jean are anxiously awaiting the birth of their first child. What emotional qualities do you see in them that would make them good parents?

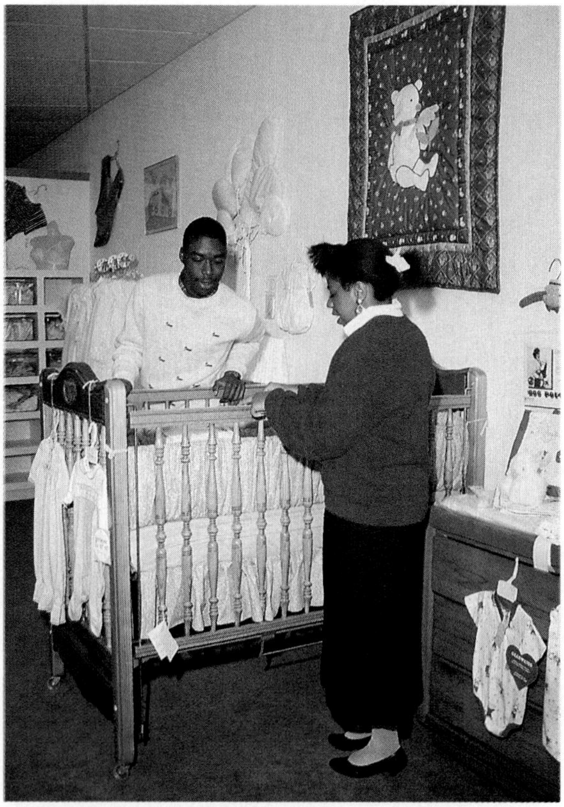

Some couples are more ready for parenthood than others. What signs do you see that this couple is ready to face the challenge?

More About Emotional Adjustments. Many new parents experience feelings of anxiety, fear, jealousy, depression, and worry over finances. These feelings are normal. The ability to cope with these feelings depends on parental attitudes toward varying situations. New parents need support from family and friends.

When couples share in the care of a child, neither parent needs to feel neglected or overburdened. What child care tasks do you think are especially important to share?

Jean and Ralph are in their early thirties. Both are successful in their jobs and feel really good about what they have accomplished. Maturity has increased their patience and flexibility. Recognizing that parenthood will drastically change their lifestyle, Jean and Ralph have decided that the sacrifices they must make will be well worth it. They agree that children will enhance their already strong relationship. Jean and Ralph readily exchange their feelings and concerns about parenthood. They truly appreciate each other and are committed to developing a strong, healthy family.

An infant changes the relationship of its parents. Before birth, partners can give full attention to each other. When the baby arrives, that changes. A baby may take all of the attention of one parent, making the other feel left out. Sharing equally in the care of the infant reduces the feeling of neglect.

Infants demand love and attention; however, they do not give back much love for awhile. Caring for them may seem like a one-way street. Parents need to be emotionally mature enough to give love without receiving any in return. They must be secure enough to think of the needs of someone else instead of their own needs.

Because babies are demanding, parents face dramatic limits on their personal freedom. Time with friends, away from the baby, becomes very valuable. Parents who are mature recognize that this will change in time.

Discussion. Ask students to consider their current health and physical maturity. What healthful habits have they developed that promote physical wellness? What changes should they make in their lives to improve their physical health in preparation for parenthood in the future?

◆ Physical Factors

Physical maturity and health are important considerations for parents-to-be. Physical checkups for both partners before pregnancy may identify any potential health problems that could affect the child or the parents' ability to care for the child.

Age is a health consideration for women. Women under age twenty and over age thirty-five are more at risk during pregnancy. Age may also have serious implications for the health of the unborn child.

Healthful eating habits are important, especially for mothers. What are your eating habits like? If you are female, will your body be able to supply the nutrients needed for a healthy baby?

Activity. Have students investigate the risks involved in having children before age twenty and over age thirty-five. What physical factors are a concern? Why? Can these risks be prevented? Why or why not?

I CAN ◆◆ Choose Parenthood

Young couples must make many decisions as they begin their lives together. Sometimes they feel pressure from their families to do things a certain way. Doug and Tonya were in this situation.

"When Doug and I graduated from college, we decided to get married before starting on our new careers. We had many goals for our future. I've always wanted to own a house. Doug and I felt we needed to establish some financial stability and pay off our college loans before thinking about children. We also wanted the freedom to experience life together for a while—just the two of us.

"Things were going well until my mother started putting pressure on us about children. Every time we were around her she would say something like, 'Tonya, when are you and Doug going to make me a grandmother?' The more often we heard these questions and comments, the more uncomfortable Doug and I became. We didn't feel ready for all the responsibilities of parenthood. We also didn't like the pressure.

"Finally, we just addressed the issue head-on. We told my mother that we were not ready emotionally or financially for parenthood. Any decisions we had to make about parenthood would have to wait for awhile.

"Surprisingly, my mother took it well. She seemed to understand. If she still hopes and dreams about becoming a grandmother, she is now quietly waiting for that possibility."

- Why do you think Tonya's mother was pressuring them to have children?
- Do people sometimes have children for the wrong reasons? What might some of these reasons be?
- What would you tell your own family in a similar situation? Why is it often difficult for young people to take a stand under such pressures?

◆ Financial Factors

The cost of raising children is a surprise to some young parents. Doctor and hospital bills are just the beginning. Babies need special equipment and furniture as well as diapers and clothing. Because of a child's rapid growth, food and clothing expenses increase rapidly. By some estimates, it can cost as much as $200,000 or more to raise a child to the age of eighteen. Just think about the cost of raising more than one!

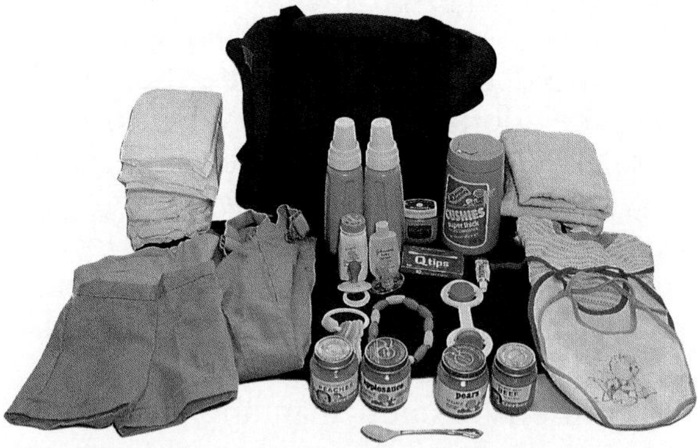

Even the basic needs for a baby can be costly. If you use cloth diapers, the cost will be lower than for disposables. Are there ecological advantages to this too? What are the disadvantages?

Life Management Skills. In pairs, have students brainstorm every possible financial factor parents need to think about. Provide each pair with a situation card describing their family, monthly income, and several fixed expenses. Have each pair develop a monthly budget using the allotted income.

Life Management Skills. In pairs, have students make a list of all equipment, furnishings, diapers (cloth vs. disposable), and clothing that will be needed during the baby's first year. Ask students to do some comparison shopping. Students should consider cost and safety. Have them report their findings to the class.

Young families often find that more housing space is needed as children become part of the family. Moving to a larger home adds more expense. If both parents must return to work, child care is an added cost. Careful financial planning before children enter the family can help ease the financial burden often felt by young families.

◆◆◆

Planning for Parenthood

Once the decision to have children is made, couples begin to think about when and how many children they will have. With advances in medical science, they are able to plan and space pregnancies if they wish.

◆ Understanding Conception

Although you will read more about reproduction in the next chapter, you need to be familiar with a few terms now in order to understand how contraception works.

Every month in the female body an **ovum**, or egg, is released. This is a single cell that determines half of what a person will be. The ovum travels through one of two tubes, called the **fallopian tubes** (fuh-LOW-pee-uhn), heading toward the **uterus** (YOOT-uh-russ), a muscular, pear-shaped organ. The male body produces **sperm**, also single cells that provide half of a person's heritage. Sperm enter the female body from the external male reproductive organ, the **penis**. Sperm are deposited in the internal female reproductive organ, the **vagina** (vuh-JI-nuh). The sperm then begin to work their way toward the fallopian tubes. If a sperm unites with the ovum in a fallopian tube, the ovum is said to be **fertilized**. The ovum then travels into the uterus where it attaches to the uterine wall to grow and develop. **Conception** has occurred, marking the beginning of pregnancy.

Discussion. Have students read the section on planning for parenthood. What factors may affect the choice and use of contraceptive methods for couples planning families? Emphasize there are no right or wrong choices.

◆ Contraception

Contraceptives are devices or methods used to avoid pregnancy. The primary objective of contraception is to prevent a sperm and ovum from uniting. This can be done in several ways. The chart on page 334 describes the most common effective methods of contraception. When used properly, contraceptives are highly effective. Remember, however, that the only 100 percent effective method of pregnancy prevention is abstinence from sexual intercourse.

Choosing a contraceptive method or device is a very personal decision for a couple to make. Often couples base their decision on values and religious principles. Whatever method is chosen, the best results occur when couples are comfortable using the method and committed to its proper use. Many couples use some form of contraception in planning their families.

◆ Problems with Infertility

Some couples are unable to have children. This condition is called **infertility.** Unsuccessful attempts to have a child can be frustrating and emotionally difficult.

The reasons for infertility vary. Infertility can have a physical or emotional reason. When no apparent explanation exists for infertility, emotional or stress factors need to be considered. Talking with a psychologist or psychiatrist can be helpful. Sometimes physical problems in the man or woman prevent pregnancy from occurring. In situations like this, surgery or medications often solve the problem.

Sometimes alternatives offered by medical science are not effective or are not acceptable to the couple. In cases like these, some couples adjust to the idea of remaining childless. Others may choose to adopt children.

Discussion. After students read the section on infertility, discuss the options available to infertile couples. Ask students what controversy surrounds many options. You may want to have the students do some library research on options for infertile couples.

Methods of Contraception

Method of Contraception	Function	Disadvantages	Effectiveness Rate
Abstinence	No sexual intercourse.	None	100%
Oral Contraceptive	Prevents monthly release of fertile egg.	Prescription needed. Can cause weight gain, headaches, mood changes. Increased risk of high blood pressure in women over 35 who smoke.	94-97%
Diaphragm: A dome-shaped latex cup stretched over a flexible ring.	Provides a barrier, preventing sperm from reaching the ovum. Most effective when used with spermicide.	Reduces sexual spontaneity. Increased risk of urinary tract and bladder infections. Must be fitted by trained medical professional.	84%
Cervical Cap: Vaginal insert.	Fits over **cervix** (SUR-viks), narrow end of uterus connected to vagina, and provides barrier. Used with spermicide.	Requires prescription. Difficult to insert.	73-92%
Condom: Latex sheath that fits over penis.	Provides barrier by trapping semen. Can reduce pregnancy and sexually transmitted diseases.	Can break or slip off. Reduces spontaneity.	86%
IUD (Intrauterine Device): Small plastic or metal device inserted into uterus by doctor.	Prevents pregnancy by interfering with implantation of fertilized egg.	Increases risk of pelvic infection. May increase menstrual flow and cramping. May be expelled from body without user's awareness.	94%
Implant: Six matchstick-shaped capsules placed under the skin of the female's upper arm.	Secretes hormone that prevents ovaries from releasing eggs. Effective for five years.	Requires doctor visit. Initially expensive. May cause irregular periods, nausea, headaches.	99%
Injection: Shot of synthetic hormone drug, Depo-Provera.	Prevents egg cells from being released. Effective for three months.	Requires doctor visit. May cause irregular periods, nausea, headaches.	99%
Spermicide: Vaginal suppositories, foams, creams, and gels.	A chemical that kills sperm. Works well with diaphragm or condom.	Easy to use incorrectly. Not very effective when used alone. May cause allergic reaction in some people.	79%
Sterilization: Tubal ligation in female (involves sealing off fallopian tubes). Vasectomy in male (involves cutting or tying vas deferens).	Prevents sperm and ovum from meeting in both methods.	Some risk of infection. Cannot be easily reversed. May require major surgery to reverse, often without success.	99%
Natural Family Planning: Involves charting temperature and noticing changes in vaginal mucus.	Prevents pregnancy by avoiding intercourse during fertile period.	Errors easily made. Demands accurate record keeping. Illness or irregular menstrual cycle can throw off calculations.	80%

Note: Effectiveness of contraceptive methods is based on proper use.

◆◆◆
Teenage Parenthood

Every year in the United States, approximately 500,000 teenage girls have babies. More than half of these teenagers are single mothers. A small number of children live with teenage fathers. For teen parents the responsibilities, readiness factors, and rewards of parenthood are the same as for older parents; however, teens face special problems.

Many of the difficulties teenagers have as parents directly relate to physical and emotional maturity. Teenage women may not have finished their physical growth. Most teens are still developing emotionally and need guidance from responsible adults. They may not be ready to take care of another person when they are still learning to be responsible for themselves. Sudden responsibility for the life of another person can be overwhelming for the young teen.

A Slice of Life

For three years it had just been Alise and her mother at home. Mrs. Handley worked long hours and seemed burdened by the responsibility of caring for the two of them. Sometimes Alise wanted her mother's attention, but her mother either wasn't there or was too distracted to become involved in Alise's concerns. Alise had not seen her father in three years. She missed him.

Because sixteen-year-old Alise was an only child, she spent many hours by herself. She had few friends. Bo was one of her friends, but he only came around when he didn't have anything better to do.

Lately Alise had been wishing she had a baby sister. How sweet and cuddly she would be. She could love it and dress it up in pretty clothes. Alise knew her mother wasn't going to have any more children. "Maybe I . . . ," thought Alise. The thought both delighted and frightened her.

Thinking It Through

- What do you think is on Alise's mind? Why is she thinking this way?
- How does Alise's thinking contrast with what you have read in this chapter?
- What other options does Alise have that might help her solve her problem?

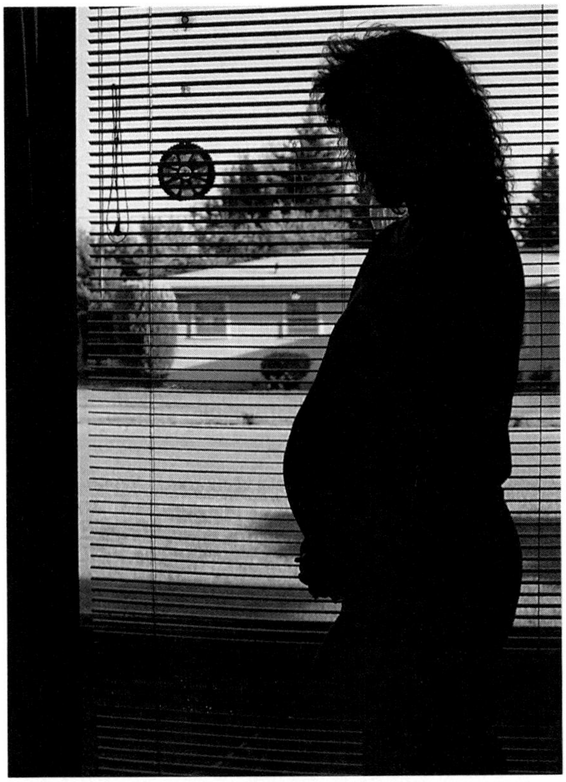

Teens are often not ready for parenthood. Can you think of some reasons why?

Photo Focus. Ask students what thoughts this teen may be having at this time. How will her life change? If possible, have students interview a teen parent about the changes in life after becoming a parent.

Problem Solving. Parenthood requires physical and emotional maturity as well as some financial stability. Discuss the issue of teen parenthood with the students. Are teens ready to be parents? Why or why not? If not, what solutions do you suggest for reducing the number of teen pregnancies yearly? Examine all possibilities. Students should think critically, carefully weighing pros and cons, biases, opinions, and facts found in resources.

◆ Health

Many teenagers experience a normal, uncomplicated pregnancy. Others do not. The likelihood of health problems during pregnancy is much greater for teens than for women in their twenties.

During pregnancy, the mother's body supplies the baby with nutrients needed for growth. Many teens have poor eating habits. As a result, their bodies are not prepared for the development of a healthy baby let alone the development of their own bodies. The chances are great that a teen mother will give birth to an infant with a low birth weight. Underweight babies run a high risk of developing health problems during their first year of life.

Smoking, drinking alcohol, and using other drugs also endanger a mother and baby. Teens with any of these habits are more likely to experience complications during pregnancy and birth. Anemia, a low red blood cell count, and abnormal bleeding are examples of such complications. You will read about other complications in the next chapter.

◆ Education

Tara was finding it difficult to return to school after the birth of her daughter Kyla. She felt cut off from friends and school activities. "Basketball and everything else that's fun seems over for me," Tara thought. "Where can I fit in? My friends and I have nothing in common to talk about anymore. They can date and go out with friends whenever they want. With Kyla in my life, I am pretty much tied to home."

Tara's feelings are similar to those of many other young mothers. To her it seems as though part of life has vanished. Others like her feel as though they are caught in a time warp: too young to truly be an adult, yet having too many adult responsibilities to be a carefree teenager.

Although many teens drop out of school after becoming parents, most want to complete their education. Lack of child care is often the reason teen parents stay away from school. Many schools across the country have developed programs to meet the special needs of teen parents. Programs with on-site child care facilities and parenting classes, as well as full high school course offerings, help teen parents complete their education. Programs such as these help young parents become self-reliant and prepared to take on the challenges of adult life.

Even though many schools have programs to help young parents, some teens become discouraged and quit school. Dropping out

Teen parents are more likely to stay in school and complete their education when the school has an on-site child care facility. How easy do you think it is to provide such programs?

Activity. Divide students into groups of two or three. Have each group research one of the following factors that affect human fetal development: nutrition, alcohol and drugs, smoking, infections and disease, and age of the mother. What special implications do these factors hold for pregnant teens?

Life Management Skills. Ask students to make a list of their long-term goals for the next five years. How would an early pregnancy interfere with their goals? Ask students to write a personal commitment statement regarding their goals and avoiding pregnancy.

of high school severely limits the kinds of jobs available to young moms and dads. Most of these jobs are low-paying, limiting the income of young families. Much evidence shows that if teen parents stay in school, their chances of success in life are greater.

◆ Money

Caring for an infant is expensive for parents of any age. Teen mothers and fathers may have to make decisions about where to live. If they decide to live on their own, they will have to pay for rent, food, and utilities. There may not be any money for clothing or recreation. As Willie said, "It's hard. You have to go without so that your kids can have the things they need."

Sources of help are available for young families; however, even these may be inadequate in meeting a young family's needs. Sometimes a combination of resources may be necessary.

Jennifer's parents were able to help her out when the baby came by providing a place for her to live. "One of my friends wasn't as lucky as I am," said Jennifer. "Her parents can't help with expenses. Actually, I don't think they want to. They feel that Carla has to be responsible for herself now."

Other resources available for young families include Aid to Families with Dependent Children (AFDC) and the Women, Infants, and Children (WIC) program, which provides money for milk and living expenses. Generally, these monthly payments are not very large. Some government agencies assist in providing child care for young parents who remain in school.

Young mothers often find it hard to work and take care of their babies too. Even young fathers who work are likely to have trouble supporting themselves and their families, especially if they have not finished high school.

Work and Family. Discuss with the students the special difficulties teen parents must face in balancing work and family issues. For teen parents, work may include a part-time job as well as going to school. Family may include their child as well as other family members. Include in the discussion items such as child care, finances, leisure time activities without children, etc. How may coping with these issues differ for more mature parents?

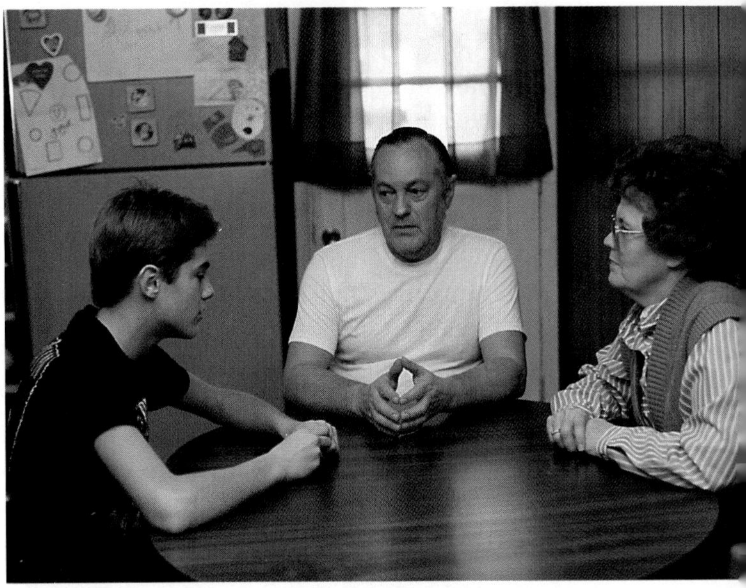

Some teens who face unexpected parenthood rely on their families for help. How do you think this might affect a young couple's desire for independence? Will there be any long-term effects?

◆◆◆

Unplanned Pregnancy

Unplanned pregnancies can happen to anyone. Many who are sexually active, both younger and older, fail to use effective contraceptive methods. Up to 50 percent think pregnancy won't happen to them. The result of this thinking is unexpected pregnancies.

Some deal with unexpected pregnancy positively, reporting that the experience has brought the partners closer together. Many eventually marry. The opposite is true for many others. Some women experience rejection from their partners, leaving them to face pregnancy alone.

Several choices are available to those who face unplanned pregnancies. Whatever decision is made, the seriousness of every choice needs to be considered. What will happen with each choice, both now and in the future?

How will these choices affect everyone involved emotionally and physically? What facts are available concerning each choice? Think about these questions as you read about the options:

- **Keeping the Baby.** Many women complete their pregnancies and keep the baby to raise with or without a father. Parenting is a challenge for two parents and even more of a challenge for a single parent. Money can be a real issue for single parents. At this time in our country, women and children make up a great number of the poor. On the brighter side, though, some single-parent families are happy and successful even with limited resources.
- **Adoption.** Completing a pregnancy and offering the infant for adoption is another choice. Although releasing a child for adoption is very hard, many birth parents feel that this is best for the child. Other couples may be more prepared physically, emotionally, and financially to raise a child. Parents who adopt accept the legal responsibilities of parenthood rather than the birth parents. Adoptions are generally arranged by local or state agencies, religious organizations, and some other public or private groups. Sometimes adoptions are arranged by attorneys or physicians.

Adoptive parents are screened very carefully to be sure that they can provide a child with a good environment. In open adoptions, birth parents and adoptive parents get to know each other and often remain in contact throughout the child's life. Identifications are not revealed in a closed adoption. Professionals who deal with adoptive parents advise them to tell the child about the adoption. This information can be upsetting if it comes as a surprise.

Adoptive parents truly appreciate the birth parents' courage in placing their child up for adoption. It's a difficult but loving thing to do.

People who wish to adopt a child are screened carefully before the adoption takes place. These people are usually placed on waiting lists until a child is available.

Photo Focus. Ask students to carefully examine the above photo. Ask students the following questions: What thoughts come to mind when you think about adoption or foster care? If you are a pregnant teen, what kinds of questions would you want a social worker to ask possible parents? You may want to invite a social worker to talk with your class about adoption procedures. Invite parents who have adopted as well as an adopted teen to talk with your class about the adoption experience.

- **Ending Pregnancy.** Some women decide to end their unplanned pregnancies by having an abortion. The term "abortion" means to end a pregnancy on purpose. Doctors may use one of several methods to end the pregnancy. Performed before the thirteenth week, abortion is considered safe for the mother. After the first twelve weeks of pregnancy, abortion involves greater risks for the mother.

Although abortion can be simple and safe, some women experience discomfort physically, emotionally, or both. Women who have abortions before age sixteen are more likely to have problems with their reproductive organs later in life. Repeated abortions increase the risk of infection, sterility, and later pregnancy failure. Guilt, anger, and depression are emotions that may be felt by some following the procedure. On the other hand, there are those who feel a sense of relief in having the situation resolved.

The right to abortion is a hotly debated subject. Some believe that every woman should have the right to decide what to do with her body. Others are concerned about the right to life of the unborn child.

Decisions about abortion are difficult. Every person must take into consideration personal values as well as what has been learned from parents and possibly religious training, the objective facts on both sides of the issue, and any moral or legal implications.

Challenges and Rewards

Many parents feel that raising children enriches their lives. They take satisfaction in watching children grow into happy, healthy, well-adjusted, and productive individuals. They find pleasure in teaching children about the world and what they value. Through sharing time and experiences, parents and children form a special lifelong bond sealed with love.

At the same time, any parent will tell you that raising children has its challenges. Parents must make sacrifices, personal as well as financial. The day-to-day care required as children grow and develop takes much of the parents' time and energy. Still, most parents say that the long-term satisfaction and joy is worthwhile.

Now, what about you? Think about these questions as you look ahead to the future:

- What expectations do you have about parenting?
- How would you evaluate your readiness for parenting?
- If you plan to have children, how are you preparing yourself for this role in life?

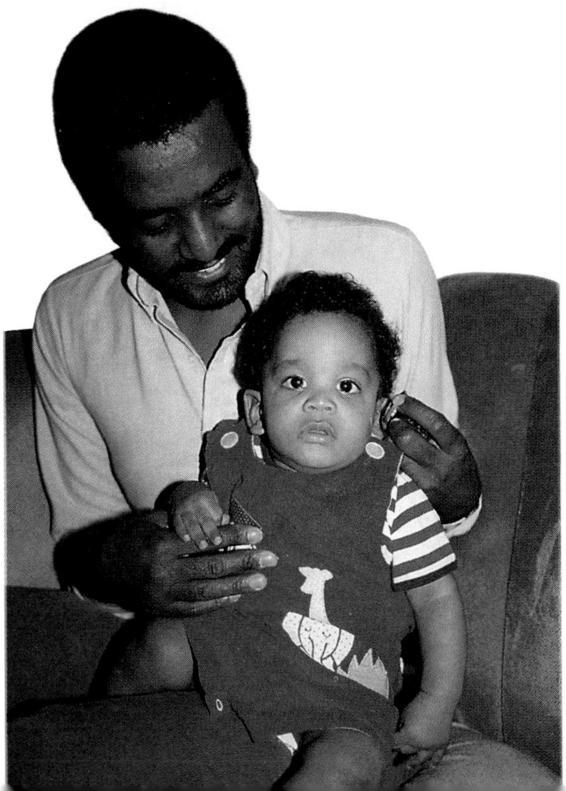

Raising a child can be rewarding when you are ready for the responsibility. It takes energy and devotion, but most parents feel their lives are enriched by the experience.

Activity. Have the students interview parents of several generations. What rewards do they find in parenting? What challenges? What were their expectations of parenthood? How ready were they to be parents? What advice would they give to people thinking about parenthood? Compare responses for similarities and differences. Were there generational differences? How can students apply this information to their own lives?

CHAPTER

23

Review

Answers
Testing Your Memory

1. Families have changed in attitudes toward marriage, size, form, and functions of family members. **Any two:** Larger families no longer needed to manage farms and businesses; costs of raising children; career interests and needs; economic needs.
2. A person should have high self-esteem; patience; flexibility; willingness to make sacrifices; desire to talk about feelings; commitment to developing a strong family; a desire to share responsibilities; willingness to give love without receiving any in return; and concern for the needs of others.
3. Physical maturity and a healthy body contribute to the development of a healthy child. Women under 20 and over 35 are more at risk during pregnancy, as is the health of the unborn child.
4. It is very costly to have a child; costs include doctor bills, equipment, food, clothing, and housing.
5. Abstinence.
6. Physically immature bodies; poor eating habits; bodies not ready for the development of a healthy baby; risky behaviors, such as smoking and drinking.
7. **Any two** of the difficulties described on pages 336 and 337.

Summarizing the Chapter

- Trends in parenting today include smaller families, single-parent families, and blended families.
- People who are planning for parenthood need to be physically and emotionally ready. They also need some financial stability.
- Parenthood changes the lifestyle of the parents.
- There are two ways to avoid pregnancy: abstinence from sexual intercourse and using an effective contraceptive correctly.
- Many teenagers become pregnant every year. Most of them are not mature enough physically or emotionally to provide for a child.
- When dealing with an unplanned pregnancy, decisions must be made very carefully, thinking about the effects on all concerned.
- Although parenthood requires great sacrifices on the part of parents, its rewards and joys are great.

Testing Your Memory

1. How have families changed over the years? Name two reasons why these changes have occurred.
2. What characteristics may indicate that a person is emotionally ready to be a parent?
3. Explain how physical maturity and health affect prospective parents.
4. Why do people need to be financially ready for parenthood?
5. Which birth control method is 100 percent effective?
6. Why is a teen mother more likely to have health problems during pregnancy than a woman in her twenties?
7. List two difficulties teen parents face.
8. How do open and closed adoptions differ?
9. What are two rewards of parenthood?

Thinking Critically

1. Healthy self-esteem is necessary for parents and children. How may low self-esteem in a parent affect a child?
2. Who do you think should be responsible for contraception, the male or the female? Why?
3. Some couples decide *not* to have children. What contraceptive choices might be best for them? Why?
4. Describe the responsibilities of a teenage mother and father. Why do some teen fathers feel that they have no parental responsibilities?
5. Why may having a child strengthen an already strong marriage but weaken an already weak marriage?

Taking Action

1. Interview a teenage parent about life as a parent. What are the difficulties? The joys?
2. Research the methods used to help infertile couples. What choices are available? What legal, moral, or ethical implications might there be?

Making Life Choices

In the middle of her junior year in high school, Katrina found out she was pregnant. Although her parents were willing to help her in any way they could, Katrina knew that there really wasn't enough money to feed another child. Her parents worked hard, but they needed their money to support Katrina's younger brother and sister. Katrina had been planning a bright future for herself. Her goal was to go to college and work toward a teaching degree. Now she had other things to think about.

What options does Katrina have? How will each option affect her life? List all the people who are involved in Katrina's decision. How does the decision affect each of them? What could Katrina have done to avoid the situation she is in?

Using Your Journal

As you have just read, parenting involves many responsibilities as well as many rewards. What are your feelings about being a parent? Use your journal to examine your thoughts about having children. Do you want to have children? If so, how many? When? How will you know when you are ready for parenthood? How will you make sure you don't have children before you are ready?

8. In ***open adoption,*** the adoptive parents and person placing the child for adoption meet and discuss the adoption. In ***closed adoptions,*** the adoptive parents do not know the birth parents.
9. **Any two** of the rewards described on page 339.

Thinking Critically

1. Answers will vary but should center on communication, demonstrating affection, ability to set guidelines for children.
2. Answers will vary. Ask students to defend their answer with sound reasoning. Point out to students that both males and females need to share in this responsibility.
3. Answers will vary but may include oral contraceptives and sterilization.
4. Answers will vary.
5. Answers will vary.

CHAPTER 24

Becoming a Parent

Chapter Challenge

Resources. Refer to the Teacher's Classroom Resources box and Student Workbook for materials related to this chapter.

Look for These Answers...

- How are babies conceived?
- What changes occur as an embryo and fetus grow and develop?
- What signs tell a woman that she may be pregnant?
- How should a woman care for herself when she is pregnant?
- What can mothers and fathers do to prepare for the birth of their baby?
- Describe the birth process.

Look for These Terms...

- amniotic sac
- chromosomes
- embryo
- fetus
- genes
- obstetrician
- placenta
- trimester
- ultrasound

Kirsten paced anxiously in front of the telephone, waiting for the call from her doctor's office. She and Daniel had been thinking about starting a family; however, she didn't think it would happen this soon. As she waited, Kirsten thought about having a baby and all the responsibilities of becoming a parent. The whole process was truly amazing, even overwhelming.

The telephone rang. It was the nurse from Dr. Thompson's office telling Kirsten that the results of her test were positive. As she hung up the telephone, Kirsten thought about telling Daniel her exciting news.

The human body and all its systems are so amazing. Even though Kirsten felt no different than she ever had, in about eight months she and Daniel would have a baby. It seemed incredible that a baby could result from something that starts out so small. What changes would occur in her body? What would childbirth be like? How would she and Daniel handle the changes in their relationship? What would this child be like? Could they meet its needs?

It was a day of waiting for Kirsten. When Daniel arrived, she would tell him the news, and they would begin another waiting process that would lead them through some wonderful and challenging experiences.

Chapter Opener. Ask students to read the opening scenario to the chapter. In small groups, have the students brainstorm all the possible changes that may occur in this couples' relationship. In what ways can any couple use the months of pregnancy to process through some of the changes that will occur? What kinds of issues can be discussed and perhaps resolved prior to the birth of a child? How may couples anticipate and work through some of the emotions that often accompany pregnancy and parenthood, such as fear and anxiety?

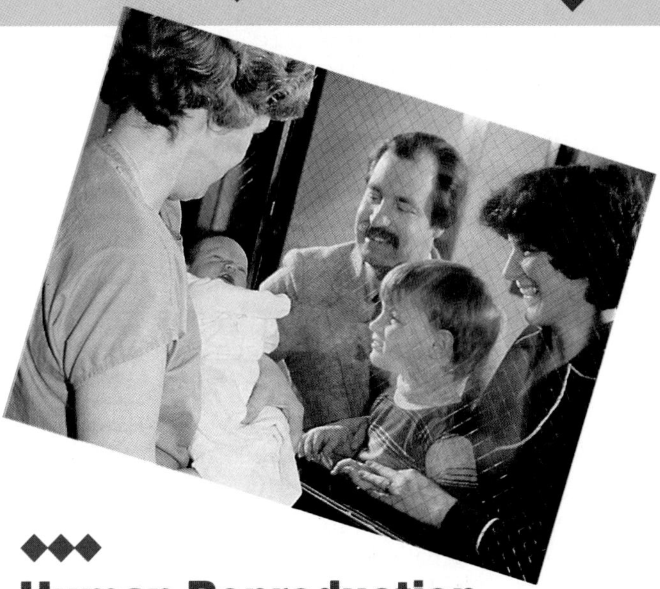

Human Reproduction

Understanding how children are conceived, nourished, and born is part of becoming a parent. The male and female reproductive systems are responsible for creating human life. Developing an understanding of how these systems work can help you understand yourself and your partner better. You read a little about the process in the last chapter. Now you will learn about reproduction in more detail.

Male Reproductive System

The purpose of the male reproductive system is to produce sperm cells. When male sperm cells unite with female egg cells, or ova, a fertilized ovum results. The two small glands that produce sperm are called testes (TES-teez), or testicles. They are suspended in a sac of skin, called the scrotum (SKROT-uhm). Each gland is continuously producing sperm at the rate of hundreds of millions per day.

Sperm cells look like tiny tadpoles, having a head (the actual cell) and a tail, which is used for mobility. The head contains half of the genetic material needed to form human life. It is the only part that will enter the ovum.

Once they are produced, the sperm travel through the vas deferens (vas-DEF-uh-runz) and other tubes and glands, where they are mixed with milky fluids called semen. Semen protects and nourishes sperm and gives them mobility.

Before leaving the male body, sperm must travel through the penis by way of the urethra (yu-REE-thruh). The penis is a tube-like organ made of spongy tissue, which is normally soft and flexible. During sexual arousal, the spongy tissue of the penis becomes filled with blood. When the penis becomes straight and enlarged, an erection has occurred. If an erection is followed by ejaculation (ee-jack-u-LAY-shun), semen is discharged from the penis. The body does not allow urine to pass through at this time. Each ejaculation contains less than an ounce of semen but as many as four hundred million sperm.

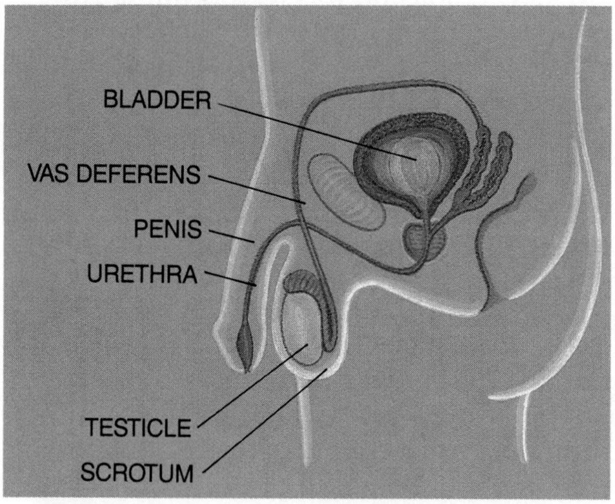

Sperm are produced in the male reproductive system.

◆ Female Reproductive System

Most of the female reproductive system is internal. Part of its purpose is to produce and develop eggs, or ova. If an ovum is fertilized, the female system is capable of nourishing and protecting that ovum as it grows into a fully formed baby.

The ova are contained in two organs, called ovaries. Located in the lower abdomen, ovaries are small, almond-shaped organs. Unlike the male, females are born with all of the ova they will ever produce. The ova remain in the ovaries until puberty, when they are most often released one at a time.

In adult females an ovum is released regularly from one ovary or the other about every 28 days. This process is called ovulation (ah-vu-LAY-shun).

As an ovum is released from an ovary, it enters one of two fallopian tubes. This tube provides a passageway for the ovum. Fertilization (the joining of ovum and sperm) generally occurs in the fallopian tube as the ovum travels toward the uterus.

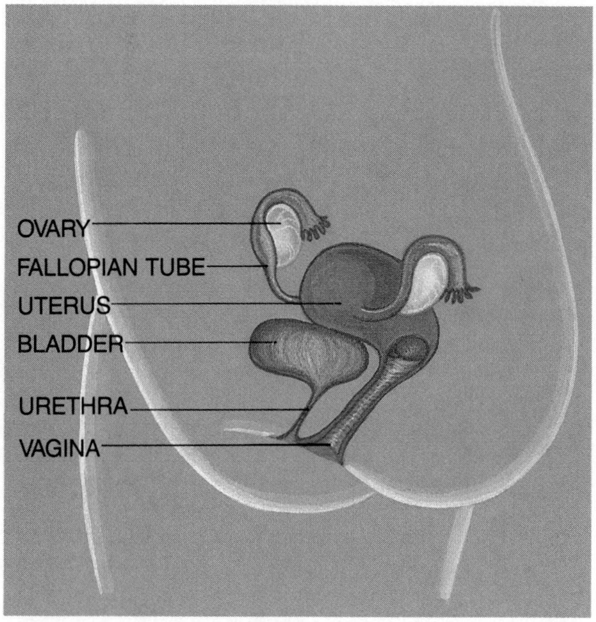

Ova, or eggs, are produced in the female reproductive system.

Activity. Ask students to write a word picture describing the development of sperm cells and the path they take through the male reproductive system. In addition, ask students to write a word picture describing the release of the ovum and the path it takes through the female reproductive system. (Note: a word picture is a thorough, creative written explanation using words.)

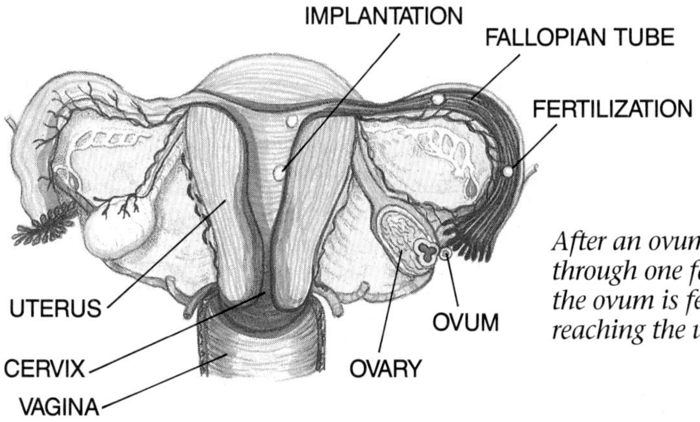

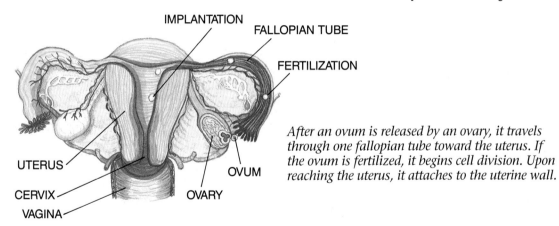

After an ovum is released by an ovary, it travels through one fallopian tube toward the uterus. If the ovum is fertilized, it begins cell division. Upon reaching the uterus, it attaches to the uterine wall.

The uterus, a pear-shaped, muscular organ about the size of a fist, is connected to the fallopian tubes. The uterus develops a thick, blood-rich tissue on its walls in preparation for a fertilized ovum. If the ovum is not fertilized by a sperm, it passes through the uterus, along with the blood-rich tissue, during menstruation (men-stru-WAY-shun). Menstruation, or the passing of the uterine lining, generally occurs once every 28 days.

The cervix is the narrow, lower end of the uterus connected to the vagina. The vagina, often called the birth canal, is a tubular passageway that connects the uterus to the outside of the body. During intercourse, it allows the male penis to deposit sperm near the cervix. Menstrual discharge leaves the body through the vagina. During the birth process, the vagina provides an exit for the baby.

◆◆◆

Conception

When a sperm fertilizes an ovum, conception occurs and a new life begins. This is not as simple as it sounds.

Although thousands of sperm may be released during an ejaculation, many of them remain in the vagina. Those that do enter the uterus through the tiny opening in the cervix swim into the fallopian tubes. Only one sperm penetrates the tough surface of the ovum. Once a sperm enters an ovum, the surface seals out all other sperm.

Sperm can live in the female reproductive system for several days. If intercourse occurs before the ovum is released, the sperm can still fertilize the ovum when it arrives later. This is possible for several days. Eventually, the sperm die.

Once an ovum is fertilized, it starts to divide immediately. By the time it reaches the uterus, it is a ball of cells. In the uterus, the ovum attaches itself to the blood-rich wall and continues to develop.

Sometimes a newly fertilized ovum divides into two fertilized eggs. When that happens, identical twins develop. Identical twins are the same sex and have the same physical traits. Other times, two separate eggs are fertilized at the same time by two separate sperm. In that case, fraternal twins will be born. Fraternal twins are not identical, and not necessarily of the same sex. Multiple births, in which three or more babies are born at the same time, are unusual, but have been more common in recent years.

More About Conception. Fertilization occurs shortly after the sperm enters the vagina. After fertilization, it takes about three to five days for the fertilized ovum to reach the uterus. During the next five days, the ovum becomes implanted in the wall of the uterus. At this point, the ovum produces hormones that signal the stop of the menstrual period. Sometimes implantation occurs in a place other than the uterus (usually the fallopian tube). These pregnancies often end in natural miscarriages or require other medical procedures to end the pregnancy due to risk to the mother.

◆ Genetics

Every human being carries 46 chromosomes (KROH-muh-sohms). The sperm and ovum each contribute 23 chromosomes to the new life. **Chromosomes** are tiny structures inside the nucleus of a cell. They are made up of smaller structures, called genes.

Genes determine the physical characteristics of a baby — for example, hair and eye color, body shape, and sex. Many personality traits are also determined by genes.

A Slice of Life

When Babette discovered that she was pregnant, both she and her husband Tony were very happy about the news. They had been planning to start a family for about a year. Babette didn't feel very prepared for pregnancy, so she took every chance to talk with her friends and relatives who had already had babies.

Her sister warned her about morning sickness. She suggested that Babette rearrange her schedule so that she could go to work late, after the nausea passed. She told Babette to avoid eating citrus fruits, which helps cut down on the queasiness.

Babette's best friend Leah also talked about food. She told Babette about her own urges to binge on double chocolate fudge sauce. With some women, food cravings are common.

Tony's mother, who had seven children, advised Babette to start supplementing her regular diet with extra servings of dairy products, dark green vegetables, and liver!

Anna, Tony's sister, called Babette to warn her to be careful what she said during pregnancy because of the baby's ability to hear everything.

Babette's mother offered to come over every day to clean and cook for Tony so that Babette could conserve her strength.

Madge, a woman who works with Babette, told her not to take anyone's advice without asking her doctor. Madge asked her doctor about every little thing.

Babette was frustrated and confused by all the advice. "Pregnancy is more complicated than I realized," she thought.

Thinking It Through

- What was the best advice Babette received?
- Which advice may be considered a myth? Why?
- How should a pregnant woman deal with all the advice and information that comes from friends, relatives, television, magazines, and other sources?

Activity. Have students brainstorm a list of inherited traits. What types of inherited traits do they see in themselves? Their family members? Have students explore the significance of dominant and recessive genes. What factors control genetic defects?

Life Management Skills. Have students select and research one birth defect. How do parents of children with birth defects cope? Can some birth defects be prevented? If so, how? What are some ways these parents manage family life?

Defective genes may cause genetic diseases that affect the development and function of the body. Each human being carries a few defective genes. Since everyone has at least 50,000 genes, however, the defective ones rarely cause problems. Genetic disease results when both parents carry the same gene for the problem. Some couples undergo genetic testing to identify any possibility of passing a genetic disease on to their children. Some of the more common genetic diseases are sickle cell anemia, hemophilia, cystic fibrosis, and Down syndrome.

◆◆◆

Signs of Pregnancy

A woman may not realize she is pregnant until one or more signs appear. Some of the early signs of pregnancy are:

- **Missed Menstrual Period.** This is usually the first sign of pregnancy, especially in women with regular periods.
- **Unusual Tiredness.** New demands on the body are sapping the mother's energy.
- **Swelling and Tenderness of the Breasts.** These glands are preparing to produce milk for the newborn infant.
- **Frequent Urination.** As the uterus begins to expand, it presses on the bladder.
- **Nausea, or "Morning Sickness."** This can happen at any time during the day for the first three or four months. Many women do not experience any queasiness during pregnancy.

All of these signs may occur for a reason other than pregnancy. Taken alone, they cannot be used to diagnose pregnancy. Blood and urine tests should be taken to confirm pregnancy.

Problem Solving. Ask students: What can a pregnant woman do to cope with morning sickness? Can morning sickness ever interfere with normal growth and development during pregnancy?

Activity. Invite a doctor or nurse practitioner in to discuss the importance of proper prenatal care. You may want to have them discuss what a woman can expect during her first prenatal visit.

◆◆◆

Pregnancy Tests

A woman who suspects she may be pregnant may confirm the pregnancy in two ways:

- **Home Pregnancy Tests.** These tests can be purchased at a drug store. They analyze urine and detect pregnancy about two weeks after a missed menstrual period. They are about 75 percent accurate when used correctly. When used too soon or mishandled, these tests do not give accurate results. Sometimes they may tell a woman that she is not pregnant when she really is or, occasionally, indicate a pregnancy that does not exist.
- **Physician Testing.** Visiting a doctor for a pregnancy test has several advantages. The blood samples taken and analyzed in a laboratory are more reliable than home pregnancy tests. At the time of testing, the doctor performs a complete physical exam and begins to discuss the woman's health during pregnancy. The earlier she begins to care for her own health, the better the chances of delivering a healthy baby.

◆◆◆

Development of the Embryo and Fetus

Approximately twenty days after conception occurs, the fertilized ovum attaches itself to the wall of the uterus (implantation). The inner layer of cells forms the **embryo** (EHM-bree-oh), the developing child in its earliest state, and the outer layer of cells makes up the placenta (pluh-SENT-uh). The **placenta** is a blood-rich organ that provides nourishment and oxygen to the embryo. It also removes waste materials from the growing embryo. The embryo is joined to the placenta by the umbilical cord (uhm-BILL-uh-cul). It serves as the passageway from the placenta to the embryo so the placenta may carry out its functions.

During the first four weeks, the embryo grows faster than at any other time in life. As soon as implantation occurs, the **amniotic sac** (am-knee-OT-ic) forms around the embryo. The fluid in the amniotic sac maintains an even temperature and protects the growing embryo from jars and bumps.

A pregnancy is generally divided into three-month periods, called **trimesters**. In the first trimester, body organs form. The heart, lungs, and brain begin functioning, and facial features become apparent. The heart starts beating by the end of the fourth week. The head is very large as the brain develops. From the eighth week until the time of birth, the developing child is called a **fetus** (FEE-tus). By the end of three months the fetus is about three inches long and weighs about one ounce. It can move and its organs are functioning.

In the middle trimester, the fetus grows longer and stronger. Muscles begin to function and bones harden. The mother can feel kicking. Fingernails and hair appear. By the end of this period, the fetus can breathe. If born now, it may be able to live on its own outside the mother's body.

During the last three months, the fetus puts on fat that will protect it after birth. It grows to about twenty inches in length. At this time, fetal demands on the mother's body are great. All organs begin to function in preparation for life on its own.

During the last month, the fetus turns to a head-down position in preparation for birth. Since it fills the amniotic sac, there is little room for movement. Just before birth, the fetus acquires temporary immunities from disease and infections. This natural protection will last for several months after birth.

More About Prenatal Development. In addition to oxygen and nutrients, the embryo (later, fetus) also receives immunity against some diseases. Nourishment, water, and immunities pass through the membranes in the placenta. The bloodstreams of the mother and infant are not directly connected; however, some diseases (rubella, sexually transmitted disease) and drugs (crack, alcohol, even prescription drugs) do pass through these membranes and can affect the embryo (fetus). The most damage may be done during the first trimester when a woman often doesn't know she is pregnant.

◆◆◆

Healthy Pregnancy

Before a woman even knows she is pregnant, a baby may be growing rapidly, forming essential body organs. The developing baby is easily affected by outside influences during this time. Some outside influences that may interfere with normal development include alcohol and other drugs, tobacco, sexually transmitted diseases, and radiation such as x-rays produce. Birth defects may result from any of these. Maintaining health before and during pregnancy provides the best guarantee that the baby will be healthy too.

◆ Medical Care

Regular visits to a doctor are a routine part of a pregnant woman's schedule. Some women choose an **obstetrician** (ahb-stuh-TRISH-un), a specialist in prenatal and postnatal care of mother and baby. Others stay with their family doctor. In a normal pregnancy, a woman visits her doctor once each month for the first eight months, then once a week until delivery.

During the first visit, the doctor performs a thorough medical examination. Blood is tested for nutrient reserves as well as diseases like diabetes, which can affect pregnancy. A doctor also looks for any disease, such as sexually transmitted diseases, that may be passed to the baby. A likely delivery date is also determined at this time.

The doctor discusses nutrition and weight gain. Vitamin or iron supplements may be recommended if a blood test shows these are lacking. The doctor also discusses the hazards of smoking, use of alcohol, and taking other drugs.

Blood pressure and weight checks are a regular part of the monthly visit to the doctor. In some cases, the doctor checks the fetus, using high-frequency sound waves, or **ultrasound**. Ultrasound pictures show the position of the fetus and give information about its general development.

Development of Embryo and Fetus

Each drawing below shows development at the end of the designated month. Lengths and weights are approximate.

Month One	**Month Two**	**Month Three**
	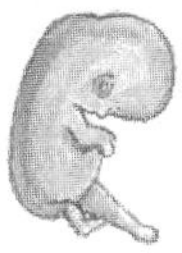	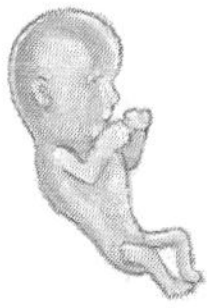
• Embryo length: $\frac{1}{4}$ inch. • Brain, heart, lungs forming. • Arm and leg buds appear. • Heart starts beating. • Digestive system, back bone, spinal cord begin forming.	• Embryo length: $1\frac{1}{8}$ inches. • Weight: $\frac{1}{4}$ ounce. • Has face. • Eyelids are fused. • Muscles, skin developing. • Limbs forming. • Vital organs starting to develop. • Brain taking shape.	• Length: 3 inches. • Weight: $1\frac{1}{2}$ ounces. • Now called a fetus. • Taking on recognizable form. • Can open and close mouth and swallow. • Heartbeat detectable with instruments. • Nails start developing.
Month Four	**Month Five**	**Month Six**
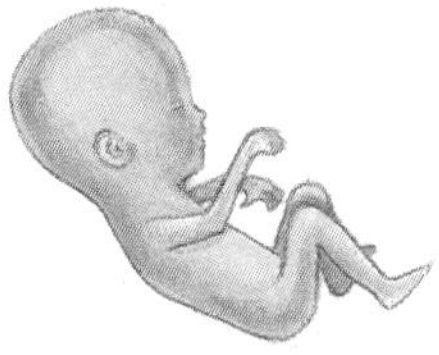	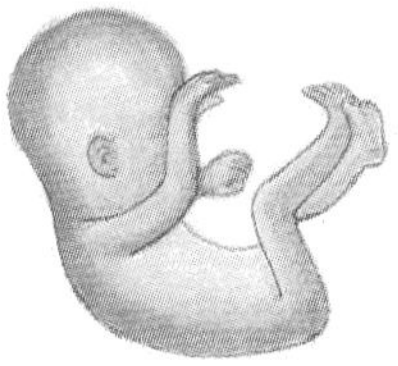	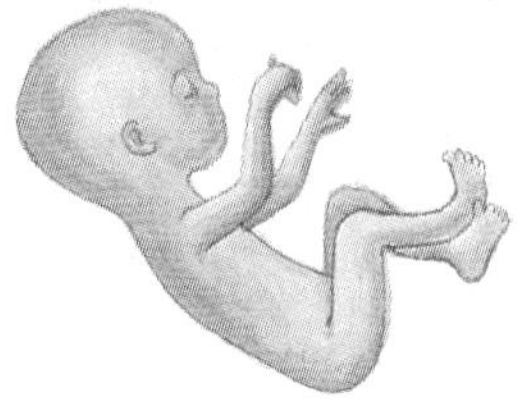
• Length: $6\frac{1}{2}$-7 inches. • Weight: 7 ounces. • Mother can feel movement. • Heartbeat is strong. • Head is large compared to body. • Ears, eyes, nose, mouth take on final appearance. • Skin bright pink and furry.	• Length: 10-12 inches. • Weight: 1 pound. • Internal organs maturing. • Eyebrows and hair on head have appeared. • Eyelids still fused.	• Length: 11-14 inches. • Weight: $1\frac{3}{4}$ pounds. • Can kick and cry. • Can hear sounds. • Might hiccup. • Skin wrinkled and protected by coating. • Eyelids separate. • Eyelashes form. • Fingernails complete growth.
Month Seven	**Month Eight**	**Month Nine**
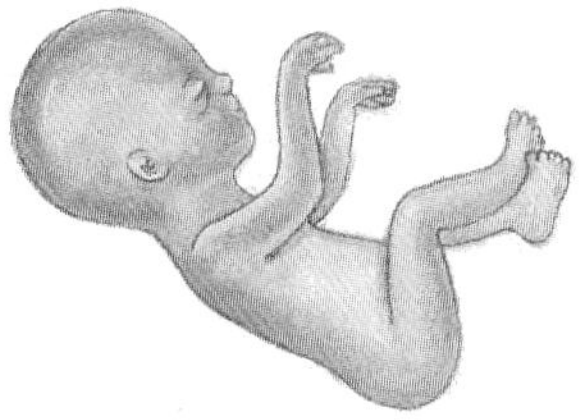	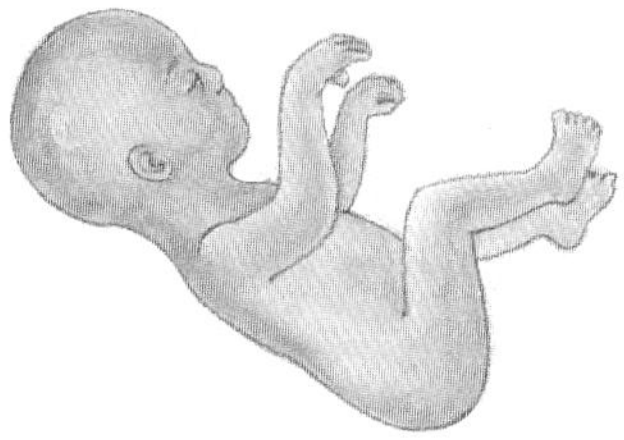	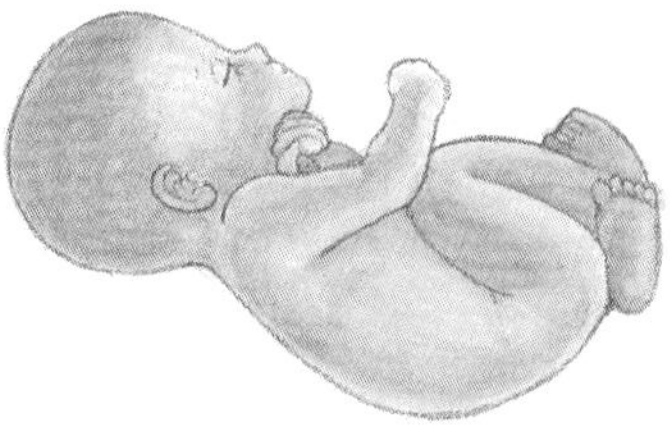
• Length: 14-17 inches. • Weight: $2\frac{1}{2}$-3 pounds. • Can move arms and legs freely. • Eyes are now open. • Skin wrinkled and red. • Organs fully formed.	• Length: $16\frac{1}{2}$-18 inches. • Weight: $4\frac{1}{2}$-$5\frac{1}{2}$ pounds. • Hair gets longer. • Skin gets smoother as a layer of fat develops. • Head bones soft and flexible.	• Length: 18-21 inches. • Weight 7-9 pounds. • Organs can function on their own. • Fine hair on skin gone. • Ready for birth.

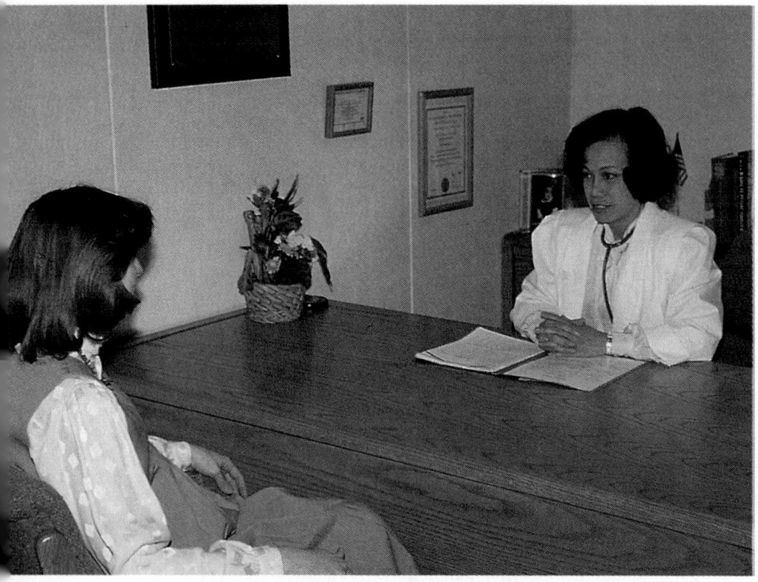

Regular visits to a physician are an important part of prenatal care for a pregnant woman.

◆ Nutrition

Good nutrition is important to good prenatal development. The diet of the mother must provide all nutrients for the baby as well as for herself.

As Kendra discussed nutritional guidelines for pregnancy with her doctor, she found they were about the same as for all people, with a few additions for pregnant women:

- Extra calcium for bones and teeth.
- More iron for blood formation.
- More protein for development of all cells.
- Extra water and other fluids, such as juice, soup, and milk.

Her doctor explained that her diet should include extra amounts of certain nutrients, while her calorie intake should only increase by approximately 300 calories above what is normal. Kendra's doctor said that her weight would be carefully monitored. A gain of 20 to 30 pounds was recommended.

Activity. Have students keep track of their food intake for three days. Using any computer diet analysis program, have students determine their daily intake of nutrients. Are their eating habits healthful? How should their habits change? How can poor nutrition affect the embryo/fetus?

◆ Exercise

At one time it was thought that pregnant women should do as little as possible. Doctors now advise moderate exercise. Activities such as walking and swimming tone muscles, improve appetite, and contribute to better sleep. In general, whatever activities a woman has participated in before pregnancy can be continued, with few exceptions.

◆ Rest

As a woman's weight and the demands of the fetus increase, she will tire more easily. She should be sure to get eight to ten hours of sleep each night and rest during the day, especially during the third trimester.

◆ Complications

During pregnancy, many prospective mothers report better health than ever before. Others suffer one or more mild complica-

Moderate exercise is important for pregnant women. A physician can suggest the best kinds of exercises for each stage of the pregnancy.

tions. These include nausea, shortness of breath, varicose veins, muscle cramps, lower back pain, hemorrhoids, and heartburn.

Although mild symptoms can wait until the next regular appointment, severe problems require immediate attention. A mother should report any unusual thirst; abdominal pain; headaches; vomiting; fever; dizziness; blurred vision; painful urination; swelling of the face, hands, or feet; rapid weight gain; vaginal bleeding; or lack of fetal movement.

◆ Drugs

Alcohol, nicotine, and drugs of all kinds are hazardous substances that can permanently damage the fetus. They, like food eaten by the mother, reach the fetus very quickly through the placenta. Using these substances can cause brain damage and physical deformities. The greatest damage is done in the first trimester, often before the mother knows she is pregnant.

If a woman smokes during her pregnancy, the chances of losing her baby to miscarriage or stillbirth increase. With miscarriage the body expells the fetus, usually between weeks 12 and 28. A stillbirth is the birth of a dead fetus. Those babies who survive run a very high risk of being smaller than normal at birth. They also have a greater chance of dying right after birth.

The drug alcohol has been proven hazardous to unborn babies. Fetal Alcohol Syndrome (FAS) is a condition caused by a woman drinking alcohol during pregnancy. Even one ounce is toxic to a fetus. The permanent effects of FAS may include mental retardation; facial, heart, and other physical defects; and learning disabilities.

Any drugs taken during pregnancy pose a risk for the baby. A woman should never take any drug, even aspirin, without checking with her doctor. Doctors now routinely caution pregnant women against taking drugs of any kind.

More About Crack Babies. If a pregnant woman uses crack, oxygen may be cut off to the embryo. If these babies survive, they may develop more slowly and have permanent brain damage and severe learning difficulties.

SIDELIGHT

Unusual Circumstances

The majority of pregnancies are uneventful and most babies are born healthy. As many as 20 percent of all pregnancies, however, involve some complications.

Sometimes a pregnancy ends when the body expels the embryo or fetus before it can live on its own. Called a *miscarriage*, this may happen because the fertilized ovum did not implant correctly in the wall of the uterus. This includes ova that implant in the fallopian tubes.

Another cause of miscarriage may be a problem with the mother's body. Scar tissue, tumors, and infection are some problems. Sometimes the cervix is too weak to carry the fetus growing in the uterus.

Alcohol, tobacco, and other drug use can prevent a pregnancy from developing normally. Rarely is a healthy pregnancy disturbed by falls or minor accidents.

Premature birth occurs when a baby is born too early and at a weight of less than five-and-one-half pounds. The body is not fully developed. Problems with breathing, digestion, and body temperature are common in premature babies. Specially controlled cribs, called incubators, provide the support necessary until the baby can survive on its own.

Sometimes babies cannot or should not be born through the birth canal. In these cases, delivery is done surgically by cutting into the uterus through the abdomen. This is a *cesarean section*. Some cesarean sections are performed because the baby is too large to pass through the birth canal or is in the wrong position for delivery. Sometimes the umbilical cord is in a position to cut off oxygen to the baby if normal delivery is attempted. If tumors are present or diseases may be contracted by the baby as it passes through the birth canal, a cesarean section may be performed.

◆◆◆

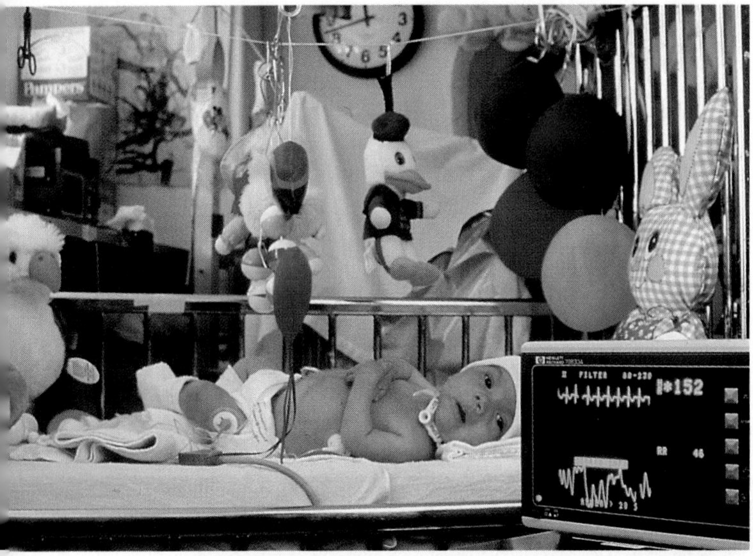

Seeing your newborn child at risk is frightening, yet some women increase the chances for this when they smoke, drink alcohol, or take other drugs.

Illegal drugs, such as cocaine and heroin, cause serious birth defects. Addicted women give birth to addicted babies. Babies are much less able to survive withdrawal than adults.

◆ Sexually Transmitted Diseases

Sexually transmitted diseases, such as syphillis, gonorrhea, genital herpes, and AIDS, can have devastating effects on a growing embryo or fetus. Many can affect the heart, brain, and other body organs. Some can cause death.

Treatments and drugs can cure diseases like gonorrhea; however, at this time there is no cure for genital herpes or AIDS. Doctors should be informed of the possibility of sexually transmitted disease so treatment can begin immediately. There is no special cure for the damage caused by sexually transmitted disease to the newborn.

Work and Family. In preparation for childbirth, when should a woman quit working outside the home? Why?

Photo Focus. Have students look at the photo at the right. How do couples benefit from childbirth preparation classes? Have students examine some of the different approaches to childbirth.

◆◆◆

Preparation for Birth

At one time, mothers giving birth in a hospital were given an anesthetic that made them unconscious during birth. Fathers were required to stay in the waiting room. The birth of a child was left to doctors and nurses. Today, more childbirth choices are available. Most often mothers are awake during birth, and fathers are present to give support to the mother.

Yolanda and Tim Rodriguez enrolled in a childbirth preparation class at their hospital. Learning what to expect during labor and delivery relieved some of their anxiety. The instructor talked about the pros and cons of different prepared childbirth methods, such as Lamaze and Leboyer. She also explained that all methods emphasize relaxation, control of body functions, and understanding the birth process.

As Yolanda and Tim continued with their classes, they learned breathing and relaxation techniques. Tim learned how to help Yolanda during labor and delivery. They felt much more prepared for delivery as they looked forward to the birth of their child.

Most couples find that childbirth preparation classes of some kind are very helpful. Knowing what to expect and how to handle it gives them confidence and makes the experience a more positive one.

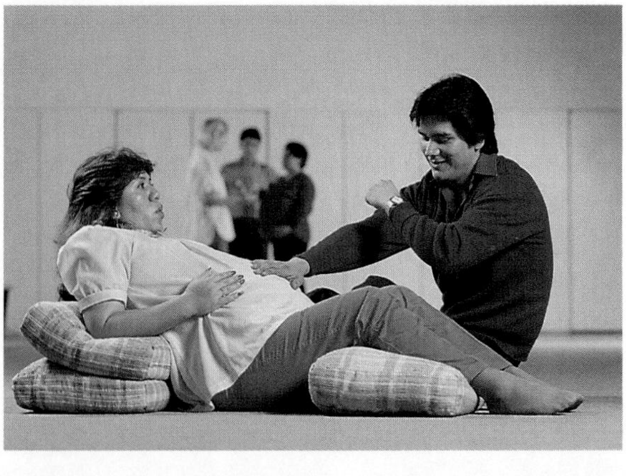

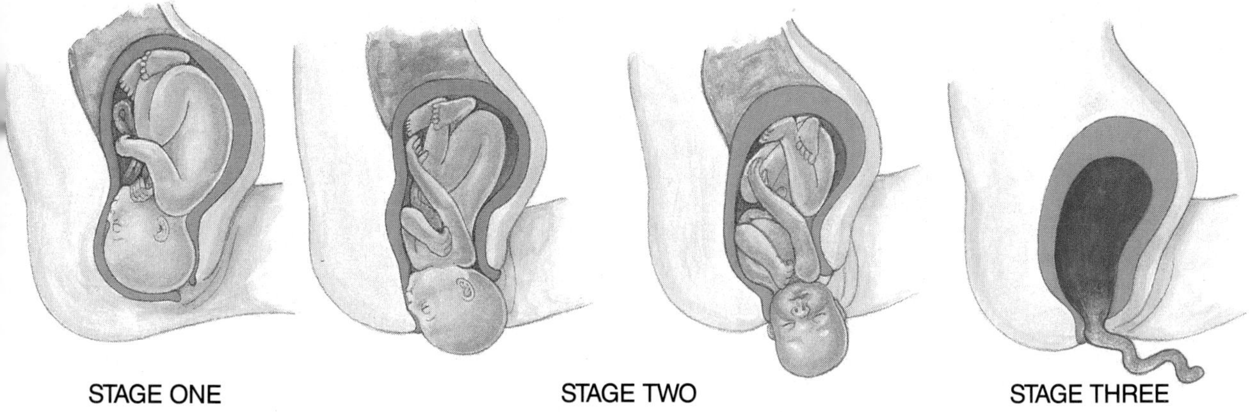

The birth process has three stages. In the first, the cervix opens to get ready for the baby to pass through. In the second the baby is delivered. In the third the placenta and remainder of the umbilical cord are expelled.

♦♦♦

The Birth Process

After nine months of developing, the baby is ready to be born. In the labor process, the muscles of the mother's uterus push the baby from the mother's body. The beginning of labor may be signalled by one or more of the following:

- **Slight Cramps and a Backache.** These cramps, or contractions, may be mild at first and 15 to 20 minutes apart.
- **Small Discharge of Blood and Mucus.** This tissue has been sealing off the cervix during pregnancy.
- **Breaking of the Amniotic Sac.** This results in a sudden flow or small trickle of clear fluid from the vagina.

The muscles of the uterus continue to contract in order to force the baby out. The contractions become stronger and closer together as birth approaches. Relaxing between contractions helps a woman keep her strength as the birth process progresses.

The birth process has three stages. The first is the longest and averages about 12 hours for first-time mothers. With each contraction of the uterus, the cervix is forced to open, or dilate. Once it expands to about four inches, the baby can pass through.

Discussion. Discuss the pros and cons of delivering a baby at home.

The second stage of labor had begun as Ruben was coaching Cindy through a contraction. Dr. Nguyen was present and said that this would be an intense period for Cindy, although it should last only 20 minutes to one hour. During the next contraction, Dr. Nguyen asked Cindy to push, or "bear down," to help the baby through the birth canal. Ruben was really excited when the head appeared. Dr. Nguyen said that one or two more strong contractions would deliver the baby.

As Cindy and Ruben were admiring their new son, Dr. Nguyen asked if Ruben would like to cut the cord. Cindy was in the third and final stage of labor. Soon the remainder of the umbilical cord and the placenta were delivered as Cindy pushed with a strong contraction, ending the third stage of labor. Cindy and the baby were closely monitored for the next few hours to be sure no complications occurred.

Like all new parents, Cindy and Ruben spent the next few days learning how to care for their new baby. Bathing, diapering, and feeding can be awkward for new parents. At the same time, these experiences provide parents with an opportunity to get to know the new person in their lives.

Discussion. Invite a midwife or Lamaze instructor to discuss the stages of childbirth with the students. What roles do mother, father, doctor (midwife), and nurse play in delivering a baby? Encourage students to ask questions.

CHAPTER 24

Review

Answers

Testing Your Memory

1. Sperm produced in the testes travel through the vas deferens and other glands and are mixed with semen. The sperm then travel through the penis and are discharged into the female vagina. The ovum is released from the ovary and travels through the fallopian tube where fertilization may take place.
2. When an ovum is not fertilized, it passes through the uterus along with the blood-rich tissue during menstruation. This usually occurs once every 28 days.
3. Defective genes. **Any two:** sickle cell anemia, hemophilia, cystic fibrosis, and Down syndrome.
4. **Any three:** missed menstrual period; unusual tiredness; swelling and tenderness of the breasts; frequent urination; nausea or morning sickness.
5. *First trimester:* formation of all body organs; heart, lungs, brain begin functioning; at end of 3 months the fetus is 3 inches long and weighs one ounce. *Second trimester:* fetus is longer; muscles begin functioning, bones harden; mother feels kicking; fingernails and hair appear; may live outside mother's body if born at the

Summarizing the Chapter

- Male and female reproductive systems together are responsible for creating new life.
- Early signs of pregnancy should be confirmed by a doctor.
- Good prenatal care greatly improves a woman's chances of giving birth to a healthy baby.
- The use of alcohol, tobacco, and other drugs during pregnancy can result in serious permanent mental and physical damage to the unborn child.
- Sexually transmitted disease can cause serious problems for the embryo or fetus. Doctors should be informed so the pregnant woman may be treated.
- Mothers and fathers can prepare for the birth of their child by attending classes.
- There are three stages of labor in the birth process.

Testing Your Memory

1. Trace the path of sperm and ovum from their origins to fertilization.
2. Explain the process of menstruation.
3. What causes genetic disease? Name two genetic diseases.
4. List three early signs of pregnancy.
5. Describe the growth and development of the embryo and fetus during each trimester.
6. How should a woman care for herself to insure a healthy pregnancy?
7. Name two serious complications that may occur during pregnancy.
8. Why are alcohol, tobacco, other drugs, and sexually transmitted diseases especially dangerous during pregnancy?

9. Describe what happens during each stage of labor during the birth process.

Thinking Critically

1. Why is it valuable for people to identify their reproductive body parts by the correct names?
2. How might a father-to-be support a woman during pregnancy?
3. Why do you think so many women continue to smoke and drink during pregnancy when warnings about the bad effects are so clear? What can be done to change attitudes about this?

Taking Action

1. Tour the obstetrics department at a hospital. Be sure to make all the arrangements necessary with hospital officials. Ask to have an obstetric nurse explain the process parents go through when having a baby at the hospital.
2. Develop a pamphlet to inform parents-to-be about healthy pregnancy and childbirth. Include information about diet and nutrition, harmful substances, sleep, and exercise. Include sample menus and perhaps recipes for foods high in calcium and iron. Addresses and telephone numbers of resources for new parents would be helpful.

Making Life Choices

Tina and Cecil are a happy couple ready to raise a family. They love each other and both have plenty of love to give to children. When discussing their plans with the family doctor, he suggested genetic testing. The tests revealed that they both carry defective genes for sickle cell anemia, a condition resulting in severe anemia; pain and swelling of joints; frequent infections; and damage to bones, kidneys, lungs, and heart.

Why did the doctor suggest genetic testing? What might Tina and Cecil be thinking and feeling? What are their options? What would you do in this situation?

Using Your Journal

One of the best ways to ensure the birth of a healthy baby is for the mother to take care of her own health before and during the pregnancy. Make sure that you have understood the rules of good health that a pregnant woman should follow by listing them in your journal. You may wish to organize your thoughts by preparing a list of "Do's" and a list of "Don'ts."

end of the trimester. *Third trimester:* fetus puts on fat; moves to head-down position; grows to about 20 inches; gains temporary immunities from mother.

6. Regular visits to the doctor; proper nutrition; moderate exercise; get 8-10 hours of sleep per night; stay away from drugs of all kinds.
7. **Any two** of the complications listed on page 351.
8. Any drug may pass through the placenta and cause brain damage or deformities. STDs can affect heart, brain, and other body organs.
9. Refer to the illustration and text on page 353.

Thinking Critically

1. Answers will vary.
2. Answers will vary but may include understanding mood swings, providing moral support, and giving positive encouragement.
3. Answers will vary.

CHAPTER 25

Parenting the Young Child

Chapter Challenge

Resources. Refer to the Teacher's Classroom Resources box and Student Workbook for materials related to this chapter.

Look for These Answers . . .

- Why is bonding critical to a child's development and how is it established?
- What should parents know about patterns of human growth and development?
- How do children develop physically, intellectually, socially, and emotionally from birth through age six?
- How do children develop morally?

Look for These Terms . . .

- bonding
- object permanence
- parallel play
- reflexes
- separation anxiety
- stranger anxiety

"Isn't she beautiful?" Gloria said to Lee. Little Jena was only 20 minutes old. Lee was speechless. He couldn't quite believe how small and fragile she looked. This new little creature was part of him, and yet he didn't even know her yet.

As the happy couple examined their baby, they felt relieved to learn that all was well. Lee laughed while Gloria counted every toe and finger. "I just want to be sure," she said, smiling back at him. "Her fingers are so tiny. She's like a little doll. Now it's your turn to hold her."

Lee was a little nervous as the nurse told him how to position his arms correctly. He didn't want to drop Jena. "Look," Lee said, as he held his daughter for the first time. "I think she just smiled at me." He watched Jena intently as the tiny facial features changed from one unidentifiable expression to another. "She has your eyes, Gloria. I'm glad."

As Gloria watched her husband and her brand new daughter, her eyes grew moist at the thought of what had just happened. She was very tired, but thrilled at the same time. Now they were three, not just two. This little seven-pound bundle was going to change their lives. They had much to learn about the way Jena would develop and what she would need from them. "Lee and I will learn together," Gloria thought.

Chapter Opener. Have students read the opening scenario. Ask the students to describe the emotions Gloria and Lee were experiencing. Discuss the following questions: How do emotions affect attitudes toward parenting? How does life change with the birth of a child? Do new parents automatically love their newborn, or does love take time to develop? How may parental self-esteem affect emotions and attitudes toward a newborn? What excitement does parenthood bring to new parents?

Bonding

Soon after birth, a link begins to form as parents and baby interact. Many experts feel that this link is needed for family health. Developing emotional ties, or **bonding**, gives security to infants. Bonding occurs when parents cuddle and touch, stroke, or talk to a baby.

Both Gloria and Lee felt it was going to take some time to get to know the new person in their lives. One of the nurses at the hospital reassured them that this was a normal feeling. He suggested that both Gloria and Lee spend time holding and cuddling Jena. Because Gloria planned to breast-feed Jena, they would make sure that Lee had opportunities to hold Jena before and after feeding whenever possible. Developing an attachment with the father is just as important to children as bonding with the mother. For Gloria, Lee, and Jena, the roots of love were established. The bonding process would develop from those roots.

Understanding Development

Often parents feel unsure of themselves when it comes to raising a child. Some may even wish that children came with instruction books. Understanding some basic facts about human development provides people with the confidence needed to raise children.

Patterns of Development

Human development follows a similar pattern. Babies all over the world, regardless of how they are raised, will lift their heads before their bodies, swing their arms before reaching for an object with their hands, and stand before they walk.

Development is also a building process. Every skill or task a child accomplishes provides a foundation for the next skill. Development follows a step-by-step pattern. Billy Joe said his first word at age one. By age two, he had mastered some simple two- and three-word sentences.

Although every child goes through similar stages of development, each child proceeds at an individual rate. Parents are less anxious if they realize this. Every child is unique and special. Heredity, nutrition, prenatal experiences, and environment all contribute to the rate of development.

Children develop physically, intellectually, socially, and emotionally at the same time. Each area affects all the others. As an example, a child who is learning how to walk needs a certain amount of muscle development and coordination. At the same time, the child may be more successful when provided with encouragement, reinforcement, and love. The chart on the next page indicates some general developmental characteristics for each age.

Discussion. Ask students to define "bonding." Have students describe how the bonding process occurs in new families. What implications does bonding have for the development of the child? The family?

The Newborn

For about the first month after birth, a baby is considered to be a newborn. During this time, immature body systems develop coordination, and parent-child relationships begin to be established. Physical, intellectual, social, and emotional growth begin at birth.

◆ Physical Development

Newborn babies can do more than you might think. They communicate by crying. In this way, you know if a baby is hungry, needs attention, or has a soiled diaper. Responding to a baby's cry gives the infant needed comfort and reassurance. This is not spoiling the child, at least not for newborns and young infants.

Newborns have a large head, fat cheeks, and a short flat nose. Right from birth, they can see, hear, and even learn. They depend on parents for physical needs and loving care.

Typical Characteristics of Children: Birth to Preschool

Physical	Mental	Social	Emotional
Newborns			
Hand closes tightly. Strong sucking. Lifts head when on stomach.	Follows object with eyes. Cries to communicate. Turns toward bright light or sound.	Needs parental attention.	Bonding is important. Contented when nursed or fed. Shows excitement by crying.
Three Months			
Reaches for toys. Turns head freely. Puts things into mouth.	Babbles and coos.	Smiles in response. Looks toward someone talking. Expects to be held.	Develops trust. Cries, kicks, and waves arms when upset. Feels delight.
Six Months			
Rolls over. Sits with support. Transfers objects from one hand to the other. Eats soft foods. Gets first tooth.	Recognizes objects. Repeats sounds. Recognizes own face in mirror.	Enjoys attention. Waves "hi" and "bye bye." Has some sense of self. Recognizes own name. Enjoys games like "peek-a-boo." May begin to fear strangers.	Laughs and smiles. Shows anger when doesn't get own way. Displays disgust.
Nine Months			
Creeps and crawls. Picks up objects with thumb and forefinger. Throws a ball.	Says words. Remembers objects when out of sight. Begins to understand "no."	Wants to be with parents. Loves attention. Likes games of chase and pick-up. May fear strangers.	Shows high spirits. Shows affection for family.
Twelve Months			
Walks independently. Drinks from cup. Pushes, pulls, and dumps things. Points with one finger. Climbs out of crib. Pulls off shoes, socks, and mittens.	Can say three to five words. Uses words to make needs known. Brings things to you when you ask. Follows simple instructions. Scribbles with crayon.	Likes to be center of attention. Enjoys games. Tolerant of strangers.	Shows affection for adults. Has beginning sense of humor.
Two Years			
Swims a little. Kicks a large object. Runs, jumps, and climbs stairs. Begins toilet training. Walks sideways and backwards. Eats with a fork.	Points to things when named. Has curiosity about everything. Touches, tastes, smells, and listens to everything.	Loves applause. Participates in parallel play. Imitates adults.	May have temper tantrums. Self-centered. Shows frustration. Seeks love and affection.
Three Years			
Goes to bathroom without help, but has some accidents. Climbs, hops, and skips.	Helps dress self. Uses zippers and buttons. Cuts with scissors. Listens to and repeats stories. Talks in sentences. Figures things out. Has longer attention span.	Has simple good manners and grooming skills. Likes to be with adults. Takes directions. Likes to talk. May have separation anxiety.	Less frustration and fewer outbursts of temper. Imaginative and may be easily scared.
Four-Six Years			
Rides tricycle. Balances on one foot. Takes a bath without help.	Plays with clay. Paints with brushes. Repeats rhymes, songs, and stories. Does simple puzzles. Asks questions and gives answers.	Plays with others. Plays games with rules. Learns fair play. Becomes more independent. Has a special friend.	Shows many emotions, often loudly.

Newborns can focus their eyes on a face and distinguish some sounds. They can even taste. In addition, they have several built-in **reflexes**. These are automatic responses that are used until the baby learns more. Have you ever noticed what happens when you touch a newborn's cheek? The baby turns its head toward the touch in search of food. This is called the rooting reflex.

◆ Intellectual Development

During the first month after birth, newborns begin the learning process that will last throughout life. Following moving objects with their eyes, responding to familiar voices, and crying to indicate needs are all part of the newborn's intellectual development. Most learning takes place through the senses.

◆ Social and Emotional Development

As described earlier, the attachment that forms between a newborn and its parents is critical to future social and emotional development. The evidence shows that most newborns who develop an early attachment to their parents feel more emotionally secure. These babies tend to cry less often. The trust that develops between baby and parents allows the child to become independent and able to form relationships with others more easily.

◆◆◆

The Infant

During the first year of life, an infant grows more rapidly than any other time. Dramatic changes occur in all areas of development as the infant matures.

◆ Physical Development

As a baby grows, increases in height and weight indicate health. During his first year, Nathan tripled his birth weight of ten pounds and grew nine inches in height. He was thirty inches tall by the end of his first year.

As he grew, Nathan began to gain control of his muscles. By six months, he had mastered rolling from side to side, reaching for objects, and sitting without support. During the second half of his first year, Nathan gradually learned to feed himself some foods, crawl, and walk around furniture with a little help. By twelve months he could stand alone and take a few

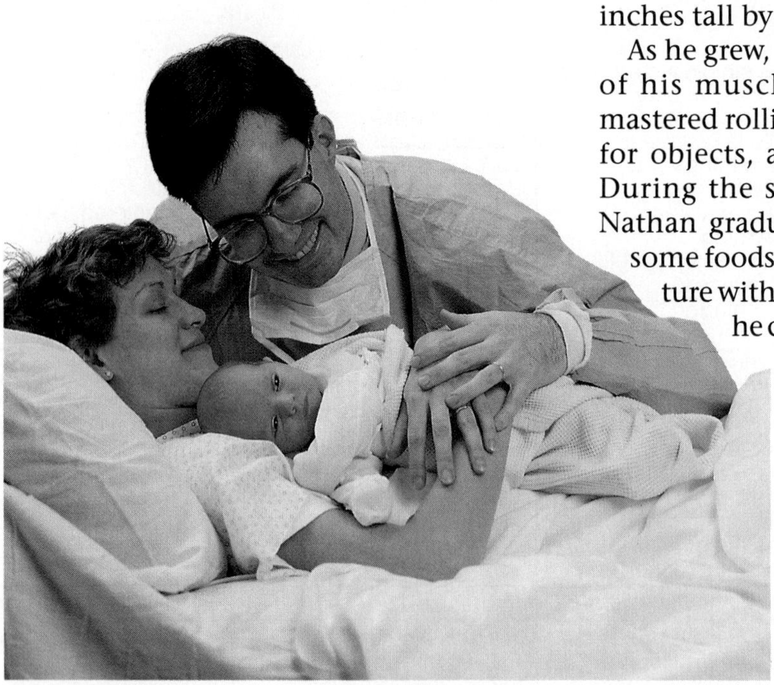

A sense of belonging together is strengthened when parents touch and hold the baby.

Problem Solving. Many schedule adjustments need to be made when a newborn enters a family. Ask students to describe some ways new parents can handle crying, hunger, comfort, and reassurance of a newborn.

More About Postpartum Blues. Many new mothers experience a mild form of depression called postpartum blues. This is a normal experience. Some contributing factors to postpartum blues may include: change in the mother's hormone levels; tiredness, soreness, and healing from the birth experience; anxiety over caring for baby.

steps as well as pick up small objects with his thumb and forefinger. Nathan's physical growth will continue, but at a slower pace, during the next year. The chart on this page shows what Nathan's growth pattern will probably be like over the next few years if he is close to the average.

◆ Intellectual Development

Crying continues to be an infant's way of communicating during the first year. Those who know an infant well are able to distinguish among different cries. Some indicate hunger, yet others may say the infant needs some attention.

Growth in language develops as an infant learns to imitate sounds, babbles, and eventually says several words by the end of the first year. Many experts feel that infants understand many more words than they are able to say at this time. Avoiding baby talk will help them learn correct speech patterns.

Babies crawl before they learn to walk. Many learn to crawl at surprising speed. This means caregivers must be alert, as babies can move swiftly into dangerous territory.

Average Heights and Weights At Ages One to Six

Age	Height (Inches)	Weight (Pounds)
1	29.8	22.5
2	34	27.7
3	37.7	32.4
4	40.8	36
5	43.5	40.5
6	46	45

By three months, Sherrie was actively getting acquainted with her world. Often she would smile and laugh when her parents came near. She explored everything by touching and tasting. By bringing objects to her mouth, Sherrie was developing eye-hand coordination, a skill necessary in future development. Her parents had to be careful to keep small objects away from her to prevent choking.

Sherrie's curiosity about cause-and-effect relationships was apparent. She liked to shake a rattle to make a sound and push a soft ball to see if it would move. As she got a little older, she tried dropping objects to see if they would fall. She continued to drop her toy rabbit from the high chair even when it was returned to her. This was an interesting experience that turned into a game. Her father never became upset by it. He simply put the rabbit away when he was tired of playing.

By the time an infant reaches nine or ten months, the concept of **object permanence** becomes a reality. At this time, an infant understands that an object continues to exist even when it is no longer seen. Playing games like pat-a-cake, looking at picture books, responding to some words, and knowing the parts of the body are typical of a child closing in on twelve months of age.

Activity. In small groups, have students trace the patterns of development (physical, social, emotional, and intellectual) for children birth through age six. You may want to assign each group one area of development to research. Each group member is responsible for contributing to the research project. When the research is completed, have each group share their findings with the class. Ask students the following questions: How do the patterns of development interact and overlap? Is it possible for children to excell in one area of development and be average or slow in others? What role do parents play in nurturing development?

Babies love to watch things drop. If you will play pick-up, they can play the game "forever."

An infant's personality begins to show early. Some are fussy and irritable, needing more than the average amount of love and tenderness. Other infants are very easygoing, rarely becoming upset by changes in daily routines. Some strong-willed babies are aggressive from birth. They like activity and rarely are afraid to try something new. Aggressive children sometimes show more anger than others. Whatever the personality pattern, infants need much love, support, and encouragement from those who care for them.

◆ Social Development

Early social development occurs as an infant responds to a soothing voice or a familiar face. By three months, an infant will smile and desire companionship. These smiles are very pleasing to parents. Social interactions gradually increase throughout the first year.

By six months, Spencer began to recognize that he was a separate person from his parents. He still loved their company and attention. He was particularly delighted with games like peek-a-boo.

◆ Emotional Development

Early infant emotions are reactions to parents and family. Trust continues to develop when infants feel loved and secure. Feelings of warmth, affection, and delight are promoted through positive interaction with others. If needs are met, the infant is more likely to show contentment. If not, frustration and withdrawal may result.

Around the age of six months infants may show **stranger anxiety**, a fear that causes them to cry or pull away from unfamiliar faces. Giving the child time to adjust to new faces without force is probably the best way to handle such situations.

Work and Family. Caring for an infant may present some special complications to the lives of new parents. Ask students to brainstorm some issues new parents may need to face in balancing work schedules and family. What pros and cons do students see regarding issues faced by dual-worker families?

During the first year the baby grows rapidly, physically, mentally, and socially.

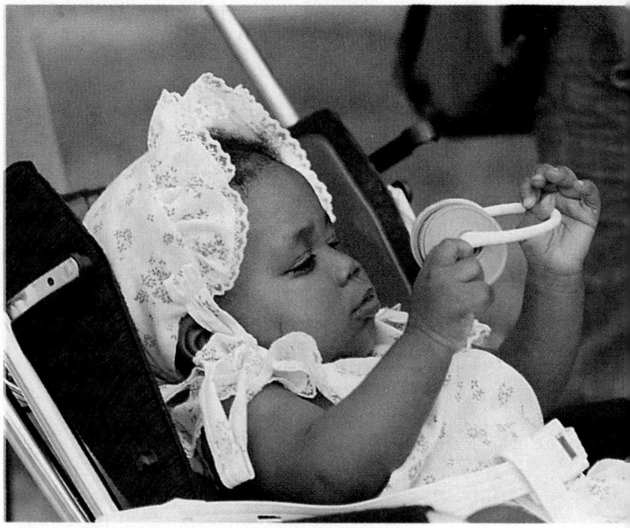

Photo Focus. Ask students to examine the photo at the top of the page. Have them describe the changes that are occurring in this infant's intellectual development.

◆◆◆

The Two- and Three-Year-Old

Two- and three-year-olds are at an in-between age. They are neither babies nor preschoolers. At this age, also called toddlerhood, children show rapid intellectual and social growth.

◆ Physical Development

Two- and three-year-olds continue to grow taller and stronger. They can run, jump, and climb. By age three, the child can throw and kick a ball as well as begin to ride a tricycle. Safety becomes even more of a concern as children at this age are more independent yet unable to fully control their motions.

Fine motor skills, such as buttoning and zipping, become easier for the two-year-old. By age three, Susie was cutting with safety scissors and stringing large beads.

Toddlers like to test their abilities. Often they attempt to lift objects larger than themselves. They may even try to lift another small child.

During this time, children are toilet trained. The actual age of training varies from child to child. Experts agree that toilet training should generally begin around the second year of age or when the child shows signs of readiness. When a child shows regularity in urination and bowel movements and awareness of these functions, the time may be right for toilet training. Keeping a chart helps identify readiness. If a child resists toilet training, you may want to wait awhile. This can save frustration for you and the child.

◆ Intellectual Development

The surge of intellectual growth continues as children discover their world. Size, color, and weight, as well as concepts like more, less, and soon, become a regular part of a child's quest for learning.

Michael, at age three, enjoyed using sentences. He would often ask many questions as stories were read to him by his sister.

Three-year-olds have very active imaginations. Pretending to be doing things that adults do helps them learn about the world. They often create elaborate games and find new uses for household items. A pan cover may become a steering wheel or a chair may become an airplane for a child in search of adventure. Children may even dream up imaginary friends. Sensitive adults do not make fun of children who use their imaginations this way for awhile. Instead they are accepting and supportive.

Buttoning up a coat becomes possible at age two. The child must have developed fine motor skills to accomplish this.

Discussion. Explain the function of each part of the brain. Ask students to draw conclusions about the relationship between intellectual and physical development (primarily the five senses). What role does the brain play in physical development?

Activity. Have students brainstorm a list of activities parents can participate in with their children that are fun and foster intellectual development.

SIDELIGHT

Handling a Temper Tantrum

Although temper tantrums are common among two-year-olds, they can still be disruptive to the family and harmful to the child. When children have tantrums often, try to identify the circumstances that triggered the behavior. Sometimes children have tantrums when they are tired or hungry, their normal routine is changed, or the limits set for them are unrealistic for the age. How can you prevent tantrums or cope with children who have them? The following suggestions may help:

- Set appropriate limits for children. Let them know what behavior is expected.
- Enforce the limits. Giving in tends to encourage repeated tantrums.
- Keep calm.
- Ignore the tantrum. Without an audience, the child soon learns that there is no reward for this behavior.
- Prevent the child from becoming hurt or hurting others. You may need to use restraint.
- Use soothing talk to help the anger subside.
- Isolate the child if the tantrum occurs at home. Time out in a quiet room away from others often ends the problem.
- Remove the child if a tantrum occurs in a public place, such as a store.
- When the tantrum is over, acknowledge the child's feelings but explain the reason why the child's demands could not be met. Make sure the child feels loved and accepted.

◆◆◆

Problem Solving. Divide students into small groups of two or three. Have each group investigate a fear that commonly appears during toddlerhood, such as fear of the dark, separation anxiety, fear of a "monster" under the bed, etc. Have each group research and make recommendations for handling each situation.

Activity. Have students observe toddlers in a play situation. Ask students to keep a running record of emotions they observe while the toddlers are playing.

◆ Emotional Development

At age two, children are struggling with independence. "Me do it!" is a phrase often heard as children attempt to do everything for themselves. Sometimes children are not coordinated enough to do what they want to. Frustration can result in anger or temper tantrums. Extra patience is needed with children at this age.

By the age of three, cooperation is more likely. With more physical skills, the toddler has fewer frustrations and less anger. A marked difference can usually be seen from what the child was like as a two-year-old.

Sometime between the ages of one and four, children may develop **separation anxiety**. They are afraid to be away from a close caregiver, usually one or both parents. Closeness and loving reassurance help the child get through this stage. Leaving a crying child can be difficult for a parent. Be calm, tell the child that you will be back, and leave without showing your concern. In time, the child will learn that you do come back and leaving once in awhile is just part of the routine. For most children the crying stops soon after the parents are out the door.

◆ Social Development

Two-year-olds love attention and socializing with family members. They like playing in the company of other children but often not with them. This is called **parallel play**. Each child plays separately alongside the other.

Three-year-olds are much more capable of completing tasks without frustration. They like friends and now play together with others. Three-year-olds like to be part of a group. At this time, they begin to learn simple manners and how to get along with others.

A common question asked by three-year-olds is "Why?" If you have ever been around a child of this age, you may have heard something like this:

Discussion. Ask students to explain how parents can tell that their toddler is developing socially.

Parallel play is common with two-year-olds. Three-year-olds will play together. Which age do you think is represented in this photo?

"Mommy has to scrub the floor," Trisha said.

"Why?" asked Laine.

"Because it's dirty."

"Why is it dirty?"

"We walked on it with muddy shoes."

"Why did our shoes get muddy?"

"Because it was rainy outdoors."

Such conversations can go on and on with a three-year-old. A patient adult knows that the child is learning through the exchange. A distraction may help if the "whys" never end. Eventually Trisha gave Laine the mop to try her hand at scrubbing. This changed the conversation.

Children are curious and enjoy the sound of talking even when they may already know the answer to the question. Taking time to listen to, and talk with, children when they are young sets the stage for open discussion later when children are older and questions are more complex.

Life Management Skills. Once children learn to walk, more of their world becomes accessible. Ask students to brainstorm ways in which parents can provide a safe environment for their toddler. What should a parent think about when making the home environment safe?

Activity. Have students work with partners to explore the nutritional needs of preschool-age children. What foods are appropriate for children? What serving sizes are needed? How does proper nutrition affect a child's physical, intellectual, social, and emotional development?

The Preschooler

By the time a child reaches age four, physical, intellectual, social, and emotional growth progress at a more even rate. Some child development experts feel that a large proportion of what children learn is gained before they enter school.

◆ Physical Development

Physical growth of preschoolers progresses at a slower, steadier pace than infancy or toddlerhood. Children are bigger and stronger. Along with more physical ability, they gain more control over their bodies.

Preschoolers can run, skip, hop, and jump. Dressing and undressing, tying their shoes, and throwing and catching a ball with ease and accuracy become a regular part of the preschooler's daily routine. Small muscle skills, such as painting with brushes and working with clay, become easier for preschoolers as their muscles develop.

◆ Intellectual Development

Preschool children are active thinkers. Many explore their world by asking questions and thinking about what they see and hear.

Preschoolers look different than toddlers. Can you describe the differences? They also have more skills. What are some of these skills?

Participating in dramatic play allows children to imitate real-life situations, which will help them socially. Parents who look for opportunities to talk with their children about what they are doing encourage interest and new ways of thinking.

Preschoolers are skillful conversationalists. Their language is more adultlike as they prepare for school. Many children are able to name colors, count, say and recognize the letters of the alphabet, and print their own names.

Why do you think some preschoolers develop faster intellectually than others? Environment and nutrition may be the answer. Children who haven't had experiences like going to the zoo or library may appear to be at a different intellectual level than others of the same age. Lack of experience does not necessarily mean low intellectual ability. Many children, when provided with more experiences, catch up to their peers after entering school.

If money and transportation are unavailable, concerned parents can still give children learning experiences. Simple items in the home promote creativity. A cardboard box, for example, can become a house, a car, or a spaceship. Talking with a child about what you see on television is better than just letting the child watch for long periods of time. Also, community programs may be available to help children learn new skills.

◆ Emotional Development

Preschoolers are learning to be more independent. They like to feel "big." As a result, they may be looking for ways to assert themselves — with tall tales and silly humor. As they grow closer to school age, they become more able to follow rules and accept instruction.

Activity. Have students observe preschool children in a child care or nursery school setting. Ask students to keep an anecdotal record (writing down what they observe) concerning emotional and social development. Students should pick out two children of different ages and watch them closely for one class period. In processing, ask students to describe the differences in emotional and social responses they observed in the children.

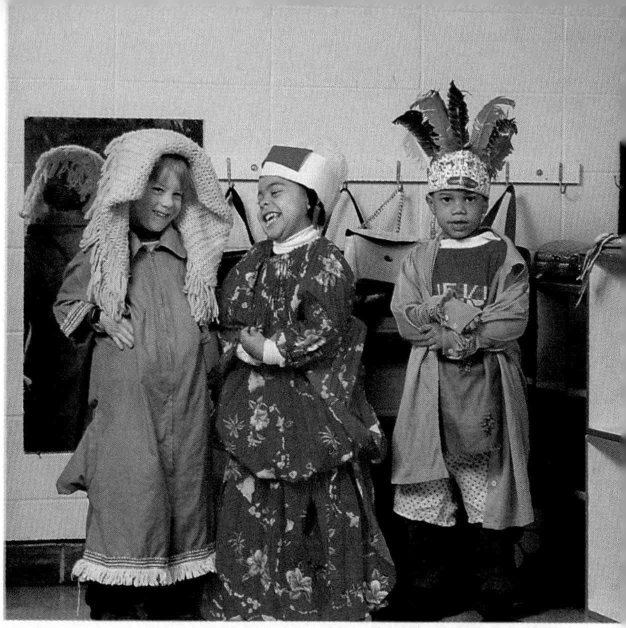

Fantasy play is good for the imagination. Besides, it's fun too.

With fantasy play preschoolers learn about the real world. At this time, most children recognize the difference between fantasy and reality but enjoy the fun of imaginative play.

◆ Social Development

Children need to learn how to make friends and get along with others. As preschoolers, they start to form close, long-lasting friendships. When they spend time with others, they learn to share. They also discover that consideration for others is part of getting along. Moreover, they learn to solve problems and compromise, skills that will help them for the rest of their lives.

Games with rules become part of a preschooler's play. Children enjoy competing with each other. Although winning is important to them, they need to see that enjoying the game, even when losing, is important too. Learning to play fair isn't always easy, but it is part of growing up.

Discussion. Divide students into small groups and ask them to brainstorm ways parents can encourage moral development in their children.

Activity. Give each student an index card with a moral issue parents may need to address with their children. Include items such as lying, stealing, hitting, biting, etc. Ask each student to suggest positive ways in which parents can deal with these issues.

◆ Moral Development

Moral development goes along with all other growth. Children need to develop a sense of right and wrong based on rules taught by families and society. The rules they learn help children guide their own behavior. Think about how Sarah handled what she had learned about correct behavior.

Sarah was looking forward to lunch at school. Her favorite foods were on the menu, along with an ice cream bar for dessert. As she was eating, Sarah became full very quickly. She thought about eating her dessert before finishing the rest of her meal. Sarah knew that in her family, dessert would not be served unless the meal was finished. Sarah decided not to eat the ice cream bar.

Upon arriving home from school, Sarah's mother asked her about her day. "How was your favorite lunch?" asked her mother. Sarah talked about what had happened with her lunch. Sarah's mother praised her for following the family rule even though no one would have known if she hadn't. She was proud of Sarah for doing the right thing.

Herein lies the key to successful parenting. Love and positive reactions mean so much to children. This is part of responsible parenting.

Learning to share is an important part of social development. Can you think of ways to help children learn to share?

A Slice of Life

Libby and Allison are two five-year-olds in the same kindergarten class. Libby, an outgoing, interested child, is making excellent progress. Her teacher feels that she is very bright, although she has no more natural intelligence than Allison. First to raise her hand, Libby tackles new projects with enthusiasm. She works well with the other children and is a popular playmate. She takes papers, art projects, and books home to show her parents. During the evening meal, she happily describes her day to attentive parents.

Allison isn't doing well in kindergarten and seldom volunteers answers. When called on, her usual response is, "I don't know." She follows directions willingly but with little enthusiasm. If a project is too difficult, she just stops working and sits quietly. When her teacher offers help, Allison says, "I can't." She usually sits on the sidelines during group projects. Allison talks very little in class and on the playground. Although she talks more at home, most of her time is spent watching television. Not expected to help around the house, she waits to let others do things for her. A parent checks to see that she is properly dressed in the morning, has the right school supplies, and knows when to leave for the bus.

Thinking It Through

- Libby and Allison have the same natural ability. What makes the difference in the way they respond at school?
- Experts generally agree that a child's experiences during the first three years are critical to all future development. If you could turn back the clock, how would you change this story for Allison?
- Make a list of ideas on how parents can help their children become independent and capable.

CHAPTER 25

Review

Summarizing the Chapter

- Bonding between parents and infant is important.
- Human growth follows a similar pattern in all children, but each child develops at his or her own rate.
- Parents can expect children to develop certain skills within a given range of time. For example, most infants can sit on their own without support around six months of age.
- Children develop physically, intellectually, socially, and emotionally all at the same time.
- Growth occurs in some areas more rapidly than in others.
- Moral development occurs as children begin to guide their behavior based on family and societal rules for conduct.

Testing Your Memory

1. What is bonding?
2. List three characteristics that parents should know about patterns of growth and development.
3. Describe a newborn infant. List at least five characteristics of a newborn.
4. By age one, what capabilities does an infant have physically, intellectually, socially, and emotionally?
5. How do two- and three-year-olds differ in development? Describe at least four characteristics of each age.
6. What is parallel play? At what age does it occur?
7. Why are temper tantrums common in two-year-olds?
8. In what way does a four-year-old use imagination to learn about the world?
9. How do preschoolers differ socially from two- and three-year-olds?
10. What is moral development?

Answers
Testing Your Memory

1. Bonding refers to emotional ties between parents and baby that occur when parents cuddle, touch, stroke, or talk to the baby.
2. **Any three:** human development follows a similar pattern; development is a building process, each skill building upon the last; each child develops at his or her own rate; development occurs in all areas at the same time.
3. Newborns communicate through crying; focus their eyes on a face; distinguish some sounds; have built-in reflexes for survival, such as the rooting reflex or search for food. Refer to chart on page 359 for five characteristics.
4. Refer to chart on page 359.
5. Three-year-olds have more advanced physical skills and are taller and stronger than two-year-olds. They are more imaginative and less frustrated due to improved capabilities. Refer to chart on page 359 for four characteristics of each age.
6. Children play separately near other children. Age two.
7. Temper tantrums are common in two-year-olds often because the children are physically unable to do what they want.

Thinking Critically

1. What might parents of a two-year-old do to help the child have fewer tantrums?
2. How may understanding the pattern of human development help eliminate child abuse in society?
3. After reading about newborns, what toys would you suggest to stimulate their intellectual development?
4. How would you expect children to use a crayon at the following ages: six months; one year; two years; four years?

Taking Action

1. Make a list of words that describe a child at each of these ages: newborn; infant; age two; age three; preschool.
2. Contact a representative from the La Leche League to find out more about breast-feeding. Report your findings to the class or arrange for someone to come and speak to your class.
3. Create a collage of pictures of children at each age: newborn; infant; two- and three-year-olds; four- to six-year-olds. Look for pictures that show children accomplishing skills typical for their age.

Making Life Choices

Ronette and William are the proud parents of ten-month-old Lamar. He has been a happy, quiet baby since birth. When he was born, he weighed just under six pounds. He began to eat well and put on weight. Now he weighs over 18 pounds. Lamar's favorite toy since birth has been a rabbit mobile which hangs above his crib. He spends hours each day watching the rabbits twirl around. He cries very little, making no trouble for his parents. They can take him places without worrying about what he will do. He smiles at them and responds to their love.

How is Lamar similar to and different from other ten-month-old infants? What concerns should William and Ronette have about Lamar's development? If you were Ronette and William, what would you do to encourage Lamar's development? What information can you use to support your answers?

Using Your Journal

In this chapter you have learned about young children's physical, intellectual, emotional, social, and moral development. Now figure out how you can apply that knowledge. Focus on one young child you know. Use your journal to explore the stage of development that the child has reached, and identify ways you can help the child develop successfully.

8. Four-year-olds use imagination and dramatic play to imitate real-life situations.
9. Preschoolers form friendships. They are learning to share and to consider others.
10. Developing a sense of right and wrong based on what is taught by family and society.

Thinking Critically

1. Answers will vary but may include setting up situations for children to feel successful.
2. Answers will vary. Understanding patterns of development encourages realistic expectations.
3. Bright toys in primary colors; toys that fasten to the crib and make noise, have push buttons, and dials; musical toys; rattles and squeak toys.
4. A six-month-old could not handle a crayon. From scribbling at age one, the child's skills will advance.

CHAPTER 26

Responsible Parenting

Chapter Challenge

Resources. Refer to the Teacher's Classroom Resources box and Student Workbook for materials related to this chapter.

Look for These Answers . . .

- What are the responsibilities of a parent to a child?
- Describe three parenting styles.
- How can a parent help a child grow physically, intellectually, socially, and emotionally?
- What are some guidelines for handling discipline?
- In what ways do children need to be protected?
- How does parenting a child with special needs compare to parenting other children in a family?
- What should parents think about when selecting child care?
- Where can parents get help with parenting problems?

Look for These Terms . . .

- conscience
- immunization
- nurturing
- pediatrician
- unconditional love
- vaccinations

"Angela came into our lives nearly four years ago," thought Paul. "How our lives have changed!" As he watched the little bundle of energy fly across the front yard, Paul realized that neither he nor Julie had really understood what parenting would be like. New challenges seem to come up every day.

Paul's attention returned to the magazine he was holding. It was a beautiful spring day, one of the first really nice ones of the season. Angela had been so eager to get outside to ride her new tyke bike. "Look, Daddy, I'm a race car!" Angela called out. As Paul looked up, he saw Angela peddling as fast as she could and heading down the driveway right for the street. Paul jumped up. With heart racing, he ran to catch Angela just beyond the curb. A car whizzed past them only a few feet away.

As Paul lead Angela back into the front yard, he said, "Angela, you know the rule about riding your bike into the street. What could have happened just then?"

Angela thought for a moment and then replied, "I almost got hit by a car."

"That's right," said Paul. "Since this is the second time you have ridden your bike into the street, we will have to put it in the garage for the rest of the day. You may either play in the house or in the back yard," explained Paul.

As Angela trudged toward the back yard, Paul thought, "Thank goodness I looked up when I did. Sometimes I feel like I can't take my eyes off that child for a minute. At least I know how to deal with things better now. The parenting class Julie and I took has really helped. Angela's behavior is much better when we are consistent in setting limits and enforcing them." Paul pushed the bike into a corner of the garage and closed the door. "I just hope that's the last major challenge for today," he thought.

Chapter Opener. Before reading the opener, have students describe a responsible parent. Read the opening scenario. Ask students to react to the way Paul handled the bike situation with Angela. Identify pros and cons. Why is it important to set consistent limits for young children? How may limits change as children grow older?

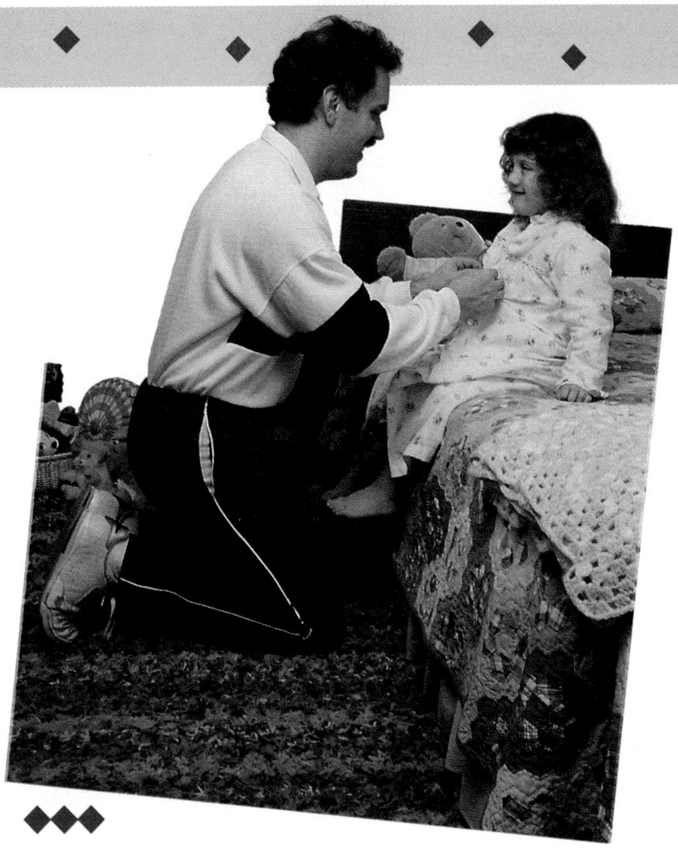

Parenting Responsibilities

Good parenting means taking responsibility for meeting the physical, intellectual, social, and emotional needs of children. Parenting is not the same as parenthood, which simply means being a biological mother or father. In the past, people assumed that anyone who had a child knew how to be a parent. Now, however, people recognize that parenting requires skills and knowledge that can be learned. Knowledge about children and how they grow is the best resource a parent can have. The more you know and apply, the better you can become as a parent.

Parents must provide a **nurturing** (NUR-chur-ing) environment, which includes love, attention, support, and encouragement as well as boundaries to grow in. Sometimes parents must put off their own wants and needs in order to nurture their child.

Effective communication is essential for good parenting. The communication skills you read about in Chapter 6 are needed in parenting. Communication skills are the same whether you are dealing with peers or children.

Certain personal qualities contribute to effective parenting. Patience, understanding, and gentleness are among them. All of these help parents as they guide their children toward appropriate behavior. A parent listens to children and considers their wants and needs. A mature parent uses good judgment to make decisions for the entire family.

◆◆◆

Parenting Styles

Studies of parents and children have identified three general parenting styles. The personalities of both parent and child, as well as values and philosophy, determine the parenting style used in a family. Most parents use a combination of these styles, although one may stand out more than the others:

- **Authoritative Parenting.** With authoritative, or democratic, parenting, adults communicate well with children. They set limits and base their expectations on what children are able to do at their stage of development. At the same time they are willing to discuss issues with children. Authoritative parenting is warm and loving. Independent behavior is expected from children. Planned activities with children are part of this parenting style.
- **Authoritarian Parenting.** There are many expectations on children with this type of parenting. Rules are set and made very clear to children, usually with little or no discussion about them. Children must follow rules without question. If misbehavior occurs, children are generally disciplined without much explanation.

Activity. Have students look up the words "authoritative" and "authoritarian" in the dictionary. Point out that although these words are similar, they have different meanings.

- **Permissive Parenting.** Permissive parenting provides few rules, if any, for children. Inappropriate behavior is accepted or overlooked, and communication with children is generally limited.

When asked if one parenting style is better than another, most child development experts say no. This may be because the styles are usually blended to serve different needs. Moreover, one style may work when another does not. For example, Blake needed some strict rules at a young age, so his parents used some authoritarian techniques. When he was older, Blake's parents felt that he could make decisions quite well, so they became more permissive.

Only when carried to an extreme is a parenting style likely to be harmful. For example, if parents are too permissive, children can become impulsive and aggressive. Without rules, these children do not learn how to set internal rules for themselves. They may be less mature and independent than they should be.

Most parents are able to find a blend of parenting styles that works for them and their children. Studies reveal that their success probably hinges more on other factors. Well-adjusted children usually come from families with:

- A strong parent-child bond.
- A stimulating environment, including freedom to explore places and ideas.
- Opportunities for quiet time away from noise and confusion.
- Frequent social experiences both in and outside the home.
- Reasonable limits.
- Praise and encouragement for successes.
- Parents or caregivers who give and receive love freely.

More About Parenting Styles. Many factors influence parenting styles. Often times ethnic background, culture, and society play a role in parenting styles. Experiences that people have as children and adults can affect the way they parent. More important than the style of parenting is the parents' ability to meet the needs of a child physically, socially, emotionally, and intellectually. Children need loving, nurturing parents who provide guidance and a supportive atmosphere in the home.

◆◆◆

Providing for Physical Needs

A primary concern of parents is to provide food, clothing, rest, and a safe environment for their children. When physical needs are met, children are better able to grow intellectually, socially, and emotionally.

◆ Food and Nutrition

A baby's diet is simple at first. Whether through formula or breast milk, an infant receives the correct balance of vitamins, minerals, protein, and carbohydrates.

As the infant grows, the need for food changes. Solid food is added to the diet gradually. This enables the infant to adjust to each addition. Also, any food allergies can be more easily identified. A **pediatrician** (PEE-dee-uh-TRISH-un), a doctor who specializes in the care of children, will usually suggest a plan for introducing a baby to new foods.

As children become old enough to feed themselves, foods should be cut into small enough pieces for children to handle. They enjoy finger foods because they can feed themselves. This gives them a feeling of independence and increases their self-esteem.

When choosing foods for children, select a variety from the food groups so that nutritional needs are met. Serving sizes will need to be smaller than for older children and adults. For example, an adult serving of peaches is one-half cup. For a toddler, half this amount is appropriate. Avoid foods that are highly spiced, fried, or high in sugar, salt, and fat. Remember that foods like weiners, raw carrots, seeds, nuts, and popcorn may cause choking.

When parents spend time with children, the bond between them grows stronger.

◆ Clothing for Children

Clothing for infants primarily consists of diapers, t-shirts, and sleepwear. Sleepwear for children should be labeled flame-retardant according to standards set by the federal government. Avoid garments that have buttons. These come off easily and can be swallowed by the infant.

As children grow, select clothing that encourages self-dressing. Clothing should fit comfortably but allow freedom of movement. Comfort, safety, and washability are factors to consider when making clothing purchases for children.

◆ Sleep and Rest

The need for sleep and rest varies from child to child. Active babies may require more sleep than quiet infants. As children get older,

Activity. In small groups, have students research the nutritional needs of young children. Have them examine serving sizes and safe foods for children.

Life Management Skills. Ask students why keeping children in clothing during the preschool years is often a problem for parents. What are some ways parents can keep their children in clothing and live within the budget?

they spend more time awake; however, regular morning or afternoon naps may be necessary until children start school. Because children tend to be very active, their bodies demand rest.

Good sleep habits promote health and well-being. When children don't get enough sleep and rest, they may become cranky, irritable, and more likely to become ill.

Lively children may have trouble settling down at bedtime. Sheldon's three-year-old son Brett didn't like to go to bed at night. Sheldon found that a regular routine, including putting on Brett's pajamas, brushing his teeth, and listening to a story, helped him settle down. The bedtime routine became a special time for Sheldon and Brett.

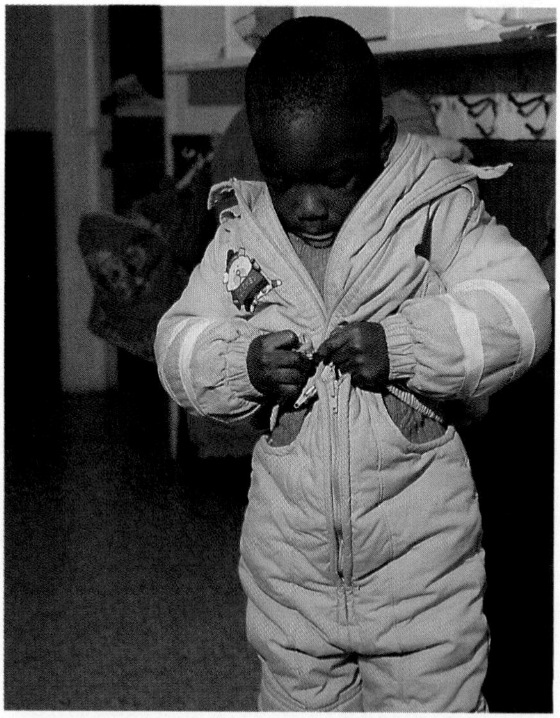

Children feel good when they can dress themselves. A large zipper is easier for a three-year-old to handle. A patient parent will let the child do the zipping himself.

Discussion. Have students debate the pros and cons of a regular schedule and early or late bedtimes. What are the benefits for parents and children? How could lack of regular rest affect a child's disposition?

♦ A Safe Environment

Parents must protect their children from harm. All safety hazards that are ordinarily found in the home must be removed while the child is small.

Children, especially toddlers, see and touch objects that are at a different level than adults. When child-proofing your home, crawl from room to room, looking for anything that could be harmful. Your eyes will be at the same level as a toddler. Remove objects that can fall or break. Plug up unused electrical outlets. Fasten kitchen cabinets so that they cannot be opened by children. Poisons should be out of reach in a locked cupboard. Check children's toys for sharp edges and loose parts that can be swallowed.

To prepare for emergencies, every family should have a well-equipped first aid kit within easy reach of adults. Adults need to know simple first aid procedures. Post emergency telephone numbers next to each tele-

Small children are curious and quick. Make the home a safer place for them by locking poisonous substances in a cabinet.

Life Management Skills. Have students work with partners to develop checklists for making a home safe for young children. Students may want to check references from the *U.S. Consumer Product Safety Commission* for ideas. Have students share their ideas with the class.

phone in the house. Include police, rescue squad, hospital, and poison control center. Poison control centers can tell you how to treat accidental poisonings.

◆ Medical Care

A baby's first medical checkup occurs within hours after birth. The doctor evaluates the newborn for everything from the number of toes, to muscle tone, to the sound of a baby's cry.

After about six weeks, the doctor will want to see the baby again. The doctor repeats many of the items on the original list. In addition, the doctor talks with parents about the child's eating and sleeping habits, bowel movements, and motor abilities. All of these help indicate whether the baby is developing normally. Babies are generally examined several more times during the first year. As children grow, they need fewer checkups.

Vaccinations (vak-suh-NAY-shuns) are given to children orally and through injection in order to prevent them from getting certain childhood diseases. This protection is called **immunization** (im-yuh-nuh-ZAY-shun). Look at the chart below to identify what vaccinations are necessary as well as when they must be given. Each disease is serious enough to kill.

Most states offer free or low-cost immunization programs. Some public "well-baby" clinics offer free physical examinations as well as advice by telephone. Your public health agency offers details on services available to new parents.

◆◆◆

Promoting Intellectual Development

If you had a child, what would you do to promote intellectual development? Many parents don't realize just how much they can do. Sitting a child in front of the television set for hours on end is not the answer. Children learn through play and communication with others. You can do much to make the most of these activities.

Immunization Schedule

Age	Diphtheria-Pertussis-Tetanus	Polio	Measles	Rubella	Mumps	Tetanus-Diphtheria
2 months	●	●				
4 months	●	●				
6 months	●					
15 months			●	●	●	
18 months	●	●				
4 to 6 years	●	●				
14 to 16 years*						●

* Tetanus-Diphtheria should be given every ten years after age 14–16.

More About Immunization. Immunizations are normally given as soon as the body is able to produce antibodies against the disease. For most diseases, more than one vaccination is needed. Despite the availability of effective vaccines, the incidence of some childhood diseases has been increasing. Parents may underestimate or be unaware of the damage these diseases can do. Many child care centers and schools now refuse to admit children who have not received the recommended vaccinations.

◆ Play

Play is a child's work. Through play, a child learns about the world as well as how to socialize with other children. A stimulating environment for children should be filled with things that encourage children to explore and be active.

Babies learn by looking, smelling, touching, and tasting. As children grow, their curiosity leads them to investigate, discover how things work, and solve problems for themselves.

Imagination plays an important role in child's play. Through imagination, children try out ideas about real life.

As a preschooler, Bobby had a very active imagination. One day his father found him carefully examining the washing machine in the basement. The next thing he knew, Bobby was banging around on the machine. When asked what he was doing, Bobby replied, "I'm fixing the washing machine." Bobby was mimicking some of the actions he had observed when the repairman fixed the washing machine a day earlier.

To encourage curiosity and imagination, provide children with the right playthings. Toys should be safe and fun. Look for toys that are multipurpose or require a child to do something. Household objects make good toys. A plastic mixing bowl, some sand, and water can keep a child interested for hours. The chart on the next page indicates some appropriate toys for each age level.

◆ Language Development

Parents encourage language development from the day a child is born. Talking to children about everyday things contributes to their understanding of words. First responses to language include body movements, facial expressions, and gurgles and coos. As a baby gets older, he or she babbles and imitates sounds made by adults. Vocabulary develops as people describe objects to the baby and talk about what is going on.

Language skills develop when children listen to stories that others read to them. Busy parents appreciate when older children in the family take the time to read to younger siblings.

Choosing the Right Toys

Age and Ability of the Child	Suggested Toys
Infancy Through One Year Babies learn through their senses. Few toys are needed at one time. They like to handle, bite, rattle, throw, and squeeze the things they play with. Toys should not have sharp edges or removable parts.	Toys in bright, primary colors. Hanging toys. Teething toys. Toys that squeak or play music. Cuddly dolls or stuffed animals. Soft, colorful, rubber balls. Floating bath toys. Large, colorful, plastic rings. Sturdy cloth or cardboard books. Push/pull toys.
Two Through Three Years Children are learning to run, skip, jump, and play with others. They like to take things apart and put things together. They love to explore and climb. Toys should be stimulating, age appropriate, and sturdy.	Bright, colorful, picture books. Stacking toys. Sturdy, simple puzzles. Building blocks. Toy telephone. Riding toys (tricycles, wagons). Dress up clothes. Puppets. Sing-a-long records and tapes. Modeling clay. Large crayons with large sheets of paper. Small wading pools.
Three Through Six Years Children are active, independent, and agile. Children like to imagine and pretend at this age. Toys should encourage large and small muscle development.	Story and picture books. Sturdy building blocks. Drawing and painting materials (finger paint, chalk, watercolor). Sandbox and toys that don't rust. Hammer, nails, saw, pliers (safe, sturdy tools that work with supervision). Simple games (lotto, matching). Swings and climbing toys. Small sports equipment. Wagons, sleds, and roller skates.

Many experts suggest that reading to children, regardless of age, encourages language growth. The words become familiar as children learn to listen and concentrate. Eventually they can follow a story line. Playing games and responding to a child's questions reinforces language development.

Activity. Divide students into small groups to investigate play activities and equipment that encourage physical, social, emotional, and intellectual development in children. How may parents provide for a balance of play activities (active play, passive activities, large motor, fine motor, imaginative)?

More About Language Development. Language begins as babies begin imitating the sounds that they hear. Some say that crying is the first language. By one or two years, children work at learning new words. Children like to learn the names of everything. Language is a wonderful challenge to them. In beginning language, one word may express a thought. As children get older, their patterns of speech and grammar become similar to others. Many experts agree that the best thing that parents can do to encourage language development is to talk with their children about everyday events and use clear speech. Generally, speech difficulties that appear in early childhood often disappear when children enter school.

Promoting Social Development

As you read in the last chapter, children need to learn how to make friends and get along with others. What can parents do to help children develop socially? They can begin by making sure children are around others from an early age, even infancy. A baby who is used to being around people is more likely to be a child who is not fearful in social settings. By leaving the baby with other trusted adults once in awhile, parents can have some time to themselves. Moreover, the baby learns to be social.

As the child grows, playmates are needed. Parents can invite children over or form play groups. Even exchanging child care with a friend gives children a chance to be together. When conflicts between children arise, and they will, give them a chance to settle their own differences as long as no physical or emotional harm is done.

Promoting Moral Development

The first lessons in moral development often come hard. A child hits a playmate and gets a return punch as well as disapproval from a parent. An observant child quickly learns that hitting others is against the rules. Gradually, parents need to help children see the reasons why actions can be either right or wrong. This knowledge will help guide their behavior. Eventually, they will form a **conscience**, an inner sense that promotes correct behavior and causes guilt feelings for inappropriate behavior.

When teaching children about right and wrong, consider the child's age and ability level. Providing children with good examples for expected behavior is very effective, since children learn by imitating. Even when children make mistakes in this learning process, knowing their families love and support them encourages children to try again.

Promoting Emotional Development

Providing **unconditional love** is the responsibility of every parent. Children need to know that their parents love them no matter

Preschoolers need friends. By playing with others, they learn the rules for getting along. They will use these skills throughout life.

Activity. Invite a preschool teacher, kindergarten teacher, or other early childhood professional to speak with the class about social development of children. What kinds of social activities should parents provide? Can children have too much social stimulation? Should parents intervene when conflicts arise between children?

Problem Solving. Have students investigate how a breakdown in family relationships may affect the moral development of children. Students may wish to focus on one type of breakdown, such as death, divorce, chemical usage by parents, abuse, etc. Have students share their findings with the class.

what they say or do. Love should be expressed in ways that are easily understood by children. Can you think of some?

When asked by her babysitter why her children were always so happy every morning, Karma had a ready response. "Every morning, before the children get out of bed, we have hugs and kisses and talk about the day. Sometimes I talk about what I do at work and what the children will do at the babysitter's. I want my children to know I love them and am interested in them. Even when I have to discipline the children, I make sure that they know I love them although I may not be pleased with their behavior at the time."

Encouraging healthy self-esteem, a sense of confidence and worth, is an essential goal for every parent. Parents can do much to encourage healthy self-esteem. By creating conditions for success, parents allow children to build confidence in their abilities.

Although Mr. Pruitt knows he could button Rachel's coat faster than she can, he lets her do it. He sometimes has to remind himself to be patient, even when they are in a hurry. When fixing lunch, he lets Rachel pour her milk into a plastic cup. She is even responsible for carrying her plastic plate to the sink after eating. Sometimes she spills a little, but each time she does her "job," she becomes more skillful and confident. Rachel's toys are stored on a low shelf that she can reach, so she is learning to return them to the right place after playing. She can do this all by herself. All of these techniques help build Rachel's self-esteem. Adults have to remember that young children take great pride in what may seem insignificant to someone older. Watch what happens when you praise a child for a simple accomplishment. It will make you both feel good.

Activity. Develop a list of items, such as a rosebud, house, hammer, an old shoe, or just about anything you can think of. Write the items on the list on separate index cards (one per student). You may also want to include a small picture of the item. Give each student a card. Ask students to describe to the class how the item on the card is like a child's self-esteem. What are some ways parents can build self-esteem in their children? What destroys self-esteem?

A Slice of Life

As Mrs. McDonald began to feed six-month-old Dougie, her mind wandered. She hoped this wouldn't take as long as usual because she had so much to do. "I can't wait for the day that Dougie can feed himself," she thought. Because Dougie ate so slowly, Mrs. McDonald placed a book on her lap. Maybe she would make a phone call after finishing the chapter. She didn't notice the little coos of satisfaction Dougie was making. If he cried or started to choke, of course, she responded to him.

Later Mrs. McDonald's daughter Ariel came running to her mother. "Look; I tied my shoelaces by myself!" she cried. "What a good girl," Mrs. McDonald said. "That's the kind of girl Daddy and I like." Mrs. McDonald thinks she has the secret for bringing up children. When they are good, she rewards them with her love. When they are bad, she takes it away.

When Ariel knocked over a plant as she was climbing up to look out the window, Mrs. McDonald frowned and cried out in an angry voice, "Shame on you! How could you be so clumsy?" Ariel realized with a sinking feeling that she had done it again. Why was she such a bad girl all the time? Mrs. McDonald had very little to say to Ariel for the rest of the day.

Thinking It Through

- How is Mrs. McDonald's attitude toward parenting affecting the self-esteem of her children?
- Rewrite this story to include ways to build self-esteem in the McDonald children.

Problem Solving. Have students react to the following: Jennifer is a single parent with low self-esteem. She is unsure about raising a child by herself. How may Jennifer's feelings about herself affect her child? How may this family be helped? Students should offer ideas.

Ridicule, put-downs, and negative labels do just the opposite. They can easily tear down a child's self-esteem. Even when children misbehave, you must separate what they did from who they are. When parents threaten to withdraw love as punishment, they end up with a child who is anxious and insecure. Love and acceptance must always be understood. The message should be something like: "I love you, but I can't let you throw your toys in the house. I want you to sit in the time-out chair for five minutes while you think about better ways to play with toys." Discipline is easier for children to accept when they are secure in parental love.

Guidance and Discipline

Parents can help children get along in the world by providing behavior guidelines, or rules, that are acceptable and safe. Children need and want guidance. Some child development experts suggest that guidelines for behavior can be compared to a fence around the school yard. When children know the fence is there, they are free to run around and throw a ball in all directions. Because the fence is there, children feel safe. When a real fence was taken away at one school, teachers found that the children huddled at the center of the playground. Their boundaries, or guidelines, had been taken away. They no longer felt safe.

Rules provide security for children. Rules that are in line with a child's abilities encourage the child to behave in an accepted manner. Discipline helps a child move from control by others to self-control.

As their children were playing in the sandbox, Vickie and Hannah were discussing behavior problems. Hannah was discouraged. She just didn't know how to react when her son refused to do what she wanted him to. "He's always into things," said Hannah. "Sometimes I just give up and let him do what he wants."

"I was having some problems with Shawn too," responded Vickie. "I finally talked to my pediatrician and asked for some advice. He gave me a book that had some good ideas in it about guiding behavior. First of all, you should ask yourself if a rule is reasonable for a child to follow. Can you really expect a child at this age to be able to do what you're asking? I really hadn't thought much about my expectations before. The book also said to make the rules clear. I had to ask myself if I

Parents are less likely to resort to physical punishment when they have alternatives in mind. Can you think of behavior situations that would call for having a child spend some time sitting quietly?

More About Using Time-Out. Using a time-out chair can be an effective method for curbing misbehavior in children. Parents should identify a consistent place in the home for time-out. Avoid using a place that the child enjoys. For example, if a child enjoys playing in the bedroom, the bedroom would be an ineffective place for time-out. The amount of time spent in time-out varies from child to child. A general rule of thumb is to allow one minute of time-out per year of age for children under five years. Older children may need to be in time-out for longer periods of time (15-30 minutes for eight years and older) in order for time-out to be effective.

was using language that Shawn could easily understand. I started thinking about it. Shawn wasn't doing what I expected because I really hadn't explained anything to him. I just expected perfection and got really frustrated when he didn't follow through."

"That sounds like my situation," confessed Hannah. "Do you mind if I borrow that book?"

In addition to Vickie's suggestions, parents should also be consistent in setting rules and following through with consequences when rules are broken. Even when rules have been clearly explained, sometimes a series of warnings is more appropriate than punishment. It may take young children longer to grasp some concepts. Terms like "soon" may have a different meaning for a child than an adult.

In some cases, a parent may feel that a child's misbehavior needs some kind of consequence. Before punishing a child, find out why the behavior occurred. Was the misbehavior intentional or unintentional? Is there an acceptable explanation? Gather all the facts when making decisions about punishment.

The form of punishment should fit the misbehavior. If a child throws a toy car in anger, you might take the car away for an hour. When a child chases a ball into the street, put the ball away for a specific period of time. Sitting in a time-out chair may be appropriate for a child who can't settle down indoors. In all cases, children should have a brief, clear explanation of what they did wrong. The only way children can begin to take responsibility for their actions is when they understand what is expected.

Some parents use spanking as punishment for misbehavior. This rarely teaches children anything. It can even cause children to become angry and defiant rather than remorseful. It may demonstrate a kind of action that parents do not want to encourage in children. As one parent put it, "If I hit Travis, how can I expect him not to hit others?"

Activity. Have students brainstorm some expectations and rules parents may have for two-, three-, four-, and five-year-olds. Students should defend their responses. You may wish to invite an early childhood professional or child psychologist in to discuss appropriate expectations for various ages of children. What are some ways parents can be consistent in their expectations?

◆◆◆

Protecting Children

A responsibility of parents and caregivers is to protect children from harm. This can be time-consuming when children are very young. One young mother expressed this thought when she said, "Sheena is like an accident waiting to happen. I have to watch her all the time."

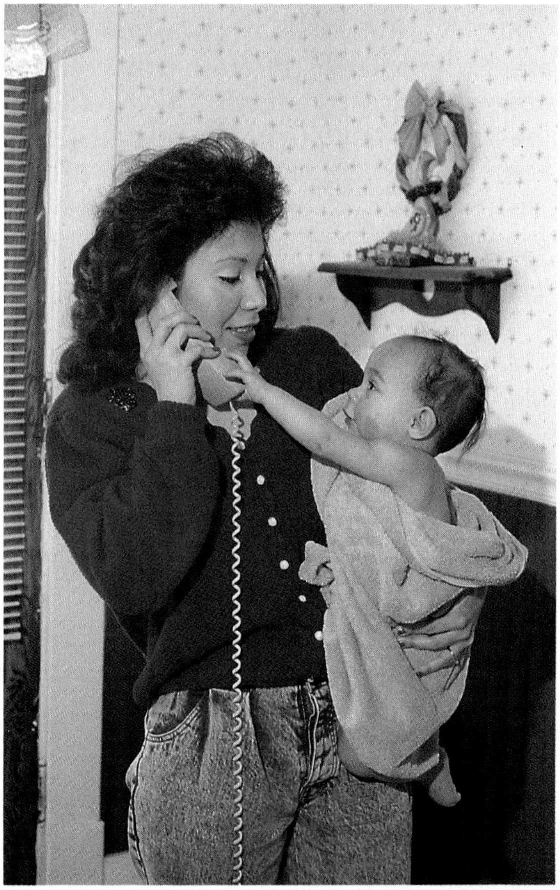

Even when a caregiver leaves for only a minute or two, a child can drown in the bathtub. If the phone rings or you need to leave the bathroom for some other reason, take the baby with you.

When children are very young, they cannot be left alone. This means you cannot run to answer the phone and leave a baby or small child in the bathtub. You cannot run to the neighbor's for a few minutes and leave a child unattended at home. You can't even leave a child alone in another room until he or she is old enough to play safely without your watchful eye. For a parent this can feel overwhelming at times. You may think that you will never ever have a moment to yourself again — but you will. When a child is small, safety is a priority. If you need time to yourself, find someone to take over for awhile. This is much better than ever putting a child in a risky situation.

Because children tend to be trusting, they are also vulnerable. Unfortunately, children cannot trust everyone. How do you teach them this without frightening them? This is a dilemma. Keeping children safe without destroying their trust in humanity is a challenge.

This grandfather wants to read a story to his granddaughter, but she is afraid to sit with him. How can you teach children to be cautious about trusting others without making them fear someone they can love and trust?

One way to help prepare children for unsafe situations is to play the "What If" game. You can play it anytime and anywhere. Questions about any situation may be included. The main goal is to prepare children for unsafe situations without creating an unreasonable amount of fear. Some questions to include might be: What if the house caught on fire? What would you do? What if you were lost in a store? What if someone in a parked car asked you for directions? There are many other questions you could ask. Can you think of some?

One young mother suggested keeping such games on the light side. After she asked too many questions about unsafe situations, her daughter didn't want to play outside for fear that someone would take her.

Some of the harm that comes to children is not from strangers. People they know, even family members, may abuse them. This cannot be allowed to happen.

As you read earlier in the text, child abuse can be physical, sexual, or emotional. Even neglect is a form of abuse. Abuse, in all cases, is against the law; however, there is help for troubled families.

Any parent who feels at risk for abusing a child should get help. Support groups and professional counselors can help people learn how to deal with anger and frustration in appropriate ways.

Parents should listen to children. Nickie tried to tell her mother about something that was bothering her, but her mother wouldn't

Discussion. Discuss the issue of using car seats with young children. Why should car seats be used? How are they used? You may want to show several examples of car seats designed for various ages of children. Emphasize that most states now have laws regarding the use of safety restraints for young children. Ask the students what they would do if someone close to them repeatedly transported their young child in a car without placing the child in a safety restraint.

pay any attention. Perhaps Mrs. Williams thought Nickie was making something out of nothing. Perhaps Nickie's mother was too busy to listen. Perhaps she was afraid to face the truth. She may have even feared for her own safety. Nickie's father was abusing her. For whatever reason, Mrs. Williams did not respond and the abuse continued.

If you observe or suspect that someone is abusing a child, take action. You may not be able to intervene yourself, but you can get help from the authorities. Law enforcement agencies, community and state social service agencies, and most hospitals are able to help. Many agencies have hot-lines for receiving child abuse reports as well as providing help for the abuser. Some communities have shelters for women and children who need to get out of an abusive situation.

◆◆◆

Children With Special Needs

Some children need extra special attention as they grow and develop. Physical impairments, emotional problems, or learning disabilities may occur at birth or because of an accident or illness. In most cases, these children can be helped to develop to their fullest potential.

Children with special needs are like everyone else in many ways. They require love, attention, friendship, and family. Like other children, they have strengths and weaknesses. With proper education, equipment, and encouragement, children with special needs can develop their strengths.

Many experts agree that parents are often first to identify a child's disability. This may be accompanied by mixed emotions. Some may feel anxiety, anger, or guilt. Generally, these feelings are quickly given over to ones of concern and a desire to do the best for and with the child. Most parents of special needs children are proud of what their children are able to accomplish.

Mia was born with Down syndrome. She is a bright and bubbly young girl, who is a delight to her family. Because her parents and brother are so encouraging, Mia has been very successful at school. She reads a little and runs in the Special Olympics. When asked about his sister, Kurt responded, "Sure, she has some limitations, but Mia is great. She always tries

Children with special needs want love, attention, friendship, and family ties just like anyone else. They contribute to family happiness in significant ways.

Problem Solving. Have students brainstorm a list of possible problems parents may face if their child has a disability. What are some ways these parents may cope with problems? What services are available to parents of exceptional children? Have students investigate how PL 94-142 benefits families of exceptional children?

Work and Family. Have students discuss the issue of child care and children with special needs. What challenges may dual-worker families face in finding appropriate care for their special needs child? What qualifications might these parents look for?

and never gives up. She asks a million questions and is very sweet and gentle. Mia loves everyone. I can't imagine having anyone else for a sister.''

Raising children today is a complex and challenging job. Although they bring special joy to others, children with special needs often require extra care, attention, and nurturing. Many communities have support groups and services that can help. Social service agencies, non-profit organizations, hospitals, and schools have useful information for families.

◆◆◆

Choosing Child Care

One of the responsibilities of parenting is to find good child care when needed. Trusting someone else to care for and nurture children is not easy for many parents. Finding quality people and programs makes it easier.

Good child care can be found, although it isn't always easy. A responsible parent knows what to look for and what questions to ask. Can you suggest some ideas?

How can families find such care for their children? Talking with friends, relatives, neighbors, and co-workers is a start. Information is also available from doctors, childbirth classes, social service agencies, and telephone directories. Social service agencies often have lists of licensed child care providers. These people must meet state and local guidelines.

Parents may choose from several forms of child care. *In-home care* is provided in the child's home. This tends to be least disruptive for the child. With *family day care* the child is cared for in someone else's home, perhaps a neighbor or friend. This is usually a homelike atmosphere. Often other children are present, giving an opportunity for socialization. *Child care centers* have planned activities and a regular routine for children. They are closely regulated by authorities. *Nursery schools* generally have an educational program in morning or afternoon sessions several days per week.

Kym Le, a single father, needed to find a caregiver for his two-year-old son Ho. Kym wanted his son to be cared for in a familylike setting. Kym set up several interviews based on recommendations from friends. He planned questions to ask during each. At each place Kym spent some time getting to know the caregiver, looking for warmth, friendliness, and open communication. He wanted to know if he and the caregiver agreed on child-rearing attitudes and methods of discipline. He watched how the caregiver and Ho got along, since he wanted Ho to be happy. He even took note of the cleanliness at each place. About the program itself, he asked questions concerning the number of children enrolled, the quality of the meals, indoor and outdoor activities, rules and routines, naptimes, and how illness is handled.

Activity. In small groups, have students examine the pros and cons of each type of child care listed above. What are the benefits to children and parents?

Activity. Have students select and examine in depth one form of child care. After researching one form of child care, ask students to assume they are professionals working at a child care facility. How would they describe the program to parents seeking quality care for their children? What questions should be answered?

Like most parents, Kym has many concerns about child care. He was determined to find the very best for his child.

◆◆◆

Additional Resources

Sometimes parents need help with problems. Most communities have state and local agencies prepared to help parents with child-rearing problems, financial difficulties, or other family crises. To locate the agencies in your community, check the telephone directory. Another way to find out who can help is asking your doctor, friends, neighbors, or others who may have had similar problems.

Many hospitals offer counseling services, support groups, and child care classes for new parents. Child welfare agencies can help with questions about adoption, child abuse, and financial aid situations. Public schools may hold child care classes for parents as well as sponsor child care programs.

Libraries have information for parents about raising children. Many good books and pamphlets are available. The United States Government Printing Office has a free catalog of booklets on all subjects. (U.S. Government Printing Office, Washington, D.C. 20402) Whatever your need, assistance is within reach if you will take the time to seek it. If it helps make you a more responsible parent, the effort is worthwhile.

Balancing *Work & Family*

Making Time for the Family

How can working parents make more time for their family? Many are looking into ways to modify the hours that they work. This helps them be home when they want to be, not just in the evenings. Here are some examples of ways parents are changing the way they work.

- **Flex time.** Parents whose companies offer flex time can make their own schedules, as long as they work a required number of hours. Some may choose to work from 7 A.M. to 3 P.M., so that they can be with their children after school. Others may prefer to start work later. Some may also be able to get a day off during the week by working four ten-hour days instead of five eight-hour days. Companies vary in the flexibility they allow with flex time. Some companies require employees to be at work during certain core hours each day.
- **Job sharing.** Under this arrangement, two people share one job. One employee may work mornings and the other afternoons. Some parents who share jobs also share child care.
- **Part-time work.** Part-time employees work fewer hours than a full work week. Some employers allow part-time workers to choose the hours they work — an arrangement that allows parents to fit their working hours around family schedules and needs.
- **Working at home.** More and more parents are working from home. They work when the children are at a child care center or in school. They may work after the children have gone to bed, too. Working at home allows them to arrange their working hours to suit the family schedule.

Not every job offers these opportunities, of course, but those that do provide a great benefit to families — more time to spend with each other.

Think About It

1. What benefits do workers and employers get from flexible working hours?
2. What types of jobs are best suited to job sharing? To working at home?

Life Management Skills. In small groups, have students develop a pamphlet for new parents that describes all the community services available. You may wish to divide the pamphlet into sections, such as health services, child care, parenting classes, etc. Have each group work on one section.

Problem Solving. Ask students to respond to the following situation: Lee and Andrea live in an economically depressed area. Both have recently lost their jobs. They have three young children. How can this family meet its needs? What services are available? What recommendations do they have for this family?

CHAPTER 26

Review

Summarizing the Chapter

- Parenting skills can be learned.
- Parenting styles are not the same in every family. Often a blend of styles works best.
- Parents must provide for their children's physical, intellectual, social, emotional, and moral development.
- Physical needs of children include food, clothing, sleep, medical care, and a safe environment.
- A stimulating environment promotes intellectual growth.
- Children need unconditional love if they are to develop self-esteem and independence.
- Children want and need guidance.
- Many children with physical, mental, or emotional disabilities have special needs.
- Selecting quality child care is challenging for parents.

Testing Your Memory

1. Describe the three parenting styles that have been identified.
2. List four characteristics of families that produce well-adjusted children.
3. How can parents child-proof their home?
4. How can parents promote intellectual development?
5. Why do children need a healthy self-esteem?
6. How can parents build self-esteem in their children?
7. Why are rules important for children?
8. Describe two ways that children need to be protected.
9. List four considerations when choosing child care.
10. List three resources for people who need help with parenting.

Answers
Testing Your Memory

1. Authoritative, authoritarian, permissive. See page 372 for detailed characteristics.
2. **Any four:** strong parent-child bond; stimulating environment; quiet time; social experiences; reasonable limits; praise and encouragement; parents/caregivers who give and receive love freely.
3. Look at rooms from a child's point of view. Remove harmful objects; plug up unused electrical outlets; use safety fasteners for kitchen cabinets; lock up poisons; examine toys carefully for sharp edges and small parts that are easily swallowed.
4. Provide a variety of play experiences that stimulate all areas of development; talk with and read to children; encourage curiosity and imagination.
5. By encouraging healthy self-esteem, parents allow children to build confidence in their abilities and their worth as a person.
6. Provide unconditional love; discipline with love; allow children to do simple tasks within their abilities that help children feel skillful and confident.
7. Rules provide boundaries for behavior. Rules provide security for children.

Thinking Critically

1. If you have children someday, what parenting style would you use and why?
2. Mrs. Ferguson often punishes her son and then apologizes to him afterwards because she is afraid he won't feel loved. What do you think about this?
3. Four times Mr. Rosenthal told his three-year-old son Robbie to stop pulling the cat's tail. He then told Robbie to go to his room, but Robbie didn't go. Ten minutes later Robbie started teasing the cat again. How do you feel about this situation?

Taking Action

1. Develop a recipe book of healthful snacks that children can make themselves. Include all food groups.
2. Construct a checklist to evaluate toy safety. Use your checklist to analyze ten toys that are popular right now.
3. What does "mainstreaming" for handicapped children mean? Identify reasons why some parents are in favor of it and why some are opposed to it. Share your findings with the class.
4. Many are concerned about how television affects young children. What does the latest research say? What advice would you give to parents about television and children? Put this in poster or pamphlet form.

Making Life Choices

Freida Stein, 24, lives in a small one-bedroom apartment with her four-year-old daughter Kaitlin. Freida works Monday through Saturday as a waitress from 2 to 10 p.m. Salary and tips barely meet her expenses. Freida has very little time to spend with Kaitlin. Instead, she buys her extra toys to keep her happy. Kaitlin plays alone most of the time or watches television while her mother sleeps.

Is Freida meeting all of Kaitlin's needs? Explain your answer. How could Freida improve her parenting skills? What kind of child care might be helpful for Freida?

Using Your Journal

What are your thoughts about being a parent now that you have read about the responsibilities that parents have? What kind of a parent would you be? Use your journal to write about the kind of parenting you have received and the kind you would wish to give to your own children. Make a list of the skills and qualities that you believe good parents need. How many of those skills and qualities do you already have? Which ones do you need to work on?

8. Children should be protected from potentially harmful situations and from people who might harm them.
9. **Any four** of the considerations described on page 384.
10. **Any three** of the resources described on page 385.

Thinking Critically

1. Answers will vary.
2. Answers will vary. Point out that Mrs. Ferguson may be sending her son conflicting messages.
3. Answers will vary. Point out that Mr. Rosenthal should explain why he didn't want Robbie to pull the cat's tail and should follow through with disciplinary action instead of just telling Robbie to go to his room (perhaps take him there).

Reaching Out

Michelle reaches out to a friend in crisis.

Michelle

"I'll never forget that day in class. Mrs. Randall was talking about parents who have personal problems. She explained that sometimes these problems can cause parents to physically or emotionally abuse their children. I looked over and saw Karen, a close friend who sat next to me, crying. After class I took her aside and asked what was wrong. She hesitated. I said, 'You know you can talk to me if you want. I'm your friend.' Finally Karen admitted, 'I can't hold it in anymore.' She told me her father had been abusing her. Her mother was scared to defend her and afraid of her father as well. We talked for a long time. 'I think you should talk to an adult you trust. Your family needs help,' I told her. A week later, Karen went to Carol, her aunt. I was relieved."

Carol Miller

"I knew it took a lot of courage for Karen to open up and share her crisis at home. I also knew it wouldn't be easy to confront my sister and brother-in-law, but I asked them to come over the next day, and the three of us sat down and talked. A lot of feelings came out and we all got emotional. Karen's dad realized how much he was hurting his family. He agreed to get professional counseling. They also realized how Karen's plea for help was an attempt to heal their conflicts. Later when I told this to Karen, she said, 'They should thank my friend Michelle. If it wasn't for her, I would have just kept the pain inside.'"

Don Haft

"When I first heard that Karen had gone to her aunt, I was upset. I didn't want anybody outside our home to know about my problem, but as we talked, it became clear that Karen was only trying to help. I wasn't being a responsible father or husband, and it took my daughter to make me see that. When I asked Karen what prompted her to go to her aunt, she told me what had happened at school. It bothers me that Michelle had to be the one to help us get back on track, but I'm glad she did."

Karen

"I kept the problem inside as long as I could. I didn't think anyone would understand, and I thought it was my fault that Dad was treating me the way he did. The slightest thing I'd do would set him off. After that day in class, Michelle let me know she was there to help. As soon as I got the words out, I felt a great relief. I knew Michelle was right: I had to talk to an adult. Sometimes now when I think about how things have changed at my house, I think of Michelle. She made a big difference in our lives."

You can make a difference too.

- What are some qualities that make people responsible parents?
- How can trusted adults outside the home help a teen in crisis?
- If you had a problem at home, who would you turn to? Why?
- Michelle helped Karen and her parents with a serious problem. In what other ways could a teen help people who are parents?

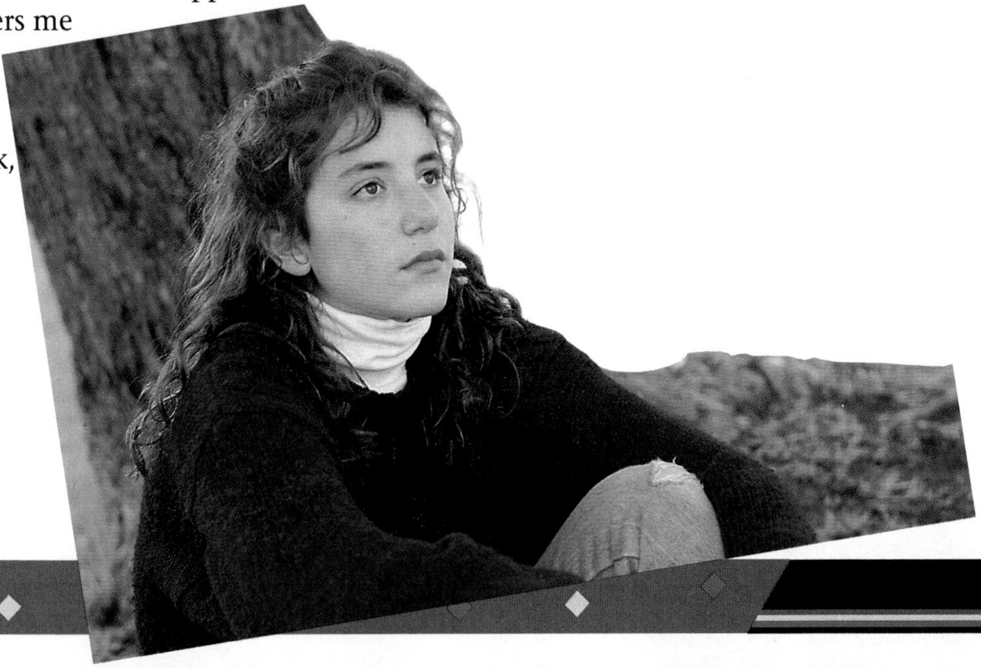

UNIT

8

What Will Your Life's Work Be?

CHAPTER

CHAPTER 27

Finding the Right Career

Chapter Challenge

Resources. Refer to the Teacher's Classroom Resources box and Student Workbook for materials related to this chapter.

Look for These Answers . . .

- What will the jobs of the future be like?
- What can you do to plan for a career?
- Where can you go for education and training?
- How should you go about getting a job?

Look for These Terms . . .

- apprentice
- entrepreneurs
- interview
- resume

"He's lucky to be alive," the doctor said. "Not many who come in with injuries like his survive. It will be a long haul from here, but he will make it."

Mrs. Mulligan looked down at her son. The tubes and equipment frightened her, but it was all part of saving lives in the Intensive Care Unit. All of a sudden Nat looked so fragile. Where was the big strapping son she knew so well? From this point on, he would have no use of his arms and legs. "How can this be lucky?" she thought.

Nat did recover, but his life was one of struggle for many years. Not only was he challenged to try to find ways to function, but he was also frustrated by a feeling of uselessness — until the day a friend gave him a paint brush and easel.

"What am I supposed to do with that?" Nat asked scornfully.

"Paint with it," Emily replied, as she gently placed the brush in Nat's mouth.

Five years later Nat's work was being sold all over the country. His notepaper designs were only one example of his artistry. He had developed his own booming business — even though he could not use his arms and legs. He found a sense of worth through work. His self-esteem soared. Although many people had helped him along the way, he was very proud to be making it on his own.

Emily too was proud of Nat and her role in his success story. On the wall of her apartment hangs one of her most precious possessions — the first painting ever created by Nathanial Mulligan.

Chapter Opener. Have students read the opening scenario. Then ask the following questions: How did Nat overcome his disability? Give an example of someone you know who has become successful after many struggles. What do you think made Nat so successful? What character traits allow for success? Failure? What should you think about when career planning?

Attitudes Toward Work

Work is the core of most people's lives. People work for many reasons, not just survival. Check your reactions with these:

- **Status.** The working person earns the respect of others.
- **Accomplishment.** Satisfaction comes with doing a job completely and correctly.
- **Improvement.** Most people are willing to work so things can be better and easier for themselves and their families.
- **Fulfillment.** Many want to be active for personal satisfaction.
- **Mental health.** In the words of one, "I'd go crazy if I didn't work."
- **Fun.** Happy are those who make a living doing something they enjoy.

Jobs of the Future

Today's changing job market will influence your future life. Technology is creating new jobs and eliminating old ones. For example, the computer field continues to provide careers, including programmers, analysts, consultants, operators, and technicians. Computers have also reduced the need for clerks, bookkeepers, and other office personnel.

According to the U.S. Department of Labor, employment in manufacturing jobs is continuing to decrease while output from the factories continues to grow. This means that machinery is becoming more and more efficient and is replacing workers.

On the other hand, employment in service industries is growing fast, especially in health services, business services, social services, and legal services. The service sector is now the largest and fastest growing division of the labor market. Employment in services is expected to rise by 40 percent by the year 2005 and will account for almost two thirds of all new jobs.

◆◆◆

Planning for a Career

Have you ever thought about what you will be doing in ten years? Sandra has. She wants to be an actress, even though she cannot sing, has never taken a speech course, and has earned only minor roles in high school plays. Recently her English teacher complimented her on a class report, saying, "Sandy, you did an excellent job of arranging your facts and presenting them clearly. You know, you might think about becoming a teacher. I think you would be a good one."

Surprised, Sandra did some serious evaluating. She did not give up her acting dream, but she did change her plans. She decided to major in English and concentrate on speech and dramatics. Then if a career in the theater does not work out, she will be prepared to teach.

Like so many others, Sandra needed a game plan for her future. It never dawned on her that what she wanted to be had to be based on what she could be. Her English teacher helped her see this.

◆ Analyze Yourself

In planning a career begin by looking at yourself. What are your interests, abilities, and aptitudes? Make a list of these, including your strong points and weaknesses. Writing it down on paper helps. Keep these in mind as you explore career options.

◆ Look at Job Characteristics

Just as you have distinctive qualities, jobs have characteristics that make them different too. A job that suits one person is not necessarily right for another. When you look at specific careers, examine more than just the work itself. Your job satisfaction will be affected by many other factors.

◆ Work Settings

Work takes place in all sorts of environments — indoor/outdoor, solitary/social, structured/informal, and calm/busy, to name a few. If you are an outgoing person, chances

Before you take a job, make sure the work setting is one you will be happy with. This firefighter would not be happy sitting behind a desk all day.

More About Finding the Right Career. According to the Bureau of Labor Statistics, some of the fastest growing jobs in the 1990s include medical assistants, paralegals, travel agents, computer service technicians, home health aides, and physical therapists. Have students choose and research one of these jobs, and write a brief report on the qualifications, training, and salary potential of that job.

Photo Focus. Have students look at the photo above. What do you think the firefighter finds challenging in this career? Rewarding?

are you would not be happy chained to a desk all day. Before you choose a career, think carefully about the work setting that would please you the most.

◆ Schedules

Some jobs require longer hours than others, including overtime that affects weekends and evenings. A job that is structured by shifts may mean always working evenings or nights. If the job is seasonal, you could have periods when you work long hours and times when little or no work is available.

On some jobs, part-time schedules are possible. People who have other responsibilities and need less income from the job may welcome the shorter hours. Working at home may even be a possibility.

With flexible hours employees can control their own schedules to some extent. This enables them to work at their more productive times and to schedule their hours to fit with other responsibilities. For example, parents must meet the needs of their children, and this is not always possible when rigid work schedules are required.

Do you like travel? Would you want to travel regularly? Some jobs require this in different degrees. If you live some distance from the job site, commuting may be necessary. A job may require occasional trips, or you could be on the road all the time.

◆ Income

The amount of money earned means more to some than others. Would you choose a job that doesn't pay very well if you love the work, or is the dollar the main motivator for you? Think about what you want in order to lead the kind of life you prefer. Remember that some incomes are more stable than others. If you work seasonally or on a commission, your income will not be the same all the time. Check to see what expenses are connected with the job. For example, if you must buy uniforms or pay for parking, this will reduce your income.

Flexible schedules enable parents to handle child care. These parents work different hours so that they do not have to use outside child care.

Discussion. Some companies have flexible work schedules. For example, an employee can work four ten-hour days and be off one day. Ask students how this might benefit employees who have children. What are some other ways employees might schedule their work time?

Photo Focus. Ask students to look at the photo above. How may this arrangement benefit a family in comparison to taking a child to a care facility on a daily basis? If one parent doesn't work, how may this affect their income? Leisure time activities? What are some ways to make a family income stretch to meet family needs?

An entrepreneur manages his or her own business. Some people start small and eventually work into bigger and better ventures.

◆ Entrepreneurship

Although risk is involved, people who work for themselves, **entrepreneurs**, (ahn-truh-pruh-NOORS), find certain satisfaction in what they do. Owning your own business often involves a large investment in time, money, and work. Such businesses can fail if careful planning is not done. The hours can be long and the income is not guaranteed, but the pride and sense of accomplishment that come with being your own boss can make such ventures worthwhile.

◆ Stress

Few jobs are without some degree of stress. Learning to manage stress is important to everyone. If you choose a job that has a high stress level, you will need to learn how to prevent this from harming your health. Otherwise, another line of work is the answer.

◆ Personal and Family Life

Always ask this question of yourself when considering a job: How will the job affect my family and me? If you don't know the answer, then find out. People have careers, but they also need fulfilling personal lives in order to be happy. A job that does not allow you to take care of your responsibilities or that prevents you from enjoying other aspects of your life could cause problems. Your willingness to stay on the job and your long-term feelings about the job depend at least in part on the answer to this question.

Work and Family. Ask students to respond: After college, Dell plans to live on his own and check out several cities around the country for employment. His sister, Delilah, plans to marry her boyfriend and raise a large family — but she will have to work part-time. Drew, their younger brother, plans to settle in their home town and find a job that allows him to help people. What jobs would be ideal for each sibling? What jobs should each avoid? Have students brainstorm choices.

◆◆◆

Explore Career Possibilities

As you consider your future career, think about this. There are more than 30,000 types of work to choose from. Although you cannot consider them all, you have many options. The problem is where to start looking. One way to narrow down the field is to consider jobs within a cluster. The U.S. Office of Education has organized all jobs into fifteen clusters shown in the chart on the next page.

Career Clusters

Cluster	Job Examples
Agriculture	Beekeepers; fruit harvesters; plant farmers; animal farmers.
Arts, Humanities, and Sciences	Librarians; teachers; editors; musicians; photographers; psychologists; chemists; economists; commercial artists.
Business and Office	Typists; accountants; computer programmers; bank tellers; secretaries; general clerical workers.
Communications and Media	TV announcers; sound and video engineers; disk jockeys; telegraph operators; line and instrument installers; public relations people.
Construction	Architects; carpenters; bricklayers; building contractors; plumbers; construction workers.
Health	Physicians; nurses; dentists; veterinarians; medical assistants; medical technicians; lab workers; pharmacists.
Family and Consumer Sciences	Dietitians; clothes designers; nutritionists; consumer specialists; homemakers; child care workers; interior designers; food scientists.
Hospitality and Recreation	Restaurant and hotel managers and workers; athletic coaches and trainers; airline flight attendants; amusement park workers.
Manufacturing	Mechanical and electrical engineers; tool designers; market analysts; factory workers.
Marine Science	Marine biologists and engineers; fish farmers; lab technicians; divers; others who work with marine life and ocean resources.
Marketing and Distribution	Sales and advertising managers; salesclerks; truck drivers; others involved in selling and distributing goods.
Natural Resources and Environment	Petroleum and mining engineers; miners; oil field workers; foresters; loggers; wildlife workers.
Personal Services	Hairstylists; butlers; domestic workers; funeral workers.
Public Service	Fire fighters; police officers; military personnel; street cleaners; probation officers; prison guards; social service workers; politicians.
Transportation	Airline pilots and mechanics; train engineers; ship captains; bus drivers; others involved in transporting people and goods.

Fortunately, the government constantly updates information on employment opportunities. You may want to study the *Occupational Outlook Handbook* published by the Bureau of Labor Statistics. Your school or public library has copies. This publication describes hundreds of careers. It includes information about job duties, educational requirements, employment outlook, and salary levels.

One career area you might want to explore is that of family service. As society changes, families do too. Since people are living longer, elderly people need more services. Many households have two employed parents, resulting in a demand for more and better quality child care. With complex family situations today, some need outside help to solve problems.

Activity. Have students write a job description for each of their classmates. Students should not share their lists with other classmates. They should list and justify their choices. The teacher should read some of the job descriptions to the class without revealing any names. Have the class guess who belongs to each job. Do the jobs suit the individuals? Why or why not?

Activity. Have students brainstorm ten possible careers they might be interested in. Have them look these careers up in the *Occupational Outlook Handbook* to find more information about each.

What qualities do you need to work in this area? People who like to help others and are good listeners may fit well into one of these careers. Also, if you are good at solving problems, you might be able to help others solve theirs.

Here are some careers that you might like to explore if the field of family service interests you: therapist; psychologist; social worker; child care worker; and geriatrician (one who provides medical care for the elderly).

According to a survey of 250 job placement directors across the country, many young people do not think about their own future careers until they finish high school or college. Why not begin planning your career now? Once you have found a career choice that has possibilities, give it a trial run first.

- Read books, pamphlets, and magazine articles that describe the job. Does it sound interesting?
- Talk to people who work in the profession. Are they like you? Find out what they like and don't like about the job. How did they get into the field? What qualities are necessary for success?
- Try to get some on-the-job training. Perhaps you can be an aide for one day, either helping or watching. Maybe the company offers an internship or work-study program that would offer a more extended training session.

Check out several career options if you can. Anything you do now to prepare for the career decisions you must make later will be helpful. You may save yourself from making a costly mistake.

If you like the idea of working with children, you might consider a career as a child care worker. It is just one of many careers in the field of family service.

Activity. Ask students to identify someone who works in a career of interest to them. Have them write a brief biography about the person selected. What were the subject's long-range goals? What were the subject's short-range goals? Students should list the steps this person followed in meeting his or her goals.

More About Career Choice. Part-time jobs, internships, and volunteer work help students discover both what they *do* want in a job and what they *don't* want. For example, a student who works part-time in a store might discover that she really enjoys the variety that retail work offers while another might find the same work dull and monotonous.

◆◆◆

Set Goals

Part of the career planning you do should include setting short-range as well as long-range goals. You may even want to put them in writing.

Kerri worked out a career plan with her school guidance counselor. Her long-range goal was to own her own insurance agency some day. Her road map included these short-range goals:

- Take all the business-related courses available.
- Continue working part-time for an insurance firm.
- Take on more office duties. Observe sales techniques. Attend insurance discussion meetings whenever possible.
- Study business administration in college and try for part-time work in an insurance company office during free hours.
- Apply for a full-time sales job with a major insurance company after graduation.

Whether Kerri keeps to her plan or not, she realizes the value of setting goals. You can do the same as you look ahead to your adult years.

◆◆◆

Planning for Education and Training

Education and training can give you an edge in the job world today. A college diploma can add between a quarter-million and a half-million dollars to your lifetime earnings. The average salary of a college graduate is about 30 percent higher than that of a high school graduate. Moreover, career advancement is often easier for those with experience and a college degree.

Discussion. Have each student develop a list of short-range and long-range career goals. Where do they plan to be in five years? In ten years? Do they plan to change careers at some point in their lives? How does post-secondary education fit into career plans?

On the other hand, technical training is valuable too. In the United States, four out of five jobs do not require a degree from a four-year college. For some occupations, technical training provides better earning power than a four-year bachelor of arts degree. The average plumber, for example, earns more than some bank employees and high school teachers. A computer technician out-earns many nurses, journalists, and business managers. Getting education and training can make a big difference in your life.

Many different kinds of jobs require computer skills. People who work in stores, offices, warehouses, and in many other places need to be able to use a computer. Take advantage of the computer courses offered at your school.

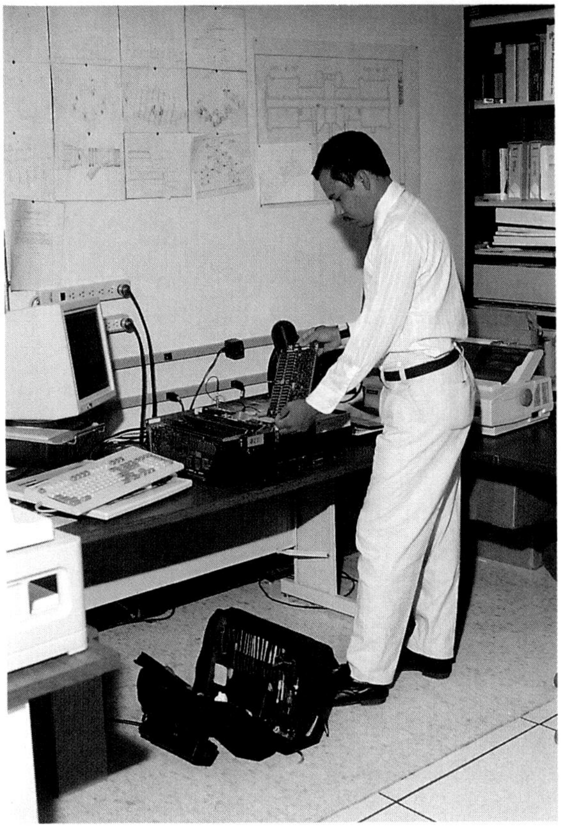

Many jobs that do not require a college education provide a good income. This computer technician trained on the job and now makes a good income due to the demand for his skills.

Activity. Have students ask their parents, relatives, and friends about how they obtained their jobs. What schooling and experience was required for employment? How do these individuals think the job market has changed in recent years? Is education and training more important now than in the past?

A Slice of Life

At age nineteen Leann was an unwed mother. She survived, but not easily, on the money she received from welfare. "I know I made some mistakes," she thought, "but do I have to pay for them for the rest of my life? I want something better for me and my boy, but I don't know what to do."

A woman who lived next door to Leann had not been employed for many years. She was raising a daughter and somehow finding ways to get by with aid from the government. To Leann she said, "You don't have to work, honey. Just sit back and relax. It will all work out."

Last year Leann was put in touch with Lilly Carlisle through someone in the welfare office. Mrs. Carlisle teaches in a special program at the junior college. Students can apply for aid to help them get through a training course that prepares them for jobs. The program provides child care and even helps the students find transportation if they need it. Leann applied and learned to do word processing and handle data bases on the computer. She now has a job with a future at a mail-order company. She is proud to be making it on her own and has high hopes for her son's future as well as her own.

Thinking It Through

- Why do you think Leann's neighbor felt as she did?
- What do you think is ahead for Leann's neighbor? What about Leann and her son?
- Explain the relationship between work and self-esteem.

◆ Where Can You Go?

When Alex graduates from high school, he plans to enroll in a welding course at a technical school. Before making this decision, he thought about several options. Do any of these sound right for you?

- **Colleges and Universities.** A bachelor's degree can be obtained in four years at a college or university. Advanced degrees are possible with additional years of study. Junior, city, and community colleges offer two-year programs. Students may study for an associate's degree or prepare to transfer to a four-year college later.
- **Technical and Business Schools.** Private technical schools offer concentrated training. Business schools also offer a wide range of courses from accounting to sales. Graduates attend classes for one to two years and graduate with a specialized certificate.
- **Correspondence Schools or Courses.** State universities offer correspondence courses to those who cannot attend classes on a campus. Required work is done at home. Remember, however, that studying through the mail requires self-discipline for completion. This can be difficult.
- **Apprenticeship Programs.** These are available in industry and through state-sponsored agencies. An **apprentice** (uh-PRENT-us) is a trainee who receives two or three years of supervised, on-the-job experience along with related instruction. Programs are offered in the fields of carpentry, auto mechanics, auto body repair, airplane mechanics, banking, barbering, bookbinding, bricklaying, cosmetology, plumbing, electrical work, cooking, and other interesting trades.

Activity. Invite someone from a social service agency to discuss ways in which single parents can further their education. What other community organizations may be able to help single parents develop career skills?

Problem Solving. Have students choose a possible job interest and research the education and training required for the job. Is a college degree necessary? Technical training? Have them identify facilities that provide proper training.

An apprenticeship program is a good way to learn a trade.

- **Continuing Education.** Colleges and public schools offer off-campus adult courses in the evening. A good reading program can help make up for a lack of formal education. National companies continually sponsor improvement courses and on-the-job training. Many have schools within their plants where employees can train for promotions to higher paying positions.

SIDELIGHT

Cutting the Cost of College

If you are thinking about going to college, consider these options:

- **Cooperative Programs.** These alternate several months of study with stretches of work experience. Students can earn while they learn.
- **Employer-Paid Tuition.** Some companies pay your tuition if you work toward a degree during off-hours.
- **Combining Colleges.** Begin at a less expensive two-year school and transfer to complete your degree.
- **Advanced Placement.** Some qualified students can enroll in college-level courses during high school.
- **Shortened Program.** Go to summer school classes, or see if you can eliminate some required courses by taking tests to prove your competency.
- **Military.** You can learn technical skills and continue your training at the college level.

◆◆◆

◆ Cost Considerations

The cost of education and training can be high. Knowing that long-term rewards await, however, makes finding a way to get what you need important.

If you plan to go to college, check to see which schools offer the program you want. Then compare tuition, room and board, and fees. A college in your home state is likely to be less expensive than one out of state. Apply for scholarships. Some are based on academic performance and some on need. Athletic scholarships are available too.

Activity. Have students make a list of area or state colleges that offer programs they are interested in. Have students record tuition fees as well as fees for room and board. Compare the costs with out-of-state colleges offering similar programs. What are the advantages and disadvantages of area colleges and out-of-state colleges?

Ask your school counselor about government-sponsored financial aid programs for college students. Less money is available for these than there used to be, but help is available for some. Students must begin repaying a loan after graduation.

You don't have to be college-bound to be eligible for government-sponsored educational programs. Some programs address the needs of young people who have dropped out of school or are about to. Some provide jobs for students who must work to remain in high

Discussion. Have students discuss options for meeting the financial requirements of post-secondary education. You may wish to invite a high school counselor to discuss applying for financial aid as well as government-sponsored educational programs.

Before selecting a college, you will probably want to visit several campuses in order to do some comparing.

school. Others provide education, vocational training, counseling, and health care. To find out about the programs available in your area, check with your school counselor or call the closest state employment office. You may find a list of government agencies to call by looking up your state name in the business section of the phone book.

◆◆◆

Getting the Job

Sooner or later the time will come to look for a job. Classified ads are a good place to begin, but the yellow pages in the phone book and the Chamber of Commerce may offer alternatives as well. Since many jobs aren't advertised, sometimes you need to call a company and ask about any openings. Temporary employment agencies can also be helpful. Today's temporary job may be tomorrow's permanent position.

Life Management Skills. Explain to students that networking often helps people find jobs through contact with people who may know of job possibilities. Instruct students to keep a network inventory and have them talk to people they know about possible job leads. Students should share the results in class.

◆ Applying for the Job

To apply for a job, send a letter of application and a resume. A letter of application, should be addressed to the employer named in the ad and should include your source of information about the job, the position you are applying for, and your qualifications. In closing, request an interview and give a phone number where you can be reached. Make sure the letter is neatly typed and all spelling is correct. Remember that your letter can determine whether or not you are granted an interview.

A **resume** (REZ-uh-may) summarizes your education and work experiences to a prospective employer. Make sure your resume sells you. List your name, address, telephone number, and age as part of the personal data. Your education, honors and awards, and date of

Activity. Select several students to act out job interviews. One student should take on the role of interviewer and the other the applicant. Have the class rate the applicant's body language. Does the person sit up straight? Make eye contact? Act positive? Are answers clear and direct? Discuss student reactions.

graduation should be listed next. Also include any extra-curricular activities, interests, or hobbies. These too describe who you are. If you have any work experience, list it. If you don't, list any volunteer work you may have done. Finally, give the names of two or three people who will be references. Check with these people before you list them on your resume to make sure they are willing to write a letter of recommendation for you.

◆ The Job Interview

Sometimes one short conversation can determine whether or not you get the job. An **interview**, a conversation between an employer and a potential employee, is usually the last step taken before a person is hired for a job. Employers are watching not only what you say but how you say it. Be pleasant, friendly, and businesslike. Maintain eye contact as you speak, and answer questions as thoroughly as possible. Relax, be yourself, and think positive. When possible, emphasize your strong points. In addition, show an interest in the company, and let the employer know you are willing to learn.

Be prepared to answer these commonly asked questions:

- Why did you apply for this job?
- What are your strengths and weaknesses?
- What are your career goals?
- What courses did you like best in school?
- How does your education or experience relate to this job?
- How would you describe yourself?

Also show some initiative by preparing a few questions of your own:

- What are the responsibilities of this position?
- Who would be my supervisor?
- Is there a training program?
- What opportunities are there for advancement?

Problem Solving. Ask students to respond to the following situation: You have applied for a job in response to an ad. The job sounded compatible with your skills. You were called for an interview. Halfway through the interview, you discover the job is different from what was described in the ad. How would you handle this situation?

If you are not offered the job during the interview, ask when you can expect to know about the decision. After the interview, write a follow-up letter to the interviewer, thanking him or her for the opportunity and expressing your interest in the job. This letter may give you an edge over other applicants or, at the very least, will leave the interviewer with a positive impression of you.

◆◆◆

What's Ahead?

Getting that first job is just the beginning. You are likely to have several jobs in your lifetime, so the skills you gain through one can be carried on to the next. What will life be like on the job? What skills will you need to be successful? The next chapter will give you some answers.

Putting your best foot forward during an interview means presenting a good appearance, making eye contact, showing confidence, and asking and answering questions in a businesslike manner.

More About Teens and Jobs. Many employers in the fast-food industry report that some teens are irresponsible when it comes to holding a job. Teens often say that jobs are too demanding. Although many jobs are demanding, most provide a learning opportunity and should be taken seriously.

CHAPTER 27

Review

Answers
Testing Your Memory

1. Status, accomplishment, improvement, fulfillment, mental health, fun.
2. Technology creates new jobs and eliminates old ones.
3. A work schedule must be appropriate for your personal and family life.
4. A self-employed person.
5. A person needs a fulfilling personal life and must be able to take care of family responsibilities.
6. A government publication describing hundreds of careers. It includes information about job duties, educational requirements, employment outlook, and salary levels.
7. **Any two:** good listener, willing to help others, good at solving problems.
8. Colleges and universities; technical and business schools; correspondence schools or courses; apprenticeship programs; continuing education. See pages 400-401 for descriptions.
9. A written document that summarizes your education and work experiences for a prospective employer.

Summarizing the Chapter

- People work for several reasons, not just survival.
- Jobs of the future will be different due to new technology and the need for many services.
- When planning for a career, you need to analyze yourself.
- Jobs have different characteristics that must be examined before you know what appeals to you.
- Setting goals can help you as you select and move toward a specific career.
- Education and training is important and should be examined carefully in terms of what is right for you and the costs involved.
- In order to get a job, you must put your best foot forward, on paper as well as in person.

Testing Your Memory

1. Name six reasons why people work.
2. What is the effect of new technology on the job market?
3. Explain why you should think about the work schedules before taking a job.
4. What is an entrepreneur?
5. Why should you think about how a job will affect your personal and family life?
6. What is the *Occupational Outlook Handbook*?
7. Name two qualities a person should have for work in family service.
8. List and describe three kinds of education and training that are available.
9. What is a resume?
10. Explain what you can do to make a job interview go well.

Thinking Critically

1. Some people get stuck for many years in jobs that they do not like. Why do you think this happens?
2. Do you think that there are people who prefer not to work at all? If so, why do you think they feel this way?
3. Name two jobs that you think would be very stressful. Explain why. What could people on these jobs do to manage stress?
4. Which do you think is more important, the amount of money you make or job satisfaction? Explain your answer.

Taking Action

1. Make a list of your interests, abilities, and aptitudes. Then list three careers that fit these qualities.
2. Research two careers that interest you. If possible, talk to people who have these jobs. Share your findings with the class with a short oral presentation.
3. List some short-range and long-range goals that might help a person toward the following careers:
   - Ownership of an auto repair business
   - Veterinarian
   - Computer consultant
   - Manager of a fast-food restaurant

Making Life Choices

For 25 years Clyde's father has been in the bakery business. Mr. Gustafson started the business himself in a small shop below the apartment where he and his wife first lived. Clyde has always loved the smell of fresh bread baking and enjoys helping his father turn out the pastries that are Mr. Gustafson's specialty. Clyde would like to take over his father's business someday, but his father has other plans. He wants Clyde to go to college and learn a profession. "Go to school," he says. "Be somebody. Make lots of money." Clyde listens, but his heart is not in this plan.

Clyde is faced with a difficult situation. Why do you think Mr. Gustafson feels as he does? What about Clyde? What do you think Clyde should do?

Using Your Journal

Some people seem to know from a young age what they want to do as a career. Others take a long time to decide what their work should be. Have you made any decisions yet? Use your journal to explore your thoughts about your future work. Look back on ideas you had in the past and then rejected. Look at some of the ideas you have now. List any questions you have about careers, then decide who can give you the answers you need. The more information you have, the better placed you will be to make the best decision for you.

10. Be pleasant, friendly, and businesslike. Maintain direct eye contact. Answer questions thoroughly. Relax, be yourself, and think positive. Emphasize strengths and show interest in the company and a willingness to learn.

Thinking Critically

1. Answers will vary. Point out that lack of self-confidence often keeps people from leaving jobs they don't like.
2. Answers will vary.
3. Answers will vary.
4. Answers will vary.

CHAPTER

28 On the Job

Chapter Challenge

Resources. Refer to the Teacher's Classroom Resources box and Student Workbook for materials related to this chapter.

Look for These Answers . . .

- What adjustments will you have to make when you join the work world?
- Why should you set career goals?
- What factors will affect the development of your career?
- Describe what it takes to be successful on the job.
- How do personal ethics play a part in the work world?

Look for These Terms . . .

- benefits
- discrimination
- ethics
- professionalism
- unemployment compensation

“Be patient, Mingh. When you are young, time seems to pass slowly. You will be out in the work world soon enough.”

Mingh’s grandmother always seemed to have a few words of wisdom for him. It was true. He was very anxious to finish his high school years and get on with his life. He was looking forward to finding a job that would bring him his own income. His eyes sparkled as he told his grandmother about the new car he would buy and the nice clothes he would get for her.

“Mingh, you have much to learn,” she said. “A job is more than just a way to earn money.” As she spoke, she glanced down at her hands, rough and scarred from many years of work at Chan’s Laundry. The work was respectable, but it had been hard. She had raised her grandson, and she was proud, but she wanted something better for him.

As Mingh watched his grandmother, for the first time he understood things about her that had never occurred to him before. Her life had not been easy. What would his life be like? This job that he longed to have — would it bring him more than just income? Could it please him as well? “Yes, Grandmother,” he thought, “I have a lot to learn, and I will begin today.”

Chapter Opener. Have students read the opening scenario to the chapter. Ask students to respond to the following: What did Mingh’s grandmother mean when she said: “A job is more than just a way to earn money”? What kinds of questions should Mingh be asking himself about his future work? How may further education and training beyond high school affect future employment and income?

Looking Ahead

Like Mingh you may be looking forward to your future. College or technical training may be the first step. Eventually, however, the work world will be part of your life.

Take a look around you. How many of the adults you know are satisfied with the careers they have chosen? You will be working for about one-third of every day for about two-thirds of every week of your life. The time you spend on the job will far surpass the time you have spent in school. You can learn to make the most of that time, first by choosing a job carefully and then by learning how to do well on the job.

Activity. Have students identify and report on two people in the news — one newsworthy for job success, the other for being fired. Have them research media resources to find out why one has succeeded and the other has not. What does it take to succeed on the job?

◆◆◆

Adjusting To the World of Work

Moving from the high school or college setting into the work world will require some adjustment. You will need to rely on old skills and develop new ones as you learn to function in your new role.

During your school years, you have been surrounded by peers. On the job this will be different. People of all ages will be your colleagues. You may be challenged to relate to others in ways that are new to you.

Your schedule will also probably change. As a student, what are your days like? You may have shorter hours than employed adults. You may have more days off. You may also have more opportunity to socialize during the day. The work world is likely to be more regimented, depending, of course, on the type of job you choose. At any rate, you need to be prepared to follow a regular routine and take responsibility for sticking to it.

◆◆◆

Developing Your Career

The average American worker stays on the same job three and one-half years. This means you will probably change jobs many times throughout your career. Some people change jobs because they are not happy with the pay, the work, the environment, or the people. Sometimes they simply make a change because it is a good career move. A switch to another company can mean new opportunities as well as a chance to increase your salary.

Life Management Skills. Divide students into small groups. Have each group interview an adult who has changed jobs or careers more than once. Have each group share the experiences and advice offered by each individual with the class. What would he or she do differently? Is the current job or career more satisfying than the previous? What affected the decision to change? What are the disadvantages and advantages of changing jobs or careers? What conclusions can the students draw based on the experiences of others?

◆ Setting Goals

Once you have taken a job, you will want to set goals that guide you in developing your career. Think about the positions you would like to hold. Then set small goals that will help you achieve what you want. Revise your goals as necessary along the way.

Ebony had been a file clerk in an office for several months when she began to take note of other jobs that she would like. The data entry position looked like a good place for her to go next. This could eventually lead her to some higher level positions working with computers. Eventually, she thought, she would like to hold a supervisory position.

When a notice came around that the company was offering a data entry class for employees, Ebony was one of the first to sign up. She had her goal in mind and seized the opportunity. Later she thought she might

The person who wants to get ahead keeps a sharp eye open for opportunity. A large office may post notices of job openings within the company.

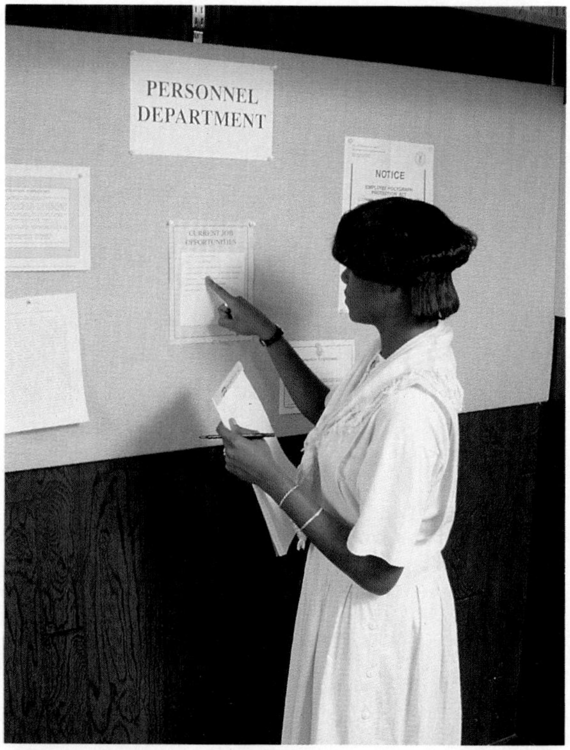

take some courses at the junior college to help with her communication skills. A talk with her supervisor made her realize that a computer class would help too.

Ebony always watched the bulletin board at work for notices of job openings within the company. When a data entry position opened up, she applied for the position. With her goals in mind, she had prepared herself for this opportunity. This fact, along with her enthusiasm, landed her the promotion she wanted and put her one step closer to her long-range goal.

◆ Pay Increases

Improving your skills and advancing your position usually go hand in hand with pay increases. Many companies give automatic raises once or twice a year. The percentage of increase is based on merit and/or cost of living.

If your company does not give scheduled raises, then you may have to ask for a raise. In preparation, keep a file of your work history. Note extra courses you've completed, letters of recommendation, and praises for special tasks. Check to see what your skills are worth to other companies. If you know your value elsewhere, your confidence will help convince your boss of your worth where you are.

Discussing a raise with your boss should always be done in private and at your boss's convenience. Also make sure the timing is right for your department or company. Ask for a raise when the company has reported a profit or finished a peak season. Avoid asking for a raise during a business slump.

Remember that you often receive more on a job than just your pay. **Benefits**, in the form of life and health insurance, retirement funds, and paid holidays are all costly to an employer. The quality of these benefits should be considered along with the wages you receive on a job.

Balancing *Work & Family*

Using Commuting Time

Commuting is a way of life for many Americans. They travel to school or work by car, bus, or train. People who use their commuting time productively can free up more time for other activities.

If you travel by bus or train you can catch up on news by reading the paper. You can make lists of things you need to do at school, at work, or at home and figure out the most efficient way of doing what needs to be done.

If you drive, you can't read or write. You can still make mental notes of plans for the day. You can also figure out what your priorities will be.

No matter how you commute, you can also use the time to relax. It may be the only time during the day that you can do so.

Think About It

1. What could you do during a walk to school or work?
2. What are some other productive ways of using commuter time?

◆ Evaluations

Periodically your employer will evaluate the job you are doing. You can profit from the information you are given, and the company can too. Use what you learn to make improvements. That way, you are more likely to get promotions and pay increases.

◆ Relocation

For many people the development of a career involves relocation. Jason's company transferred him when he became a district manager. Moving usually means promotion and more pay, but there can be drawbacks.

Problem Solving. Ask students to respond to the following situation: Thuy works for a company that does not give scheduled pay raises. He has been with the company for two years and has added many improvements to his department. In this situation, how would a supervisor be approached about a raise?

Discussion. Discuss the following situation with the class: Steve was just given a promotion, providing he transfers to another state. His wife Lorna has a great job and makes a salary comparable to Steve's. Their children will finish school in three months. Should Steve accept the promotion? What are possible solutions?

Uprooting your family and asking your spouse to leave a job are major considerations. Being able to sell your house and buy another is also a factor. Some firms make this easy on transferred employees by buying their present home and selling it for them. Some companies also cover moving expenses or help compensate for higher mortgage payments. If the cost of living is higher where you are going, compare this to the salary increase you will receive. Then decide if the move will really benefit you and your family.

◆ Are You Dependable?

Showing dependability is really quite easy. Arrive at the job on time and stay until the work day is over. Keep absences to a minimum and call when you are ill or have another problem. When you are asked to get something done, follow through. Your employer will soon learn that you can be counted on.

◆◆◆

Success on the Job

Imagine for a moment that you are the owner of a business. You must hire someone to work for you. Take a moment to list the qualities you would want in that person. Remember that these are the same qualities that an employer will be looking for in you. How do you measure up as a potential employee? Answer the following questions to see.

◆ Do You Have a Positive Attitude?

Few people want to share a portion of every day with people who are very negative. These people are the complainers, the ones who are never satisfied and always finding fault with others. Often they are angry and unhappy. Smiles are few and far between. By contrast, those who have positive attitudes are cheerful and easy to get along with. They are thoughtful of others and have an enthusiastic spirit with a sense of humor too. They also have good things to say about others and the company they work for.

Work and Family. Conflicts between work and family can be extremely stressful unless members communicate openly. Ask for volunteers to act out the following, with each person defending a position: a husband wants to take an out-of-state job and his wife has just started a job she loves; a single parent has to work late hours and his teenage son needs to assume more responsibility at home; a parent with a new job plans to move the family and a teen wants to finish the year at school; both parents work and have two small children — they feel they should spend more time with the children.

A Slice of Life

"This company doesn't care about you, me, or anybody else," Marlie said to her friend Christa. They had come in early to work, before anyone else.

"How Ms. Silverstein ever got to be a supervisor is beyond me," Marlie continued. "All she does is talk on the phone all day, and then she expects me to keep my phone calls short. She says I miss too much work too. Who wouldn't with all the boring jobs she gives me to do! What time did we get here this morning, Christa? Seven-thirty? Let's put seven on our time cards. That's close enough."

Thinking It Through

- Is Marlie the kind of employee you would want to have? List the flaws that you see.
- If you were Christa, how would you react to Marlie?
- What do you think is ahead for Marlie on the job?

Problem Solving. Some people haven't learned the importance of a positive attitude and dependability. Have the class brainstorm steps to take to turn around a person's negative attitude or lack of dependability. Students may want to use library materials to support their ideas.

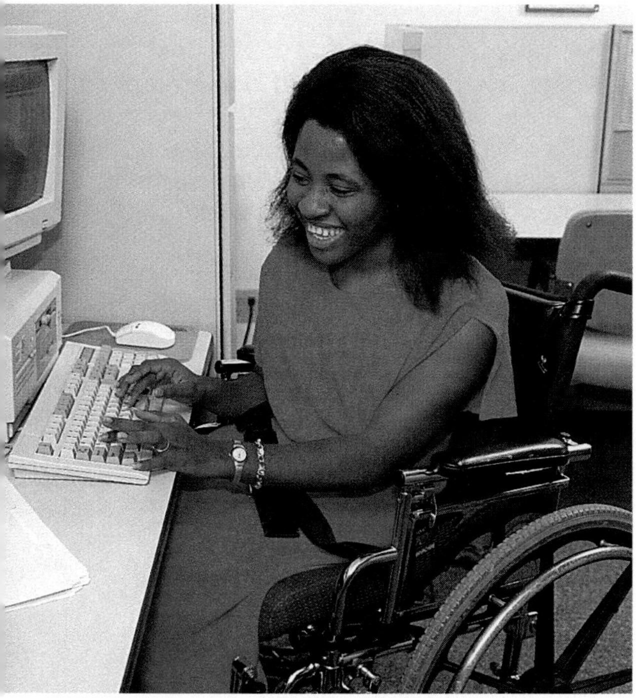

People who have a positive attitude on the job are likely to do well. After all, isn't that the kind of person you would prefer to work with?

SIDELIGHT

Criticism Can Be Constructive

Perhaps it is just human nature, but few people like to be told that they are wrong, that they have made a mistake. On the job, however, people must learn to accept such criticism. With it, you learn to do your job better. Without it, you may never see the ways that people expect you to improve.

How should you react to criticism? Avoid the defensive response. Some people automatically want to place the blame elsewhere, often looking for excuses. Accepting responsibility is much better. Say something like, "I'm sorry this happened. Now that I understand, it won't happen again." Remember that all people make mistakes. Stay confident, and constructive criticism will help you, not hinder you.

◆◆◆

◆ Are You Honest?

Using your working hours for anything other than work is as dishonest as taking supplies home with you at night. You expect honesty from your employer and others. You must give it as well.

◆ Are You a Willing Worker?

Some tasks that you will be asked to do on the job may not be fun but they are necessary. Doing your assignment well and without complaint makes life easier for your employer. Eventually, this can result in rewards for you. Show that you can take on responsibility without being told. Try to learn new tasks. Listen to directions and carry them out correctly. When you do something wrong, admit that you made a mistake and do better the next time. Soon you will have the reputation of being a willing worker. When it comes time for raises and promotions, you should be at the top of the list.

◆ Can You Get Along with Others?

You don't have to like everyone you work with, but you can get along with them. Adopting an attitude of tolerance is a first step. People are very different, and you can learn something from each and every one. Try looking for the good qualities in others and letting the rest go by. Let the gossip go by too.

Activity. Have students list ten important personal traits or qualities that are useful in getting along with others. Then ask: How are good relationships helpful in a job? What boundaries or limits should co-workers have? Should co-workers be friends? Mates? Why or why not?

Life Management Skills. Ask students how learning to be more tolerant in the workplace can benefit interaction with family at home.

When others have disputes, remain neutral. Getting involved in petty differences is a waste of time. Good relationships with others can be very helpful to you, because you need that cooperation in order to get your job done. Remember that when you are willing to pitch in and help others, they will do the same for you.

If someone seems impossible to get along with, first put yourself in his or her shoes. Then take some extra steps. You will be surprised to discover how many people you can win over by simply making an effort, by showing some understanding. Losing your temper will not help. If all else fails, limiting your contact with the person or seeking the counsel of a supervisor may be the solution.

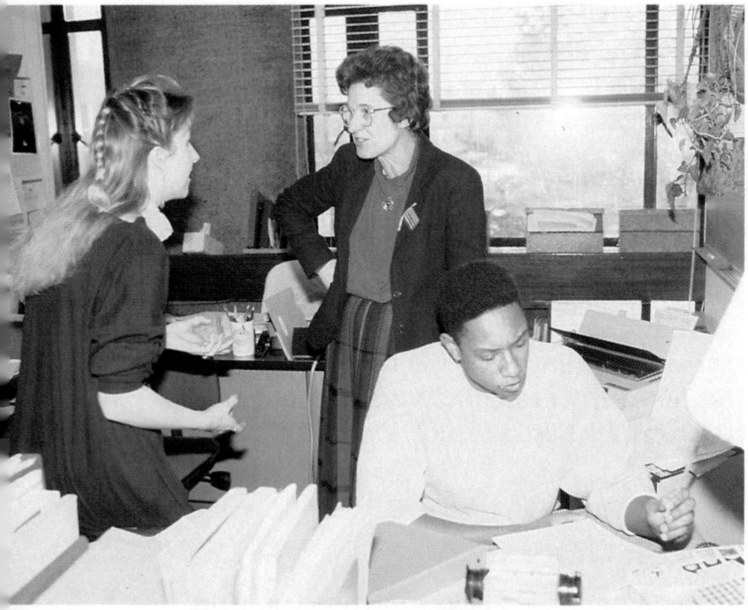

Can you let the petty disputes of others go right over your head?

Photo Focus. Ask students to look at the photo above. Stress is part of any job. Working with a negative person may add more stress. What coping skills could be used to avoid taking on more stress in this situation?

Discussion. Ask students to describe the ideal workplace. What would the work atmosphere be like? Is it realistic for the workplace to be pleasant at all times? Why or why not?

Employee Wanted

Wanted. A person for hard work and rapid promotion. Individual must:

- Find things to be done without help.
- Get to work on time and not imperil the lives of others in an attempt to be first to leave.
- Be neat in appearance.
- Not sulk because of an hour's overtime in emergencies.
- Listen carefully when spoken to and ask only enough questions to insure accuracy in the work.
- Move quickly and make as little noise as possible.
- Look you straight in the eye and tell the truth every time.
- Not pity himself or herself for having to dig in and hustle.
- Be cheerful, courteous to everyone, and determined to make good.

If interested, apply any hour, anywhere, any place, to anyone.

◆◆◆

Challenges on the Job

In your working life you may encounter some challenging situations. Thinking about them ahead of time can help prepare you just in case.

◆ Job Loss

As you read in Chapter 12, losing a job can be very difficult. The most immediate concern usually centers around the need for income. Ninety-seven percent of all workers in the United States are covered by **unemployment compensation**. This is money received by eligible people who have recently become unemployed. Terminated employees should file for unemployment benefits immediately. The waiting period varies from state to state.

More About Job Loss. Unemployment is not easy on any family. Homelessness may result from extended unemployment.

Benefits vary too. In most states you'll receive about half of your last salary, up to a specified maximum. Most states pay benefits for 26 weeks.

Not all terminated employees are eligible for unemployment benefits. If you quit your job without good cause or you were fired for a good cause, you are not eligible. Local employment offices make the final decisions.

◆ Discrimination

When people are treated differently based on some reason other than individual merit, this is **discrimination** (dis-krim-uh-NAY-shun). Because some companies knowingly disobey discrimination laws, the Equal Employment Opportunities Commission (EEOC) enforces anti-wage-discrimination laws. These laws protect a person's right to equal pay for equal work, regardless of race, creed, color, or sex. This means that two employees who work side by side on the same job for the same length of time should make similar wages.

If you ever think you are being discriminated against, first talk to your employer. If you don't get results, contact your union or company grievance committee. Another option is writing to your district or regional EEOC office. It is probably located in the capital city of your state.

Losing a job is hard on the ego. The effects extend to all family members. What steps should people take when faced with this situation?

More About Job Situations. Stereotypes, or common beliefs about groups of people, often affect the way some people expect others to perform on the job. For example, some may think a woman can't or shouldn't perform the same job responsibilities as a man. Others may think that a minority job candidate is less qualified and deserving than another. Ask students to brainstorm: Where do such beliefs come from? Are they true? If not, what can be done to change untrue beliefs?

◆ Sexual Harassment

Just as the law protects you against discrimination, it also protects you against sexual harassment on the job. Sexual harassment occurs when somebody makes unwelcome sexual advances. The person may ask for sexual favors in exchange for a raise or a promotion. The person may touch, pinch, or stroke in a sexual way. Sometimes, the person just makes suggestive comments or tells an obscene joke.

Victims of sexual harassment often feel unable to do anything about it, especially if the harasser is a supervisor. They are afraid that they will lose their job if they say something. They may also feel guilty or confused, thinking that they may have caused the behavior.

An increasing number of victims of sexual harassment have filed complaints in recent years. In so doing, they have raised people's awareness of this workplace problem. As a result, many companies now publish guidelines for acceptable behavior. More importantly, more people have become aware that certain types of behavior are simply not acceptable.

Discussion. Ask students why it is important to find a balance between work and home life. What may happen in a family when one or more of the persons involved spends a disproportionate amount of time at work?

◆◆◆

Balancing Work and Home Life

One of the biggest challenges you will face when you first start working is achieving a balance between your work life and your home life. Work takes up more hours a week than school did. It also takes up more weeks in the year. That means that you will automatically have less time available to spend with friends and family, and less time for yourself.

Some people make the mistake of trying to keep up with all their old activities when they start working. They may sacrifice sleep and relaxation in order to make time for friends, sports, parties, and so on. As a result, they don't do their best at work.

Others make the mistake of devoting all their energies to the job. They think, mistakenly, that they will advance more rapidly if they sacrifice time spent with family and friends. They underestimate the importance of a satisfying social life to good performance on the job.

Achieving a balance between work and home life means finding a way to mesh both worlds so that your life runs smoothly. Often it means making a conscious effort to organize your personal time. With limited time available you will need to make choices about who you will spend your time with and how you will spend that time. Making those choices with the demands of the job in mind will help you find the balance you need.

I CAN ◆◆ Stand By My Convictions

Zak's first job was only part-time, but he was very happy to get it. He needed money to pay tuition at the junior college and hoped to make enough sales to take care of it.

"Before I could actually start going door to door with the books, I was put through a training session. They told me several things to say in order to get inside people's homes. Not one of them had anything to do with the children's books I was selling.

"For my first day on the job, I used the ploy about a survey. I told a lady that I was taking a short survey on products for children and asked if she had time to answer some questions. If she said 'no,' I was equipped with several persuasive comebacks.

"My first job lasted one day. I just couldn't handle the dishonest tactics I had been taught in order to make a sale, and that's exactly what I told my supervisor. Leaving that job felt good. I know what's right, and that's what I'm going to do."

- Why do you think Zak quit the job when he needed the money so much?
- Do you think people would stay on a job like this very long?
- Have you ever been subjected to pressure or unethical practices when you were considering a purchase?
- If you were selling something, how would you get people to buy?

Life Management Skills. Emphasize that students need to make time for physical activity when they start working. They will be moving from an environment where sports teams and facilities are readily available to one where they will have to make their own arrangements.

Discussion. Have students share a situation in which they or someone they know failed to do what they felt was right according to their convictions. What happens when a person fails to stand by his or her convictions? How may this affect self-esteem?

◆◆◆

Professionalism and Ethics

How do you feel about the following situations?

- Marlon uses the company's computer equipment to keep track of records on his bowling league.
- When Karen wanted to take a vacation, she contacted one of her company's suppliers in hopes of using their Florida condo.
- TJ takes credit for the ideas suggested by his employees.
- Shaylyn writes advertising copy for products, making them sound better than they really are.

The principles of conduct that people work by are known as **ethics**. Sometimes companies explain in writing what is right and wrong behavior. Covering every possible situation, however, would be impossible. Sometimes you, as an employee, must act according to what you know is right.

Professionalism is needed in today's world. This means conforming to ethical work standards. Too many people quickly cry "foul" when they are wronged but readily find ways to justify their own unethical actions. They may say: "Everybody does it," or "They owe me this." Eventually, a price is paid as standards go down. Products do not work. Service is poor. People feel cheated, angry, and frustrated.

Fortunately, there is a solution to this problem. It begins with you. When you are on the job and faced with an ethical question, act according to what you know is right. If you are not sure, consult with someone you respect. Ask yourself how your decision will affect others. If you were them, how would you want to be treated? Don't be afraid to stand up for what is right. In the end you will gain the respect of your colleagues, and your professionalism will take you far in your chosen career.

Have you ever tried to put together something you bought only to find that parts were missing or the instructions were incomplete? Well-made products show that the people who manufactured them care about their workmanship. A lack of ethics, on the other hand, can result in the opposite situation.

Activity. Invite a businessperson or employer to talk with the class about the importance of ethics and professionalism in the workplace. Ask the speaker to share examples of ethical and unethical behavior in the workplace. What may be the long-term effect of unethical behavior in the workplace?

Activity. Ask students to report on someone honored for ethics on the job at the present time or sometime in the past. Students should give examples showing how this individual performed job duties in an ethical fashion.

CHAPTER 28

Review

Summarizing the Chapter

- In order to develop your career, you will need to set goals that lead you to the positions you want.
- Job changes are a part of career development. Weigh all pros and cons before you make a move.
- For job success, you need to be positive, dependable, honest, cooperative, and willing to work.
- Most workers are entitled to unemployment compensation if they lose a job.
- The Equal Employment Opportunities Commission (EEOC) handles discrimination cases.
- Your work life affects your home life, and vice versa.
- Ethical behavior in the work world can have beneficial effects for everyone.

Testing Your Memory

1. List two adjustments you will face as you move from the academic to the work world.
2. Explain how setting goals can help with career development.
3. When is a good time to talk to your boss about a raise?
4. Describe what it means to have a positive attitude.
5. List three suggestions for getting along with others on the job.
6. What is unemployment compensation?
7. What action should be taken if you feel you have been discriminated against?
8. Why is it necessary to achieve a balance between work life and home life?
9. What is meant by ethics?
10. What does professionalism mean?

Answers
Testing Your Memory

1. **Any two:** more responsibility, rely on old skills, develop new skills, relate to others in new ways, changed schedule that is more regimented, regular routine.
2. Goals will guide you in developing your career. Small goals that you set and revise along the way can help you reach large goals.
3. At your boss's convenience; in private; when company has reported a profit or finished a peak season.
4. Cheerful and easy to get along with; are thoughtful; have sense of humor; have an enthusiastic spirit; speak well of company and other employees.
5. **Any three:** having an attitude of tolerance; avoiding gossip; remaining neutral when others have disputes; pitching in to help; putting yourself in the other person's place; making an effort to get along; showing understanding.
6. Money received by eligible people who have recently become unemployed.
7. Talk to your employer. If you can't resolve the dispute, contact the union or company grievance committee or write to district or regional EEOC office.
8. Work performance is affected by social demands; a

Thinking Critically

1. Suppose a young married couple both have careers. One is offered a wonderful opportunity in another state. How should they handle this?
2. If you repeatedly saw a fellow employee taking office supplies home at night, what would you do?
3. How will tolerance help you get along with others?
4. If your supervisor often asked you to do things that are unethical, what would you do?

Taking Action

1. Assume that you are starting a new business and looking for employees. List five questions that you could ask in order to help you determine which applicants you want on the job.
2. You and your spouse are both employed. You feel that your spouse does not handle enough home responsibilities. Write a dialog that shows how you reach agreement on this problem.
3. In a group of two or three people, talk about the television programs you have watched recently. Determine two situations that resulted in unethical behavior. Decide what the characters should have done to behave ethically. Share the results of your discussion with the class.

Making Life Choices

Elena has worked for an advertising agency for two years. During that time she has not received a raise or a promotion. Curtis was on the job in a similar position for about a year before moving up in the organization. Elena's friend Juanita, who was hired at the same time, received a pay increase several months ago.

Do you think Elena has any concerns at this time? If so, what are they? What explanation might there be for this situation? What should Elena do?

Using Your Journal

Reread the questions on pages 410 and 411. They focus on the qualities that employers look for. Now use your journal to answer the questions. For those questions to which your answer is "yes," write about how you will convince an employer that you have that quality. For those questions to which your answer is "no," write about actions you can take to develop that quality.

satisfying social life contributes to good performance on the job.
9. Principles of conduct that people work by.
10. Conforming to ethical work standards.

Thinking Critically
1. Answers will vary. Point out that the couple should think about career opportunities for each partner, the possibility of living on one income until the other partner finds work, and the job satisfaction of both persons.
2. Answers will vary.
3. Answers will vary. Point out that tolerance allows a person to be more patient and understanding of others and their opinions.
4. Answers will vary. Emphasize that not following through with what you believe is right causes inner conflict. This may affect self-esteem.

Dennis reaches out in an after-school job.

Dennis

"When I needed some extra cash, I decided to get a part-time job after school. After looking around, I found a job as a sales assistant in a clothing store. I didn't know how the job would turn out, but I thought I would give it a try. Now after two years, it's part of my daily routine. I help customers and other salespeople, write up purchase orders, and track down merchandise in the stock room. I really like learning about how the store operates. I'm even thinking a career in a retail business may be the right goal for me. I enjoy doing what's needed around the store, but the best part is helping customers find exactly what they want."

Ted Rankin

"I have to admit I wasn't sure about hiring a teen for the job, but Dennis has a great attitude. He is friendly and perfectly natural, which makes it easy for him to deal with people. He is also willing to learn. I think if a teen wants to grow in a new job experience, he or she has a good chance of getting ahead. Dennis asks questions, and his genuine curiosity has made me want to teach him more. The more he learns, the more I give him to do. I like the way he gives me advance notice when he is going to be late for some reason. I am flexible because he is responsible. Dennis knows he has a place to work if he goes to college in the area. It's a pleasure to have him around."

Carolyn Hall

"Taking Galen, my ten-year-old, shopping for clothes is an endurance test — for me and the salespeople. He loves to run around — and around — the store, but Dennis knows how to handle him. Last week he took Galen in hand and showed him clothes he might like, and I was able to relax and make sure we got what we needed. Dennis was both kind and patient, and when I left, I told him he'd racked up a new customer."

Susan Kestler

"I can see my son's part-time job has been a positive choice. With this job, Dennis has learned to balance school and work and still have time for a social life. It's not easy, but he manages pretty well most of the time. He's also more talkative at home now, more outgoing. I think that's partly because he is proud of himself. He set a goal — he got a job to give him extra money, and he met his goal by doing the job well. Every once in awhile I run into someone who has been in the store where Dennis works. They always have something nice to say about how pleasant and helpful he was. It makes me feel proud of him."

You can make a difference too.

- Are there some jobs you would rather do than others? What are they?
- How does being open to new experiences make you grow?
- Why do setting and reaching goals raise your self-esteem?
- How can your attitude on the job make a difference in your life as well as the lives of others?

UNIT 9

Will You Be an Informed Consumer?

CHAPTER

CHAPTER

29

Managing Your Money

Chapter Challenge

Resources. Refer to the Teacher's Classroom Resources box and Student Workbook for materials related to this chapter.

Look for These Answers . . .

- How do taxes, Social Security, inflation, and recession affect your income and spending plan?
- Describe the steps for developing a spending plan.
- How do you establish the saving habit?
- How do you manage a checking account?
- What is credit and how does it work?
- When should you borrow to buy something and how should you shop for a loan?
- What are important keys to successful money management for families — and for roommates?
- Where could you go to get help with financial problems?

Look for These Terms . . .

- bankruptcy
- budget
- credit
- down payment
- gross pay
- inflation
- investments
- net pay
- recession
- Social Security
- tax return

"I can't believe that," Becca said. "Are you serious? You really live on only half your income?"

"That's right," replied Emil. "I have plans. I want to make some investments eventually. You know those storage units that people rent? I have a friend in Florida who wants me to go into a partnership with him on a 24-unit building. If all goes well, I should be ready in two more years. I may be skimping today, but someday it will be different."

Becca had heard of saving money before, but this was the first time she had met anyone who put away so much. How could she live on half her income? "Most people couldn't do that," she thought, "but I guess it shows that some type of savings plan can work for anyone — if you have the will and you discipline yourself. I wonder how much I could spare for savings. I'm not sure how I might want to use it yet, but I think it would feel good to have money in savings. Emil is going to use his money to make more money. That's not a bad idea."

Chapter Opener. Have students read the opening scenario. Ask students to respond to the following questions and statements: Why do you think Emil is able to live on half of his income? What are the benefits of developing the saving habit? What are your reactions to not having money in savings? Brainstorm some ways in which people can determine how much money to save each month.

More About Managing Your Money. People have strong emotions about money. These influence their spending habits. Some people use money to fill emotional needs. Ask students to think about what money means to them. Have them list and explain five feelings they might have if they were rich. How would they feel if they had no money?

Discussion. Have students explore their feelings about taxes. Ask them to list the benefits and services paid by taxes. What would their lives be like without taxes?

The Money You Earn

Before you can plan for spending and saving, you must think about your income. Notice that the money you earn, **gross pay**, is not the same as money you take home, **net pay**. This is because federal, state, and Social Security taxes are taken out of your pay before you receive your check. Factors such as inflation and recession also affect net earnings.

Taxes

Taxation has been with us since early times. In general, services provided by the government are paid for by taxes. When Congress passed the Sixteenth Amendment to the Constitution in 1913, the income tax became a regular part of American life.

Personal income taxes are collected on the pay-as-you-go system. Every employer is required to subtract income tax from each employee's paycheck. You must fill out a withholding form that determines how much is to be taken out. This tax goes directly to the government. On every April 15 each employee must file a **tax return**, showing the income for the year and the tax due on that amount.

When Jolene filed her income tax return, she figured out how much she owed by locating her income on an Internal Revenue Service (IRS) tax table. Since the money withheld over the year totaled more than she owed, Jolene received a tax refund from the government. When she filed last year, the amount withheld did not cover what she owed, so she had to pay the difference.

◆ Social Security

With **Social Security**, our nation provides some continuing income for retirement or disability. These payments are not intended to replace all lost earnings at such times.

The way Social Security functions is simple. During working years, employees, their employers, and self-employed people pay Social Security taxes. A percentage of your pay is deducted each payday. Your employer matches your payment and sends the combined amount to the IRS.

When workers reach retirement age or become disabled, the benefits paid are figured by a specific formula. When a worker dies, survivor benefits are paid to the spouse and children under eighteen years of age. Each person's benefit rate is based entirely on the earnings covered by Social Security. Those who paid in the most in their working lifetime will receive larger benefits.

◆ Inflation

In the United States today, some families might spend $500 per week just to maintain a modest standard of living. A similar family could live on $500 per year in 1893. When your dollar will not buy as much as it used to, this is **inflation.** To put it simply, inflation increases the cost of most goods and services. Unless your income increases in proportion, you may have difficulty with the budget.

Many people who have retired have some income from Social Security. Unfortunately, Social Security is not intended to provide for all their needs, and they may have little else to live on.

How does inflation affect the budget? Assume the annual inflation rate is 5 percent. An item that costs $100 this year will cost $105 next year. In ten years with inflation at 5 percent, that same item would cost $163. A salary at $15,000 this year would need to be at $24,400 in ten years just to keep even. Even if a raise occurs, federal, state, and Social Security taxes take a portion of that raise. Careful budget adjustments need to be made if purchasing power is to be maintained.

◆ Recession

The effects of a **recession**, also called deflation, are the opposite of inflation. Unemployment increases as productivity and prices go

Life Management Skills. Familiarize students with state and federal tax forms. Offer examples of different income tax rates. Invite an income tax accountant to explain the basics of filing yearly taxes to your students.

Activity. Have students choose a favorite product and gather ads from newspapers or magazines to determine the retail price increase over the last five years. What percentage is the increase? How does it compare to the local yearly inflation rate?

down. Some prices and incomes go down more than others. The best personal safeguard against money problems is never to overextend your use of credit.

◆◆◆

Using Your Management Skills

If you are like many American teenagers today, the income you have is spent on entertainment, hobbies, snacks, cosmetics, and clothing. With your basic necessities provided, you may be free to spend as you please on wants rather than needs. Once you are on your own, however, you will have many other expenses. A place to live, furniture, insurance, food, and clothing will be your responsibility.

As you learn to manage money, thinking about your real needs first is best. After the essentials are met, then dream about getting the extras. By using your management skills to set up a budget and a savings plan, you will take a major step toward achieving your goals.

Teens do not usually manage money for basic needs. They are more likely to handle money that is spent on entertainment, hobbies, snacks, cosmetics, and clothing.

Discussion. Ask students if money management is more important for someone with a high income or low income. *(People at all income levels need to learn good money management.)*

◆◆◆

Making a Spending Plan

A **budget** is a plan for managing your money. It compares your income with how much you spend. It also sets aside funds for future goals. Some people cringe when they think of budgeting, often confusing it with penny-pinching. A well-planned budget, however, can give clear direction and a certain amount of freedom in financial situations.

There are four basic steps in planning a budget:

1. Determine your financial goals for the next five years. Include plans for major purchases and savings.
2. Write down expected income for the year. Use the take-home pay amount, not the salary before deductions.
3. Write down all "fixed" expenses to be paid each month. Include rent or house payment, insurance premiums, telephone, loan payments, utilities, and savings. Add all these expenses. Subtract the total from the amount of income in Step 2 above.

Problem Solving. Ask students to keep a record of every expense for one week. Share and evaluate examples through class discussion. Ask students how their expenditures fit into their personal budget. Have students brainstorm ways to manage money better.

Discussion. Ask students to discuss how living with a well-planned budget can allow a certain amount of financial freedom.

4. List all expenses that change every month. These expenses may include food, clothing, recreation, and medical care. Set aside some money to cover costs that you don't expect. Total these expenses. Compare them with the balance from Step 3. If the costs in Step 4 equal more than this amount, you have two choices. You can either cut your spending or you can figure out a way to make more money. To keep your budget working you will need to update it whenever your income or your expenses change.

Writing a budget is a good start toward better money management. Living with the spending plan you set up may be difficult at first but satisfying once you adjust to it. You will know how much you can spend each week, and you will gradually see your savings build up.

The Saving Habit

Most people need to save money in order to reach future goals or deal with unexpected emergencies. Experts generally suggest putting aside a set amount from each paycheck.

Savings Options

When you start saving, you will need to decide what kind of savings plan is best for you. Some of the options available to you are listed below.

Savings Accounts

With a savings account at a bank you can make deposits and withdrawals at any time. The bank pays you interest for the use of the money in the account. Interest rates are generally quite low.

I CAN ◆◆ Manage My Money

When Clarice graduated from high school and started working, she felt rich.

"I was earning my own money and could finally buy the things I really wanted. With my first check, I bought designer jeans and a new sweater. I went out to eat with my friends and enjoyed all the latest movies.

"I soon realized that I'd like to rent an apartment of my own, buy a car, and maybe take a vacation, but I didn't have money for these things. Saving some money for the future became a priority.

"Keeping track of all expenses for a few months proved to be very surprising. I was spending a lot of money on unnecessary things. I set up a budget and actually stuck to it! I still enjoy spending, but now I'm also saving for my future."

- Why do you think Clarice spent so much money right after getting her first job?
- Will budgeting allow Clarice to obtain everything on her list of wants?
- What are your goals for this month? Next year? Five years from now? Fifteen years from now?
- How can you manage your money in order to achieve your goals?

More About Interest on Savings. Two kinds of interest are available on savings accounts. They include simple and compound interest. Simple interest is paid only on the principal. Compound interest is paid on the principal plus any simple interest accumulated on the principal. Interest = principal x rate x time (i = prt).

Problem Solving. Have students respond to the following problem: George borrowed $600 from the bank to buy a CD player. He agreed to repay the loan in 2 years at an interest rate of 11%. How much interest will George have to pay? (i = prt; 1 = 600 x 0.11 x 2; 1 = 132; George will pay $132.00 in interest.)

Certificates of Deposit

Once you have set aside money for emergencies, you may want to consider a longer-term savings plan. Certificates of deposit are available for set periods of time at a guaranteed interest rate. In general, the longer the time period, the higher the rate of interest. Withdrawing money early results in a penalty.

Money Market Accounts

A money market account is different from a savings account in that it does not have a set interest rate. Rather, the interest rate changes daily to reflect rates paid on investments. Depending on the type of account, it may or may not be insured by the government.

Savings Bonds

When you buy a savings bond, you earn interest over a period of time. Bonds are issued in various denominations and are guaranteed by the government.

A checking account offers the conveniences of not having to carry as much cash with you and the ability to pay bills easily through the mail.

Managing a Checking Account

A checking account allows you to pay bills easily without carrying around much cash. It also provides a record of your spending. Many kinds of accounts are available today. When you get ready to open an account, compare several banking services to find the plan best suited to your needs.

When writing a check, fill in the date, the name of the person or business receiving the money, and the amount to be paid. Then sign the check. When the bank pays the check, the amount of money in your checking account will be reduced.

At regular intervals, bank statements are sent that show any activity in the account. You must then check your records against those of the bank to be sure you agree. This is called reconciling the checkbook register with the bank statement. Doing this regularly will help prevent overdrafts, writing checks that are not covered by money in the account.

Bad checks are said to "bounce." This means the person who writes the check does not have enough money in the account to cover it. Writing bad checks is illegal.

Today, 24-hour banking is available in many places through Automated Teller Machines (ATMs). Money can be deposited or withdrawn any time of the day or night.

Joint Checking and Savings Accounts

Checking and savings accounts can be opened either individually or jointly. If the account has one name on it, only that person can write checks or make withdrawals from the account. If the account is a joint account, both people named on the account may make

Life Management Skills. Have students visit local banks and gather information about opening checking and savings accounts. What are the differences in various checking and savings plans? What benefit may there be in "bank shopping"?

Activity. Prepare a sample bank statement and checkbook register. You may want to ask a local bank for a sample copy. Make copies for each student. Have students practice reconciling the checkbook register with the bank statement.

transactions. Single people may want to consider having a trusted individual also named on their account. In this way, someone will have access to the money in emergencies.

◆◆◆

Making Investments

Money available for long-term saving can also be used to invest in stocks, bonds, and mutual funds. **Investments** like these can provide a higher return on your money than you would get from a savings account. When considering investments, however, do your homework. Look at the risks involved. Are you willing to lose some of your money for a chance at a greater return? Discussing investment opportunities with a reputable financial counselor may help you make the right decision.

◆◆◆

Understanding Credit

"Credit has done a thousand times more to enrich mankind than all the gold mines in the world," noted the famous orator Daniel Webster. **Credit** may be defined as the current use of future income. It lets you spend money now that you will earn later.

When used wisely, credit can be an important financial tool. It can allow you to invest in your education or buy a house or a car. At the same time, when credit is not used wisely, it can cause financial problems and stress. Failure to keep up the payments may result in repossession of purchased items.

Before buying something on credit, ask yourself if the payments fit into the budget. Will something needed have to be done without in order to pay the bill? Also, consider the cost of credit. Would it be better to pay cash or postpone the purchase?

Discussion. Have students brainstorm wise and unwise uses of credit. Then ask: What are some reasons why people have credit problems? What should you think about before making a credit purchase?

A Slice of Life

Consider Mark's plight. A lab technician for four years after graduating from high school, he found himself increasingly in debt to stereo shops, clothing stores, and department stores. He spent his salary as soon as he received it. His credit cards took him deeper into debt.

He was engaged to be married, but his future wife gave him an ultimatum: All accounts, totaling more than $2,200, had to be paid before she would agree to a wedding date.

Unable to get out of debt on his own, Mark turned his paychecks over to his father, who let him have only enough for lunch, transportation, and incidental expenses. The rest of the salary was used to pay old debts. Charge accounts were cut off.

It was nearly a year before the wedding date could be set, but Mark started out his married life with a new set of values, a realistic budget, and clear goals.

Thinking It Through

- Can you see how Mark could get into debt so quickly and so easily? What could he have done to prevent this from happening?
- What are some signs that could warn you that you're using your credit cards too often?
- If you find yourself over your head in debt, what steps can you take to help stretch your dollars and pay your bills?

Discussion. Point out to students that some people do not use credit. Ask them to give advantages and disadvantages for this.

◆ Buying with Credit

Buying items on credit can be done in several ways. The most common methods include using credit cards and installment loans. Both are a consumer convenience allowing purchases without much cash.

Credit Cards

The credit card is most commonly used to buy goods and services on credit. Many cards are available to consumers. All-purpose cards, such as Mastercard, Visa, and American Express, can be used at most places of business around the world. Some places of business offer their own credit cards and only accept those for credit purchases.

Credit card companies may offer two different plans for payment. Both types of payment plans will have credit limits based on ability to pay.

- Regular charge accounts require payment of the full amount charged within thirty days of billing.
- Revolving charge accounts allow the consumer to pay the bill in full or pay a portion of the bill. If only a portion of the bill is paid, a service charge is added to the unpaid balance.

Credit cards can be used to make many purchases. During the month, each purchase is added to your account for future payment. Why do you think many people get into financial trouble with credit cards?

More About Managing Money. One way to gain credit is with a student credit card issued in his or her name. A parent co-signs and guarantees payment. Have students share ideas about this plan. Should credit cards be issued to students? Why or why not? Do your students have credit cards? How do they manage them?

Installment Loans

Installment loans allow consumers to purchase large items like cars and major home appliances. The installment credit contract states the purchase price, the amount of interest to be paid, the monthly payment, and the length of the agreement.

As with all purchases, you need to consider how the installment loan purchase fits into the budget. Financial experts advise keeping installment payments at or below 20 percent of your net annual income. Consider the cost of credit carefully. Compare lending rates and ask to have the true interest rate explained in terms of dollars and cents.

Some purchases, such as a car, cannot be easily made without credit.

Commercial banks, industrial banks, savings and loan associations, small loan companies, credit unions, and some insurance companies offer loan services.

◆ Mortgages

In a mortgage contract, a person borrows money and offers property as security. Real estate is most commonly offered as security. If the borrower does not pay back the money, the lender may take the property.

Mortgage loans are made by banks, savings and loan associations, mortgage companies, and individuals. The borrowers provide a **down payment**, which is a percentage of the full value of the property. The lenders provide the remainder of the cost. This sum is called the principal. The borrower pays interest for using the money. The monthly payment covers part of the principal and part of the interest.

SIDELIGHT

Checking Your Own Credit

If you are ever turned down for credit and you don't understand why, ask. Sometimes credit bureau files can be inaccurate or out of date. Most credit bureaus are able to prevent this from happening, but if it does, you should call them to straighten out any problem. The Fair Credit Reporting Act gives you the right to do this.

◆◆◆

Discussion. Ask students to explain what people should do when they lose a credit card.

◆ Establishing Credit

When a person applies for credit, a credit check usually takes place. Here is how it works.

Vince applied for a credit account at Stanford's Department Store. He filled out an application that asked about employment, the size of his family, stores where he charges or buys on installment, and banks where he has accounts. It also asked if he rents or owns a home. Before extending credit to Vince, the store called the credit bureau to get a report on what Vince owes to other businesses and how he pays his accounts.

Based on the report they received from the bureau, Stanford's decided to extend credit to Vince. They felt that his credit rating was quite good. That is, he has a steady job, pays all his bills on time, and has no financial problems. Sometimes items of public record are contained in a file, such as a notice of court action against a borrower. A wage assignment, taking money from an individual's paycheck for payment of debts, is an example. There was nothing like this in Vince's file.

Sometime in the months ahead the credit bureau will probably call Stanford's Department Store to see whether or not credit was extended to Vince and how well he is handling that account. This information will be added to the file and be part of the next report when Vince applies for credit with another business.

Vince's good credit rating is important to him. By maintaining a good rating, he should be able to get credit whenever needed.

Problem Solving. Explain to students that sometimes people have difficulty obtaining credit when a situation arises that has given them a bad credit rating (bankruptcy due to unemployment, etc.). Have students investigate how people can go about clearing up problems with their credit rating. You may wish to invite someone from the credit bureau to talk to the students.

◆◆◆
Sharing a Household and Expenses

For married couples financial decisions need to be made as a team. Communication is a key to successful money management, whether the household has one or two incomes. No budget will work if one or the other partner decides to go it alone.

To reach a satisfactory financial arrangement, couples may have to compromise on things they feel strongly about. Resolving money conflicts isn't always easy, but solutions are usually possible. In two-income families, the partners may decide to pool their money and set aside certain amounts each payday for savings and paying bills. As an alternative, they may keep their incomes separate and assign specific expenses to each. Two-income families tend to spend more money than one-income families. Adjusting the budget may be necessary to cover additional expenses for such items as convenience foods, clothing for work, transportation, and perhaps child care.

As with married couples, any people who share a household need to communicate well. Some may choose joint bank accounts for household expenses, and others keep separate accounts and agree to divide food and miscellaneous expenses. Writing down the division of responsibilities toward household expenses is one way of avoiding conflict. When making joint purchases, such as furniture, decide ahead of time who will own the items or what the buy-out cost will be if one person moves away from the household. This way, everyone knows what was discussed and agreed to.

◆◆◆
Solving Money Problems

Even with careful planning, emergencies may keep you from making payments on an account . When Doreen could not make payments on her new CD player, the lender was about to repossess it. Doreen could have lost the player and what she had already paid.

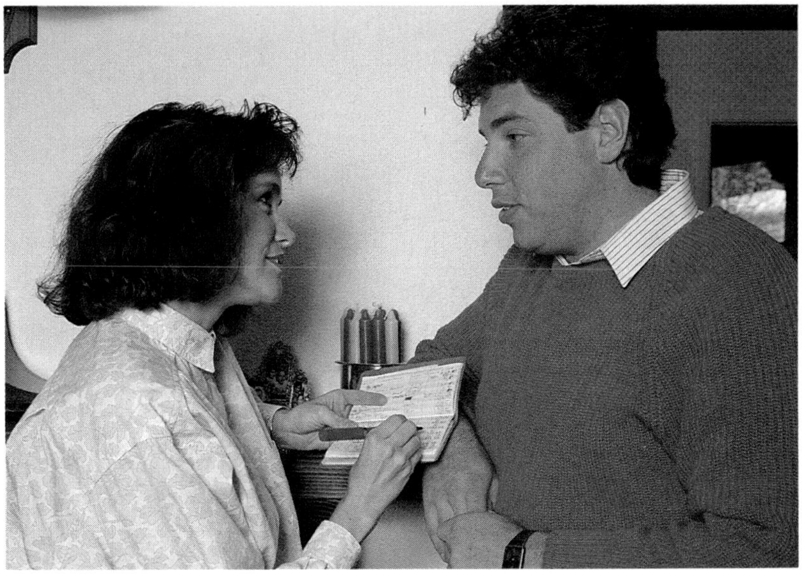

Money management decisions need to be shared and made carefully. What might eventually happen if one partner is excluded from this process?

Work and Family. Emphasize to students that many families with working parents have additional wage earners. According to the U.S. Bureau of Labor Statistics, over 50 percent of U.S. teens now work part-time. Why do so many teens work today? Ask how many students have paid jobs. Why do they work? What is their reaction to teens sharing household expenses? What are some ways that teens can contribute to household expenses?

Photo Focus. Have students discuss the role communication plays in managing household expenses.

After explaining her problem to the lender, however, she was able to work out a new payment method. Since she had a good credit rating, the creditor was willing to help her find a way to solve the problem.

When financial problems occur, people may need outside help. Few, however, know about the services available to them.

Consumer credit counseling services, which are open to everyone, help families get out of debt. Consultation takes only a couple of hours. After filling out forms regarding income and expenses, a counselor looks for ways to get more for the dollar. If a stack of unpaid bills is the first worry, a counselor will cut expenses to the minimum so these can be handled. The counseling office may get a small fee for this service.

Consult an attorney when considering any major legal financial commitment. This may eliminate problems in the long run.

◆ Bankruptcy

The last step to take in solving debt problems is **bankruptcy.** In straight bankruptcy, Chapter 7 of the current law, the court sells your property and pays creditors part of the amount due them. Chapter 13 of the law outlines how to repay debts in installments. This wage-earner plan protects an individual's salary and property from creditors while providing time to pay back debts gradually. Both bankruptcy plans tend to carry a stigma and may make it difficult to get credit when needed in the future.

Credit counseling services are available to those who need help solving money problems.

Activity. Divide students into pairs. Provide each pair with a situation card similar to the example of Doreen above. One teen — the consumer — should try to work out a new payment method with the partner — a lender, merchant, or credit card officer. The situation and purchases may vary. Have students act out their situation for the class. Ask the rest of the class to critique each pair.

Discussion. Have students discuss reasons for using bankruptcy only as a last resort in solving financial problems.

When families do not have enough money, the welfare office can provide money for basic needs.

Not Enough Money

When a family or individual has little or no money and needs help right away, a call to the welfare office usually brings immediate assistance. The following help is available:

- Food Stamps help families with low incomes buy the food they need.
- Aid to Families With Dependent Children (AFDC) provides a monthly payment for the basic needs of children and their families. AFDC-Emergency Assistance is a source of financial help in emergencies.
- General Assistance (GA) provides financial aid to persons who are not eligible for other financial assistance programs and who lack the income needed for the basics of life.

Other programs provide funds for medical needs or heating fuel, food, and shelter in emergency situations.

Federal, state, and local assistance organizations have representatives in most communities. Information about community services should be available at the nearest courthouse.

Activity. Invite a social worker or a financial assistance case worker to talk with the class about financial help available to families in your community. Ask the speaker to discuss ways in which families are helped to manage their finances as well as obtain financial assistance.

CHAPTER 29

Review

Answer
Testing Your Memory

1. Tax refunds are received when amount of tax withheld totals more than what is owed. When taxes are owed, not enough was withheld during the year.
2. During inflation, the dollar does not buy what it once did. If income doesn't increase with rate of inflation, budgets are difficult to meet. Recession is the opposite of inflation — prices and incomes go down.
3. Budgets help manage money. Ways of developing a budget are outlined on pages 425-426.
4. **Any two for fixed:** rent, mortgage, insurance, loan payments, utilities, and savings. **Any two for expenses that change:** food, clothing, recreation, medical care.
5. Advantages of checking accounts: pay bills easily without cash; record of spending. A check "bounces" when the funds in the account do not cover the check.
6. Does the payment fit into the budget; what is cost of credit; is it better to pay cash or delay the purchase?
7. Any two: credit cards, installment loans, mortgages. See pages 429-430 for details.
8. Credit ratings tell what a person owes in debt and how payments are made.

Summarizing the Chapter

- Your income is affected by taxes, Social Security, inflation, and recession.
- By using your management skills you'll take a major step toward achieving your goals.
- Credit is the present use of future income. It can allow you to invest in your education or buy a house or a car. Unwise use causes financial problems.
- The cost of credit varies widely, so it's important to compare lending rates.
- A good credit rating is important. The credit bureau keeps an up-to-date record of how you pay accounts.
- Credit counseling services are available to people who need help in stretching their dollars. Community and welfare programs can aid those who have little or no money and need help right away.

Testing Your Memory

1. Explain why some people must pay income tax every year, yet others get a refund.
2. Explain the difference between inflation and recession. How do each affect your income?
3. What is the purpose of a budget? How can one be developed?
4. Give two examples of "fixed" expenses and two examples of expenses that change from month to month.
5. What are the advantages of a checking account? What does it mean when a check "bounces"?
6. Before you decide to buy something on credit, what should you ask yourself?
7. Describe two methods of buying on credit.

8. What is a credit rating? Why is it important?
9. How can people who share a household avoid differences over money?
10. What can people who are having problems with managing their money do?

Thinking Critically

1. What might happen to someone who planned on income only from Social Security during the retirement years?
2. Why is it important to develop a saving habit? List some ideas on how you can save for your long-range goals.
3. Name one advantage and one disadvantage of credit. List two purchases and services you might charge, two you might pay cash for, and two that you would postpone buying until you have the money.
4. David and Brenna are planning marriage. They are both employed and not sure how to manage the two incomes. What would you suggest?

Taking Action

1. Figure out what you would need to spend on food, utilities, and basic household expenses if you were to move into an apartment of your own. Ask a parent to help you prepare your numbers.
2. Look at newspaper advertisements from credit card companies. Prepare a comparison chart showing the interest rates charged and the annual fees. Share your findings with the class and with adults in your family.

Making Life Choices

You have just graduated from high school, have landed your first full-time job, and have decided to join three friends in renting a single-family house as roommates. Look through the classified section of the newspaper to find a house to rent. Estimate the additional costs of utilities, furnishings, and food. Divide the money into equal shares.

How much money would you be responsible for each month? How would this fit into your overall budget and long-range goals? What else should be discussed before moving in?

Using Your Journal

Managing your money means knowing what you can afford and controlling what you spend. Start building your money management skills by keeping track of everything you buy over the next few weeks. Keep a list in your journal, then examine the list. Identify the items you really needed, and those you could have done without. Doing this will raise your consciousness about your spending habits.

With a good credit rating, credit should be available when needed.

9. Communicate. Write a list of responsibilities toward household expenses. With joint purchases, decide who will own the items or what buy-out cost will be.
10. Call the lender and try to work out new payment schedule. Consult a consumer credit counseling service.

Thinking Critically

1. They may not have money to meet basic needs.
2. Savings allows freedom to make purchases; allows financial backup when a crisis occurs. Answers will vary.
3. Answers will vary.
4. Answers will vary but may include consulting a financial planner or a bank representative.

CHAPTER 30

Buying Know-How

Chapter Challenge

Resources. Refer to the Teacher's Classroom Resources box and Student Workbook for materials related to this chapter.

Look for These Answers...

- How do your personal values and goals influence what you will buy?
- What are your rights and responsibilities as a consumer?
- What influence does advertising have on buying?
- What precautions should you take when deciding where to shop and who to buy from?
- How do labels and warranties help the consumer?
- What steps can you follow that will help you make smart purchases?
- How do you complain effectively if something you bought does not work?

Look for These Terms...

- comparison shopping
- consumer
- high-pressure sales tactics
- impulse buying
- warranty

The man at the door was well dressed and clean cut. He smiled at Amber and spoke in a friendly manner, making her feel quite comfortable with him.

"Would you like to have your house number painted on the curb?" he asked. "It's really helpful when people are trying to find your home. The cost is $5, and my crew will be here to do the painting next month."

"Why not?" Amber said. "Just a second. I'll get my purse."

As she stepped away to reach for her purse, Amber had a thought. "This is October. These people are coming back to paint the curb in November? There could be snow on the ground. Doesn't it make more sense to pay them after the job is done?"

Instead, Amber turned back to the stranger. "I've changed my mind," she said. "I don't believe we need to have this done."

It was several weeks later when Amber heard a news report that caught her attention. People were complaining about paying someone to have house numbers painted on their curbs, but the job was never done. "Umm hmm," Amber thought. "My instincts were right. That man almost got my $5 too."

Even though the dollar amount was not high, Amber was glad that she was not taken in by this con artist. "He was so nice," she thought. "People lose a lot more than $5 all the time, and I can see how easily it happens."

Chapter Opener. Have students read the opening scenario. Ask them to respond to the following questions: What are some other examples of situations in which unsuspecting people have lost money to con artists? How should you respond to someone who comes to the door offering services for payment? Did Amber handle this situation in the best possible way? Why or why not? What kinds of questions should you ask of people who are selling something door to door?

You Need To Know

Everyone is a **consumer**, a person who uses goods and services to satisfy individual needs. Knowing how to be a skillful consumer today is not an easy task. Every day consumers are faced with making decisions that require knowledge, good sense, and, as in Amber's situation, a little wariness. This is more important today than it has ever been.

Your Values and Goals

When making decisions about spending, your choices are based on several concerns, including personal values and goals. Values help you choose what is most important to you. Goals provide motivation for an end result. You may spend your money on a new car, yet your friend takes a "dream" vacation. You may save your money for education, while a friend buys furniture for an apartment. One person might look for prestige, the other at practicality. One might choose the latest style, while another chooses lasting quality. As you make spending decisions, let your values and goals be your guide. Combined with consumer awareness, they will serve you well.

◆◆◆

Consumer Rights and Responsibilities

In order to get the most from your buying dollar, become aware of your rights as a consumer. In 1962, President John F. Kennedy helped launch the consumer movement by outlining four basic rights:

- **The Right To Safety.** Products should not be hazardous to life or health.
- **The Right To Be Informed.** Accurate information about products should be available so all can make wise choices.
- **The Right To Choose.** A selection of products and services should be available at fair prices.
- **The Right To Be Heard.** Consumer interests are important. Action may be taken if products are not safe, if they are of poor quality, or if a consumer has been a victim of fraud.

Consumer responsibilities accompany consumer rights. You will read more about some of the following responsibilities later in the chapter:

- Become informed about products and services so that you make wise choices.
- Read labels and follow manufacturers' directions on how to use and care for products that you buy.
- Follow safety standards in using a product.
- Save sales receipts, labels, and guarantees. If an item needs to be returned, the necessary records will be available.
- Identify the quality of the product and file a complaint if the product is unsatisfactory.
- Deal with reliable businesses.
- Report any unfair and illegal practices to the proper authorities.

◆◆◆

Understanding Advertising

The competition for your attention in the marketplace is intense. Companies use different media approaches for advertising their products. These methods range from brightly colored newspaper ads to 30-minute television "info-mercials." Some cable television networks sell products 24 hours per day. Magazines, radio commercials, and even billboards tempt consumers to buy. Whatever the medium used for advertising, the goal is always the same. Companies want to sell products, and advertising works!

Advertisements surround us. How often do you think you are influenced by advertising without even realizing it?

Life Management Skills. Have students list five "wishes" for short-term financial goals, such as a clothing item, stereo, or vacation. Have them brainstorm steps they could take to reach one goal. Have them keep a chart of any progress made toward the goal during the semester.

Activity. Ask students to choose and report on one concrete result of President Kennedy's "consumer bill of rights," such as a safety law, new product label, or consumer action that has effected change. Are consumer rights more strongly protected today? Why or why not?

Good ads provide information on products and give important facts to help with buying decisions. In today's world, most advertising claims are truthful. A few, however, are designed to confuse the consumer. It is the consumer's job to recognize the difference in true and false advertising.

When looking at ads, identify the facts first. Look for price, color, size, contents, and quality. Watch for half-truths and vague promises. If the product is guaranteed, who guarantees it, what is it guaranteed against, and for how long? A good store will be specific about the guarantee.

If an ad claims something is "25 cents off," ask "off what?" Is an "all-new" product really new? If an item is free, are you required to buy another item to receive it? Is a sale really a sale, or are the regular prices so high that the sale prices aren't really a bargain?

Some ads tempt people to buy unneeded or unaffordable items. Suppose Long-Legs Lindley, the "famous basketball player," promotes a certain basketball shoe. Soon every thirteen-year-old wants to wear that brand. After all, they work for Long-Legs! What happens when Petula Perfection, the "famous movie beauty" advertises her line of makeup? Using it will make women look flawless, just like Petula. Right? Wrong! Many ads appeal to your emotions, your desire for success or stature. Hardly anyone can play ball like Long-Legs. Look around you. Does anyone look as perfect as Petula? Advertisements can subtly raise false hopes and dreams that the products will not satisfy. Be wary about spending your money this way.

Most companies try to make sure that their ads provide accurate, easily understood information. Let the advertiser know if you have a problem with an ad. Most companies appreciate constructive consumer criticism and strive hard to correct any misunderstandings.

A Slice of Life

Sixteen-year-old Tracy saw an ad for a half-price jeans sale. The jeans were an expensive brand, but she had been saving her money. At half-price, they would be a real bargain. Eagerly, she bicycled to the store after school.

Asking for the advertised brand, Tracy was told the jeans had not arrived in time for the sale. A helpful clerk suggested another expensive brand: "We're selling lots of these," she said, "but not on sale." Tracy wasn't sure she liked the cut or fit, but two smiling salespeople assured her the jeans looked just great. An expensive pink shirt was added to complete the outfit. It brought more compliments from the clerks.

Tracy spent three times what she had planned. When trying her purchases on again at home, she wasn't sure she liked them at all.

Thinking It Through

- Why do you think Tracy made the purchases that she did?
- Have you ever heard of "bait and switch" advertising? Does the situation described above fall into this category? Why?
- What steps should Tracy take now?

Problem Solving. Ask students to choose a recent example of consumer fraud, local or national, and write a short report. Have them examine resources, such as newspapers, magazines, and TV programs, to describe and evaluate the scheme. Have students offer ideas for avoiding consumer fraud.

Activity. Ask students to watch four or five commercials on television at various times during the day. Ask them to evaluate the commercials for the following: factual information about the product; prices; half-truths; special claims; audience the commercial is directed at. How do these commercials affect the desire to buy products? Do commercials take advantage of consumers? Is all advertising ethical?

Activity. Divide students into teams and have them create an ad. Their goal is to create an irresistible pitch for a healthful food or consumer product. They can write a magazine ad, tape record a radio commercial, or videotape a TV sport. Share results in class. Have the students evaluate the ads for effectiveness.

Environmental Awareness

In recent years consumers have become increasingly aware of the need to protect the environment and to use resources carefully. People are shopping with the environment in mind.

You can join this movement by looking for items that will not damage the environment. Choose products that are reusable rather than disposable. Seek out packaging that you can recycle or that is made from recycled materials. Don't buy products that are overpackaged. Look for energy efficiency when buying appliances.

Some manufacturers have responded to this environmental awareness by redesigning their products. Others have introduced new product lines that are "environment-friendly." When buying such products read the small print carefully. Make sure that you understand what the labels say.

Consumer Magazines

Advertisements and product labels tell you what the manufacturer wants you to know. They don't necessarily give you all the facts you need. That's where the consumer magazines can help.

Consumer magazines provide unbiased comparisons of similar products. They rate the products in terms of price, quality, durability, and other factors that a consumer needs to know about. The ratings enable you to make direct comparisons and to choose the product that's right for you, given your particular needs and circumstances.

You can generally find back issues of the main consumer magazines in your local library. You'll find them particularly helpful when you need to choose expensive or complicated items such as new speakers or a used car.

Before making any major purchasing decision, check the consumer magazines and find out how the different brands compare.

Discussion. Have students identify three places they shop for consumer products in the community. Why do they like each store? What is the store's reputation? Have them report on the store's special services and refund policies.

Work and Family. Have students brainstorm ways in which families determine how and when to shop. Is this different for families with two workers? For singles? How?

◆◆◆

Where Will You Shop?

Once you've decided what to buy, you need to decide where to buy it. The modern marketplace is full of places that compete for your purchasing dollar. Department stores, discount stores, supermarkets, specialty stores, convenience stores, factory outlets, and warehouse clubs all have appealing merchandise.

Ordering products through catalogs, by mail, over the telephone, or from door-to-door salespeople offers additional convenience to consumers. Some companies are even using computers to dial telephone numbers at random in selling products to consumers!

When deciding where to make a purchase, deal only with businesses that truly want you as a customer and stand behind everything they sell. Find out about the refund policy of the store. Check to see if special services, such as alterations on clothing or delivery of appliances, are available. When ordering from catalogs or by mail, read item descriptions carefully to be sure you are getting what you want. Before buying from an unfamiliar business, check out a company's reputation, especially if the purchase is to be made from a door-to-door salesman or over the phone. The Better Business Bureau, Chamber of Commerce, or local consumer protection agency can supply helpful information to wise consumers.

Before ordering goods from a catalog, read the item description carefully and make sure you understand the company's policies for returns and exchanges.

Activity. Have students bring in catalogs from home and share their experiences dealing with different catalog companies. Compare shipping and handling costs, return policies, and other factors that affect the cost of shopping by catalog.

◆◆◆

Resisting Pressure and Gimmicks

Be as careful about who you buy from as where you buy. Smart shoppers learn to resist **high-pressure sales tactics** wherever they are encountered. These are techniques that are used to convince people to buy. What would you think if a salesperson made these remarks to you?

- "This is the last chance you will have to buy at a price this low."
- "You won't find a range that has any more features on it than this one. It will do everything for you."
- "Several of your neighbors have purchased this water purification system. Mrs. Wittry down the street suggested your name to us."
- "This is the last one we have. It's hard telling when we will get in some more."

Sales gimmicks, such as "free" prizes, real estate bargains, and unbelievably low prices, are designed to catch the consumers' attention. If a deal is just too good to be true, chances are it will be a poor purchase.

Harlan ordered a small keyring flashlight for the "low, low price of $2.95 and a money-back guarantee." When the flashlight stopped working after two weeks, he threw it away, figuring that it wasn't worth his time to return it for a refund. Do sellers know that some people will not take the time to go after a small refund? Unfortunately, the answer is "yes," and some will take advantage of this.

◆◆◆

Reading Labels and Warranties

Before buying any product, read the label for instructions as well as use and care of the product. A garment that requires special costly cleaning techniques, for example, will cost you additional money beyond the purchase price. This may affect your buying decision.

The **warranty** is a legal statement of rights and responsibilities agreed to by the consumer and store or manufacturer when the product is purchased. Everything purchased carries an implied warranty, an unwritten protection that the item will operate as it is supposed to. A microwave oven must heat food; a VCR must record television programs and play tapes; a clock must tell time. If the item doesn't work, the seller must repair it, replace it, or give a refund.

Products may also carry full or limited written warranties. A full warranty provides the most protection. It states that the seller will repair, without charge, an item that doesn't work or give the buyer a choice between a refund or a replacement. A full warranty generally has a time limit, such as 90 days to one year.

Limited warranties often exclude certain parts of a product from coverage or require the buyer to pay some costs. Seller responsibilities are often limited. Limited warranties provide less protection than full warranties.

The warranty also includes information on servicing the product. It will note which expenses are covered and which are not. Buyer responsibilities, such as registering the product with the company and proper maintenance, are often required to keep the warranty in force. A warranty may be void if the item is misused.

Some clothing must be dry cleaned for proper care. If an outfit costs $30 to buy and $5 to dry clean, how long might it take to double the cost of the garment?

Activity. Ask students to bring to class one product or store warranty from home. Is it a limited or full warranty? Does it offer adequate protection? Does it omit any important seller rights or responsibilities? How could this warranty be improved to better protect consumers and manufacturers?

Problem Solving. Have students respond to the following situation: Sarah bought a microwave oven at a discount store. Thirty days after the purchase, the microwave no longer heated food. Sarah did not get satisfaction when she returned the microwave to the store. What should she do?

◆◆◆

Making Purchases

When you decide that you want to buy something, take some steps to help you. Follow these tips for making purchases:

- Decide whether or not the purchase is necessary.
- Check consumer magazines for information.
- Obtain recommendations from friends who have purchased the same product.
- Compare prices and quality at several different stores. This is called **comparison shopping**. Remember that a high price does not guarantee the best quality.
- Look at different brands, features, qualities, and styles.

Products are evaluated and rated by some consumer organizations. The information can help you when the time comes to make a purchase.

I CAN ◆◆◆ Comparison Shop

How do you get the most from your buying dollar? Do you buy the first item you see at the first store you visit? Dan had saved some money to buy a television set to take with him to college next year, and he was ready to make a purchase.

"I knew I would have to do my 'homework' first. On a trip to the library, I looked up some information in a consumer magazine to see how the main brands were rated. I also checked ads and visited several stores to compare the features of different television sets. Some of the prices were high, so I talked to salespeople about when they might have a sale. I decided exactly what qualities I wanted for the price I could pay.

"Within a couple weeks, I bought a good set at a store with an excellent reputation. I knew that if I had any problems with it, they wouldn't let me down. Even before turning the set on, I read the instruction booklet. Knowing that I got the best buy I could for my money made me feel good."

- It is said that an ounce of prevention is worth a pound of cure. How does this relate to the situation above?
- Do you think every purchase Dan makes should be made in the manner described? Why or why not?
- What have you purchased using comparison shopping? Describe what you did. What will you purchase in the next year or two using this method?

Life Management Skills. Have students work in small groups. Ask each group to choose a high-price product they'd like to buy, such as a car, piano, or appliance. Have them apply the consumer tips above to report on a "best buy" model or brand. Have students justify their reasons for the selection.

Discussion. Ask students to discuss the pros and cons of comparison shopping. Is there ever a time when a person should not comparison shop? Have students defend their answers.

- Decide what specific features will best meet your needs.
- Watch for sales and specials.
- Decide how much you are willing to pay and what will fit the budget.
- Inspect articles thoroughly. Look for quality in construction whether you are buying furniture, clothing, or anything else.

◆◆◆

Impulse Buying

If you follow the tips above, you are not likely to regret the purchasing decisions you make. People who buy on impulse, however, often do. When **impulse buying**, people purchase without any thought beforehand. They simply react in some way to the product and decide to buy on the spot. Researchers at Georgia State University asked 1,600 shoppers to identify the point when they decided to purchase the items they had just bought. The results showed that 40 percent of purchasing decisions were made after entering the store. A similar survey of nearly 7,000 persons in six areas across the country found that 30 percent of those shoppers did the same.

Impulse buying is often encouraged by companies who are eager to get you to buy. These companies employ experts who study consumer shopping habits. They know which colors are most likely to catch the eye and why one type of package is appealing over another. When Mr. Tremont is buying groceries, his four-year-old son Will always begs for every children's cereal he sees. All of these are displayed on a low shelf in the store. Do you know why?

People who have a problem with impulse buying need to develop some new habits. Carrie does several things to control her spending. First, she tries to shop only when she has a purpose in mind. Simple browsing often results in unnecessary purchases for her. Usually she carries a list with her and sticks to it. This way she buys only what she needs. Carrying just what money she needs also helps avoid unplanned buying.

SIDELIGHT

Figuring Cost Per Unit

Many products come in different sizes. For example, shampoo may be sold in bottles containing 8, 12, and 16 ounces. How can you tell which to buy? Some stores mark the cost per unit (ounce in this case) on the shelf along with the price. Then you can compare each bottle size to see which has the lowest cost per ounce. If this information is not provided, use your math skills. Simply divide each price by the number of ounces to get the unit cost.

◆◆◆

Discussion. Have students share personal anecdotes of impulse buying. What factors made them buy the item? Do they regret the purchase? Why or why not? Ask them to imagine they are store managers. What products would they display at the cash registers?

The impulsive shopper often regrets making purchases. Have you ever been in such a situation?

Photo Focus. Ask students what they feel this consumer is thinking. How can people avoid impulse buying?

Solving Consumer Problems

Even with careful shopping, there are times when products don't work and need to be returned. Registering complaints effectively often has satisfactory results.

An effective complaint is supported by organized records. LaToya needed to return the radio she purchased because it didn't work. She took her dated receipt and warranty information back to Harrison's Department store, the place where she purchased the radio. Because the sales clerk was unable to help LaToya, she requested to see the store manager. After explaining the problem and showing the manager her sales receipt and warranty information, LaToya was able to receive a refund for the radio.

The VCR Shane bought six months ago was not working correctly. Knowing it was still covered under the warranty, Shane read the warranty information carefully to find out if the seller made repairs or if repairs were done elsewhere. After discovering the seller made repairs, Shane took the VCR and a copy of the warranty and sales receipt to the seller. Because Shane was organized and followed the warranty specifications, the repairs were made quickly. He was soon able to enjoy the VCR again.

Sometimes it is not possible to get satisfactory results from the seller. If this happens, write to the manufacturer. Describe the problem with the product, indicate the purchase date, and request specific action within a set time period. Be sure to include your name, address, and daytime telephone number. Be firm and reasonable, not angry or threatening. If the results are still unsatisfactory, take the complaint to the Better Business Bureau and local or state consumer protection agency. Explain the problem, steps already taken, and what results would be most fair in the situation.

If you were mistakenly billed for an item, send a letter to the creditor, indicating the reason the error may have occurred. The letter must reach the creditor within 60 days after the first bill containing the error is received. Include your name, account number, and the amount in error in the letter. Most billing errors are cleared up quickly to consumer satisfaction.

When you buy something that doesn't work, take the merchandise, the warranty, and the sales receipt back to the store. You may be entitled to repairs or a replacement.

Activity. Ask for three students to volunteer as judges to hear "consumer complaints." On index cards, write down consumer problems regarding a variety of purchased products. Put one issue on each card. Give one card to each of the remaining members of the class. Ask a student to register a complaint about a fictional product, and have each judge offer a solution. Have the class identify the best solution offered.

CHAPTER 30

Review

Answers
Testing Your Memory

1. Values help you choose what is most important to you. Goals help provide the motivation for the end result.
2. **Any two consumer rights:** right to safe products; right to be informed; right to choose; right to be heard. **Any two consumer responsibilities:** be informed about products and services; read labels; follow manufacturers' instructions; follow safety standards; save receipts; identify product quality — file complaint if unsatisfactory; deal with reliable businesses; report unfair and illegal practices.
3. Look for facts, half-truths, or vague promises; guarantees; special claims; sales really being sales.
4. **Any three:** deal with reputable businesses that stand behind products; check on refund policy; find out if special services are available; read catalog descriptions carefully; check out any unfamiliar companies with the Better Business Bureau or Chamber of Commerce.
5. **Any one:** free prizes; real estate bargains; unbelievably low prices; a deal too good to be true.

Summarizing the Chapter

- Your values and goals influence the purchases you make.
- As a consumer, you have certain rights, but there are responsibilities that go along with these too.
- To be a wise consumer and good money manager, evaluate advertising claims, product quality, pressures to buy, and sales techniques.
- Good ads provide important facts to help consumers, yet they can also tempt people to buy items that are not needed or are unaffordable.
- Buy from businesses that you trust and are familiar with.
- Read labels and warranties before you buy.
- To make the best buying choices, do some product research, evaluate your needs, and compare products and services.
- Learn to think before you buy.
- You should register a complaint when you have a problem with a purchase.

Testing Your Memory

1. Explain how values and goals affect buying.
2. List two consumer rights and two consumer responsibilities.
3. What should you look for when reading an advertisement?
4. List three considerations when deciding where to shop.
5. Give an example of a high-pressure sales tactic.
6. Why should you read labels and warranties?
7. List four tips to follow when making purchases.
8. What is impulse buying?
9. What should you do if a product you buy does not work correctly?

Thinking Critically

1. Explain any problems you see in these advertising statements:
   a. "Lose all the weight you can in just two weeks with our weight-loss system."
   b. "You have been selected to receive one of four prizes, including a brand new automobile."
   c. "Only people with good taste drink Larchmont soda."
2. Is buying on sale always better than buying at regular price? Explain your answer.
3. How does comparison shopping help you get the most for your money?
4. What are the advantages and disadvantages of ordering by mail? What should an informed consumer watch out for?

Taking Action

1. List five small items that you buy frequently. Compare prices at several different stores. Where would you buy and why?
2. Bring five ads to class. Explain the method each ad uses to convince the consumer to buy the product or service.
3. Write a sample letter registering a complaint about a product with the manufacturer. Explain that the product did not measure up to the expected quality.
4. A 12-ounce bottle of detergent costs $1.13, a 22-ounce bottle costs $1.68, and a 42-ounce bottle costs $2.99. Which one is the best buy?

Making Life Choices

"We are going to have a representative in your neighborhood tomorrow doing free roof inspections. Could we check yours for you?" the man on the phone asked. Marla didn't catch the name of the company he was with, but she agreed anyway. After all, it was free. "I guess it's a good thing he did check it," Marla thought on the following day. "He says the roof won't last through another winter, and we could have a mess on our hands by January. They can repair it now for $3,000. He says it will cost a lot more if we wait."

Is there anything about Marla's situation that bothers you? If so, explain why. What would you do if you were Marla?

Using Your Journal

How would you rate yourself when it comes to making informed consumer decisions? Use your journal to write about the way you generally go about buying important items. What do you do right? What do you need to change about your buying patterns? Make a list of things you need to learn more about in order to be a wiser consumer. Refer to the list before you make your next major purchase.

6. To be informed about proper use and care of a product and the protection offered.
7. **Any four** of the tips listed on pages 443-444.
8. Making purchases without thought beforehand.
9. Take receipt, warranty, and product back to store. Discuss problem with manager or customer service office. If not satisfied, write to the manufacturer. If results are unsatisfactory, call the Better Business Bureau or consumer protection agency.

Thinking Critically

1. Answers will vary.
2. No. Regular prices may be so high that the sale price isn't really a bargain.
3. By comparing cost and features you get the best product for your needs.
4. Answers will vary. Look out for sales gimmicks, fraudulent sales, etc.

CHAPTER 31

Making Consumer Decisions

Chapter Challenge

Resources. Refer to the Teacher's Classroom Resources box and Student Workbook for materials related to this chapter.

Look for These Answers. . .

- Why is responsibility part of being a good consumer?
- When you're looking for housing to rent or buy, what should you consider?
- What are some guidelines for purchasing furniture?
- How should you shop for a car?
- How can you save money on food, clothing, and recreation?
- What are the different types of insurance and why are they important?

Look for These Terms. . .

- beneficiaries
- condominium
- dependent
- deductible
- lease
- liable
- permanent life insurance
- term insurance
- will

As Mr. Antonini's eyes scanned the room, the look of dismay on his face quickly turned to one of anger. "How could they do this?" he cried. "What did I do to deserve this? It will cost me hundreds of dollars to repair the damage. My only choice then will be to raise the rent for the next tenants."

The building was small, with only four apartments. Mr. Antonini had owned it for two years and already three tenants had left apartments in terrible condition.

"Don't worry, Pop. I'll help you fix things up again — just like we always do." Tony was concerned about his father. His health was not good. He didn't need problems like this, nor did he need another financial blow. Every time this happened Tony wondered why. Why didn't the people care? Didn't they realize that rents go up when these things happen? Tony reached out to put his hand on his father's shoulder. They exchanged wistful smiles, knowing that together they would make the best of another tough situation.

Chapter Opener. Have students read the opening scenario. Discuss the following issues: What responsibilities do tenants have in taking care of the property they have rented? Describe the connection between irresponsible tenants and the high cost of rent in many areas. How may this hurt everyone in the long run? What does it mean to be a responsible consumer?

Discussion. Ask students: If you were a judge, what would you order Mr. Antonini and his problem tenants to do to resolve the situation above? What responsibilities do tenants owe a landlord, and vice versa?

The Responsible Consumer

As an adult, you will face many consumer decisions. You will choose housing, transportation, professional services, and insurance. You will buy food, clothing, and products of all kinds. You will also spend money on entertainment. Too often consumers think only about their own interests when making such decisions. There is more to the picture.

Responsibility is an important part of being a good consumer. Think about Mr. Antonini's tenants. The few who were not responsible created a situation felt by all. Because of damage to his apartments, Mr. Antonini must raise the rent. Eventually, everyone pays the price. After Carlin bought a new coat, he returned it to the store because of a rip that he caused. Incidents like this cost the store. This cost is eventually passed on to all consumers, including Carlin.

As you read about making smart consumer decisions in the rest of this chapter, think about the other side of the coin too. First, how can you get the most for your money, but, second, what responsibilities are also yours?

◆◆◆

Housing

With the cost of houses today, many people are finding that buying a "dream" home is not easy. Other housing options are often considered first.

◆ Renting an Apartment or House

Ninety-two percent of all young people who leave home for the first time — for school, work, or marriage — choose rental housing. Since many move several times during the first ten years on their own, rental living can be both practical and economical. When looking for housing to rent — whether a house, an apartment, or a single room — consider the following points:

- **Cost.** Know just how much you can afford each month before you start looking. That amount will be based on income, other expenses, and the type of housing you want. Be sure to include related housing costs, such as utilities, insurance, telephone, and maintenance.
- **Space.** The amount and type of space needed depends on your own personal lifestyle. A one-room efficiency is right for some people, yet a five-room house is better for others.
- **Location.** Check such things as easy access to work, public transportation, shopping, and general safety.
- **Services.** Facilities vary greatly. A refrigerator, range, dishwasher, carpeting, drapes, air conditioning, and disposal may be included. Some rental units are completely furnished to the last frying pan. Others have none of the above.
- **Lease.** A **lease** is a legal document that describes the terms by which the property is rented. Be sure to study it carefully before signing it so that you'll know your rights and your responsibilities.

◆ Buying a House

To buy a house, you will usually need a down payment. Since down payments are costly, most people need time to save for this expense. Few young people can afford a house right away.

For many people the cost of home ownership is always out of reach. The down payment is the first hurdle, but beyond that there

Home ownership can be costly. Plumbing work, for example, can be expensive if you have to pay someone to do the work for you.

Activity. Have students check newspapers and "choose" a desirable rental unit in the community. Have them list five reasons why the unit would suit their needs and explain what jobs they would need to meet annual housing expenses.

More About Renting. When renting a house or apartment, remember that the lease protects the landlord. Renters should not rely on oral commitments regarding terms of the lease. If repairs or alterations need to be made in the rental unit, be sure these are indicated in writing.

are other costs. Insurance, property taxes, and upkeep all add to the cost of a home, as do the expense of appliances and furnishings.

If owning a home is in your plans, you can look for ways to make this possible. Starting to save early for home ownership will help you reach your goal. A very small house might be a good start. One that needs some work may be a good choice if you have the skills, time, and energy to fix it up. Choosing a house that will increase in value can help you sell your way to a bigger and better home.

How do you select a home that suits you and will be a good candidate for resale later on? First, think about the location. Where do you want to live — in a city, a suburb, or the country? How close is the house to work, schools, police and fire protection, and shopping areas? Take a look at the neighborhood. Do the other residents take care of their property? Your property may decrease in value if they don't.

Whether you choose a new house or an older home, look at the construction and the condition. How many rooms — and what special features — do you want? Make sure the structure is sound and the appliances work. If you're thinking of buying an older house, you might want to have it inspected by an expert to see if any repairs are necessary.

◆ Buying a Condominium

Buying a condominium (condo) provides some ownership advantages, often at less cost than buying a house. A **condominium** is one unit in a multi-unit structure, such as a high-rise building downtown, a community of townhouses in the suburbs, or a cluster of one- or two-family houses in a larger compound. The buyer owns the unit he or she lives in and shares the ownership of surrounding grounds, landscaping, and parking areas, as well as the elevators, lobby, and halls. To cover upkeep of these areas, each owner pays a monthly maintenance fee.

◆ Buying a Manufactured Home

Many people find low-cost housing in manufactured (mobile) homes. As Ryan put it when he and Amelia bought a manufactured home shortly after they were married, "There's a lot of housing packed into a small space." From a wide range of sizes and prices, they were able to find one to suit their needs. It was compact, well-designed, and equipped with built-ins. They set up housekeeping with very little furniture and few appliances. Since they did not have enough money for a down payment on a house, this was a good alternative for them. Although they know the manufactured home will not hold its value the way a house does, at least this way their money will go for more than just rent.

A manufactured home is less costly than most houses, and it provides an opportunity for home ownership.

Life Management Skills. Have students make a list of housing needs for themselves. They should identify the number and types of rooms (bedrooms, bathrooms, living space, closets, etc.) Students should give reasons supporting their needs. Have them compare the cost of buying versus renting a home that meets their needs.

Problem Solving. Divide students into small teams and assign each a fixed sum of money for annual housing costs. Have teams investigate the best housing choice possible — rental or buying a home, condominium, or manufactured home. Students should defend their choices with supporting evidence.

◆ Buying Furnishings

Acquiring furnishings can be expensive. When you are just getting started, you may want to look for ways to economize.

Check the family storage area first. This is a common source of first furnishings for many young people. One father commented, "I not only lost a daughter, I lost the dining room set, the guest bedroom furniture, and a comfortable couch!"

Garage sales, newspaper ads, and used furniture shops offer possibilities. A little fixing and refinishing can turn discards into fine furniture. Inspect carefully for quality and condition.

Before buying anything in the stores, do some window shopping. Look through stores, magazines, books, newspapers, and decorating brochures. Browse through decorated room displays in furniture stores as you study styles, colors, sizes, and designs.

Before buying in a used furniture shop, check the item carefully for quality and condition. By looking inside and underneath, you can see how sturdy the construction is.

Life Management Skills. Ask students to choose one piece of furniture and comparison shop to decide on the best buy. How can an outlet store's deferred payment program benefit them in making their choice? Have the students report their results to the class.

A Slice of Life

In an older building Joy found an apartment that she could afford. She liked the charm of the long, narrow living room with paneled wood low on the walls and around the windows. The high ceilings and old-fashioned, red brick fireplace suited her taste.

Joy decided to put a couch and two chairs around the fireplace for a conversational group. She chose a couch that converted into a bed. Big pillows added extra seating for guests.

Like other budget-minded, first-apartment dwellers, Joy searched everywhere for furniture. Her old room yielded a dresser and bookshelves. Her parents sent along her bedroom rug. An attic search turned up an old wooden spool used for heavy wire. It became a lamp table. Joy bought two lamps at a discount store. She brought her clock and stereo from home. In a thrift shop she found a sturdy table and chairs. After sanding and staining, Joy discovered what other first-home dwellers have learned: almost any old piece of furniture can be fixed up to fill a need.

Finally, Joy was ready for the finishing touches. She used American Indian baskets, weavings, photographs, and a beautiful blanket, all collected on family trips out West. She filled the baskets with plants, dried flowers, and reeds. The colors were picked up in pillows for the couch and in the geometric patterns on the shades. Even an Indian-patterned beach towel became a wall hanging. With everything in place, Joy surveyed the results with pride.

Thinking It Through

- How did Joy save money in furnishing her first apartment?
- How did she add personal touches to make it a home?
- Why do you think Joy is proud of her living space? Do you think pride is possible in a modest setting? How do people show pride in their living space?

Wait for sales to make major purchases, and furnish in stages, perhaps over several years. Concentrate on the necessary big items first — furniture for sleeping, eating, and lounging. Begin with a combination of good mattress and box springs on legs; both can be used later with a new bedroom set. Use a folding card table and chairs for dining if you need to; they're always usable when replaced later. Then add stuffed chairs, occasional tables, shelves, and chests as your budget allows. Finally, choose accessories to give accent and personality. Throw pillows, plants, pictures, and knickknacks can add such emphasis.

◆ Energy

When renting or buying a home, think about the energy cost — the cost of heating and cooling plus electricity. To save money, first make sure your house is well insulated. Try lowering the temperature a few degrees during the winter. If you have air conditioning, keep the temperature a little higher during the summer. You might also use an automatic setback device that changes the temperature setting during the day when no one is home or at night when everyone is asleep. Also keep furnace and air-conditioning units clean and have them checked periodically.

To save electricity, turn off lights, radios, and television sets when you're not using them. Wash only full loads in your washing machine or dishwasher to save energy. Can you think of other ways to save energy in the home?

◆◆◆ Transportation

Next to a house, an automobile is one of the most expensive purchases people make. The total cost — price, financing, insurance, maintenance, and gasoline — continues to increase. Choosing a car carefully can make a difference.

When buying a used car, read consumer publications that rate different models for different years, and compare prices at several dealers.

Mason had looked forward to buying his first car. When the time came, he was eager to do it right. His cousin Todd had gotten stuck with a real lemon, so Mason hoped to learn from Todd's mistakes.

Mason did two things to get started. First, he read about car models in consumer publications at the library. He studied car sizes and styles and checked safety and repair records. Second, he talked to friends about their experiences with different cars.

At first Mason thought he might buy a new car. He could get a good price on a current model when the new models come out. As he talked to dealers, however, he decided this was still too expensive for his budget. Instead he would settle for a used car. In comparing used cars at several dealers, he test-drove many.

Problem Solving. Have students do some research to answer the following: In general, which saves more energy — a bath or shower; electric heat or blazing wood fire in fireplace; conventional gas oven or microwave; electric ceiling fan or air conditioner?

Discussion. Have students brainstorm some ideas for buying the best used car possible for their money. How can students be sure a car runs well and is worth the money?

One salesperson seemed too pushy, so Mason eliminated him. He especially liked another salesperson who had been recommended to him and who had won several company awards. It took a few weeks, but Mason finally settled on one of her cars. He had it checked by a mechanic he trusted just as extra insurance.

Before buying, Mason read the warranty and financial papers carefully. Later, he also read the car-care manual. Mason's efforts paid off. The car he bought runs well and needs few repairs as long as he maintains it well.

SIDELIGHT

Saving on Transportation

You can save transportation costs by following a few simple suggestions:

- When driving, start smoothly, accelerate steadily, and maintain a steady driving speed. This saves gas.
- Keep your car engine well tuned. A faulty carburetor, bad spark plugs, burned-out ignition points, dirty radiator, or clogged air filter can decrease gas efficiency as much as 20 percent.
- Limit your use of air conditioning to save gas.
- Be your own mechanic when you can.
- Whenever possible, car pool or use public transportation.

◆◆◆

Make a list before you shop. Not only does it help you remember what you need, but you are less likely to buy items that you don't need.

Discussion. Have students discuss how making a plan for grocery shopping can help save money. Does clipping coupons help save money? How?

◆◆◆

Food

Good meal planning and good eating habits will pay dividends throughout your life. To stay healthy, look attractive, and have the energy for an active life, you will need to make good food choices.

Shopping for the food is as important as planning and preparing it. To get the most for your food dollar:

- Make a shopping list to save time, help you keep within your budget, and cut down on impulse buying. Take advantage of sales and store specials by checking newspaper ads in advance.
- As often as possible, clip and use coupons for items you like and need.

Life Management Skills. Ask students to write a list of at least six favorite foods or food products they eat every week. Have them comparison shop at several community stores to discover the best buy for each food choice on their list. Share results in class.

- Become a comparison shopper. Visit several different stores to compare prices. Within the stores, compare items for quality, weight, and contents. Read the labels to do this. Store brands or generic foods cost less than nationally advertised brands, but food value may be the same.
- Remember that you pay extra for convenience foods, even though you may need them at times because of a busy schedule. Compare the prices with homemade foods to see the difference in cost.

◆◆◆

Clothing

People always compliment Carmella on her appearance. Although her budget is limited, careful planning and shopping help her get the most for her clothing dollar. Perhaps some of Carmella's techniques could be useful to you.

Carmella creates different looks day after day. She does this by putting garments together in different combinations along with inexpensive accessories. Her wardrobe was planned around two basic colors that go well together — navy blue and dark red. She buys what will go with these colors, giving her many options for outfits.

When Carmella shops, she looks for quality garments at reasonable prices. Watching for sales helps. She has discovered that good quality means a garment will last longer, need a minimum of upkeep, and require few repairs. Carmella looks for close, even stitches and strong thread. She checks seams for reinforcement at points of strain and makes sure that fasteners and trims are firmly attached. She also checks labels and looks for fabrics that are easy to clean and resistant to soil and wrinkles. Before buying, she always tries garments on to see that they fit correctly and look good.

Life Management Skills. Invite a retail clothing professional to talk with your class about purchasing quality clothing for reasonable prices. What should students look for in regard to quality characteristics? Is price an indicator of quality? Why or why not?

◆◆◆

Recreation and Entertainment

The more free time Americans have, the more they spend for recreation and entertainment. Such expenses can push budgets out of balance.

To help cut costs, rediscover your own community. Schools, libraries, public parks, zoos, playgrounds, camping facilities, and community classes all offer things to do. The newspaper has ideas for free and inexpensive events. You might be surprised at the interesting places that are just a short trip away. Camp-outs, walking trips, and picnics are other ideas. Simple entertainment might include a potluck dinner with friends, each bringing something for the meal. Save money by going to the movies during bargain hours or renting a tape and inviting friends over to watch it.

Entertainment does not have to be expensive to be fun. How do you enjoy time with friends without spending much money?

Activity. Have students research community resources and report on free or inexpensive recreation events. Have them give details and any special highlights of events. What are some other inexpensive or no-cost recreational activities students can become involved in?

◆◆◆

Professional Services

From time to time, you will need professional services — medical, dental, or legal. If you move to a new community, check with neighbors, friends, or professional organizations for recommendations. You will want professionals who are knowledgeable and up-to-date in their fields. Choose people you trust. When you have limited funds, check for medical and legal clinics in the area. You can probably find the help you need for reduced rates.

◆ Wills

One legal service you will need at some point is help with drawing up a will. Legal authorities recommend that both singles and couples make a will as soon as they have accumulated even limited assets. A **will** is a legal document. It assures that property will be split according to the wishes of the person who died.

When a will is drawn up by a lawyer, you can be fairly certain that it conforms to the laws of your state, that it's witnessed correctly, and that your wishes are clearly understood. For a family, a will can name a guardian for the children in the event both the husband and wife die together in an accident. If you fail to make out a will, the state will decide how your property will be divided.

People who have dependents need life insurance. This guarantees that the dependents will have financial support if the provider dies.

More About Making Consumer Decisions. There are several kinds of health insurance. A *group policy* is often offered by an employer and covers the employee and immediate family. *Individual* insurance is often tailored to particular needs. *Basic protection* and *major medical* policies vary in their conditions. Have an insurance agent talk with your students about insurance options in preparation for comparison shopping.

◆◆◆

Insurance

Insurance protects you against the high costs of unexpected incidents, such as the death of a wage earner, a serious illness, an automobile accident, a serious fire, injury to another person, or damage to property. The main types of insurance are life, home owners', automobile, and health/accident.

People who have dependents, such as an elderly parent, need life insurance. This guarantees that the dependent will have financial support if the provider dies.

◆ Life Insurance

Experts generally recommend that anyone with dependents purchase life insurance. A **dependent** is someone, such as a husband, wife, child, or elderly parent, who relies on another for some degree of financial support. The cost of life insurance depends on the age of the policyholder. The younger the person, the longer he or she is expected to live, and the lower the annual cost.

Basically, there are two types of life insurance: those that provide financial protection only and those that provide financial protection plus savings, or cash value.

The simplest type of coverage is **term insurance**. It is temporary, running for a specific period of time, say five or ten years. If the policyholder dies within the term of the insurance, the **beneficiaries** (ben-uh-FISH-ee-air-eez), who are named by the policyholder, receive the value of the policy. Term insurance has one major advantage: rates are low for young families that generally need the protection most. As you grow older, the rates rise.

Permanent life insurance, such as whole and universal life, may be kept for a lifetime. These policies double as a savings account, building up cash value. Although the cost is higher than on term insurance when you are young, it usually remains the same as you grow older.

◆ Homeowners' Insurance

With a homeowners' insurance policy, you can protect yourself against loss of your house and possessions as a result of such tragedies as fire, burglary, theft, vandalism, windstorms, hail, hurricanes, explosions, lightning, or falling aircraft. Most people buy what is called all-risk coverage, which usually excludes damage by war, floods, or riots.

A policy that offers replacement protection is best. It covers the amount needed to rebuild your home or replace your possessions. Liability protection is also important in case someone is injured on your property and decides to sue. When you are liable, you are responsible according to the law.

Because renters have the same need to protect their personal property, they buy a renters' policy for protection.

◆ Automobile Insurance

If you drive a car, you'll need automobile insurance. Most policies cover car repairs, hospital and doctor bills, and property damage in the event of an accident. Comprehensive insurance covers loss from theft, vandalism, fire, or storms. Liability insurance covers damages if you are sued after causing the death or injury of another person.

Insurance policies generally have a **deductible**, an amount that you would pay — perhaps $100 or $250 — before the insurance policy takes over. You can save money on insurance by increasing the deductible amount.

Activity. Ask students to do some comparison shopping for car insurance. What kind of accident coverage should they have? How are payments made? How can having good grades influence insurance premiums for students?

The cost of automobile insurance varies, so shop around. Many companies give discounts to students who have passed driver's education courses and to those who have good grades in school.

◆ Health and Accident Insurance

An illness or an accident can be very costly today. If you find yourself facing a long stay in the hospital, major surgery, and doctor bills, your savings could disappear and debts pile up in a hurry. Thus, a good health insurance policy should be part of your overall insurance plan.

Basic hospital-surgical-medical plans cover most of the medical care that families need. Major medical or catastrophe insurance provides protection against the high cost of major accidents or prolonged illness. A young couple needs a family plan to cover the costs of pregnancy and birth.

Many companies offer health insurance as a benefit to their employees. In some cases, the employer pays the full premium; in others, employees pay a portion. A group plan may also include disability insurance, which pays a percentage of a worker's salary while he or she is recovering from illness or accident. Dental insurance is also now a part of some group plans.

Companies over a certain size are required to offer employees HMO coverage as an alternative to regular health insurance. An HMO (Health Maintenance Organization) charges a set monthly fee for each member, no matter how much or how little the member uses the HMO's services. HMO members are required to use physicians associated with the HMO. They may have to pay a small payment for each visit.

Yet another alternative is the PPO (Preferred Provider Organization). PPO members are encouraged by lower costs to use physicians who belong to the PPO.

Activity. Have students investigate reasons for high health and accident insurance rates. What can be done to make insurance affordable for everyone?

CHAPTER 31

Review

Answers

Testing Your Memory

1. Renting a house or apartment; buying a house, condominium, or a mobile home.
2. Cost, space, location, services, lease. Refer to page 450 for details.
3. Home ownership is expensive due to down payment, insurance, property taxes, up-keep, appliances, and furnishings.
4. **Any three:** obtain unused furnishings in family storage; shop garage sales; look carefully at stores, magazines, brochures before making purchases; wait for sales on major purchases; buy large necessary items first and add other items as the budget allows.
5. **Any four:** insulate home; lower heat temperature in winter; raise cooling temperature in summer; use automatic setback device to alter settings; keep furnace and air conditioning units clean; turn off lights and appliances when not in use; wash full loads of dishes and laundry.
6. Read about car models in consumer publications; talk to friends; determine what your budget will allow for a car; read warranties and instruction manuals.

Summarizing the Chapter

- Major expenses that you will have in the future include housing and furniture, transportation, food, clothing, recreation and entertainment, professional services, and insurance.
- When looking for housing to rent or buy, consider the cost, the location, the size, and the special features you would like to have.
- Inexpensive furniture options are possible at garage sales and through newspaper ads and used furniture shops.
- Before you buy a car, do some research first. Then visit several dealers and test-drive the cars of interest.
- Eating right will help you stay healthy and energetic. Smart shopping will help you get the most for your food dollar.
- By carefully planning new purchases, shopping sales, and looking for quality in garments, you can not only look well-dressed but also stay within your budget.
- To save money on recreation and entertainment, look for low-cost events in your own community.
- Insurance protects you against the high costs of unexpected incidents.

Testing Your Memory

1. What different types of housing options are available today?
2. What should you look for when renting an apartment?
3. Explain why home ownership is expensive.
4. List three ways to cut costs on home furnishings.
5. List four ways to save on energy costs at home.
6. What homework should you do before you go shopping for a car?

7. List three tips to follow when shopping for food.
8. Name three ways to identify quality in a garment.
9. What are the four main types of insurance?

Thinking Critically

1. Compare home ownership to apartment rental. What are the advantages and disadvantages of each?
2. What attitudes do people have about cars? What causes these feelings? Do attitudes affect how often people trade cars? What are the economic results?
3. How might good eating habits and staying physically fit save you money over your lifetime? Suggest some ways to stay physically fit.
4. Mr. Danforth is 45 and has never been to a doctor. "I don't need health insurance," he says. "I'm as healthy as a horse." How do you feel about this situation?

Taking Action

1. To get an idea of the cost of housing, collect information on the different types of homes in your community. Check with lenders to see what incomes would be needed to pay for each.
2. Suppose you wanted to buy a $70,000 house. A 20 percent down payment is required. What would this amount be? What would it be on an $85,000 house?
3. Suppose the deductible on your car insurance is $200. An accident causes $650 damage to your car. What amount will the insurance company pay?

Making Life Choices

Eric wants to live on his own. He has been living at home, but he now has a job as a computer programmer and wants his own place. Eric has no money saved because of many medical bills. He has looked at three apartments. None will accommodate his wheelchair.

If you were Eric, what would you do?

Using Your Journal

If you are like most young people, you are probably looking forward to moving into a place of your own. Now that you have read about different kinds of housing options, think about the options available to you. Use your journal to analyze your housing needs and wants, short term and long term. Once you've compiled your wish list, figure out how much it will cost and how you will achieve your goals.

7. **Any three:** make a shopping list; clip coupons for items you use; comparison shop; compare the cost of convenience food to homemade.
8. **Any three** of the qualities described on page 455.
9. Life insurance; homeowners' (renters') insurance; automobile insurance; health and accident insurance.

Thinking Critically

1. Answers will vary. With home ownership, money is invested in own property. When renting, there is no worry about maintenance but property is not yours.
2. Answers will vary.
3. Answers will vary. Healthful habits prevent disease and save medical bills.
4. Answers will vary. Point out that one major illness or accident could wipe out Mr. Danforth's savings.

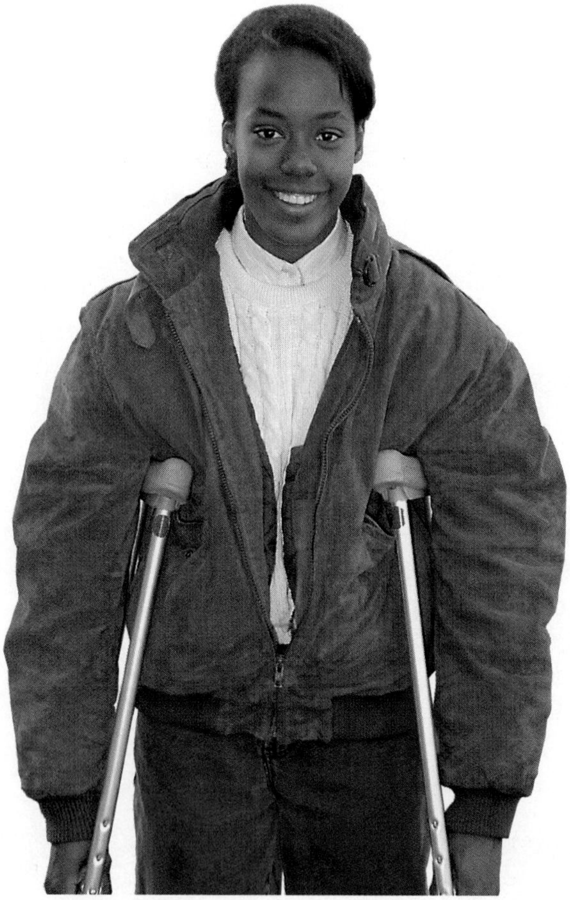

Libby reaches out to her neighborhood through a community project.

Libby

"I see so many people who don't care about the environment, but I do. At school we learned that by cutting down the rain forests, we put the world's climate in danger. We wrote to influential people who can help make some vital changes. That gave me the idea to try to do something at home. I decided to start a recycling program in my neighborhood. A friend and I researched the idea through phone calls. We canvassed every house on our block and the streets next to us. Many neighbors were gung-ho on the idea. For the next few weeks my friend Jenna and I worked before and after school to organize the project. It took time and effort, but most people were helpful. We are real proud of how it has all worked out."

Jenna

"Libby just takes it for granted that when there's a problem, you take action to resolve it. She has such a high self-esteem that she is always reaching out to others. Almost everywhere we went for this project, people were polite. Some neighbors didn't go for the idea, but most loved it. We learned a lot as consumers by setting up this recycling program. Now I see that if you have a good idea, one that seems reasonable to others, there are people out there willing to be supportive. First you need to do your homework to see what it will take to put your idea into action. Then you have to reach out and make it become a reality."

Dean Walters

"One afternoon not long ago two teenagers knocked on my door and asked if they could explain their idea to start a neighborhood recycling program. I was skeptical at first, but they were so well-mannered and organized that I soon became very enthusiastic. A few of us on the block had talked about recycling our trash, but nobody took the time to get it off the ground — pun intended. We decided to take action.

"According to the plan, each family recycles trash at home. It is then properly collected by private companies. The girls provide extra trash bags to each family and check each house to make sure the trash is properly separated. They also make sure it is picked up. Then they collect money to pay the truckers.

"When everyone saw how well the program was working, they decided to set up a neighborhood association for other such projects. Everybody even chipped in to start a small fund to finance them. In fact, things have worked out so well that I've agreed to become the first president of our neighborhood association. As far as I'm concerned, Libby and Jenna are my joint chiefs of staff."

You can make a difference too.

- Why do you think some people care more about making the world a better place to live in than others do?
- What choices can you make as a consumer that would benefit the environment?
- Can you think of any community projects that would improve the quality of life in your neighborhood? How could you help?

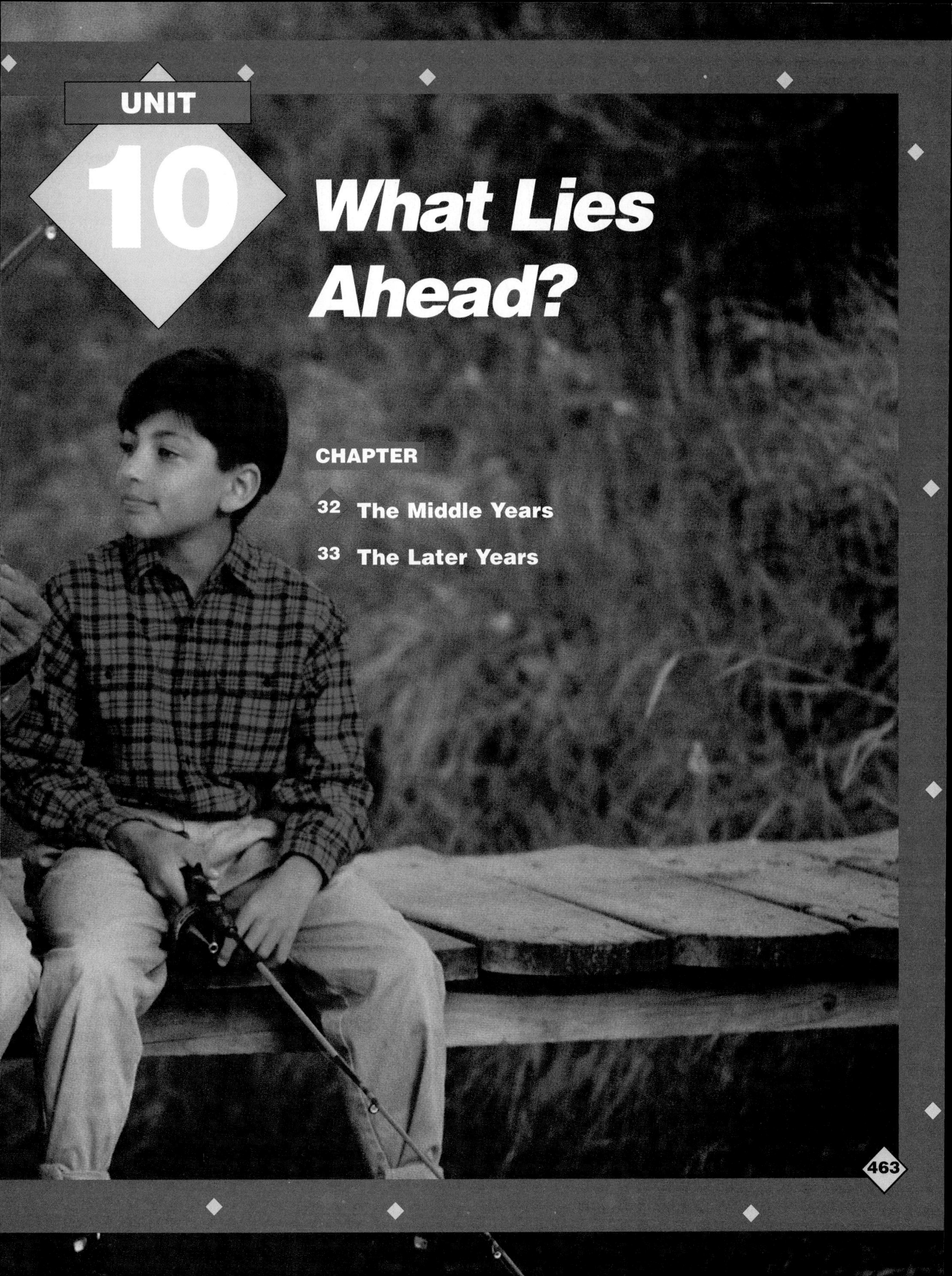

UNIT

10 What Lies Ahead?

CHAPTER

CHAPTER 32

The Middle Years

Chapter Challenge

Resources. Refer to the Teacher's Classroom Resources box and Student Workbook for materials related to this chapter.

Look for These Answers . . .

- Why are the middle years called a time of transition?
- What are some of the lifestyle changes that many people experience in their middle years?
- Why do people in their middle years find themselves assessing their goals?
- What are some of the challenges that people may experience during their middle years?
- What kind of planning for the future should people in their middle years be doing?

Look for These Terms . . .

- empty nest stage
- mammogram
- menopause
- osteoporosis
- sandwich generation
- transition

When Maria and Tony went into John's room, Maria burst into tears. "It looks so empty and forlorn. Look, he even took his comic book collection with him." Maria's and Tony's only child had just left for his first year of college, and they knew that he had probably left home for good.

John had been excited about leaving home but a little scared about living on his own for the first time. His parents were scared too. Did John really know how to take care of himself? Would he eat too much junk food or stay out too late or not study enough? What if he started hanging around with students who used drugs?

After John had been gone for a month, Maria and Tony began to relax. John sounded happy and busy when he called home, so they were less worried about him. At the same time, they began to realize that there were benefits to having the house to themselves. "I must admit it's nice not having to share the car with John anymore," observed Tony one evening. "Yes, and I can't believe how clean the house stays with just the two of us in it," Maria said. "And I don't feel guilty about eating out when neither of us wants to cook." Tony smiled at her and then had an idea: "Why don't we go away this weekend? The change will be good for both of us — and we won't have to worry about leaving John home alone. I didn't like to do that when he was still in high school."

Maria and Tony are adjusting to being alone together for the first time in many years. They will have many other adjustments to make during this new phase of their life.

Chapter Opener. Have students read the opening scenario to the chapter. Ask the following questions: Why are John's parents upset about his leaving home? In what ways do their lives change after John's departure? What kinds of adjustments do parents have to make when their children leave home? What other changes happen to people during their middle years?

Transition Time

Leaving home is a rite of passage for young adults and a milestone for parents. When the last child moves out, the parents are effectively finished with active parenting. Usually, too, they have reached their middle years.

The middle years start at about age 45 and last until about age 65. It is a period of **transition** — or change — for all adults. Whether married or single, parents or childless, adults experience a number of emotional, social, and physical changes as they move from young adulthood through to their later years. Some find their middle years exciting and fulfilling. Others struggle to come to terms with growing older.

Emotional Changes

People experience various new emotions as they approach and experience the middle years. They become aware of their own mortality during this time, especially if they experience the death of their parents. They also become aware that they are growing older and slower, and that they don't have the energy that they once did. For many people, though, the middle years are a time of contentment. They enjoy being settled and having time to explore new interests. Some of the emotional changes of the middle years are linked to physical changes. Changes in hormone balances can cause unpredictable mood swings for a while.

Parents experience a variety of emotions when their children leave home. They have to adjust to a new lifestyle. The home is quieter, and there is less activity and fewer demands on the parents' time. This period, often called the **empty nest stage**, affects people in different ways. Some feel relief and contentment that the children have moved on to the next phase in their lives. Like Maria and Tony, they enjoy discovering the greater freedoms that they now have. Others find the adjustment very difficult. They miss the children's company and find it hard to adapt to the empty nest. For some parents, even learning to buy and prepare food in smaller amounts can be a big adjustment.

Most couples now have more time to spend either together or on outside activities. Those who no longer have to support their children may enjoy having more money to spend. However, those who are helping their children establish a home or continue their education may actually have less money for a while.

The empty nest stage can be especially hard for single parents. When the last child moves out, single parents find themselves living alone for the first time in many years. Without a partner to help with the adjustment, they need to make a special effort to adapt to their new lifestyle. On the other hand, some single parents enjoy their newfound freedom and build a whole new social life once the children move out.

◆ Social Changes

In general, people in their middle years have more free time than they had when they were younger. Parents whose children have become independent can now spend their time and money on their own interests. Single people are more settled and selective about how they spend their time.

Discussion. Ask students why they think the middle years are the "now or never" time for many people. What kinds of things might people have this attitude about? What aspects of the midlife stage might contribute to this feeling?

Some people get involved in new interests such as travel, volunteer work, or sports and hobbies. Some develop a "now or never" attitude about things they have always wanted to do.

Married couples whose children have left home have more time to spend with each other. For some, this is a welcome change that helps strengthen the marriage. Others find that with the children gone they have little left to talk about. Couples who cannot rebuild their relationship may separate or divorce.

◆ Physical Changes

Certain physical changes are inevitable during the middle years, although most people can still pursue an active lifestyle. Both men and women begin to "go gray," and many men start losing their hair. The skin becomes less elastic, resulting in wrinkles. The knees and other joints may stiffen, and the circulatory system becomes less efficient.

In women, **menopause**, or the cessation of menstruation, is the most dramatic sign of the arrival of the middle years. It usually occurs between the ages of 45 and 52 and may cause both emotional and physical symptoms. The emotional symptoms may include depression and anxiety. The physical symptoms may include irregular periods, headaches, and hot flashes (sudden increases in body temperature). These symptoms all indicate that the body's production of estrogen, the female hormone, has slowed down.

Reduced estrogen levels increase a woman's risk of developing **osteoporosis**, a disease characterized by brittle, porous bones. Some health professionals recommend estrogen replacement therapy or other kinds of hormone therapy for women in their middle years. Women who get regular exercise and eat a calcium-rich diet are less likely to develop osteoporosis as they age.

More About Menopause. About 25 percent of women notice few changes at menopause apart from the cessation of periods; 50 percent experience slight changes; and the remaining 25 percent experience symptoms that cause serious discomfort and inconvenience.

Regular exercise, a balanced diet, and regular checkups are recommended for both men and women in their middle years. People who take care of their health are more likely to remain strong and active. Of course, no efforts can entirely halt the physical aging process. However, exercise and healthy eating can help maintain good muscle tone and circulation, and regular checkups may make it possible to detect and treat diseases before they become serious. For this reason, women are advised to get a **mammogram** (X ray for the detection of breast cancer) every year after the age of 50.

Regular exercise, combined with other healthful habits, helps people stay strong and active in the middle years and beyond.

Activity. Ask students to take a survey of older adults they know to discover how many of the adults experienced a midlife crisis. What did these people do as a result of the crisis? What changes did they make in their life? Have students report their findings and compare results.

◆◆◆

Midlife Decisions

Many people, both parents and nonparents, decide to take stock of their lives during the middle years. As they become aware that they are growing older, they feel a need to reexamine priorities. This process may, in turn, lead them to make significant changes before it is too late.

◆ Personal Reassessment

The process of taking stock may be calm and measured, or it may be highly emotional. Some individuals go through a period of intense self-examination during their middle years, often called a midlife crisis.

Not everyone experiences crisis, of course. Some people in their middle years are at the height of their career achievement. If they enjoy their work and have been successful at it, they experience great satisfaction. They look forward to continuing along the same track and to achieving the rewards that go with career growth. Other people in their middle years experience satisfaction from seeing the achievements of family members or from making progress in personal interests.

Others find themselves less satisfied, however. They may feel trapped in unsatisfying or low-paid work or in an unhappy home life. They might ask themselves, "Is this what I want to do for the rest of my life?" or "Is this the person I want to spend the rest of my life with?" Such questioning often leads to decisions to make changes.

◆ Career Changes

Midlife assessments often lead to career changes. Sometimes people decide that this is their last chance to pursue a type of work that they have always wanted to do. Some leave well-paying jobs to pursue work that they

Work and Family. Point out that midlife career changes affect the whole family, not just the person making the change. Ask students to give examples of career changes that people might make and then brainstorm the effects of those changes on family members.

Midlife assessments may lead to career changes. This man left his job as a computer salesperson to establish his own restaurant.

believe will be more satisfying, even though it pays less. For example, a successful advertising executive left her job so that she could teach in a preschool. Others seek a new and challenging career after many years spent in routine work, such as the 45-year-old salesman who decided to open his own home repair service.

For some people, however, the career change is not voluntary. In recent years, in an effort to save costs or operate more efficiently, many large companies have laid off workers at all levels. For people in their middle years, the layoffs call for them to make an unexpected and often difficult adjustment. Unlike people entering the work force today, many people who are now in their middle years grew up thinking that if they found a job they liked and were good at, they would keep that job until retirement. These people are having to become more flexible in their ideas about work in order to make successful career changes in their middle years. Often, this involves going back to school to learn new skills.

◆ Continuing Education

People in their middle years are going back to school in greater numbers than ever before. They are enrolling in colleges and technical schools to prepare for new jobs or to learn new skills so that they can move up in the workplace. Sometimes they need new skills simply to help them keep their present jobs. Some parents who stayed home to raise families are going back to school to learn skills that will enable them to get a job.

Most people who are now in their middle years completed their educations before the use of modern technology was widespread. They are realizing that if they want to compete in the workplace, they must learn how to operate computers and other electronic equipment.

In addition, people in their middle years return to school because they are interested in learning for its own sake. Most communities have adult education programs where people can take courses ranging from foreign languages through woodworking and drawing to gourmet cooking. Now that they have fewer responsibilities or are more secure financially, people in their middle years feel free to pursue such interests.

Many people in their middle years go back to school, either because they have to or because they want to.

More About Career Change. Some companies that lay off executives arrange for them to receive "outplacement counseling." They get help with preparing a resume and with preparing lists of potential employers to contact. Some outplacement companies also help job candidates prepare for a job interview.

Activity. Have students examine the catalogs of adult schools and community colleges in the area. Ask what kinds of courses seem to be designed for people in their middle years.

◆◆◆

Becoming a Grandparent

During their middle years many parents become grandparents, although this happens much later for some. Most grandparents derive great happiness and satisfaction from their grandchildren. They enjoy being around young children without having the responsibilities of parenthood. Grandchildren who live nearby can visit often. Some grandparents willingly accept the role of primary caregiver during the working day.

Some grandparents miss out on many of the pleasures of grandparenting, however. The children may live too far away for more than occasional visits. In some cases, a divorce causes problems. When the grandchild's parents are divorced, grandparents may find it hard to spend time with their grandchildren. Some grandparents have gone to court to secure the right to see their grandchildren.

When the grandchildren's parents are, for some reason, unable to care for their children, the grandparents often accept this responsibility. Some would prefer not to take such an active role in their grandchildren's lives, but they do so out of a sense of family responsibility.

For grandparents who see their grandchildren regularly, grandparenting brings the joys of parenting without the responsibilities.

Discussion. Have students discuss the ways in which their relationship with their grandparents (or with some other older person in their lives) is different from their relationship with their parents. Do they talk about different things or participate in different activities? Why do they think the relationships are different?

Discussion. Ask students to suggest ways grandparents can stay in touch with their grandchildren if they do not live close by. Encourage students to think about how technology can be used for communication.

◆◆◆

Midlife Challenges

As if the emotional, social, and physical changes of the middle years weren't enough to deal with, some people face additional challenges. They may have to deal with adult children who return home, or they may need to take care of elderly relatives.

◆ Continuing Care of Children

Some parents who thought they had an empty nest find their adult children returning home after having been on their own for some time. In fact, adult children are returning home in record numbers. Sometimes the reason is an upset in the children's lives such as a divorce or the loss of a job. Sometimes young adults return home after completing college because they have no other place to go until they find a job. In other cases, young adults want to live at home for a while to finance further education or save money. Some children, especially those with certain disabilities, never leave home because they cannot live independently.

Having a grown-up child return to the home can be a source of both joy and friction for parents and the child. Parents may tend to forget that the child is an adult. They may want to make rules about what to eat and what to wear and what time to get home at night. Sometimes the child, too, forgets that things have changed and may expect to have meals prepared and laundry done by mom or dad the way it was before.

Families need to resolve such conflicts before they become serious problems. They need to establish ground rules and boundaries so that all family members know what is expected of them.

When an adult child returns home to live, both generations need to agree on rules and responsibilities.

Problem Solving. Ask students to consider the following situation: Luann is 25 years old, and has been living on her own and working full time for 5 years. Now she wants to move back in with her parents so that she can save money to go back to school full time. Her parents are in favor of this idea, but they want to write an agreement about living together. Have the students suggest items that should be included in the agreement.

◆ Care of Elderly Relatives

Many people in their middle years have elderly parents or other relatives who need care. In the past, it was generally expected that each generation would take care of the previous generation. In those days, families were larger and family members tended to live in the same community. Their proximity made it possible for family members to share the responsibility of caring for aging relatives.

Today things have become more complicated. Families are smaller, and family members often live at great distances from one another. Better health care has increased life expectancy so that people live longer. In addition, many of today's elderly people are poor. Their Social Security payments and savings are not enough to keep up with rising costs. As a result, many can't afford to pay for the help that they need as they become less capable of caring for themselves.

Care for such people often needs to be provided by younger relatives. An elderly widowed mother may move in with her daughter. A son may visit his aging parents every

People in their middle years may become responsible for the care of an aging parent — a situation that calls for compromise on both sides.

evening on his way home from work. Adult children who live at a distance from their aging parents may feel guilty if they cannot do much to help.

When an elderly parent moves in with a son or daughter, both generations need to adjust to the changing circumstances. Often, once the adjustment is made, families are happy to have the grandparent in the home and enjoy the company and help that the grandparent provides.

◆ The Sandwich Generation

Some people in their middle years find that older relatives need their help before their own children have left home. This is particularly true of people who married and started families late. These people are often referred to as the **sandwich generation**. Caught between the needs of their children and the needs of their parents, they have to find ways of coping with the demands placed upon them. Women are more likely to be affected than men since elderly people often turn to their daughters when they need help.

Activity. Have students write and role-play scenarios about families who have an elderly relative who can no longer live alone. Have students take turns playing the roles of the elderly relative, the parent generation, and the younger generation.
Photo Focus. Have students study the photo on this page. Do students think the grandfather feels welcome in this home? Why or why not?
Discussion. Have students identify some conflicts that might arise in a three-generation household and suggest ways of resolving the problems they identify.

A Slice of Life

Michelle Baker helped her elderly mother through the door. "Just one more step, Mom," she said encouragingly. Michelle gently guided her mother through the hallway into the living room, where a chair was ready for her near the television.

At age 84, Michelle's mother was no longer able to live by herself. She needed help getting dressed and could no longer prepare her own meals. The doctor suggested two options — nursing home care or living with a family member. Unable to bear the thought of a nursing home, Michelle discussed the second option with her family. Her husband and two teenage sons were supportive. They loved Michelle's mother and wanted to help her.

There were adjustments to make, of course. Robby moved into Danny's bedroom, so his grandmother would be able to have her own room. The Bakers bought a wheelchair so that they could take Michelle's mother out with them. Michelle hired a part-time nurse who would stay with her mother when no one else could be there. On weekends, the family planned to share that responsibility.

As far as Michelle was concerned, the look on her mother's face was reward enough for the family's efforts. "I can tell I'm going to enjoy it here," she said as she squeezed her daughter's arm. "It's nice to be with family."

Thinking It Through

- Why does the whole family need to support a decision to take in an elderly parent?
- How do you think Michelle felt about having her mother move in?
- How do you think your family would cope with a situation like Michelle's?

Balancing Work & Family

Taking Time Out

When Margaret found out her father was seriously ill, she didn't know what to do. The doctors said he would probably live for only a short time, but he couldn't care for himself. Margaret didn't want her father confined to the hospital in his last days. The local hospice program would help care for him at home if someone else lived with him full-time. She was determined to be there, even if she had to quit her job. Luckily, she didn't, because of the Family and Medical Leave Act.

Enacted in 1993, the Act allows people to leave work for up to twelve weeks each year to take care of family matters. Although employers aren't required to pay employees' wages during this time, the company is required to save their job — or one at a similar position and salary.

Margaret qualified for leave under provisions of the Act. She had worked at the company for at least a year. Her reason for taking leave fit one of the criteria in the Act — to care for a parent with a serious health condition. Because of the sudden and terminal nature of the illness, Margaret needed to provide only a week's notice to her boss. Normally, thirty days' notice would be required.

Knowing that her job was secure helped Margaret to focus on making her father comfortable. She was determined that his last weeks would be as happy as possible.

Think About It

1. Why do you think the Family and Medical Leave Act was passed?
2. For what other family reasons might people take leave from work?

More About the Family and Medical Leave Act. The purpose of this act is "to balance the demands of the workplace with the needs of families" by entitling employees "to take reasonable leave for medical reasons, for the birth or adoption of a child, and for the care of a child, spouse, or parent who has a serious health condition."

Older people who need help are more likely to turn to their daughters than to their sons.

Planning for the Future

It is during the middle years that many people first start thinking seriously about what their life will be like after they reach the age of 65. As they see their own parents age and cope with retirement, they begin to see that they, too, need to plan for the future.

What do they need to plan for? Basically, they need to figure out how they will support themselves and what they will do when they no longer have a regular income from a job. They may also start thinking about where they want to live after they retire. Many people move into a different kind of housing or even to a different part of the country after retirement.

◆ Financial Planning

Social Security benefits are a substantial part of most people's retirement plans. Right now a worker can begin to collect a monthly benefit at the age of 62. A worker who waits until age 65 collects a bigger benefit. The worker's spouse is also eligible for a benefit, even if he or she has never worked. The age at which a person is eligible to collect Social Security benefits is gradually being raised. People who are young today will have to wait until they are at least 67 to receive their benefits.

Social Security benefits are not, however, enough for most people to live on after they

More About Social Security. Wage earners have Social Security payments deducted from their paychecks; their employers pay an equal amount on their behalf. Self-employed people pay a tax that is equal to both the employer's and employee's contributions.

It is during the middle years that many people start to think seriously about how they will support themselves after they retire.

stop working. When people reach their middle years, they often start figuring out how much other income they might need in retirement. Ideally, this planning should begin earlier. In fact, however, most people don't take their financial planning seriously until they reach midlife.

Many people belong to company pension plans to which both the employer and the employee can contribute. Employees often choose to increase their contributions during their middle years. People who work for companies that do not have pension plans can build retirement savings through various private plans.

Having private savings also brings peace of mind. You may have heard that some Americans are concerned about where all the money will come from to pay Social Security benefits in the future. The "baby boomer" generation is large, and is moving toward retirement age at a time when population growth has stabilized. The future of government-sponsored health care programs, such as Medicare, is also uncertain. Consequently, every adult needs to plan carefully for the future. The amount of retirement income people have will greatly affect many aspects of their retirement years.

◆ Retirement Planning

The middle years are also the time to start thinking about how retirement time will be spent. Many people use the relative freedom of their middle years to sample the kinds of leisure and volunteer activities that give them satisfaction. Some get involved in outdoor activities such as hiking, bird watching, or working in community gardens. Others are interested in sports such as golf, bowling, and tennis. Opportunities for volunteer service are everywhere. People involve themselves in tutoring projects, or in volunteering at senior citizen centers or child care centers.

Getting involved early makes the transition to retirement easier. It means that people have already built a network of acquaintances with similar interests. They have also sampled different activities and chosen the ones that suit them best.

Many people make time during the middle years to practice activities that they plan to devote time to during their retirement.

Life Management skills. Have students discuss the benefits of putting some retirement savings away in the early working years. Ask them to think about various stages in a person's earning life and to suggest reasons why more money is available for saving at some stages than at others.

More About Volunteer Opportunities. People in their middle years are particularly welcomed as volunteers because they have so many skills to offer. Some communities have job banks or registers so that people can volunteer to trade skills. For example, a person skilled in bookkeeping could trade work with someone who offers home repairs in return.

CHAPTER 32

Review

Summarizing the Chapter

- The middle years are the period in life between the ages of about 45 and 65.
- Most people experience emotional, social, and physical changes during this time of transition.
- Parents going through the empty nest stage react to the departure of their children in different ways.
- The middle years are a time when many people reassess their life goals and their jobs.
- Becoming a grandparent is usually a pleasure for those who get to see their grandchildren often enough.
- Some people in their middle years need to cope with the needs of both the younger generation and the older generation.
- Midlife planning for both the financial and social aspects of retirement is critical to happiness in later years.

Testing Your Memory

1. What event often makes parents aware that they have reached their middle years?
2. What kinds of emotional changes do people experience during their middle years?
3. Why do people in their middle years often develop new interests?
4. List three physical changes that happen in the middle years.
5. What health habits can women practice to lower their risk of developing osteoporosis as they age?
6. What kinds of changes often occur as a result of midlife reassessments?
7. What aspects of their future life do people need to plan for during their middle years?

Answers

Testing Your Memory

1. The departure of the last child from home.
2. Awareness of own mortality; awareness of growing older and slower; emotional changes linked to physical changes; adjustment to new lifestyle when children leave home.
3. They have more time and money to devote to new interests; they may think this is their last chance to pursue a new interest.
4. **Any three:** "graying," hair loss; wrinkles; stiffer joints; less efficient circulatory system; menopause in women.
5. Regular exercise and a calcium-rich diet.
6. People might decide to change career; they might go back to school; they might get involved in new interests.
7. They need to plan for their financial future and for their retirement activities.

Thinking Critically

1. Answers will vary but may include the idea that in our youth-oriented culture people feel that they must try to look younger in order to remain attractive.
2. Answers will vary but may include rules about chores, cooking, grocery shopping, contributions to household

Thinking Critically

1. Why do you think that many people in their middle years are anxious to hide the effects of aging by using hair coloring, makeup, hairpieces, and so on?
2. Give some examples of rules that families would have to agree on when an adult child returns to the family home.
3. Why do you think that so many people don't start thinking seriously about their financial future until they reach their middle years?

Taking Action

1. Work with several classmates to write a play about a family in which an adult child returns to live at home. Make your play focus on both amusing and serious aspects of the return.
2. Bring to class information about adult education programs in your community. Discuss the kinds of courses offered and reach conclusions about the interests of adults in your community.
3. Imagine that an elderly relative is going to move into your family home. Write a list of the actions you would need to take and the things you would need to discuss as a family to make the relative feel welcome.

Making Life Choices

Janna is 50 years old. She is divorced and has two teenage sons. She has worked for the same company since she was 30, gradually rising to a well-paid supervisory position. Her parents, who are in their late 70s, and her two brothers both live nearby. Janna and her sons spend a lot of time with their family. Her company is relocating to another town 600 miles away and has offered her a job there. She has to decide whether to accept the offer or try to find another job.

What are the factors Janna needs to consider in making her decision? Who might she consult for advice? What do you think her sons would want her to do?

Using Your Journal

You have just read about some of the emotional, social, and physical changes that people experience during their middle years. Now think about how what you have learned applies to someone you know. Use your journal to write about a relative or friend who is in his or her middle years. Write about the changes you have observed in that person. You might prepare a list of questions you would like to ask the person. Then talk to the person about what you have read in this chapter and ask your questions.

expenses, use of telephone, use of garage, and so on.

3. Students may suggest that younger people often don't feel that they earn enough money to be concerned about saving for the future. Also, people in their middle years are more aware of their approaching retirement, so they are more likely to think about financing it.

CHAPTER 33

The Later Years

Chapter Challenge

Resources. Refer to the Teacher's Classroom Resources box and Student Workbook for materials related to this chapter.

Look for These Answers . . .

- Into what two periods can the later years be divided?
- What are some of the physical aspects of aging?
- What are some common emotions that older people experience?
- List some of the main concerns of older people.
- Describe the housing options that are open to older people.
- What are the stages of dying?

Look for These Terms . . .

- ageism
- Alzheimer's disease
- arthritis
- congregate housing
- continuing care retirement community
- fixed income
- hospice
- living will
- respite care
- retirement community

"I didn't know what it would be like to be retired. I'd worked ever since I was 18 years old and now I'm 68. One thing I do know now though — it's different from what I expected."

Jay is talking to a friend who is about to retire. "I had to make a lot of adjustments. The first one was getting used to not having a paycheck. I have Social Security and a pension so I have enough money, but the money doesn't seem to go as far as it used to.

"The biggest adjustment for me was figuring out what to do all day. When I was first retired, I had a list a mile long of things to do. I cleaned out the garage, painted the kitchen, fixed the broken shutters, and so on. Pretty soon, though, all the projects on my list were done and I needed to find something to do besides watching TV and reading the newspaper.

"I always swore that I wouldn't go to the Senior Center. I thought of it as a nursery school for old people. But I changed my mind when I found out that they needed me more than I needed them. My friend Gus works there as a volunteer. There are a lot of people who need help with small household repairs. Gus is an electrician, and I'm pretty handy too. We go together now to someone's house a couple of times a week. We do little things like fixing a broken step or rewiring a lamp. Sometimes I take my grandson along so he can learn how to do these things too. He helps do things that Gus and I don't do anymore, like getting up on a ladder to clean someone's gutters.

"Gus and I meet some pretty nice people that way. I don't feel the same way about the Senior Center anymore either. And I'm much happier now that I'm busy again."

Chapter Opener. Have the students read the opening scenario to the chapter. Ask the following questions: How did Jay feel about retirement when he first retired? In what ways was it different from what he expected? What has Jay done to make his retirement happier? What did he need in order to feel happier?

The Aging Population

The middle years are generally said to end at 65, but many people dispute the idea that 65 is the beginning of old age. Traditionally, 65 was considered the start of the later years because it was the age at which most people retired from their jobs. Today, with many people continuing to work beyond age 65, and with countless men and women enjoying active and vigorous lives many years longer, definitions of old age are changing.

For many people, the later years are divided into two periods — the active later years and the more frail later years. The period from 65 to 75 or beyond is, for many, an active extension of the late middle years. After 75 or 80, many elderly people — but by no means all of them — do become frail.

Today, a larger percentage of the population than ever before is over age 65. Improved health care and medicine have contributed to the fact that people live longer. In the 1990s, about 1 in 8 Americans is more than 65 as compared to 1 in 25 in 1900. The percentage of older Americans will increase dramatically between the years 2010 and 2030, when the baby boomer generation reaches age 65.

The large number of older people is also responsible for the political and economic power of this age group. Older people vote

As older people became more numerous, they gain political strength, especially since they are more likely to use their votes than younger people.

more regularly than any other age group. Manufacturers and providers of services also know that older people make up a growing segment of their market.

People like Jay and his friend Gus are discovering that retirement does not have to mean inactivity. More and more retirees are finding useful ways to spend their time — as volunteers, as part-time workers, and as active participants in a variety of activities.

◆◆◆

Physical Aspects of Aging

Most people between 65 and 75 are healthy and active. There are, of course, some limitations that occur as part of the aging process. As people age, their reaction time slows down. Also, their joints become less flexible, their muscles become weaker, and their memory may not be what it once was. Changes in the inner ear and in the blood supply to the brain may affect the sense of balance — which is why Jay and Gus no longer want to get up on a ladder.

Discussion. Explore with students the changing definition of "old age." Point out that earlier this century life expectancy was shorter than it is today. Today, when many people live well into their eighties and nineties, it is not realistic to define old age as beginning at age 65.
More About the Aging Population. It is estimated that by the year 2000, the part of the American population that is over 65 will be as big as the entire population of Canada.

As people age, their vision tends to get weaker, especially their ability to see at night. This explains why many older people do not like to drive after dark.

Most older people also experience some loss of hearing. Many are reluctant to admit to it at first. Fortunately, modern hearing aids are less noticeable and more efficient than older models were. They have helped countless older people stay connected with the people around them.

Many people "shrink" as they get older. Their posture becomes stooped as bones and muscles lose strength. Women who have osteoporosis are particularly likely to develop a stooped posture.

Still, for most older people, physical aging does not prevent them from leading normal active lives. If they eat properly, get enough exercise, get regular checkups, and get treatment for minor medical problems, people without serious health problems can continue to be physically active for many years.

Growing older does not prevent most people from leading active useful lives — they just have to move more slowly and rest more often.

◆◆◆

Mental and Emotional Aspects of Aging

There is still a lot to discover about the effects of aging on people's mental capabilities. Some capabilities, such as short-term memory, do decline with age. Experts are not so sure about others, such as problem-solving, creativity, and the ability to learn. Some people used to think that these abilities declined with age. Recent studies suggest, however, that any apparent decline may, in fact, just be a result of slower reaction time. Some experts believe that certain abilities, such as verbal comprehension and reasoning, actually improve with age.

Emotional reactions to aging vary widely. We live in a culture that places a great emphasis on youth and youthful attractiveness. This emphasis tends to make many people fear old age. They may become depressed as they see unmistakable signs of aging when they look in the mirror.

Older people are often victims of **ageism**. Ageism, like racism and sexism, is based on stereotypes. It depicts older people as incapable, childish, complaining, and demanding; or as "cute" and stupid. Such stereotypes, which abound in TV commercials and magazine advertisements, are misleading and harmful.

In general, a person's emotional health during the later years will depend on that person's interests. The more interests a person brings to old age, the happier that person is likely to be. Even people who live into their eighties and become quite frail are emotionally better adjusted if they still take an active interest in the world around them. People with a high level of interest in various activities are actually likely to live longer too.

◆◆◆

Retirement

Retirement at age 65 used to be required by law. Now federal laws prohibit employers from forcing workers to retire at a specific age, except in certain job categories such as airline pilots or police officers. Many companies pressure older workers to retire, however,

While some mental skills decline with age, others actually improve. Older people may be slower, but they may also be more patient and more careful.

Discussion. Discuss with students the idea that physical deterioration is not something that happens to people abruptly at 65. In fact, eyesight, circulation, and reflexes all begin to go downhill in the early forties. Hearing reaches its most acute level at the age of 20, and declines thereafter.

Problem Solving. To help students understand ageism, have one student role-play the part of an older person who wants to rent an apartment and another student the part of a landlord who tries to discourage the person because of his or her age. What can the older person do? How can the landlord's attitude be changed?

A Slice of Life

Maggie woke up at 7 A.M., as always. She didn't need an alarm clock. After all, she'd been waking up at the same time for the past 50 years. Only before, she had had a reason to get up — to go to work. Now that she was retired, she couldn't seem to train her body to sleep just a little bit longer. At least that would take up some of her newfound free time.

Maggie had really looked forward to her retirement. She'd made investments and saved money to be sure she could live comfortably. She'd dreamed about having lots of time to herself to do anything she wanted. She could spend time with her children, grandchildren, and friends. She could sleep late. She could go to the movies in the afternoon. There was no limit to what Maggie could do once she didn't have to work.

Now after several months, Maggie wasn't sure retirement was all that great. Sure, she had plenty of time, but her children and grandchildren had work and school commitments. They also had plans with their friends. She only saw them occasionally. Maggie did get together with her friends to play cards and talk, but that's about all they did these days. Traveling to new places or doing new things cost money, and Maggie's friends were reluctant to spend money on nonessential items.

During her free time, Maggie thought a lot about work. She missed the sense of accomplishment that came from doing a good job. Hadn't she felt more important when she was working? It seemed as if work had given her a purpose in life. She had been able to make a difference. Now each day dragged on, the same as the last. Maggie read a lot of books, watched television, and complained about not being useful anymore.

Her friends, content with retirement, kidded Maggie. They said she was so desperate for something to do she would go back to work for free. Maggie laughed with the rest of them, but later she thought about it some more. It wasn't such a bad idea.

Thinking It Through

- In what ways did Maggie fail to prepare properly for retirement?
- What kinds of things can Maggie do to fill her schedule and make retirement more enjoyable?
- How might family members help retirees adjust to their new schedules?

either by offering them financial incentives or by using social pressures.

People who continue to work after age 65 do so for two reasons. Some of them love working and have no desire to stop. Others cannot afford to stop working. They simply do not have enough money saved to support themselves in retirement. Some older people wish they could work but they cannot. Either their health does not permit it, or they cannot find suitable employment.

Many people over age 65 retire from their regular job and then find different employment. Employers have been discovering that

Discussion. Ask students to suggest reasons why airline pilots and police officers are still required to retire at age 65. What qualities do people who do these jobs need? What are some other jobs that might justifiably require retirement at a specific age?

More About Retirement. Nearly 25 percent of newly retired Americans now take seasonal or part-time jobs. **Activity.** Have students examine the employment pages of the local newspaper. Do any of the ads call for older workers? What jobs do the students think older workers would enjoy most or be especially good at?

hiring retired workers makes sense. Employees over 65 tend to be very reliable. As a group, they have lower accident rates, fewer absences, better judgment, and more ability to handle responsibility than some younger employees.

For people who do retire, the retirement years may be relaxing and enjoyable, or they may be boring and depressing. Much depends on the individual's state of health, financial situation, and preparation for retirement. The person's lifestyle before retirement also plays a significant role. In general, those who led a full and active life in their earlier years are more likely to enjoy a satisfying retirement. Still, no one can be prepared for everything, and many older people do experience serious problems.

A large percentage of elderly Americans worry about finding the money to pay for basic necessities.

◆◆◆

Problems That Some Older People Face

In survey after survey, older people cite money and failing health as their two main concerns. Many are afraid they won't have enough money to support themselves or that they will suffer a debilitating illness. Other concerns that rank high include lack of transportation, fear of accidents, emotional problems, and the problems associated with the death of a partner.

◆ Financial Problems

About 12 percent of all Americans over age 65 have incomes below the poverty level. This percentage has declined steadily since the introduction of the Social Security program in 1935. Nevertheless, a large percentage of elderly people — while not officially below the poverty level — do not have enough money for basic needs.

Social Security payments provide an income for about 90 percent of Americans over 65. However, Social Security does not, and never was intended to, provide enough for a retired person or couple to live on. People need personal savings or a pension in addition to Social Security. Many just don't have these resources.

Even those who have savings or a pension often find that the amount they receive is not enough. Most are on a **fixed income** — an income that stays the same for the rest of the person's life. An income that seems adequate when a person retires becomes less than adequate as time goes on and as prices rise.

◆ Health Problems

Although many older people are conscious of the effects of their advancing years, they do not necessarily suffer from major health problems. They can continue to go about their daily lives — they just have to do so at a slower pace.

No matter how healthy they are, however, most older people eventually develop one or more of the health problems associated with old age.

Life Management Skills. Discuss with students the role of inflation in eroding the resources of people living on a fixed income. Have them do research to compare the costs of certain basic items today and 20 years ago. Emphasize that people who are 85 today retired 20 years ago, when prices were much lower.

More About Health. Point out that regular exercise brings numerous benefits to older people. Exercise reduces the risk of heart disease and stroke; lowers the risk of certain cancers; reduces the risk of bone fractures from osteoporosis; helps maintain normal body weight; helps people overcome depression; helps people sleep better.

I CAN ◆◆ Plan Ahead for Retirement

Most young people just starting work don't think about retirement. But when Shelley was given a chance to join her company's pension plan, she didn't even hesitate.

"I think about retirement a lot, every time I run into my next door neighbors. They're a couple in their seventies, and they've worked hard their whole life. The problem is they never put away money for retirement. Now they barely scrape by. Their son visits each week to give them some money. They live on that plus a small Social Security check. They never get to go anywhere or buy anything that's not absolutely necessary.

"I thought retirement was supposed to be a great part of your life. You don't have to work, so you have time to do anything you want. You just need the money to do it. I'm going to make sure I have more than enough when I retire.

"I'm not going to count on getting Social Security checks, either. There are more older people now, because people live longer. By the time I retire, people may live past 100. With all those extra people, there may not be enough Social Security money for everyone.

"That's why I'm choosing a deduction from each of my paychecks to go toward the company pension fund. All of that money, with interest, will be there waiting for me when I'm ready to retire."

- Why might young people not think about saving for retirement?
- How can starting early help you save more money in the long run?
- When will you start saving for your retirement? Explain your reasoning.

- **Arthritis.** Although it can strike at any age, **arthritis** is the most common disability of older people. This degenerative joint disease causes pain and limits mobility in such areas as the fingers, knees, hips, and back. If it is severe, it can be disabling. Modern joint-replacement operations have helped many people overcome severe arthritic conditions.
- **Dietary Deficiencies.** Older people generally use less energy and need fewer calories. They still need all the essential nutrients, however. Some older people skip meals or snack on foods that are low in nutrients. This is particularly true of people who are suddenly on their own after the death of a spouse and who dislike eating alone. Meals on Wheels, which delivers prepared meals to people who are unable to shop or cook for themselves, offers one solution. Programs at community centers that combine good meals with social activity are a better solution.
- **Osteoporosis.** This condition, in which the bones become brittle, porous, and weak, occurs mainly in women. Brittle bones are more likely to break and take longer to heal.
- **Alzheimer's Disease.** People with **Alzheimer's disease** suffer from confusion and forgetfulness. As the disease progresses, they become severely disoriented and, eventually, unable to function from day to day. About 5 percent of all elderly people suffer from this disease.

Problem Solving. Have students suggest actions that can be taken to help older people eat properly. What can communities do to help them? How might volunteers help? What about supermarkets and processed food manufacturers? Encourage students to think of creative ways of getting the message across.

Discussion. Point out that independent adulthood in America is often related to the ability to drive a car, at both ends of the adult years. Getting a driver's license marks the beginning of real adulthood for most American teenagers in the same way that having to stop driving defines the onset of old age for many older Americans.

Other diseases associated with advanced years include the two leading causes of death in adults — cardiovascular disease and cancer. Both diseases can develop over many years, during which time there may be no symptoms. By getting regular checkups, people can detect these diseases in their early stages and get the necessary treatment.

Hand in hand with concern about health problems is concern about paying for medical treatment. Medicare and Medicaid programs cover some of the costs of medical care, but paying the remaining costs can be difficult, especially if medical problems are severe, frequent, or long-term.

◆ Transportation

A large percentage of Americans rely on the automobile as their main means of transportation. For many older people, losing the ability to drive is the real onset of old age. Some people can no longer drive because of failing eyesight or slowed reactions. Others can no longer afford to own a car. Whatever the reason, the loss of the freedom and independence that the car represents is a severe blow.

Family members or friends may help provide transportation, but seniors are often hesitant to ask for help. In urban and suburban areas, most mass transit systems have programs that offer reduced fares to people over 65 at off-peak hours. However, some older people cannot physically manage mass transit, and others are afraid to use it. In some cities, towns, and rural areas, social service agencies provide vans to transport those unable to drive.

Older people in good health who are still able to drive are, statistically, the safest drivers of all. They have the lowest rate of automobile accidents of any age group.

More About Depression. People who do not go outside much in the wintertime may suffer from a form of depression known as SAD, or Seasonal Affective Disorder. It can often be treated by spending some time outside every day or, if that is not possible, by sitting under a special light for a while every day.

◆ Accidents

Older people are, however, subject to other kinds of accidents. Falls, and the broken bones caused by them, are especially dangerous for older people. Their bones break more easily and, once broken, heal more slowly. The immobility that can result from a broken bone can also cause serious health problems. Most falls happen in the home, and the most common cause is tripping. Some safety measures that minimize the risk of falls in the home are listed on page 485.

◆ Emotional Problems

Depression is a common emotional problem for older people. Some feelings of sadness, grief, and loneliness are to be expected as older people experience the loss of friends and loved ones. Exercise, activity, and maintaining a sense of self-worth are the best guards against depression. People who have a part-time job or are involved in community projects are less likely to suffer from prolonged depression.

Many older people find that having a pet to take care of helps them feel more needed and more cheerful.

Serious depression in the elderly is a treatable illness, just as it is for younger people. Some older people suffer severe depression as a result of the medications they take. This is most likely to happen when a person is taking several medications that interact with one another. A seriously depressed older person needs medical attention.

Fear is another emotion that is common in old age. Many older people, particularly those who live in high-crime areas, are afraid to go out. They know that they are especially vulnerable to crime. Some people are also afraid of becoming lonely and useless, or of running out of money.

People who live alone may be afraid of getting hurt or sick and not being able to get help. Family and friends can help by calling regularly. Older people can also help themselves by wearing emergency call buttons. Many communities have introduced programs that make sure that older people make or receive a telephone call every day to let someone know they are all right.

The telephone can be a lifeline for older people who are unable or afraid to go out.

Problem Solving. Have the students write brief summaries of all the different ways people who live alone can make sure that someone else will know if they are hurt or sick and cannot call for help.

◆ Death of a Partner

Eventually, in any partnership, one person dies and the other must deal with the loss. Women usually live longer than men, and in most married couples, the husband is older than the wife. The surviving partner, then, is more often the woman than the man.

It is not only widows who have to survive alone, however. The survivor of any two people who have lived together for a long time — whether they are friends, siblings, or other relatives — has to make the same kind of adjustment.

The death of the partner has a profound effect on the survivor. It makes the surviving partner aware of his or her own impending death. It can also have significant practical and financial effects.

When two people live together, they develop routines for their days. They are accustomed to sharing activities and responsibilities. One person may not know how to prepare meals or do the laundry. The other may not know how often the oil in the car or the air filter in the furnace should be changed. When one partner dies, the other has to learn new skills.

The financial impact of a partner's death depends on the sources of the couple's income. If the partner was still working, his or her income is gone. If the couple was married and both were receiving Social Security, the amount the survivor receives can be as little as one-half of the couple's combined income. If there was a long, expensive illness before the death, the couple's assets may be substantially reduced.

The death of a partner often leads to a change in living arrangements. This is especially true if the couple continued to live in their own home after retirement. The surviving partner may not be able to manage the home alone.

Discussion. Have students discuss the ways in which the survivor partner of a couple is similar to a young adult who has to learn to live on his or her own for the very first time.

◆◆◆

Housing Decisions

Some older people make key decisions about housing shortly after they retire. Others wait until widowhood or failing health oblige them to make a change. When choosing from the available options, people need to consider their financial position, their state of health, their personality, and their lifestyle.

A housing decision made by an older person is often more critical than one made by a younger person. The older person may find it more difficult to move again once the decision has been made.

◆ Staying at Home

Most older people prefer to stay in their own home if they can manage to do so physically and financially. Those who are active in their community are especially reluctant to move.

There are federal, state, and local programs that help older people remain in their own homes. Some help older people to pay heating and utility bills or make their homes more energy efficient. Local community-sponsored services may help with the minor repairs and chores. Some alterations, such as installing a wheelchair ramp or a handrail on steps, may be needed to make the home safe and accessible for an older person.

◆ Moving in with Grown Children

In some cases, both the older and the younger generation welcome the idea of an older parent or relative moving in. In other cases, the move is prompted by medical or financial necessity.

Whether or not both generations welcome the move, it calls for major adjustments. Just as when a younger person returns to the family home, the family needs to establish ground rules. They need to discuss roles and responsibilities, financial arrangements, and other matters that could cause friction.

One reason that friction is likely is that there is a role reversal — the older person who was once in control of the family home is now in the home of the younger generation.

SIDELIGHT

Safety for Seniors

Falls in the home are a common cause of broken bones in older people. Older people's homes and homes that they visit frequently need to be accident-proofed. Here are some measures you can take to make a home safer for an older person:

- Make sure there is adequate lighting, especially on stairwells and near steps. Install night lights in all rooms.
- Remove hazards underfoot such as loose rugs or place nonskid pads under the rugs.
- Check that there are no trailing electric cords or telephone wires.
- Make sure that carpeting on stairs is tacked down securely.
- Install grab bars and handrails in the bathroom and place a nonskid mat in the bathtub.
- Install handrails on all steps, indoors and outdoors.
- Replace faucets and doorknobs that are difficult to turn.
- Provide seating that is firm enough and high enough for an older person to get up from.
- Move furniture so as to create clear, wide passageways.

◆◆◆

Discussion. Have students discuss why the average American woman can now expect to spend more years caring for her parents than she did caring for her children. Do they think this is also true for men? Is the situation likely to change?

More About Safety for Seniors. Interested students can send for a free publication, *Safety for Older Consumers: A Home Safety Checklist*, from the Consumer Product Safety Commission, Office of Information & Public Affairs, 5401 Westbard Avenue, Bethesda, Maryland 20207.

The older person may be tempted to tell his or her adult child how to wash the car or clean the house. The son or daughter may be tempted to treat the parent like a child or deny the parent privacy. Both generations need to be prepared to compromise.

When an elderly person who needs constant physical care or supervision lives with children or other relatives, the younger generation must meet their own needs for privacy and recreation too. Home health aide programs and adult day care programs can give the caregiver a break, either on a regular or occasional basis. **Respite care** programs provide temporary nursing home care for a person who needs constant supervision so that the caregivers can have a vacation. As in any other family life situation, good communication is the key to avoiding or minimizing serious problems.

Retirement communities provide the kinds of facilities that older people need — like transportation to the nearest shopping center.

◆ Retirement Communities

Retirement communities are groups of housing units designed for older people. They come in every style and price range. There are single-family homes, condominiums, apartment buildings, and mobile home communities.

Some retirement communities offer subsidized rents for low-income residents. Most communities provide services and social activities that are suited to older residents. Health care facilities, transportation such as minibuses, and maintenance services are often available too.

A person who is thinking about moving into a retirement community should investigate several communities. It's a good idea to get a clear idea of the accommodations, the services, and the costs. Different communities operate in different ways.

Activity. Have students gather literature on various types of retirement communities in the area where they live. Have them compile a chart comparing the costs of living in the different places and the services provided. They could make the chart available to interested senior citizens.

◆ Continuing Care Retirement Communities

Continuing care retirement communities (CCRCs) differ from regular retirement communities in that they require a fixed sum as an entrance fee as well as a monthly fee. These fees entitle residents to the use of a living unit and medical care for life.

In most CCRCs, the residents live in independent units or apartments as long as they are able. They may then move into a nursing facility, often on the same premises, if they become unable to live independently.

A person who is considering moving into either a conventional retirement community or a CCRC should exercise the same care as anyone who is signing a significant financial contract. An attorney, preferably one who has had experience with retirement community contracts, should review the contract and explain exactly what the person is agreeing to.

◆ Shared Housing

Informal shared housing arrangements have always been around, but since the 1980s programs to match people with suitable roommates have been available. Some of these programs focus on older people. They enable older people to stay in their own homes by renting space to another person. Often the renter is another senior citizen, but sometimes it is a younger person who needs inexpensive housing and is willing to exchange help with chores and maintenance for part of the rent.

Congregate housing (KAHN-gri-gate) is an innovative kind of shared housing where a number of people live in a building and share chores, meals, and some living space. Congregate housing arrangements vary from those where the residents themselves do almost all the chores such as cooking and cleaning to ones that have full-time managers and staff.

Shared and congregate housing have many advantages for older people. They cost less than living alone or in a retirement community. They provide companionship and security. Most important, these arrangements give people a degree of control over their lives that they might not otherwise have.

◆ Nursing Homes

A nursing home is sometimes the only option for a frail elderly person who needs skilled nursing care. Nursing homes can be expensive, and the quality of care in them varies a great deal. The person's family needs to take time and effort to investigate the alternatives and make the best possible decision.

The family of an elderly person who has to go to a nursing home often suffers from emotional stress, particularly guilt at "abandoning" the parent. Many good nursing homes offer counseling for the families of patients.

Congregate housing arrangements provide seniors with companionship, security, and a sense of being in control.

Activity. Divide students into groups of six. Each group is to imagine that they are the residents of a shared or congregate house. Members of each group should come up with a list of the chores that must be done and decide who is to do them. The groups should then discuss how they went about allocating chores. What did this activity tell them about shared living?

More About Nursing Homes. About 5 percent of all people over 65 are in nursing homes. Of these, about 50 percent are over 80. Almost 50 percent of the people in nursing homes are childless. More than two-thirds of them are women. Discuss with students the reasons for these statistics.

◆◆◆

Death and Dying

The end of life is death. People in a modern society sometimes would rather not think about this. Medical progress, better health care, and better health habits have increased the human life span. Nevertheless, everyone dies in the end.

Medical advances sometimes create the impression that a person who follows all the "rules" for healthy living can escape death. This may make people feel guilty when they develop a terminal illness such as cancer or heart disease. There is an unspoken implication that if the person had lived differently or had "taken better care of himself," he or she would not die.

Realistically we know this isn't true, but part of the cultural emphasis on youth in America is a denial of inevitable death. Denial is often a person's first response to the news of impending death. The denial is followed by a series of feelings and reactions called the stages of dying.

◆ The Stages of Dying

Although we know that eventually everyone dies, learning that death is actually coming in the near future is a shock. Most people go through a series of predictable stages when they learn that they have a terminal illness:

- **Denial:** "This can't be happening to me."
- **Anger:** "Why is this happening to me? Why can't the doctors make me better?"
- **Bargaining:** "I will do anything you tell me to if only I can live long enough to go to my granddaughter's graduation."
- **Depression:** "Since I am dying, there is no point in caring about anything anymore."
- **Acceptance:** "I have reached the point where I can deal calmly and openly with the idea of my death."

The stages of dying were first described by Dr. Elisabeth Kübler-Ross, who studied the needs of dying people. Many people believe that these emotional stages have a broader application. They believe that humans go through similar emotional stages whenever they have to deal with any major loss or disappointment.

◆ Living Wills

Most dying people, if they are asked, say that their wish is to die with dignity and comfort. Indeed, many people express that wish long before they expect to die. Two social developments that seek to satisfy this wish are the living will and the hospice movement.

A **living will** is a document that outlines a person's wishes about the medical measures to be taken to sustain life when there is no chance of recovering. In some states, the living will has the force of a legal document. In others, while it expresses the person's choice, it has no legal force.

◆ The Hospice Movement

The **hospice** movement strives to make sure that people with a terminal illness will die in as comfortable a situation as possible. Hospice care emphasizes the right of a dying person to be free of pain and to remain in his or her own home if possible. Trained hospice workers help the family to care for the dying person. The program emphasizes physical, emotional, and spiritual support for both the dying person and the family.

People whose families cannot look after them at home may spend their last few weeks in a hospice facility. Here, the surroundings are more pleasant and homelike than those of a hospital. The specially trained staffs know how to deal with the needs of dying people.

Activity. Bring a living will form to class and share with students the wording of the document. Point out that since it encourages people to list specific medical treatments that they do not want, a knowledge of medical procedures is necessary.

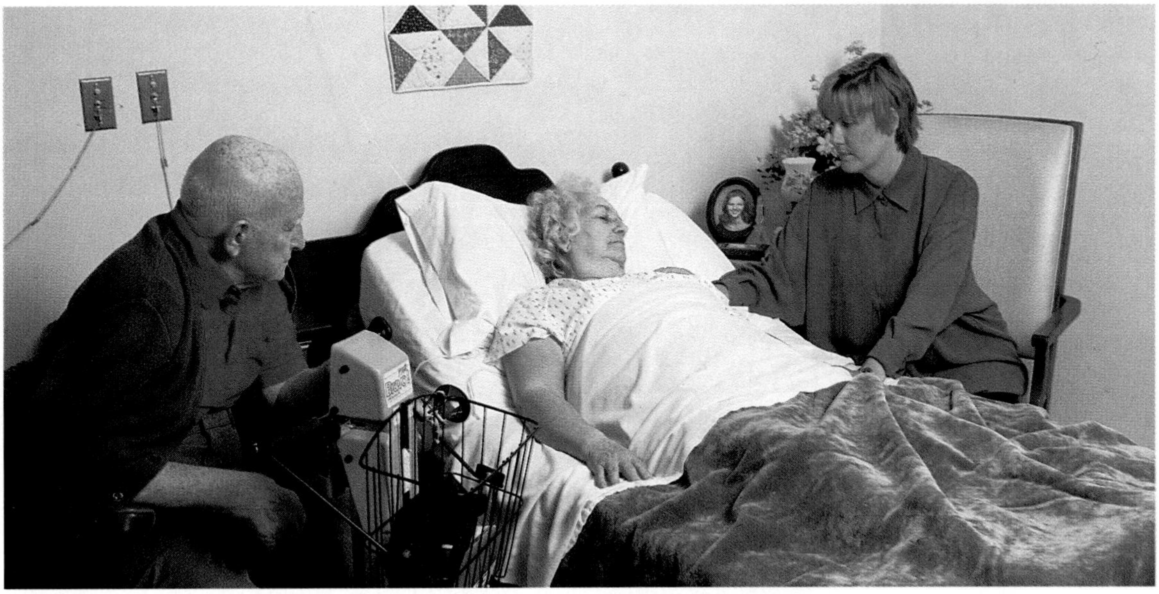

The hospice movement focuses on pain control and skilled support for the patient and the family.

◆◆◆

Grieving

Grieving is the process by which people adjust to the loss of someone important to them. Grieving is a necessary experience that proceeds in stages. In fact, the stages of grieving are very much like the stages of dying. When people lose a loved one, they experience a similar series of emotions from denial through acceptance.

Older people, naturally, become more used to grieving than younger people. In the course of a long life, they will lose many friends and close relatives. As more of the people they have shared experiences with die, older people tend to feel more and more isolated.

Understanding the stages of grieving will help you prepare for the loss of a loved one. It will also help you understand what others are going through when somebody close dies. Survivors need the support and comfort of their family. They need to be able to talk about the person they have lost. Often they want to talk about the good times they shared as they slowly come to terms with their loss.

People who have lost a loved one need the support and comfort of family members as they go through the stages of grieving.

Discussion. Have students discuss the idea of memorials for the dead. What importance do they attach to memorials? What are some of the memorials in your community? What kinds of memorials do something to benefit the living?

CHAPTER 33

Review

Summarizing the Chapter

- The later years can be divided into two periods — the active later years and the more frail later years.
- Physical changes during the later years include slower reactions, stiffer joints, weakening of eyesight, loss of hearing, and stooped posture.
- Older people may experience problems related to money, health, transportation, accidents, depression, and death of a partner.
- Housing options for older people who do not stay in their own homes or move in with their children include retirement communities and shared housing.
- The stages of dying are denial, anger, bargaining, depression, and acceptance.
- Grieving is the process by which people adjust to the loss of a loved one.

Testing Your Memory

1. Name three of the changes that happen to the human body as people get older.
2. What are two reasons that some people work beyond the traditional retirement age?
3. Why do some employers prefer to hire older workers?
4. List three things many older people are afraid of.
5. What are some of the housing options available for older people?
6. How do programs like adult day care and respite care help people who have an elderly relative living with them?
7. What are the stages of dying?

Answers

Testing Your Memory

1. **Any three:** slower reaction time; stiff joints; weaker muscles; reduced sense of balance; weaker vision; loss of hearing; stooped posture.
2. Some people continue to work because they love what they do; others work because they need the money.
3. Older workers are stable and reliable, with lower accident rates, better attendance, and better judgment than some younger employees.
4. **Any three:** Fear of being a crime victim; of becoming lonely; of becoming useless; of running out of money; of getting hurt or sick and not being able to get help.
5. Staying at home; moving in with relatives; retirement community; shared housing; congregate housing.
6. These programs allow the caretaker to have some free time or vacation.
7. Denial, anger, bargaining, depression, acceptance.

Thinking Critically

1. Answers will vary. Possible advantages: lower cost of living; better climate; more services. Possible disadvantages: leaving com-

Thinking Critically

1. What are the advantages and disadvantages of moving to another part of the country upon retirement?
2. Why is ageism harmful, and what can be done to prevent it?
3. What kinds of things do families need to discuss and agree on when an older person moves in?

Taking Action

1. Find out about the services available to older people in your community. Make a resource pamphlet that can be made available at the local library or senior citizens' center.
2. Work with several classmates to write a play about an older person who moves in with his or her children. Show some of the ways in which both generations would benefit from the situation and some of the ways they might have to make compromises to get along.

Making Life Choices

Elena is a single parent, 22 years old, with a 6-year-old son, Miguel. She works for minimum wage as a supermarket checker and lives in a one-bedroom apartment in a housing project. Elena would like to go back to school so that she could get a better job and move into a safer neighborhood. Elena has an aunt, Marcy, who is 75 years old and who lives alone in her own small house in a nearby town. Aunt Marcy can no longer manage on her Social Security money, the only income she has. She needs someone to help share the cost of the household and has asked Elena if she would like to move in with her. She and Elena have always gotten along fairly well, but sometimes Elena thinks her aunt is "too bossy." Aunt Marcy thinks that Elena is a nice girl, but "sometimes she isn't strict enough with Miguel."

What do you think Elena should do? If she moves in with her aunt, what problems might they have? What kind of agreements should they make before they try sharing a household?

Using Your Journal

In this chapter you learned about some of the problems that older people face. What could you do to reach out to older people in your family or neighborhood? Use your journal to write about some of the older people you know. Describe their situation and list the problems they might be dealing with. Then prepare a plan for spending time with them and talking with them. What might you talk about? What actions could you take that would make their lives easier? You might want to add new ideas to your plan after your first few visits.

munity; having to learn about a new area; cost and stress of moving.

2. Answers will vary. Ageism is harmful because it promotes misunderstanding. People can help prevent it by speaking out against ageism and by giving older people more opportunities to express their opinions.
3. Answers will vary. Possible answers: mealtimes; preferred foods; responsibilities for chores; use of family car; sharing of household costs.

Gina reaches out to an elderly neighbor.

Gina "For a long time I noticed that no one came to visit the elderly lady who lives across the hall from us. One day she and I entered the building together and I said hello. After that, we talked a little in the hall. In time I learned that Mrs. Tyler's husband is dead and her daughter lives far away. She has a few friends but they don't get around much. We've been friends for several months now, and if I don't see Mrs. Tyler for a while, I knock on her door to make sure she is all right. She invites me in, and I can tell she is grateful for my concern. Sometimes I do little things for her — pick up prescriptions, get groceries. I get a lot from her too. She has taught me about traditions I'd never heard of. She even bakes a tray of cookies every week just for me. I go over to talk and watch TV with her. She's a special friend to me."

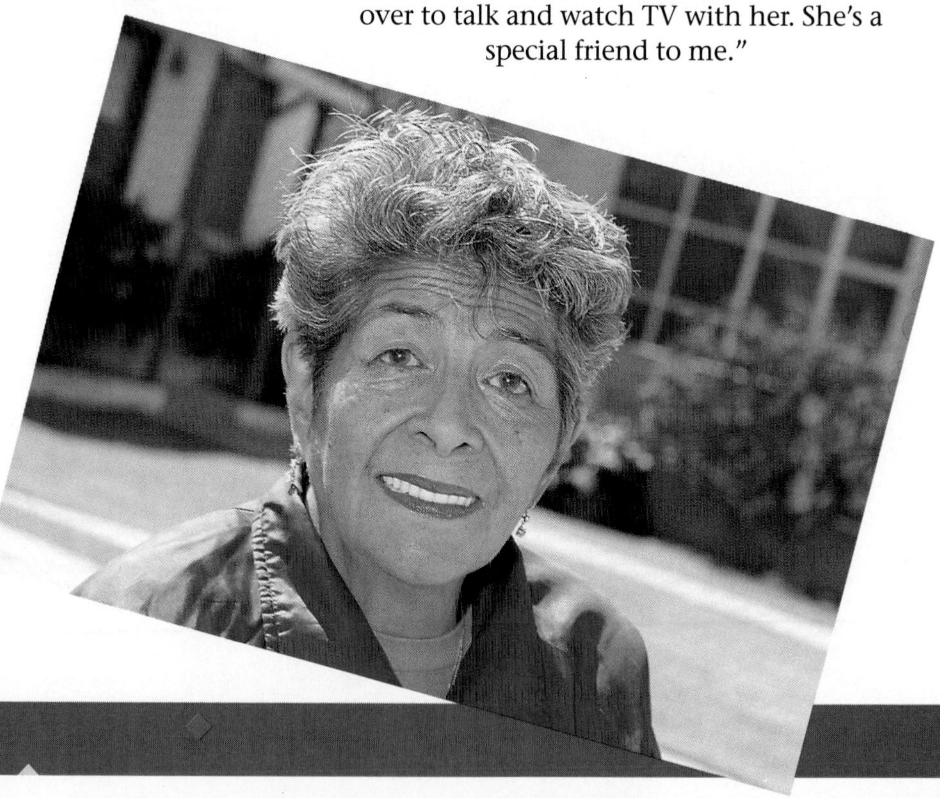

Roselyn Tyler

"The newspapers are full of stories about the troubles that young people have. Just as teens often have the wrong image of older people, we sometimes have the wrong image of them. Gina is the perfect example of a teen who is on the right track. We've shared some good talks with each other, and now I think we're both more in tune with how another generation looks at the world. That has helped us both. Gina has been a godsend for me. She is honest and dependable, and we have fun together. Most important, I can count on her as a friend."

Victor Perez

"I've been so busy at work I haven't been able to spend as much time with my daughter as I'd like. My wife told me about Gina and her friendship with Mrs. Tyler. I was surprised and touched. I felt proud to know that Gina is growing up to be a genuine, caring person. She's able to give of herself to other people. I think this experience will help her become successful at whatever she chooses to do with her future. Right now she's laying down the building blocks of her character."

Sarah Ogden

"In a conversation I had with Mrs. Tyler, she told me all about Gina, how helpful she was and what a good friend. I said, 'Do you think Gina would like to earn a little extra money every week running simple errands for me too?' Roselyn talked to Gina, who was eager to get started. That was just the beginning. Now she has a regular business going. Several of us use Gina as a 'girl Friday,' and we've all come to care about her welfare — as she does for ours. If more people like Gina reached out to others, imagine how different the world would be."

You can make a difference too.

- What are some ways Gina can communicate positively with her elder neighbors?
- What are steps Gina can take to manage her business efficiently?
- Have you ever made the first move to begin a friendship with a neighbor?

Glossary

A

abstinence (AB-stuh-nuns). Refraining from sexual intercourse.

abuse. When a parent, guardian, or other caregiver harms or threatens a child's physical or mental health.

active listening. The message receiver hears what is said and supplies nonverbal or verbal reactions.

addiction. A physical and/or psychological dependence on a substance or behavior.

adolescence (add-uhl-ES-uhns). The stage of life between childhood and adulthood.

affection. The warm and tender feeling you have for another person.

affinity (uh-FIN-uh-tee). Relationship by marriage.

ageism. Prejudice against older people based on groundless stereotypes.

AIDS (Acquired Immune Deficiency Syndrome). A communicable disease that destroys the body's ability to fight disease and leaves its victims without any defense against life-threatening illness.

alcoholic. Someone who is addicted to alcohol.

alimony (al-uh-MOH-nee). A monthly living payment sometimes paid by one spouse to another after a divorce.

alternatives. All the choices that are possible for a decision you must make.

Alzheimer's disease (awlts-HY-murz). A disease that affects older people and that is characterized by steadily worsening mental confusion.

amniotic sac (am-knee-OT-ic). The membrane containing the fluid that surrounds and protects the developing baby during pregnancy.

annulment (uh-NULL-ment). A legal decree stating that no valid marriage was contracted because the legal requirements of marriage were not met; the marriage did not exist.

apprentice (uh-PREN-tus). Trainee who receives two or three years of supervised, on-the-job experience along with related instruction.

aptitudes (AP-tuh-toods). Natural talents a person has.

arthritis. A disease that affects many older people and that is characterized by pain in the hips, knees, and other joints.

assertiveness (uh-SURT-iv-ness). Speaking up for yourself without offending others.

B

bankruptcy. A legal declaration of the inability to pay debts. When a person files bankruptcy, he or she usually has more debits than credits.

beneficiaries (ben-uh-FISH-ee-air-eez). Upon a person's death, the people designated to receive the income or benefits of an insurance policy or a will.

benefits. "Extras," besides salary, that an employer offers an employee, such as paid holidays, vacation, life insurance, health insurance, or retirement funds.

betrothal (bee-TROTH-uhl). An agreement to marry. In the past it included a father's approval of a man to marry his daughter. The man had to pay the father's demanding price with gifts and other goods.

bigamy (BIG-uh-me). Marrying a second person, even though you are already married. This practice is illegal.

blended family. A family in which both spouses have children from previous relationships.

blind dates. Dates arranged by others for people who have never met before.

body language. Communication using facial expressions and movements of the head, arms, hands, and body to convey messages.

bonding. Strong emotional ties between parents and infant. Bonding occurs when parents cuddle and touch, stroke, or talk to their baby.

budget. Plan for managing your money.

C

casual acquaintances. Speaking friends; you may exchange greetings and a few words whenever you happen to be with these people.

cervix (SUR-viks). The entranceway between the vagina and the uterus.

character. Moral maturity. It includes your actions, your personal code of ethics, your attitudes, and your ability to assume responsibility.

child support. Money paid by the noncustodial parent for part of a child's living expenses.

chlamydia (kluh-MID-ee-uh). A sexually transmitted infection that attacks male and female reproductive organs.

chromosomes (KROH-muh-sohms). Tiny structures inside the nucleus of a cell. They carry genes, which determine heredity.

civil. A type of ceremony where a couple is married in a courtroom or some location that has no religious connection.

close friends. People who have come to know and trust one another. They have shared a variety of experiences and have common interests.

code of ethics (ETH-iks). Clear set of rules or principles to guide your actions and decisions.

co-dependency. A common reaction in which the dependent person is the alcoholic and the co-dependents are those who are close to the alcoholic and feeling powerless.

commitment to a relationship. A promise or pledge of loyalty to another person.

commitment to family. A willingness to work together and sacrifice for the benefit of the whole family.

communication. The exchange of information, thoughts, and feelings.

comparison shopping. Comparing prices and quality at several different stores.

compatible (kum-PAT-uh-bull). Existing together in harmony.

compromise. A solution that requires both parties to give in on certain points and allows them to have their way on other points.

conception. The union of an ovum and a sperm, resulting in the beginning of a new life.

condominium. An apartment or dwelling in a multi-unit structure; it is individually owned.

conflict. Disagreement or struggle between two people or groups with opposing points of view.

conformity (kun-FOR-mut-ee). Changing in order to be like others.

congregate housing. A shared housing arrangement in which a number of people live in a building and share chores, meals, and some of the living space.

consanguinity (kahn-san-GWIN-uh-tee). Marriages between blood relatives.

conscience. Inner sense that promotes correct behavior and causes guilt feelings for inappropriate behavior.

consequences (KAHN-suh-kwen-sez). The results that come from a decision.

consumer. A person who uses goods and services to satisfy individual needs.

contentment. A feeling that you are satisfied with your life or the situation you are in.

continuing care retirement community. A retirement community that provides residents with housing and medical care for life.

contraceptives. Devices or methods used to avoid pregnancy.

conviction. Something that a person believes strongly in and takes very seriously.

coping skills. Techniques that enable you to handle the stress and conflicts in life.

cottage industries. Families who worked together at home to make clothing, textiles, or other products for market prior to the Industrial Revolution.

credit. Current use of future income.

culture (KUL-chur). A set of learned and shared beliefs, customs, skills, habits, traditions, and knowledge common to members of a society.

custody (CUS-tud-ee). Authorized care and control of a child or children following a divorce.

D

date rape. Unlawful sexual intercourse by force or threat and taking place in a dating situation.

deductible. Clause in an insurance policy stating how much the insured will pay before the insurance company pays the rest of the bill.

defense mechanisms. Reactions to stressful situations.

delayed marriage. Postponed union between two people for different reasons.

dependents. People, such as husbands, wives, children, or elderly parents, who rely on another for some degree of financial support.

desertion. When one partner walks out on the other without notice.

discrimination (dis-krim-uh-NAY-shun). Unfair treatment of certain people based on their race, religion, handicap, or point of view.

distractions. Something, such as a noise or action, that makes it hard to pay attention.

down payment. Money paid for property — a percentage of the full value of the property.

dual-earner families. Families in which both parents work.

dysfunctional family. A family that has a negative environment which contributes little to the personal development of family members.

E

egalitarian family (ih-gal-uh-TER-ee-un). A family in which power is shared by spouses.

embryo (EHM-bree-oh). The developing child in its earliest state within the womb.

emotions. Feelings experienced in reaction to thoughts, remarks, or events.

empathy. Seeing another person's point of view.

empty nest stage. A period of adjustment that parents go through after their children leave home.

engagement. The announced intention of two people to marry one another.

entrepreneur (ahn-tru-pru-NOOR). A person who is self-employed in his or her own business.

environment (in-VY-run-munt). Surroundings, including family, friends, and associates at school, work, and in the community. All of these affect your personality.

ethics. Principles of conduct that people live and work by.

exclusive dating. Partners date only each other.

extended family. A family that includes relatives other than parents and children, such as grandparents or cousins.

extroverts (EK-struh-vurts). People who like to be around other people and communicate with them.

F

fallopian tubes (fuh-LOW-pee-uhn). The passageways connecting the ovaries to the uterus in the female body.

family life cycle. The stages of life a family goes through.

family nest. An individual's family as it lends support in times of hardship. A person will sometimes return home during these times.

feedback. Verbal listener responses.

fertilized. United sperm and ovum.

fetus (FEE-tus). Term given to the developing child in the womb from the eighth week until the time of birth.

fixed income. An income, particularly a retirement income from a pension fund, that does not increase over time.

Food Guide Pyramid. A nutrition guide that recommends certain numbers of daily servings from the five main food groups.

functional family. A family that has a positive environment, nurturing personal development.

G

genes. The parts of the chromosomes that determine all inherited characteristics.

genital herpes. A sexually transmitted disease that produces blisters and sores in the genital region.

genital warts. A sexually transmitted disease in the form of small growths found on the male and female genitalia.

goal. Something you plan to be, do, or have, and you are willing to work for.

goal setting. When goals are carefully selected and clearly stated.

gonorrhea (gahn-uh-REE-uh). A sexually transmitted disease caused by bacteria that live in moist, warm areas of the body, such as the male urethra lining and the female cervix.

gross pay. Money that you earn before taxes are taken out.

grounds. Valid reasons for divorce.

H

heredity (huh-RED-uht-ee). Traits that are passed to you at birth from your parents.

hierarchy (HY-uh-rahr-kee). Ranking from most essential to least.

high-pressure sales tactics. Techniques used to convince people to buy certain merchandise.

HIV (Human Immunodeficiency Virus). The virus that causes AIDS.

hospice. An organization that provides care and guidance for terminally ill patients and their families.

human resources. Useful assets related to people — time, energy, ability, attitude, and people themselves.

hygiene (HY-jeen). Practicing cleanliness.

I

immunization (im-yuh-nuh-ZAY-shun). Protection against certain childhood diseases.

impulse buying. Purchasing without any thought beforehand.

impulse decisions. Decisions made without any thought or planning.

incest. Sexual activity between persons who are closely related.

infatuation (in-fach-uh-WAY-shun). A love experience that is based on a sudden, intense attraction.

infertility. A couple's inability to have children for physical reasons.

inflation. An economic condition in which the dollar will not buy as much as it used to. Inflation increases the cost of most goods and services.

integrity (in-TEG-rut-ee). Honesty.

intellectual love. Love that involves mutual respect — valuing the beliefs, opinions, and life goals of the loved one.

interfaith marriage. A marriage in which the partners come from different religions.

interracial marriage. A marriage in which the partners are of different races.

intervention. When people step in and take action in order to stop abuse.

interview. A meeting between an employer and a potential employee.

intimacy. The closeness that comes from deep, personal conversation, loving gestures, and displays of affection.

introverts (IN-truh-vurts). People who find satisfaction in being alone.

investments. Money available for long-term savings.

J

joint custody. Parents share in the care of children once a divorce has been finalized.

L

lease. Legal document that describes the terms by which property is rented.

liable. Held responsible according to the law.

lifelong friends. Close friends for whom the ties have lasted over time.

living will. A document that outlines a person's wishes about being kept alive when there is no hope of recovery.

long-range goals. Goals that have a time span of one year or more.

M

mammogram. An X-ray of the breast, taken to detect breast cancer in its earliest stage.

management. Planned use of resources in order to reach goals.

manipulators (muh-NIP-yuh-layt-urs). People who appear to be a friend but are not. They take advantage of the weaknesses of others.

material resources. Useful assets that have physical form — money, property, supplies, tools, and information.

matriarchal family (may-tree-AHR-kul). A family in which the mother is the head of the household.

mature love. Love that lasts.

maturity (muh-TUR-uht-ee). A state of full development.

menopause. The cessation of menstruation that occurs when a woman reaches her middle years.

mentor. A loyal, wise adviser.

mobility. Tendency to move often.

modeling. When adults and older siblings show children what to say and do.

monogamy (muh-NAHG-uh-mee). Being married to only one spouse at a time.

N

needs. Things that are required for survival.

neglect. Where a child does not receive enough food, clothing, or supervision.

net pay. Money you take home after federal, state, and Social Security taxes are taken out.

no-fault divorce. A divorce in which both spouses agree that the marriage has broken down and is irreconcilable. No blame is placed on either spouse.

nonverbal communication. Messages that are sent in visual ways; body language.

nuclear family. A family that consists of members of two generations: parents and children.

nurturing (NUR-chur-ing). Atmosphere of love, attention, support, and encouragement.

nutrition. Eating the right food for proper health and development.

O

object permanence. An object continues to exist even when it is no longer seen.

obstetrician (ahb-stuh-TRISH-un). A specialist in prenatal and postnatal care of a woman and her baby.

osteoporosis. A disease that tends to affect older women and that is characterized by brittle bones that break easily.

ovum. A single cell or egg in the female body that is released from the body each month during the female menstrual cycle. If the egg unites with a sperm (fertilization), pregnancy results. The ovum determines half of what a person will be.

P

parallel play. When young children play independently but side by side, rather than interacting with each other.

paraphrasing. Summarizing what is heard.

patriarchal family (pay-tree-AHR-kul). A family in which the father has the most power.

pediatrician. A doctor who specializes in the care of children.

peer pressure. An attempt to influence someone of similar age.

peers. People you associate with who are a similar age to you.

penis. External male reproductive organ.

permanent life insurance. Insurance, such as whole and universal life, that may be kept for a lifetime. This insurance doubles as a savings account, building up cash value.

personality. The sum of all characteristics that make a person unique.

phobias (FO-bee-uhs). Extreme fears.

physical love. Love that refers to the intimacies expressed by two people.

placenta (pluh-SENT-uh). A blood-rich organ that provides nourishment and oxygen to the embryo. It also removes waste materials from the growing embryo.

polygamy (puh-LIG-uh-mee). Marriage with more than two partners. This is illegal in the United States.

prejudice (PREJ-ud-us). An unfair or biased opinion, often about a certain religious, political, racial, or ethnic group.

prenuptial agreement. A contract drawn up by a couple before they are married to handle their property and income should they ever go separate ways.

prioritizing (pry-OR-ut-eye-zing). Ranking in order of importance.

professionalism. Conforming to ethical work standards.

proximity (prahk-SIM-ut-ee). Nearness.

puberty (PYOO-burt-ee). The time when males and females begin to mature sexually.

R

rape. Unlawful sexual intercourse by force or threat.

recession. Also called deflation, a period of reduced economic activity. Productivity and prices go down, unemployment increases, and some prices and incomes go down more than others.

reflexes. Automatic responses, such as sneezing or sucking, that infants possess before learning more at a later stage.

resourceful. Good at recognizing and making the best use of resources.

resources. Assets that are available for use in reaching goals.

respect. Honor and esteem shown for others.

respite care. Temporary nursing home care of an elderly relative so that caregivers can take a break.

responsible freedom. Making decisions independently and taking responsibility for the consequences.

resume (REZ-uh-may). A brief history of a person's work experience and qualifications usually prepared by an applicant seeking a job.

retirement community. A group of housing units designed to meet the needs of older residents.

role. The socially expected behavior pattern determined by a person's status in society.

role anticipation. Thinking about your future roles.

role expectations. Certain behaviors that people look for in the roles that people have.

role model. The person imitated.

role strain. A pull between familiar behaviors of the past and the unknown challenges of the future, such as changing from the role of a child to the role of an adult.

romantic love. Love in which you get to know and cherish all the wonderful things about a person.

S

sandwich generation. Middle-aged adults who need to take care of elderly parents and of children who have not yet left home.

secured building. Dwellings that often have locked exterior doors and an intercom system.

selective attention. Taking from a message only what catches a person's attention.

self-actualization (self-ak-chuh-wuh-luh-ZAY-shun). The process of becoming all that one is capable of becoming; reaching one's highest potential.

self-concept. The image a person has of himself or herself.

self-esteem (self-is-TEEM). The way you feel about yourself.

separation. When one spouse moves out with notice. Although still married, they live apart.

separation anxiety. A child's fear or stress when away from a familiar environment or familiar people.

sex. Intercourse.

sexuality. What it means to be a male or female. Includes how you handle yourself sexually in all areas of development.

sexually transmitted disease (STD). A communicable disease that is spread from one person to another through sexual contact.

short-range goals. Goals that have a time span of days, weeks, or months.

sibling. A brother or sister.

singlehood. Living without a marriage partner.

single living patterns. Living arrangements of unmarried individuals, such as living alone, living with family, having a roommate, or living together without marriage.

single-parent family. A family headed by one parent who has never married or who is left alone after a death, divorce, or desertion.

socialization. Learning how to relate to other human beings.

Social Security. Plan where employees, their employers, and self-employed persons pay Social Security taxes that are used to pay benefits to eligible people. When a worker retires, becomes disabled, or dies, monthly benefits are paid to replace part of the earnings the family has lost.

sperm. A male cell capable of fertilizing a female egg or ovum. This cell will determine half of what a person will be.

stepfamily. A family that includes children from a previous relationship.

stereotyping. Prejudging people on the basis of personal characteristics or group associations.

sterility (stuh-RILL-uh-tee). The inability to have children.

stranger anxiety. A baby's fear of strangers that is characterized by anxiety expressed through crying. It usually appears between the ages of six months to ten months.

stress. Physical, mental, or emotional strain or tension.

suppression (suh-PRESH-uhn). Storing all feelings inside to avoid conflict.

syphilis (SIF-uh-lus). A sexually transmitted disease which, if left untreated, may lead to mental illness, blindness, paralysis, heart disease, or even death.

T

tantrum. A state of violent or uncontrolled behavior that occurs when a person is angry, frustrated, or upset.

tax return. A form filed annually by taxpayers, reporting annual income and the tax due or the amount that you should get back from the government.

term insurance. Insurance that is temporary, running for a specific period of time, such as five or ten years.

tolerance (TAHL-uh-runts). The ability to accept people as they are.

traditional family. A family in which the man is the primary breadwinner and the woman concentrates on motherhood and household management.

transition. A change to which an individual needs to adapt.

trends. General directions of change.

trimesters. Three-month periods of a pregnancy.

U

ultrasound. Technique of using sound waves to make a video image of an unborn baby to show the position of the fetus and check for health problems.

unconditional love. Love that is given without limitations.

unemployment. Lack of a job.

unemployment compensation. Money received by eligible people who have recently become unemployed.

uterus (YOOT-uh-russ). A muscular, pear-shaped organ in the female body in which a baby develops during pregnancy.

V

vaccinations (vak-suh-NAY-shuns). Small amounts of a disease germ administered by injection or orally to protect against certain childhood illnesses.

vagina (vuh-JI-nuh). Internal female reproductive organ. This organ is also known as the birth canal because it is the passage leading from the uterus to the external opening.

values. Beliefs and feelings about how important someone or something is to you.

verbal communication. Communication that uses spoken or written words.

volunteerism. Practice of offering services of one's own free will.

W

wants. Things that you would like to have or do, but that are not essential.

warranty. Legal statement of rights and responsibilities agreed to by the consumer and the store or manufacturer when the product was purchased.

wellness. Way of living each day that includes choices and decisions based on healthy attitudes.

will. A legal document disposing of a person's property upon his or her death.

Index

Credits

Barbara Alper/Stock Boston, 481
George Ancona/INT'L Stock Photo, 105
Jeff Andrew/Keystone, 33
Arnold & Brown, 65, 72, 113, 115, 126, 145, 150, 151, 160, 165, 181, 190, 201, 205, 207, 228, 230, 257, 455
Bill Aron/PhotoEdit, 294
Bill Bachman/Stock Boston, 468a
James L. Ballard, 19, 24, 36, 78, 79, 122, 126, 136, 195, 204, 223, 237, 244, 330, 336, 352, 356, 360, 365, 366, 384, 460
Paul Barton/The Stock Market, 71, 80-81
Bill Bateman, 275
Roger B. Bean, 28, 68, 119, 141, 192, 196, 203, 224, 225, 393
Peter Beck/The Stock Market, 284
Ed Block/The Stock Market, 5, 11, 18
Jim Bradshaw, 304, 307, 342
Robert Brenner/PhotoEdit, 168, 172, 193, 310
Michael Bridwell/PhotoEdit 484
Uzi Broshi, 112, 312, 315, 423, 442, 444, 452
Barbara Caldwell, 163, 258, 329, 373, 412, 413, 429
Campbell's Soup Co., 358
Jose Carillo/PhotoEdit, 281
Joe Carini/The Image Works, 479
Melanie Carr/Zephyr/Picture Perfect, 473a
Jim Cummins/FPG International, 14-15
John Curtis/The Stock Market, 471
Bob Daemmrich, 31, 97, 124, 472
Bob Daemmrich/The Image Works, 157, 411
Bob Daemmrich/Stock Boston, 42, 137b, 247a, 437, 467
George W. Disario/The Stock Market, 117
Eastcott/The Image Works, 483
Eastcott/Momatiuk/Woodfin Camp & Associates, 44
Anthony Edgeworth/The Stock Market, 469
Myrleen Ferguson/PhotEdit, 215, 216, 303
David R. Frazier Photolibrary Inc., 9b, 13a, 82, 83, 136-137, 146, 188, 206, 213, 217, 240, 245, 270, 296, 299, 335, 370, 398, 427, 453
Tony Freeman/PhotoEdit, 17, 29, 87, 111,140, 176, 210, 218, 277, 295
Jim Gaffney, 48, 102, 272, 287, 288, 318, 321
Rob Gage/FPG International, 441
Ann Garvin, 23, 32, 60, 70, 86, 114, 130, 162, 212, 252, 288, 298, 314, 318, 328, 330, 339, 365, 392, 403, 408
Art Gingert/Comstock, 63
Grand Illusions/Rick Burdette, 142, 143, 147, 148, 149, 177, 179, 253, 255, 256, 259
Dorothy Little Greco/The Image Works, 303
Tom Grill/Comstock, 9a, 186-187, 238-239
Charles Gupton/Stock Boston, 465, 468b, 487
John Henley/The Stock Market, 10, 197, 268, 477
Michal Heron/The Stock Market, 489
Ellis Herwig/Stock Boston, 473b
Hewlett Packard, 352
Willie L. Hill Jr./The Image Works, 8, 189
Willie L. Hill Jr./Stock Boston, 268
Chuck Hofer, 47, 98, 202, 350, 357, 374
Bill Horsman/The Stock Market, 486
Richard Hutchings, 88, 106, 194
Impact Communications, 229
Interco Inc., 219
Steven W. Jones/FPG International, 367
Catherine Karnow/Woodfin Camp Associates, 104
Michael A. Keller/The Stock Market, 280
Russ Kinne/Comstock, 420-421
Grant LeDuc/Monkmeyer, 470
Bob Llewellyn/Uniphoto, Inc., 12, 290-291
David Lissy/FPG International, 2a, 13b, 462-463
Mike Malyszko/FPG International, 464
March of Dimes, 383
Julie Marcotte/Stock Boston, 350
Paul Markow/FPG International, 432
Stephen McBrady/PhotoEdit, 154
Robert McElwee, 50, 55, 300, 337, 399, 425, 450
McLaughlin/The Image Works, 478b
Toni Michaels, 123
Lawrence Migdale, 93, 137t
Lawrence Migdale/Stock Boston, 407
Roy Morch/The Stock Market, 226, 376
Suzanne Murphy, 305
Suzanne L. Murphy/FPG International, 476
Joseph Nettis/Stock Boston, 136b
Michael Newman/PhotoEdit, 200, 440
North Wind Picture Archives, 155, 269
Tony O'Brien/Stock Boston, 424
David Owen, 158
Richard Pasley/Stock Boston, 37, 261
Pedrick/The Image Works, 173
Jose L. Pelaez/The Stock Market, 7, 456
Mike Penney/David R. Frazier Photo Library, 489b
Norm Peterson, 332
Brent Phelps, 58, 69, 242, 243, 401, 422
Phyllis Picardi/Stock Boston, 249
Stacey Pick/Stock Boston, 247b
Proctor Community Hospital, 331, 343
Liz Purcell, 344, 345, 349, 353
Ross Laboratories, 361
Chuck Savage/The Stock Market, 242a
Shackman/Monkmeyer, 246
James Shaffer, 22
R. Sidney/The Image Works, 128
Vicki Silbert/PhotoEdit, 211, 223
Frank Siteman/Stock Boston, 338
Ariel Skelly/The Stock Market, 326-327
Special Olympics International, 127
Tom Stewart/The Stock Market, 1, 138-139
Les Stone/Sygma, 478a
Kevin Syms/David R. Frazier Photolibrary Inc., 222
Texas Highways, 114
Topham/The Image Works, 156
Peter Vandermark/Stock Boston, 317
Mel Waters, 380
Dana White Productions, 16, 78, 125, 184, 185, 236, 237, 257, 264, 265, 286, 297, 306, 316, 320, 324, 325, 388, 389, 402, 418, 419, 431, 460, 492, 493
Tom Wilson/FPG International, 3, 266-267
Nancy Wood, 362, 363, 374, 381, 382, 445
David Young-Wolf/PhotoEdit, 311
David Young-Wolf/Tony Stone Images, 54
Zefa/The Stock Market, 2b, 40
Duane R. Zehr, 6, 34, 41, 43, 50, 61, 78, 85, 86, 89, 91, 96, 99, 101, 103, 110, 132, 175, 191, 233, 241, 255, 260, 273, 283, 284, 302, 315, 371, 394, 395, 396, 406, 415, 429, 433, 436, 438, 443, 448, 449, 451, 454, 461

Special thanks to the following individuals, schools, businesses, and organizations for their assistance with photographs in this book. In Peoria, IL: B'nai B'rith Apartments; Crime Stoppers, Officer Jay Sauer; Maria Diaz; Fairchild's Ltd.; David Holt; Manual High School; Peoria Camera; Tri-County Urban League; Woodruff High School, Mary Lou Schlesinger; YWCA. American Indian Center, Chicago, IL; Bloomington Normal Adult Education, Bloomington, IL; Chicago Antiques Center, Chicago, IL; D.A.R.E., Officer John T. Bailey, Creve Coeur, IL; Limestone Community High School, Linda Ragain, Bartonville, IL; Parkview School, Creve Coeur, IL.

Models and fictional names have been used to portray characters in stories and examples in this text.